SOUTH AFRICA:
A PLURAL SOCIETY IN TRANSITION

South Africa: A Plural Society in Transition

Editors

DJ van Vuuren
NE Wiehahn
JA Lombard
NJ Rhoodie

Butterworths
Durban

ISBN 0 409 11083 3

THE BUTTERWORTH GROUP

South Africa
Butterworth Publishers (Pty) Ltd
8 Walter Place, Waterval Park, Mayville, Durban 4091

England
Butterworth & Co (Publishers) Ltd
88 Kingsway, London WC2B 6AB

Australia
Butterworths (Pty) Ltd
271–273 Lane Cove Road, North Ryde, NSW 2113

Canada
Butterworth & Co (Canada) Ltd
2265 Midland Avenue, Scarborough, Ontario MIP 4S1

New Zealand
Butterworths of New Zealand Ltd
31–35 Cumberland Place, Wellington

USA
Butterworths (Publishers) Inc
80 Montvale Avenue, Stoneham MA 02180

Cover design by Jenny Exton
Set and printed by Creda Press (Pty) Ltd

Foreword

During the course of history, intergroup relations in South Africa have been characterised on one hand by increasing economic integration and on the other by political segregation, with the Whites dominating the central institutions of decision-making power. By means of apartheid, the Whites, particularly the Afrikaners, endeavoured to accommodate the economic integration of South Africa's disparate communities without putting the political dominance required to safeguard their vital interests at risk. To this effect a policy was designed which provided, in theory at least, for the self-determination of the major Black ethno-historical group — an attempt at political Balkanisation without economic fragmentation and without relinquishing White hegemony at the political centre.

In narrow sense this policy was partially successful politically — witness the emergence of four independent Black states and six self-governing Black national states. The political aspirations of many Blacks, especially those living permanently in the major urban areas of South Africa, and also those of the Coloureds and Indians were, however, not met, since they enjoyed only limited civil and constitutional rights despite deeming themselves full-fledged citizens of an undivided South African state. In the final analysis, apartheid failed to enhance the self-determination of the so-called Non-Whites, primarily because it conflicted with the realities of a permanent Non-White population determined to attain equal rights with Whites. If anything, apartheid sowed the seeds of a potentially catastrophic power struggle polarised along racial lines.

Current changes in South Africa are an adaptive response to the reality of a joint political and economic destiny for the different population groups and the right of all South Africans to free social and political expression, to full participation in a free market economy and to full protection of human dignity. During this process, as is evident in the contributions to this book, major discriminatory practices spawned and perpetuated by the apartheid policy are being removed. The incumbent National Party Government today accepts that all South Africans, irrespective of race, class, or ethnic or cultural background, constitute one nation sharing a common state territorium and destined to live under a single constitution providing for a democratic reconciliation of particularistic group rights and universalistic individual rights. The latter involves recognition of the necessity to design a socio-political order that will provide for self-determination in respect of basic group rights balanced with power sharing at all levels of decision making involving matters of common interest.

Contemporary developments in South Africa indicate that the ultimate political model for ordering the country's plural society is that of a variant of federalism limited to the unique needs and conditions of the Subcontinent. Regional group and geographical considerations will play a major role in designing and operationalising such a federal dispensation. The current debate on South Africa's socio-political future is thus expected to switch progressively to constitutional options conceptualised in terms of federalist and consociationalist principles.

The editors wish to thank Mr TW Steward and Miss M Prinsloo of the HSRC for their assistance. Also, a special word of thanks to Miss M Hills of Butterworths, who acted as internal editor.

THE EDITORS
October 1985

Statement by the Human Sciences Research Council

As was the case with *Change in South Africa* (Butterworths 1983), *South Africa: A Plural Society in Transition* is an attempt to provide details of the changes taking place in different fields in South Africa and to offer an analysis of these changes.

As a whole, the publication cannot be evaluated in terms of a coherent and interdependent set of generalised propositions regarding change and development, although the South African situation, as it emerges in these pages, does in fact provide material for the formulation of such propositions.

The editors and co-workers are thanked for their interest in and contributions to the project. It is our conviction that this publication will serve *inter alia* as an important source of reference with regard to change in South Africa.

A special word of thanks is extended to the Advisory Committee for Political Science Research (Prof JC van der Walt (chairman), Dr GME Leistner, Profs CJ Maritz and GC Olivier, Drs P Smit and DJ van Vuuren and Prof M Wiechers) for their continued involvement in the activities of the Division for Political Science Research.

The views expressed in this work are those of the authors and not necessarily those of the HSRC or the Advisory Committee for Political Science Research.

JG Garbers
President
October 1985

Contents

1 The RSA Constitution: Continuity and change[1]

LJ Boulle

INTRODUCTION

The years 1983, 1984 and 1985 have been noteworthy in the restructuring of the South African constitutional system in that they witnessed, respectively, the enactment of a new Constitution Act, the formation and convention of its main institutions and the early stages of its being put into operation. These developments have entailed a transition from a relatively extended phase of constitutional planning, debate and rhetoric to one of legal-institutional and political innovation. They have been occasioned by deep strains in the country's political economy and institutional infrastructure and have been attended by real and perceived shifts in Government policy, as well as adaptations in substantive areas of social and economic life. These changes are epitomised by the announcements in April 1985 that the Prohibition of Mixed Marriages Act 55 of 1949 and s 16 of the Immorality Act 23 of 1957 would be repealed and that Blacks would qualify for freehold rights in urban areas. The ideology of apartheid has begun to dissolve and be replaced by the associated ideologies of the free market, privatisation, consensus, depoliticisation and technocratic administration, although there have been significant variations in the practical implications of these notions. The period has produced discrepancies between justificatory theory and reality, contradictions and disjunctions in the constitutional process, and themes of continuity and discontinuity.

Constitutional developments during the period under review can be approached in terms of a basic duality. For Blacks the 1983 Constitution continued to bar participation in the central institutions of government and the separatist political institutions for Blacks remained substantially intact. There was, however, a comparative lull in the implementation of the homelands programme and attention was directed towards Black local government and other modifications of prevailing policies. The exclusion of Blacks from the new Constitution was its most controversial feature. For non-Blacks, on the other hand, there emerged a unified constitutional

1

structure, the most salient feature of which was the extension of the parliamentary franchise to two statutorily-defined subordinate groups, namely the Coloureds and the Indians. Great symbolic significance attached to the facts that for the first time in South African history over 40% of the national Parliament was Non-White and Indian and Coloured membership of the national Cabinet and subsidiary bodies was both entertained and realised. The two parts of this dualist system comprise South Africa's constitutional whole.

The constitutional developments of the recent past were intensely politicised, both locally and abroad. The enactment and implementation of the 1983 Constitution in particular was attended by frenetic political activity and civil instability, which confirmed the fractious nature of the reformist option. It also elicited diverse and conflicting perceptions and interpretations of its significance, exacerbated by both the volatile circumstances of its appearance and its inherent ambiguity and flexibility. From the official vantage, the new Constitution was portrayed as an evolutionary extension of democratic rights, underwritten by the principle of ethnic autonomy, to those hitherto not accommodated in the political system. More critical, but still favourably-disposed interpreters advanced a 'reform by stealth' theory which acknowledged the system's structural inadequacies and inconsistencies, but emphasised the intentions of the system's operators and the goods it promised. The Constitution was negatively evaluated by conservatives and from a range of progressive perspectives. For the former it portended an imminent loss of White authority and privilege and eventual Black majority rule. For the latter it was designed to entrench some elements of apartheid at the same time that it was reversing others and was conspicuous in not being accompanied by significant socio-economic changes or improvements in civil liberties. From this perspective there was considerable emphasis on the underlying reasons for, and therefore determinants of, the constitutional changes, *inter alia* deep-rooted problems pertaining to legitimacy, security, political stability and the economic system. The nature and implications of Black constitutional developments were also differently construed — as an extension of participatory rights or a process of authoritarian co-optation and as providing a basis for pluralist co-operation or new forms of class domination.

From within this broad and varied subject matter, this contribution will focus on the key legal-institutional aspects upon which any evaluation of the emerging Constitution must be based. It deals with the process of constitutional change, the 1983 Constitution, Black constitutional developments, sub-national proposals and aspects of state-subject relationships before attending to some intrinsic themes in the contemporary constitutional politics of South Africa.

2

THE CONSTITUTIVE PHASE: 1976 to 1983

The period between 1976 and 1983 may be identified as a constitutive phase with regard to the new Constitution for Whites, Coloureds and Indians. The year 1976 witnessed three discrete but cumulatively significant events for constitutional change: the publication of the Theron Commission Report, the enactment of the Status of Transkei Act, and disturbances in Soweto and other Black townships. Whatever the precise causal relationships, there was a clear temporal coincidence between these events and the early emergence of the plans for a new constitutional dispensation. The first official proposals were formulated by a Cabinet committee and in its early stages the Constitution was part of the ruling party's political manifesto; it was endorsed as such by the White electorate in 1977. In 1979 it was adduced in a legislative bill and considered by a parliamentary select committee, which became the Schlebusch Commission. Although it was selectively endorsed by the Commission, it was never considered by Parliament, but was instead submitted to the President's Council, which had been designed and constituted especially for this purpose. The Council duly deliberated and reported on the bill, as well as on wider constitutional and related matters. However, significant consultations occurred simultaneously outside the President's Council, most importantly within the National Party and appropriate State institutions, but also with selected outsiders, in particular individual Coloured and Indian elites. A second bill was promulgated in early 1983 and later that year the Constitution was enacted by the White House of Assembly and validated by the State President. Although the Constitution's gestation was protracted, its birth was sudden and induced — parliamentary debate on the bill was attenuated by Government-sponsored guillotine motions which resulted in only one third of the individual clauses being considered during the committee stage. Commentators attributed this expedition to the important factor of timing within the complex and rigorous circumstances of its introduction. Finally, the Constitution received the plebiscitory ratification of the White electorate in late 1983.

The constitutive phase has several short-term implications for the new Constitution. The composition and enactment processes were effectively unilateral, the external consultation serving to legitimise and secure participation in the system rather than to allow negotiation on its essential elements. Although the final product was significantly different from the earliest prototype, the changes were the outcome of deliberations within the dominant group and not concessions to outsiders. This factor was epitomised by the Government's rejection of several President's Council recommendations which conflicted materially with its intentions (see

below) and the commitment of key Coloured and Indian elites to participate in the system even before its final form was known. As a result, the new
Constitution was partly an extrapolation and partly a modification of the
Government's long-established constitutional policy. The unilateral enactment process was one of the factors which affected its acceptability and
credibility among the Coloured and Indian electorates. It also entailed that
even participants did not endorse its basic premises, nor see it as more than
a short-term instrumental framework for more enduring political ends. The
legal continuity which the processes entailed denied the new system any
constitutional autarchy and raised several theoretical problems relating to
the termination of the old parliament's legislative supremacy and its
transfer to the new parliamentary institutions. Finally, they reinforced
prevailing notions of contingency in the constitutional process insofar as
constitution-making was presented as normal legislative activity, susceptible to the whims and wishes of the prevailing party. The 1984 amendments to the Constitution Act were enacted unilaterally by the White
legislature before its implementation.

For Black constitutional development, the constitutive phase was more
limited and comprised mainly administrative consultations with appropriate groups and unilateral legislative and at times executive action by
the State. Some attempts to broaden the process were unsuccessful. The
Schlebusch Commission recommended the establishment of a Black Citizens' Council to function as a counterpart to the President's Council, but
intense Black opposition to the body led to its still-birth. In February 1983
a special Cabinet Committee was appointed to investigate a range of issues
affecting urban Blacks and in 1985 its membership was opened to all
parliamentary parties. Although the Committee has consulted homeland
leaders, local authorities and other Black representatives, it has no Black
members and according to its original terms of reference is bound by the
framework of National Party policy. Finally, in opening the 1985 session of
Parliament, the State President announced the formation of an informal,
non-statutory forum in which Blacks and representatives of relevant
government bodies could deliberate on an *ad hoc* basis and by invitation on
a wide range of constitutional and related matters. While the ruling group
remained in firm control of the constitutional process, it was compelled to
widen its consultative scope.

The shortcomings in the constitutive process during the period under
review are a function of the conflicting demands of constitutional reform —
the need for the dominant group to countenance changes which would win
support and draw outsiders into the system without endangering its own
dominance and control. Apart from affecting the legitimacy of the constitutional process, these conflicting demands have resulted in specific
inconsistencies in the 1983 Constitution.

4

THE CONSTITUTION ACT OF 1983

Basic elements

Since the final form of the 1983 Constitution was largely predictable in the light of its protracted genesis, it is not described in any detail here. There is already convenient literature on the subject. All the main institutions of government, including the three Houses of Parliament, Ministers' Councils, State President, Electoral College and President's Council were instituted as previously envisaged, subject to variations in nomenclature, composition and size. In only one respect did the final product provide a significant surprise. Although the Government had consistently set itself against the President's Council's recommendation of a wholly non-parliamentary executive, its committee-stage amendment to the Constitution Act requiring Cabinet Ministers to be Members of Parliament, subject to a 12-month grace period, had not been anticipated. This Westminster principle seemed to reflect concern on the part of the ruling party and its caucus that the executive should not stray beyond its reach and ultimate control. In other, lesser respects the Constitution fell short of hopes and expectations, for example in not regulating the composition of committees (remedied by the standing orders), in eschewing a bill of rights and judicial review and in leaving several matters vague and ambiguous. Beyond this, however, the Constitution was not innovative in its essential elements. Moreover, for those familiar with the Constitution of the first Republic, it displayed a strong sense of continuity in matters of both substance and ornamentation.

From the perspective of constitutional law, clarity was obtained on several basic issues on which there had been speculation previously. The Constitution is semi-rigid as far as the structures of government are concerned, highly rigid in respect of the official languages and flexible for the rest. It does not constitute supreme law and there is no bill of rights or judicial review. The doctrines of parliamentary sovereignty and legislative supremacy have survived, albeit in modified form. So, too, has the principle of parliamentary government in that there is a weak separation of powers and Parliament can, within limits, bring the Cabinet down, but elements of presidentialism contribute towards a hybrid executive. The Constitution can be classified as unitary, although there is nominalistically a new diarchical division of functions based on the own affairs/general affairs distinction. In this respect it can be said to have corporative-federal elements. Past conventions and practices are retained to the extent that they are consistent with the new system.

Ambiguity and flexibility, however, characterise the more politically salient distribution of power under the new system. Thus Parliament is

5

definitionally flexible in that it consists either of all three Houses, or of such Houses as are actively operating, and it is functionally flexible in that there are five basic methods by means of which Parliament can legislate, some of them with subsidiary variations and one involving the participation of the President's Council, which is not included in the flexible definition of Parliament. These variations are designed to frustrate threats to the operation and efficiency of the legislative process occasioned by the non-participation or recalcitrance of subordinate groups. The element of flexibility is epitomised in respect of the own affairs/general affairs distinction around which the Constitution revolves. Finding its justification in theories of ethnic pluralism and the principles of self-determination, the distinction purports to allow each of the three groups exclusive control over matters of specific concern to it while allowing joint deliberation on matters of common concern. To this end definitional primacy is given to own affairs (s 14), all other matters being regarded as general. However, there is an incongruity between this definition and the list of own affairs matters contained in the first schedule: while the former links the concept to factors of culture, tradition, custom and way of life, many of the scheduled matters (e.g. agriculture and water supply) are not ethno-culturally determined. The definitional primacy of own affairs, moreover, is misleading in that the first schedule subordinates many such matters to general affairs law, either comprehensively or in relation to norms, standards and financial arrangements. This repugnancy principle is of significance in that all pre-existing enactments have been characterised as general laws, which entails umbrella constraints for the new own affairs institutions. The restricted potential scope of own affairs is illustrated further by the limited sizes of the Ministers' Councils and the nature of the portfolios — apart from the budget (a service function) and local government (a co-ordinating function which is in turn controlled from Pretoria), the only matters of substance are education, health services, housing and welfare, all of which are subject to overriding general affairs legislation. Above all, the absence of independent revenue sources and financial autonomy emphasises the precarious status of the crucially important concept of own affairs — a concurrent conclusion of several commentators. Ultimately, only culturally-determined matters can be conceived of as own affairs, as the s 14 definition logically implies. However, cultural affinity does not necessarily coincide with the statutory definitions of the participating groups.

Much attention has been given to a further source of flexibility in this area, namely the State President's competence to designate a matter as the own affair of a particular group. This was motivated in terms of the probable future need to rectify deficiencies in the schedule, thereby expanding the own affairs category. In the light of the above analysis this is a highly remote possibility. Instead, commentators have seen it as a thinly-disguised reserve power to enable the State President to launder contentious matters through the House of Assembly, the courts being expressly excluded from intervening in this discretionary process. Such high-handedness, however, would not only violate the spirit of the system and refute its internal logic, but would have high transaction costs as far as Coloured and Indian participants are concerned. It is also an unlikely eventuality in the light of the other avenues open to the dominant group for the implementation of its social designs.

The most plausible conclusion on this matter is that the own affairs concept has more of a justificatory, ideological and logistical than a functional role. It serves to validate an elaborate institutional superstructure, including separate legislative and executive bodies based on the 4:2:1 ratio, which allows continued political control by the dominant group. While its practical significance is likely to decrease steadily, there being few matters of importance to Whites, Coloureds or Indians exclusively, the concept is likely to be retained, even if as a constitutional fiction only. Ironically, this entails an in-built contradiction for social reform: as the own affairs matters have an immediate bearing on apartheid practices in residence, education and welfare, they circumscribe the scope of reform in these areas.

Implementation

Comprehensive transitional and empowering provisions in the 1983 Constitution facilitated its implementation over a relatively short period. General elections for the House of Representatives and for the House of Delegates were held in August 1984 amid intense political activity and media attention. The percentage poll for the House of Representatives was 29,6% and for the House of Delegates 20,2% (that is 19,3% and 17,9% of all potential voters respectively).[1] No elections were held for the new House of Assembly, the succession principle entailing that members might serve for almost nine years before facing re-election. The Electoral College was constituted and duly elevated the former Prime Minister to the office of State President. In turn, the State President nominated members to the four Cabinets, distributed portfolios among the ministers and deputies and appointed nominated parliamentarians to each House. The various components of the President's Council were designated by the State President and three Houses. Other functionaries, such as the Speaker and House Chairmen, were elected as constitutionally prescribed. The reorganisation of the bureaucracy was neither immediate nor visible, although the

7

allocation of State officials to general and own affairs departments and the integration of the public service will be crucial features of the new system. It was later indicated that Coloureds and Indians would be appointed to statutory boards and tribunals.

The two election results produced early complications for the new system, but for diametrically opposed reasons. In the House of Representatives elections the Labour Party won 43 of the seats, which result raised the potential anomaly of the two-member Peoples' Congress Party nominating all three Coloured opposition members of the President's Council. The issue was resolved by agreement, with the PCP assigning one seat to the LP. However, the gross numerical imbalance in the House led to speculation that the Labour Party would form a counterfeit 'opposition' from among its members so as to capture the spoils (albeit frugal) of the official opposition. The project was abandoned, apparently after Government intervention, but the imbalance continues to undermine the principles of parliamentary government in the House, as well as the operation of the committee system. In the House of Delegates, in contrast, the election results left the National Peoples' Party and the Solidarity Party in a closely balanced position. Vacillation among independent members and speculation of defections from both sides left the identity of the majority party in doubt until the day on which the Cabinets were announced. However, once its slight majority position had been confirmed, the NPP was decisively advantaged by the appointment of indirectly-elected and nominated members to the House; for the first time this controversial constitutional feature, first introduced in 1980, was seen to have a real influence on party dynamics.

Probably the most striking feature of the constitutional transition has been the accompanying continuity of personnel.[2] The perpetuation of the White chamber has already been referred to, as well as the accession of the Prime Minister to the Presidency. In addition, no fewer than 15 members of the new 18-person Cabinet were members of its predecessor and there has been no indication that the composition of crucial Cabinet committees, such as the State Security Council, has been affected yet. Thus, while the institutional framework within which it operates has been altered, the same core of policy-makers dominates the constitutional system. This is likely to have significant consequences for both the emergent practices of the system and its political outputs.

Early indicators

The executive function

The executive function will be the crucial feature of the new Constitution.

Executive dominance, if not sovereignty, is the hallmark of the modern administrative state and the control and accountability of the executive is the predicament of modern constitutionalism. Not surprisingly, the role and power of this estate received considerable attention from constitutional lawyers during the genesis of the new Constitution and much of the critical evaluation was unfavourable.[3] The executive function will revolve around the institution of the presidency, which incorporates elements of parliamentarism and presidentialism. The State President's mandate is not popular but parliamentary, although only in a limited sense of the term. The composition of the Electoral College, the concurrent majority principle and the dissolution procedures entail that his effective accountability will be to the majority White party. The Constitution requires all ministers to be parliamentarians, subject to the 12-month grace period, which circumscribes presidential choice. In fact, the resignation/dismissal provisions assume a compatibility between the executive and legislature which is intrinsic to the Westminster system. Each of the Ministers' Councils, moreover, comprises a one-party Westminister Cabinet with parliamentary principles governing its relationship with the relative House of Parliament. The executive function does not, therefore, have a presidential foundation.

In addition, the Westminster bias will be evident in the practice of the executive function. The presidency combines the roles of titular head of State and head of Government, but as far as own affairs are concerned the State President is required by law and convention to follow the advice of the relevant Ministers' Council (of which he is not a member), as was the case with the previous head of State. In respect of general affairs, a terminological innovation in the Constitution Act requires the State President to consult the Cabinet, but not necessarily to comply with its recommendations. This arrangement provides the institutional leeway associated with presidential government; the State President is more than *primus inter pares*. In early practice, however, the change should have less significance. The continuity of personnel already alluded to and the consolidating function of the party are likely to render the style of policy making similar to previous patterns. In respect of own affairs, the Ministers' Councils can also be expected to follow Westminster conventions and practices in performing executive functions. Again the presidential bias of the executive function is not pronounced.

Nevertheless, the nature and style of the executive function will be determined by political practice and organic development to an even greater extent than is the case with the legislative function. The executive head's ability to delegate and redelegate ministerial functions in disregard of statutory allocations of power (a competence predating the new Constitution) is now extensive. On one hand it enhances administrative flexibility and efficiency (it pre-empts boycott tactics), but on the other it erodes principles of ministerial responsibility and potentially undermines the own affairs/general affairs distinction. Whether such statutory empowerments are used or abused will depend on political exigencies. A strong possibility is that the centre of gravity in policy making will shift from the Cabinet to a super mini-cabinet, the State President and his staff, or important Cabinet committees such as the State Security Council. An early indication of such proclivity was given in the 'Coventry four' incident, where it was acknowledged that an important and much-publicised decision affecting foreign relations was taken by only a small group of ministers.[4] The institutional and political vantage of the State President was further exemplified in his appeal to Parliament (and indirectly the citizenry) not to debate the politically contentious handling of public disturbances in early 1985 pending the findings of a commission of enquiry.[5] Further developments along these lines, together with increased centralisation and executive sovereignty, could lead to the gradual emergence of a more presidential style of government.

Collective responsibility

The new Constitution Act explicitly retains the constitutional conventions which supplemented its predecessor, including those pertaining to ministerial responsibility. Past patterns of parliamentary government have not produced strong conventions of individual responsibility, partly because of the restricted franchise and rigid party system. On the other hand, the convention of collective responsibility has been strong insofar as Cabinet solidarity has been maintained and has served to shield refractory ministers. Historically, these developments have occurred within the context of predominantly single-party Cabinets. Although multi-party Cabinets are not wholly alien to South Africa's constitutional experience, in the past they have been preceded by political coalitions or pacts.

Under the new Constitution each of the three Ministers' Councils is a single-party executive and the Houses have the same mechanisms of control and accountability in respect of individual ministers as they did under the old. A striking innovation, however, is the composite nature of the national Cabinet in the absence of any pre-election political alliance. Although Cabinet appointments are discretionary, these features are likely to endure because it will be difficult for the State President to exclude the chairmen of the Indian and Coloured Ministers' Councils, ex officio, from future Cabinets and pressure for additional Indian and Coloured ministers must increase. The individual responsibility of ministers will be significantly circumscribed in respect of the legislative chambers of which they are not members, despite their ability to participate.in the proceedings of

10

these bodies. As far as collective responsibility is concerned, structural factors, political realities and comparative experiences suggest that this would also be placed under strain. Because several Cabinet Ministers, including those of both Non-White groups, are simultaneously members of Ministers' Councils, the principle could not operate comprehensively in both bodies unless the Councils were to act as submissive imitators of the Cabinet. The greater the heterogeneity of the Cabinet and the constituency pressures applied on Non-White ministers, the less feasible the principle would become. The fact that the majority Coloured and Indian parties are simultaneously in partnership with and in opposition to the Government would be a major underlying cause of tension. The doctrine will become even more unacceptable if power tends to shift away from the national Cabinet as a joint institution.

In anticipation of likely conflicts in this area, the State President was compelled to announce in September 1984 that the doctrine of collective responsibility would be applied less vigorously henceforth. In respect of Cabinet decisions, it would be suspended where the dissenting minister clarified his position with the Cabinet Chairman and they issued a joint statement on the matter. Public criticism of ministerial colleagues should not be undertaken without prior intimation. These guidelines could not accommodate some of the early strains. A minister without portfolio in the national Cabinet participated in his party's call for the dismissal of a fellow minister; the House of Delegates, including its ministers, unanimously rejected the Minister of Finance's proposals for a special account for the South African Police; and both the Labour Party and National People's Party expressed reservations about their leaders' continued membership of the Cabinet. While these issues were all inconclusively resolved, it is apparent that this is an area in which established and comparative norms of constitutionalism are unlikely to guide the practice of government.

Government/opposition and the party system

The new Constitution Act makes several conspicuous allusions to political parties and the party system has been prominent in the early days of its operation. The system revolves largely around stable majority parties in each House and places a premium on the non-circulation of party leaders. Inevitably, the bias in favour of majority parties has been transferred from the old Constitution to the new and is reflected in the electoral system, the supernumerary Members of Parliament and the composition of the Electoral College. There is also a bias among the three groups. Thus its dominance in the White House of Assembly has enabled the National Party to acquire a working majority in the electoral college, to elect the party leader to the presidency, to appropriate the White Ministers' Council and dominate the Cabinet and to control several other key positions. The predominance and control extends to the new President's Council, which has a more overtly party composition than did its predecessor. Moreover, most posts are held by members who are well-established in the party hierarchy, the continuity in Cabinet membership emphasising the influential force of party in government. The party dominance entails a practical fusion of political power in negation of its constitutionally enjoined dispersion.

The fusion is exemplified by the institution of the state presidency. The President's Council recommended that the incumbent should be partly insulated from party politics, which would be the preserve of an intermediary post of premiership, but early practice suggests direct and regular political involvement. After his inauguration the State President performed the ceremonial opening of Parliament, occupied his old seat in the House of Assembly, chaired the newly-constituted Cabinet, was re-elected Cape chairman of the National Party and participated in the Party's other provincial congresses. This institution, buttressed by the party system, provides a decisive link between the congresses, caucus and executive, again in emulation of Westminster patterns of government. The main threat to this convergence is the legislative committee system, to which attention is given in the following section.

For the first time the Constitution refers expressly to opposition parties, yet their likely role is somewhat ambivalent. In respect of own affairs, the opposition parties have limited potential significance within the context of majoritarian elections, one-party executives and non-consensual decision making. In respect of general affairs, the majority Indian and Coloured parties are, at one level, in opposition to the Government, but because of their minority position they do not constitute an alternative to it. Moreover, the incorporation of the party leaders into the national Cabinet has rendered them minor partners of the Government, which involves a partial political co-optation of the respective parties. While this co-optation situation prevails, it is improbable that the parties will propose a motion of no confidence in the national Government. By definition they would also not do so with respect to the respective Ministers' Councils, which they control. It is therefore the minority parties in each House which will have a more conventional opposition role, although their institutional position is even less favourable despite the repeal of the Prohibition of Political Interference Act 51 of 1968, which formerly precluded a range of co-operative ventures. Moreover, with the debate shifting away from Parliament and the public eye and the shortcomings in executive responsibility, the opposition function is likely to be generally restricted and there is little likelihood of leaders of the non-ruling parties coming to contribute to, let alone share control in, the political agenda. However, members of the non-ruling party will be in a numerical majority in the legislative committees and although they will not wield a conclusive veto over the legislative process, they may have significant influence at that level. The Constitution thus blurs traditional notions of government and opposition. Even for the majority White party, the normative principle of consensus undermines the mandate theory of government. The non-inclusive franchise also entails that much of the political opposition to the Government will be extra-parliamentarily located.

The committee system

The shift to a committee-based Parliament is one of the main innovations of the 1983 Constitution. Although it is unusual for national constitutions to accord any prominence to committee systems, in constitutional practice they have developed to an important position in many countries of the world. In their study of national legislatures, Lees and Shaw found that committee systems are strongest in the context of presidentialism (or continental parliamentarism) and weak party control.[6] There is also a high coincidence between a developed committee system and federalism. Committees can have wide-ranging functions, *inter alia*, legislative, financial, investigative, housekeeping and administrative oversight. To the extent that they contribute to the diffusion of and control over political power, committees constitute an important check and balance in contemporary constitutional systems. However, their efficacy depends significantly on their relative autonomy from the legislature, political executive and party structures.

Although in the new system the parliamentary committees have a constitutional foundation, their practical significance will depend on political practice and convention. Section 68 of the Constitution prescribes the establishment of at least one joint committee of the three Houses for general affairs bills and entertains the creation and management of several other committees by joint rules and orders. The first orders were promulgated before the inception of the Constitution and make provision for select and standing select committees for each House and its domestic affairs. For Parliament as a whole, there are composite joint committees and standing committees, the latter being constituted for the duration of a Parliament and providing the fulcrum of the tricameral system. Each standing committee comprises all members of the three corresponding standing select committees and a chairman and deputy chairman appointed by the Speaker. Standing committees have been established in respect of each ministerial portfolio for general affairs and there are also committees on private members' bills, specially designated matters and internal arrangements. The portfolio committees deliberate on all bills within their jurisdiction before the second reading. Once a decision has been taken on a bill, each component of the joint committee reports to its respective House. The proclaimed objective of the joint committees is to secure agreement on legislation within the sanctuary of their confidentiality. This would ease its subsequent passage.

The dynamics of the committee system are likely to revolve around several factors. Not unexpectedly, the position of chairman is, with a single unimportant exception, held by a member of the dominant White party; the monopoly is almost as extensive in respect of the deputies. The comparative precedents show the importance and potency of this position in a committee system and it mitigates the risk factor to which the dominant group is exposed in the multi-party committees. While the arithmetic of the joint committees might seem to place the ruling group in jeopardy, it should be borne in mind that the majority Coloured and Indian parties are, by virtue of their leaders' Cabinet status, part of government and the 'government' parties have a vast numerical superiority.[7] Furthermore, there is no individual voting in the committees in that consensus is deemed to have been attained when the majority of members from each component committee is in support of a measure. This 'concurrent majority' principle provides, on one hand, a minority veto for each majority party, but on the other prevents voting alignments across the colour barriers. It is also not possible for opposition parties to present minority reports.

The committee system thus reinforces the influence of the three majority parties. The system is being grafted onto a long tradition of party- and caucus-based policy making which will not easily accommodate a transition to committee dominance. Even if the committees do educe some initiative from the political executives and party leaders, their decisions are made before Parliament deliberates on legislation and they are susceptible to reversal by the State President and President's Council. Thus the institutional circumstances of the committees suggest that they are geared to executive action and organisation and are unlikely to be assertive sources of policy in their own right.

However, several other factors could, over time, lead the committee system to acquire a significant degree of autonomy from other institutions in the legislative process. First, the minister responsible for legislation is not a member of the relevant joint committee, the 'ministerial' function being assumed by the respective committee chairmen. Thus, while the minister might be able to ensure principled approval for legislation in the Cabinet, he will forfeit his former direct control over its detailed consideration. In one of the early public indications of committee dynamics, it was reported to Parliament that committee consensus could not be obtained on the South African Police Special Account Bill.[8] This entailed that the minister would have to either suspend the bill in its existing form, or prevail on the State President to manoeuvre it through the President's Council. (The latter procedure was subsequently adopted.) Secondly, the practice of summonsing top officials before the committees to explain and justify aspects of their legislation soon developed and, while it might not make the bureaucracy significantly more accountable, it should at least produce better legislation. Thirdly, although the concurrent majority principle is a patent safeguard (or minority veto) for the dominant White party, it could be mitigated by convention and does not in itself prevent minority parties from contributing to the technical improvement of legislation. Finally (although it is only indirectly related to the committee system), all bills are now accompanied by explanatory memoranda which serve to explicate their purpose and objectives to the committees and public — a practice which has proved beneficial in other jurisdictions.

Apart from these potential legislative functions and the inevitable housekeeping duties, it is unlikely that the parliamentary committees will, in the short term, assert the administrative oversight which characterises their counterparts elsewhere. Here the role and control of the fourth estate has also been omitted from the equation.

The Constitution and constitutionalism

Constitutionalism, in its most immediate sense, denotes the practice of limited and accountable government and in its modern manifestations it is closely associated with legality and the judicial function. Besides containing political power maps, modern constitutions are characterised by three associated features: the constitution comprises basic law, there is an entrenched bill or charter of rights, and judicial review is explicitly conferred. These features entail direct or mediated roles in the constitutional process for the courts and many jurisdictions establish special constitutional tribunals for some or all of these functions.

The 1983 Constitution does not incorporate this judicial package. While it provides detailed descriptions of the legislative and executive functions, little attention is given to the judicial counterpart. The brief references to the courts are inherited from the 1961 Act. The omission of organisational detail is not in itself significant in that the Supreme Court's composition and powers are regulated by a separate organic statute. However, the omission symptomises inertia in the role of the South African courts in that the new Constitution does not, at a time of significant institutional change, enhance their public power. In this respect the norms of constitutionalism are not advanced. Again one encounters a fundamental principle of the Westminster constitutional system in the local setting.

The Constitution does portend a more prominent judicial function in certain respects. It expressly provides that the courts may supervise the legislative process, parliamentary rules and orders excepted, and although this power existed under the old Constitution, the new, more complex legislative procedure entails an enhanced scope of review. Changes are also implied by the existence of four legislative authorities within a single territorial jurisdiction and it is inconceivable that the courts should not be required to police their jurisdictional boundaries. All enactments of these bodies are of nominally equal legal status, which will require that the courts apply the lex posterior derogat priori principle to conflicting provisions, even where the earlier law is on general affairs and the later on own affairs. A more intrusive judicial role is implied by the repugnancy doctrine: the own affairs laws which are subject to norms and standards contained in general affairs laws will require restrictive interpretation and application by the courts.

These are, however, parsimonious accretions of judicial power. The absence of a bill of rights and a substantive yardstick against which to measure the validity of legislative and executive action entails, in the words of a leading commentator, a failure to 'strive towards the attainment of a higher constitutionality'.[9] In two crucial areas the Constitution leaves policy making legally unchecked and unbalanced. First, the State President has the exclusive competence to determine what are own affairs and to certify that a proposed amendment to a bill extends beyond the relevant group's own affairs. Secondly, once the procedural prerequisites have been satisfied the content and scope of legislation is unbounded. Legislative supremacy also entails that the executive can use Parliament instrumentally to obtain the extensive and largely unreviewable discretionary powers which characterise the modern administrative state. In these areas the courts cannot intervene in executive or legislative actions.

Intellectual support for the non-inclusion of a justifiable bill of rights was provided in the second constitutional report of the President's Council.[10] Paradoxically, the argument was couched partly in terms of this institution's incompatibility with parliamentary sovereignty, a basic feature of Westminster government. In addition, it was asserted that already in South Africa 'human rights are to a large extent protected by the substantive law and the law of procedure . . .', a rationalisation which the commentators rigorously exposed.[11] Despite its commitment to a group-rights thesis, the Government was not even prepared to allow any guaranteed own affairs for each of the participating groups. Instead, the Council recommended the

16

incorporation of certain principles in the preamble to the Constitution, a course which was subsequently followed, as were suggestions that provisions regulating the size and composition of the key institutions be entrenched.

One of the main political obstacles to a reviewable bill of rights is that it could not be non-discriminatory without subverting the institutional basis of the Constitution itself. Although Act 110 of 1983 contains few references to race or ethnicity, these are indispensable factors for the continuation of the system. Basic civil rights, such as due process or habeas corpus, are not conflictual with a group-based constitution, but would involve curtailments of executive power and an increased judicial role. The reform option in South Africa has been not only compatible with, but also partly dependent upon, the continuation of authoritarian patterns of government which do not permit increased power for the judiciary.

The judicial role could, however, be augmented by the courts themselves. In the first place, with the disruption in the unity of the legislative process and the shift of law-making power to committees, the doctrine of legislative supremacy could lose some of its mystique and sacrosanctity as far as the courts are concerned. Judicial autonomy was won in England in the 17th century once the courts had acknowledged the supremacy of a parliament rejuvenated after the clandestine committee-based rule of the Stuarts, during which it was forced into submission.[12] In South Africa, judicial autonomy is an established tradition and this might provide the basis for a more assertive judicial function vis-à-vis the modern committee-based system. In the second place, the uncertain definition and scope of parliamentary controls over the executive and in particular the likely adulteration of ministerial responsibility to which the courts have deferred in the past, might render the courts more assertive in reviewing and controlling executive power and developing principles of administrative law. Such developments have already materialised as a consequence of the litigious strategies of public interest law firms. In the third place, the shortcomings in the political institutions will result in more issues being packaged as legal problems for resolution by the courts. In at least one recent decision, the court acknowledged that deficiencies in political redress were a motivating reason for the court's predisposition to adjudicate on controversial issues. Therefore, while the prospects for constitutionalism are not demonstrably improved by the 1983 Constitution, the judicial role could be a hidden factor in its operation.

BLACK CONSTITUTIONAL ARRANGEMENTS

Homelands and citizenship

During the period under discussion the Government remained committed to the homelands programme, although a preoccupation with the non-Black Constitution caused a lull in its implementation. While a 'hidden agenda' hypothesis suggested that a fourth chamber for Blacks could be added to the tricameral Parliament, this was consistently denied by the Government and was never a realistic option. Official commitment to the homelands policy was evidenced by the events relating to KaNgwane and Ingwavuma in 1982 and 1983. Here the executive set in motion the cession of the KaNgwane homeland and parts of KwaZulu, together with their respective citizens, to the adjoining Kingdom of Swaziland, notwithstanding the opposition of the Black governments of the two territories. The initiative was suspended after the courts had invalidated various executive actions[13] and it was referred to a commission of enquiry, but the commission was subsequently disbanded and the project discontinued. The position in early 1985 was that four homelands had attained legal independence and the remaining six were at the second stage of self-government provided for in the Black States Constitution Act.

In certain matters judicial actions have led to the materialisation of the postponed consequences of the homelands system. In decisions on matters of jurisdiction and procedure, the legal independence of the national states became an established feature of South African law.[14] Moreover, after a period of vacillation on the issue, several judicial decisions applied the full legal consequences to the compulsory denationalisation of Black South Africans.[15] In both civil and criminal matters, homeland Blacks were depicted as foreign aliens and are subject to the deportation sanctions and visa requirements laid down in the Admission of Persons to the Republic Regulations Act 59 of 1972, where these are administratively applied. Some judgments have been criticised for adopting too restrictive and legalistic an interpretation of the relevant statutory provisions and in some matters inconsistent decisions have been taken by different courts. However, the indications are that the citizenship status of individuals will assume a more prominent legal-political role in the future.

Local government

Significant attention was given to Black local government during the course of the past three years. This was part of a revised official policy towards qualified urban Blacks in matters concerning residence, housing and employment. The Black Local Authorities Act 110 of 1982 came into effect in August 1983 and in general terms envisaged a Black municipal system similar to that for Whites. It provides for the phasing out of the over 200 community councils and their replacement by city, town or village

18

councils. The latter have greater status and autonomy than the former, deriving their powers directly from statute and not from the relevant minister. They also assume many functions formerly vested in the Administration Boards. However, the new bodies are still subject to Central Government supervision. The relevant minister establishes each council, determines its composition and area of jurisdiction and retains close control over numerous financial and other functions. The Administration Boards have been transformed into Development Boards which continue to exercise control functions with regard to urban Blacks, particularly in matters of township and housing development.

The first elections for the new village, town and city councils were held in late 1983 under voting criteria which were more liberal than previously: both nationals of independent homelands and contract workers were eligible to participate. Popular support for the councils, as measured by electoral registration and participation, was very low.[16] In the majority of elections, percentage polls were lower than those of the last elections for the corresponding community councils and it became apparent that despite the significant upgrading of their status, the new bodies had inherited the credibility problems experienced by their predecessors. This was comfirmed by the urban disturbances of 1984 and early 1985, when prominent councillors were often the targets of local residents. As a result many of the new councils ceased to function and this posed problems for the Government's higher-tier proposals for Blacks. The performance of the elected councils was adversely affected by their dependent and uncertain financial position and this led to renewed attention to possible revenue sources. Legitimacy and economic viability remain the twin vulnerabilities of the new Black local authorities.

New directions

While remaining committed to the above twin channels of Black constitutional development, the Government has recently shown greater flexibility in this area. This is a function of several factors, inter alia the intense pressure on the established institutions and contradictions between them. The special Cabinet Committee appointed in early 1983 to investigate the political status of urban Blacks (see above) became the main policy maker in this area. Thus, in late 1984 it was announced that the Western Cape would no longer be a Coloured labour preference area and that Blacks would be eligible for urban property rights. A more recent indication of Government thinking in this area was provided by the State President in his opening address to the 1985 Parliament.[17] The matters referred to indicate medium-term priorities for Government attention:

19

- *Co-operation with the independent national states within the multilateral dispensation will be extended so that the homeland governments are given a say regarding actions by the RSA that affect them.* This appears to refer to the constellation of states proposals which date back to 1979 but have fallen from prominence, apart from the establishment of the Development Bank of Southern Africa in 1983.
- *Independence will remain the goal for all self-governing homelands, but this will not be forced upon individual states and the granting of further stages of autonomy between self-government and independence will be considered.* While the first proposition reflects a basic rigidity in official thinking, the second suggests a re-evaluation of the principle of 'special status regions' advocated by the Quail (Ciskei) and Buthelezi Commissions, but at the time unfavourably received by the Government. Although the notion is not new even in official circles, it demonstrates the State's need for a way out of the impasse created by those homelands resisting the independence option, as well as problems of homeland consolidation and financial autonomy.
- *Structures must be developed for Black communities outside the national states through which they themselves can decide on their own affairs up to the highest level.* This is based on the Government's acceptance of the political inadequacy of local government structures for Blacks outside the national states. To this end an informal, non-statutory forum is to be established in which interest groups and representatives of government bodies can participate by invitation on an *ad hoc* basis. Although this recalls such failed institutions as the Native Representatives' Council and Black Citizens' Council, it could be used to generate a category of Black 'own affairs' for central regulation.
- *To avoid unnecessary fragmentation at the constitutional level, efforts will be made to co-operate on matters of common interest within the same overall framework with the various political entities that find themselves within the South African context.* This enigmatic statement appears to reflect official concern about the shortcomings of the homelands system and alludes to the constellation and regionalist policies favoured by the Government.
- *Clarity must be reached soon on the question of citizenship, the special Cabinet Committee being mandated to report on problems of terminology and content surrounding it.* These matters, however, were investigated by an earlier commission whose findings were not publicised. Substantial changes to Black nationality and citizenship arrangements would disturb the symmetry of the Government's constitutional policy and cannot, therefore, easily be envisaged, although the State President subsequently intimated that homeland independence need not, in the

future, entail automatic deprivation of citizenship.

On one hand these pronouncements testify to a continuing commitment to the fundamentals of Black constitutional arrangements, but on the other to increased Government flexibility and ambiguity in their evolution.

SUB-NATIONAL GOVERNMENT

Several steps were taken towards the reorganisation of regional and local government during the period under review, partially at the initiative of the President's Council and a nominated advisory Council for the Co-ordination of Local Government Affairs established in 1983.[18] At the local level, the statutory basis for a uniform system of government for Whites, Coloureds and Indians, based on separate voters' rolls and separate councils has been provided. The municipal franchise will be identical in each province. It extends to both natural and juristic persons and a multiple vote system weights it in favour of property owners and business. The system revolves around the concept of local 'own affairs' for each group and is based on the same principles which underlie the national Constitution for Whites, Coloureds and Indians. It could be operational by 1986. Reference has already been made to the separate system of Black local authorities and its current predicament.[19]

At the regional level, the anticipated demise of the provincial councils was finally announced in November 1984. Current proposals entail a network of Regional Service Councils throughout the country. Their jurisdiction and membership will be determined by the provincial administrators. While local authorities will be represented on the councils in proportion to their size and financial resources, no one body will be entitled to more than five members or 50% of the total vote. Although Black local authorities were excluded from the ambit of the 1984 draft bill, subsequent ministerial pronouncements indicated that the final enactment will make provision for them on the councils, although whether there will be sufficient to involve remains unclear. The proclaimed object of the Councils is to facilitate joint decision-making on affairs pertaining to more than one local authority (local general affairs) in the region or metropolitan area concerned. However, they are also a consequence of the practical difficulties inherent in institutionalising 'own affairs' at the local level. A parallel system of Black Development Boards (formerly Administration Boards) is already in operation and they are required, *inter alia*, to develop Black local government within the areas under their control.

Despite these developments, the status and significance of sub-national government remains unclear. In particular, questions of financial resources, political and administrative relationships with Central Government and the nature and extent of regional and local policy making remain to be determined. There is also uncertainty as to the extent of decentralisation it will provide. Nevertheless, the activity at this level has resurrected the federal debate in South Africa and there have been recent indications that the Government is reconsidering the Buthelezi Commission recommendation of an autonomous Natal-KwaZulu entity within the Republic as an alternative to its regional policies.

THE STATE AND ITS SUBJECTS

No overview of the living constitution in South Africa can neglect referring to State-subject relationships, since issues of civil liberty are axiomatic to modern constitutional government. The absence of a bill of rights in the new Constitution already alluded to has deprived the relationship of the courts' mediating role. The most important State powers in this area were consolidated in the 1982 Internal Security Act, which now provides a statutory and administrative framework for the control of individuals, organisations, gatherings, publications and other politically-related activities. It introduced various administrative safeguards for those affected by State actions, but in many instances judicial remedies were expressly precluded. A rudimentary index of the use of the power conferred by the Act is provided by the number of authorised detentions: 181 persons in 1982, 238 in 1983 and 339 in 1984. These figures are significantly lower than those for 1980 and 1981, but the difference is offset by an increase in homeland detentions and the use of other devices, such as the denial of bail to accused persons for long periods. Invariably, those on the receiving end of such actions are outside existing constitutional structures, whether by statutory exclusion or their own volition. While all conflict is not constitutionally structured, coercive measures will continue to be necessary to stabilise the State system.

Apart from security-related matters, State control over the movement and residence of Black subjects has been the most focal area of civil liberties concerned. Here the Government has continued to enforce its resettlement and influx control policies, the two most contentious forms of Black control. It was officially revealed in early 1985 that over 160 000 Blacks had been arrested in the previous year for pass offences[20] and other sources have computed that about three million Blacks have been resettled during the past two decades.[21] Both these realities present a direct challenge to the constitutional reform process. For those affected the Constitution is fundamentally authoritarian, since they experience the sharpest edge of State power without any participation in or control over it. In both areas, however, reforms have been propounded. A reinvestigation of influx control measures has been in progress for some time and their enforcement has been transferred from administrative bodies to the regular lower courts pursuant to the recommendation of a commission of enquiry into the court system. A tentative moratorium on the forced removal and resettlement of Black persons has also been proclaimed. The significance of these measures will depend on future developments in Black urban rights, political institutions and homeland consolidation.

Within the parameters of their competence the South African courts have given several civil liberty-oriented decisions. In this they are able to draw on common law principles as developed by the judges, at times in apparent defiance of parliamentary intent. Ironically, one of the most prominent decisions involved the interpretation of the Bophuthatswana Bill of Rights, where the Appellate Division refuted often-expressed concern that it would adopt a restrictively positivist approach to such matters. There is also evidence of judicial activism in other areas where the State has acquired vast discretionary powers — the control of Black movement and residence, individual liberty and the provision of benefits.[22] However, executive-minded decisions are also apparent. Ultimately the courts lack the institutional basis and normative orientation for developing civil rights on a systematic and consistent basis.

THEMES OF CONTINUITY AND DISCONTINUITY IN CONSTITUTIONAL DEVELOPMENT

South Africa's recent constitutional development displays a complex farrago of conflicting and reinforcing themes.

At the *structural* level, the 1983 Constitution can be seen on one hand as the continuation, or even culmination, of grand apartheid policy in its political dimension. The Constitution not only excludes Blacks from the parliamentary franchise, but self-evidently complements the homelands political structures and implicitly precludes the future incorporation of Blacks on its existing terms. It has not only evolved out of the institutions of separate development, but is based on the same justificatory theory and purports to be the ultimate institutional expression of self-determination for the participating groups. On the other hand, the new Constitution itself has exposed the inconsistencies in that theory. The contingent nature of the own affairs concept undermines the principle of self-autonomy and thereby the rationale for much of the institutional superstructure. Moreover, just as the design-board symmetry of the 1983 Constitution and homelands system could be demonstrated, key aspects of the latter became discredited, even from the official vantage. These included consolidation, resettlement, influx control, citizenship and even independence. As the apartheid State was fulfilled at the legal-institutional level, so deeper organic forces in the political economy caused the elimination or at least undermining of separatism in many areas of social and economic life. If the 1983 Constitution is the last phase of political apartheid, it is juxtaposed with the first stage of social and economic integration. It has opened the mainstream political process to Coloureds and Indians and provides a rudimentary basis for power-sharing among these groups and Whites. It simultaneously fulfils and contradicts the premises of separate development.

From a historical perspective, the 1983-5 developments are notable for addressing, in the most formal sense, the *franchise issue*. In taking the highly symbolic step of extending parliamentary participation to Coloureds and Indians, the dominant group has conceded that the franchise should avail all inhabitants, regardless of race or colour. However, the overall institutional context within which electoral rights are exercised entails vast discrepancies in their weight and significance, particularly between Blacks and non-Blacks, but also between Whites, Coloureds and Indians. In relation to comparative constitutional developments in Africa, the Republic is at the 'fancy franchise' stage of political incorporation. Thus, with 42% of the members of the tricameral Parliament, the National Party is able to control the legislative and executive functions and vast areas of the administrative state; this control could endure until its strength declines to 29% and the plurality electoral system entails that this might constitute a much smaller percentage of direct electoral support. Conversely, other participants have no institutional means to challenge or obstruct the dominant group, although they can make its unilateral exercise of power more costly. This determinant of constitutional reform was candidly conceded by the President's Council when it indicated that reform should not threaten the institutional position of the dominant group.[23] This inherently contradictory factor resulted in both the extension of democratic participation and the retention of residual powers for crisis management.

The new Constitution is predicated on normative standards of consensus and consociational patterns of policy making. However, its implementation was attended by extensive social upheavals, some of which could be attributed to the Constitution itself (in its comprehensive sense). The new terrain led to political realignments among White political parties and among Coloureds and Indians it caused divisions between participants and non-participants and among the participants. For those excluded from its ambit it constituted a negative factor of unification, most notably in a loose political alliance, the United Democratic Front (UDF), which by definition has been in extra-parliamentary opposition to the system. Generally there

24

has been a dialectical relationship between the emerging Constitution and the political process — while the Constitution has attempted to restructure political claims, it has been subjected to intense pressures by various claimants and has generated a range of new claims in which it has become a focal issue. As far as policy-making is concerned, it is notable that in respect of own affairs consensus is not an institutional requirement and in respect of general affairs it will be a concessional, but not a negotiational outcome. The flexibility in its structures and processes entails that power-sharing among participating groups could materialise, but that the institutional basis for strong, decisive and non-consensual government remains. Consensus and consociationalism are features of the prescriptive rather than the legal-institutional plane.

Finally, one of the consistently proclaimed intentions of recent constitutional changes has been to effect a systematic *decentralisation* of authority throughout the political system, whereas several of the institutional changes presage greater centralisation of power. The list of own affairs of each House and Ministers' Council entailed the eventual emasculation of the provincial system, the abolition of which will occur in 1986 after a history of 76 years. Centralisation of functions, in the context of growing corporatism and administrative power, entails increasing executive sovereignty in South Africa. The proposals for sub-national government referred to above are all premised on the need for a future devolution of administrative and policy-making functions. However, closer analysis reveals that the newly-constituted Indian and Coloured local authorities will have to surrender to a Regional Services Council (RSC) any function which the Council decides to exercise itself and that there is a potential conflict in the division of functions between the RSCs and national own affairs. Effective control will be retained by Pretoria in the person of the Minister of Constitutional Development and Planning, the extent of such power being reflected in the decision to defer all local government elections until 1988. Moreover, the system will be based on Central Government policies of separate development and its statutory adjuncts, such as the Group Areas Act. The reform/control paradox is also evident in this area. The system seems less concerned with the decentralisation of functions from national to sub-national level than with the rationalisation and co-ordination of the functions of a plurality of local bodies at the supra-local level.

The most consistent feature of recent constitutional developments is their indeterminancy. Factors of legitimacy, effectiveness, fiscal reality and economic imperatives will determine the constitutional progressions which succeed them.

25

NOTES

1 For the purposes of this chapter, the author has taken note of events up until 15 April 1985.
2 See *Social Indicator*, vol. 2, no. 3, 1984, pp. 8-11.
3 Cf R Schrire's paper *Decision-Making and the Constitution*, which was presented at the HSRC Symposium on the Constitution of the RSA in Pretoria 1985.
4 Cf Dean, WHB. The Government's Constitution Proposals 1982 in Dean and Van Zyl Smit (1983: 90 at 102 ff.).
5 Namely not to allow four South Africans to return to Britain to stand trial on charges of export control violations in retaliation for the British Government's refusal to terminate the occupation of its Durban consulate by six political activists.
6 The Kannemeyer Commission of Inquiry into police shootings at Uitenhage, Govt. Not. No. R 726, *Government Gazette* 9 674, 22 March 1985 and see *House of Assembly Debates*, vol. 9, col. 2 825-9, 22 March 1985.
7 Lees and Shaw (1979: 383 ff.).
8 The committees comprise 23 members, seven of whom are from the National Party. However, nine others are from its junior coalition parties and only seven are from the opposition parties.
9 See *House of Assembly Debates*, vol. 4, col. 1 108-9, 19 February 1985.
10 Wiechers, M. Constitutional requirements for an open society in *Codicillus*, vol. xxiv, no. 1, 1980.
11 PC 4/1982, 70-77.
12 Cf Boulle (1983: 182).
13 See Aylmer (1975: 213, 229).
14 *Government of KwaZulu v Government of the RSA* 1982 (1) SA 387 (D); *Government of the RSA v Government of KwaZulu* 1983 (1) SA 163 (A).
15 *S v Maseki* 1981 (4) SA 374 (T); *S v Magxwalisa and others* 1984 (2) SA 313 (N); cf *ex parte Registrar of the Supreme Court, Bophuthatswana* 1980 (1) SA 572 (BSC).
16 *Ex parte Moseneke* 1979 (4) SA 884 (T); *SA Television Manufacturing Co v Jabati and others* 1983 (2) SA 14 (E); *Minister of Police v Magida* 1984 (3) SA 102 (E).
17 SAIRR *Survey of Race Relations*, Johannesburg: SAIRR, 1983.
18 *House of Assembly Debates*, vol. 1, col. 14-16, 25 January 1985.
19 Cf the *Promotion of Local Government Affairs Act*, 1983 (Act 91 of 1983).
20 By January 1985, elections had been held for 34 Black local authorities under the 1982 Act (*House of Assembly Debates*, vol. 7, col. 617, 14 March 1985), but at the time of writing no more than six were still operating.
21 *House of Assembly Questions and Replies*, vol. 7, col. 563-5, 12 March 1985.
22 In early 1985 a comprehensive work on influx control — *Up Against the Fences* by H Giliomee and L Schlemmer — was published. It argues from a reformist perspective that it is impossible to soften or deracialise influx control and that the system should be abolished.
23 *S v Marwane* 1982 (3) SA 717 (A).
24 Amongst these, the decision in *Oos-Randse Administrasieraad en 'n ander v Rikhoto* 1983 (3) SA 585 (A) was pre-eminent. As a consequence, 24 330 Blacks were granted section 10 rights in 1984 — see *House of Assembly Questions and Replies*, vol. 5, col. 303-4, 26 February 1984.
25 PC 4/1982, 54.

BIBLIOGRAPHY

Aylmer, GE. *The Struggle for the Constitution.* (4 ed.) London: Blandford Press, 1975.

Baxter, LG. *Administrative Law*. Cape Town: Juta and Company, 1984.

Booysen, D and Van Wyk, D. *Die '83 Grondwet*. Durban: Butterworth, 1984.

Boulle, LJ. *South African and the Consociational Option — A Constitutional Analysis*. Cape Town: Juta and Company, 1984.

Centre for Applied Social Studies *Social Indicator*, vol. 2, no. 3, 1984.

— *Social Indicator*, vol 2, no. 4, 1985.

Dean, WHB and Van Zyl Smit, D. *Constitutional Change in South Africa — The Next Five Years*. Cape Town: Juta and Company, 1983.

Forsyth, M. *Federalism and the Future of South Africa*. (Barlow Series Paper.) Johannesburg: South African Institute of International Affairs, 1984.

Giliomee, H and Schlemmer, L. *Up Against the Fences — Poverty, Passes and Privilege in South Africa*. Cape Town: David Philip, 1985.

Lees, J and Shaw, M. *Committees in Legislatures*. Oxford: Martin Robertson, 1979.

President's Council, South Africa. *Local and Regional Management Systems in the Republic of South Africa*, Cape Town (1982) (PC 1/1982);

Worrall, D. (Chairman.) *First Report of the Constitutional Committee*, Cape Town (1982) (PC 3/1982).

Van der Merwe, SW. (Chairman.) *The Adaptation of Constitutional Structures in South Africa*, Cape Town (1982) (PC 4/1982).

Van der Merwe SW. (Chairman.) *The Adaptation of Constitutional Structures in South Africa — Final Report*, Cape Town (1984) (PC 4/1984).

The Buthelezi Commission, South Africa, Schreiner, GDL. (Chairman) *The Requirements for Stability and Development in KwaZulu and Natal*, Durban, 1982.

South African Institute of Race Relations. *Survey of Race Relations*. Johannesburg: SAIRR, 1983.

South African Research Service. *South African Review I and II*. Johannesburg: South African Research Service, 1983 and 1984.

Saul, J and Gelb, J. *The Crisis in South Africa — Class Defence, Class Revolution*. New York: Monthly Review Press, 1981.

Schrire, R. *Decision-Making and the Constitution*. (Paper presented at HSRC Symposium on the Constitution of the RSA). Pretoria: 1985.

Stultz, N. *Interpreting Constitutional Change in South Africa*. New Haven: Yale University, 1983. (Unpublished paper.)

Van der Vyver, J. *Die Grondwet van die Republiek van Suid-Afrika*. Johannesburg: Lex Patria, 1984.

Van Vuuren, DJ, et al. *Change in South Africa*. Durban: Butterworths, 1983.

Van Wyk, DH. 'n 'Nuwe' Grondwet vir Suid-Afrika. *Codicillus* 40, vol. xxiv, no. 2, 1983.

— The New Constitution: Some Unresolved Questions. *SA Yearbook of International Year*, 104, 1983.

Wiechers, M. Constitutional requirements for an open society. *Codicillus* 40, vol. xxiv, no. 1, 1983.

27

2 Political reform in South Africa

DJ van Vuuren

INTRODUCTION

Societal change or reform is a practical reality in South Africa and may be analysed and compared by the constitutional legal analysis of formal documents such as the Constitution of the Republic of South Africa Act, 1983 (Act 110 of 1983), as amended. However, reform implies more than merely the formal, institutional aspects which come strongly to the fore in such documents and therefore the analysis of these is only partially satisfactory.

The dynamic concept of a transitional political system provides a more accurate model of political reality and has been dealt with in greater depth by scientists such as Almond, Easton, Coleman, Verba, Pye, Powell and Wiseman. Blondel also recognises the importance of this concept.

Important aspects that emerge from this approach are the emphasis on the functional in juxtaposition with the institutional on one hand and the analysis of more traditional communities in contrast with modern communities on the other. Concepts such as state, government and nation, which could otherwise be applied only to modern communities, are now replaced by concepts of a more universal nature (e.g. action, behaviour and political culture) because, according to Almond (1963:7), all systems suffer from similar problems, namely international accommodation, internal segregation, the mobilisation of resources and participation and distribution. Almond and Powell (1966:218-219) therefore state that although it is difficult to analyse this process in primitive political systems, the functions of a political system exist and are carried out nevertheless (see also Coetzee 1985:26).

In order to operationalise the political system approach, attention must be paid to *action* (i.e. empirically discernible political behaviour) and the norms or institutions that affect this behaviour. Political behaviour comprises the deeds and actions of a person who plays a specific political role. More specifically, it concerns political actions, convictions, motivations, attitudes and values. In addition, it includes the actor's perception of the role allocated to him, of what society's norms for such actors are (i.e. what it demands from the actors) and of the interrelationship between actors, decision makers and society.

The unique identity of a political system lies in its monopoly on the physical power to maintain law and order in a specific area. Almond defines a political system as '. . . the patterned interaction of roles affecting decisions backed up by the threat of physical compulsion' (Almond 1956:395).

Also important is the *orientation* of political action. Any political system has a characteristic pattern of orientation for political action. This pattern consists of distinct components, namely perception or cognition; preference, involvement, or effect; and evaluation or choice through the application of standards or values to the cognitive and effective components. Almond (1956:396) calls it the political culture. Pye (1965:5) lays particular stress on political culture as a phenomenon with a view to a general theoretical framework. Verba (in Pye and Verba 1965:513) also emphasises political culture (in a narrower sense) as part of the political system, for it incorporates empirical convictions, exposed symbols and values within which political actions take place. Institutions are not excluded and it is rightly admitted that a close relationship exists between culture and institutions (see Almond and Powell 1966:18 and Wiseman 1966:33).

Wiseman (1966:34) summarises the concept of political culture in an operational sense. He states that it investigates the orientation of individuals in respect of the general political system (patriotism or alienation) and the various components of the political system (the specific roles or structures of, for example, the legislative authority; the executive authority, bureaucracy and political parties; the office bearers; and specific directions of policy, decisions and implementations — that is the input and output process). It also investigates the individual's views on rights, powers and obligations.

Three types of political culture may be distinguished, namely parochial, subordinate and participating cultures. In any of these we find attitudes of loyalty, apathy or alienation which, as will become evident later, can be related to political stability.

In view of the above one must take note of Western political culture in the South African context. This political culture (which has become the dominant one in South Africa) developed over several centuries and created the *national state* distinct from other subsystems. An important feature in the origin and development of the national state, especially the democratic form of government, was the restriction of the arbitrary powers of the absolute monarchs of the 17th and 18th centuries. Restrictions may be given legal status in the form of constitutions.

29

Closely connected with the above and another important characteristic of Western political culture is the restriction on the wielding of authority in the political sphere effected by the division of government functions into executive, legislative and juridical institutions. This institutional division does not, however, prevent dictatorial and totalitarian conduct. A parallel development is the territorial division of government functions, which finds expression in the federal form of government. This is, in essence, democratic, but is also characteristic of a dictatorship.

In addition, the Western political culture (and the development of the state from an initially undifferentiated classification of society) is characterised by the increasing importance of the state (both unitary and federal). The State can be employed as a means of promoting certain values of a comprehensive nature — in the political and socio-economic sense — which include both democracy and dictatorship. Therefore in terms of Almond and Verba's classification, it may be either a participating culture with a democratic political structure, or a subordinate culture with a centralised authoritarian structure.

In the case of a democracy, we are dealing with a specific form of authority which expresses rights and liberties in a particular way. They are spelled out, for example, in the Universal Declaration of Human Rights (1948), the International Treaty concerning Economic, Social and Cultural Rights (1966) and the International Treaty concerning Civil and Political Rights (1966). These documents give us an idea of the individual's rights and liberties, which include physical and juridical rights; rights referring to the individual and the community; religious rights and liberties; political rights; and social, economic and cultural rights.

Apart from the individualistic liberal-humanist element which came strongly to the fore, the exercising of these rights must also be seen within the group context. Compare, for example the Capotorti Report (1979) and Van Dyke's view (1974:729-741) that groups often have status and rights within the State regarding politics and groups, the law and the administration of justice, education and culture, property ownership and residence and economic opportunity.

In their original forms, the political cultures of Africa and certain parts of Asia differ radically from the above. Coetzee (1985:26) points out that Southern Africa is characterised by traditional communities having very little central order and no clearly recognisable and distinguishable institution or person in authority. In these groups communality exists in a common language and culture and the size of the unit often varies. However, communities such as the tribe are also to be found. These inhabit their own areas, have arrangements regarding law and order and a figure of authority, namely a tribal head, who fulfils a variety of roles which collectively bring about the creation and maintenance of order (Coetzee 1985:28). The tribal head is assisted by a tribal council, the composition of which may vary from tribe to tribe. Coetzee maintains that 'draft legislation' is initiated and deliberated on by this tribal council, which has, therefore, a distinguishable controlling function (1985:32). An important feature is the fact that the paramount chief (who holds the highest office) nevertheless governs by means of consensus.

In Southern Africa the trend has been and still is towards a consolidation of tribes, a development which can be attributed to the efforts of tribal leaders and external factors such as colonisation. However, despite consolidation, the decision-making process remained the same as it had been for separate tribes. The most important characteristics of the process must surely be that decision making was by means of consensus (opposing parties did not occur); that if differences continued the results were fatal; that officialdom traditionally related to the royal family and high offices were inherited; and that legislation was not an important function — action was taken within the framework of legal tradition as a result of discussion and decision making. The *trias politica* did not develop and the political system is not characterised by renewal and change (Coetzee 1985:37-38).

Under colonial rule, with the exception of France, these regions were governed separately (the inhabitants were treated as subordinates) and not on an integrated basis so that the traditional communities could gain experience of democracy and the process of democratisation of the West (Coetzee 1985: 39). According to Almond and Verba, therefore, the main type of political culture was the parochial-participating type.

In my handling of the political system of South Africa, attention is paid to convictions, values and structures and it is shown that the initial paradigm undergoes a change (to become more in line with generally accepted Western values). Groups having different political cultures are accommodated in one political system, confirming their existing economic accommodation and upward mobility in the West-orientated structures. However, before discussing the South African situation it is necessary, first, to draw attention to the problems of change.

THE PROBLEMS OF CHANGE

The political scientist finds it difficult to explain how Western democratic procedures and values and modern political institutions may be transferred to new environments. Certain patterns are recognisable, for example the emergence of an elite culture and a mass culture and a fusion of these two. In some instances the distinction between rural and urban segments is maintained, as is the case in developed and developing regions. Political culture may also be adjusted by means of the deliberate manipulation of values.

Pye points out that the process of development does not simply entail a lessening of traditional behavioural patterns and an increase in rationality and efficiency:

> The problems of development, viewed in terms of political culture, involve less the gross elimination of old patterns and values and more the successful discovery of how traditions can contribute to, and not hamper, the realisation of current national goals. Effective political development thus requires that a proper place be found for many traditional considerations in the more modern scheme of things (Pye 1965:19, see also Binder et al 1971:53).

In political theory, concepts of change presuppose linear development. However, although he admits that there are indications of a change of system in respect of some developments, for various reasons Almond (1963:3-6) rejects linear development (see also Lowenthal in Ehrmann 1965:177-178 and Almond and Powell 1966:215). He points out that political systems do not necessarily have similar problems and that problems are not necessarily of the same order or intensity and may be solved in different ways. He is of the opinion that the systematic characteristics of political systems — their structural, cultural and performance properties — are determined by the way in which problems or challenges are encountered and experienced and that change can be brought about by internal or external pressure.

More recent studies confirm the view that the process of change is not at all easy to explain and that the uniqueness of each situation must be accepted (see Coleman in Binder et al 1971:74; Stulz 1983:288 and Emmett in Kotze 1983:23-50).

The South African situation illustrates Verba's view that certain political/cultural aspects are important in a situation of change (Verba in Pye and Verba 1965:529-543). These are national identity, identification with fellow-citizens and expectations and the nature of the decision-making process (see also Pye 1965:22-23 and Binder et al 1971:53). The process of national integration is therefore closely connected with these aspects and theoretical deliberation on political development and stability is usually from the perspective of the integrative process within states. Lijphart (1971:4-9) points out that according to virtually all theories on integration, cultural homogeneity is more conducive than cultural diversity to a stable democracy. He cites the research by Deutsch (1953), Northrop (1954), Almond (1956, 1963 and 1966), Coser (1956), Lipset (1963), Truman (1951), Binder (1964) and Coleman and Rosberg (1964) to substantiate his argument. Even Haas (1958), who initially held the view that the process of community formation in the North Atlantic region was promoted by economic pragmatism, later (1967) recognised the importance of normative aspects.

Etzioni (1965) propounds that a common culture is not necessarily a prerequisite for unification, because certain cultural traits may not be politically relevant. As examples of national communities which do not have a common culture, he quotes Canada, South Africa, Switzerland, Belgium, Nigeria and India. According to Lijphart (1971:7), however, of all these states only Switzerland's political unity is not threatened by a fragmented culture. And although Etzioni does not consider a common culture to be a prerequisite for unification, he does regard it as vital to the promotion of the process.

In their analysis of federations, Wheare (1964) and Riker (1964) do not deviate much from common norms as an important factor for integration. Rhoodie (1982:483) also refers to this concept, but arrives at the conclusion that, calculated purely in terms of probability, a territorial consociational federation of the asymmetrical type is the only democratic pluralistic system that has any chance of successful implementation in South Africa.

Lijphart (1971:9) posits that theoretical deliberation on political stability (in which a distinction is made between elite and mass political culture) deviates from the negative views above in that stability is possible in culturally fragmented systems, provided that the leaders of the subcultures pledge themselves to co-operation. He calls this pattern of mass culture and elite behaviour *consocialism* and analyses Austria (second Republic), Switzerland, the Netherlands, Belgium and the Lebanon in terms of this. Lijphart extended this model still further (see his contributions in 1975, 1977 and 1981). Contributions towards a model of a plural society were made by *inter alia* Van den Berghe, Bekker, Kuper, Furnivall, Smith, Conner, Glazer, Friedrich and Horowitz as well. In a study on community autonomy in Estonia, Cyprus and Belgium, Cloete (1984) also points out the possibility of reducing conflict in a democractic manner in an ethnic, plural society.

In the literature on the developing states with fragmented cultures this model is held up as a possibility, especially where there are obvious problems in the functioning of the Western democratic national state as far as structural (executive, legislative and juridical) and value-orientated (individualism, equality, liberty and popular sovereignty) aspects are concerned.

The realisation of democratic values among developing peoples in both individualistic or group contexts varies. A comparative study of the analyses of the constitutions of these states, as quoted in the Europa

33

Yearbook, indicates that for the democratic unitary system in Northern, Central and Southern Asia, a parliamentary form of government is more applicable. Preference is given to one-chamber, proportional electoral and multi-party systems. Most states are republics and are orientated towards capitalism.

The democracies in Africa, on the other hand, are characterised by parliamentary, extra-parliamentary or mixed forms of government, one-chamber and geographic electoral systems. These democracies generally have multi-party systems and are, on the whole, republics. Restricted democracies such as those in Egypt, Uganda, South Africa, Transkei and Venda, are also found.

Pye (1966:87) has a negative attitude towards the realisation of democracy in the new states. Linz (1978:62) also has his doubts and considers consociation to be a possible solution. The problems concerning these states include *inter alia* the matter of original loyalties, i.e. the question of internal integration referred to above (see Apter 1968:55; Linz 1978:62; Lowenthal in Ehrmann 1965:198; and Ake 1967:1-16). South Africa, with its complex society, presents a unique problem. The Western political model and the recognition and realisation of rights and liberties (see above) demand loyalty in the wider national context which must at least also be realised in a consociational context, whether unitary or federal.

Naturally, there are states in Northern, Central and Southern Asia which do not advocate and express democratic values. This is also true of states in the Middle East and Africa. In the latter, for example, there are 14 one-party dictatorships and 20 military governments.

Change (a central problem in political theory) is constantly part of the democratic process. In this regard, Neumann (in Ehrmann 1965:9-21) points out the importance of popular sovereignty, the shift of power between presidential, parliamentary and extra-parliamentary institutions, a free choice between alternative directions in policy, a governing party's ability to absorb the ideas of its opponents, the necessity for responsible leadership which must take increasing account of pressure groups (extra-parliamentary), the maintenance of supreme power, the amendment of undesirable legislation through representation and direct action (but also by means of anticipatory adjudication), the role of the party rather than other elements to change the voter into a *zoon-politikon* (a problem among the developing nations), the recognition of the plural nature of the society and the inclusion of all in the process of change and the involvement of the individual and the recognition of his rights and liberties.

Change may also promote destabilisation and important questions in this regard are the relationship between stability and certain values and whether there is a connection between social and economic requirements for the institutionalisation and maintenance of democracy. The matter of the level of political differences, attitudes and structures should also be considered.

The above aspects are all closely related to development in South Africa and the creation of a new political culture.

THE SOUTH AFRICAN SITUATION: 1910-1976

As was pointed out earlier, in South Africa we have to contend with both developed and developing political cultures (see Pye and Verba 1965:15). In addition to factors such as language, race and ethnicity, level of development complicates the South African situation. The White and his Western political culture initially showed — as far as survival was concerned — little faith in the other population groups in the country. This led to the development of a hierarchical political system in which the Non-White was in a subordinate position. Political and civil rights (in a certain sense) on the basis of equality was unacceptable to the Whites, especially the Afrikaners, who gained positions of power. The political system was not characterised by identification with the Non-Whites, but by segregation and apartheid that was enforced by statutory measures.

Important characteristics of the system are separate areas for the different population groups, the control of the influx of Blacks from their areas to the so-called White areas and control over the movements of Blacks in the White areas, non-recognition of the permanence of Blacks outside their own areas, the introduction of separate voters' rolls (for Blacks in 1936 and for Coloureds in 1955) and the creation of political institutions with limited powers and functions in Black areas.

Thus, Non-White access to the general political process in 'White areas' was blocked. However, the conduct of the Blacks since the inauguration of Union in 1910 has, in a certain sense, been characterised by a national awareness in the sense that *Blacks consider themselves to be part of the South African political system and believe that, as such, they have certain rights.* Thus, by means of an instrument of Western political culture — the political party — they oppose the legislation that hampers their political freedom and their freedom of movement.

However, the national awareness among Blacks described above does not necessarily mean that they identify with the country's other citizens. For example, the concerns of the South African Native National Congress (1912) were the handling of Black political and socio-economic interests and Black unity (see Kotze 1975:4-5). With its change of name to the African National Congress (ANC) in 1925 came a change in its concerns — apart from opposition to Government policy (which advocates White exclusivity) — to Black exclusivity (compare the objectives of the All Africa Convention (1935) and the Youth League of the ANC, which operate within the frame of reference of Black nationalism and socialism (instead of individualism)). This illustrates that values, attitudes and political differences that are directly opposed — and therefore prejudicial to stability — are to be found in South Africa. The Coloureds and Indians were obviously part of the hierarchical political system at this stage (compare the Coloureds' position in the Transvaal and the OFS and that of the Indians in Natal).

When the National Party came to power in 1948, the White Government endeavoured to strengthen these separation measures politically, economically and socially. Consider, for example, the Population Registration Act, 1950 (Act 30 of 1950) as amended, the Black Homelands Citizenship Act, 1970 (Act 26 of 1970) and subsequent legislation, the Prohibition of Mixed Marriages Act, 1949 (Act 55 of 1949), the Immorality Act, 1950 (Act 21 of 1950) as amended and the Group Areas Act, 1950 (Act 41 of 1950) as amended.

The indirect representation which Blacks had had in the White Parliament came to an end in 1959. Democracy (values and institutions) thus occur mainly within the group context, with recognition of the traditional political culture.

Eventually, this led to the creation of the Black national states, some of which have since gained independence (i.e. Transkei, Bophuthatswana, Venda and Ciskei). The rest (i.e. Lebowa, Gazankulu, KwaNdebele, Kangwane, Qwaqwa and KwaZulu) now have self-governing status.

The explicit (theoretical) object of this exercise was not to expand the limited democracy of the Whites over the whole of South Africa, but to effect separate freedoms (see Verwoerd in *Hansard*, 27/1/1959, columns 64-70) in accordance with the principle of groups' right of self-determination. This action evoked violent reaction abroad because it was seen as a violation of the basic human rights as laid down by the Charter of the United Nations (articles 55 and 56) — compare India's conduct at various sessions of the United Nations. Locally, too, the National Party Government's policy and the recognition given to the traditional political culture as a point of departure for change elicited Black reaction.

This reaction included a greater inclusivity (more noticeable among Non-Whites at present), which may be seen in the convening of the Congress of the People (1953), which involved both Indians and Coloureds and the creation of the Freedom Charter, in which Whites and political parties such as the Communist Party of South Africa were also involved. In 1958 the ANC declared itself in favour of a multiracial society based on friendship, equal rights and mutual respect. This illustrates, more clearly than during the period before 1948, an 'identification' with fellow citizens in South Africa. This attitude is also illustrated by further developments such as the All-in Conference of 1960, which included Whites, Coloureds and Indians. Such nationalism and identification with fellow citizens cannot, however, be interpreted as illustrative of a common political culture — the values of the various groups are too divergent, a characteristic which does not promote stability — as was proved by, among other things, actions towards a multiracial convention in 1961.

Despite the trend towards inclusivity among Non-Whites, the tendency towards exclusivity continued by way of a radical movement among the ANC youth which advocated Black domination and eventually led to the foundation of the Pan Africanist Congress (PAC), which officially expounded its objectives as full citizenship for Blacks, a multiracial South Africa, Black independence and a United States of Africa. A further radical movement under the PAC (Poqo) is a purely Black organisation which advocates a socialist democratic state. The movement also evinces the break with the objectives of the 'modern' and the more traditional Black. In reality, it opposes the traditional elements. (See Swanepoel in Kotze 1983:97-113), in which the matter of Black communalism and its connection with Black consciousness, which plays an important role in the Blacks' future vision of South Africa, is discussed.)

As far as the Coloureds and Indians were concerned, the Whites continued to implement the hierarchical system — with the difference that these two groups did not have to and could not realise their group rights within an own territory, as was the case with the Blacks.

In a way this political system was acceptable to the Coloureds and Indians, for, despite maintaining an own identity, they had consistently identified themselves with a national objective which included all groups.

In the economic sphere, the different population groups became more and more integrated. However, insofar as Non-White involvement is concerned, the economic system is characterised by differentiation and therefore discrimination which, in addition to existing ethnic and cultural differences, also promotes differences in prosperity. For example, the Erika Theron Commission (see Terblanche 1977:20-30) found that Coloureds in the upper income group experience more problems than those in the lower group and that certain statutory measures entail a real and/or potential loss of a material nature. The Commission also found that an important problem for Coloureds is their lack of effective participation in the decision-making process, which results in their being unable to bargain effectively for improvement in their socio-economic position.

Despite a generally positive attitude, the Commission highlighted various problems to do with work opportunities and conditions of service, employment, training and remuneration in the institutional labour market, in which about 50% of Coloureds find themselves (Terblanche 1977:35-53).

Regarding the natural labour market, in which no significant labour arrangements and government institutions exist, the Commission found that the poor wages and employment positions of low-income Coloureds could be attributed to personal, institutional and circumstantial factors. Personal factors include voluntary unemployment, work-shyness, a high turnover of labour, idleness, unreliability, etc. Institutional and circumstantial factors include poor housing conditions, vast distances between home and place of work, inadequate transport facilities, scholastic and technical inadequacy and lack of in-service training (Terblanche 1977:91).

Subsequent commissions of inquiry, namely the Riekert Commission (1979), the Wiehahn Commission (1979, 1980) and the Strydom Commission (1983), identified problems that impede the achievement of prosperity not only by Coloureds, but also by other Non-White groups. These include poor vertical and horizontal mobility, wage levels, the restriction of economic growth and development in certain regions and sectors, job reservation and poor training (or the lack thereof and therefore a shortage of skilled manpower).

To summarise: Due to their developed, differentiated culture and technical development, Whites have at their disposal the political structures and the power to enforce their values (at least in the areas that they occupy). In the Black areas, the Western state serves as structural model. Citizens of colour were treated unequally in both the political and economic spheres in White areas. They were not accepted in the political sense and Whites did not identify with persons of colour. Economically, Non-Whites were undoubtedly part of the system, a fact which was both advantageous and disadvantageous to them.

THE NEW PARADIGM: 1976-1985

Socio-economic development among Blacks, Coloureds and Indians can be seen to be an important determinant in the realisation of the new paradigm — in fact, this development is already part of the new paradigm.

In South Africa there is upward socio-economic mobility. Suchard (1984: 195) points out that the gap between Black and White incomes is narrowing in four sectors, namely the mining industry, construction, agriculture and manufacture. He compares Black and White incomes during the years 1960, 1970, 1973 and 1975 and comes to the conclusion that a redistribution of prosperity among Blacks and Whites is taking place. He points out, however, that this positive trend is negated by rapid population growth and widespread unemployment among Blacks. During the years mentioned above, Blacks were the only people to obtain any real increase in income and Suchard ascribes this phenomenon to higher wages, increased skills and promotion to better-paid work. If this redistribution continues, Blacks should receive the highest percentage total personal income by the turn of the century (Suchard 1984: 199). Therefore, the urban Black's income will increase and the concomitant improvement in his life-style will be accompanied by increased expenditure on sophisticated consumer goods and housing. Already, Blacks have an increasing share in the market (see also De Klerk 1984:4-5).

Suchard also shows that Blacks have developed greater mobility in respect of technical and professional posts in the mining industry, manufacturing and trade. The gap between semi-skilled and skilled White and Black employees has narrowed, while the gap between unskilled White and Black employees increased between 1982 and 1983.

Since 1969, more Blacks than Whites have entered the technical, professional, clerical and sales divisions, excluding management and administrative posts (Suchard 1984:199). In their study of structural changes in medium-level manpower, Terblanche and Jacobs (1983:17-22) report that during the period 1965 to 1981 the percentage of White clerical workers, salesmen, foremen, supervisors, tradesmen and apprentices decreased, while the percentage of Indians, Coloureds and Blacks in these positions increased significantly. The percentage of Whites in medium-level positions dropped from 82,2% in 1965 to 65,5% in 1981. Except in the case of tradesmen and apprentices, the drop was in the vicinity of 20%. In most instances the percentage participation by Non-Whites doubled over the period. As far as the vertical career mobility of the population groups is concerned, it was found that a higher percentage of Whites move to management posts or professional or semi-professional careers than is the case for the other three population groups (Terblanche and Jacobs 1983:15-32).

According to 1977 statistics, 85% of the Black population were still in the uneducated category. However, education is improving and the number of Black pupils increased by 14,7% between 1980 and 1983 (see Verwey et al 1984 and Suid-Afrika (Republiek) 1983b). Terblanche and Jacobs (1983:53-54) indicate that, except in the case of Whites, the growth rates for the number of pupils in Std 8 and Std 10 exceed the rate of population growth by a considerable margin and they are of the opinion that the number of White pupils who pass matric will drop to approximate population growth more closely, as is the case with Std 8 pupils. For some time, the number of Std 8 and Std 10 Indian, Coloured and Black pupils entering the labour force will exceed the rate of population growth. This situation naturally makes exceptional demands, especially if the current economic situation and the lack of employment opportunities are taken into account.

It has been pointed out that social mobility (which involves Non-Whites in particular in South Africa) generates tension because it activates those whose power is eroded to destroy the new order (Ake 1967:97). The developments among the Whites, especially the Afrikaners, who have been sharing their political power with Non-Whites since the implementation of the new Constitution in 1984 (in terms of Verba and Pye's views as explained above), clearly illustrate this. (Valuable contributions concerning social mobility have been made by Huntington and Dominquez, Horowitz, Conner, Flanagan, Schlemmer, Kuper and Lijphart.)

As a result of the deployment of the new policy, which involved Coloureds and Indians in a plural democracy with Whites, a group that was part of the governing National Party broke away from the Government. In February 1982 this group formed the *Conservative Party* (CP) and since then has entered into agreements with another White political party — the *Herstigte Nasionale Party* (HNP) — for the contesting of certain by-elections. These two parties have the following objectives:

- The maintenance of White self-determination
- Separate homelands for the different peoples
- The rejection of co-responsibility and co-participation between the different population groups
- The querying of agreements of co-operation such as that with Mozambique (the Nkomati Accord), since to their minds it implies that South Africa relinquishes its sovereignty. (They also believe that it will endanger the South African economy and support Russian imperialism.)
- The rejection of the new constitutional dispensation. (On the other hand, the CP has not, however, refused to participate in the new constitutional dispensation and admits that it will only be possible to amend the dispensation in a democratic manner and with the agreement of the Coloureds and the Indians.)
- The rejection of a federal form of government for South Africa
- That Blacks should have no rights in the so-called White areas
- Assistance to Black states on certain conditions only
- Economic apartheid by means of own business districts in own areas for each population group.

From the results of by-elections contested on the basis of the above policies, it appeared that the parties advocating them could, separately and jointly, count on significant White support. The CP and the HNP polled more votes than the National Party in six by-elections. This is significant in view of the considerable number of positive votes during the Referendum on 2 November 1983 (66,3% in favour and 33,7% against). It must be borne in mind that the Referendum could have painted an over-optimistic picture, since many non-NP supporters voted 'yes', there was a significant stay-away vote and a large number of spoilt ballot papers (10 669).

The adverse reaction to the new dispensation was further strengthened by the emergence of organisations and groups such as the *Afrikaner Volkswag*. This organisation, which considers the new dispensation to be a risk to the maintenance of the uniqueness of each population group in South Africa, has as its specific objective the uniting of the Afrikaner ethnic group in a new cultural organisation. Unlike other cultural organisations such as the *Federasie van Afrikaanse Kultuurverenigings* (FAK), it operates on a broader base.

Although the Afrikaner Volkswag professes to be a cultural organisation, both the CP and the HNP figured strongly in the founding of the organisation on 5 May 1984, as did other political organisations such as the Afrikaner Weerstandsbeweging. It has since become evident that it is an organisation which is very strongly opposed to the new political dispensation — in fact, one of its objectives is to oppose it.

Such attitudes held by organisations of this nature obviously create divisions among Afrikaners in all fields. This is evident in its actions in respect of the Broederbond, the Ruiterwag, Education, the FAK and the Church. At the inaugural meeting of the Afrikaner Volkswag, some speakers assumed a militant attitude. Through its leader in Parliament, the CP dissociated itself from such militant actions (Treurnicht in *Hansard*, 9/5/1984, column 6 173), while the leader of the new organisation took a stand against violence (see Boshoff in *Beeld*, 10/5/1984).

Other organisations that are actively opposed to the new political dispensation include the Vereniging van Oranjewerkers, the Wit Tuislandaksie and the Afrikaner-studentefront. These groups of Whites reject identification with Non-Whites in the broad national context. Among another group of Whites, however, there is a different view, as was proved by the results of the Referendum of 2 November 1983 and attitude surveys.

The Whites are not, however, the only ones to display a certain dualism. Indeed, it is also evident in the actions and demands of persons of colour.

Among Blacks there is considerable agreement concerning the rejection of the new constitutional dispensation, as statements by the ANC, Inkatha and the South African Council of Churches (SACC) illustrate. However, they differ in the following respects:

- The extent to which they identify with the other groups in South Africa and therefore in respect of a broad national consciousness — the matter of inclusivity and exclusivity referred to above. (See, for example, the

Black Consciousness Movement, the Azanian People's Organisation (AZAPO) and the National Forum (NF) on one hand and Inkatha on the other.)

- The way in which they should achieve their objectives. The ANC, for example, is in favour of violence, while the SACC views it as a possibility. The latter organisation also advocates disinvestment. Inkatha, on the other hand, favours non-violence and is opposed to disinvestment.

The Coloureds and Indians are also not all in agreement, as their involvement with the United Democratic Front (UDF) and with parties participating in the new constitutional dispensation (the Labour Party, the People's Congress Party, the National People's Party and the Solidarity Party) show. Although a number of them do work within the official structures (i.e. the Inkatha National Movement, Inyandza National Movement, Transkei National Independence Party, Democratic Progessive Party, Ciskei National Independence Party, Venda National Party, Venda Independence People's Party, Lebowa People's Party, Bophuthatswana Democratic Party and the Dinkwankwetla Party), some of the Blacks resent the Coloureds' and the Indians' participation in the new dispensation. However, both of these groups agree with the Blacks as far as most of the demands that are made and which are normally related to social mobility are concerned (see Ake 1967:97, Neumann in Ehrmann 1965:8, Schlemmer 1977:5, Welsh 1978:29-38 and Flanagan in Almond, Flanagan and Mundt 1973: 62-63).

These include the rejection of the new constitutional dispensation (despite the fact that Coloureds and Indians are participating), the advocation of a federal dispensation, the rejection of independent national states, the demand that South Africa develop on a non-racial basis and that one man one vote must apply. South African citizenship is regarded as non-negotiable and Blacks must be incorporated in the political system.

A better socio-economic dispensation is demanded, as are higher wages and more job opportunities. Schlemmer (SA Digest, 28/9/1984) finds that capitalism is not rejected outright, since 75% of Black factory employees accept the present industrial system. There is, however, a tendency to perceive the free enterprise system as one which is beneficial to Whites only (see School of Business Leadership 1984:12).

The following aspects of the current paradigm are rejected: enforced population movements, the Group Areas Act, influx control, detention without trial, separate amenities, the Prohibition of Mixed Marriages Act and section 16 of the Immorality Act (the last two Acts have since been repealed). There are also demands concerning education, training and housing.

Under the circumstances the conflict potential is high (as Coleman 1971:88 shows) and violence and an increasing degree of violence exists in South Africa. The gravity of the situation lies in the receptiveness of Non-Whites (especially youths) to this type of action. Apparently, a certain percentage of Non-Whites do not find peaceful means of change acceptable. In this regard the Coloured groups are in agreement to a certain extent and co-operative acts of violence have been organised on a country-wide basis. This unity is also apparent in the overlapping membership of political parties and pressure groups such as the ANC and the UDF. Acts of terrorism are also aimed at fellow Blacks who are participating in the process of change within the system.

Politically, the trend of violent action stems from the exclusion of Blacks from the new constitutional dispensation for Whites, Coloureds and Indians. However, dissatisfaction with the general economic situation (including increases in rent for Blacks and increased transportation tariffs and sales tax) has resulted in lower expectations among Non-Whites and causes frustration and revolt. This is evident in strikes for higher wages. This situation creates the opportunity for organisations (based locally and abroad) to incite Non-Whites to action which often leads to violence. The most important organisations are the ANC and the UDF. Also, compare the actions of the SACC, the PAC, the All-Africa Conference of Churches and the World Council of Churches (WCC). Trade unions are apparently involved in the struggle, their contribution being the organisation of country-wide strikes.

From the action of Non-Whites it is clear that their plan of action is to make demands in all spheres and to incite everyone to action. Foreign governments and organisations are also influenced to exert economic and diplomatic pressure on the South African Government. Foreign action is evident in the support which the SACC receives from organisations in West Germany, Switzerland, Denmark,* America, Sweden,* Britain, Canada, Norway, Finland* and the Netherlands,* as well as from the World Council of Churches. (See the Report of the Commission of Inquiry into the South African Council of Churches (South Africa (Republic) 1983a).) The Commission of Inquiry into the South African Council of Churches, under the chairmanship of Judge CF Eloff, found the process of change advocated by certain groups and their means of bringing about radical socio-political and economic changes in South Africa to be of a clearly revolutionary nature (1983a:427-428).

Therefore, the process of change in the South African political system is characterised by a certain degree of tension among Whites, among Non-Whites and also between Whites and Non-Whites. At the same time,

---

* In these instances the support comes directly or indirectly from the various governments.

however, there are also positive aspects, as is evidenced by Government action and attitude surveys among Whites and Non-Whites.

The situation is aggravated by the fact that changes occur against a background of economic problems such as increased imports, a strong dollar, a weak rand and the fluctuating gold price, an increasing rate of inflation, the collapse of exports (minerals, diamonds and uranium), unemployment (see the Annual Report of the National Manpower Commission (Suid-Afrika (Republiek) 1983b)), efforts to bring about disinvestment, increasing numbers of educated Blacks entering the labour market and poor economic growth against the background of a high population growth rate.

As has already been indicated, foreign pressure is an important factor in the process of change.

A way must be found to ensure maximum stability during this time of change. The conclusions of several studies indicate that there is a relationship between prosperity, industrialisation, education, urbanisation and stability (see for example Barry 1970:65 and Hurwitz 1972:476). It is easier to prove or disprove the above than it is to prove the existence of a correlation between values and stability. In a multivariate correlation analysis, Hurwitz (1972:482) found that he could not give an outright and final answer (see also Barry 1970:75 et seq.).

There is substantial agreement about the importance of the structures of a system (see Planematz 1956:115, Ake 1967:98-101 and Almond 1963:4). What is important in this regard is the role of the political party (see Barry 1970: 164), through which the citizenry has a voice in political decision making. There are, however, contradictory findings concerning the most suitable party system for stability (see Hurwitz 1972:479 and Venter 1984:19). Attitudes, or a combination of attitudes, play a vital role (see Barry 1970:48 and 126).

Misgivings about the realisation of democracy in the new states have already been expressed (see Ake 1967:101 and Lewis and Dahl in Verba 1967:125). Because of the complexity of plural societies, the view (already indicated) is held that a say for all in the central government must be assured by, amongst other things, coalition government and proportional representation.

In accordance with the views on the arrangement of complex plural societies, we find that the new paradigm in South Africa is characterised by democratic pluralism. That is, efforts are made to recognise individual and group rights on one hand and to extend rights and liberties by recognising the communality of the South African situation, on the other. This means that, in addition to extending rights and liberties, a broader national awareness and greater identification with fellow citizens are recognised

44

and applied. This national consciousness and identification with fellow citizens and the *democratic right to participate in decision making* are illustrated by the new constitutional dispensation, which includes Whites, Coloureds and Indians (see figure 2.1).

The abovementioned groups are involved at the *first level* of government in an executive capacity in a multi-ethnic Cabinet for general affairs and in Ministers' Councils for own affairs. These groups also form an electoral college for the election of a State President, who must qualify to be a member of at least one chamber of Parliament.

The multi-ethnic nature of the Cabinet does away with an important characteristic of the previous Westminster system, namely that all members of the Cabinet should belong to the same political party. Indeed, the new Cabinet consists of members of the National Party, the Labour Party and the National People's Party. The arrangement is that the members may differ as in a coalition government (see Botha in Press Conference, 15/9/1984).

The legislative authority consists of a Parliament with three Chambers, namely the House of Assembly (Whites), the House of Representatives (Coloureds) and the House of Delegates (Indians). An important characteristic of the composition of the Houses is that they consist of directly and indirectly elected members. There are both separate and joint sessions. Decision making concerning an own or general matter occurs separately in a specific House of Parliament. In respect of the own affairs of a group, the procedure is straightforward. As far as general affairs are concerned, a procedure is laid down for handling the type of legislation and differences that may emerge.

In this regard, the most important instrument is a committee system which, in addition to the select committee for the specific session for each House, consists of a select standing committee for the duration of Parliament. These committees have the task of identifying differences in legislation for general affairs during their sessions, which are held in camera. These standing committees include representatives of the majority and minority parties in each House. A second instrument for the solution of problems regarding *inter alia* legislation for general affairs is the President's Council, in which the various groups are represented.

From the above it should be clear that coalition, consensus and elite co-operation between Whites, Coloureds and Indians are important elements of the new political culture for the various segments of society. These alter the hierarchical nature of the previous paradigm drastically.

The juridical authority has retained an important characteristic of the earlier system, namely that it cannot try the law. There are, however, proposals for change (see the Constitutional Committee of the President's

DIAGRAM OF CONSTITUTION, 1983: CENTRAL LEVEL

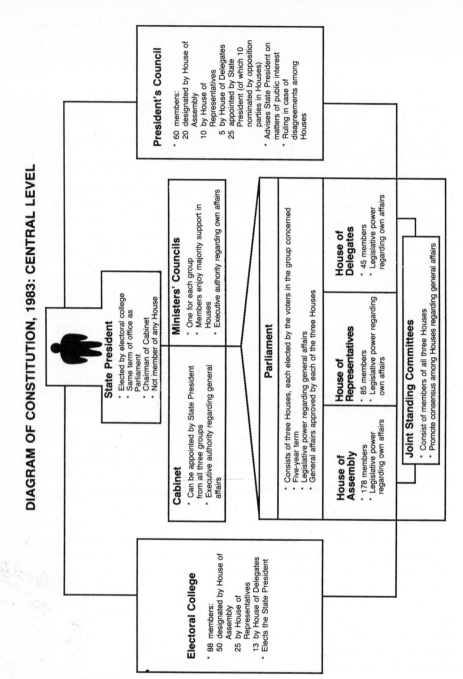

State President
* Elected by electoral college
* Same term of office as Parliament
* Chairman of Cabinet
* Not member of any House

President's Council
* 60 members:
  20 designated by House of Assembly
  10 by House of Representatives
  5 by House of Delegates
  25 appointed by State President (of which 10 nominated by opposition parties in Houses)
* Advises State President on matters of public interest
* Ruling in case of disagreements among Houses

Cabinet
* Can be appointed by State President from all three groups
* Executive authority regarding general affairs

Ministers' Councils
* One for each group
* Members enjoy majority support in Houses
* Executive authority regarding own affairs

Parliament
* Consists of three Houses, each elected by the voters in the group concerned
* Five-year term
* Legislative power regarding general affairs
* General affairs approved by each of the three Houses

House of Assembly
* 178 members
* Legislative power regarding own affairs

House of Representatives
* 85 members
* Legislative power regarding own affairs

House of Delegates
* 45 members
* Legislative power regarding own affairs

Joint Standing Committees
* Consist of members of all three Houses
* Promote consensus among Houses regarding general affairs

Electoral College
* 88 members:
  50 designated by House of Assembly
  25 by House of Representatives
  13 by House of Delegates
* Elects the State President

Fig 2.1 Diagram of Constitution, 1983: Central level

46

Council (Suid-Afrika (Republiek) 1984a:120-138)) and the Hoexter Commission's recommendations on one set of courts independent of race (Suid-Afrika (Republiek) 1983a:346).

The right to participate in the decision-making processes also found expression in the *third level* of government. Special investigations were made in respect of electoral qualifications, the delimitation of geographic areas of jurisdiction, the criteria for viable local authorities, joint provision of services and regional authorities, personnel and control over local authorities. Important legislation concerning this level of government was passed during 1984 and included, for example, the Local Government Bodies Franchise Act, 1984 (Act 117 of 1984). This Act created uniform voting qualifications for the different local authority bodies. Parliamentary franchise and land tenure now forms the basis of the right to vote for the local authorities of Whites, Coloureds and Indians. The qualifying value of property may differ in urban and rural areas and also as far as the categories of existing local authorities are concerned. There is no such restriction for the different groups at the first level of government.

The Promotion of Local Government Affairs Amendment Act, 1984 (Act 116 of 1984) empowers the Minister to lay down a uniform set of criteria for the determination of the autonomy and viability of local authorities for the three race groups concerned. The provincial authorities retain the power to create, disband or unite such authorities.

The Regional Services Councils Act (still to be promulgated) envisages the introduction of regional services councils which will provide for joint decision making by Whites, Coloureds, Indians and Blacks at local government level. This will include decisions concerning services provided by local authorities and which can be regarded as general affairs, e.g. transport and transport services, traffic matters, water supply, sewage purification, storm-water drainage, electricity, fresh-produce markets, ambulance and fire-brigade services and health services. The regional services councils will be extensions of third-level authorities and will therefore be controlled by provincial authorities. A regional services council will not have the right to impose property tax, since this is considered to be an own affair. Revenue will be obtained from the services supplied to a local authority and will also form the basis for the determination of a local authority's voting strength on a regional services council. However, one member will not be able to dominate such a council, since a member's votes will be limited to 50% of the total number of votes.

Other legislation concerning third-level authorities includes the Labour Relations Amendment Act, 1984 (Act 81 of 1984) and the Group Areas Act, 1984 (Act 101 of 1984).

Devolution of power is an important characteristic of the new dispensation and the proper institutionalisation of third-level authorities, through which the different groups will gain greater control over own affairs, is important. Joint decision making in respect of common affairs, as already indicated, also received attention.

In the meantime, Minister JC Heunis (Heunis in *Hansard*, 6/5/1985) has also announced that the right to participate in the decision-making processes will also find expression at a *proposed second level of government*. This body will replace the four provincial councils and will consist of an administrator and an enlarged executive committee which will have a say in general affairs. Both the administrator and the executive committee will be appointed by the State President from the ranks of serving politicians for each province. In future own affairs, currently handled by the provincial councils, will be handled by the Ministers' Councils for own affairs of the three Houses of Parliament. Further particulars, which will indicate whether this proposed body signifies greater centralisation or decentralisation, is still awaited.

A second right, which is important in a democratic sense, is the right to participate in the country's administration. The new dispensation makes provision for a central public service for general affairs, while each group has a separate administration for own affairs, namely the Administrations of the House of Assembly, the House of Representatives and the House of Delegates. It can be expected that in future Coloureds and Indians will have a greater share in the general public service as far as general affairs are concerned. In fact, they are already insisting on this (see *Rapport*, 2/11/1984).

A third right, which is important politically, is the right to periodic and honest elections. An important deviation from the earlier standpoint that party-political rights may only be exercised within the group context (see De Klerk in *Hansard*, 13/3/1984, columns 2 862-2 867), has been introduced. It has since been announced that the Prohibition of Political Interference Act, 1968 (Act 51 of 1968) is to be amended so that no restrictions will be placed on groups as far as membership of political parties is concerned. This could eventually have a stabilising effect in that representatives of the various Houses of Parliament can belong to the same political party and therefore subscribe to the same political principles. It could also have a beneficial effect on loyalties.

The new dispensation differs from the Westminster model, in which the majority party governs, in that members of the three majority parties form the Government (thus creating a type of coalition government), representatives of the majority parties form an electoral college for the election of the State President and Speaker, majority and minority parties are represented in the President's Council and in the standing committees and decision making takes place by consensus.

The fourth right is, according to democratic principles, the right to equal franchise. The Electoral Amendment Act, 1984 (Act 42 of 1984) ensures a uniform system of voting for Whites, Coloureds and Indians.

The political/constitutional changes thus denote a political culture that differs from the previous one. The national aspirations of the different population groups are recognised and there is some identification with fellow citizens on the part of the Whites. This also finds institutional expression in basic rights and liberties.

Regarding the Blacks, who are excluded from the new constitutional dispensation, there is development on the basis of the existing paradigm in the sense that four of the Black states (KwaNdebele also applied for independence) that gained independence and the rest (including Kangwane) that have self-governing status, are retained. This signifies participation by Blacks in the decision-making process in their own self-governing states.

On the other hand, an important aspect of the new paradigm applies in respect of Blacks in White areas; their permanence is accepted. (See Heunis in *Hansard*, 25/5/1984, column 7 379; Botha in *Rapport* 27/5/1984 and *Hansard*, 25/1/1985, column 12.) This indicates recognition of the fact that, in addition to the Black states (independent and self-governing), there is an area permanently inhabited by all four race groups. This is a common area and no longer the 'White' area of the old paradigm. Association with persons of colour is an important aspect of the new paradigm and naturally has political consequences, especially for Blacks, who are in a certain sense excluded from the new Parliamentary dispensation. However, the Government does not see the acquisition of property as necessarily equal to the granting of political rights (see Botha in *Hansard*, 26/4/1984, column 5 347 and Morrison in *Hansard*, 11/6/1984, column 8 554). A distinction is made between these two aspects.

Political rights at the first level of government are apparently not to be found in a fourth chamber in the new constitutional dispensation (Botha in *Rapport*, 27/5/1984) or in a federal system (Heunis in *Rapport*, 27/5/1984). The Progressive Federal Party's federation of universal franchise without group identity is thus unacceptable to the present White Government (Botha in *Hansard*, 26/4/1984, column 5 344 and Heunis in *Hansard*, 24/5/1984, column 7 315).

Political expression is seen in a confederal system (which, as shown above, is not accepted by Blacks) by means of which the problems of citizenship and nationality can also be solved (see Botha in *Hansard*, 26/4/1984, column 5 347; Heunis in *Rapport*, 27/5/1984; Botha in *Beeld*, 17/8/1984 and De Klerk in *Beeld*, 17/8/1984). Attention is being paid to the concept of confederation through *multilateral co-operation*, according to which all interested parties will have a say. The following diagram indicates the way in which multilateral and regional co-operation between South Africa, Transkei, Bophuthatswana, Venda and Ciskei have been institutionalised. (See figure 2.2.)

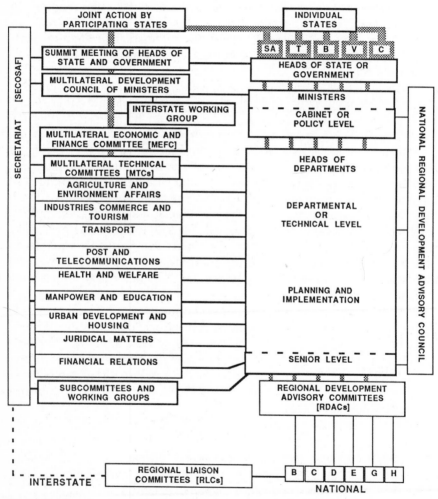

Fig 2.2 Multilateral and regional co-operation between the SATBVC States

Apart from the viability of this vision, it is evident that the Government is sincere in its efforts to make provision for the Black population of South Africa outside the national states (see Botha, *Speech* at Bloemfontein, 29/10/1984, in *Rapport*, 2/9/1984 and in *Hansard*, 18/9/1984, column 10). In a speech in Parliament on 25 January 1985, the State President, Mr PW Botha, declared *inter alia* the following (*Hansard* 25/1/1985, columns 14-15):

In the constitutional field certain decisions have been taken in the light of the investigation and negotiations of the Special Cabinet Committee:

The Government accepts the permanence in the RSA in large numbers of members of the Black population communities who find themselves outside the national states. After thorough investigation it is also accepted that not all these peoples can express themselves politically beyond the local level via the government structures of the national states. The intensive promotion of the local government system for Black communities and steps to increase the credibility of existing local authorities are vital. It has therefore been decided to treat such communities, for constitutional purposes, as entities which in their own right, with retention of the principle that no population group should be placed in a position to rule over another, must be given political participation and a say at higher levels. Structures must therefore be developed for Black communities outside the national states through which they can themselves decide on their own affairs up to the highest level. The same bodies can serve, at the various levels, as links for co-operation on matters of common interest with government bodies of the RSA, the independent former national states and the self-governing national states.

To avoid unnecessary fragmentation at the constitutional level the Government has further decided that in the longer term efforts should be made to co-operate on matters of common interest within the same overall framework with the various political entities that find themselves within the South African context.

The decisions reached regarding the constitutional position of Black communities indicate that clarity must be reached soon on the question of citizenship. The Government confirms that it is its intention to do so. For this reason the Special Cabinet Committee has been directed to submit a report and recommendations, to be based on investigation and negotiation, on the problems of terminology and content that surround the question of citizenship.*

---

* On 11 September 1985 the State President announced that the Government was prepared to restore South African citizenship to the peoples of the Transkei, Bophuthatswana, Venda and Ciskei. In effect, this means dual citizenship for the peoples of the independent Black states and eliminates a major stumbling block to political reform in South Africa. It is an important deviation from the previous paradigm.

At a news conference on 24 May 1985, the Minister of Constitutional Development and Planning, Mr JC Heunis, explained the Government's points of departure concerning the political rights of Blacks as follows:

- The creation of democratic institutions to give substance to Black claims for political rights
- Co-operation with all those involved in the search for peaceful solutions
- Sustained democratising and socio-economic reform
- The granting of self-determination to groups (without one population group dominating another)
- Acceptance of the principle of the rule of law
- Rejection of discrimination on the grounds of race, ethnicity or origin
- The maintenance of stability
- The use of negotiation as a means of creating a new dispensation.

It appears from earlier statements that the Black population in South Africa presents not only a political problem for the Government, but also a socio-economic one that is related to urbanisation and that an urbanisation policy also necessitates a regional development strategy (see Heunis in *Rapport*, 27/5/1984, Botha in *Hansard*, 26/4/1984, column 5 348 and Heunis in *Hansard*, 25/5/1984, column 7 380).

The Black Local Authorities Act, 1982 (Act 102 of 1982), in terms of which Black town councils are created, makes provision for Black participation in own affairs in the *common area* at the third level of government. These Black town councils obtain financial support from taxes that are imposed on commerce and industry and not on the consumer.

As indicated above, Black municipalities will be able to participate in the regional services councils. A regional services council can provide municipal services (within or outside the RSA) to a Black government body. The development of local governments, which includes those of the Blacks, must be seen to be in accordance with the Government's policy of the decentralisation of political rights and the devolution of power.

The above discussion indicates *inter alia* the extent to which political rights find institutional expression and the degree of association between the different population groups. However, it is also accepted that in addition to *political rights, there are social, economic and cultural rights* to which the individual as a member of a community can lay claim. These include the right to work, to a certain standard of living, to education and to participation in the cultural life.

In terms of the new constitutional dispensation, Whites, Coloureds and Indians are jointly involved in financial and economic matters (see the State President's Committee on National Priorities Act, 1984 (Act 119 of 1984) and the Revenue Accounts Financing Act, 1984 (Act 120 of 1984)).

Principles that come to the fore are a joint say and consent on the basis of negotiation and consensus — an important deviation from the old paradigm in respect of the handling of financial and economic affairs.

As far as the development of Black financial and economic affairs is concerned, it has already been pointed out that although the Whites are in a strong position in management and administrative posts, more Blacks than Whites have entered the technical, professional, clerical and sales fields since 1969. This indicates an upward mobility and eventually a bigger say in economic affairs. The Government's attitude regarding social, economic and cultural rights is characterised by steps towards *equal opportunities* for all. Compare, for example, changes in *labour affairs*: workers of all population groups may now be members of registered trade unions; statutory job reservation has been abolished; the State is encouraging the training of employees through trade unions and employer organisations; the differences drawn between the various population groups in the Unemployment Insurance Act have been done away with; restrictions on facilities have been lifted through mutual consultation; important principles such as industrial self-management by employers and employees have been introduced; and there is minimum intervention by the State, maximum decentralisation of decision making and autonomy for employers and employees in matters of common interest.

Of particular importance is the attempt to create *equal education* and *equal educational opportunities*. The realisation of this objective is impeded by the large numbers of the developing groups at present (5,5 million Blacks, including those in the TBVC and national states, see Verwey *et al* 1984), the fact that there are too few trained Black teachers to handle the situation and the historically backward position and lack of funds. All of these put a great deal of pressure on the Republic's budget. However, from the Government's actions in this matter it is clear that it is doing everything in its power to create an equitable situation for all. This is evident not only in the allocation of funds for more facilities, but in the creation of parity in education as far as salaries and conditions of service are concerned.

The Education and Heraldry Laws Amendment Act, 1984 (Act 6 of 1984), is a step in the direction of greater co-ordination and standardisation of examinations and qualifications at post-school level. A Joint Matriculation Board lays down the standards. The new constitutional dispensation makes a distinction between general matters such as financing, examinations and standards, while each population group has its own schools and education departments. Culture-related education serves as point of departure. Own universities therefore remain part of the new paradigm, although there is modification in the sense that the permit system for admission to a university other than one in the group to which a person belongs was abolished in 1983 and replaced by a fixed-quota system. However, all groups are represented on national educational bodies, for example the Committee of University Principals. Own residential areas, schools and universities are a part of the old paradigm which has been retained.

Closely linked with equal opportunities in a democratic dispensation is the promotion of prosperity. Government action in this sphere and in respect of developing groups concerns both the RSA and the independent and self-governing states.

The new paradigm in the common area emphasises the development of Black communities (rather than administration only) and has as its objective the prevention of economic and social degeneration. This is evident from the following developments:

- The replacement of Administration Boards with Development Councils in terms of the Black Communities Development Act, 1984 (Act 4 of 1984)
- The introduction of Black town councils
- Stability in respect of domicile in the common area
- The creation of better residential areas, for example Khayelitsha in the Cape Peninsula
- The upgrading of existing residential areas in the Eastern Cape
- The provision and subsidisation of Black housing
- The acceptance of a firm strategy for the provision of employment (see White Paper WPC 1984:7)
- The promotion of trained manpower (see White Paper WPC 1984:12)
- The opening of central business districts to all groups.

The Government nevertheless maintains its views on residential segregation, although there is the possibility that some of the Acts concerning this may be substantially amended or repealed. These include the Group Areas Act, 1966 (Act 36 of 1966), the Community Development Act, 1966 (Act 3 of 1966), the Reservation of Separate Amenities Act, 1953 (Act 49 of 1953) and section 28(1) of the General Laws Amendment Act, 1969 (Act 101 of 1969). The Strydom Committee, which recommended the repeal of these Acts, suggested that residential segregation be maintained by means of the title-deed conditions for land (see South Africa (Republic) 1983b:65-66).

Concerning the independent Black national states and self-governing Black states, the Government maintains its views in respect of important aspects of its policy such as the consolidation of the Black states, which it hopes to complete within four years (see Morrison in Hansard, 11/6/1984, columns 8 557 and 8 562 – 8 566). In recent times some 4 900 000 hectares were acquired at a cost of R789 million in terms of the Development Trust and Land Act, 1936 (Act 18 of 1936). As early as 1979, it was decided that the 1936 quota could be exceeded.

There is also the matter of the resettlement of persons, which the Government sees as an aspect of the consolidation of peoples and their right to express themselves as such (see Morrison in *Hansard*, 13/6/1983, column 8 551). An important objection is the control of the influx of Blacks from the Black states to the common area. This control can be attributed largely to the fact that the Black states do not have the ability to absorb their own growing labour force, with the result that 20% of their population is unemployed. This has caused poverty to assume vast proportions in these areas (see Koornhof 1982:63-72 and the White Paper on the creation of job opportunities in the RSA (WPC 1984:2)). South Africa has to cope with migrant labourers (1,4 million) and daily commuters (773 000) from the various areas. Thus, for political, social and economic reasons, the Government follows a policy of control of the influx to the common area, conditions for entry being adequate housing and the availability of work (see Badenhorst in *Hansard*, 23/3/1984 column 3 669).

However, judging from the new legislation envisaged and the investigations of a select committee into the matter of influx control, it would appear that the emphasis has shifted to orderly settlement in the common area. The fact that the Western Cape has been opened to Blacks is a significant modification. The Government has accepted that the Black states do not offer a complete answer. This is clear from such actions as the introduction of third-level authorities; the right of domicile; recognition of the permanence of Blacks in the common area; the emphasis on community development, education and the training of manpower; and the creation of job opportunities.

The RSA still assists with the development of Black states and this assistance, together with the wages of migrant labourers and commuters, constitutes an important contribution to their total revenue. Ligthelm and Coetzee (1984: 10-11) advocate a shift of emphasis in assistance to small-farmer development, the establishment of small-business enterprises, the development of the informal sectors and technological development. The development aid is closely related to the Government's view on decentralisation and regional development and an increase in productivity.

All of the above point to a broader South Africanism in which there can be a greater deployment of the political, social, economic and cultural rights of the various population groups; that is, to a widening of democracy. This would focus on the political institutionalisation of certain groups which are already well-accommodated economically — and to a certain extent also socially — so that a completely democratic, parallel system could evolve. South Africa is, therefore, on the road to reform, the emphasis being on, amongst other things, equal participation by its citizens in the social, economic and political dispensation, without ethnic group domination.

The proposed democratic framework and the principles according to which the different groups are to be kept in equilibrium and harmony, namely elite co-operation, mutual veto, proportionality, segmental autonomy and joint responsibility, are by no means a generally accepted framework or a prelude to stability. Plural democracies that were characterised by instability in the past are Northern Ireland, Cyprus and Lebanon. However, there are plural democracies which maintain an important degree of stability, for example Switzerland, Israel, Luxemburg and Canada.

Although predictions are obviously difficult, the question nevertheless remains: what are the chances of stability in a system such as that in the RSA, in which efforts are being made to plan the relationships of the different multi-ethnic groups in a democratic and parallel manner? As was indicated, the literature concerning empirical democratic theories bring different views to the fore. However, the success of the entire process of change and the maintenace of stability must ultimately depend on four factors, namely the extent to which a new political culture can be established, the emergence of a loyalty in the greater national context, the legitimacy of the new system and efficient control and the nature of a new economic dispensation.

BIBLIOGRAPHY

Ake, C. A theory of political integration. Homewood, Illinois: Dorsey Press, 1967.
Almond, GA. Comparative political systems. Journal of Politics, vol. 18, 1956.
— Political systems and political change. The American Behavorial Scientist, June 1963.
Almond, GA and Powell, B. Comparative politics — a developmental approach. Boston: Little, Brown and Co, 1966.
Almond, GA, Flanagan, SC and Mundt, RJ. Crises, choice and change: historical studies of political development. Boston: Little, Brown and Co, 1973.
Apter, DE. Some conceptual approaches to the study of modernization. Englewood Cliffs, New Jersey: Prentice-Hall Inc, 1968.
Badenhorst, PJ. Hansard. 23 March 1984.
Barry, B. Sociologists, economists and democracy. London: Macmillan, 1970.
Benyon, JA. Constitutional change in South Africa. Pietermaritzburg: University of Natal Press, 1978.
Binder, L, et al. Crises and sequences in political development. Princeton, New Jersey: Princeton University Press, 1971.
Boshoff, CWH. Beeld. 10 May 1984.
— Rapport. 26 February 1984.
Botha, PW. Beeld. 17 August 1984.
— Hansard. 26 April 1984, 18 September 1984, 25 January 1985.

— *Press Conference.* 15 September 1984.
— *Rapport.* 27 May 1984, 2 September 1984.
— *Speech.* Bloemfontein: 29 October 1984.
Capotorti, F. *Study on the rights of persons belonging to ethnic, religious and linguistic minorities.* Report of the United Nations subcommission for prevention of discrimination and the protection of minorities. New York: United Nations, 1979.
Coetzee, JH. *Eienskappe van en raakpunte tussen Westerse en Suider-Afrikaanse politieke kulture.* Pretoria: Raad vir Geesteswetenskaplike Navorsing, 1985.
Conner, W. Nation building or nation destroying. *World Politics,* vol. 24, no. 55, 1972.
Cloete, GS. *Gemeenskapsoutonomie in Estland, Ciprus en België.* Pretoria: Raad vir Geesteswetenskaplike Navorsing, 1984.
De Klerk, FW. *Beeld.* 17 August 1984.
— *Hansard.* 13 March 1984, 4 May 1984.
De Klerk, GJ. Swart koopkrag: 'n Swart dag of goue geleentheid? *Woord en Daad,* vol. 24, no. 265, 1984.
Ehrmann, HW. *Democracy in a changing society.* London: Pall Mall Press, 1965.
Heunis, CJ. *Beeld.* 27 October 1984.
— *Hansard.* 17 February 1984, 24 May 1984, 25 May 1984, 6 May 1985.
— *Press conference.* 24 May 1985.
— *Rapport.* 27 May 1984.
— *Speech.* Political Science Association, 2 October 1984.
Hurwitz, L. Democratic political stability. Some traditional hypotheses re-examined. *Comparative Political Studies,* vol. 4, January 1972.
Koornhof, GW. *The economic consequences of urbanisation in Lebowa.* Pretoria: University of South Africa, 1982 (D. Comm. dissertation).
Kotze, DA. *African politics in South Africa 1964-1974. Parties and issues.* Pretoria: Van Schaik, 1975.
Kotze, DA (Ed.) . *Development policies and approaches in Southern Africa.* Pretoria: Academica, 1983.
Ligthelm, AA and Coetzee, SF. An appropriate development strategy for Southern Africa. *Development Southern Africa,* vol. 1, no. 1, 1984.
Linz, JJ. *The breakdown of democratic regimes — crises, breakdown and re-equilibration.* Baltimore: Johns Hopkins University Press, 1978.
Lijphart, A. Cultural diversity and theories of political integration. *Canadian Journal of Political Science,* vol. iv, no. 1, March 1971.
— *The politics of accommodation: pluralism and democracy in the Netherlands.* 2nd ed. Berkeley: University of California Press, 1975.
— *Democracy in Plural Societies.* New Haven: Yale University Press, 1977a.
— Majority rule versus democracy in deeply divided societies. *Politikon,* vol. 4, no. 2, 1977b.
— *Consociation: the model and its applications in divided societies.* Belfast: Queen's University of Belfast (A paper presented at a study conference), March 1981.
Morrison, G de V. *Hansard.* 11 June 1984, 13 June 1984.
Planematz, J. Cultural prerequisites to a successfully functioning democracy: a symposium. *The American Political Sciences Review,* vol. L, 1956.
Pye, LW and Verba, S (Eds). *Political culture and political development.* Princeton, New Jersey: Princeton University Press, 1965.
Pye, LW. *Aspects of political development.* Boston: Little, Brown and Co, 1966.
Schlemmer, L. Theories of the plural society and change in South Africa. *Social Dynamics,* vol. 3, no. 1, 1977.
— *The stirring giant.* (Original manuscript), 1978.
SA Digest. 28 September 1984.
School of Business Leadership. *Project free enterprise.* Pretoria: University of South Africa, 1984.
South Africa (Republic). Commission of Inquiry into the South African Council of Churches. (Eloff Commission.) *Report.* Pretoria: Government Printer, 1983. (RP 74/1983.)
— Technical Committee of Inquiry into the Group Areas Act, 1966. The Reservation of

Separate Amenities Act, 1953 and related legislation. (Strydom Committee.) *Report*. Pretoria: Government Printer, 1983.

— Local Government Bodies Franchise Act, 1984 (Act 117 of 1984). Promotion of Local Government Affairs Amendment Act, 1984 (Act 116 of 1984). Labour Relations Amendment Act, 1984 (Act 81 of 1984). Group Areas Amendment Act, 1984 (Act 101 of 1984). Promotion of Local Government Affairs Act, 1983 (Act 291 of 1983). State President's Committee of National Priorities Act, 1984 (Act 119 of 1984). Revenue Accounts Financing Act, 1984 (Act 120 of 1984).

Stulz, NM. Interpreting Constitutional Change in South Africa. *Journal of Modern African Studies*, vol. 22, no. 3, 1984.

Suchard, H. Changes in Black personal income and expenditure in South Africa. *Africa Insight*, vol. 14, no. 3, 1984.

Suid-Afrika (Republiek). Kommisie van Ondersoek na Arbeidswetgewing. Wiehahn-kommissie.) *Verslag*. Pretoria: Staatsdrukker, 1979 en 1980. (RP 47/1979 en RP 38/1980.)

— Kommissie van Ondersoek na Wetgewing Rakende die Benutting van Mannekrag (Uitgesonder die Wetgewing Geadministreer deur die Departemente van Arbeid en Mynwese). (Riekert-kommissie.) *Verslag*. Pretoria: Staatsdrukker, 1979. (RP 32/1979.)

— Kommissie van Ondersoek na die Struktuur en Funksionering van die Howe. (Hoexter Commission.) *Verslag*. Pretoria: Staatsdrukker, 1983. (RP 78/1983.)

— Nasionale Mannekragkommissie vir die Tydperk 1 Januarie 1983 – 31 Desember 1983. *Verslag*. Pretoria: Staatsdrukker, 1983. (RP/41/1984.)

— Grondwetkommittee van die Presidentsraad oor die Aanpassing van die Staatkundige Strukture in Suid-Afrika. *Verslag*. Kaapstad: Staatsdrukker, 1984. (RP 4/1984.)

— *Witskrif oor 'n strategie vir die skepping van werkgeleentheid in die Republiek van Suid-Afrika*. Pretoria: Staatsdrukker, 1984. (WPC 1984.)

Terblanche, S. *Gemeenskapsarmoede. Perspektief op chroniese armoede in die Kleurlinggemeenskap na aanleiding van die Erika Theron-verslag*. Kaapstad: Tafelberg-uitgewers, 1977.

Terblanche, SS en Jacobs, JJ. *Struktuurverandering in middelvlakmannekrag*. Pretoria: Raad vir Geesteswetenskaplike Navorsing, 1983.

Treurnicht, AP. *Beeld*. 5 May 1984, 29 June 1984, 16 August 1984.

— *Hansard*. 17 February 1984, 25 April 1984, 26 April 1984, 9 May 1984, 23 May 1984, 26 June 1984.

— *Rand Daily Mail*. 9 August 1984.

— *Rapport*. 28 October 1984.

Van Dyke, V. Human rights and the rights of groups. *American Journal of Political Science*, vol. 18, November 1974.

Van Vuuren, DJ en. Kriek, DJ (Reds). *Politieke alternatiewe vir Suider-Afrika*. Johannesburg: Macmillan, 1982.

Venter, AJ. *Koalisieregering in plurale samelewings*. Pretoria: Raad vir Geesteswetenskaplike Navorsing, 1984.

Verba, S. Some dilemmas in comparative Research. *World Politics*, vol. 20, October 1967.

Verwey, CT, *et al*. *Educational and Manpower production*. Research Institute for Educational Planning, UOFS, 1984.

Verwoerd, HF. *Hansard*. 27 January 1959.

Welsh, D. The nature of racial conflict in South Africa. *Social Dynamics*, vol. 4, no. 1, 1978.

Wiseman, HV. *Political systems. Some sociological approaches*. London: Routledge and Kegan Paul, 1966.

3 Administrative change in South Africa

WLJ Adlem

INTRODUCTION

The constitutional changes of the past decade have inevitably had an important effect on administrative and institutional change. With a view to making provision for the Coloured, Indian and Black population groups in particular, the existing government institutions and administrative arrangements have been subjected to scrutiny and, in the course of time, been changed. For the purposes of this discussion, the focus will be on the most recent administrative and institutional changes introduced into the South African governmental hierarchy at the central, regional and local levels.

NATIONAL TIER OF GOVERNMENT

The national or central tier of government may be regarded as the first or primary level of government. In order that administrative and institutional change at this level may be traced, in this section a brief historical review and the guidelines for constitutional change will be given. The legislative institutions will be discussed briefly, with attention to the legislative process, and the executive institutions responsible for the implementation of parliamentary legislation will be dealt with.

Historical perspective

Initiatives for the present constitutional dispensation can be traced back as far as 1973, the year in which the Theron Commission (the Commission of Inquiry into Matters Relating to the Coloured Population Group) was appointed. The Commission's findings and recommendations led to the appointment of a Cabinet committee under the chairmanship of the Prime Minister. This committee investigated ways of taking the political development of Whites, Coloureds and Indians a step further and its findings and recommendations led to the Government's Constitutional Plan, which was

59

referred to a select committee whose task it was to take the matter further. The select committee was subsequently converted into a commission.

One of the recommendations of this commission was that a specialist advisory body, the President's Council, should be established to investigate the political development of the country further. In May 1982 the President's Council brought out its findings and recommendations, which were to serve as the framework for the formulation of what were termed the Government's guidelines for constitutional development.

A Constitution Bill was introduced in Parliament on 5 May 1983 and, after the second reading debate, was referred to a select committee for further investigation. This committee added further touches to the Bill, which was passed in Parliament by a two-thirds majority in September 1983. At a referendum on 2 November 1983, the White electorate voted in favour of the implementation of the new Constitution by a two-thirds majority. Coloured and Indian members of the new Parliament were elected in August 1984, the new Constitution Act coming into operation on 3 September 1984.[1]

The Government's constitutional guidelines

In the light of the findings and recommendations of the President's Council and of the debate that followed, the Government laid down specific guidelines which were to serve as the basis for constitutional renewal. These guidelines may be summarised as follows:[2]

- It was to be a democratic dispensation, under which all were to have an effective voice in matters affecting their interests.
- One group should not be dominated by another.
- The rights and legitimate aspirations of all should be guaranteed.
- The self-determination of each separate group should be ensured.
- Provision should be made for joint responsibility in affairs of general interest on the basis of consultation and co-operation between equals.
- Political and constitutional adaptations and adjustments should be based on thorough deliberation and aimed at promoting a stable society.
- Constitutional change should be accompanied by change in all other spheres of society and a healthier balance should be maintained in this regard.
- The successful implementation of a new constitutional dispensation becomes possible only through sustained consultation and negotiation between the groups concerned.

Within the framework of these guidelines, the Government proceeded to adapt the legislative, executive and judicial institutions to changing circumstances.

Legislative institutions

The Republic of South Africa Constitution Act, 1983 (Act 110 of 1983, section 301), that is the new Constitution, vests the legislative power of the Republic in the State President and Parliament, providing that it shall be the sovereign legislative authority in and over the Republic. The State President and Parliament have full power to make laws for the peace, order and good government of the Republic.[3] It appears, therefore, that the primary function of Parliament is the promulgation of laws.

Parliament is composed of three Houses, namely the House of Assembly (for Whites), the House of Representatives (for Coloureds) and the House of Delegates (for Indians).[4] The House of Assembly consists of 178 members; 166 of these are elected by White voters from the candidates nominated by the political parties in the 166 electoral divisions, eight are elected by the 166 members and four are appointed by the State President.

The Coloured voters elect 80 members to the House of Representatives from candidates nominated by the political parties in the 80 electoral divisions. A further three members are elected by the 80 members and two more are appointed by the State President. The House of Delegates consists of 45 members. The Indian voters elect 40 members (also on the basis of electoral divisions), these 40 members elect three members and the State President appoints two members.[5] The period of office of Members of Parliament is five years. The Speaker of Parliament is elected by the electoral college which elects the State President.[6]

The main object of the new Constitution is to achieve joint participation by Whites, Coloureds and Indians in the government of the country. In order to accomplish this, various structural adjustments were made to the previous Constitution. These may be summarised as follows: Whites, Coloureds and Indians will henceforth have an equal vote and will participate together in the legislative and executive functions of the Government as far as general affairs are concerned. A functional distinction is drawn between the 'own affairs' of a particular population group and general affairs, which concern more than one population group. In each of the Houses each group decides separately on its own affairs, while general affairs are decided upon jointly, but in separate sittings, by all three Houses. In cases where the three Houses cannot reach consensus on general affairs, the draft legislation in question is referred to joint standing committees, which consist of members from all three Houses.[7]

Executive institutions

The nature of the functions to be executed determines which institutions and individuals will be involved. Thus, whenever general affairs are at issue, the executive consists of the State President, the Cabinet and those departments of State designated for general affairs and whenever 'own affairs' are at issue, the three Ministers' Councils, the State President and those departments designated for 'own affairs' constitute the executive.[8]

When the Cabinet accepted the broad constitutional guidelines in 1982, the Commission for Administration was requested to investigate the reclassification of governmental functions. An inevitable consequence of the distinction drawn between 'own' and general affairs was that it became necessary to create new structures and groups of structures and to redistribute governmental functions among 'own' departments on one hand and 'general' departments on the other. To accomplish this, the horizontal and vertical devolution of power had to be effected within the governmental hierarchy as a whole. A horizontal devolution or transfer of powers and functions to the various population groups and the private sector, to ensure the population groups' right to self-determination, is envisaged. These are matters that affect each of the population groups concerned separately as far as the preservation of its identity and the maintenance and promotion of its way of life, traditions and customs is concerned.

In February 1984, the Cabinet decided that it was necessary to create three groups of administrative executive institutions for 'own affairs'. These were to be in the form of administrations and each one was to have a number of departments. Apart from these 'own affairs' administrations, provision had to be made for the administration of general affairs as well.

However, the South African governmental hierarchy was to be reorganised in accordance with the provisions of the Constitution Act, which embodies two important principles that have to be upheld, namely nations' right to self-determination in their own affairs and co-responsibility for general affairs. Consequently, *four* groups of executive institutions came into being at the level of the central government. These are the institutions for general affairs, White own affairs, Coloured own affairs, and Indian own affairs.[9]

As has been shown, the 'own' functions of Whites, Coloureds and Indians were brought together under three groups of administrations. Each of these administrations is divided into a number of departments. In the Administration for the House of Assembly (Whites) there are five departments: Health Services and Welfare; Education and Culture; Budgetary and Auxiliary Services; Local Government; Housing and Works; and Agriculture and Water Supply. The Administration for the House of Representatives (Coloureds) and the Administration for the House of Delegates (Indians) each have only four departments. In these institutions, the functions of local government, housing, works, agriculture and water supply are grouped under one instead of two departments, namely local government, housing and agriculture.[10]

Each of these 'own affairs' departments is headed by a Minister. Together, the Ministers form the Ministers' Councils for the House of Assembly, the House of Representatives and the House of Delegates.

Only seven of the existing departments of State were affected by functions being relinquished to the 'own affairs' Administrations. For general affairs, following consultation with the Cabinet, the Office of the Commission for Administration recommended that almost all the former central departments of State should be retained in one form or another. Consequently, 25 departments of State (including the Office of the State President) under 18 Cabinet Ministers (including the chairmen of two Ministers' Councils, namely those of the House of Representatives and the House of Delegates, who are without portfolios) came into being. These departments of State include:[11]

- The National Intelligence Service
- The South African Transport Services
- The Department of Transport
- The Department of Constitutional Development and Planning
- The Department of Foreign Affairs
- The Department of Home Affairs
- The Department of National Education
- The Office of the Commission for Administration
- The South African Police
- The Department of Posts and Telecommunications
- The Department of Public Works and Land Affairs
- The Department of Health and Welfare
- The Department of Co-operation and Development
- The Department of Education and Training
- The South African Defence Force
- The Department of Manpower
- The Department of Trade and Industry
- The Department of Justice
- The Department of Agricultural Economics and Marketing
- The Department of Mineral and Energy Affairs
- The Department of Finance
- The Office of the Auditor-General
- The Department of Environment Affairs.

REGIONAL TIER OF GOVERNMENT

The functions of regional authorities are determined and influenced largely by their particular organisational position within the governmental hierarchy as a whole. In South Africa, regional authorities form part of a group of authorities which individually, but also jointly, seek to promote the general welfare of society as a whole.

Further, the organisational position of regional government institutions is influenced by the nature and status of the institutions that function at this level of government. At the level of regional authorities, regional government and administration are carried out by various governmental institutions such as provincial authorities, regional offices of departments of State, State-controlled corporations and agricultural product control boards, divisional councils, peri-urban areas boards and committees, regional services councils, etc, the nature and status of which vary considerably. The great variety (especially in nature and status) of governmental institutions functioning at the regional level, makes it extremely difficult to establish a meaningful conceptual framework for these institutions.

Any attempt to give meaningful organisation to all the governmental institutions functioning at the regional level and to ensure that the resultant scheme will offer advantages is fraught with numerous difficulties, due mainly to the distinctive character of the various institutions. The nature and scope of these varied institutions is summarised below.

Provincial authorities

Provincial authorities may be regarded as truly regional *government institutions* as opposed, for example, to regional offices of departments of State, the power base of which lies at the central government level. The regional status of provincial authorities was originally enshrined in the Constitution Act.[12] Despite the constitutional 'protection' enjoyed by the provincial authorities, their right to existence has been questioned repeatedly and their abolition advocated. Closer examination of the main functions of the provincial authorities, such as control over local authorities, roads, hospital services and education, reveals that these functions could be accommodated at the level of national government.[13] It seems, therefore, that the present provincial system has merited re-appraisal within the total framework of regional government and administration. The argument of those opposed to the abolition of the provincial authorities — i.e. that these institutions should be retained for considerations of democracy, as well as for certain other reasons — is not a valid one, since there are other regional authorities that can fulfil these needs.[14] A re-appraisal of the provincial system should take the regional tier of government in its entirety into account and should assess all the functions of each participant in government at this level together.

On 6 May 1985, during the debate on his Vote in the House of Assembly, the Minister of Constitutional Development and Planning announced that provincial authorities would have to be adapted to fit in with the reforms at the other two levels of government.[15] The need for adjustments at the level of provincial government was mainly due to factors of the following kind:[16]

- Only Whites are elected to provincial councils, the other population groups being excluded.
- Provincial autonomy is limited to only a few functional spheres.
- National policy on these matters is almost invariably embodied in Acts of Parliament or Cabinet decisions, the provinces merely promulgating ordinances for the execution of such functions and the ordinances of the various provinces showing considerable similarity.
- Provincial authorities perform functions of general interest and also deal with matters of 'own' interest, which conflicts with the current principles of constitutional renewal.
- Provincial authorities are already receiving about 85% of their revenue in the form of a subsidy from the central government.
- The Administrators are appointed statutorily as the State President's official representative at the provincial government level.
- The provincial executive committees and provincial departments are concerned largely with carrying central government policy into effect.

From the foregoing it is evident that at the level of provincial government the legislative function has not proved fully justified and investigations have shown that certain governmental functions could be carried out more successfully and effectively at the lower levels of government. Consequently, the reform of the provincial system has been proceeded with.

Following discussions with the respective Administrators and MECs, consensus on the broad guidelines for a new two-tier dispensation was reached during February and April 1985. These may be summarised as follows:[17]

- The present provincial dispensation should be terminated between 29 April 1986 and 30 June 1986.
- Vacancies on the provincial councils should be filled by the political party whose seat has fallen vacant.
- The 'own affairs' which have been assigned to the various Ministers' Councils by the Constitution Act, should be transferred as soon as possible.
- The new system at the second level of government should deal with general affairs only.
- The existing provincial councils should be abolished.

- Administrators and Executive Committees should be vested with extensive statutory and subordinate legislative and executive powers to deal with general affairs. These institutions will be directly accountable to Parliament and their members will be nominated by the State President from among the ranks of politicians.
- There is a need for advisory councils which will liaise with the voters and advise the second-tier executive authorities.
- The present provincial administrations should continue to exist as second-tier administrations on the understanding that 'own affairs' will be transferred to the central tier of government and general affairs to the provinces.
- Transfers of staff and funds will coincide with the transfer of functions.
- A rationalisation between the functions of the regional offices of departments of State and those of second-tier governmental institutions will be carried out.
- Proposals regarding those functions that are to be transferred to the lower tiers of government should be submitted to the Cabinet as soon as possible.

Peri-urban areas boards and committees

These boards and committees perform their functions in specific regional areas, their main purpose being to assist in the provision of services for smaller communities in the peri-urban areas and, where possible, to guide such communities towards the development of autonomous local authorities. As these boards and committees have the expertise, experience and equipment to help smaller communities to develop into independent local authorities, the contribution they can make to the development of local authorities for population groups other than the White group should be taken into account in the evaluation of the entire spectrum of regional government and administration.

In the Transvaal there is the Transvaal Board for the Development of Peri-urban Areas. Its functions are aimed at developing the area committees in its area into fully-fledged local authorities as quickly as possible, or at incorporating local areas into the area of jurisdiction of an adjoining local authority. In the Cape Province there are the divisional councils, which were originally established to provide services, especially roads, in the rural areas of the Cape Province. In Natal, the Development and Services Board was established. This Board's area of jurisdiction is made up of semi-urban and rural areas which do not form part of the municipal areas of local authorities and within which the Board is able to provide such services as are required. In the Orange Free State, mainly because of the development of small-holding areas, it was decided to establish a Small-holding Areas Board of Control. This Board is also responsible for the orderly development of small-holding areas.[18]

Metropolitan co-operative agreements

In the strict sense of the word 'authority', as yet there can be no question of metropolitan authorities existing in South Africa. However, in various metropolitan areas it is common practice, for metropolitan co-operative agreements to be entered into on a regional basis. This points to development towards metropolitan politics and administration, which may in time develop into metropolitan authorities. At present it is mainly matters such as planning, transport, sewage and certain medical services that are involved in metropolitan co-operative agreements on a regional basis.

It is necessary to adopt a very cautious approach to the creation of metropolitan authorities, since this will necessitate a further group of governmental institutions at the regional level, which is already characterised by its great diversity of institutions. Because of the costs involved in creating metropolitan authorities, it is necessary, first, to establish whether there is in fact any need for such authorities. Some of the representatives of the local authorities involved in metropolitan co-operative agreements are not in favour of metropolitan authorities, while others consider such authorities to be desirable.

Rural co-operation

There are various reasons for there being a need for local authorities, particularly the smaller rural ones, to co-operate and in this connection considerations of cost are of cardinal importance. Co-operation between local authorities in certain regional areas is considered particularly desirable in cases where a single regional abattoir or fresh produce market can serve the region concerned, making it unnecessary for each local authority in the region to provide these services, sometimes at great expense. Co-operation in this regard is mainly informal, usually on an *ad hoc* basis. The potential advantages of such co-operation to the rural local authorities merit further consideration within the framework of regional government and administration.

Regional offices of departments of State

The regional offices of institutions such as departments of State, State-controlled corporations (Escom), agricultural product control boards and

State commercial undertakings (transport services and the post office) are also involved in regional government and administration. These governmental institutions may be distinguished from the abovementioned institutions which operate at the level of regional government. This distinction is based mainly on the organisational interrelation of regional offices and national governmental institutions. Because of this situation, regional offices can appeal to authorities at the national level for assistance and support in the performance of their functions. Especially in the light of views expressed in favour of greater decentralisation to the lower tiers of government, it is desirable to give careful thought to the nature, substance and scope of the functions of regional offices within the framework of the overall regional government and administration process.

Regional services councils

To pave the way for future metropolitan authorities, the President's Council recommended the establishment of joint services committees.[19] These committees were supposed to assist in making the nascent local authorities viable and in guiding them towards independence. Seen in terms of the definition of an authority as given above, it appears that one school of thought holds the view that the joint services committees should develop into full-scale authorities — therefore an alternative 'tier of government' — while another regards such committees as merely executive institutions of the local authorities concerned. Certain functions, chiefly those of bulk water supply, bulk electricity supply, sewage mains, sewage purification works, regional passenger transport services, regional roads, regional planning, regional cemeteries, regional refuse dumps, regional fresh produce markets and regional abattoirs, could then be earmarked for such joint services committees.

However, the establishment of joint services committees was dispensed with by the introduction of the Regional Services Councils Bill (p. 127-84) in 1984. This Bill provides for the joint performance of duties and exercise of powers by local authorities. To this end, certain regions are identified, regional services councils are established for them and the councils' composition, functioning, functions, powers and duties are set forth.[20]

In general, therefore, it appears that regional government and administration are passing through a phase of change at present. However, it should not be forgotten that the creation of regional government structures is not to be seen as an end in itself, but as a means to an end, namely the promotion of the general welfare of society in a regional context.

THE LOCAL GOVERNMENT TIER

The constitutional changes of the past year may be regarded as being amongst the most important in the history of local authorities in South Africa. Since Union (1910), local authorities have been under the supervision and control of the provincial authorities.[21]

The strongly centralised union-based system of government that developed over the years had an important influence on the status, powers and general development of local authorities. The subordinate character of local authorities within the strongly centralised governmental hierarchy was to have an adverse effect on the 'autonomy' of local authorities in South Africa. In addition, local authorities were hampered by inadequate sources of revenue.

Another important feature of the local government system in South Africa was the subordinate status of the Coloured, Indian and Black local 'authorities', at one stage or another, to the White local authorities. The Non-White local authorities could be regarded as mere appendages to the White local authorities. Within the local government system it was possible, therefore, to distinguish four subsystems, the White system acting as guardian to the others. Furthermore, the system was characterised by scant interest and participation in local government affairs on the part of the Non-White communities.[22]

The beginnings of constitutional change at the local government level can be traced back largely to the findings and recommendations of the Browne Committee,[23] the main function of which was to inquire into the need for additional sources of revenue by local authorities. The reaction, particularly the protest, elicited from local authorities in particular by these findings and recommendations, led to the formation of the Croeser Working Group, which had to inquire into and make recommendations on the findings of the Browne Committee.[24] At the same time, a committee of the President's Council[25] investigated regional and local government systems in South Africa. In the midst of these investigations and numerous debates, discussions and negotiations, specific guidelines within which the system of local government was to develop in South Africa began to emerge. These guidelines may be summarised as follows:[26]

- Constitutional change should be based on maximum devolution of powers and decentralisation of 'administration' to local authorities.
- The minimum of administrative control necessary should be exercised over local authorities.
- Separate local authorities should be established for the different population groups wherever this is at all possible.
- Certain services should be provided jointly by all the population groups on a regional basis.

- Effective co-ordination should be instituted at central government level.

In 1983, the Minister of Constitutional Development and Planning announced that the Government had accepted the President's Council recommendation regarding the establishment of a Council for the Co-ordination of Local Government Affairs to advise the Minister on any important local government affairs.[27] From the composition of this Council it appears that for the first time in the history of local government in South Africa, an earnest attempt was made to co-ordinate local government affairs in South Africa at the macro-level. A wide variety of representatives from all local authorities, the provincial authorities and certain departments of State are represented on the Council.[28]

At its first meeting in 1984, the Council for the Co-ordination of Local Government Affairs appointed six committees to conduct in-depth investigations into and make recommendations on six matters. These are discussed below.

Municipal franchise qualifications[29]

The committee that went into this matter put forward 13 recommendations. Included among these are recommendations concerning the qualification and disqualification of voters and candidates, the removal of councillors from their seats, the delimitation of wards and councillors' terms of office. It was recommended that the adoption of a code of conduct for councillors should be investigated in all provinces. The principle of uniformity of municipal franchise systems for Whites, Coloureds and Indians, as well as uniformity among the provinces, was advocated. It was also recommended that no natural person should be disenfranchised. Further, it was suggested that the recommendations should be brought into operation systematically.

Pursuant to the report and recommendations of this investigation committee, legislation which culminated in the promulgation of the Local Government Bodies Franchise Act 117 of 1984[30] in July of the same year was prepared. This Act implies that local voters themselves will decide directly, by means of democratic elections, who their elected representatives will be. As for the voters, they are divided into two categories, namely natural persons and juristic persons. Natural persons are also parliamentary voters, which means that they must be South African citizens, 18 years of age or older, White, Coloured or Indian with registered addresses within the area of the local authority of which they are members. As for juristic persons, companies, trusts and deceased estates owning ratable immovable property of a certain value in the area of jurisdiction of a local authority also have the right to vote in the ward in which such property is situated.

Depending on the circumstances, for each vacancy in a particular municipal ward a person may have one, two, or even three votes. If an individual's name appears on the parliamentary voters' list and he or she is resident in a ward but owns no immovable property, he or she has one vote; if an individual is resident in the ward and also owns immovable property, he or she has two votes; and if an individual is resident in the ward, owns property and is also authorised by a company to vote on behalf of that company, he or she has three votes.

The demarcation of geographic areas of jurisdiction of local authorities[31]

The committee charged with this investigation recommended that a demarcation board be established to fulfil the function of demarcating the areas of jurisdiction of both local authorities and group areas. Certain procedures for the demarcation of geographic areas of jurisdiction are laid down. The Committee recommended that regional services boards should determine their own boundaries and that where it was not possible to reach agreement in this connection, the Demarcation Board should be requested to conduct an independent investigation. The committee also recommended that the following criteria be taken into account in the demarcation of municipal areas of jurisdiction:

- The principle of 'own' homogeneous areas for the various population groups should be upheld in the demarcation of areas.
- The interests of the population group for which a particular local authority is to be established should be served in the area.
- The historical background, life-styles, cultural interests and traditions of the communities concerned should be taken into account and upheld.
- The present group areas, existing local government structures and degree of development already achieved, as well as the development potential of the area, should be taken into account.
- The area should meet the criteria laid down for a viable independent local authority.
- The needs of modern society should be satisfied.
- The local authorities envisaged should have the ability and the means to provide services for their residents.
- Economies of scale should be carefully considered in order to ensure that the geographic area can be efficiently and economically administered.
- Adjacent local authorities should take account of co-responsibility for matters of common interest.
- The areas of jurisdiction of local authorities should preferably consist of single, contiguous areas.

- Free trade zones should be established if the local authority concerned so wishes and the Government approves.
- The density and size of the population and the expected increase or decrease in population should be taken into account.

As the local authorities grow, their boundaries will have to be adjusted in order to meet their spatial requirements. The committee also recommended that guidelines for development in such areas be provided in the form of structural plans through which development in the respective geographic areas can be co-ordinated.

The laying down of criteria for the viability of local authorities[32]

This investigation committee was called upon to lay down criteria for viable local authorities which could serve as the basis for decisions concerning the establishment of new local authorities (especially for the Coloured and Indian population groups) and the grading of local authorities into different categories.

The committee began by defining two key concepts, namely viability and autonomy. Viability was defined as the functional and political capacity of a community to meet its physical, economic, social and cultural needs in an acceptable manner at local government level, with a reasonable prospect of improving its standard of living. Autonomy, on the other hand, was defined as the degree of independence of a local authority. From this it appears that different levels of autonomy or independence of local authorities can be distinguished. However, a particular community's level of autonomy correlates closely with its degree of viability.

The committee distinguished further between decision-making autonomy and executive autonomy. A local community might have limited means, but may, nevertheless, have certain statutory responsibilities assigned to it, even though it continues to be dependent upon some other regional or local governmental institution or a 'mother' local authority for the provision of capital-intensive services. In such a case the community has decision-making autonomy, but is dependent upon other authorities for the execution of its decisions. As soon as a local authority has executive autonomy, it will of necessity also have decision-making autonomy. Executive autonomy therefore signifies the highest level of viability and independence that may be achieved by a local authority.

The committee laid down guidelines for the existence of viable local authorities, a summary of which is given below:

- There must be a homogeneous community that requires the provision of certain municipal services. Numbers should not play any part in viability, but only in the grading of local authorities.

- A body of voters which can exercise control over the actions of its representatives by means of elections and in other ways, must exist.
- To be viable, a community must have a sufficient number of community leaders to constitute a representative institution.
- The existence of a demarcated area over which the representative institution of the community has jurisdiction is a further requirement.
- A range of basic services and facilities of a minimum prescribed standard should exist for each separate case if a community is to be viable. These include facilities and services such as water supply, health services, roads, sewerage, electricity, housing and other services such as transport, refuse dumps, traffic control, fire protection, etc.
- Trained personnel comprising a minimum nucleus of full-time or part-time administrative staff must be available.
- A local authority should have access to sufficient funds to enable it to fulfil its basic functions. The community should also be prepared, within reasonable limits, to generate its own funds for the provision of local authority services.

Control over local government institutions[33]

The committee charged with the investigation into control over local government institutions was required to go into the matter giving due regard to the principle of maximum devolution of power, the decentralisation of administration at the local government level and the reduction of administrative control over local authorities. Further, the committee was required to make recommendations for possible adjustments to the current system of prescriptive administrative control over local authorities, so as to provide for a system of constitutional and electoral control. Accordingly, the committee made the following recommendations:

- Constitutional control over local authorities should be exercised by circumscribing the functions and powers of local authorities in legislation. No further provisions regarding local authorities should be added under Item 6 of Schedule 1 to the 1983 Constitution Act and general functions and powers should be circumscribed in general legislation and 'own' functions and powers in 'own' legislation.
- Electoral control should be promoted by the laying down of procedural rules compelling local authorities to give public notice of a particular municipal decision in order to afford interested parties the opportunity of lodging objections. With a few exceptions, meetings of the council should be open to the public and the general media. Moreover, voters

should be given the right to exercise control over local authorities through access to independent authorities for the settlement of disputes. Such authorities include the courts, the Advocate-General, the Auditor-General, appeal bodies and tribunals.

- Overall control should be exercised by the central government to ensure that local authorities function within the framework of national administration as a whole.
- All authorities in all three tiers of government should take appropriate steps to ensure better understanding of and interest in local authorities in the political sphere. A comprehensive information programme would effect this.
- In view of the wider powers envisaged for local authorities, municipal tribunals to settle possible differences between local authorities, between the participating local authorities in a regional services council and a local authority and the residents, should be established. Municipal tribunals would act as independent quasi-judicial tribunals and the rules of natural justice would apply.
- The Advocate-General's present powers of investigation regarding the handling of public funds by local authorities should be retained and extended so as to enable him to investigate, on the grounds of a complaint lodged with him, the administrative actions of local autorities that amount to irregularity.
- There should be financial control over local authorities, such control being dependent upon the degree of independence and autonomy of each local authority. The records and accounts of all local authorities should be audited and an auditor's report should be submitted to an elected higher authority.
- General legislation to determine matters such as property rates, tariffs, budgets, macro-financial control, etc should be passed in Parliament.
- Regarding central government control over local authorities, a matter having many ramifications, the committee recommended that it be investigated further by all departments of State in consultation with the Department of Constitutional Development and Planning and the Commission for Administration.
- Constitutional control over the elected provincial councils should be phased out along evolutionary lines and their legislative powers should be replaced by legislation ('own' affairs) passed by the respective Houses and legislation (general affairs) passed by Parliament.

Personnel for local authorities[34]

The provisions being made for the establishment of autonomous local authorities, particularly for Coloureds, Indians and Blacks, but also for Whites, has, insofar as the greater autonomy envisaged for local authorities is concerned, given rise to an urgent need to prepare councillors and municipal officials. To create the possibility of the mobility of staff between local authorities, the committee recommended that equivalent training should be provided throughout the country on a co-ordinated basis and that use should be made of an overall structure operating country-wide to co-ordinate and constantly keep an eye on matters such as the recruitment, training, utilisation and retention of staff, as well as the orientation of councillors.

The committee also found that the image of local authorities as employers compared unfavourably with that of employers in the private sector and it recommended, therefore, that a dynamic publicity campaign be launched to improve the image of local authorities. In addition, it suggested that a policy for the recruitment of candidates should be formulated within the framework of such an improved image of local government in South Africa.

The committee also considered that staff selection should be done in an accountable way, preferably by individuals and institutions suitably trained for this purpose.

The committee emphasised the importance of training personnel. As far as in-service training is concerned, existing White local authorities in particular should be encouraged to employ members of other population groups and to train them for eventual placement in the developing local authorities.

The committee also recommended that the Council for the Co-ordination of Local Government Affairs should create a national training committee to co-ordinate training on a nation-wide basis. It suggested that the country be divided into four regions, these to coincide with the boundaries of the existing provinces, and that for each of these regions there should be a regional training committee and a regional co-ordinator. The four regions could be divided into subregions, with subregional training committees consisting of, inter alia, a subregional co-ordinator and a training office. Through this proposed structure, it would be possible to reach and involve all local authorities and to offer training at comparable levels.

Further, it was recommended that a fund be established to assist in the financing of training. Such a fund would be under the control of the Director-General of Constitutional Development and Planning, who would exercise control over disbursements from the fund as well as the assets (and liabilities) of the fund.

Another recommendation was that a practical manual on procedures be prepared under the direction of the National Co-ordinating Training Committee and that this manual be adapted from time to time. Such a manual would be necessary if the committee found that there was a serious lack of procedure manuals for functional officials and supervisors in local authorities.

Joint services and regional services[35]

The Council for the Co-ordination of Local Government Affairs requested that a committee go into the question of the joint rendering of services and the rendering of regional services. The findings and recommendations of this committee led to the tabling of the Regional Services Councils Bill in 1985. The object of the Bill is the creation of institutions for the joint rendering of services at the local government level. Whites, Coloureds, Indians and Blacks will be represented in these institutions on a proportional basis in accordance with their financial contributions to the institutions.

In terms of this draft legislation the Administrator, in consultation with all interested parties, is empowered to delimit a region, to combine two or more regions, to include part of the area of any region in that of another region, or to revoke the delimitation of a region. These regions are to be instituted to render cost-effective and efficient joint services in certain regions.

The committee recommended that, among other matters, the following should be considered in the delimitation of regions:

- The communality of general interests of all the residents of a region.
- The requirement that the region should be functional.
- Services should be based on optimum efficiency and cost-effectiveness.
- Natural boundaries should be respected.
- Existing boundaries should not, as far as possible, be disturbed.
- The area concerned should, as far as possible, constitute an economically sound unit.
- The area should, as far as possible, be financially self-supporting as regards the joint provision of services.
- The development potential of the area concerned should be borne in mind.

After consultation with the parties concerned, the Administrator may establish a regional services council for the area concerned and determine which representative institutions of the Whites, Coloureds, Indians and Blacks should constitute the council. Such a council is to be a juristic person and a wide variety of services (mainly bulk services) may be assigned to it, including the following:

- Bulk water and electricity supply

- Sewage purification works
- Land use and transport planning
- Roads and stormwater drainage
- Passenger transport services
- Traffic affairs
- Abattoirs
- Fresh produce markets
- Refuse dumps
- Cemeteries and crematoriums
- Ambulance and fire protection services
- Airports
- Civil defence
- Library services
- Museum services
- Recreation facilities
- Environmental conservation
- Promotion of tourism.

These services are of a general nature and as general affairs are provided for all the residents of the region. The council is further empowered to perform any function or duty by agreement with any local authority or administrative or representative institution, or acting as an agent on behalf of such an institution. Services rendered by the council must be accepted by the participating parties, which may not refuse such services, or render them themselves.

The regional services council is to consist of a chairman, appointed by the Administrator, and a number of members. Each local authority in the region appoints as its representative one member of the council for every 10% or part thereof of the total number of votes which such an institution has in the council. No local authority may have more than five members on the council. In this way, the domination of one group by another is obviated. The term of office of the members is five years. The number of votes which the members of a regional services council have is determined on a financial basis. The number of votes each local authority has is apportioned on the basis of its contribution to the total revenue of the regional services council derived from the provision of regional services.

From the foregoing discussion of local government institutions, it appears that the six investigating committees of the Council for the Co-ordination of Local Government Affairs have made important contributions to changing and reforming local and regional government in South Africa in their efforts to provide for the accommodation of all racial groups in the rendering of joint or general services and the individual rendering of these services.

SUMMARY

During the past decade South Africa has seen unprecedented changes and new departures in the constitutional sphere. These changes, introduced mainly as a result of pressure from abroad and the rising political aspirations of the Coloured, Indian and Black groups in South Africa, have led to the development of a new constitutional dispensation which, in the main, would involve the adaptation of existing governmental administration and institutions so as to provide for the joint rendering of general services to all population groups together, at the same time ensuring the separate rendering of services peculiar to each population group. With this broad fundamental principle in view, a start has been made with the creation at the central, regional and local tiers of government, of legislative and executive governmental institutions designed to meet the needs of a new South Africa administratively and institutionally.

NOTES

1 Commission for Administration. *Publico*, vol. 4, no. 4, December 1984, p. 4.
2 South Africa (Republic). Department of Foreign Affairs and Information. *Constitutional guidelines: A new dispensation for Whites, Coloureds and Indians*, Pretoria: Government Printer, 1982.
3 South Africa (Republic). *Republic of South Africa Constitution Act, 1983* (Act 110 of 1983), section 30.
4 *Ibid*, section 37.
5 South Africa (Republic). Department of Foreign Affairs and Information. *The New Constitution: The 1984 Elections*, Pretoria: Government Printer, 1984, p. 1.
6 Commission for Administration. *Publico, op cit*, p. 14.
7 *Ibid*, p. 15.
8 South Africa (Republic). *Republic of South Africa Constitutional Act, op cit*, section 19(1).
9 Commission for Administration. *Publico, op cit*, pp. 6-7.
10 *Ibid*, p. 10.
11 *Ibid*, supplement.
12 South Africa (Republic). *Provincial Government Act, 1961* (Act 32 of 1961), Part IV.
13 South Africa (Republic). *Joint Report of the Committee for Economic Affairs and the Constitutional Committee of the President's Council on Local and Regional Management [sic] Systems in the Republic of South Africa*, Cape Town: Government Printer, 1982, pp. 114-5.
14 Cf Cloete, JJN. Deug die provinsiale stelsel nog in hedendaagse omstandighede? *The Public Servant*, July 1970.
15 House of Assembly. Opening speech by the Hon JC Heunis during the debate on his Vote in the House of Assembly on 6 May 1985, p. 2.
16 *Ibid*, pp. 3-7.
17 *Ibid*, pp. 10-16
18 Cloete, JJN. *Munisipale regering en administrasie in Suid-Afrika*, Pretoria: Van Schaik, 1976 pp. 166-81.
19 South Africa (Republic). *Joint Report . . ., op cit*, pp. 116-7.
20 A full discussion of regional services councils appears under a subsequent head.
21 South Africa (Republic). *Provincial Government Act, 1961, op cit*, section 84(1).

22 Adlem, WLJ. Konstitusionele verandering: Die munisipale raadslid en amptenaar. *Politeia*, jg. 3, nr. 1, 1984, pp. 51-2.
23 South Africa (Republic). *Report of the Committee of Inquiry into the Finances of Local Authorities in South Africa*, vol. 1, 1980.
24 South Africa (Republic). Department of Finance. *Report of the Croeser Working Group on the Report of the Committee of Inquiry into the Finances of Local Authorities in South Africa*, Pretoria: Department of Finance, 6 May 1982.
25 South Africa (Republic). *Joint Report . . .*, op cit.
26 Haygarth, G. *Metropolitaanse ontwikkeling in 'n nuwe staatkundige bedeling*. Paper delivered at the Twenty-seventh Congress of the Institute of Town Clerks of Southern Africa, Port Elizabeth, 1983.
27 Heunis, JC. Notes used by the Hon JC Heunis, Minister of Constitutional Development and Planning, for his address to the joint meeting of five municipal associations in Cape Town on Monday 14 February 1983 at 14h30.
28 South Africa (Republic). *Promotion of Local Government Affairs Act*, 1983 (Act 91 of 1983).
29 South Africa (Republic). Council for the Co-ordination of Local Government Affairs. *Report and Recommendations of the Committee of Inquiry into Municipal Franchise Qualifications*, April 1984.
30 South Africa (Republic). *Local Government Bodies Franchise Act*, 1984 (Act 117 of 1984).
31 South Africa (Republic). Council for the Co-ordination of Local Government Affairs. *Report and Recommendations of the Committee of Inquiry into the Demarcation of Geographical Areas of Jurisdiction of Local Authorities*, April 1984.
32 South Africa (Republic). Council for the Co-ordination of Local Government Affairs. *Report and Recommendations of the Committee of Inquiry into the Determination of Criteria for Viable Local Authorities*, April 1984.
33 South Africa (Republic). Council for the Co-ordination of Local Government Affairs. *Report and Recommendations of the Committee of Inquiry into Control over Local Government Institutions*, April 1984.
34 South Africa (Republic). Council for the Co-ordination of Local Government Affairs. *Report and Recommendations of the Committee of Inquiry into Personnel of Local Authorities*, March 1984.
35 South Africa (Republic). Council for the Co-ordination of Local Government Affairs. *Report and Recommendations of the Committee of Inquiry into the Joint Provision of Services and the Provison of Services on a Regional Basis*, April 1984.

79

4 A Fragile Plant: The judicial branch of Government and the Hoexter Report

H Corder

... [A] legal system does not exist for the sake of academics, advocates, attorneys, public servants or any other particular group. It exists for the sake of the general public. It is therefore of overriding importance that our existing court system and all proposed adaptations to the system be subjected to this fundamental test: does it or will they enjoy public confidence or credibility?

Professor JPJ Coetzer, SC, at 23-4 of his 'Opening Speech' at the *Conference on the Practical Implications of the Recommendations of the Hoexter Report*, held at Pretoria in November 1984 (unpublished).

INTRODUCTION

It has long been accepted wisdom in government and opposition circles, both within South Africa and abroad, that the independence of the judiciary and the freedom of the press shine forth as beacons of liberty and fearlessness in this country. Although the image of the latter has become tarnished in the recent past due to considerable inhibitions placed on the daily press by legislation,[1] as well as direct and indirect Government action against the more outspoken newspapers,[2] the administration of law through the courts has held more tenaciously to its reputation for independent action. Despite the 'constitutional crisis' due to the removal of South Africans classified as 'Coloured' from the voters' roll in the mid-1950s, in which the Appellate Division of the Supreme Court succumbed in the face of considerable resolution on the legislature's part, the South African judiciary has continued to be greatly esteemed by the majority of commentators.[3]

In the second half of the 1970s, however, it seems that a two-fold process was taking place with regard to the administration of the country's laws. Firstly, there developed in South Africa an increasingly insistent school of thought which refused to take the judicial process at face value and trenchantly criticised the exercise of judicial power, particularly in sensitive political fields such as race and executive power.[4] Sentencing practices and the judicial interpretation of legislation were studied and often led to disquieting conclusions. In addition, the notoriety achieved by the outcome of the inquest into the death in detention of Steve Biko and the startling absence of procedural and substantive justice in the courts administering the influx control and other racially discriminatory laws contributed to public scepticism about the role of the lower courts at least. Continuing urban unrest after 1976 indicated that direct executive action was no longer as effective a control as it had been in the 1960s. It could be expected, therefore, that the courts would assume greater significance as a comparatively peaceful mechanism of social control, in addition to being seen as a means whereby subjects could attempt to protect their interests.

Secondly, it appears that there was at that stage a growing crisis in the operational efficiency of the Department of Justice (the State department responsible for the administration of the court system) and the legal profession in general.[5] There was a chronic shortage of suitably qualified and trained officials, especially at the junior levels of the prosecutorial and administrative staff of South Africa's courts. The courts themselves were overworked, with resultant delays in bringing matters to trial and inadequate opportunity for judicial officers to prepare for and consider thoroughly the issues at stake. Moreover, private legal practitioners appeared impervious to calls for limits to already high legal fees and legal education at universities and through the profession tended to display a smugly self-satisfied approach to warnings[6] that legal remedies were unattainable (and thus irrelevant) for the overwhelming majority of South Africa's population.

There were piecemeal attempts by State commissions[7] and the South African Law Commission to redress the grievances, but by the end of the 1970s it seems that the point had been reached at which a major overhaul of the courts of the country was needed if a complete breakdown in public confidence was to be avoided. It was into this set of circumstances that the Hoexter Commission was thrust.

SUMMARY OF THE MAIN FINDINGS AND RECOMMENDATIONS OF THE HOEXTER COMMISSION

The 'Commission of Inquiry into the Structure and Functioning of the Courts'[8] was appointed by the State President on 29 November 1979. Originally five members were appointed,[9] under the chairmanship of Mr Justice GG Hoexter, (t)o inquire into the structure and functioning of the courts of law in . . . South Africa and to report and make recommendations on the efficacy of that structure and functioning and on the desirability of changes which may lead to the more efficient and expeditious administration of justice and a reduction in the cost of litigation . . .

In addition, the Commission was requested to rule on the desirability of certain specific matters[10] such as an intermediate court, a Family Court, the restriction of appeals, the settlement of minor civil disputes and the incorporation of several 'non-Justice' courts under the responsibility of the Minister of Justice.

The Commission heard an extraordinarily wide-ranging and substantial body of evidence, as appears in Annexures AI and AII of the Final Report. It issued four interim reports at various stages and signed its fifth and final report in December 1983. This document was tabled in the House of Assembly in April 1984. The first three interim reports[11] dealt with particularly urgent shortcomings in the court system, to which the Government responded promptly.[12] They will not be discussed further here. The Commission's views on the subject of the fourth interim report of May 1982, the Small Claims Court system, and the chief matters of interest in the extensive final report[13] will be described in cursory fashion below. Thereafter, any implementation of the proposals thus far will be discussed and the whole exercise evaluated.

Small Claims Courts

In the fourth interim report[14] the Commission gave detailed attention to the provision of 'special machinery for the settlement of minor civil disputes in an informal manner', as it had been specifically enjoined to do.[15] In the 14 chapters of this report the Commission provides evidence of considerable research into the procedures for the settlement of small civil claims in Australia,[16] England and Wales[17] and the United States,[18] some of which had been visited by members of the Commission. After listing the main problems inherent in the normal court process as the costs involved, the time-lag before resolution of the dispute and the psychological barrier presented to many would-be litigants by the present courts,[19] the Commission concluded that the present Magistrates' Court procedures were not satisfying the requirements of small claims settlement,[20] these being accessibility, speed, low cost, simplicity, self-representation, fairness and effectiveness.[21]

In the light of the generally favourable reaction to the idea evidenced in submissions to it,[22] the Commission decided that South Africa needed a

Small Claims Court, to be introduced on an experimental basis.[23] In selecting a form of settlement of minor claims appropriate to the country, the Commission took note of the inescapable facts that most potential litigants were likely to be 'poor, ill-educated, and unsophisticated' and that there was a severe shortage of trained lawyers in relation to the perceived needs of the country.[24] Consequently, the Commission recommended, among other things,[25] that the Small Claims Courts should form part of the series of lower courts, with civil jurisdiction over several types of liquid claim up to half that of the Magistrates' Courts;[26] that presiding officers in these courts should be unpaid volunteers drawn from the ranks of the practising and teaching legal profession;[27] that adjudication, rather than conciliation, should occur informally and inquisitorially[28] as the presiding officer's prime function;[29] that legal representation should not be permitted because of its effect on the costs and expedition of proceedings,[30] but that in its stead specialised pre-trial assistance by full-time, salaried, legal and para-legal staff should be provided (senior and recently-graduated students could be employed in this way);[31] and that there should be no appeal against judgments of the courts, but limited grounds for review of the proceedings.[32] The Commission stressed the fact that the Small Claims Courts should be open to all litigants, irrespective of race or colour[33] and they facilitated its accessibility by suggesting that no award for costs should be made (other than a minimal filing fee)[34] and that court sessions should be held in the evening.[35]

The independent administration of justice

Part I of the Final Report provides a substantial and complete review of the main findings and recommendations contained in that report. Under the heading 'Efficient Administration of Justice', Part II includes seven chapters on various subjects which the Commission considers to be vital to the achievement of efficiency. Of these issues, two seem to be of special relevance to present purposes and will be outlined here and in the next section.

In discussing the independent administration of justice, the Commission proceeded upon the understanding that the doctrine of the separation of powers, formally interpreted, was recognised in South Africa[36] and it noted that the fusion of executive and judicial functions in the office of Magistrate had 'frequently given rise to severe public criticism of the lower courts . . .'[37] The Commission felt that the formal separation of offices was not a sufficient safeguard[38] and that a 'proper method of choosing proper men' was necessary.[39] With regard to the appointment of Supreme Court judges, the Commission referred to several 'indications . . . that . . . individual merit ha(d) not always been the decisive factor'[40] and opined that

> . . . it is prejudicial alike to the efficient administration of justice, the image of the Bench and public confidence if the manner in which judges are appointed leaves any room for gossip about the independence of those elevated . . .[41]

In its consideration of Professor John Dugard's contention that only a small group of judges presided in trials involving State security in the Transvaal,[42] the Commission came to no firm conclusion, but expressed several revealing thoughts:

> It is vitally important that the general public should have confidence that our courts will maintain absolute impartiality at all times and especially in cases involving subject and State. Judges should guard against a belief that those somewhat exalted notions regarding the administration of justice which they themselves may cherish are shared by the general public. The latter . . . often regard the administration of justice with a jaundiced and even cynical eye. Confidence in the law is a fragile plant.[43]

The Commission went on to review the method of determination of judges' salaries,[44] pensions and age of retirement,[45] the reasons for the reluctance of some eminent senior advocates to accept appointment to the Bench[46] and the extra-judicial functions of judges.[47] In the last instance, the Commission warned against too liberal a use of judges as members of Government commissions, for, besides possible loss of efficiency and dislocation, involvement in sensitive political issues both embarrassed the judge and damaged 'the image of independence of the administration of justice'.[48] Concerning the protection of judicial independence in the lower courts, the Commission had less to say and contented itself with pointing out the several ways in which their position as members of the Public Service detracted from the independent image of magistrates.[49]

In order to remedy these defects, the Commission suggested a detailed process of consultation by the Minister of Justice with the relevant Bench, enforceable by statute, before any judicial appointment or transfer was carried out.[50] In addition, it recommended as small a difference as was practicable between the salaries of judges in different offices '. . . so . . . as to satisfy the public that judicial aspiration to higher office is not prompted by the possibility of financial betterment'.[51] As for the office of Magistrate, the Commission recommended that it be made independent of the Public Service and that the conditions of service be protected in all respects by statute.[52]

Accessibility of the courts

After discussing the exercise of the executive functions associated with the administration of justice and recommending the creation of a Council of Justice to advise the Minister of Justice in the carrying out of such duties,[53] the Commission moved on to consider the extent of the accessibility of the courts in South Africa. It identified five major factors which hamper access to the courts, these being the excessive costs of litigation, delays in the administration of justice, the limited availability of legal aid, the geographical distribution of courts and a lack of legal information and guidance.[54]

The Commission reviewed each of these aspects in turn[55] and concentrated its gaze on the question of excessive costs, which it regarded as 'the most important reason why access to justice for most people exists in theory only'.[56] Advocates' fees in particular were closely scrutinised,[57] but, after some startling evidence, the Commission could only conclude that it was '. . . unable to find that advocates in general charge excessively high fees . . . however . . . certain advocates do err in this respect'.[58] On the question of the possible fusion of the two branches of the private practising legal profession, which seems from the report to have been more strongly supported than continued separation,[59] the Commission somewhat cautiously concluded that it was not 'in the interests of the public to grant attorneys the right of audience in the Supreme Court'.[60] Severe defects in the State legal aid scheme were apparent to the Commission.[61]

In order to attempt to lower some of these considerable barriers to access to the courts, the Commission recommended any number of adjustments to the costing and taxing practices of private legal practitioners,[62] one of which was the scrapping of the compulsory briefing of a junior advocate when a silk was briefed in a trial matter, which had been the rule in certain divisions of the court.[63] Further, it put forward the idea that 'the provision of legal representation to accused persons of limited means' should be the final goal of the legal aid scheme[64] and that steps such as the official recognition of legal clinics should be taken towards this goal.[65] Finally, in order to work towards the accessibility of the courts, the Commission recommended the immediate establishment of a State information service, its aim being to inform all South Africans about the structure and functioning of the courts.[66]

Restructuring of the Magistrates' Courts

The next issue to which the Commission paid particular attention was the lower court system, which falls under the administrative responsibility of the Minister of Justice.[67] Here the existing situation with regard to the geographical distribution, the jurisdiction and the staffing of the bench of Magistrates' Courts, as well as the relationship between those courts and the executive branch, were outlined.[68] As far as the functions of magistrates were concerned, the Commission found that generally their criminal jurisdiction was satisfactorily carried out,[69] but that the same could not be said for the exercise of their civil jurisdiction.[70] In addition, the Commission was of the opinion that the evidence before it overwhelmingly supported the conclusion that the judicial aspect of the magisterial function suffered as a result of the range of administrative duties which magistrates were expected to perform.[71]

In its consideration of the submissions made in relation to the training and recruitment of magistrates,[72] the Commission highlighted the acute and chronic shortage of trained personnel and the rapid turnover of staff with concomitant low levels of experience, especially in the prosecutorial ranks.[73] The Commission felt that this was primarily ascribable to inadequate remuneration, although several other factors, most of which flowed from magistrates' status as members of the public service, contributed to the problem.[74] To move towards a cure for these ills, the Commission set out detailed and far-reaching proposals through which there runs a constant refrain — that judicial officers in Magistrates' Courts should be relieved of their 'agency' functions on behalf of the executive so that they can be placed more firmly within the judicial branch of government.[75]

To this end, the Commission recommended that administrative and judicial work in Magistrates' Courts be separated as soon as possible;[76] that in time all judicial officers be made independent of the public service;[77] that in future administrative functions be performed by public servants known as 'resident magistrates'[78] who would nevertheless retain very limited judicial jurisdiction;[79] that an independent Regional Courts Advisory Board and a similar District Courts Advisory Board be created, their duties encompassing recommendations for the appointment, transfer, and disciplining of regional and district magistrates;[80] that recruitment for the magistracy be eased by the active pursuit of candidates of all racial groups in the private sector and by improved remuneration and conditions of service;[81] and that practical legal training be carried out independently of the public service at a 'National Law School'.[82] In addition, the Commission suggested several means whereby court procedures could be smoothed, as well a marked increase in the limits of imposable fines and civil jurisdiction and a re-delimitation of the geographical boundaries of district courts.[83]

Special courts for Blacks

There can be little doubt that the existence of separate courts to hear matters concerning Black South Africans has been a source of constant debate and, more often than not, trenchant criticism of the legal system in South Africa. Accordingly, the Commission devoted substantial attention to this matter.[84]

In a full exposition of the origins and current structure of special courts for Blacks,[85] the Commission shed light on the deadlock which had existed between the Departments of Justice and Co-operation and Development with regard to Blacks in non-homeland areas, as well as the uneasy compromise to which these divisions of the public service eventually came.[86] While the Commission did not consider it part of its brief to pronounce upon the desirability of a separate system of law which could give expression to traditional customary practices,[87] it was prepared to state repeatedly and categorically that there ought to be a single hierarchy of courts for all the inhabitants of South Africa.[88] In putting forward this conclusion, the Commission was able to rely on the support of almost all those who submitted evidence to it on this matter.[89]

As a result, the Commission felt able to recommend strongly that, with the exception of Chiefs' Courts,[90] all courts especially for Blacks should be abolished as soon as possible, the judicial function of the Commissioners' Courts being transferred to District Courts[91] and that of the Black Divorce Court to the proposed Family Court.[92]

The establishment of a Family Court

The fourth substantial structural change of which the Commission approved (after the introduction of Small Claims Courts, the reorganisation of the Magistrates' Courts and the abolition of separate courts for Blacks) was the institution of a Family Court.[93] As was the case with the investigation which preceded the fourth interim report, the Chairman of the Commission and its chief researcher travelled abroad to gain insight into the operation of such courts in other countries.[94] Further, the Commission relied extensively on the work of an academic in order to aid its analysis of the issues surrounding such a concept.[95]

The Commission started from the premise that a Family Court should seek to synthesise the approaches and functions of courts of law and social experts and proceeded to discuss the therapeutic and integrative potential of such a court in contrast to the adversarial and fragmentary nature of the existing approach to family matters in the South African court system.[96] Up till that point, however, several investigations into the desirability of a

South African Family Court had not supported such an idea[97] and the bulk of legal opinion submitted to the Commission was in the same vein, while social scientists were overwhelmingly in favour of such a court.[98]

The Commission concluded that the present fragmentation of jurisdiction adversely affected the adjudication of family matters[99] and that separate court systems based on race were 'morally indefensible, and incompatible with the fundamental principle that all are equal before the law'.[100] In addition, the Commission found that theoretical standards had been substantially relaxed or ignored in the practical adjudication of divorce, childrens', juvenile and maintenance matters,[101] that the working relationship between the courts and welfare agencies left a lot to be desired[102] and that there was an urgent need for more legal aid and advice in this sphere of legal relations.[103] In the light of these and other factors, the Commission decided that South Africa was in need of a Family Court 'with comprehensive jurisdiction in respect of all family matters'.[104]

In recommending this course of action, the Commission suggested that the Family Court should be a lower court functioning at the level of the Regional Court[105] and consisting of a social component (counselling service) and a court component.[106] The Family Court should have wide-ranging jurisdiction over family matters, including divorce actions and the status of juveniles and aged persons,[107] although jurisdiction in divorce and ancillary actions was to be concurrent with that of the Supreme Court.[108] The Commission proposed several alterations to procedure in divorce actions to bring practice in line with theory,[109] including the creation of the office of 'Children's Friend' in order to protect the interests of minor and dependent children at public expense.[110] The Commission felt that this new system for the adjudication of family matters ought to be preceded by one or more pilot projects.[111]

Additional important matters considered by the Commission

Besides the six pre-eminently relevant issues described above, it is necessary to draw attention to four other matters dealt with at some length by the Commission in its final report.

In the first place, the structure and operations of the Supreme Court were reviewed with an eye to their efficacy.[112] Here the Commission concentrated on the Court's workload[113] and several factors affecting expeditious action in this regard, including staff shortages,[114] inefficiency of private practitioners[115] and the system of automatic review of magistrates' decisions.[116] The Commission recommended that operators of recording machines be supplied for lower courts (a task at present performed by presiding officers).[117] Its suggested solution for the relief of the workload of the Provincial Divisions in civil cases was to increase the jurisdiction of the Magistrates' Courts;[118] the number of judges should not be increased to a great extent as the exclusivity of the Supreme Court ought to be maintained.[119] In addition, a permanent Rules Board representative of each branch of the profession should be constituted, with the task of bringing uniformity to the rules of court.[120]

Secondly, the Commission had been asked specifically to determine the desirability of the introduction of an intermediate court between the lower and superior courts.[121] Opinion before the Commission was divided, the vast majority of the practising private legal profession being against the idea and the magistracy and a fact-finding committee of the Department of Justice supporting it.[122] It seems, in the end, that factors such as cost, the proliferation of courts and the 'potential threat to the prestige and independence of the Supreme Court' convinced the Commission that such an intermediate court was not desirable.[123]

Thirdly, in Part VIII of the report the Commission reviewed the status and position of 'Officers of the Court' at some length. It stressed its belief in the fearless independence of the office of Attorney-General and his supporting staff and deplored the lack of experience often to be found amongst the latter, mainly due to the poor remuneration offered.[124] In this regard the Commission recommended greater security of tenure for Attorneys-General and salaries for state advocates more in keeping with their potential earnings in private practice.[125] Similar sentiments were expressed about the work of registrars and clerks of the courts, concerning whom no criticism whatsoever had been submitted to the Commission.[126]

Finally, in Part IX of its report the Commission considered several sundry items such as the status of courts under the administrative responsibility of Ministers other than the Minister of Justice, bail and the recording of court proceedings.[127] Its most provocative statements were left to the last and its consideration of the 'enormous size of South Africa's prison population'.[128] The Commission disclosed that the prisons were overcrowded to the extent of 46% and maintained that 'hordes' of Blacks, in prison as the result of influx control measures, should not have been there at all. In its words,

> they are the needy victims of a social system that controls the influx of people from the rural to the urban areas by penal sanction. The reason for this virtually unstemmable influx is poverty.[129]

The overcrowding of prisons bred contempt for the court system among Blacks and frustrated penological and sentencing policies.[130] In the view of the Commission, this situation severely affected the image of justice and could not be allowed to continue.[131]

REACTION TO AND IMPLEMENTATION OF THE COMMISSION'S PROPOSALS

From the outset it was clear that the Hoexter Commission's reports were not such that the Government could afford to ignore them. The fact that large proportions of the existing corps of judges, advocates, attorneys, magistrates, legal academics and other interested parties had testified before the Commission lent weight to its considered opinions.[132] Swift measures were taken to remedy the defects pointed out in the first three interim reports[133] and these seem to have had the desired effect. The Small Claims Courts Act[134] substantially incorporates the recommendations of the fourth interim report, although the planned launching of pilot projects has been postponed because of financial stringency.[135]

The final report was accorded extensive analysis and comment in the daily press and a special parliamentary debate on its findings and recommendations was held soon after publication.[136] The main speaker, the Minister of Justice, generally welcomed the report on behalf of the Government, stating that it was predicated on

> ... die vasberadenheid ... om te verseker dat ons regspleging vanweë sy doeltreffendheid steeds die waarborg is ... vir die regte, belange en voorregte van alle onderdane van hierdie land.[137]

He confirmed the Government's adherence to the doctrine of the separation of powers, but was not prepared to accede to the request for legislation to make consultation with the Bench prior to new appointments mandatory, as this was the practice by which he was already bound, he said, and appointments were made on merit.[138]

Further, the Government welcomed the ideal of splitting the judicial from the administrative magisterial functions, the 'rationalisation' regarding special courts for Blacks and the concepts of a Family Court and a Council of Justice, although in each case vested interests and the financial cost of implementation were inhibiting factors.[139] With regard to the prison population, the Minister differed from the Commission as to the extent to which influx control laws contributed to overcrowding and added that measures already taken had reduced overcrowding to 41,8% and that the Government was building more prisons.[140]

The reactions that this speech and the final report elicited from other members of the House of Assembly were fairly predictable — the PFP saw the Hoexter criticisms as an indictment of the Government and the Minister;[141] the Conservative Party called for a series of family courts for the different 'population groups';[142] and the NRP regarded the report as part of the 'reform process'.[143] Other National Party speakers tried to defend the Government's record with regard to the administration of the courts of the country.[144]

Since that debate it appears that several of the recommendations of the final report have, in fact, been implemented by the Government. Commissioners' Courts have been transferred to the control of the Minister of Justice[145] and the civil jurisdiction of Magistrates' Courts has been increased,[146] as has the punitive jurisdiction in respect of fines imposed in Magistrates' Courts.[147] In addition, a Divorce Amendment Bill and a Family Court Bill have been referred to a joint committee of all three Houses of Parliament in order that further evidence and comment may be heard[148] and the Department of Justice 'proposes to establish a uniform rules board for all courts'.[149]

It seems, therefore, that the Government has shown a serious commitment to the adoption of at least the structural and some of the functional alterations put forward by the Hoexter Commission. Whether changes in form will be sufficient to ensure the efficient and expeditious administration of the laws of the country remains to be seen.

COMMENTS AND CRITICISMS

The Hoexter Report is an impressive document and its well-argued, clearly-expressed findings and recommendations stand to be ignored only by the foolish or the short-sighted. It presents a frequently chilling indictment of the lamentable shortcomings present in parts of the South African judicial branch of government. The Commission is uncompromising in its propagation of the catch-phrase 'equality before the law', a sentiment with which each chapter of its final report is infused. In this respect it is worthwhile and probably indispensable to quote just three passages from the report which starkly indicate the Commissioners' approach:

> That inhabitants of the same country should purely on the grounds of race be criminally prosecuted in separate courts is . . . by any civilised standard, unnecessary, humiliating and repugnant.[150]

> Separate court systems on the grounds of race are morally indefensible, and incompatible with the fundamental principle that all are equal before the law.[151]

> The Commission accepts as a fundamental principle that the proposed family court should be open to all the inhabitants of the Republic regardless of race or colour.[152]

Naturally, the Commission's report may be criticised on a number of grounds, the thrust of which will depend upon the perspective of the critic. For the writer, there is sometimes a perceived tendency for the Commissioners to be overly legalistic in their approach, which stems perhaps from a too-secure belief in the majestic potential of the law and the Supreme Court. Certainly, the prestige and exclusivity of the latter institution are jealously guarded, as the following quotations indicate:

> An important safeguard of the independence of the Judiciary in this country is the fact that the Bar serves as the primary source of appointments to the Supreme Court Bench.[153]

> The Commission holds the view ... that the exclusiveness of the Supreme Court should be preserved as regards both the limitation of the size of its Bench and selectivity in determining the nature of the cases to be heard by it.[154]
> And

> In consequence of the establishment of an intermediate court the Supreme Court would lose prestige both in the eyes of the inhabitants of our country and in the eyes of the outside world.[155]

For this reason, perhaps, the Commission failed to recommend the establishment of further courts (or even tribunals) to relieve the Supreme Court in the area of administrative law.

In addition, when it came to a consideration of the activities of the Industrial Court, the Commission seemed to assume that 'true judicial independence' could occur only under the aegis of the Department of Justice.[156] It appears, also, to have taken too complacent an attitude to the matter of limiting legal costs.

However, these remarks must be read in the context of a remarkable willingness on the part of the Commissioners, given the 'inherent conservatism of the legal fraternity in this country',[157] to borrow from the court systems of other countries,[158] to cast out dysfunctional though traditional practices,[159] to introduce bold new concepts[160] and to learn from academic writings.[161] On occasion, the Commission was also prepared to disregard the views of the overwhelming majority of legally-trained deponents before it.[162]

It is still too early to say whether the type of structural and functional changes proposed by the Commission will succeed in eliminating many of the defective aspects of the South African court system. Certainly, if fully implemented in the spirit of the report, the changes will restore much-needed credibility to the courts as a mechanism for conflict-management, and even conflict-resolution, in South African society.

But this touches the heart of the matter. No doubt can remain in the mind of the reader of the Hoexter Final Report that the crisis of the legitimacy of the courts referred to in the Introduction to this chapter is an acute reality. Once more, the anxiety of the Commissioners on this score shines clearly through their comments:

> The image of criminal justice in our lower courts is impaired by the observance of administrative arrangements incompatible with the standards of judicial aloofness expected of magistrates.[163]

> [Poorly-prepared] legal representatives not only make the task of the judicial officers more difficult, but also create a poor impression in the public mind of the administration of justice.[164]

> [T]he image of the administration of justice in South Africa in general is seriously impaired [by the 'political' duties of magistrates].[165]

> It is a cardinal maxim of our law that justice should not only be done but should also be seen to be done. Accordingly, it was argued that it was monstrous and quite untenable for officers of the very department which lays down the policy with regard to Blacks to preside at the trial of a Black for offences directly connected with the implementation of that policy.[166]

> And

> [Prison sentences for influx control offenders] breeds in many Blacks . . . contempt for the administration of justice and the criminal courts in particular.[167]

These and similar utterances[168] convey a strong sense of an attempt to rescue the courts and legal system from complete identification with the manifestly discriminatory laws which they interpret and apply daily. This awareness of the parlous position of the judicial branch of government must be juxtaposed with the ever-increasing attention devoted to the judicial function by South African legal writers in the years of the Commission's existence.[169] The gist of most of these contributions is that the judicial branch of government has a duty to uphold the basic principles of justice and that it had too often failed to do so, a tendency which was on the rise.

The question which must be posed in the light of the critical position in which the courts of South Africa find themselves is this: Is it in any sense a realistic expectation that the law and the courts of a political system which, by most standards, does not meet the requirements of justice can, in some remarkable way, remain untainted by the activities of the legislative and executive branches of government? More concretely, will the implemented Hoexter proposals ensure the administration of 'justice' in South Africa?

The answer to these questions is likely to be in the negative for several reasons. The nature of law as a system for social ordering, the position of the courts in the constitutional structure of South Africa and, most important-ly, the ideological role which law and the courts fulfil in the maintenance of the interests of the authorities all play their parts in limiting the judicial branch of government to a strictly circumscribed contribution to initiative for social change. There is no necessary connection between the existence of an efficient and expeditious system of courts and the maintenance of the principles of what is commonly called 'justice'.

But this does not necessarily dispose of the value of the Hoexter enterprise. There is a school of thought which propagates the notion that the fact that power is exercised through pre-publicised laws and a well-established and functioning system of courts is in itself a curtailment of the arbitrary use of that power and a protection for those living under the wielders of that power.[170] According to this argument, the changes to the courts proposed by the Commission are significant, not in that they create justice, but in that they constitute a framework which accords attempts to remedy injustices a better chance of success than if it had not existed. There are those who would deny this, arguing that the imposition of an apparently fair court system and sufficient propaganda about 'equality before the law' on an inequitable political system is counter-productive in that the dispossessed do not realise their true position and are thus less likely to attempt to alleviate it.[171]

In assessing the proposals of the Hoexter Commission in the context of their potential for change in South Africa, the former argument is preferred. There are signs that there is increasing awareness that efforts to achieve social change can be invested with an important and sometimes vital status if confirmed in law by a court.[172] There can be no doubt, too, that many legitimate interests continue to be ignored in South Africa through the lack of this sanction of the law only because those entitled to these interests are ignorant of the way in which to go about their confirmation. In addition, the pre-Hoexter court system was decidedly unsympathetic to the needs of the poor and the illiterate.

Without idolising law or the legal process, it can probably be claimed that the Hoexter Report has given a great boost to the adaptability of the court system in the light of the changing needs of the inhabitants of South Africa. On the other hand, whether the courts and law are to be given a chance to participate or are to be made redundant by the rapidity of the process of change depends ultimately on factors in the socio-economic sphere. But lawyers can play some part and therein lies the challenge.[173]

94

NOTES

1 See particularly the catalogue of controls listed in Stuart, KW. *The Newspaperman's Guide to the Law.* 3rd ed. Durban: Butterworths, 1982.

2 For example, the banning of the *World* newspaper in October 1977; regular action against the student press under the Publications Control Act, 1974 (Act 42 of 1974); as well as the prosecution of individual reporters and editors and the founding with State funds of a Government-supporting newspaper, *The Citizen.*

3 There were some dissenting voices. See, for example, International Commission of Jurists, *Erosion of the Rule of Law in South Africa.* Genéve : ICJ, 1968; Millner, Apartheid and the South African Courts (1961) 14 Current Legal Problems 280; and Sachs, A. *Justice in South Africa.* London: Chatto Heinemann, 1973.

4 See particularly the work of Professors Dugard and Van Niekerk in several contributions to the *South African Law Journal,* and Dugard's book *Human Rights and the South African Legal Order.* Princeton: Princeton University Press, 1978. For a review of the literature on this issue, see Corder, HM. *Judges at Work.* Cape Town: Juta, 1984, pp. 231-237.

5 As was to be confirmed in submissions to the Hoexter Commission (see below).

6 Which often emanated from student ranks in the form of publications such as Corder, HM. *Lexis.* Cape Town: NUSAS, 1978.

7 Such as the Botha Commission of Inquiry into Criminal Procedure (1971), the Viljoen Commission of Inquiry into the Penal System (1976) and the Galgut Commission of Inquiry into Civil Proceedings in the Supreme Court (1980).

8 Referred to as 'the Commission' below.

9 Representative of the bench, the bar, the side-bar, the Department of Justice and the academic profession. As a result of death and resignation, only three of these five signed the final report.

10 See (a) to (g) of the Commission's terms of reference at 1-2 of its Final Report.

11 These reports were submitted in January 1980 and February and April 1981.

12 In the form of the Supreme Court Amendment Act, 1980 (Act 46 of 1980); the payment of additional allowances to certain employees of the Department of Justice; and the Appeals Amendment Act, 1982 (Act 105 of 1982).

13 The fifth and final report appears in nine parts contained in three volumes, plus one volume of annexures (RP 78/1983). Unfortunately, the pagination differs in the English and Afrikaans versions of the report, so reference will be made here to the chapter, section and paragraph numbers within each part under discussion.

14 RP 52/1982.

15 In par. (f) of its terms of reference.

16 Chapters 6 and 7.

17 Chapters 8 and 9.

18 Chapters 10 and 11.

19 Chapter 2.

20 Chapter 4.

21 Chapter 3.

22 Chapter 5.

23 Chapter 12.

24 Chapter 13.1.

25 Chapter 14 of this report provides a very good summary of the findings and recommendations.

26 Chapter 13.2.

27 Chapter 13.4.

28 Chapter 13.8.

29 Chapter 13.6.

30 Chapter 13.9 to 13.12.

31 Chapter 13.13 to 13.15.

32 Chapter 13.35 to 13.40.

33 Chapter 13.44 and 13.45.

34 Chapter 13.21.
35 Chapter 13.23.
36 Par. 1.1.1.
37 Par. 1.1.8.
38 Par. 1.2.1.
39 Par. 1.2.3.
40 Par. 1.3.2.
41 Par. 1.3.5.
42 Par. 1.3.8.1.
43 Par. 1.3.8.4.
44 Par. 1.3.9.
45 Par. 1.3.10.
46 Par. 1.3.11.
47 Par. 1.3.12.
48 Par. 1.3.12.3.
49 Par. 1.4.
50 Par. 3.1.1.
51 Par. 3.1.2.
52 Par 3.2.
53 See Chapters 4 and 5 of Part II.
54 Par. 6.1.2.
55 See parr. 6.2 to 6.6, in which the Commission makes much use of the works by Cappelletti, M and Garth, B. *Access to Justice* (1978/1979) Alphenandenrijn: Zijthoff and Noordhoff and Zander, M. *Cases and Materials on the English Legal System.* 3rd ed. London: Weidenfeld and Nicolson, 1980.
56 Par. 6.2.1.6.
57 Par. 6.2.2.
58 Par. 6.2.2.2.8.
59 See par. 6.2.4.
60 Par. 6.2.4.19.
61 See par. 6.4.
62 See parr. 7.1. to 7.9.
63 Par. 7.4.
64 Par. 7.13(a).
65 Par. 7.13(c).
66 Par. 7.14.
67 See Part IV of the final report.
68 Chapter 1.
69 Par. 2.2.1.2. Remarkably, 85% of criminal cases in South Africa in 1980 were heard at district magistrates' court level (par. 2.2.1.2.1).
70 Par. 2.2.1.3.
71 Par. 2.3.
72 Chapters 3 and 4.
73 Par. 4.1.
74 Par. 4.2.
75 Chapter 5 *passim*, particularly 5.1.2 and 3.
76 Par. 6.4(a).
77 Par. 6.4(b).
78 Par. 6.5.
79 Parr. 6.6 and 6.7.
80 Par. 6.13.
81 Parr. 6.14, 6.17 and 6.18.
82 Par. 6.15.
83 Parr. 6.18, 6.19 and 6.21 and Annexures B, C and D.
84 Part V of the report.
85 Chapter 3.

86 Parr. 3.13 to 3.20.
87 Par. 4.1.
88 Parr. 4.3 and 4.4 and Chapter 6.
89 Chapters 4 and 5.
90 Par. 7.1.
91 Par. 7.2.
92 Par. 7.3.
93 Part VII of the report.
94 Chapter 1.
95 Chapter 2, the work of Dr ID Schäfer.
96 Chapters 3 and 4.
97 Chapter 5.
98 Chapter 6.
99 Par. 7.1.
100 Par. 7.2.
101 Par. 7.3.
102 Par. 7.4.
103 Par. 7.5.
104 Par. 7.8.
105 Par. 9.1.
106 Par. 9.4.1, further defined in parr. 9.4.2 and 9.4.3.
107 Par. 9.6.1.
108 Par. 9.7.2.
109 Parr. 9.7.1 and 9.8.1.
110 Par. 9.8.2.
111 Par. 9.14.
112 Part III of the report.
113 Par. 2.1.3.2.6.
114 Par. 2.2.1.2.
115 Parr. 2.2.1.1 and 2.2.2.2.
116 Par. 2.1.4.
117 Par. 2.2.2.
118 Parr. 2.1.3.3. and 3.1.
119 Par. 2.1.3.2.8(e).
120 Parr. 3.5 and 3.7.
121 Par. (a) of its terms of reference and Part VI of the report.
122 Chapters 2, 3 and 4.
123 Chapters 5, 6 and 7.
124 Part VIII, Chapter 1.
125 Chapter 2.
126 Chapters 3 and 4.
127 Chapters 1, 2, 3 and 4.
128 Chapter 5.
129 Par. 5.2.
130 Parr. 5.3.2 and 3.
131 Parr. 5.4.1 and 2.
132 The lists of deponents which appear in Annexures A(I) and A(II) are impressively representative of South African legal opinion.
133 See note 12 above.
134 61 of 1984.
135 Statement by Minister of Justice, 1 March 1985.
136 *Hansard*, Thursday 12/4/1984, cols 4965-5023.
137 Col. 4 966.
138 Col. 4 967.
139 Cols 4 968-4 970.
140 Cols 4 971-4 972.

141 See DJ Dalling (cols 4 972-4 981); H Suzman (cols 5 002-5 006); and HH Schwarz (cols 5 016-5 020).
142 See LM Theunissen (cols 4 988-4 991).
143 See PC Rogers (cols 4 995-4 997).
144 See HMJ van Rensburg (cols 4 982-4 987); L van der Watt (cols 4 998-5 001).
145 As from 1 September 1984, by Proc R 131 of 1984 in GG 9367.
146 By the Magistrates' Courts Amendment Act, 1984 (Act 56 of 1984), which came into force on 2 May 1984.
147 By the Criminal Procedure Matters Amendment Act, 1984 (Act 109 of 1984), which came into force on 1 September 1984.
148 Both bills were introduced by the Minister of Justice on 11 March 1985.
149 Bekker, JC. and Pannell, PC. Amendments to Legislation on Courts in the wake of Hoexter, paper presented at a conference on the practical implications of the Hoexter Report. Pretoria: November 1984, at 6 (unpublished).
150 Part V, par. 6.1.
151 Part VII, par. 7.2.
152 Part VII, par. 8.18.
153 Part II, par. 1.3.11.7.
154 Part III, par. 2.1.3.2.8(e).
155 Part VI, par. 6.1. In par. 7.2 the Commission also recommended that the official designation 'judge' be reserved exclusively for members of the Supreme Court Bench.
156 Part IX, Chapter 1, par. 2.
157 Part II, par. 6.1.4.
158 Albeit perhaps, slightly inappropriate first-world models considering South African conditions.
159 Such as the two-advocate rule.
160 Such as the Small Claims and Family Courts.
161 See notes 55 and 95 above.
162 Approval of the Family Court idea is a good example.
163 Part I, par. 3.4.2.8.
164 Part IV, par. 2.2.1.3.13.
165 Part IV, par. 4.2.1.(g)(ii) (author's paraphrase).
166 Part V, par. 4.3.6.
167 Part IX, par. 5.3.2.
168 For example, part II par. 3.2.(d), part IV parr. 5.1.3 and 5.7.1.1, part VII par. 8.12.3 and part VIII par. 1.8.
169 See here the list of articles cited at footnote 1 on page 242 of Corder, HM. Judges at Work (1984).
170 The modern origins of this argument can be traced to the work of Thompson, EP. Whigs and Hunters. London: Allen Lane, 1975 and subsequent writings which have built on that base.
171 See, for example, Bankowski, Z. and Mungham, G. Images of Law. London: Routledge and Kegan Paul, 1976, passim.
172 This is particularly evident in the field of Labour Law, through the Industrial Court — ironically, one of the courts which does not fall under the control of the Department of Justice.
173 It is readily acknowledged that the issues and criticisms contained in this last discussion raise problems which are symptomatic of long-standing and crucial disputes about the existence of law and its role in society. It is not possible nor within the scope of this chapter to do full justice to the several points of view in this wide-ranging debate. However, it is thought to be important to situate any consideration of the Hoexter Report within such a context.

5 Urbanisation: A South African perspective

PC Kok and WP Mostert

INTRODUCTION

Urbanisation is inevitable and occurs world-wide wherever there is potential for further urbanisation and socio-economic development is taking place. No country has ever been able to escape this process in the course of its development and therefore it is a process that must be accepted as inevitable in South Africa, too. Urbanisation has already taken place among some of the population groups in the country (viz the Whites, the Indians and the Coloureds) and is under way at present among the Black population.[1]

What must be fully appreciated, however, is that South Africa, although not yet experiencing any urbanisation problem[2] worth mentioning, is already weighed down by its population problem. The magnitude of this problem becomes clear if one considers that South Africa's total population (along with those of Ethiopia and Zaire) is the third largest in Africa — only Egypt and Nigeria have larger populations. Moreover, only 24 countries in the world have populations exceeding South Africa's in size — there are two in Africa, 12 in Asia, one in North America (the USA), two in Latin America (Mexico and Brazil) and seven in Europe (including the USSR). (See Population Reference Bureau 1983.)

Any reference to the 'problem' of urbanisation usually brings to mind the phenomenon of metropolitanisation (especially in a country's prime metropole). It is in the metropoles that the rate and extent of urbanisation are at their greatest and, due to the media coverage given to these matters, at their most visible. The distinction between urbanisation and metropolitanisation is not merely an academic manipulation of words, but is fundamental to a proper understanding of the problem. Therefore, when the problems concerning urbanisation are referred to in this chapter, what

99

is actually meant are the metropolitanisation problems experienced by the Third World in general and South Africa in particular.

Notwithstanding the often difficult living conditions in the city (the lack of job opportunities in the formal sector, poor housing, etc), it is now clear that migrants from rural areas are better off than they would be if they did not migrate (see, for example, United Nations 1984: 41). In the formulation of an urbanisation strategy, this fact should be taken into account.

It is also important to remember that mortality, fertility, migration/ urbanisation and socio-economic development cannot be compartmentalised. These four phenomena are inseparably bound up with each other and any factor influencing one will also influence the others. Therefore, in a democratic country there can be no question of socio-economic development in the absence of urbanisation, while socio-economic development is — with a few exceptions in communist or autocratic countries, for example, China and Indonesia (see Freedman 1979) — essential to the abatement of the population increase.

THEORETICAL PERSPECTIVES

Introductory remarks

Before discussing the expected future trends in urbanisation, it is necessary to obtain a theoretical perspective. It is necessary to know what the motives for migration are, which members of the population show the highest tendency to migrate, which impeding factors apply to migration and what we can learn from the theories relating to mobility transition regarding the urbanisation trends imminent in the Third World (of which South Africa is part). The literature affords important insights into this phenomenon. In Kok (1985: chapter 4) we have a fairly detailed exposition of the present 'state of the art' in migration theory. A few relevant aspects are touched upon briefly in this discussion.

Migration stems from certain motivating and influencing factors at the micro-level (the individual and/or family), the meso-level (the local community) and the macro-level (the region or country). Because of this, migration is a singularly complex phenomenon which poses great challenges to research.

Selective and motivational aspects

International empirical research reveals that it is particularly the young adult who has a relatively high potential occupational and social status

100

who tends to migrate. Empirical research in South Africa comfirms this. The conclusion to be drawn is that the rural areas subject to large-scale out-migration may be losing their best human material to the metropolitan areas during phases of metropolitanisation.[3]

Analyses of the selectivity of rural/urban migration indicate that it is mainly those who have a lesser capacity for achieving success in the city who prefer alternative opportunities in agriculture and other fields in the countryside. This conclusion is confirmed by recent findings overseas and in South Africa that it is the 'pull' factors of the city that may be decisive and not the 'push' factors of the rural areas as was previously believed. One of the implications of this is that the motivation to migrate (which is based on personal needs and aspirations) does, after all, justify in-depth research. The particularly relevant influence of family and friendship ties in decision making about migration, especially in the choice of destination, is also not to be underrated. Information transmission and dissemination, as well as information processing and evaluation by the decision maker, are therefore important.

As far as migration forecasting models are concerned, an evaluation of the various types of models indicates that the macro-level models have little to offer in the way of improving the policy maker's insight into the process of migration. On the other hand, the micro-level models, although not without operational problems, are far more suitable to the purposes of policy formulation. The type of micro-level model that is aimed at quantifying people's value-expectations concerning possible migration destinations — for example, with a view to forecasting — has the greatest potential for policy formulation and is therefore being investigated by the HSRC at present.

Resistance factors

Distance (in any of its forms — geographic, social, psychological, etc — and as a substitute for time, income, social and other losses) is an important resistance factor in the migration process. There is a theory that migration often takes place in steps — people move from a rural environment to a nearby town (largely as a result of the distance resistance factor), from there to a larger town or a city, thence to the regional prime city and perhaps eventually to the national prime metropolis. This theory was originally formulated in the 19th century, but so far it has not been possible to find universal proof for it. Indeed, empirical research in South Africa shows that the Black population does not go through these processes, but simply migrates straight to the metropoles from rural environments. This phe-

101

nomenon is probably largely due to the absence of any intermediate cities worth mentioning in South Africa — a matter which certainly merits attention in the formulation of an urbanisation strategy.

Mobility transition[4]

At this stage it is necessary to consider the mobility transition theories in broad outline in order to form an idea of the position of South Africa's population on a mobility continuum.[5]

The mobility transition theories put forward by Zelinsky (1971), Brown and Sanders (1981) and Kelly and Williamson (1984) have the following in common: Large-scale urbanisation may be expected in the Third World (and therefore also in South Africa) in the decades to come as a result of high levels of urban in-migration and a subsequent decline in the contribution of rural–urban migration to total urban growth. Although these transition theories cannot be regarded as nomological, since a country may not necessarily develop along exactly the same lines suggested in the theories, they do, nevertheless, indicate the most probable future course of mobility and are useful in that they give a perspective on a country's relative position on the urban development continuum.

Discussions of these transition theories are also contained in Kok (1985: paragraph 2.4) and therefore it is not necessary to go into detail here. However, what is important to further discussion is Kelly and Williamson's theory (1984), which indicates that the urbanisation level of a 'typical' Third World country over time will be in the form of a logistic curve (an extended S-curve) with a relatively steep positive incline between the years 1980 and 2020. (The curve is illustrated in figure 5.1.) This suggests that, although urbanisation is expected to increase sharply in the Third World, later (from about the year 2020) it will tend to become asymptotic to a saturation level of 85%, which Kelly and Williamson consider to be an 'urban limit' for non-island states. They believe that the relative contribution of natural increase to the growth of the urban population may increase slowly, but that urban in-migration (as a percentage of total urban population increase) will initially rise sharply to about 40% a year and thereafter begin to decline sharply, eventually tending to become asymptotic to a level near zero.

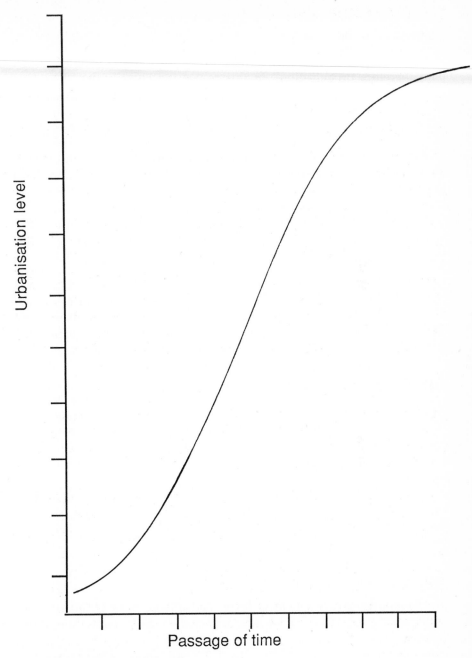

Fig 5.1 Normal pattern of urbanisation

EXPECTED FUTURE URBANISATION

Introductory remarks

In Mostert et al (1985), it is shown how difficult it is to predict migration (and therefore urbanisation). In this report the authors also show that urbanisation is closely related to income, literacy and female participation in labour (all three of these being elements of socio-economic development) in Third World countries. If the rate of socio-economic development in the country were to increase, there would probably be an increase in the urbanisation rate and vice versa. Therefore, forecasting is out of the question. All that can be done is to indicate what the urbanisation level might be expected to be if existing trends were to continue, or if there were to be certain changes in existing trends.

As far as Whites, Indians and Coloureds are concerned, the future course of urbanisation is more predictable than that of the Black population, since the urbanisation levels of the first-mentioned three groups are already close to the theoretical saturation levels and there is therefore greater clarity regarding probable future trends in urbanisation. However, in the case of the Black population, which at present is still very far from the saturation level as far as urbanisation is concerned, scientifically-based forecasts of future levels of urbanisation are not possible and any projections or forecasts for this population group are obviously highly speculative.

Expected urbanisation of Whites

Application of the modified exponential curve to White urbanisation levels from the beginning of the present century has shown an expected saturation level of 94,2%. This saturation level has been built into a logistic regression equation (see Mostert et al 1985) and the result is illustrated in figure 5.2.

It is clear from the figure that White urbanisation has already entered the saturation phase, the point at which the level of urbanisation begins to become asymptotic (and urbanisation is replaced by increased metropolitanisation).

Expected urbanisation of the Indian population

The theoretical saturation level for urbanisation among Indians is estimated at 97,4%. Figure 5.3 shows the expected trend of urbanisation among Indians.

Fitting the logistic curve to the urbanisation of Indians is less satisfactory for the 1970 and 1980 census years, but, viewed as a whole, it does offer a

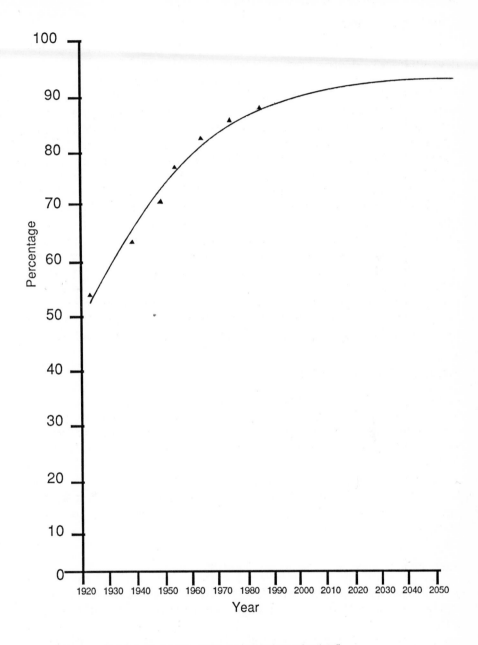

Fig 5.2 Expected urbanisation levels: Whites (percentage urbanised)

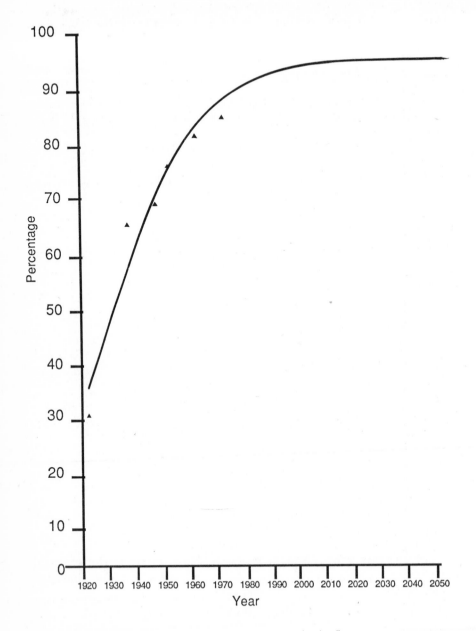

Fig 5.3 Expected urbanisation levels: Indians (percentage urbanised)

good approximation of the historical course of urbanisation of the Indian population. It is clear from figure 5.3 that the Indians, like the Whites, have virtually reached the saturation phase, at which urbanisation is replaced by increased metropolitanisation.

Expected urbanisation of the Coloured population

The present and expected urbanisation levels of the Coloureds, whose saturation level of urbanisation is estimated at 91,4%, are shown in figure 5.4.

According to this graph, the Coloured population may be expected to reach the theoretical saturation level towards the end of the second decade of the next century if present trends continue. However, that phase may be reached sooner, depending on prevailing socio-economic conditions in the country in general and in relation to the Coloured population in particular. A levelling off in the rate of urbanisation among this group is, however, already evident.

Possible future urbanisation of the Black population

General orientation

As stated previously, a forecast with regard to Black urbanisation is highly problematic. Figure 5.5 shows the historical course of the urbanisation of the Black population (derived from the various censuses).

The levelling off that has manifested itself since 1951 is not in accord with the theoretical transition models, nor is it possible to find any economic or other related explanation for this change in trend, which must therefore be attributed to one or more of the following factors:
(a) Unreliable census data owing to
  (i) a lack of interest among the Black population (possibly owing to political considerations, etc),
  (ii) the exclusion of the great majority of 'illegal' urban Blacks and other 'backyard lodgers' who cannot be traced and/or
  (iii) unsatisfactory definitions as to which areas are urban and which are not — which exclude, for example, settlements with relatively high population densities, such as Winterveld outside Pretoria.
(b) Influx control measures, which hamper the rural — urban migration of whole families, although not necessarily that of the male members of families.
(c) The observed fact that urban Blacks' children are often brought up

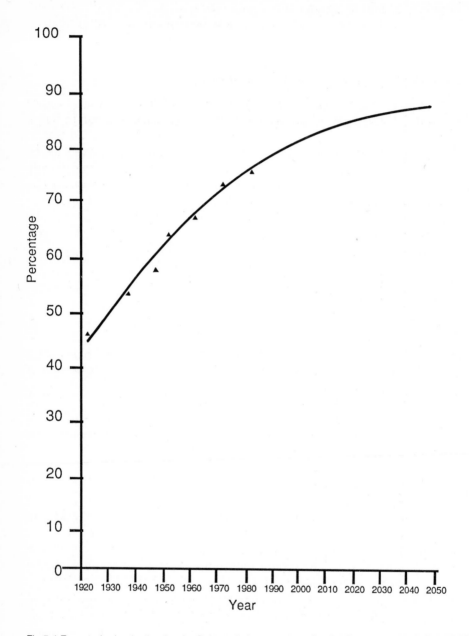

Fig 5.4 Expected urbanisation levels: Coloureds (percentage urbanised)

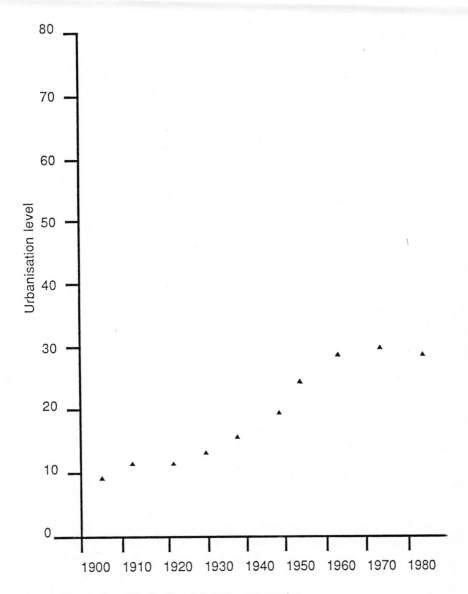

Fig 5.5 Urbanisation of Blacks: Trends based on census data

elsewhere (see Simkins 1983: 67 and Van Zyl 1983). Consequently, these children are not classified as 'urban' because they are said to be living with relatives in rural areas. In addition, many Black men are migrant labourers who work in the cities while their wives and children remain in the rural areas. The migrant labour system contributes to unnatural urbanisation patterns, because natural increase is not fully reflected in the urban population figures.

(d) The effect of resettlement actions and the removal of 'Black spots' from urban areas have apparently involved a large number of Blacks during the period 1960-80 (see *SPP Reports* 1983).

The effect of South Africa's policy of 'under-urbanisation' with regard to the Black population, which results in migrant labour and commuting becoming substitutes for permanent migration (see Fuchs and Demko 1981: 73), could be that the potential urban population is being 'dammed up' in rural areas at present, or that 'illegal' urban residents simply refuse to become involved in census or other (especially official) surveys (as was in fact confirmed by personal interviews conducted by HSRC staff with 'illegal' Black residents in Pretoria and its environs during 1984).

According to the transition theories, Black urbanisation should have been more or less in accordance with the broken line in figure 5.6, but because it is impossible in practice to determine the trend of that line with any degree of reliability, it is also not possible to deduce expected future trends from it. Therefore other approaches are necessary if one is to get some idea of the outlook for the future. Attention is given to this in the subparagraphs that follow.

Continuance of existing, officially observed trends

It is assumed that if the official census data relating to Black urbanisation are reliable — and, in the light of what has been said, there is little reason to make such an assumption — future Black urbanisation may be as shown in figure 5.7.

This logistic regression line has been determined on the basis of a broad estimate of the saturation level of Black urbanisation at 83,7%.[6] As is evident from figure 5.7, there can hardly be any question of a levelling off in the rate of Black urbanisation until the middle of the next century, since the present (official) urbanisation level is so far from the theoretical saturation level. The implication is that if the official figures did reflect the true position and the urbanisation rate were to accelerate again in the future (as may be concluded from the transition theories), then the urbanisation level of the Black population would increase in any case until approxi-

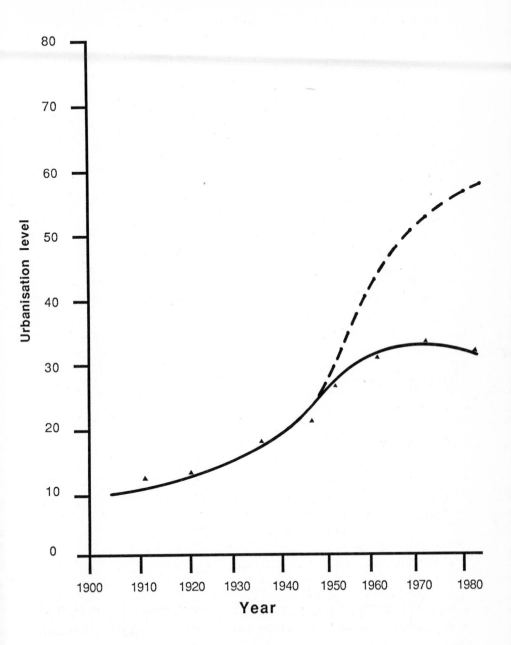

Fig 5.6 Urbanisation of Blacks: Possible actual trends

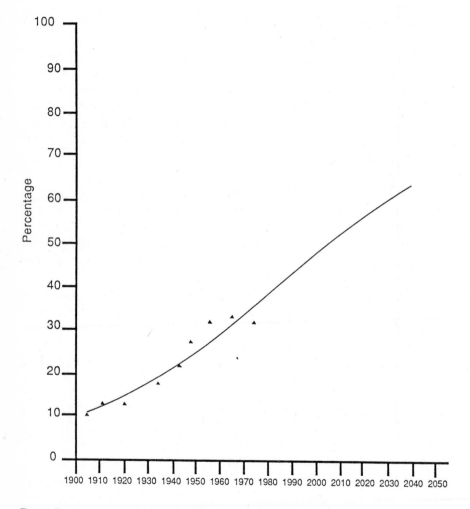

Fig 5.7 Possible urbanisation trends of Blacks (percentage urbanised)

mately 2050 at roughly the same rate as (according to official sources) it increased during the period 1921 to 1970, i.e. at approximately 2,0% per annum.

Maintaining the status quo with regard to migrant labour and influx control

An alternative to accepting that the official figures are correct in every respect would be to make the following assumptions:

(a) The 1980 urbanisation levels in the *respective Black 'states'* were correct. There is considerable justification for this assumption, since it might be expected that in these 'states' under-enumeration due to 'illegality' would have been far less likely than in the common area (often referred to as the 'White area', which is, of course, a misnomer).

(b) The 1980 urbanisation levels of the various Black 'states' will be maintained at the same level for the entire projection period. Although urbanisation levels may actually rise within the various Black 'states', it is quite possible that the 1980 levels will be maintained, since urban development in these 'states' has been mainly the result of artificial township establishment actions consequent to resettlement and will therefore not necessarily continue.

(c) In the Black 'states' the ratio between migrant labour and the population will remain the same. From Mostert *et al* (1985), it appears that the populations of the individual Black 'states' will continue to increase at a high rate and that migrant labour (particularly men) will assume large proportions in the common area. The disadvantages of this system are partly dealt with by Kok (1985: paragraph 2.3).

(d) All migrant labourers in the common area are in urban areas. This assumption is relatively logical, since migrant labour attracted to farming and other rural activities is probably minimal in comparison with the migrant labour absorbed in urban areas. In some cases, migrant labourers employed in rural areas may also be living in towns.

(e) The number of Blacks living in the rural part of the common area will be maintained at a constant level. Rural and particularly agricultural development in the common area will probably be accompanied by a certain measure of mechanisation which, at most, will keep the demand for unskilled labour at its present level.

In table 5.1 the adjusted 1980 urbanisation pattern, as well as the possible population figures and urbanisation levels during the projection period, is given in terms of the abovementioned assumptions. The last column of the table, which shows the possible pattern for the year 2100, is included to give the necessary long-term perspective.

Table 5.1 Possible urbanisation of the Black population of South Africa, if the status quo with regard to influx control were to be maintained

Description	1980	1990	2000	2010	2020	2030	2100
Total Black population (in millions)	20,8	27,2	36,2	48,2	65,0	87,7	845,5
Urban Black population (in millions):							
Black 'states'	1,5	2,0	2,7	3,4	4,8	6,6	60,1
Rest of SA	6,6	9,5	14,6	19,2	26,3	35,6	203,2
Total	8,1	11,5	16,3	22,6	31,1	42,4	263,3
Urbanisation level	39%	43%	46%	47%	49%	49%	31%*

* This marked decline in the urbanisation level may be due to unrealistic assumptions reflected in this table, since it is not in accordance with the theories of mobility transition (cf. the paragraph entitled 'Mobility transition').

From the urbanisation figures in table 5.1, it would appear that there may be a saturation level of about 50% in the urbanisation of the Black population. Such a situation could come about only if the policy of 'under-urbanisation' of the Black population were to be continued. However, the population-increase implications of such an approach point to its short-sightedness. This aspect will be discussed further in the next section.

If influx control were to be abolished

An alternative approach to the assumption that the status quo in Black migrant labour trends will be maintained in the future is to try to determine what the effect on the extent and rate of urbanisation will be if all restraints on Black migration and urbanisation are removed.

In this case, however, two different scenarios are involved. In one scenario it is assumed that the abolition of influx control and forced resettlement will take place without actual urban development in the Black 'states', while in the other it is assumed that purposeful, actual stimulation of development will take place in those 'states' (cf. Mostert et al 1985). These scenarios accord with the last two scenarios (numbers 3 and 4 in the report) postulated by Mostert et al 1985.

With regard to these alternative scenarios, the following assumptions are made:
(a) The official 1980 urbanisation levels in the respective Black 'states' were correct. The same levels of urbanisation will be maintained in

114

those 'states' in future (cf. the section entitled 'Maintaining the status quo with regard to migrant labour'), except in the case of the second scenario, where the increase in the number of persons aged 20 years will be accommodated in the developing cities of the Black 'states' (see Mostert et al 1985).

(b) Migrant labour will be replaced by permanent in-migration to towns and cities within the common area, except in the case of the second scenario, where it will be possible to accommodate the increase in the number of persons aged 20 years and older in the Black 'states' as large-scale urban development takes place there — in accordance with the time schedule given by Mostert et al (1985).

(c) The number of Blacks living in the rural part of the common area in 1980 will be maintained at a constant level (cf. the section entitled 'Maintaining the status quo with regard to migrant labour').

The possible patterns of urbanisation in terms of these scenarios are given in table 5.2.

Table 5.2 Possible urbanisation of the Black population of South Africa, if influx control were to be abolished: Two scenarios

Scenario/Description	1980	1990	2000	2010	2020	2030	2100
A Little development in the Black 'states':							
Total Black population (in millions)	20,8	27,0	34,9	44,2	53,8	63,8	130,8
Urban Black population (in millions):							
Black 'states'	1,5	1,3	2,7	3,4	4,8	6,7	10,6
Rest of SA	6,6	13,7	18,8	25,0	31,1	36,5	47,8
Total	8,1	15,0	21,5	28,4	35,9	43,1	58,4
Urbanisation level	39%	56%	62%	64%	67%	68%	45%
B Large-scale development in the Black 'states':							
Total Black population (in millions)	20,8	27,0	34,7	42,4	49,4	55,7	73,0
Urban Black population (in millions):							
Black 'states'	1,5	1,3	1,9	3,3	5,1	6,5	8,9
Rest of SA	6,6	13,7	18,8	22,9	25,8	29,1	37,4
Total	8,1	15,0	20,7	26,2	30,9	35,6	46,3
Urbanisation level	39%	56%	60%	62%	63%	64%	63%

As in the case of table 5.1, a decline of this magnitude in the urbanisation level between the years 2030 and 2100 (from 68% to 45%) as that shown in

115

the case of scenario A cannot be scientifically justified. (The possible urbanisation pattern for the period between 2030 and 2100 was also examined and it appears that the turning-point in the rise in the urbanisation level could be at about 70% in scenario A. In scenario B, the turning-point (saturation level?) is about 65%.)

The possible effect of large-scale urbanisation on population increase emerges clearly from the table. This applies particularly to scenario B, where the assumption is that in the Black 'states' urbanisation will rise to levels above those of 1980.

As is the case with the possible future trends shown in table 5.1, the long-term picture of urbanisation in the case of scenario A in table 5.2 does not accord with the theory that there is a close relationship between urbanisation and population increase, probably because of the anomaly that a very low urbanisation level in the Black 'states' themselves is assumed. In these 'states', the lack of any urban development stimulants worth mentioning gives rise to the anomaly of a very high population increase and a low urbanisation level. In this respect, scenario B is far more justifiable.

The urbanisation levels shown here probably give little cause for concern. What should be given careful thought, however, are the numerical implications of these urbanisation levels. If this urbanisation volume is to be absorbed mainly in the four existing metropoles, and particularly the PWV area, the pressure on the infrastructure of those metropoles may be great (see Kok 1985). Scenario B undoubtedly indicates the proper approach, i.e. to endeavour, with every possible resource of available funds, knowledge and initiative, to bring about large-scale urban development in the Black 'states', i.e. an adequate number of intermediate cities between the rural areas and the existing metropoles (cf. Kok 1985: chapter 6).

SUMMARY AND CONCLUSIONS

In this chapter an attempt has been made to place urbanisation in its true perspective. It is necessary to stress that South Africa's population problem is far greater than its urbanisation problem. The dynamics of population increases in the Black 'states' have been clearly indicated in the sections entitled 'Maintaining the status quo with regard to migrant labour' and 'If influx control were to be abolished'. Whatever the strategy adopted, the momentum of growth, in both relative and absolute terms, is at present so great that future population increase on a large scale is simply unavoidable. In view of the undeniable interplay between urbanisation, development and population dynamics, a well-thought-out urbanisation strategy can do much to counter future problems. An urbanisation strategy that does not take population dynamics into account would be an extremely short-sighted approach, having only a short-term effect at the very most.

Without large-scale urbanisation, the rapid enhancement of standards of living and of quality of life and aspirations is not possible and therefore the policy of 'under-urbanisation' may frustrate any attempt to limit undesirable family sizes. It would appear that the correct approach would be to create development (and alternative migration destinations comparable to the existing metropoles) in the Black 'states'. That would make it possible to address, probably simultaneously, the possible future population and urbanisation problems. The alternatives, i.e. the continuation of the migrant labour system and influx control and the abolition of restrictions on the free movement of people without concomitant purposeful, selective and intensive development in the Black 'states', do not offer much hope of easing the population problem.

As pointed out by Mostert *et al* (1985), there is a need for urbanisation among the inhabitants of any country. Education and the communication media are increasingly preparing the youth for an urban life style and inevitably young adults will try to move to the cities in order to secure a better future for themselves and their children. Population pressures within the limited space available in the Black 'states' must be taken into account as well. Any urbanisation strategy which ignores these factors is naïve.

NOTES

1 In terms of the Population Registration Act, the South African population is divided into at least four population groups, i.e. Whites, Coloureds, Indians and Blacks (amounting to respectively 4,5; 2,6; 0,8 and 21 million in 1980). There are widespread doubts in the social scientific research community of South Africa about the empirical validity and moral acceptability of enforced racial classification. In this chapter these official categories will be used to compare certain parts of the South African population with one another. The motivation underlying this usage is not the desire of the present authors to sanctify or perpetuate these racial divisions. Rather, it is considerations such as the fact that official statistics are based on these divisions, influx control legislation applies only to Blacks, etc.

2 An 'urbanisation problem' would, for example, be constituted by the following elements as far as the urban population of a country is concerned: (a) problems with the accommodation of numbers; (b) problems in maintaining social standards; (c) problems with regard to quality of life; and (d) problems relating to the satisfaction of aspirations. (Political unrest is not necessarily a result of the process of urbanisation.)

3 Large-scale education of rural inhabitants, for example, creates a tendency among them to migrate to the cities once they have completed their schooling.

4 'Mobility' here refers to *geographic* mobility and should not be confused with social mobility.

5 Statements regarding the position of South Africa's population on the urban development continuum actually refer to the Black population group's position because of this group's numerical dominance within the population as a whole. Therefore, it is necessary to interpret the theories of mobility transition with some caution, since these theories have

been formulated mainly for societies as a whole and cannot be applied just as they are to components of national populations. It is also necessary to take into account the fact that the progress of South Africa's Black population through mobility transition has been considerably retarded relative to that of other population groups in the country. Explanations for this should not be sought in the theories of mobility transition themselves, but rather in the unique economic and political forces that have influenced the development of South Africa's Black population.

6 This estimate was based on the assumption that Kelly and Williamson's (1984) 'urban limit' of 85% is in fact valid for the total population of the country and was calculated on the projected populations of all four population groups, taking into account the expected urbanisation levels of Whites, Indians and Coloureds.

GLOSSARY OF TERMS

(a) An *urban area* is a city or town (classified by the Central Statistical Services as 'urban').
(b) The *urbanisation level* is the proportion (expressed as a percentage) of a population living in urban areas.
(c) *Urban population growth* is the change (mostly increase) in the number of persons living in urban areas as a result of natural increase (births minus deaths) and migration.
(d) *Urbanisation* is the process whereby the urbanisation level of the population increases over time.
(e) A *metropolitan area* (or *metropole*) is a major urban complex, covering various administrative (and even political) units, that has a large and relatively dense population of which the majority of working residents are involved in basic (regional and national export) activities and that is also marked by a high degree of daily movement and other forms of interaction between the different geographical components thereof.
(f) The *prime metropole* (or *prime city*) of a country (or region) is that metropolitan area (or city) where by far the greatest population and economic growth within the country (or region) takes place. (In South Africa's case, the Pretoria-Witwatersrand-Vereeniging complex — the 'PWV area' for short — is the country's prime metropole.)
(g) *Metropolitanisation* is the process whereby an ever-increasing proportion of the population is found in the prime metropole and other secondary metropolitan areas of a country.
(h) *Rural-urban migration* is the movement of persons from rural environments to urban areas to settle there *permanently*.
(i) *Migrant labour* is the phenomenon of the temporary employment of persons who settle temporarily (but continuously) at their place of work and who return to their permanent place of residence after some time. (This 'temporariness' of migrant labour can stretch over the entire working life of an individual.)
(j) *Commuting* is the regular (daily, weekly and even monthly) movement of persons to and fro between their place of work and permanent place of residence.

BIBLIOGRAPHY

De Jong, GF and Gardner, RW. *Migration decision making.* New York: Pergamon, 1981.
Hauser, PM. *Population and development: challenges and prospects.* New York: UNFPA, 1979.
Kelly, AC and Williamson, JG. Population growth, industrial revolutions, and urban transition. *Population and Development Review*, vol. 10, no. 3, 1984.
Kok, PC. *Population redistribution: a review and evaluation of theoretical contributions, strategies and policy instruments.* (In Afrikaans.) Pretoria: Human Sciences Research Council , 1985. (Verslag S-131.)
Mostert, WP, Kok, PC, Van Tonder, JL and Van Zyl, JA. *Demographic implications of alternative migration scenarios regarding the South African Black population.* (In Afrikaans.) Pretoria: Human Sciences Research Council. (Report S-133.)

Population Reference Bureau. *World population data sheet.* Washington DC: Population Reference Bureau, 1983.

Simkins, CEW. *Four essays on the past, current and possible future of the distribution of the Black population of South Africa.* Cape Town: University of Cape Town (SALDRU), 1983.

SPP Reports. *Forced removals in South Africa* (vols 1-5). Pietermaritzburg: Surplus People Project, 1983.

United Nations. *Population distribution policies in development planning.* New York: United Nations, 1981.

— *Population distribution, migration and development.* (Report on Population Distribution, Migration and Development, Hammamet, Tunisia, 21-25 March 1983.) New York: United Nations, 1984.

Van Zyl, JA. *Projected natural increase of the Black population of the PWV area for the period 1980-2020.* (In Afrikaans.) Pretoria: Raad vir Geesteswetenskaplike Navorsing, 1983. (Navorsingbevinding SN-239.)

Zelinsky, W. The hypothesis of the mobility transition. *Geographical Review,* no. 61, 1981.

6 Manpower development

W Backer

INTRODUCTION

Over the past five years, development in the sphere of manpower has taken place largely in three areas, namely labour relations, in-service training and the structure of the labour force. The changes that have occurred in the field of manpower will be illustrated by an overview of the major tendencies which have become apparent in these three areas.

In the 1983 edition of *Change in South Africa*, Wiehahn[1] described in detail the development of the trade union movement in South Africa up to the beginning of the 1980s.

This chapter is an analysis of the major changes which occurred on the labour relations front between 1980 and the end of 1984. In order to provide an understanding of the tendencies, movements and changes in labour relations, the labour relations systems presently in operation in the RSA will be described briefly in the following section.

A new era in labour relations

As a result of the amendments made since 1981 to the Labour Relations Act, 1956 (Act 28 of 1956), hereafter referred to as the Act, a new era in labour relations came into being in this country. The new, formal labour relations system has succeeded in creating order on the labour front in that it determines the rights and responsibilities of employers and employees; creates the necessary machinery for collective bargaining, the settlement of disputes and the regulation of terms and conditions of employment; and guarantees opportunities for worker development and security. This system has already proved itself to be a firm basis for job satisfaction and productivity and, above all, for labour peace as far as a significant proportion of the economically active population of South Africa is concerned.

However, the Act, specifically does not apply to the following categories of workers:
• Farm workers

- Workers in domestic service in private households
- Officers of Parliament, such as the sergeant-at-arms
- People who work in charitable institutions for no remuneration
- University students doing practical work in a firm as part of their university training
- Public servants are allowed to join unions, but they are not allowed to strike, or to use an Industrial Council or any of the labour relations machinery as determined by the Act.

The 1981 amendment removed all traces of racial discrimination from labour relations legislation and the role of the State changed from that of active party in labour relations to that of creator of the legal frame work and monitor of labour relations.

At present, labour relations in this country are characterised by industry-level or centralised bargaining, also known as the *formal system*, which exists parallel to plant-level or decentralised bargaining, also known as the *non-formal system*.

THE FORMAL LABOUR RELATIONS SYSTEM

Determining conditions of service by collective bargaining

The Industrial Council

As shown in figure 6.1, the Industrial Councils form the hub of the formal system. They can be formed on a voluntary basis only by an equal number of representatives of registered unions and employers' organisations.

Industrial councils are registered for a particular undertaking, industry, trade or occupation and for a particular area and may be established regionally, provincially or nationally. The parties to the council must, of course, be sufficiently representative of the employers and employees on each side.

The most important function of an industrial council is to endeavour to prevent the occurrence of labour disputes between employers and employees and to settle disputes that have arisen.[2] This function is performed mainly through the negotiation of conditions of service. An Industrial Council Agreement is made legally binding by publication in the *Government Gazette* by the Minister of Manpower. A breach of any of the provisions carries criminal sanctions (Jones 1984:60).

Agreements usually include provisions concerning working hours, basic wage rates, overtime payments, vacations, pensions, medical aid, training and other working conditions. No differentiation may be made on the grounds of race, colour or sex.

By the end of 1984, as many as 103 industrial councils were in existence and had administered a total of 187 agreements.

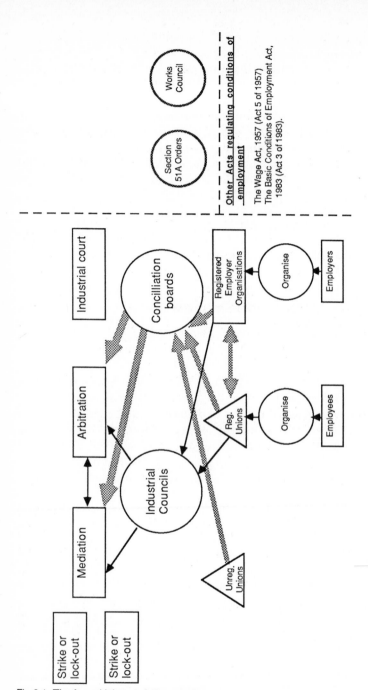

Fig 6.1: The formal labour relations system

122

Other procedures for the settlement of disputes include conciliation boards, mediation, arbitration and status quo orders made by the Industrial Court.

Conciliation Boards

Disputes often arise where industrial councils have not been established for various reasons, such as that one of the parties has not been registered in terms of the Act, or that one (or both) of the parties is simply not interested in the formation of an industrial council.

Where there is no industrial council, parties bargain privately, in good faith with one another. But when such bargaining ends in deadlock, or a serious dispute arises, a problem which can normally be solved only with assistance from outside develops. The Act makes provision for the establishment of a temporary body, namely a *conciliation board*, to perform the task that the industrial council would (Jones 1984:71). Thus, a conciliation board is a temporary body established by the Minister on application by one of the parties to the dispute.

As is the case with an industrial council, a conciliation board consists of an equal number of employer and employee members. The agreement reached is also published in the *Government Gazette* by the Minister and is also binding.

Over the past year, the Minister has approved 62 applications and refused 80. Apart from these, 56 applications were withdrawn because the disputes were settled by the parties.

Mediation

Often an industrial council or a conciliation board experiences difficulty in resolving a dispute. This is largely due to suspicion, antagonism or the unwillingness of one of the parties to reveal its full hand, in spite of the fact that a good deal of common ground may exist.

In such a case, a mediator is appointed as a third party. The Minister normally appoints a mediator who is acceptable to both parties. The mediator makes inquiries and investigations and endeavours to 'build bridges' between the two parties in order to effect a settlement. He may attend and preside over meetings, but may only suggest the directions in which possible solutions can be found — he is not meant to make any decisions or to vote (Jones 1984: 73).

Arbitration

The Act provides that when industrial councils or conciliation boards cannot resolve a deadlock, they may voluntarily refer the dispute for arbitration. The parties have the choice of appointing a single arbitrator, a number of arbitrators with an umpire, or the Industrial Court. The arbitrator(s) must come to a decision and the award that is made is binding upon all the parties involved. Where no industrial council exists, the parties may go directly to arbitration, omitting the conciliation procedure where it is agreed that a conciliation board would not be able to settle the dispute.

Where labour disputes involve essential services such as the activities of local authorities (e.g. the provision of electricity, water, sanitation, etc and passenger transport), or where the disputes involve unfair labour practices, these are subject to compulsory arbitration.

Status quo orders made by the Industrial Court

The Industrial Court has various functions such as status quo orders (employers are ordered, for example, to reinstate workers who have been dismissed while their case is heard), arbitration, industrial demarcation (i.e. of the borders between two industrial councils) etc.

Two of the court's major tasks are the adjudication of unfair labour practices and the formulation of a labour code. Disputes concerning allegedly unfair labour practice cannot be referred directly to the Industrial Court. It must first be referred to either an industrial council or a conciliation board for consideration, after which it may be passed to the Industrial Court.

Determining conditions of service outside collective bargaining

Section 51A orders

Any group or association of employers operating where no industrial council can be formed may submit proposals concerning wages and other conditions of service to the Minister and request that they be declared binding on all employers and employees in that sector or occupation. The Minister makes such 'orders' and declares these binding after consultation with the Wage Board. Employees are not consulted when these orders are made.

At the end of 1984, five orders were in force. These applied to an estimated 713 employers and 137 427 employees.[3]

124

Works councils

The Act allows for works councils to be formed largely as a communication tool between management and workers. At least 50% of the members of a works council must be elected by the workers, but the rest may be appointed by management. Decisions made by works councils have no statutory significance.

At present, works councils exist mainly in firms where there has been no, or only very little union activity. However, as a union becomes stronger in a firm, the works council usually loses support until it finally disappears. In general, works councils exist on the basis of joint problem-solving with management. As a rule, matters of pay and discipline are not dicussed, although problems in this regard may be brought to management's attention.

The benefits of registration for trade unions

Registration with the Department of Manpower holds the following benefits for unions (Jones 1984:39-40):

- Only registered unions are granted the opportunity of objecting to another union's registration application. (The principle is under review at present.)

- On registration a union becomes a body corporate — a legal entity. The rights and liabilities of members devolve upon the union. Individual members cannot be held liable for union debts, except as far as their membership fees are concerned.

- Only registered unions have access to the wage regulating and conciliation machinery (such as the Industrial Council) of the Act. (However, unregistered unions, may also request the Minister to establish a conciliation board.)

- Registered unions can obtain stop-order facilities from employers for union membership fees. No employer may provide this facility to any unregistered union, except with the permission of the Minister.

- Registered unions are protected against civil proceedings for damages due to certain wrongful acts committed during strikes — but only in the case of legal strikes.

- Various statutory bodies, such as the National Training Board or the Unemployment Insurance Board, regularly invite registered unions to nominate persons to serve on these bodies.

Acts regulating conditions of employment

As was pointed out above, in organised industries minimum wages, salaries and other conditions of employment can be regulated in terms of the Labour Relations Act, 1956 (Act 28 of 1956) by industrial council agreements, conciliation board agreements, awards, etc.

Wage Act, 1957 (Act 5 of 1957)

Where industries are only partly organised or totally unorganised, minimum wages and other conditions of employment are regulated by wage determinations in terms of the Wage Act, 1957 (Act 5 of 1957) through the Wage Board. The three members of the Wage Board are State officials. They consult with employers and employees in a particular industry with the objective of determining the profitability of the industry and what an acceptable living wage for the employees should be. It should be noted that no bargaining of any sort takes place in a wage determination.

The Wage Act does not apply to farm workers, domestic servants, apprentices and people bound by regulations in terms of the Labour Relations Act. However, an estimated 1 000 000 employees are subject to wage determinations under the Wage Act (Jones 1984:69).

Basic conditions of the Employment Act, 1983 (Act 3 of 1983)

The Act prescribes the basic conditions of employment for all workers (except farm workers and domestic servants) in the local authority and private sectors who are not already subject to the Labour Relations Act, the Wage Act, the Manpower Training Act, 1981 (Act 56 of 1981) and the Mines and Works Act, 1956 (Act 27 of 1956). Public servants and semi-state workers are also excluded.

The Basic Conditions of Employment Act does not regulate minimum wage levels, but deals specifically with matters such as maximum working hours, meal breaks, overtime work and overtime pay, leave, notice periods, etc.

Grouping of trade unions

Unions often group themselves under an umbrella organisation with a view to achieving certain objectives. Such an objective may be to have a co-ordinated strategy in negotiation with employers. In many instances in South Africa, union federations have been established on economic and political grounds.

Trade Union Federations

Although there are 12 registered union federations at present, the following four major federations have emerged:

- Trade Union Council of South Africa (Tucsa)
- South African Confederation of Labour (Sacol)
- Federation of South African Trade Unions (Fosatu) (unregistered)
- Council of Unions of South Africa (Cusa) (unregistered).

These four federations can be arranged as follows in relation to present Government's political policy:

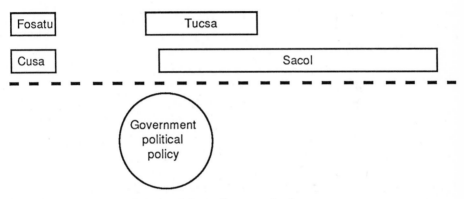

Fig 6.2 Trade union federations in relation to Government policy

The philosophies and objectives of the four federations are discussed individually below

Trade Union Council of South Africa (TUCSA)

Tucsa, formed in 1955, is a multiracial organisation unaffiliated to any political party which believes in free enterprise capitalism and rejects Communism and all forms of totalitarianism. It embraces all workers

in a system of negotiation and co-operation rather than confrontation and conflict. In pursuing its economic and social philosophies, Tucsa believes that unions can operate validly only in the workplace and should not concern themselves with issues or actions on a wider scale that are not directly connected with the relation between employers and workers. This philosophy is known as 'pure and simple' trade unionism and is closely allied to the American pattern as opposed to the European pattern where unions involve themselves in party politics and align themselves with policies, and take actions, over a wide-ranging spectrum well divorced from the specific employer-worker relation (Jones 1984:53).

Tucsa organises just under 400 000 workers in some 50 unions which recruit at all levels (approximately 55% Coloureds, 25% Whites and 20% Blacks). In the 1984 Review of the Institute for Industrial Relations Tucsa membership as at the end of 1984 is reported as 362 306 (Institute for Industrial Relations: 1985). No two sources on union membership agree on exact figures. It represents middle of the road conservatism as far as South African politics are concerned. Tucsa remains a strong and forceful federation.

It is generally believed that during the period prior to the Wiehahn Commission investigation, Tucsa was operating significally to the left of Government policy, but that the new dispensation resulted in Government policy moving closer towards Tucsa policy, as is pointed out in figure 6.2.

Federation of South Africa Trade Unions (FOSATU)

Fosatu was established in 1979. Although in its stated philosophy it has multiracial intentions, all of its members are Black. Its leadership is multiracial.

Fosatu does not believe in the benefits of free-enterprise capitalism — at least not openly — and is actually antagonistic towards capitalism. It strives to secure decent standards of living, social security and fair working conditions for all members of affiliated unions and the working class as a whole (Jones 1984:54).

Although Fosatu has been concentrating largely on organisation and recognition at plant level, a fair number of Fosatu unions have already registered and are participating in industrial councils. Fosatu has close ties with Black political movements in this country. (See the section on trade unions and politics.)

Fosatu incorporates nine unions with the following estimated membership in the major industrial sectors of South Africa (Levy et al 1985:1).

	1983	1984
Signed up	108 166	135 917
Paid up	80 841	—

Its hold as the premier organisers of Black labour is unchallenged in the engineering, auto, chemical and textile sectors. Fosatu unions all follow a strict policy of equality, and are multiracial, although the bulk of their membership is amongst Black unskilled and semi-skilled labour. They have pioneered the strategy of strong plant level organisations, and have set standards in worker education and training. Their strategic ability to mount and win campaigns has been adequately demonstrated. Their international links are well forged and important, and have proved to be invaluable to them in winning numbers of tough disputes (Levy *et al* 1984:18).

To date, Fosatu signed up well over 325 recognition agreements and by the middle of 1985 the number of factories it has organised should be approximately 600.

Council of Unions of South Africa (CUSA)

Cusa's philosphy corresponds largely with Fosatu's, except that it is a uniracial union with Black members and Black leaders. In a policy document it stated: 'We believe in developing Black leadership in order to come to grips with the exploitation of the Black worker by the more sophisticated and developed race groups' (Jones 1984:56).

Cusa's ultimate objective is the establishment of a non-racial, non-exploitative, democratic society, which it hopes to achieve by means of Black leadership.

The 12 Cusa member unions have an estimated membership of approximately 264 000. The estimated figure in 1983 was 104 592. The largest of the Cusa unions is the National Union of Mineworkers, which became the largest Black union in South Africa within a period of 18 months. To date Cusa has signed in the region of 155 recognition agreements and 40 are currently being negotiated (Levy *et al* 1985:1).

South African Confederation of Labour (SACOL)

This group comprises approximately 120 000 White workers in 11 unions. Although it started off organising mainly artisans during the earliest years in our labour relations history, it is now caring for the needs of White workers at all levels and in all functions.

As far as political orientation is concerned, Sacol comprises unions which support Government policy and unions which oppose the Government from a very right wing position. Although Sacol has been opposing equality at work, many individual firms within Sacol have made great progress towards the development of opportunities for workers of all race groups. They have adapted to most of the procedures brought about by the new dispensation — and had done so even before it was introduced.

These firms displayed an increasingly pragmatic attitude towards Black

129

unionism. Yster-en-Staal (Iron and Steel), one of the strongest unions in the Sacol grouping, was party to the metal agreement which opened skilled jobs to Blacks and negotiated on the same councils as Black unions. The other very powerful union in the Sacol camp is the Mineworkers' Union.

Some Sacol unions are now reviving its shop steward structure by the intensive training of stewards and officials. Thus they are placing strong emphasis on the development of shopfloor leadership and bargaining skills.[4]

Unaffiliated unions

Nearly 700 000 employees are members of unions which are not affiliated to any of the above federations.

The Azanian Confederation of Trade Unions (AZACTU)

Seven of the larger unions which have remained unaffiliated thus far have recently formed a new federation, Azactu, with a claimed paper membership of some 75 000 Black workers. They operate largely at plant level.

Azactu is the labour wing of the Black consciousness movement, Azapo. Wherever there is a political slant to a labour issue, Azactu polarises support rapidly and relentlessly — always in a strong and radical way. From the industrial relations point of view, it is very difficult to co-operate with this federation (Levy et al 1985:8).

Congress of South African Trade Unions (COSATU)

Progress has been made towards the formation of a federation which will encompass the vast majority of the non-racial unions in the country, i.e. the Cusa and Fosatu unions. It is envisaged that Cosatu will be fully-established towards the end of 1985. This merger will undoubtedly bring with it greater numerical strength, less competition, greater overseas muscle and more shopfloor and political clout.

It is highly likely that Cosatu will become the biggest single grouping having one political philosophy and this in itself could have major political ramifications. The independents will not become a coherent political threat because of their divergent nature.

The establishment of Cosatu will entail a restructuring of the political map in South Africa. The development of this new confederation, coupled with the increased politicisation of the trade union movement and with the broad political developments and uncertainties which characterise South Africa at this time spell out clearly what the keynotes for the immediate future in our labour relations history will be (Levy et al 1985:8).

130

The relative sizes of the federations are illustrated in figure 6.3.

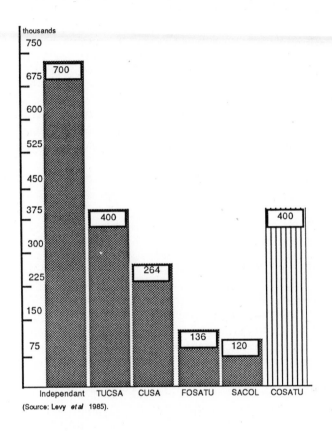

(Source: Levy *et al* 1985).

Fig 6.3 Federation size

THE NON-FORMAL LABOUR RELATIONS SYSTEM

The formal labour relations system embodied in the Labour Relations Act is by no means compulsory and employers and employees are under no obligation to register. Even though a union or employer organisation is registered, it may choose whether or not to use the machinery created by the Act.

An elegant example of such a situation is provided by the Chamber of Mines and relevant trade unions, which have never used the industrial council system in spite of the fact that the Chamber and some of the unions are registered. Bargaining takes place on a totally non-statutory basis, with some disputes being referred to a conciliation board.

However, many of the unions, particularly in the Black trade union movement, have so far refused to register with the Department of Manpower. The main reasons for their reluctance may be summarised as follows (Piron 1984:2-3):

- Most emergent unions concentrate their efforts on collective bargaining at plant level, whereas the industrial council system operates on a national or regional level.
- Industrial councils cannot deal with issues such as grievances and disciplinary procedures as well as they can be handled on the factory floor. The issue of security is of prime importance to Black workers, who can easily be replaced from the masses of unemployed.
- The political aspirations of the members of some emergent unions can be more successfully channelled through a recognition agreement than through an industrial council agreement.
- The settlement of disputes by the industrial council is said to be slow, cumbersome and time-consuming and to involve the State too closely.

In the non-formal system, the particular employer and union enter into a recognition agreement. The contents of recognition agreements may include items such as the definitions of terms, the conditions of recognition, bargaining rights, access, facilities, union subscriptions, shop stewards, disciplinary and dismissal codes and procedures, health and safety, redundancy, etc. Recognition agreements may be ordinary common law contracts, provided that the requirements for a valid contract are met (Piron 1982:25).

Many employers and unions utilise both systems; the industrial council system for basic pay rates and other conditions of employment and the recognition process for domestic issues such as incentive pay and discipline.

DEVELOPMENT IN LABOUR RELATIONS

In the new labour relations dispensation, which came into operation on 1 October 1979, a comprehensive collective bargaining machinery which allowed every worker the right to join the trade union of his choice was made available to all population groups.

Increased unionisation

The first sign of the success of the new approach to labour relations is large-scale unionisation, especially amongst the Black labour force. This tendency is clear in the increased use (by workers of all population groups) of the opportunity to establish and register trade unions and to use the official bargaining and conciliation machinery.

Since the inception of the new dispensation, a total of 58 new applications for the registration of trade unions has been received. Of these, four were for Whites-only membership, 29 for Blacks-only membership, six for Coloureds and 18 for multiracial membership. Registration was granted to 51 of the new applicants and some of the others are still being considered (one application was withdrawn).[5]

Towards the end of 1977 there were 27 unregistered unions for Blacks, with an estimated membership of between 55 000 and 70 000.[6] As far as unregistered trade unions are concerned, by the end of 1984 there were a total of 67 known ones, some of which have applied for registration. The Department of Manpower[7] calculated the total membership of unregistered unions to be 231 884 as at 31 December 1984.

Figure 6.4 provides a graphic view of the estimated strength, growth and composition of the union movement. Figure 6.5 shows Black membership as a proportion of union growth, 1980-1984 (Levy et al 1984:4). The racial composition of union membership (registered) in 1984 is illustrated in figure 6.6. If the members of unregistered unions, who are presumably largely Black, were to be incorporated, the percentage of Black members would undoubtedly be close to 50% of the total union population.

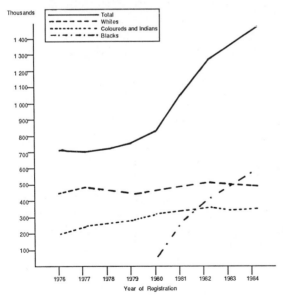

Fig 6.4 Membership of registered unions, 1976-1984

Table 6.1 Union membership

Year	Number of Unions	Membership according to population group			
		Whites	Coloureds	Black	Total
1976	173	435 836	196 450	—	632 286
1977	174	463 477	241 669	—	678 146
1978	174	444 385	254 546	—	698 931
1979	167	433 936	267 822	—	701 758
1980	188	447 466	303 850	56 737	808 053
1981	200	468 029	326 794	259 582	1 054 405
1982	199	488 044	343 900	394 510	1 225 454
1983	194	474 454	330 176	469 260	1 288 748
1984	193	470 672	338 314	578 064	1 406 302

Unregistered: 231 884

Source: Department of Manpower 1984 Annual Report and National Manpower Commission 1983 Annual Report

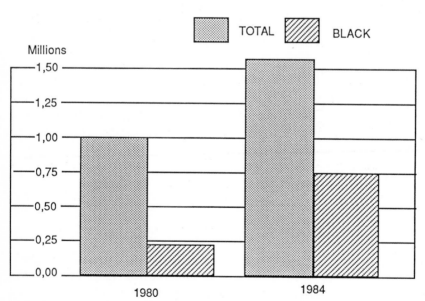

Fig 6.5 Black membership as a proportion of union growth 1980-1984

Source: Levy *et al*, 1984

134

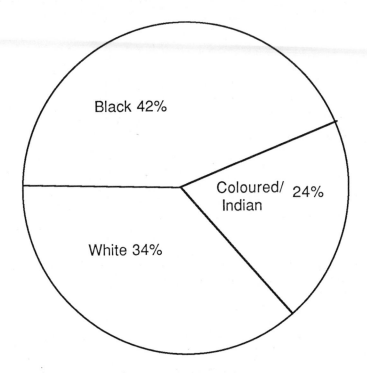

Fig 6.6 Racial composition of union membership (registered) 1984

An analysis of union membership grouping in terms of the racial composition of unions for 1983 and 1984 is set out in table 6.2. This table shows that, as was the case in 1983, the number of trade unions for Whites and Coloureds, as well as their membership, has declined. On the other hand, during the same period there was a definite increase in the number and membership of multiracial unions and unions for Black workers. The number of unions for Whites and Coloureds showed a decline largely because of the amalgamation of unions and because some of them became multiracial. There was also an increase of two registered unions for Black workers.[8]

A major indication of the increased utilisation of the labour relations system is the significant growth in the number of unions, as well as the growth in union strength between 1977 and the present. The steepest increase occurred between 1979 and 1982, but the positive increase continues. The dramatic increase in union membership has been largely in the number of Black union members.

Table 6.2 Number and membership of registered trade unions, 1983 and 1984

Scope of membership	Number of trade unions		Membership according to population group							
			Whites		Coloureds (including Asians)		Members of the Black population groups		Total	
	1983	1984	1983	1984	1983	1984	1983	1984	1983	1984
White	56	46	348 766	275 572	-	-	-	-	348 766	275 572
Coloured	35	25	-	-	63 592	46 562	-	-	63 592	46 562
Black population groups	23	25	-	-	-	-	289 578	383 018	289 578	383 018
White and Coloured	15	16	19 027	24 176	12 093	14 126	-	-	31 120	38 302
Coloured and Black population groups	17	20	-	-	56 175	50 707	83 039	55 524	139 214	106 231
All population groups	42	51	81 894	155 348	198 316	226 919	95 657	137 382	375 867	519 649
White and Black population groups	4	6	24 767	15 576	-	-	986	2 140	25 753	17 716
Membership composition unspecified	2	4	-	-	-	-	-	-	14 858	19 252
	194	193	474 454	470 672	330 176	338 314	469 260	578 064	1 288 748	1 406 302
Increase			-	-	13 724	8 138	74 750	108 804	63 294	117 554
Decrease			13 590	3 782						
Percentage Increase			-	-	4,0%	2,4%	19,0%	23,2%	5,2%	9,1%
Decrease			2,8%	0,8%	-	-	-	-	-	-

Note: The above figures and percentages denoting increases and decreases in membership cannot necessarily be accepted as valid, because trade unions did not submit their membership figures according to population group.

Source: Department of Manpower, 1984 Report, *ibid*, p. 37

Further evidence of the increasing use of the statutory institutional machinery for negotiation, collective bargaining and the settlement of disputes is the increased number of applications for the establishment of conciliation boards (see table 6.3 and figure 6.7) and the increased utilisation of the Industrial Court (see table 6.4 and figure 6.8).

As far as conditions of employment are concerned, it should be noted that during 1984 the conditions of employment of some 1 742 162 workers of all population groups were regulated by statutory measures such as industrial council agreements and wage determinations. This constitutes approximately 32,7% of the economically active population (excluding farm workers, workers in domestic service and government employees). It should be noted, however, as is pointed out in table 6.5, that between 1980 and 1984 very little growth in the number of workers whose conditions of service were regulated by industrial council agreements took place.

Union density

It is estimated that union density in South Africa is approximately 25% of the economically active population (excluding employees in agriculture, workers in domestic service and State workers), that is, almost the same as union density in the USA. Unionisation in the RSA has a long way to go to reach the level attained in Sweden and Israel (more than 80%) and the UK (between 50 and 60%).

Table 6.3 Applications for the establishment of conciliation boards, 1979-1984

Year	Applications	Approved	Refused	Withdrawn before consideration	Still receiving attention at the end of the year
1979	29	16	5	8	-
1980	23(2)	13(1)*	2(1)	8	-
1981	24(2)	8	5(2)	11	-
1982	60(25)	(9)* 28(2)**	18(7)	14(7)	-
1983	118(94)	(13)* 43(14)**	40(36)	35(31)	-
1984	279(216)	(17)* 62(10)**	80(73)	56(54)	81(62)

Figures relating to alleged unfair labour practices are indicated separately, but are included in the figure appearing alongside.

* Application approved on the basis of a dispute involving an unfair labour practice.

** Application approved on the basis of a dispute not involving an unfair labour practice.

137

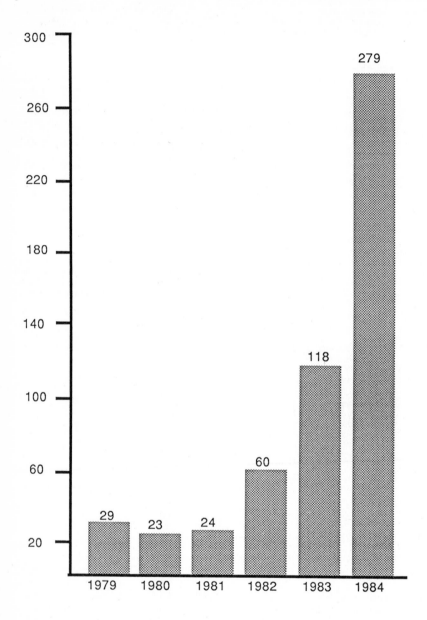

Fig 6.7 Conciliation board applications, 1979-1984

Table 6.4 Cases referred to the Industrial Court, 1984

Nature of functions	Carried forward from previous year	Received during period under review	Total for period under review	Completed	Partly heard	In various stages of progress
Court of law functions (s 17(11)(a))	6	2	8	7	1	-
Reinstatement orders (s 43)	36	318	354	209	15	130
Arbitrations (ss 45, 46 and 49)	6	11	17	11	1	5
Unfair labour practices (s 46(9))	15	51	66	36	1	29
Demarcations (s 76)	8	9	17	9	-	8
Appeals (s 21A)	-	1	1	-	-	1
Appeals (s 51(6))	5	5	10	7	-	3
Investigations (s 46(7)(c))	-	1	1	1	-	-
Referrals (s 77)	-	1	1	-	-	1
Totals	76	399	475	280	18	177
Totals (1983)	22	168	190	114	8	68

Source: Department of Manpower 1984 Report, p. 122

Table 6.5 Industrial Council wage agreements, 1980-1984

Date	Agreements	Employers	Employees				
			Whites	Coloureds (excluding Indians)	Indians	Members of the Black population groups	Total
31/12/80	98	41 280	205 885	205 143	81 590	602 854	1 095 472
31/12/81	99	46 668	212 836	249 800	82 589	719 783	1 265 008
31/12/82	77	44 811	158 234	233 347	76 972	634 902	1 103 455
31/12/83	87	46 075	182 907	239 886	85 631	663 300	1 171 724
31/12/84	94	51 031	165 976	267 379	85 494	664 550	1 183 399

Source: Department of Manpower 1984 Report, p. 383

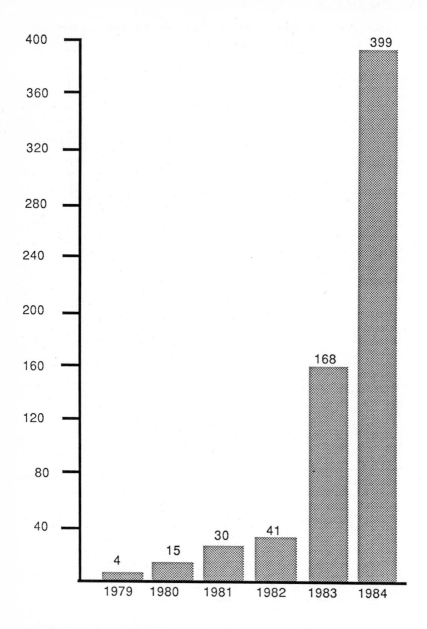

Fig 6.8 Industrial Court cases

Increased strike patterns

Strikes and unionisation go hand in hand. The greater the number of unions and union members, the greater the likelihood of strikes. Success in settling disputes should be sought by the averting of potential strikes and confrontation situations and the breaking of strikes in the shortest possible time. Unfortunately, to date less than 50 of all the strikes which have occurred since 1924, when the Industrial Conciliation Act was introduced for the first time, can be labelled 'legal' strikes.

The number of strikes is not really an index of the success of the labour relations system. What is important is the effect of the strikes (Backer 1983): Did they occur in strategic industries? What was their average duration? What triggered the strikes? Who were involved? Strike incidence is also an indication of the labour relations climate in the country. In order to grasp the nature of union activity over the past five years, it is necessary to investigate the strike phenomenon.

The incidence of strikes and work stoppages in South Africa during the past 13 years has been as follows:

Table 6.6 Strikes and work stoppages, RSA 1971-1984

Year	Number of strikes and work stoppages	Number of employees involved		Number of man-days lost		Man-days lost per striking worker
		All workers	Black workers	All workers	Black workers	
1971	69	4 451	4 067	3 437	-(a)	0,7
1972	71	9 224	8 711	14 167	-(a)	1,5
1973	370	98 378	90 082	229 291	-(a)	2,3
1974	384	59 244	57 656	98 583	95 327	1,7
1975	274	23 323	22 546	18 709	18 275	0,8
1976	245	28 013	26 291	59 861	22 014	2,1
1977	90	15 304	14 950	15 471	14 987	1,0
1978	106	14 160	13 578	10 558	10 164	0,7
1979	101	22 803	15 494	67 099	16 515	2,9
1980	207	61 785	56 286	174 614	148 192	2,8
1981	342	92 842	84 706	226 554	206 230	2,4
1982	394	141 571	122 481	365 337	298 256	2,6
1983	336	64 469	61 331	124 594	120 962	1,9
1984	469	181 942	174 897	379 712	365 096	2,1

Source: Department of Manpower and National Manpower Commission
(a) Figures not available for Black workers separately

In addition to the Department of Manpower, a large number of independent monitoring services regularly publish statistics and trends related to strikes. In many instances large discrepancies can occur between those published by the State and other sources, largely due to differences in the sources of strike reports, in the method of analysis and the interpretation of definitions such as a 'strike' or 'work stoppage' (Howe 1984).

Since the official reports of the Department of Manpower and the National Manpower Commission supply the most complete information and since by law all strikes and work stoppages have to be reported to the State, it was decided to use the official source for the purpose of this analysis.

Strike incidence

From table 6.6 it appears that strikes and stoppages reached a high point in 1973 and 1974 and dropped sharply in 1977, but immediately showed a steep increasing trend to reach an alltime high of 469 strikes in 1984. The strike incidence curve moves almost parallel to the increase in union membership curve (see figure 6.9).

The increased industrial action tendency is further illustrated in table 6.6 and figure 6.10 in terms of man-days lost per annum, as well as in the total number of employees involved between 1978 and 1984, with only a slight fluctuation in 1983. Even the average man-days lost per striking worker was much higher for the period 1979-1984 than for the period 1971-1978 (see figure 6.11).

It should be pointed out, however, that White participation in strike activity is very low. No White workers were involved in strikes from 1980 to 1982, only 11 in 1983 and 16 in 1984.

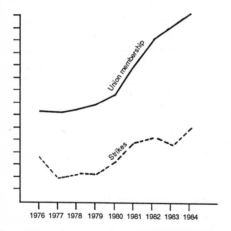

Fig 6.9 Strikes and work stoppages against union membership, 1976-1984

Fig 6.10 Total number of employees involved in strikes and number of man-days lost, 1971-1984

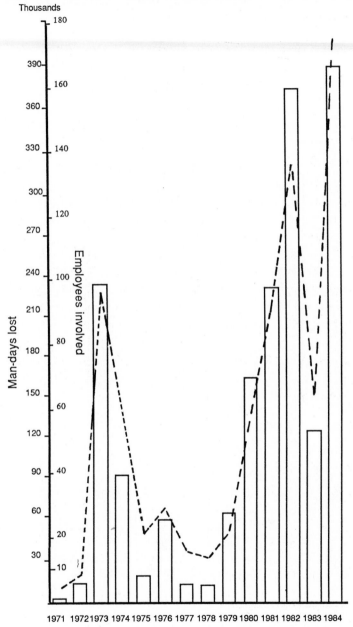

Thousands

1971 1972 1973 1974 1975 1976 1977 1978 1979 1980 1981 1982 1983 1984

Source: Department of Manpower and National Manpower Commission Reports

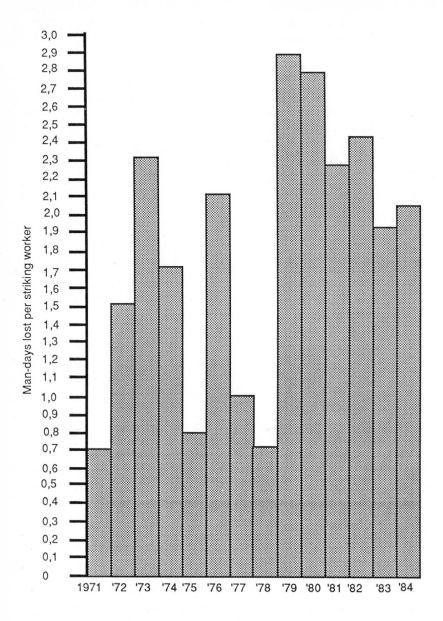

Fig 6.11 Man-days lost per striking worker, 1971-1984

Union involvement

Levy[9] observed that where a union is involved in strike action, it is likely that the strike will be of longer duration, from three to five days being the probable figure. (See his analysis of union involvement in strikes between 1979 and 1982 in figure 6.12 and of strikes by confederation in figure 6.13.)

Fosatu is still the biggest strike participant, but its share in strike activity has decreased significantly from 65,11% in 1981/82[10] to 45% (at present) (Levy *et al* 1985:33-34).

In terms of man-days lost, the lead was taken by the National Automobile and Allied Workers' Union (NAAWU) (Fosatu) and 50% behind it was the National Union of Mineworkers (NUM) (Cusa), closely followed by the Metal and Allied Workers' Union (MAWU) (Fosatu), the South African Allied Workers' Union (SAAWU) and the National Union of Textile Workers (NUTW) (Fosatu) (Levy *et al* 1985:33-34). In terms of the number of workers involved, MAWU was approximately two times ahead of its next nearest rival.

Strike length

The general trend thus far has been for strikes to last a short time only (see figure 6.14). In 1984, as many as 48,6% of the strikes and work stoppages lasted for only one day or less. During recent years, about 75% of all strikes have lasted for three days or less.

Industrial sector

From 1979 to 1984, most industrial action was seen (in rank order) in the retail, metal and food and, to a lesser extent, the automotive, building, textile and chemical industries, with small incidents occurring in the manufacturing, mining, transport and printing industries (Levy *et al* 1985: 33-34).

Strike triggers

The pattern of strike triggers shows short-term shifts due to factors such as the state of the economy and the time of the year, but an analysis of strike triggers 1979 to 1984 in general revealed domination by wages ($\pm$ 40%), grievances (19%) and dismissal (19%), as illustrated in figure 6.15 (Levy *et al* 1985:33).

Fig 6.12 Influence of union involvement on the duration of strikes

Length of strikes: no union/ union

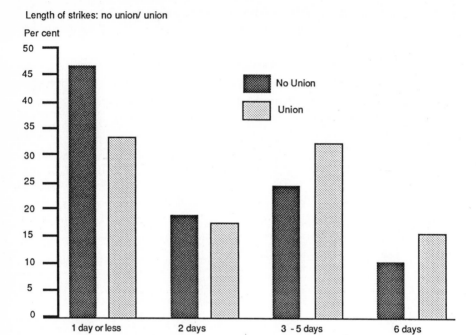

Source: IR Data, June 1983, p. 5

Fig 6.13 Strikes by confederation, 1979-1984

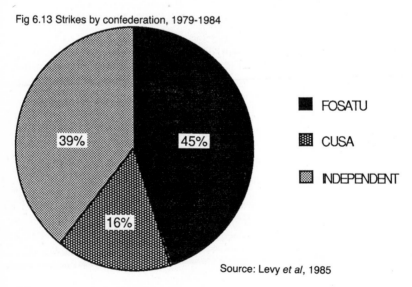

Source: Levy *et al*, 1985

146

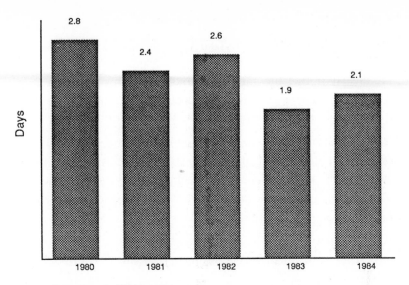

Source: Department of Manpower

Fig 6.14 Average duration of strikes

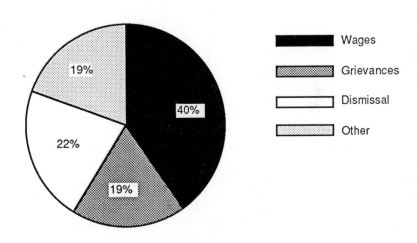

Source: Levy *et al*, 1985

Fig 6.15 Strike triggers, 1979-1984

Stages of development

The past five years have been characterised by a dramatic increase in union membership and by increased strike activity. Signs of consolidation, however, are clearly noticeable and it is unlikely that this rate of growth will continue. As will be seen in the next section, the unions have now entered a new stage in their development. Levy observed that

> Growth rates are now lower as the movement has been hampered by both the recession and the lack of organisers. At the same time a distinct politicisation is occurring at an accelerating pace, and the movement is becoming far more of a political vehicle than has been the case in the past (Levy *et al* 1985:7).

A diagram showing the main stages of the development of the union movement in this country since the beginning of the century is provided in figure 6.16.

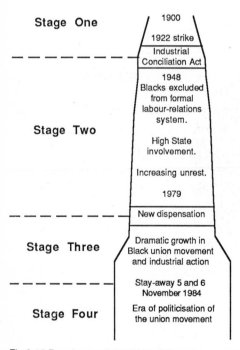

Fig 6.16 Developmental stages of the union movement

Union and politics

DWF Bendix (1983:31) pointed out that the policies, strategies and actions of unions have been and will in future be influenced by the need to serve the socio-political ambitions of their members as well. Emergent unions initially concerned themselves mainly with the establishment of their position and the achievement of benefits for their members at their place of work. They have now reached the second stage of their development, during which they must, of necessity, focus increased attention on social and political factors affecting the lives of their members (Bendix 1984:32).

There are, of course, other authors who feel that worker politics is being focused upon excessively in order to divert attention from other, more immediate, practical issues, namely the solution of management/worker conflict (Bendix in Howe 1984:30).

Cyril Ramaphosa, general secretary of the National Union of Mineworkers, expressed his view of the relationship between trade unions and the broader political struggle in South Africa as follows:

We place more emphasis on worker organisation and the workplace. We have to build that core at the workplace, then thereafter it automatically starts spilling over into other issues. If you start on other issues you are not able to build a strong union, cohesive in nature and strong enough to tackle issues outside the workplace . . . Our union's task is to arouse working class consciousness among the miners (Ramaphosa in *The Star*, 28/5/1985).

Authors like Maree (1985) are even of the opinion that politicisation of unions can only become a healthy force in the democratisation process.

The Black unions showed a definite commitment to political activity by their active participation in the November 1984 stay-away, which was a protest against the new Constitution and some unions operate directly as the labour arms of political organisations.

The fact that the political aspirations of many Black citizens will find increased expression in the union movement is certain; what is not certain is the extent and the form of politicisation that unions will undergo.

Figure 6.17 gives a schematic overview of the forces of Black politics and trade union involvement at present.

149

Fig 6.17 Forces of Black politics

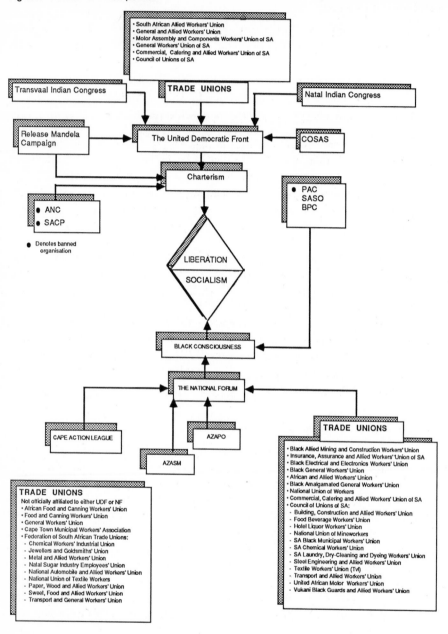

* South African Allied Workers' Union
* General and Allied Workers' Union
* Motor Assembly and Components Workers' Union of SA
* General Workers' Union of SA
* Commercial, Catering and Allied Workers' Union of SA
* Council of Unions of SA

TRADE UNIONS

Transvaal Indian Congress

Natal Indian Congress

Release Mandela Campaign

The United Democratic Front

COSAS

Charterism

* PAC
  SASO
  BPC

* ANC
* SACP

* Denotes banned organisation

LIBERATION

SOCIALISM

BLACK CONSCIOUSNESS

THE NATIONAL FORUM

CAPE ACTION LEAGUE

AZAPO

AZASM

TRADE UNIONS

* Black Allied Mining and Construction Workers' Union
* Insurance, Assurance and Allied Workers' Union of SA
* Black Electrical and Electronics Workers' Union
* Black General Workers' Union
* African and Allied Workers' Union
* Black Amalgamated General Workers' Union
* National Union of Workers
* Commercial, Catering and Allied Workers' Union of SA
* Council of Unions of SA:
  - Building, Construction and Allied Workers' Union
  - Food Beverage Workers' Union
  - Hotel Liquor Workers' Union
  - National Union of Mineworkers
  - SA Black Municipal Workers' Union
  - SA Chemical Workers' Union
  - SA Laundry, Dry-Cleaning and Dyeing Workers' Union
  - Steel Engineering and Allied Workers' Union
  - Textile Workers' Union (Tvl)
  - Transport and Allied Workers' Union
  - United African Motor Workers' Union
  - Vukani Black Guards and Allied Workers' Union

TRADE UNIONS

Not officially affiliated to either UDF or NF
* African Food and Canning Workers' Union
* Food and Canning Workers' Union
* General Workers' Union
* Cape Town Municipal Workers' Association
* Federation of South African Trade Unions:
  - Chemical Workers' Industrial Union
  - Jewellers and Goldsmiths' Union
  - Metal and Allied Workers' Union
  - Natal Sugar Industry Employees' Union
  - National Automobile and Allied Workers' Union
  - National Union of Textile Workers
  - Paper, Wood and Allied Workers' Union
  - Sweet, Food and Allied Workers' Union
  - Transport and General Workers' Union

*Some Fosatu unions have recently pledged their support to the Charterist movement.
Source: Van Staden in *The Star*, 18/10/1984

Plant-level bargaining

It is estimated that by the end of 1984 more than 500 plant-level agreements, also known as recognition agreements, were in existence. This type of agreement has become most effective in the regulation of industrial conflict.

General comments on changes in labour relations

In a summary of the major changes that have taken place in the field of labour relations during the past five years, the most important change that must be highlighted is that a labour relations system in which both the registered and unregistered unions participate, governed by the Labour Relations Act, was established. This change brought about extensive unionisation of the Black labour force, with concomitant industrial action.

Another change that took place was the rapid development of the non-formal labour relations system (the plant-level bargaining system), which in many cases operate parallel to centralised bargaining. A further major development is the successful functioning of the Industrial Court.

The labour relations situation is well in hand. The National Manpower Commission is continuously investigating the acceptability of labour laws and labour relations practices and procedures to both employers and employees. Without doubt, further constitutional developments in Southern Africa will have real and serious implications on relations between the State, employers and employees.

PROGRESS WITH IN-SERVICE TRAINING

As will be pointed out in the next section, South Africa's labour productivity is greatly influenced by the fact that a major portion of the economically active population has little or no formal schooling. The National Manpower Commission concluded that 65% of the total labour market are illiterate. Of this 65%, 29,2% have no formal education whatsoever and 35,8% have received primary school education only — 90% of this category are Black (in country areas as many as 80% of the Black adult workers can be considered illiterate) (De Vries 1984:7).

With the improvement of the general education of the entire South African population as its long-term goal, the Government decided to upgrade the working ability of the country's total labour force by massive in-service training.

Although in-service training on a co-ordinated basis was initiated in the mid-1970s the training effort finally got under way with the establishment of the Manpower Training Act, 1981 (Act 56 of 1981), which provides the basic legislative framework within which the Government's manpower training policy is executed. This Act regulates the establishment of the National Training Board; the training of apprentices; the registration of in-service training schemes, centres and courses; the training of work seekers; the provision of financial incentives for training; etc.

The National Training Board played a major role in achieving the above goals for training.

The National Training Board (NTB)

The NTB was established on 5 November 1981, its function being to advise the Minister on policy concerning the implementation of the Manpower Training Act and on any other training matters. Board members are drawn from employer bodies, trade unions or union federations and State departments. The Board's main functions are the co-ordination, encouragement and promotion of training, largely through research and investigations.

The functions of the NTB are carried out by an executive committee, a research and development committee, committees for artisan training, in-service training and regional training and full-time research and planning staff. See figure 6.18 for the institutional infrastructure for in-service training.

Apprenticeship affairs in the various industries are controlled by manpower training committees, of which there are 33 at present. These manpower committees, consisting of employer and employee representatives, are appointed by the NTB. During 1984, a total of 12 661 apprenticeship contracts were registered.

The promotion of training in all regions throughout the country is co-ordinated by regional training committees established by the NTB and chaired by the permanent regional advisers of the Department of Manpower.

The National Training Board recently published *Guidelines for Training in Labour Relations*,[11] a comprehensive manual (compendium) on training matters for employers, trainers and training advisers[12] and also completed a training course catalogue on the almost 20 000 courses registered with the Department of Manpower. Various other research projects and investigations on various aspects of training have been completed or are in progress.

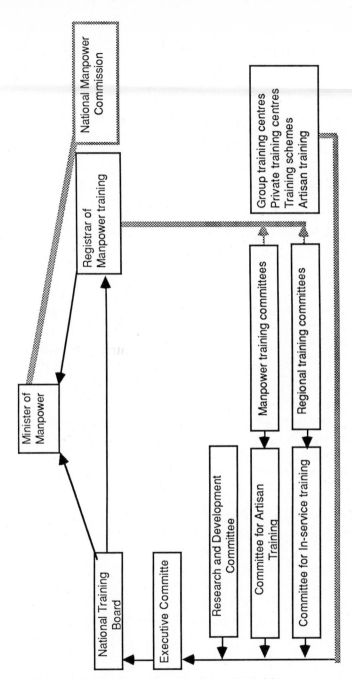

Fig 6.18 Infrastructure for institutional in-service training

Intensive research on in-service training was undertaken up to 1981 by the National Manpower Commission.[13] The findings of these investigations guided the National Training Board in assigning priorities to its vast number of projects and highlighted other urgent research needs in the field of manpower training.

Further, the NTB undertook, in collaboration with the Human Sciences Research Council (HSRC) a comprehensive investigation into the training of apprentices and artisans in the RSA. This report[14] was recently tabled in Parliament. If accepted, the recommendations made in this report could result in the dramatic improvement of the selection of apprentices and of the standards of apprentice and artisan training, in the adaptation of the course content and the trade tests to meet the needs of the specific artisan direction and specific industry and in the adaptation of teaching and learning modes and methods to meet the needs, characteristics and requirements of the various population groups in the country.

In-service training by means of training centres and schemes

In-service training is done largely by group training centres, private training centres and training schemes.

A *group training centre* is a non-profit training centre, with its own governing body, established by a group of employers in a particular industry and area. On the initiative of the Government, in 1976 eight group training centres were established in various parts of the country. One such centre serves agriculture.

At these centres employees are given training lasting from a few days to a few weeks in approved job categories through courses registered with the Department of Manpower.

The State subsidises training by paying 75% of the fees and in this way provides the incentive for employers to establish facilities for training. These are also used for the training of workseekers.

Private training centres are run by employers and other bodies to train their own and other employers' employees. Such centres must be registered with the Department. Tax rebates on training are granted to employers whose workers are trained by means of registered courses. They are given a 50% tax rebate on training costs. In decentralised areas, cash grants amounting to 37,5% of training expenses are paid to industrialists. In 1984, R7,2 million was paid to industrialists for this purpose. Some private training centres are non-profit organisations serving specific industries such as timber, sugar, clothing, steel, etc. During 1984 144 new private training centres were registered.

A *training scheme* is conducted by an employer for the training of his

154

own employees. Upon registration, private training schemes are also granted tax rebates.

Since 1980, a widespread enthusiasm for training has become apparent among employers and training facilities and incentives for training have been utilised to an ever-increasing extent. This resulted in a dramatic increase in the skills and knowledge and also in the work performance of workers.

Table 6.7 and figure 6.19 illustrate the dramatic increase in the number of people being trained on registered courses while employed between 1980 and 1984. By far the majority of workers were trained by in-company training schemes and by private training centres. (See figure 6.20.)

Table 6.7 In-service training by means of centres and schemes registered by the Department of Manpower, 1980-1984

Institution	Number of people trained in a specific year				
	1980	1981	1982	1983	1984
Training schemes	150 174	226 244	247 750	219 430	54,5% 256 141
Private training centres	25 538	77 275	164 361	202 638	42,8% 201 004
Group training centres	10 658	13 401	14 068	12 873	2,7% 12 700
Total	186 370	316 920	426 179	434 941	469 845

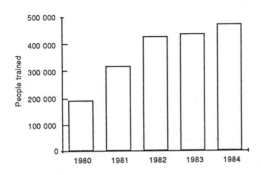

Fig 6.19 People attending in-service training courses registered with the Department of Manpower, 1980-1984

155

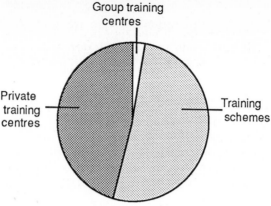

Fig 6.20 Proportion of trainees at schemes and centres

An amount of R3 542 550 was paid out from the Manpower Development Fund (in the form of low interest rate loans) to training centres and schemes, mainly to fund capital projects such as erection of training centres and the purchase of training equipment. During 1983, R958 700 was paid out and during 1982 R775 000.

Training of workseekers

During 1984, the Government spent an amount of R3,91 million on the training of workseekers at group training centres.

Table 6.8 illustrates that a high percentage of workseekers trained have been successfully trained and placed in jobs. The lower placement rate in 1984 was due to the serious recessionary situation.

Table 6.8 Training and placement of workseekers, 1982-1984

	1982	1983	1984
Person who commenced training	860	3 852	9 250
Persons who completed training	149	3 171	6 875
Persons placed	242	2 301	3 973

More information on the types and number of in-service training courses already registered is provided in the next section.

Training course catalogue or index

Employers qualify for tax rebates or cash grants where employees are trained on courses registered with the Department of Manpower. The National Training Board recently developed a training catalogue of all of the almost 20 000 registered courses available as at September 1984. This

156

catalogue can be used by employers for the identification of courses already registered and will thus avoid unnecessary duplication in the design of courses. It remains the prerogative of every course owner to decide whether he is prepared to make his course(s) available to other employers, and, if so, in what form.

Computer printouts containing information on the name and address of the course owner and the name, type and length of the course required, can be obtained from the Department of Manpower. This catalogue also assists the training advisers of the Department in the promotion of training.

The characteristics of the 19 576 courses registered by 1 385 organisations on 30 September 1984 can be summmarised as follows:

Type of courses registered

The courses can be classified as follows in terms of type of course (see table 6.9):

Table 6.9 Classification of registered courses

Type of course	Number of courses registered	Percentage
Production	4 902	25,0
Maintenance, construction and power generation	3 922	20,0
Computer	2 630	13,4
Management principles (planning, organising, controlling)	1 260	6,4
Marketing, sales, client relations	953	4,9
Transport	935	4,8
Financial	921	4,7
Personnel	509	2,6
Clerical and administrative	483	2,5
Induction and orientation	400	2,0
General skills (for example report writing)	360	1,8
Training	326	1,7
Quality control and development	284	1,5
Labour relations	284	1,5
Safety and health	224	1,1
Purchasing and stores control	219	1,1
Retail	198	1,0
Business principles, productivity, 6M*	183	0,9
Security	157	0,8
Agriculture, forestry and horticulture	114	0,6
Communication and information	96	0,5
Fire fighting	72	0,4
Services (hairdresser, steward)	68	0,3
Workstudy	58	0,3
Legal aspects	12	0,1
Aptitude test administration	6	0,03
Total	19 576	

* The course on how a modern business functions and relates to the six economic factors (e.g. money, market, machines, etc).

The above is only a preliminary analysis.

80% of the 19 576 registered courses relate to production, maintenance and construction, computing, management principles, marketing and sales, transport and financial activities — in this order.

Analysis shows that courses representing almost the entire work spectrum already exist. Employers have ample opportunity to obtain suitable courses from other employers rather than develop these themselves from the start.

Employers and employee organisations are advised to develop courses appropriate to present needs in the fields of labour relations, training of trainers and productivity.

Course level

Table 6.10   Courses by course level

Number of courses on senior and middle management levels	5%
Number of courses on first-line supervisor level	13%
Number of non-managerial courses	82%

Although large numbers of courses have been registered to date, the quality of most of these courses is by no means certain. At present, the Department of Manpower is putting a major effort into the promotion of more effective training for trainers and the continuous evaluation of the contribution of training to increased performance. Undoubtedly, this will lead to more cost-effective training.

Type of training centre that registered courses

Table 6.11   Courses registered by institution

Institution	Number of courses	Percentage
Private training centre	509	37
Training schemes	859	62
Group training centre	8	1
Total	1 376*	100

*A further nine institutions are registered under conditions outside the Manpower Training Act.

The 1 376 employers who have registered courses to date are largely from training schemes (62%) and to a lesser extent from private training centres (37%) and group training centres (1%).

Course length

The course lengths can be summarised as follows:

Table 6.12 Course length

Course length	Number of courses	Percentage
Half a day and less	1 561	8,0
1 Day	1 850	9,5
2 Days	2 275	11,6
3 Days	1 977	10,1
4 Days	249	1,3
5 Days	2 485	12,7
6 Days	635	3,2
7 Days	345	1,8
8 Days	264	1,4
9 Days	191	1,0
10 Days	1 296	6,6
11-15 Days	1 200	6,1
16-20 Days	842	4,3
Longer than 20 days	2 508	12,8
No information available	1 898	9,7
Total	19 576	

The majority of the courses last only a few days: 53% of the courses last five days or less and 14% last between five to ten days. Thus, almost 70% of all the courses last for ten days or less, 6% from 11 to 15 days and 17% for longer than 16 days. Information on course length was not provided for 10% of the courses.

Classification of employers (course owners) according to industrial index

Table 6.13 Industrial classification of employers (course owners)

Industry	Number of courses	Percentage
Manufacture of chemical products	2 787	14,2
Business services, including attorneys and accounting and auditing services	2 006	10,2
Manufacture of iron and steel and steel products	1 676	8,5
Manufacture of clothing and textiles	1 477	7,5
Educational services such as driving schools and group training centres	1 061	5,4
Manufacture of motor vehicles, parts and accessories	952	4,8
Wholesale trade (except motor vehicles)	965	4,9
Retail trade (except motor vehicles)	957	4,8
Construction and civil engineering	894	4,5
Financial institutions and insurance	717	3,6
Manufacture of food	689	3,5
Manufacture of electrical machinery and appliances	528	2,7
Petroleum refineries	498	2,5
Manufacture of machinery, except electrical	362	1,8

Table continued on following page

Beverage industries	320	1,6
Manufacture of non-metallic mineral products	286	1,4
Business, professional and labour associations	245	1,2
Manufacture of rubber products	244	1,3
Manufacture of pulp, paper and board	228	1,1
Motor trade and repair services	226	1,1
Transport services	216	1,1
Electricity, gas and steam	155	0,8
Manufacture of wood products and furniture	147	0,7
Manufacture of glass and glass products	110	0,6
Manufacture of transport equipment (except motor vehicles)	107	0,5
Large variety of other economic activities	1 723	100,0

Fifty per cent of the courses were registered by employers in the following industries:

Manufacture of chemical products	14,2%
Business services such as bookkeeping services, data processing and architects' services	10,2%
Manufacture of iron and steel and of metal products	8,5%
Manufacture of clothing and textiles	7,5%
Educational services such as driving schools and group training centres	5,4%
Manufacture of motor vehicles and accessories	4,8%

Other economic activities in which there was active course registration were the following:

Wholesale trade

Retail trade

Construction and engineering

Financial institutions and insurance

Manufacture of electrical machinery and appliances

Petroleum refineries.

Further, the analysis revealed that although in certain industries there are some independent large firms which have registered courses for their own purposes, the major part of the specific industry does not do systematic training, presumably due to the lack of suitable courses (many of these are small firms which do not have sufficiently sophisticated training sections to do their own course development). Similar information points to the urgent need for the establishment of training boards for specific industries which would initiate and co-ordinate courses and training services for their members' firms.

Geographical distribution of training establishments

The four metropolitan areas, namely the Pretoria/Witwatersrand/Vaal Triangle-area (PWV), the Durban/Pinetown area (DP), the Port Elizabeth/Uitenhage area (PEU) and the Cape Peninsula (CP), house a large concentration of firms which provide courses as illustrated in the table below:

Table 6.14 Geographical distribution of training establishments

Area	Number of courses	Percentage of total in the RSA	Bodies	Percentage of total in the RSA
PWV	11 860	60,6	816	58,9
DP	2 401	12,3	170	12,3
PEU	755	3,9	55	4,0
CP	704	3,6	79	5,7
Total	15 720	80,3	1 120	80,9

The rest of the courses, namely 3 856 (20%), fall outside the above area.

Although the place of registration of most of the courses is limited to metropolitan areas, use of the courses is not limited to the above areas, largely because many employers have branches in country areas where their courses are utilised.

General conclusion regarding progress with in-service training

The tremendous progress that has been made with in-service training is best illustrated by the following figure,[15] which indicates that in-service training increased by more than 30% between 1979 and 1983, compared to almost 6% for university training and 6,5% for technical training. One can conclude that the institutional infrastructure is working well and is well-utilised by employers.

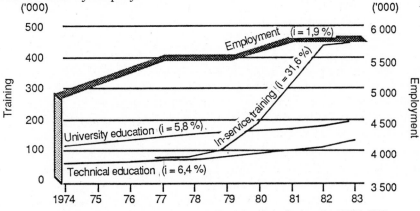

Fig 6.21 In-service training compared to university and technical education 1974-1983

161

STRUCTURAL CHANGES IN THE LABOUR FORCE*

Although organisations find it relatively easy to obtain information on their internal manpower situation, the same cannot be said about the changing external situation. The aim of this section, then, is to describe recent major changes in the macro-manpower situation.

The supply of and the demand for manpower

Labour supply

The supply of labour is a function of population growth (Terblanche 1980). Depending on assumptions about fertility, mortality and emigration, different population projections are possible. A population group's fertility rate is dependent on its quality of life. The rate at which a population group's standard of living changes thus influences the population growth rate of that group.

The different population groups in the RSA have different growth rates. Table 6.15 indicates population growth projections of the RSA population (1980-2040), given the current growth rates.

Table 6.15 Population growth projections of the RSA, 1980-2040

	Population group (1 000 000)				
	Indians	Whites	Coloureds	Blacks	Total
Growth rate	1,76%	1,55%	1,80%	2,80%	
Year					
1980	0,81	4,40	2,50	20,70	28,41
2000	1,16	5,81	3,79	36,40	47,15
2020	1,55	6,64	5,40	65,60	79,19
2040	1,99	7,03	7,57	121,60	138,19

Source: Department of Health, The Population Development Programme, 1982

*The author acknowledges with thanks information provided by Mr Pierre Joubert, lecturer in Manpower Strategy at the Rand Afrikaans University.

As is the case with population projections, different estimates of the size of the labour force are possible, depending on the set of assumptions that form the basis of the estimates. However, sources upon which to base the assumptions are very limited. For Whites and Indians we have the population census figures, while the Current Population Survey gives information for Blacks and Coloureds.

The size of the labour force is calculated by applying the activity rate (the percentage of the population that are economically active) for each age

group to the relevant population estimate. The total estimate of the size of the South African economically active population for 1977 and 1987 by population groups is given in table 6.16.

Table 6.16 Estimate of the size of the South African economically active population for 1977 and 1987 by population group

Year	Whites	Coloureds	Indians	Blacks
Growth rate	1,7%	3,1%	3,4%	2,9%
1977	1 780 851	871 991	240 206	5 771 031
1987	2 113 378	1 189 276	320 218	7 710 510

Total labour force 1977 8 664 079
1987 11 333 382

Source: HSRC Report MM-83

Creation of job opportunities

The growth in the labour force is indicative of the job opportunities that must be created. According to table 6.16, the economically active population will increase by roughly 267 000 per annum. This means that roughly 730 job opportunities have to be created each day of this period.

Estimate of the SA population 1980

Estimate of the SA population 2040

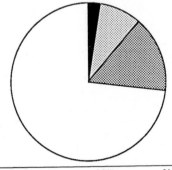

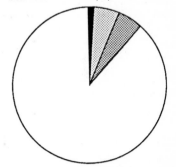

	Millions	%
Indians	0,81	2,9
Coloureds	2,50	8,8
Whites	4,40	15,5
Blacks	20,70	72,8
TOTAL	28,41	100,0

	Millions	%
Indians	1,99	1,4
Coloureds	7,57	5,5
Whites	7,03	5,1
Blacks	121,60	88,0
TOTAL	138,19	100,0

Fig 6.22 Estimate of the population of South Africa, 1980 and 2040

Bearing in mind the relationship between population growth and the supply of labour, the population group composition of labour supply will change dramatically in the future, as illustrated graphically in figure 6.22. It is estimated that the White component of the population will decrease from 15,5% in 1980 to an estimated 5,1% in 2040, while the Black component will increase from 72,8% to an estimated 88% over this period. White workers will therefore become scarcer in the future. This aspect will be referred to again when the demand for labour is analysed.

Labour demand

The demand for labour is primarily a function of the demand for goods and services and the price paid for labour. Economic growth affects the availability of jobs, as more jobs are needed when the demand for goods and services increase. Given a fixed level of technology, the demand for labour will increase as production increases. The level of economic activity is usually expressed in terms of the Gross Domestic Product (GDP). In the Economic Development Programme (EDP) for the RSA, a target for economic growth is set. From this target (4,5% growth in GDP), a certain estimate of the demand for labour is made. The total estimate of the demand for labour for 1977 and 1987 is given in table 6.17.

Table 6.17 Estimate of the demand for labour (1977 and 1987) by population group*

Year	Whites	Coloureds	Indians	Blacks
1977	1 543 093	554 258	187 372	3 069 701
1987	2 036 367	789 284	278 222	3 900 927

Total demand for labour   1977   5 354 427
  1987   7 004 800

*Domestic and agricultural workers excluded.

Source: HSRC Report MM-83

Long term estimates should be viewed with circumspection, as the variables which influence the demand for and the supply of labour change over time. Given the current population growth rates and an economic growth rate of 4,5%, the total supply of and demand for labour (domestic and agricultural workers included) for 1980, 1990 and 2000) are indicated in figure 6.23.

164

Fig 6.23   Total supply and demand for labour, 1980, 1990 and 2000.

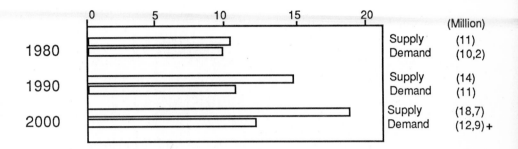

Source: Focus on key economic issues, Mercabank (agriculture and domestic services included)

Tables 6.16, 6.17 and figure 6.23 emphasise the two main manpower problems in the RSA. The first is a critical lack of job opportunities due to the fast-growing population. The analyses (figure 6.23) indicate unemployment figures of almost 800 000 in 1980, 3 million in 1990 and approximately 5 million in 2000. (Source: *Rapport* 19/5/1985.) Furthermore, the ratio of work seekers to the total population does not change during the period of prediction, which indicates that the problem of unemployment will be as severe in the future.

The second is a shortage of skilled manpower, which at present is largely a White preserve. The projections of demand (table 6.17) show an annual growth rate in the demand for White workers of approximately 2,8% per annum. On the other hand, table 6.16 shows that supply will increase at a rate of only 1,7% per annum for the same group.

The magnitude of the problem must not be underestimated, especially when the aspirations of the Non-Whites and the tendency among Whites to defend vested interests and to maintain the status quo are taken into account.

The changing occupational structure

The products and services we use are produced by a variety of skills illustrated in figure 6.24. The bi-annual manpower surveys of the Department of Manpower for the period 1965-1979[16] were used as the sources of information upon which the estimates of occupational structures and changes in manpower are based.

Figure 6.24 indicates that the changes in the occupational structure

165

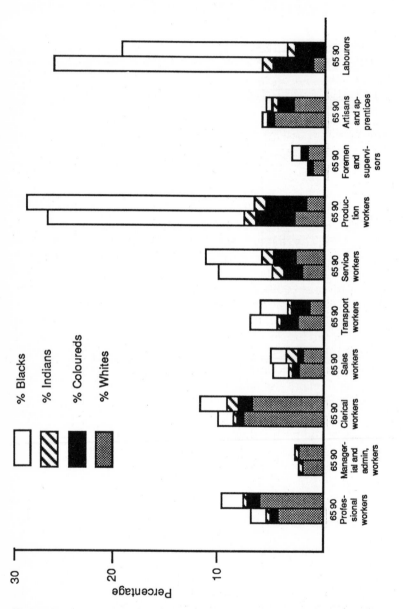

Fig 6.24 The occupational structure of the South African labour force, 1965 and 1990

follow the general trend for industrialised countries in the West. The demand for professional, managerial, clerical, service and production workers shows a definite increase for the period 1965-1990, while the demand for artisans, transport workers and labourers shows a decrease. The tertiary sector is becoming more important as a creator of jobs, while the manufacturing sector is becoming more sophisticated and capital-intensive. The racial composition of the five major occupational groups for 1965 and 1987 is illustrated in figure 6.25 and table 6.18.

Table 6.18 The racial composition of the five major occupational groups

Category	1965			1987		
	White	Black	Coloured and Indian	White	Black	Coloured and Indian
Professional	88,20	10,11	1,69	79,57	12,99	7,44
Management	97,98	0,22	1,80	94,47	1,81	3,72
Clerical	83,13	9,06	7,81	64,45	17,51	18,04
Service	24,03	59,91	16,06	20,18	65,42	14,40
Artisans and apprentices	88,45	0,40	11,15	69,30	7,82	22,88

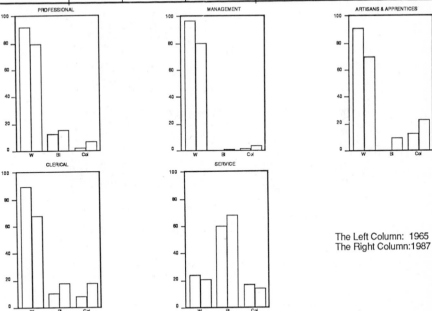

The Left Column: 1965
The Right Column: 1987

Fig 6.25 Percentage distribution of Whites, Blacks and Coloureds in the major occupational groups during 1965 and 1987

Source: Department of Manpower Utilisation, Manpower Surveys 1965-1979, Pretoria

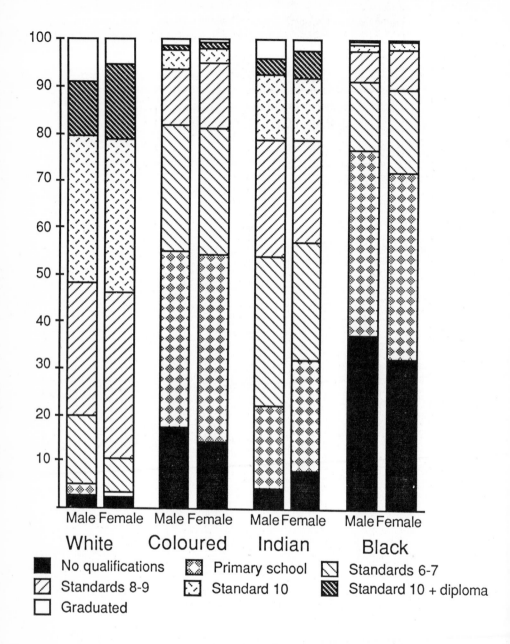

Fig 6.26 Educational level of the labour force, 1980

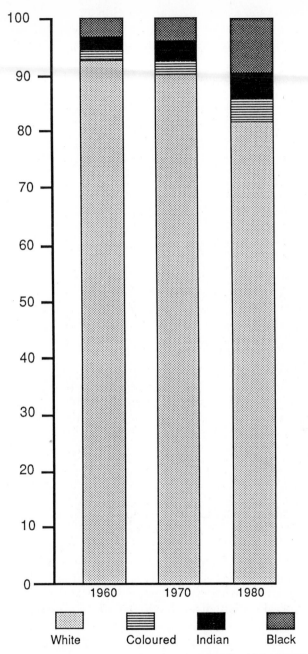

White   Coloured   Indian   Black

Fig 6.27 Distribution of the labour force with Std 10 or higher qualifications in 1960, 1970 and 1980

169

The above figures illustrate the decreasing participation by Whites and the increasing participation by Blacks and Coloureds in professional, management, clerical, service and artisan occupational groups.

The educational level of the labour force

According to Professor JC Sadie, the labour force may be classified into four socio-economic groups (De Vries 1984):

- The executive group (entrepreneurial and managerial echelons)
- The highly skilled group (professional and technical personnel)
- The semi-skilled group
- The unskilled group.

The combination of the executive and highly skilled groups represents the country's high level manpower, for they make decisions which affect economic growth. Almost all of these occupations require a minimum of two years training after Std 10.

According to figures 6.25 and 6.26 (Terblanche, Jacobs and Van Pletzen 1983), the high level manpower traditionally consists largely of White workers. The structural changes (a higher proportion of other population groups in high level manpower) depicted in these figures can be attributed to the prediction that the White population's share in the total population will decline (figure 6.26).

It seems, therefore, that the educational process is conforming to changes in imbalances within the labour force. The critical question is whether these changes occur in response to, or in anticipation of structural changes. It is clear that in future Black, Coloured and Indian employees will play an increasing role in that they will occupy higher level positions requiring matric and post-matric qualifications.

SUMMARISING COMMENT

Major strides have been made in the field of manpower over the past five years, the most important of which concern labour relations, in-service training and the manpower structure. The growth and concomitant changes that characterised these developments occurred systematically and although growth trends cannot always be predicted, the existing control mechanisms should be able to cope with any further growth that may occur.

South Africa is facing exciting challenges due to growth and development in the economic, social, constitutional and political fields and undoubtedly these will necessitate the mustering of all the available manpower. As a result of the infrastructure for labour relations created by the Government and the personal and career development of all groups in

170

the population, South Africa should be able to meet all its future manpower needs. Because of the foresight revealed by the Government in this regard and the enthusiasm with which employers and employees have greeted these initiatives, it may safely be assumed that unparalleled economic heights will soon be achieved.

NOTES

1 Wiehahn, NE. Industrial relations in South Africa — a changing scene, in Van Vuuren, Wiehahn, Lombard and Rhoodie (Eds.). Change in South Africa, 1983.
2 South Africa (Republic). Department of Manpower. Annual Report 1984 Pretoria: Government Printer, 1985 (RP 66/85), p. 60.
3 *op cit* p. 29.
4 IR Data: vol. 4, no. 1, March 1984, p. 26.
5 South Africa (Republic). *op cit*, p. 24-25.
6 Wiehahn Report. Lex Patria. Johannesburg: 1982, p. 28.
7 See note 5 above.
8 South Africa (Republic). *op cit*, p. 24.
9 IR Data: Special Report on Industrial Action. June 1983, p. 5.
10 See note 9 above.
11 South Africa (Republic). Department of Manpower, National Training Board. *Guide-lines for Training in Labour Relations*. Pretoria: Government Printer, 1984.
12 — *Compendium of Training:* Pretoria: Government Printer, 1984.
13 South Africa (Republic). National Manpower Commission. *In-service Training in the Republic of South Africa 1980-81*. Pretoria: Government Printer, 1983 (RP 2/84).
14 HSRC/NTB. Investigation into the training of artisans. Pretoria: HSRC, 1984.
15 Mercabank: Focus on Key Economic Issues. No. 36, Johannesburgh: 1985.
16 Department of Manpower Utilisation, Manpower Surveys 1965-1979.

BIBLIOGRAPHY

Backer, W. *Arbeidsverhoudinge: 'n Strategie vir arbeidsvrede*. Publikasie A152. Johannesburg: Randse Afrikaanse Universiteit, 1983 (professorale intreerede).
Bendix, DWF. Trade Unions and Politics Effects on the Company. Industrial Relations Trends SA. Occasional Publication 8/83. Pretoria: 1983.
De Vries, M. Developing skilled manpower. *Industrial Relations Journal of South Africa*, vol. iv, no. 3, 1984.
Howe, G. (Ed.). *Industrial relations in South Africa 1982-1984. A comparative review of statistics and trends*. Durban: Indicator Project South Africa, Centre for Applied Social Sciences, University of Natal, 1984.
Jones, RA. *Collective Bargaining in South Africa*. Johannesburg: Macmillan, 1984.
Levy, A and Associates. *Annual Report on Labour Relations in South Africa 1984/85*. Johannesburg: 1984.
— *Workbook for seminar The Outer Edge of Industrial Relations*, Johannesburg: 1985.
Maree, J. Swart Vakbonde: Kampregter vir Demokrasie. *Die Suid-Afrikaan*, Somer 1985.
Mercabank. *Focus on Key Economic Issues, no. 36, 1985*.
Piron, J. *Recognition or Rejection*. Johannesburg: Macmillan, 1984.
— *The South African System of Industrial Relations. SA Journal of Labour Relations*, vol. 6, no. 1, 1982.

Terblanche, SS. *An analysis of the macro-manpower demand and supply situation (1977-1987) in the RSA*. Pretoria: HSRC, 1980 (Report MM-83).

Terblanche, SS, Jacobs, IJ and Van Pletzen, J. *The Manpower Scene 1982*. Pretoria: HSRC, 1983 (Research. Finding MN-101.).

Wiehahn, NE. *Report*. Johannesburg: Lex Patria, 1982.

7 An appropriate development strategy for Southern Africa[1]

AA Ligthelm and SF Coetzee

INTRODUCTION

The poverty and development problems of the Third World gave rise to considerable stimulation of thought about development and change in development strategies during the 1970s. It was increasingly appreciated that the development models arising from the growth and modernisation experience of the First World were not applicable to the circumstances of the less developed countries (LDCs). The conventional development approach (CDA) was increasingly criticised and questioned. This process has progressed to the extent that a newly-conceived approach to development, appropriate to the circumstances of the LDCs, has begun to crystallise.

The unsatisfactory results of development efforts experienced elsewhere in the Third World, but more particularly in Africa, are also being experienced in the less developed areas of Southern Africa.[2] Ancillary to this, the typical North-South or rich-poor dichotomy characteristic of the international scene is also prevalent in Southern Africa. In spite of this dichotomy, the modern and underdeveloped sectors of the economy are functionally inter-dependent and should be approached within the context of one spatial framework. Both the typical development issues and the question of relationships are thus integral to the situation in the Southern African subcontinent.

Although in this chapter an attempt will be made to give a brief outline of the evolution of thought regarding development, it should be realised that this can be done only by means of a few guidelines. The object of the chapter, however, is to make a contribution to the quest for an appropriate development strategy (ADS) for the specific development circumstances in Southern Africa. To emphasise the urgency of a solution to the poverty problem, the first part of the chapter contains a short resumé of development experience. Thereafter, attention will be given to the unfolding of thought about development and to possible guidelines for an ADS for Southern Africa.

DEVELOPMENT EXPERIENCE

In this section attention will be given to development experience in Africa and then in Southern Africa. In the latter case, attention is given to the question from the points of view of both the typical underdevelopment problem in the national states as such and the dualistic experience in which the national states form an integral part of the economy of Southern Africa.

Africa

Despite the intensive attention which the issue of development has received during the past three decades at both the political and academic level, there is considerable disillusionment and even widespread pessimism about development in the Third World. In spite of the relatively high economic growth rates achieved in the Third World during the past 25 years, the poverty problem has begun to adopt increasing proportions. Experience has shown that the income of the greater proportion of the population of the LDCs has shown a definite decline, particularly since the start of the 1970s. Streeten & Burki (1978: 411) refer to the fact that both the scope and intensity of poverty have steadily increased in the midst of positive economic growth rates.

As far as Africa is concerned, development experience during the past two decades shows that Africa south of the Sahara has fared considerably worse than the rest of the less developed world. During the 1970s, the annual growth in per capita income averaged only 0,2% as opposed to 2,9% for the Third World as a whole (OECD 1981: 22). Even African countries which grew at rapid rates in the past have increasingly experienced problems (World Bank 1981: 1).

Together with the extremely unsatisfactory economic showing of Africa, which is already the poorest continent, an increasingly skewed distribution of income is being experienced, especially in Kenya, Swaziland and Zambia. The richest 20% of the populations of various African countries earn more than two thirds of the total income (Bequele & Van der Hoeven 1980: 382). One of the factors contributing to the poverty problem in the Third World is the fact that economic growth has been taking place mainly in the small modern sector of the economy in which highly sophisticated technology is used (Singer 1979: 3).

The implication of the economic problems is that of the 33 countries classified as the poorest countries (i.e. countries with a per capita income of less than $410) in the World Development Report of 1982, two thirds are in Africa. A consequence of this poverty problem is that the greater portion of the population has an income so low that it does not enjoy access to basic services. To illustrate this point, the literacy rate in Africa is only 28%, which is less than half the literacy rate of the Third World as a whole. The mortality rate in Africa is the highest in the world, while the lowest life expectancy is also found in Africa. The World Bank (1981: 3) also suggests that 15 to 20% of all children in Africa die in the first year of life and that only 25% of the inhabitants of Africa have access to clean drinking water.

As standard indicators of poverty, the abovementioned compare extremely poorly with the rest of the LDCs. Thus the extent of the development problem in Africa is of such a nature that it could even imply a crisis of survival in certain African countries. The conclusion drawn by Elliot Berg (World Bank 1982: 4) after an extensive study of Africa was that '. . . the continent (Africa) is in serious crisis . . . the crisis is deep, so deep as to threaten the stability and even the survival of many states of the region'.

From the above summary of the poverty or development problem of the Third World (and more specifically of Africa), it is clear that the development strategies of the past have not had meaningful development results. The growth or modernisation approach, which concentrates on urban development, advanced technology and large-scale development projects producing modern products and services, has benefitted only a limited elite in the LDCs, while very little trickling down of benefits to the poorer section has taken place. From a report of OAU (1980: 3) it is clear that the political leaders of Africa have begun to realise the extent and nature of the development problem. In the abovementioned document it is stated that '. . . Africa is unable to point to any significant growth rate or satisfactory index of general well-being in the last twenty years. . . . Successive strategies have made the continent stagnate.' It is concluded that a basic restructuring of the continent's economic basis is needed. The failed growth approach, which concentrates mainly on capital accumulation in the modern sector, will thus have to be replaced by an ADS to address the poverty problem.

The national states[3]

The development problem of the national states is broadly similar to that of African countries. However, there are certain structural questions pertinent to Southern Africa which differ from those relevant to the rest of Africa and which relate largely to the dualistic nature and close economic integration of the economic system of the former. The improvement in living standards which has taken place in the national states is, to a large extent, of external or exogenous origin. This includes the decentralisation of industries, development of border areas, the promotion of governmental spending by means of development aid, etc. There are, as is the case in the

175

rest of Africa, limited existing economic forces to stimulate endogenous growth.

Because the economies of the national states are linked into a broader economic system with the RSA, they can be regarded as part of the Southern African economy. There are strong mutual links and influences which must be taken into account. However, it remains essential that the phenomenon of a modern and a traditional system existing next to one another must be taken into account in devising an ADS. The extent of poverty in the national states and the uneven distribution of economic activity in Southern Africa are highlighted by available facts and figures.

The poverty profile of the national states

(a) The GDP per capita (at 1970 prices) of the inhabitants of the self-governing national states increased from R40 in 1970 to R46 in 1980, representing an average annual increase of only 1,3%. This is among the lowest in the world. The improvement in the standards of living in the national states during the past decade originated overwhelmingly from outside these states, because a large number of their inhabitants were employed in the RSA as border commuters or migratory workers. The income earned by these workers (R4 460 million in 1980) represented 72% of the total GNI of the national states. The consequence of this is that the real GNI per capita increased from R117 in 1972 to R176 in 1980. The rate of growth of 4,6% per year on average was thus appreciably higher than that of the real GDP per capita, which means that the proportional share of outside earnings was still increasing in importance. The contribution of internal production to the GNI in the national states thus declined from just above a third (35%) in 1972 to just more than a quarter (26,1%) in 1980.

(b) The distribution of income is exceptionally skewed. In the case of Transkei, the poorest 20% of the population earn only 4,2% of the total income, while the most prosperous 20% earn 55,5%. Furthermore, data indicate that this distribution of income is still worsening. In Transkei the real increase in income for the four-year period between 1975 and 1979 was 12% for rural households and 44% for the urban elite. Thomas (1982: 83) confirms that '... for the bulk of rural Transkeians the income gap vis-à-vis the urban elite has widened'.

(c) The absolute level of household income confirms that poverty is adopting proportions of great magnitude. In Transkei 85% of rural households are earning incomes lower than a conservatively calculated minimum subsistence level. For urban households, the corresponding percentage is only 15%. In 1979 the poorest 20% of rural

176

households in Transkei earned only R242 per annum. This is about 15% of a minimum subsistence income.

(d) The retention capacity of the national states is also extremely low. For the period 1972 to 1975, only 28% (one in every four workers) who entered the labour market in the national states could be provided with employment in those states. Indications are that this tendency continued for the rest of the decade. The rest were either migratory labourers or border commuters, or simply added to the body of the unemployed or underemployed. According to the Economic Development Programme, the unemployment rate in the national states is 20%, while the occupational participation rate is estimated at 35% for men and only 19% for women. As a result of the limited retention rate of the national states, more than two million Black workers from these states were employed in the RSA during 1982. This total comprised 773 000 border commuters and just over 1,4 million migratory workers.

(e) The agricultural sector, which is the most important resource asset of the national states, is also largely under-utilised and contributes only to a limited extent to further economic development. This is confirmed by the fact that the contribution of subsistence production to total production is still increasing. In 1973 agricultural production comprised 86,5% of subsistence production and by 1980 this had increased to 88,3%. Simkins (1979: table 3) reports that the real value of agricultural income in the national states, expressed in 1970 values, increased from R43,8 million in 1918 to R44,6 million in 1965, with greater fluctuations inbetween.

(f) Industrial decentralisation has had limited success. The development of border areas and growth points near and in the national states has been able to provide employment for only 6,8% of the growth in the de facto labour force.[4] The majority of industrial undertakings which decentralised were established within the sphere of influence of the metropoles, with 42% of the industrial employment opportunities created in the national states in Babelegi, near Pretoria. Although the new regional development policy, which came into effect in 1982, has been much more successful in creating employment opportunities in and near the national states, it is not expected that it will solve the problem.

(g) The limited economic basis of the national states is also reflected in the sources of finance of the national states' governments. Development aid from the RSA to the governments of the self-governing states in 1981/82 comprised almost 77% of the total income of those governments. In respect of the independent states, the combined contribution of the RSA payments (i.e. development aid, customs union payments and Rand monetary union payments) comprised some 65% of the total income of their governments.

(h) Poverty is assuming serious proportions as far as the quality of human resources and access to basic services are concerned. Some examples in Transkei are that almost a third of the rural population and a fifth of the urban population has received no training; that infant mortality is 130 per 1 000 births, which is among the highest in Africa; that the average distance to clinics in rural areas is 7 km, while the nearest medical practitioners are an average of 13 km away; that rural households spend an average of 3,5 hours per day fetching water, while the per capita use of water is only 10,8 litres compared with a hygienic norm of between 20 and 50 litres; that food shortages are a general occurrence and almost a fifth of all children between six months and two years show signs of the four most important nutritional diseases; and that serious housing shortages, with consequent overcrowding, are encountered, particularly in urban areas.

(i) The development problems experienced by the national states are also accentuated by the fact that these states contribute only 4% to the GGP of the space economy of Southern Africa, compared to the 65% and 31% contributed by the metropolitan core areas and the inner- periphery (RSA rural) areas respectively. This pattern is not likely to change within the next 15 to 20 years; in fact, it is expected that, as a result of urban pull and rural push factors, between 12,5 million and 17,5 million Black people will become urbanised. Some ten million of these people will be in the RSA. Thus, the process of urbanisation has become inevitable and irreversible.

From the above summary it is clear that poverty is beginning to assume serious proportions in the national states. The economies of the national states have limited existing economic forces, while the welfare which does exist there can be attributed to the achievements of the states themselves to a limited extent only. In the case of Transkei, for example, Thomas (1982: 81) states that '. . . half of Transkei's 1980 national income of R1 200 million consists of gross earnings by migrants, i.e. income created outside Transkei. Of the remaining R600 million, another 50 to 55% is made up of public-sector activities, of which about three quarters are (directly or indirectly) financed by the RSA. Thus, in essence only about 28% of the total national income is generated by the local economy.' Ancillary to the conclusion that the development of Transkei is largely a function of increased migrants' earnings and RSA transfers, the Transkei Government (1980: 44) itself states that 'one can hardly speak at present of a Transkei economy in any meaningful sense: more properly one must consider it a labour reserve.'

178

The data also confirms the fact that the human resources are generally poorly developed and under-utilised. Only a small, privileged group has reaped the advantages of economic growth in the Third World. Because in most cases labour is the only resource of the poor, the development of human resources and the consequent raising of productivity must receive particular attention in an ADS.

Development strategies of the national states

In the national states, as is the case in the LDCs, conventional growth strategies are applied with limited developmental results (Van der Kooy 1979: 21). Brand (1977: 9) confirms that in all the economic development programmes since the first one appeared in 1964, economic growth is the goal upon which the emphasis was placed.

The consequence of this approach, which is discussed in the next section, is that emphasis was laid upon the large-scale provision of infrastructure, industrial development with sophisticated technology, urban development and modern commercial and agricultural projects. Thomas (1980: 60) confirms that 'like in so many Third World countries most of the emphasis has hitherto fallen on the few urban areas . . . and on large-scale agricultural, forestry, infrastructure and industrial projects where the link with rural communities is often minimal. On the whole, grass roots rural development has actually been neglected'. Development programmes in the sphere of rural development, small farmer development, small business development, the development of the informal sector and applied technology simply received low priority in development strategies.

Ancillary to the production structure which was based on the Western pattern of growth, the majority of the rural population lacked the most basic products and services. Apart from the fact that they receive low incomes which do not grant less privileged groups access to basic products like food and clothing, governmental priorities were of such a nature that collective products like education, health and infrastructure were made available only to a limited elite (cf Beukes 1983: ch 4).

The need for an appropriate development approach

Apart from the need for eradicating poverty in the national states, there are other factors which necessitate a search for an ADS capable of assuring positive development results. From the previous section it is clear that progress in the national states originates to a large extent from outside the states. Most important in this regard are the earnings of the migratory workers and border commuters. Present indications are that the number of migratory workers from the national states is beginning to stabilise, while in the case of Transkei (the most important source of migratory labour) it is even beginning to decline. This source of employment, which in the case of Venda and Transkei, for example, provides 70% of the male workforce with employment, can thus to an ever lesser extent supplement the limited retention capacity of the national states. In addition to this historic employment sponge, in the past the subsistence agricultural sector was also an important source of employment (even a 'poverty buffer') for labour growth. In the cases of Transkei and Venda, the average size of arable land per household is only 1,9 ha, which indicates that further subdivision cannot offer meaningful additional employment opportunities.

With this reality as background and in view of the fact that the population increase in the national states doubles the numbers almost every 20 to 25 years and consequently will add another 11 million people by the year 2000, it is obvious that an ADS is essential.

In addition to an appropriate strategy geared to handling the typical problems of the less developed areas of Southern Africa, the strongly centripetal forces of the Southern African economy demand measures which will allow a more equitable regional distribution of economic activity to be attained. The functioning of the modern sector where it directly adjoins the less developed sector creates distinct problems in the development of these areas. According to Du Plessis (1973: 84), the geographic proximity of rich and poor countries/regions strengthens the polarisation effect of economic activities to the advantage of the rich country and the disadvantage of the poor countries. These economically centripetal forces contribute to the metropolitan areas being the economic concentration point in the process of economic development in Southern Africa.

These agglomerative tendencies result in the particularly disproportionate geographic distribution of economic activity in Southern Africa. Close on 97% of the GDP of Southern Africa is produced within the borders of the RSA. This 97% is also highly unequally distributed, with close on 70% of it being generated in the four metropolitan areas. The national states each produce less than 1% of the GDP of Southern Africa. With the exception of Bophuthatswana, KwaZulu and Transkei, each of which contributes in the order of 0,7%, the other states' contributions range between 0,1 and 0,3%.

The concentration of economic activity occurs particularly in industrial activity. Du Pisanie (1981: 11) found, for example, that between the two industrial censuses of 1972 and 1976 the PWV complex attracted no less than 46% of the increase in the number of industrial employment opportunites. Together, the four metropolitan areas attracted 97% of the net increase in the number of factories, while employment opportunities in the industrial sector in the rest of the region declined by more then 4 400.

Even industrial development based on internal consumer demand in the national states is extremely low. Nel (1980: 70) refers to the fact that the total domestic household consumption of the ten national states combined comprised only 8% of the total household expenditure of Southern Africa. This is equivalent to that of the Pretoria metropolitan area and less than 60% of the household expenditure of the Johannesburg metropolitan area.

These strongly polarising tendencies emphasise the necessity for the institution of programmes and instruments aimed at a better distribution of economic activity. The new and improved instruments required for the purpose, which will form an essential part of an ADS, are discussed in the section entitled 'The formulation of an appropriate development strategy (ADS) for Southern Africa: a preliminary framework'.

Summary

From the discussion thus far, it is clear that the magnitude of the poverty problem is still increasing amidst relatively high economic growth rates. Further, it is evident that from now until the turn of the century the urbanisation of Black people is and will remain the single most important factor in the Southern African economic, social and political environment. Due to the close interrelationship between all the regions in Southern Africa, an appropriate development strategy must ultimately embrace its entire spatial framework. The economy of Southern Africa has reached a stage of which the modern sector is so powerful and its influence so pervasive that it is misleading to treat the pockets of economic backwardness and poverty as separate economic entities. This reality has stimulated thought regarding development to the extent that a newly-designed and appropriate strategy for the development of South Africa has crystallised. Before this appropriate strategy is discussed, attention will be given to the development of theory on the development problem over the last three decades.

THE DEVELOPMENT OF DEVELOPMENT THEORY

The conventional development approach (CDA)

The economic bias

Since the Second World War, the development theme has received increasing and sustained attention. Although the multidimensional nature of the

181

development process was acknowledged in the early fifties in textbooks and other writings, the main emphasis in thought about development was on economic development. Earlier thought on the nature of the development process was pre-occupied with the economic transformation needed in LDCs to such an extent that the concepts of development and economic development became synonymous in the literature. Apart from the fact that the non-economic dimensions of the development process were grossly neglected, almost no attention was paid to the interplay of economic and non-economic forces. Earlier views on the 'other' dimensions of the development process centred on modernisation in areas such as education, health, etc, along the lines of Western standards and norms, which were often alien to the conditions in the LDCs. This process of modernisation or 'catching up' with the Western Countries also had the rather narrow basis of promoting the goal of economic growth.

The economic bias in thought about development in the fifties and sixties stemmed *inter alia* from

(a) attempts by developed countries (DCs) to rebuild their economies, with the aid of the Marshall Plan, following a period of destruction during the Second World War
(b) the process of decolonisation, as a result of which many nation states gained sovereign independence, but emerged as relatively poor or underdeveloped countries in which it became clear that political freedom required an underpinning of economic development
(c) the involvement of economists from the DCs in the development efforts and formulation of development plans of the LDCs.

For the DCs, the fifties were a period of optimism following their growth record immediately after the Second World War and led to rising expectations with regard to the future (Singer 1975: 6) and finally to the belief that development was founded on a process of economic growth, measured by the growth in GNP or GNP *per capita*.

Economic growth via capital accumulation — the vehicle of development

The firm belief in the merits of economic growth led to the view that it was the 'vehicle' of development. Based on the notion of the competitive equilibrium of the conventional economic analyses, it was also believed that economic growth would more or less automatically distribute its fruits to all sections of the community — the so-called trickle-down effect. This view holds that the distribution of income is virtually no problem and will take place in an automatic fashion as long as the marginal propensity to save increases with succeeding increases in income during the development process (cf Cornia 1982: 12). The aforementioned approach was based on the Harrod-Domar model, which postulated that, given the incremental capital-output ratio, the growth rate of GNP was made solely a function of the savings-income ratio. Savings thus became the critical factor in the process of economic growth (Mannur 1981 and Coetzee 1980 and 1983). Cornia (1982: 12) asserted that:

> Conventional economic theory has repeatedly claimed that lack of savings and subsequent insufficient capital accumulation are the main — if not the only — reason for economic backwardness and poverty. Savings, in turn, are low because of the low level of income of most people. As a consequence, on the assumption that households' marginal propensity to save increases with income, a highly skewed distribution of income has often been recommended, at least temporarily, as an efficient policy for promoting accumulation and growth.

Inspired by the Marshall Plan, the Harrod-Domar model and the Keynesian analysis, economists believed that economic growth could best be promoted by the accumulation of capital. The development theories (read growth theories) of the fifties can, therefore, be labelled as capital-shortage theories.

Only the most influential of these theories will be briefly presented:

(a) Based on his notion of zero marginal productivity of labour in the agriculture of LDCs, Arthur Lewis advocated a policy of transferring disguised unemployed labour in the agricultural sector '. . . to fuel capital accumulation in the modern sector' (Livingstone 1981: 1). Arthur Lewis' stance finally led to policies which regarded agriculture and the rural areas as the 'milch cow' of development and the view, which dominated thought about development for some time, that agriculture should be offered on the altar of modernisation so as to promote industrialisation.

(b) Another very influential contribution was Rostow's deterministic and historical stages theory. Taking the industrialised DCs as his background, Rostow specified the stages of economic development (from the traditional society to the age of high mass consumption) and the rise in the rate of saving and investment needed to pilot the take-off into sustained growth.

(c) Apart from the abovementioned theories, a number of theories which tried to identify the most critical factor in the growth-cum-development process of the LDCs emerged. Amongst these single instrument theories were the Big Push (Rosentein-Rodan), the vicious circle of poverty (Hans Singer), balanced growth (Nurkse), unbalanced growth (Hirschman and Singer), Nurkse's low level equilibrium trap and McClelland's achievement motivation theory (cf Strassman 1976, Livingstone 1981, Mannur 1981 and Coetzee 1980).

Development from outside — exogenous development

Almost up to the seventies, economic growth was accepted as synonymous with development. Although different components of the development process had been identified, development was reduced to primarily a growth problem (Coetzee 1980: 53 and Beukes 1983: 36) and to a rather mechanical approach. The driving force behind economic growth, after the analogy of the DCs, was the market mechanism. What was needed, according to this view, was the modernisation of the 'backward' economies and the creation of a modern sector to trigger off the growth process and the multiplier effects. Economists put their faith in trade, industrialisation, aid and, later, in planning for industrialisation and growth. This inspired the belief that development could be imposed from outside. Trade, for example, was viewed as the 'engine of growth' (cf Lewis 1977), without the relatively unfavourable position of the LDCs with regard to resources, technology and research facilities vis-à-vis the DCs being taken into account. Capital, especially foreign private investment, was needed to fill the savings-investment gap, the foreign trade gap, the tax gap, etc (cf Todaro 1981: 403-404). Once these gaps had been filled, the resources would be available to trigger off the process of sustained growth.

Industrialisation and urbanisation

Conventional wisdom emphasised capital-intensive industrialisation in urban areas or metropoles as an inherent part of growth strategies. The rationale behind industrialisation on this scale was the benefits of the agglomeration and multiplier-effects that would be created by the afore-mentioned process, taking into account the forward and backward linkages in the economy (cf Isard 1960 and Tiebout 1962). This approach promised spill-over effects to the rural economy and finally the modernisation of the whole economy — a belief that has been severely criticised in recent years.

Richardson (1978: 134) very neatly summarised the reasons for disenchantment with the aforementioned strategies:

There are many reasons why opinion has shifted so dramatically away from growth centre strategies in developing countries. First, the Western concept of growth poles (emphasising large-scale capital-intensive manufacturing) has been carelessly transplanted to developing countries without sufficient modification to the economic and social conditions prevailing in these countries (Richardson & Richardson 1975;

184

Conroy 1973). Second, growth centres have too frequently been treated as piecemeal locations for planned development rather than as an integrated element in a national urban development strategy. Third, policymakers have vacillated in their pursuit of growth centre policies, often abandoning them or changing them radically due to disappointments resulting from over-optimistic expectations of the speed of success (Richardson 1975). These problems may be correctible through a better understanding of the processes of spatial development. A fourth reason, more difficult to handle, is the switch in development policy emphasis from urban-industrial strategies to rural development. It is true that there has been an urban bias in development planning, and there is a strong case for the argument that redistributing investment from urban to rural areas would offer more prospects for spreading benefits to the target poor (Lipton 1977).

Richardson has argued that a complementarity between urban and rural development is necessary and, it may be added, that a certain compatibility is necessary between growth strategies and the modern-day development approach. This merits revision of the whole development approach.

DISENCHANTMENT WITH THE CDA: THE POVERTY CRISIS

The need for rethinking the concept of development may be attributed to the outcome of the UN's two Development Decades and growing criticism in the First and Third Worlds from academics and development 'experts' alike.

The outcome of the two development decades

While the First Development Decade (1960-1970) showed some respectability in that it achieved its target rate of growth for LDCs, the 6% growth rate set by the UN for the Second Development Decade did not materialise at all. Without elaborating on this, it should be pointed out that Morawetz (1977), Singer & Ansari (1982), the ILO (1976) and many others made it abundantly clear that there were considerable differences in the regional growth rates among LDCs and that income inequality, diseases, malnutrition, undernourishment, illiteracy, poverty and unemployment have reached proportions unknown in human history. Seers (1977: 2) stated that '. . . we have misconceived the nature of the main challenge of the second half of the twentieth century . . .' The gap between the DCs and LDCs has increased, contrary to the promises of the growth strategies.

The CDA, as was described in a previous paragraph, has a tendency towards polarisation between rich and poor which results in income inequality and differences in growth rates between different regions and countries. There is an increasing realisation today that the CDA encouraged growth without development in the LDCs. Evidence suggests that 'Income, wealth and consumption inequalities disrupt a community' and may be '. . . a major source of political instability' (Diwan & Livingston 1979: 72).

Although the newly-industrialised countries (Argentina, Brazil, Mexico, Korea, Hong Kong, Malaysia, Singapore and Taiwan) and the oil-exporting countries experienced high growth rates during the 1970s, the overall picture of world poverty and underdevelopment is still bleak (Brandt in Todaro 1983: 11-12). This is especially so in Africa and Asia. The World Bank projections indicate that the absolutely poor will number 600 million in the countries of the South by the year 2000 (Brandt in Torado 1983: 10). In some of the newly-industrialised countries (e.g. Mexico, Brazil and India) there is still a highly uneven distribution of income and economic activities (cf Henriot in Todaro 1983: 29) and there seems to be a trickle-up instead of a trickle-down effect.

Even in the DCs, the success of the CDA has been scrutinised. The polarisation of highly or overdeveloped metropoles and regions versus relatively less developed areas has led to a separate branch of study, namely regional economics. In addition, it is clear that overdevelopment has negative effects on man and the environment. Diwan & Livingston (1979: 71) remark:

> In the industrialised countries where the growth in material standards has been high it is being recognised that these high material standards have not brought greater satisfaction, happiness, and social harmony.

In the industrialised DCs there are still pockets of poverty which remain a challenge to these countries (Brandt in Todaro 1983: 11). This, *inter alia*, points to the poverty of the prevailing development theory (Sinaceur in Perroux 1983: 6).

Criticism from academics and development experts

The crises caused by the outcome of the two Development Decades initiated growing concern about the validity of the CDA. Many voices were raised against the false hopes created by the CDA and a search was initiated by authors of different schools of thought in favour of a NDA. It is generally agreed that the CDA is in a state of serious crisis.

In this regard, Todaro (1981: 99) has stated that:

> One of the principal failures of development economics of the 1950s and

'60s was its inability to recognize and take into account the limited value of the historical experience of economic growth in the West for charting the development path of contemporary Third World nations. Such theories as the 'stages of economic growth' and related models of rapid industrialisation gave too little emphasis to the very different and less favourable initial economic, social and political conditions of today's developing countries.

Furthermore, Todaro (1981: 99-107) has pointed out that the modern process of economic growth has limited value for the development of LDCs due to significant differences in initial conditions between the latter and the DCs when they (the DCs) embarked on the process of modern economic growth. Cornia (1982), amongst many others, has also scrutinised the 'misleading concepts' of conventional approaches to development. Criticism of this nature has been thoroughly discussed in the literature and will be included in part in the next section, where the new development approach will be outlined and contrasted with the CDA.

NEW DIRECTIONS IN DEVELOPMENT: A NEW DEVELOPMENT APPROACH (NDA) AND APPROPRIATE DEVELOPMENT STRATEGIES (ADS)

Introduction

It should be stated at the outset that several questions are being asked about the content of the NDA: Is economic growth included or excluded? Is it a demand approach, or is there a supply (production) side as well? Is it a universal strategy (recipe) for development, or is any differentiation allowed between countries? What about the role of aid and trade within a strategy of self-reliance or endogenous development? Without answering these questions explicitly, we shall attempt to deal with them while outlining the NDA.

Total development: A multidimensional approach, recognising the interplay of forces

It has become increasingly clear in recent years that development cannot be focused on economic development alone. In an excellent recent contribution, Perroux (1983: 14) refers in this regard to global development which

> ... describes a view of all the dimensions of a human whole and the disparity of aspects that must be accepted in their interrelationships, over and above specific analysis. The term is of course applied to entities of different sizes, such as a nation, a group of nations or the whole world.

It flows naturally from this view that development is a multidimensional process in which non-economic factors are equally as important as economic factors and sometimes even more so.

Whilst the multidimensional nature of the development process had been acknowledged in the CDA and in earlier writings, the interplay of forces was grossly neglected. Today it is accepted that the provision of a certain minimum of social and other public services (e.g. education, health, water, etc) has an important bearing on productivity and development. If a person lacks good health and nutrition and is illiterate, he can hardly be expected to be a productive worker.

Economic and non-economic factors thus cannot be separated and are integrated in the process of development, causing an interplay of forces which must be reflected in development strategies.

Based on this view of development, it is clear that the political and institutional aspects of the development process cannot be ignored. An assault on poverty and unemployment is of no use if the political will to combat these evils is lacking. Sandbrook (1982: 10) has therefore quite correctly stated that '. . . fighting poverty is as much a political as a technical problem'.

Apart from the political will to carry out development strategies, the role of political and economic power is equally important. Due to the limits set by a contribution of this nature it is not possible to elaborate on this theme. Suffice it to say that the access of people to the satisfaction of certain minimum needs is to a great extent determined by their political and economic power.

Flowing from the broader (or global) approach to development is the general recognition that development is not simply a phenomenon that involves the transplantation of Western or Eastern 'blueprints' to the LDCs, including strategies which are alien to the conditions in the latter countries. Instead, it is increasingly accepted that development takes place within a specific socio-cultural setting, or that development is a historio-cultural process (cf Beukes 1983, Perroux 1983 and Goulet 1977). Therefore, priority should be given to development from within.

Development from within: Endogenous or self-reliant development

It is common knowledge that the resource-intensive development path of the DCs is unattainable and undesirable for the LDCs. The failure of development blueprints imposed from outside suggests that development should be initiated from within and that development is endogenous in nature (Perroux 1983: 14, Beukes 1983: 42 and Coetzee 1980: ch 7). Given the available resources in LDCs or underdeveloped regions, countries should strive towards self-reliance and should be enabled to provide for their own sustenance.

Endogenous or self-reliant development should not, however, be confused with economic isolation or import substitution. John Friedmann (1981: 240) has stated that: 'In the first place, self-reliance does not mean territorial autarchy . . . It does mean that the local community (and higher intermediate levels, such as the region) should be empowered to carry out those programmes and investments which are primarily of local benefit.' Bavu (1975: 73) asserted that self-reliance '. . . is very much associated with self-determination . . . which is achieved through one's participation in making decisions that affect his or her well-being'.

It should be emphasised that self-reliant development does not exclude development aid (official or private). Such aid should, however, be toned in with local conditions, resources and development goals. After all, self-reliance is aimed at self-generating efforts in the development process (cf Friedmann 1981: 240). This implies that local physical and human resources should be used to the maximum and imports considered only in areas where resources are not available locally. Also, local human resources and energies must be employed to the maximum before outside expertise is considered. Implicit in the last statement is an emphasis on the development of human beings and their talents in the LDCs.

Development of people for people and by people: The inner meaning of development

From the foregoing discussion it can be perceived that there has been a shift in the thought about development following the failures of previous development strategies. Instead of focusing solely on economic growth, it should concentrate on people and their needs, starting with the most urgent needs in LDCs.

Development of and for people

The shift in emphasis is clear form Todaro's formulation of the three vital objectives for development in 'all societies' (Todaro 1982: 72):

(a) To increase the availability and widen the distribution of basic life-sustaining goods such as food, shelter, health and protection
(b) To raise levels of living including, in addition to higher incomes, the provision of more jobs, better education and greater attention to cultural and humanistic values, all of which serve not only to enhance

material well-being, but also to generate greater individual and national self-esteem

(c) To expand the range of economic and social choice available to individuals and nations by freeing them from servitude and dependence, not only in relation to other people and nation-states, but also to the forces of ignorance and human misery.

Although the CDA sometimes referred to the development of human beings, it stressed the material side of development (Diwan & Livingston 1979: 72). What is needed is the development of '. . . the whole man and of all men' (Perroux, 1983: 15). Development of the whole man implies the satisfaction, firstly, of the basic, predominantly physical needs of a person, as well as needs of a higher order, such as self-esteem. Development of all men includes the poorest and most needy, who are often not reached by development strategies.

Development by people

Apart from the fact that development should be directed at people, development plans and strategies cannot be executed without the participation of the leaders, communities and people of LDCs. Friedmann (1981) has asserted: 'In referring to self-reliance, therefore, the intention is to stress self-generated efforts in carrying out a political will in whose formation people take an active part'. Many development plans have failed as a result of ignorance on this score.

Development from below

The recent evaluation of the results of the UN's two Development Decades reveal that more than half of the population of the Third World cannot satisfy its primary and most urgent needs. Ever since the mid-'70s, there has been a growing body of literature supporting an approach which may be described as development from below (or grass roots development). This strategy followed from the 1970s debate and searched for a compromise between growth and distribution. It became known as the redistribution with growth (RWG) approach (cf Chenery et al 1974). Henriot (1981: 33) has written in this regard:

. . . there has been a growing dissatisfaction with a 'grow first and distribute later' strategy. This dissatisfaction has been heightened by the marked failure of such a strategy to achieve real human progress in terms of a decrease in poverty, increase in employment, and promotion of more equitable income distribution.

While some authors have embarked upon a path of radical redistribution, others have propagated a strategy which concentrates on the most urgent needs of people in LDCs or seeks to determine priorities in development and put 'first things first'. This may also be viewed as a synthesis of the growth, employment and poverty eradication (distribution) goals (cf Lisk in Todaro 1983: 95).

Instead of merely accepting a simple GNP or *per capita* GNP growth target, the upholders of a 'development from below strategy' have, quite correctly, posed the question: What kind of growth is needed to address the problems of poverty and inequality? Therefore it cannot be asserted that 'development from below' is merely a demand or needs approach. Priority is given to production for the local market, using local resources as far as possible. Production for export markets is not excluded and countries or regions can still specialise in products with a comparative advantage. The same argument applies to imports — products that cannot be produced locally may be imported. However, a strategy of exports as the engine of growth offers little hope for the typical less developed country.

In his treatise on core and periphery, Prebisch pointed out that the promised results of international trade for the LDCs did not materialise. This was due to the fact that the exports of LDCs were based mainly on primary products and that the rate of exchange deteriorated in favour of the developed, industrialised countries (Smith & Toye in Todaro 1983: 293). Prebisch also maintained that the exports of LDCs are income-inelastic, causing a small increase in export income in the event of an increase in income in DCs.

From the foregoing discussion it can be concluded that the choice of products to be produced and the choice of technology are of crucial importance for the development of the LDCs. Appropriate products should be produced and appropriate technology employed. As Morawetz, quoted by Stewart (1978: 5), has stated:

> Appropriate technology may be defined as the set of techniques which makes optimum use of available resources in a given environment.

In a less developed country with an abundance of labour it is evident that maximum use should be made of small-scale labour-intensive activities in order to combat unemployment. This does not exclude the use of sophisticated technology, because there may still be cases where the latter is necessary.

From the above discussion it can be deduced that both the private and public sectors have an important contribution to make, as well as a responsibility to combat the evils of underdevelopment and as far as the lack of basic necessities in LDCs are concerned, e.g. employment, income, education, health, food, clean drinking water, public transport and sanitation. The challenge of the future is to harmonise private and public sector involvement and strategies with the economic, social and cultural environments of the LDCs. The strategies of the future should, therefore, be aimed at formulating appropriate strategies for employment and the creation of income and for the provision of education, health etc, taking into account the prevailing conditions in the less developed countries and regions. It should be emphasised that appropriate development strategies are not static in nature and do not exclude the satisfaction of higher order needs. Given the scarcity of resources in LDCs and the world at large, the state of poverty, unemployment and famine and the frequency of disease, it is a matter of determining priorities (or putting 'first things first'). Such a strategy is not a predetermined blueprint and should be formulated according to the specific conditions of each country.

Interdependent development

From the discussion thus far, it should be clear that appropriate strategies involving both the private and public sectors and the local population are needed in LDCs. To this it may be added that changes in strategies are not only vital within the LDCs, but also with regard to external involvement. On a global scale this implies the contribution of the DCs towards dealing with the real development problems of the LDCs — especially as far as the role of multi-nationals is concerned. The same arguments apply to the Southern African development scenario. First and Third World (core and periphery) development cannot be demarcated or viewed in isolation. The two components mutually influence each other and are also mutually interdependent. Therefore, if regional development strategies are formulated, they should be applicable to the development problems of the less developed areas. In fact, what is needed is a coherent development strategy which takes into account the development needs and problems of all the development regions (First and Third World) in Southern Africa, as well as the different components (economic and non-economic) in the development process.

Rural development: an integrated approach

Whilst conventional development strategies emphasised the role of urbanisation in the development process, over the past decade a growing body of literature has accentuated the urgency of rural development. The imperative of rural and agricultural development (the former a much broader concept) is due to, inter alia, the following conditions in LDCs (cf

Friedmann 1981: 236):

- Unemployment in rural areas and cities
- The massive migration of people to the cities
- Population growth in rural areas (in spite of migration to the cities)
- The low rate of growth of agricultural production compared to population growth (declining living conditions)
- The income differential between rural areas and cities.

The underlying motive of integrated rural development (IRD) is the involvement of people in the development process; to help people to play an active and constructive role in development and to benefit the poor in the LDCs (cf Beukes 1983: 216 and Friedmann 1981: 236). According to Friedmann (1983: 236), IRD

> ... is meant to involve (a) the preparation of a territorial plan which formulates development objectives; (b) an organization capable of designing such a plan and of harmonising it with the plans of both higher and lower levels of programme integration; (c) an organisational structure for co-ordinating programme and service delivery; and (d) a political structure capable of responsibly articulating a sense of local priorities, identifying projects, and mobilising resources for development.

IRD comprises the following goals (Beukes 1983):

Economic — satisfying the most urgent needs
Technical — the use of appropriate technology
Ecological — a development approach not exceeding the inner limits (within countries) and the outer limits (on a global scale) set by available resources
Social — participation of the local population
Political — an appropriate political and institutional framework for development
Cultural — underlying motives of the development process and values and norms to be considered.

It should be noted, however, that the framework for IRD is not something different from the NDA as outlined in previous sections, but is in fact the application of the principles of the NDA in the field of rural development. IRD accentuates the importance of agricultural and rural development in the development of LDCs and less developed regions, taking into account the multidimensional nature of development and the interplay of forces. Therefore, in rural development principles such as self-reliant development, development from below, global development and interdependent development are taken into consideration.

According to the IRD approach, the position of the small farmer merits special attention — in contrast to earlier convictions with regard to modernising the agricultural sector. Agricultural development cannot be separated from the development process and should be promoted along the lines suggested above (cf the subsections 'Total development: A multidimensional approach, recognising the interplay of forces' to 'Rural development: An integrated approach') and within the framework of integrated rural development (cf Kötter 1982: 7-17). The small farmer and small landholdings are important springboards of development, using appropriate technology and improving their access to credit and marketing facilities, fertilisers and other inputs.

Instead of using the agricultural surplus to the advantage of other sectors of the economy, a strategy of IRD (or self-reliant development) suggests that such a surplus should be ploughed back into the agricultural sector. Bird (1974) pointed out that the drain of financial resources from the agricultural sector (e.g. through taxation) led to this sector becoming the 'milch cow' of development. The agricultural sector should, according to the new approach, be used as one of the corner-stones of development, helping people in rural areas to be self-sufficient as far as food is concerned. Empirical studies have shown that smallholdings have proved to be superior to large farms. According to the World Bank (1981: 51), 'Kenya's experience shows that African small farmers are very responsive to opportunities for profitable innovation, and that small farms are frequently far more productive than large farms'.

Urban development

Although the role of agriculture is being revisited and revised at present, this does not mean that the role of urbanisation is being neglected. On the contrary, there is a growing body of literature on this topic (cf e.g. Todaro 1983: ch 7). Urban development should be included in a coherent and integrated development strategy. However, an urban bias resulting in the neglect of the rural areas should be avoided.

Urban development should also be approached in terms of the NDA and the application of ADS. This means, inter alia, that urban development should also be deployed in such a way that the multidimensional nature of development is recognised and the alleviation of poverty and unemployment and their symptoms given priority.

A return to the traditional society — a word of caution

It should be clear to any objective observer that the ideas expressed in the subsections above do not imply a return to the traditional society or to 'rediscovering the wheel'. Henry (1981: 25) has stated in this regard that:

> ... self-sufficiency cannot mean a return to a traditional society which is no longer capable of meeting the needs of a humanity which is in the middle of a demographic change. It can however demand a re-examination of a situation in the process of rapid change where man taken separately and men taken as a group are calling into question the consumption model and their production methods.

Finally, a word of caution must be given with regard to the ideas expressed in this chapter, because they do not imply the solution of development problems. Sinaceur (in Perroux, 1983: 5) stated:

> We oscillate between a model that has lost its virtue and charm and an idea that has yet to demonstrate its effectiveness. This is what is usually referred to as the crisis.

We should, therefore, not be over-optimistic about the future, but realistic about the nature of the development problems. Thus it is important that we in Southern Africa take cognisance of the outcome of development approaches elsewhere in the world, as well as of the progress that has been made towards a better understanding of the inner meaning of development. The final word has not been spoken about the conceptualisation of development and development strategies and we are in need of considerably more articulation. It may be stated, however, that we have probably arrived at a better understanding of the nature of the development problems in LDCs and of the forces that should be accounted for in the formulation of development policies and strategies.

Conclusion

From the discussion in the sections 'The development of development theory' to 'New directions in development: A new development approach and appropriate development strategies' it is clear that the outcome of development strategies followed in the fifties and sixties has caused a shift in thought about development from growth as the vehicle of development towards an approach which includes economic growth, but redirects it towards the real needs of LDCs, concentrates on the multidimensional nature of the development process, gives cognisance to the interplay of forces in development, and takes the specific conditions inside LDCs into consideration. Finally, this amounts to the formulation of appropriate development strategies. If the NDA is to be applied in Southern Africa, the question may be asked: What should be done to address our development problems? This question is the theme of the next section.

THE FORMULATION OF AN APPROPRIATE DEVELOPMENT STRATEGY (ADS) FOR SOUTHERN AFRICA: A PRELIMINARY FRAMEWORK

Introduction

From the discussion in the sections named above, it is clear that:

- Southern Africa's development scenario is marked by a First World/Third World dichotomy within one economy
- the First World (developed) component is marked by a skewed regional distribution of economic activities. There is also concern as to whether the developed component can generate enough job opportunities, even during times of economic upswing (cf RSA White Paper 1984)
- the relatively small success achieved with previous strategies and the resulting poverty and underdevelopment of the Third World component is a salient feature of the latter's development performance
- Southern Africa is in need of an appropriate development strategy that should take cognisance of the evolution of thought about development and the greater clarity achieved about the concept of development.

Following this outline, a general framework is presented in the next subsection and is followed by a discussion of the dynamics of, and guidelines for, the strategy to be deployed.

The general framework

Based on the discussion in the section entitled 'The development of development theory', the general framework for an ADS comprises:

(a) *Interdependent development in Southern Africa.* The First and Third World components cannot be viewed in isolation — they mutually influence each other and are mutually interdependent. Therefore, a coherent development strategy is needed. The instruments used to deploy the strategy in the First and Third World components must be compatible.

(b) *A comprehensive development approach.* An ADS must acknowledge the role of economic and non-economic forces in development and the interplay of these forces and should finally lead to a package of policies linking these forces.

(c) Development inside the TBVC countries and other national states should be

- endogenous in nature, encouraging the use of local resources (human and physical), talents and energies

196

- directed at development of people by people and for people
- development from below, addressing the most urgent needs of the population
- within the framework of integrated rural development (IRD), but should not neglect the role of appropriate policies for urban development.

(d) *A collective political will.* In the final analysis, a collective political will is needed to address the development problems of the Southern African region. This implies the enhancement of constitutional development as well as the creation of the necessary multilateral institutional framework to execute such a collective development strategy. Many of the failures of the past may be attributed to the artificial demarcation between developed and underdeveloped areas and a lack of co-ordination between these areas.

The dynamics and guidelines of an ADS for Southern Africa

Broad perspective

An appropriate development strategy for LDCs has the specific aim of mobilising unutilised resources (particularly the unutilised labour of the less privileged groups) in the development process. This broadening in approach will result in a change in the structure of demand, consumption and production, which could result in fundamental changes in development policy and the distribution of funds (Ghai 1978: 18). Alarcon (1979: 309) confirms this when he points out that 'in general it can be argued that the two most important problems to tackle are the redirection of investment and the enforcement of measures that increase the opportunities for the working poor to raise their productivity and income'. This approach thus demands a comprehensive and integrated development effort, which can be achieved only through 'a comprehensive set of measures and not through a limited number of *ad hoc* initiations' (Hopkins & Van der Hoeven 1979: 13).

One of the most important methods whereby an increase in the income of the poor groups can be attained, is the better use of human resources through productive employment. Making sufficient employment opportunities available to the poor is regarded as an important means of eradicating poverty over the long term (Szal & Van der Hoeven 1976: 27). Some of the programmes to achieve this are, for example, the use of appropriate technology, the development of the small business sector and public works programmes. The second avenue for the attainment of increased income for the poor groups is the improvement of the resources at their disposal. These include the provision of appropriate education, health and nutrition. The programmes must concentrate to a meaningful degree on the production factors in the possession of the poor groups, their labour being the most important (Ghai, Godfrey & Lisk 1981: 72). This process of human capital accumulation (raising of productivity) cannot be achieved only through putting people into a position to earn sufficient income, because not all basic products are provided through the market. Services such as education, health and infrastructure are normally provided collectively, with the result that a satisfactory income (through a suitable employment opportunity) must necessarily also be supplemented by specific governmental programmes providing public services.

From the above it is clear that the new approach involves both supply and demand in a strategy. Thus emphasis is laid not only on a changed production structure, but also on the distribution of income emanating from it.

If the proposed approach is compared with the present economic structure, it is clear that the watchword for the implementation of the strategy is structural change. Chenery (1979: 3) declares that economic development consists of a series of interdependent changes in the economic structure and adds that these structural changes '. . . involve the composition of demand, production and employment as well as the external structure of trade and capital flows'. Chenery (1979: 4) also mentions that the planning of rapid structural changes in LDCs, in an effort to maintain sustained growth and achieve a better distribution of its advantages, must be regarded as the most important issue facing LDCs.

Although the eradication of poverty and underdevelopment has always been the central theme of all development strategies, the ways and means whereby this object may be achieved have changed continually. These changes usually assumed structural changes in the development process. During the growth-orientated approach, the structure of development was characterised by an imbalance in spatial distribution (urban-orientated), an imbalance in the utilisation of production factors (capital intensive) and an imbalance in the product market (the production of luxury and inappropriate products) (Vandemoortele 1983: 1).

The result of the abovementioned shortcomings, which concentrated the advantages of economic growth in the hands of a limited elite, was the creation of a more appropriate strategy whereby the less privileged were also able to share in the economic processes. This new approach concentrates mainly on the interrelationship between the structures of consumption, investment and production. These interrelationships are illustrated in figure 7.1, from which it is clear that the structure of consumer demand influences the production structure, which in turn influences the demand structure for production factors and eventually leads to a higher quality of life for all. In practice these dynamics of the new approach boil down to the following: the demand for and provision of more basic products and services (consumption demand) influences the production structure in the direction of smaller undertakings, local production and the use of appropriate technology. Although the climate for the last-mentioned programmes is favourable, specific instruments for its promotion are needed. In turn, this production structure influences the demand structure for production factors in favour of labour and local raw materials. Not only is the entire population's quality of life improved, but also the level of participation in the production processes.

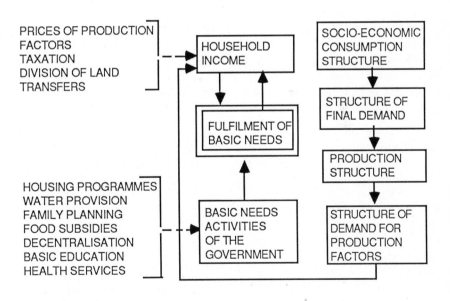

Fig 7.1: The structural interrelations in the new development strategy

From the above perspective it is clear that the following may be regarded as central conditions for the successful application of the new development approach (Fischer 1979: 763):

- Continued changes in the economic and social structures
- Participation of the less privileged section of the community in the development process (in most LDCs this group represents 80 to 90% of the population)
- A sustained process whereby economic growth can be assured.

Programmes through which the above structural changes can be accomplished are discussed below.

The nature of programmes for an appropriate strategy

Development programmes must comply with specific requirements if they are to be appropriate to the new development approach. These requirements include the following (Ghai, Godfrey & Lisk 1981: 92):

(a) They must contribute towards increased income for the identified less privileged groups (e.g. the rural population, women, etc) through, for example, the creation of employment opportunities and the raising of productivity.
(b) They must make a direct contribution to the achievement of targets set for the provision of the most urgently needed products and services.
(c) They must lead to increased production of those products and services most urgently needed by the poor groups.
(d) They must enhance decentralisation, participation and self-reliance.

Most of the projects and programmes which contribute to the achievement of the above goals have the following characteristics:

(a) The programmes are characterised by small-scale production activities.
(b) The production techniques normally show a low capital : labour ratio, whereby more employment opportunities are created for a given amount of capital than is the case with conventional or modern production methods.
(c) The required skills and training levels are more easily acquired because they are less sophisticated.
(d) The production techniques normally demand simple technology.
(e) In most cases, local raw materials are employed.

Thus, what is important in the identification of appropriate development programmes is that through the creation of income, an effective demand will arise for the most urgently-needed products and services, resulting in the production structure being geared to produce them. Ancillary to this change in the production structure, the quality of production factors (particularly labour) must also be raised so that a sufficient income can be earned.

The nature of and programmes relevant to the changed production structure and the raising of productivity will now be discussed.

Programmes for the creation of employment opportunities and income (production structures)

The aim of increasing the income of the less privileged or poor groups can best be achieved through the extension of employment possibilities. Without attempting to discuss the rationale underlying each of the possible programmes, a few appropriate programmes are identified hereunder. Appropriate programmes which comply with the requirements of the new development approach may include the following:
- agricultural development and more specifically the extension of small farmer development and food production programmes
- development of the small business and informal sector
- the implementation of appropriate technology
- the development of a capital products sector which makes appropriate technology available
- public works programmes.

The abovementioned must take place within the framework of integrated rural development and the development of an economic basis for the rapidly accelerating urbanisation process.

Programmes to raise productivity

In addition to the job creation programmes, programmes for the improvement of the quantity and productivity of human resources are also regarded as an important means of increasing the income of the less privileged target groups. There is a direct correlation between the provision of a minimum level of basic needs and economic growth. The improvement of human capital amongst the poor groups is thus regarded as productive investment and not as consumption, as was the case in the past. It is generally accepted that expenditure on increased food production, preventive health services and training in countries which show signs of malnutrition, a high disease rate and a low literacy rate, is a form of investment in human capital (Selowsky & Taylor 1973: 17 and Cornia 1982: 13).

Since the poor groups have limited access to their most urgent requirements, a shift in the distribution of services such as education and health in favour of the less privileged groups is regarded as a key element in an ADS. The programmes through which better and more appropriate provision of the abovementioned services can be activated, arise out of the specific circumstances of every country or community. Certain services must be collectively provided, while others can be acquired privately. Some examples of programmes through which labour productivity can be raised are the following:

- appropriate education and training, particularly at primary school level
- preventive and primary health care
- the provision of sufficient clean water and sanitation facilities
- sufficient nutrition
- basic housing programmes, concerning both dwellings and infrastructure.

Services which can be privately acquired, such as food and housing, can be obtained through increased income, whilst the Government must ensure that collective services are placed within the reach of the less privileged groups as well.

The important point, however, is that all programmes concerned in the new approach must be planned and handled as an integrated whole. Experience has shown that development is an integrated process and that selective measures which concentrate on single aspects such as industrialisation, agricultural development, education, or infrastructure are not capable of yielding meaningful development results.

Summary

The application of the above programmes complies with the principles of the new development approach as discussed in the section entitled 'New directions in development: a new development approach (NDA) and appropriate development strategies'. To summarise, the programmes contribute to a better division of income, the involvement of the less privileged groups in the development process and the production of products and services relevant to the needs of the poor. The approach is comprehensive in nature and thus includes both economic and non-economic aspects and can be designed to take account of the specific circumstances of every country or community. It also implies that the poorer sections of the people are empowered to take independent, collective action in order to overcome their poverty and improve their social status.

Regional strategy

The strategy described briefly above is aimed specifically at improving the living standards and raising the participation in the development process of the less privileged groups. The programmes and instruments for this purpose were also designed to solve the underlying problems of the Third World. The need for this lies in the fact that the development of the modern sector on the basis of the conventional growth theory does not automatically extend to the advantage of the poor groups. A very limited trickling down of advantages takes place and therefore an appropriate strategy must be brought into action to the advantage of these groups.

Ancillary to the abovementioned programmes and instruments, it should also be accepted that the economy of Southern Africa functions within the framework of an economic union and that the modern sector (of the RSA) is consequently able to make a contribution to the creation of employment opportunities. Thus, an appropriate strategy for Southern Africa will have to consist of programmes and instruments which accommodate both legs of the dualistic system.

As far as the modern sector is concerned, the development of the ADS takes place within the framework of the regional approach, which is aimed primarily at a more equitable geographical spread of economic activity. The most important instruments are

- the extension of financial and other support to the governments of the national states and the relevant development corporations
- the decentralisation of economic activity to the less developed areas
- the demarcation of development regions and co-operation on economic development within the regional context
- institutional development by means of which institutions for the handling of the abovementioned instruments are created.

Given the limited achievements of regional development in Southern Africa, regional development strategies should give attention to

- the formulation of a comprehensive regional development strategy (at present the emphasis is on industrial development) which addresses the economic and non-economic aspects of development
- development strategies for each one of the eight development regions in Southern Africa which promotes a bottom up approach to development
- the satisfaction of basic needs on a territorial basis
- a more limited form of industrial decentralisation which focuses on the intermediate cities and a few other centres
- the integration of urban development within the regional context and an assessment of the trade-offs between urban and rural areas in the different regions

- the utilisation of local resources (within regions) and the identification of growth factors other than industries.

The above instruments are aimed primarily at placing the geographical location of employment creation centres in, or as close as possible to, the labour sources. Thus, large-scale population movements are prevented, while the great differences in welfare between regions are reduced.

Harmonising of programmes and instruments

An ADS for Southern Africa consists of the sum total of both the new developmental approach, which concentrates on the underdeveloped sector, and the regional strategy, through which the geographical location of modern sector activities is restructured.

From the nature of the instruments and programmes relating to the ADS, it is clear that conflict can occur between the various instruments. In the case of the Third World component in Southern Africa, aspects such as small business development, appropriate technology and the production of 'basic' products and services are emphasised, while the regional strategy (industrial decentralisation programme) can include aspects such as highly sophisticated technology and the production of luxury and inappropriate products. A dualistic economic structure leads to a non-integrated economy and inherent inequalities in income. According to Singer (1979: 1), it can also lead to non-satisfaction of the basic needs of those situated outside the modern sector. It is thus essential that all instruments and programmes be harmonised as far as possible and applied within the same framework of principles.

If this is not done, the danger exists that capital-intensive development will replace labour rather than create a net increase in employment (Cornia 1982: 8). For example, a single, large manufacturing undertaking which manufactures clothing could satisfy the entire demand and consequently force existing small manufacturers out of the market or reduce the future potential for small manufacturers. Similarly, large 'foreign' construction companies could employ capital-intensive techniques and 'imported' materials and thereby force small builders using local materials out of the market. The harmonisation of instruments within the framework of the new development strategy will determine the effectiveness of the on-slaught on poverty.

In conclusion, it should be mentioned that concentration on labour-intensive and appropriate technology does not mean that large-scale production processes and sophisticated technology should be ignored.

According to Cornia (1982: 11) and Singer (1979: 4), a dual approach should be followed. In certain sectors and processes, capital-intensive technology is indicated. However, where possible, capital-saving and employment creating technology which uses local raw materials, abilities and sources of energy should enjoy the highest priority. 'In both industry and agriculture, mechanisation — unless strictly necessary — should be postponed until full employment is achieved' (Cornia 1982: 23). Thus, where possible, the regional strategy and industrial decentralisation will have to synchronise with the principles of the appropriate strategy discussed in this article.

CONCLUSION

It could be concluded that 'the problem of mass poverty is more fundamentally one of the pattern of economic growth than the rate of economic growth' (Sandbrook 1982: 2). The fact is that economic growth remains a necessary precondition, but cannot be regarded as a sufficient precondition. The unfolding of thought about development culminated in a new development approach which is (with the retention of a high economic growth rate) aimed at restructuring the production process in such a way that the whole population can benefit from the fruits of development.

McNamara (1972: 8) concluded as far back as 1972 that the

> increases in national income — essential as they are — will not benefit the poor unless they reach the poor. They have not reached the poor to any significant degree in most developing countries in the past, and this in spite of historically unprecendented average rates of growth throughout the sixties.

The package of reinforcing instruments and programmes to eradicate poverty and promote participation by all in the development process consists of satisfying the most urgent needs not by transfer payments to the poor, but by the provision of sufficient productive (and remunerative) employment and the provision of essential public services to all. This approach necessitates a change in production structure towards small-scale production with the application of appropriate technology, as well as the redirection of public investment so that everyone can have access to services such as education, training and health facilities. This approach obviously also requires a shift away from the production of non-essential products for the relatively well-off towards the production of basic food-stuffs and simpler consumer and capital goods appropriate to the low incomes of the majority.

This new approach contains certain principles that must guide any development strategy, applicable to both the development of the less developed sector and the regional co-operation policy. Essentially, these are the following:

- A comprehensive approach to development which acknowledges the importance of both economic and non-economic factors, should be followed.
- In order to create an effective demand for products and services that together constitute the fulfilment of the most urgent needs within a particular country, there should be redistribution of income by means of remunerative employment.
- There should be a new orientation of the system of production which includes aspects such as the diffusion of appropriate technology, small-scale orientation and the production of essential (urgent) goods.
- There should be sufficient provision of, and equitable access to, appropriate public services for the community at large through which productivity can be enhanced.
- The participation of the local population should be encouraged to stimulate active involvement in the planning and implementation of programmes and projects.

The new development paradigm needs a suitable political, institutional and administrative framework to carry out development plans and appropriate strategies to give the poor access to the satisfaction of their most urgent needs, to take care of the implementation of appropriate strategies in areas such as health, education, job creation, etc and to develop the political will to execute appropriate strategies and plans. Sandbrook (1982: 17) has stated that fighting poverty is as much a political as a technical problem. The problem is one of mobilising the political will to undertake the necessary change and of appropriate planning and resource allocation. Cornia (1982: 24) added that the re-orientation of policies is primarily a political, not a technocratic decision and that as long as the political cohesion to support such a strategy is nowhere in sight, it is difficult to take an optimistic view of the present situation in the Third World.

NOTES

1 Originally published in *Development Southern Africa*, vol. 1, no. 1, 1984.
2 For the purpose of this article Southern Africa is defined as the RSA, the self-governing states and the independent states. RSA refers specifically to that territory from which the independent and self-governing national states are excluded.
3 Information for this subsection was obtained from Ligthelm, AA. *'n Toepaslike ontwik-*

kelingstrategie vir Suider-Afrika. Potchefstroom: Potchefstroomse Universiteit vir CHO, 1984. (Ongepubliseerde D.Comm.-tesis.)

4 Transkei was not taken into account in this calculation.

BIBLIOGRAPHY

Alarcon, JV. Planning for basic needs in Latin America: A research proposal. *Basic needs strategy as a planning parameter.* Berlin: German Foundation for International Development, 1979.

Bavu, IK. *Tanzanian experience of self-reliance.* Michigan: University Microfilms International, 1975.

Bequele, A and Van der Hoeven, R. Poverty and inequality in Sub-Saharan Africa. *International Labour Review,* vol. 119, no. 3, 1980.

Beukes, EP. *Die ontwerp van die basiese vertrekpunte vir 'n ontwikkelingstrategie met besondere verwysing na die ekonomiese ontwikkeling van Qwaqwa.* Bloemfontein: Universiteit van die Oranje Vrystaat, 1983. (Ongepubliseerde D. Phil.-tesis.)

Bird, RM. *Taxing agricultural land in developing countries.* Cambridge: Harvard University Press, 1974.

Brand, SS. *Beleidsmaatreëls betreffende die vermindering van inkomsteverskille in Suid-Afrika.* Pretoria: Economic Society of South Africa Conference, 1977.

Brookefield, H. *Interdependent development.* London: Methuen, 1975.

Cairncross, A. and Mohinder, O (Eds.) *The Strategy of International Development. Essays in the economics of backwardness.* London: The Macmillan Press, 1975.

Chenery, H et al. *Redistribution with growth.* London: Oxford University Press, 1974.

Chenery, H. *An overview of structural change and development policy.* Washington: World Bank, 1979.

Coetzee, SF. *Die ekonomiese basisteorie geëvalueer binne die kader van resente denke oor die ontwikkelingsvraagstuk: 'n Toepassingsondersoek vir Qwaqwa.* Bloemfontein: Universiteit van die Oranje Vrystaat, 1980. (Ongepubliseerde D. Phil.-tesis.)

Coetzee, SF. Development: False hopes and new directions. *Development Studies Southern Africa,* vol. 6, no. 1, 1983.

Cornia, GA. *Development strategies for the 1980s: Old myths and new ideas.* United Nations Conference on Trade and Development. Discussion Paper No. 4. Geneva: UNCTAD, 1982.

Diwan, RK and Livingston, DL. *Alternative development strategies and appropriate technology. Science policy for an equitable world order.* New York: Pergamon Press, 1979.

Du Pisanie, JA. *Verwagte ekonomiese ontwikkeling van metropolitaanse gebiede in Suid-Afrika.* Paper read at the Conference re Metropolitan Areas, 17-18 November 1981. Pretoria: SA Institute for Public Administration, 1981.

Du Plessis, DT. *Die toepaslikheid van geykte vorms van internasionale ekonomiese samewerking op Suidelike Afrika, Deel II.* Pretoria: Universiteit van Pretoria: 1973 (M.-thesis).

Fischer, D. Problems and prospects of development planning in line with a basic needs strategy. *Basic needs strategy as a planning parameter,* Berlin: GFID, 1979.

Frank, AG. *The political economy of development and underdevelopment.* New York: Random House, 1979.

Friedmann, J. The active community: Toward a political-territorial framework for rural development in Asia. *Economic Development and Cultural Change,* vol. 29, no. 2, 1981.

Ghai, DP. Basic needs and its critics. *IDS Bulletin,* vol. 9, no. 4, 1978.

Ghai, DP, Godfrey, M and Lisk, F. *Planning for basic needs in Kenya.* Geneva: ILO, 1981.

Goulet, D. Political will: The key to Guinea-Bissau's alternative strategy. *International Development,* vol. 4, 1977.

Henry, PM. Economic development, progress and culture. *Development,* vol. 3, no. 4, 1981.

207

Hopkins, M and Van der Hoeven, R. A socio-economic framework for basic needs planning. *Basic needs as a planning parameter*, Berlin: GFID, 1979.

International Labour Office. *Employment, growth and basic needs: A One-World problem.* Geneva: International Labour Office, 1975.

Isard, W. *Methods of regional analysis: An introduction to regional science.* Massachusetts: MIT Press Cambridge, 1960.

Kötter, H. *Objectives and strategies of agricultural development in the Third World economics*, vol. 25, 1982.

Leupoldt, M. Integrated rural development: Key elements of an integrated development strategy. *Sociologia ruralis*, vol. 17, no. 1/2, 1977.

Lewis, WA. What should be the LDCs engine of growth? *Finance and Development*, vol. 14, no. 3, 1977.

Ligthelm, AA. *'n Toepaslike ontwikkelingstrategie vir Suider-Afrika.* Potchefstroom: Potchefstroomse Universiteit vir CHO, 1984. (Ongepubliseerde D.Comm-tesis).

Livingstone, Ian. 'The development of development economics.' *ODI Review*, no. 2, 1981.

Magee, B. *Popper.* Glasgow: Fontana/Collins, 1979.

Mannur, HG. Development economics and economic development — Old theories and new perspectives. *The Indian Journal of Economics*, vol. LX II, 1981.

Matthews, WH (Eds.) *Outer limits and human needs*, Uppsala: Dag Hammerskjold Foundation, 1976.

McNamara, RS. The basic problems of development. *Vital Speeches of the Day*, vol. 38, 1972.
— *Address to the Board of Governors* (of the World Bank). Washington: World Bank, 1972.

Nel, PA. Huishoudingsbesteding vergelyk maar swak. *Volkshandel*, jg. 42, nr. 5, 1980.

OAU. *Lagos plan of action for the implementation of the Monrovia strategy for the development of Africa.* Lagos: OAU, 1980.

OECD. *Critical issues in development in the 80s.* Paris: Development Centre of the OECD, 1981.

Perroux, F. *A new concept of development.* Paris: Unesco, 1983.

Richardson, HW. Growth centres, rural development and national urban policy: A defence. *International Regional Science Review*, vol. 3, 1978.

Sandbrook, R. *The politics of basic needs. Urban aspects of assaulting poverty in Africa.* London: Heineman, 1982.

Seers, D. The meaning of development. *International Development Review*, no. 2, 1977.

Selowsky, M and Taylor L. The economics of malnourished children: An example of disinvestment in human capital. *Economic Development and Cultural Change*, vol. 22, no. 1, 1973.

Simkins, C. *Agricultural production in the African reserves of South Africa*, Development Studies Research Group Working Paper No. 10, Pietermaritzburg: UN, 1979.

Singer, HW. Appropriate technology for a basic human needs strategy. *International Development Review*, vol. 2, 1977.
— *Technologies for basic needs.* Geneva: ILO, 1979.

Singer, H and Ansari, J. *Rich and poor countries.* London: Allen and Unwin, 1982.

Smit, P en Booysen, JJ. *Swart verstedeliking. Proses, patroon en strategie.* Kaapstad: Tafelberg Uitgewers, 1981.

South Africa (Republic). *White Paper on a strategy for the creation of employment opportunities in the Republic of South Africa.* Pretoria: Government Printer, 1984.

Stewart, F. *Technology and underdevelopment.* London: Macmillan, 1978.

Strassman, WP. Development economics from a Chicago perspective. *Journal of Economic Issues*, vol. X, no. 1, 1976.

Streeten, P. *Development Perspectives.* London: Macmillan, 1981.

Streeten, P and Burki, SJ. Basic needs: Some issues. *World Development*, vol. 6, no. 3, 1978.

Strong, MF. More is not enough. *Mazingira*, vol. 3, no. 4, 1977.

Szal, RJ and Van der Hoeven, R. *Income distribution and employment programmes: Inequality and basic needs in Swaziland.* Geneva: ILO, 1976.

208

Thomas, W. *Socio-economic development in Transkei in the context of Southern Africa's urban-rural nexus.* Umtata: Institute for Management and Development Studies, University of Transkei, 1982.

Tiebout, CM. *The community economic base study.* New York: Committee for Economic Development, 1962.

Todaro, MP. *Economic development in the Third World.* New York: Longman, 1981.

— *The struggle for economic development. Readings in problems and policies.* New York: Longman, 1983.

Transkei (Republic) *The development strategy.* Transkei Government, Umtata, 1980.

UNCTAD. *Development strategies for the 1980's: Old myths and new ideas.* Geneva: UNCTAD, 1982.

Van der Kooy, RJW. In search of a new economic development paradigm for Southern Africa: An introduction. *Development Studies Southern Africa,* vol. 2, no. 1, 1979.

Vandemoortele, J. *The public sector and the basic needs strategy in Kenya: The experience in the seventies.* Geneva: ILO, 1983.

Van Wyk, LA. Priorities for basic needs in economic development. *Development Studies Southern Africa,* vol. 4, no. 2, 1982.

World Bank. *Accelerated development in Sub-Saharan Africa: An agenda for action.* Washington: World Bank, 1981.

8 Recent changes in education

JP de Lange

INTRODUCTION

Change in education is a notoriously slow process. Changes enacted in the structures for the provision of education may be achieved in the short term. Changes at the coal-face, i.e. in the actual teaching and learning situation, presuppose changes in people: in their value orientations, habits and skills and this tends to be a slow process.

Review of the changes made over the last few years with regard to the provision of education in the RSA indicates that quite remarkable structural changes have been, or are being made. This does not mean that these changes meet everybody's idea of the rate of change necessary to redress disparities and take the provision of education out of the sphere of political confrontation into the sphere of political negotiation. Compared with developments internationally, there can be little doubt that the actual and continuing change constitutes a basic restructuring of education in this country.

THE IMMEDIATE BACKGROUND TO THE CHANGE

By 1980, pressures for change had built up to such an extent that in the middle of that year the Government requested the Human Sciences Research Council (HSRC) to undertake and complete, in one year, comprehensive research into the provision of education in South Africa. These pressures had three major sources: the unacceptable level of disparity in the quality of the education provided for the different population groups; the teachers' associations' growing dissatisfaction with the conditions of service in the teaching profession; and the criticism from commerce, industry and administration that the educational system was not producing the required number of adequately prepared skilled workers at all levels and that standards in the subsystems differed too much.

The research involved 600 researchers and 200 research assistants, with

500 more people involved in seminars, work sessions and memoranda. In all, 130 research projects were undertaken. The report, together with 18 supporting reports, was presented to the Government by mid-1981 and released in October 1981, together with an interim memorandum, for public comment. The deadline for comment was the end of February 1982. More than 200 organisations and individuals commented exhaustively.

The Government appointed an Interim Work Party to evaluate both the HSRC Report on the Provision of Education in the RSA and the comments thereon. The director of the original research and eight members of his Main Committee were members of the 19-member Work Party, with the director as chairman.

The Interim Work Party handed its report to the Government in October 1982 and at the same time requested the HSRC to research specific areas such as the role of computers, radio and TV in education. The *White Paper on the Provision of Education in the Republic of South Africa* was released by the Government on 23 November 1983. At about the same time, the State President requested the President's Council to investigate and advise him on the stimulation of informal and non-formal education. In the original HSRC report these areas were highlighted as fundamentally important modes of the provision of education in modern society, but could not be researched in depth within the time limit set by the Government. The President's Council presented its *Report by the Science Committee of the President's Council on Informal and Non-Formal Education in South Africa* to the State President on 18 June 1984.

In the meantime, the HSRC was doing follow-up research and presented two reports, *The Computer in Education and Training* and *The Use of Radio and Television in Education and Training*, to the Government in 1983 and 1984 respectively. At the request of the National Training Board, the HSRC did extensive research into the training of artisans, completing it by the end of 1984.

Parallel to the original research, an investigation into the status of the educator in South Africa was undertaken by the Department of National Education. The first phase, completed in 1982, focused on the remuneration of teachers.

It should be obvious that since 1980 large-scale and in-depth research attention has been and is being given to education in this country. The massive input of research-based information into the decision-making processes relating to education has stimulated confidence that both the political and technical decisions at the operational level in the provision of education will be influenced for the better by this objective data base.

THE WHITE PAPER

The *White Paper on the Provision of Education in the Republic of South Africa* was brought out by the Government after its consideration of the HSRC report, *The Provision of Education in the RSA*, the comments thereon and the report of the Interim Work Party. It gives the Government's decisions on the large number of recommendations and deals with these matters under the following headings:

- The role of the central authority in the provision of education
- The principles guiding the Government in its consideration of the HSRC Report
- The structuring of educational management at the first level of government
- The structuring of educational management at the second level of government
- The structuring of educational management at the third level of government
- Education provision.

The role of the central authority in the provision of education

The Government accepts that its main aim must be to ensure the greatest possible mental and material well-being of all citizens. This requires *inter alia* that certain services be provided.

However, the Government is also convinced that private initiative must be encouraged and that through the devolution of functions of the central authority to other levels of authority and to the private sector, depersonalisation and lack of involvement and efficiency in the administration of education can largely be avoided.

As a result of this philosophy, the Government sees its task of providing education as having two main foci:

- It must create systems for the provision of education which can be divided into subsystems into which educational bodies and institutions can be grouped.
- It must, in a co-ordinated manner, provide the systems for the provision of education with the necessary resources. This entails control over the public funds provided.

It is not the Government's task to administer these systems from the central level; this is the task of executive departments and autonomous institutions. However, a government policy regarding the aims, the structure and the working of the systems for the provision of education is still

212

necessary. Such a policy must make provision for every population group to deal with education at the functional level as an own matter.

However, it is essential that comparable standards in education are striven for by the subsystems and therefore structures for deliberation, consultation and advice must be created.

On the basis of this view of its role in education, the Government proceeds to give its decisions on the structures it considers to be necessary in a system for the provision of education.

The principles for the provision of education

The Government accepts the 11 principles proposed by the HSRC report and emphasises that their interdependence must be understood. The principles are:

Principle 1: that equal opportunities for education, including equal standards of education, shall be strived after for every inhabitant of the Republic, irrespective of race, colour, creed or sex;

Principle 2: that recognition shall be granted both to that which is common and to that which is diverse in the religious and cultural way of life of the inhabitants of the Republic and to their languages;

Principle 3: that, subject to the provisions of any law regarding the attending of a school for a particular population group by a pupil who is subject to compulsory school attendance, recognition shall be granted to the freedom of choice of the individual, parents and organisations;

Principle 4: that the provision of education shall be directed in an educationally responsible manner at the needs of the individual and those of society and the demands of economic development, and shall take into account the manpower needs of the Republic;

Principle 5: that a positive relationship shall be promoted between formal, informal and non-formal education in the school, society and the family;

Principle 6: that the State shall be responsible for the provision of formal education, but that individuals, parents and society shall share responsibility and have a say in that regard;

Principle 7: that the private sector and the State shall share responsibility for the provision of non-formal education;

Principle 8: that in providing education, provision shall be made for the establishment and State subsidisation of private education;

Principle 9: that in providing education, a balance between centralisation and decentralisation in the administration thereof shall be strived after;

Principle 10: that the professional status of the teacher and the lecturer shall be recognised; and

Principle 11: that the provision of education shall be based on continuing research.

The Government adds the following qualifications to its acceptance of these principles:

- It stands by its view that education should, broadly speaking, be Christian and national in character. Any changes will have to take this into account, while the Government acknowledges the right of each group to decide for itself.
- The Government remains convinced of the educational justification of the principle of education through the medium of the mother tongue, although it acknowledges that there are population groups which have difficulty with this principle.
- The Government reaffirms its conviction that each population group should have its own schools and departments of education. However, co-ordination and the structures to make this possible are necessary at all levels.
- Freedom of choice is limited to choice within the own structures.
- New constitutional arrangements will affect structures in education.

The structuring of educational management at the central government level

The following are regarded as common matters of policy to be decided upon by Parliament:

(a) Norms and standards for the financing of the current and capital costs of education
(b) The salaries and conditions of service of personnel and the professional registration of teachers
(c) Norms and standards for curricula and examination and for certification of qualifications
(d) The grounds on which and the limits within which digression from the principle of parity in education in separate institutions may be allowed
(e) The collection of information
(f) Co-operative support services insofar as own departments of education require these
(g) The entering into of interstate agreements on education.

The legislative power over these general matters resides with Parliament and they will be the responsibility of a minister of the Cabinet. The actual

214

provision of education for Blacks, Coloureds, Indians and Whites will be the responsibility of a minister for each of these groups.

The notion of the establishment of a South African Council for Education to advise the minister responsible for general matters in education is accepted. This Council will advise on the first four (a to d) of the general matters mentioned above as they pertain to education at the school level and to teacher education. The establishment of a separate council to advise the minister on general matters concerning universities and technikons is also accepted. Both councils will have to take the total provision of education into account and at times express views on educational matters outside their specific fields. Thus the Universities and Technikons Advisory Council Act 99 of 1983 was passed.

The National Policy for General Education Affairs Act was passed in 1984 and created the *South African Council for Education* to advise the Minister for General Affairs in Education on formal, informal and non-formal education, including teacher training. This Council may also advise every minister of a department of State responsible for education on any aspect regarding co-operation between various departments of State responsible for education. An interim Council (the previous Work Party) was created in 1984 and, according to the Minister of National Education during the tabling of his budget in the present session of Parliament, the members of the permanent Council will be made known by the middle of 1985.

In the White Paper the government accepts the need for *central registration* of all categories of staff in education. This acceptance has not yet led to the creation by law of a statutory body. The various teachers' associations, the South African Council for Teachers (White) and the executive departments have apparently recently reached a consensus and have advised the Government accordingly.

The Government accepts that there is a need for a *committee of heads of education*. The National Policy for General Education Affairs Act establishes a Committee of Heads of Education Departments consisting of the head of the department of State for general education matters (chairman), the heads of the other departments of State responsible for education and one head of a provincial education department. This Committee advises on general matters and on co-operation between departments.

The White Paper notes the Government's partial acceptance of the recommendation that the *Committee of University Principals* (CUP) be broadened. The principals of the Indian and Coloured universities are now included. This Committee has a close voluntary liaison with the Committee of University Rectors (CUR) (Black universities), which has also become a statutory body (1983) and they have reciprocal representation. The CUP has a number of standing subcommittees on matters such as finance, tertiary teaching methods, teacher training, academic planning, etc and the CUR is represented on most of these.

The Government also accepts the recommendation that a *National Council for Standards, Evaluation and Certification* be created. During the discussion of his budget in May 1985, the Minister of National Education indicated that the necessary legislation would be passed during the present session of Parliament. The Government indicated that the setting of *university entrance standards*, which is handled by the Joint Matriculation Board, would probably become the responsibility of the Committee of University Principals.

The Government accepted the need for the creation of a Committee of Technikon Rectors and the enabling law was passed during the 1983 session of Parliament.

Also accepted by the Government, but still awaiting detailed recognition, are the recommendations concerning the basic role of the professional associations of teachers in advisory and other capacities.

The Government indicates its acceptance of the principle of the establishment of certain specialised, co-operative services such as guidance, educational technology, evaluative and diagnostic help to learners with disabilities, curriculum design and development and guidelines for physical planning. The specific arrangements in this regard are still pending.

Finally, the Government accepts that while respecting the autonomy of independent and self-governing states which were previously part of the Republic of South Africa, every effort must be made to *avoid the development of undue disparities* between the standard of the provision of education in these states and in the RSA. Basically the support would have to be financial.

There has been (and the process is an ongoing one) a massive restructuring of the management of education at the first level of government. This is due partly to the recommendations of the HSRC report and the report of the Interim Work Party and partly to the new constitutional dispensation which came into operation in 1985. There can be little doubt that as the intended accommodation of Black people in the decision-making structures at all levels becomes fact, new adjustments and restructuring will take place.

The structuring of the management of education at the second level of government

The White Paper states that as the new constitutional dispensation has not been finalised, no decisions regarding the management of education at this level can be taken. The thrust of the recommendations in this regard was focused on the regionalisation of executive departments, but was necessarily vague due to the lack of knowledge regarding the exact nature of the new Constitution.

However, in addition to regionalisation, the principle of the devolution of decision-making powers to the lowest level of government commensurate with an orderly and equitable provision of education was strongly recommended. Fortunately, this approach found favour with the Government. Most departments of education have implemented at least a measure of decentralisation of administration, if not actual devolution of powers. An announcement in May 1985 that the Provincial Councils would be phased out by 1986 implies that some of their powers will move up to the first level of authority and some down to the third level. It is well-nigh impossible to indicate which at present.

The structuring of educational management at the third level of authority

Policy at the local level, the Government decided in the White Paper, is an own affair for each population group.

The Government accepts the decision-making role of representative *parents' organisations* at the school level and intends to devolve suitable powers to this level. It is also accepted that *local* raising of *funds* for schools is necessary. The practical aspects of these matters are still being considered.

Regarding *private schools*, the Government accepted and will announce by the end of 1985 measures to co-ordinate State financial support of private schools.

The importance of *rural schools* is acknowledged and the Government indicates what is being done and what it intends doing to improve rural education.

As far as *non-formal* education is concerned, the Government acknowledges the disparity existing between the population groups and indicates that the technical colleges, possibly renamed, will play an important role in this mode of the provision of education. A close coupling of non-formal and formal education must be striven for. The South African Council for Education must advise the Government on the development of non-formal education.

As was noted earlier, the State President requested that the President's Council investigate the stimulation of non-formal and informal education. The report brought out by this Council in 1984 has wide-ranging recommendations and is under consideration.

It is necessary to remark that a dramatic increase in the private and public sector's involvement in non-formal education is underway in South Africa and an informed guess is that the total 'budget' for non-formal education has increased from about R800 000 000 in 1980 to more than R3 000 000 000 in 1984. This is undoubtedly one of the most promising signs for improvement of the provision of education in the RSA.

Informal education has received a significant boost from the South African Broadcasting Corporation's growing involvement in educational television and radio. The duration of educational programmes on television will increase to 300 minutes a week sometime in August 1985. This constitutes growth from a nil-situation to major involvement in the space of three years. Sponsorship of educational TV by the private sector is being considered and could result in further growth in informal education in our society.

The provision of education

The Government referred most of the educational design recommendations to the executive departments of education for consideration and possible implementation, but accepted a number of key recommendations as matters of policy. These include *inter alia* the following:

- The Government accepts the recommendations regarding *pre-basic education*, especially that a bridge period of one or two years before formal schooling starts, aimed at the promotion of school readiness, should be instituted. This is arguably of great importance for Black children.
- Accepted, too, is the suggested *bridging module* for young school-leavers entering the work situation or non-formal, work-related education.
- Merit is seen in the creation of greater *horizontal mobility* within formal and between formal and non-formal modes of education.
- Regarding the *financing of education* at the various levels (primary, secondary and tertiary), the Government accepts the recommendation that education be financed in terms of financially realistic norms for the provision of a functionally adequate quality of education regardless of race, colour, sex or creed. These norms, relating to both current and capital costs, will probably be made known by the end of 1985. The increase in the education budget from just over R2 000 million in the 1980/81 fiscal year to just over R5 000 million in the 1985/86 fiscal year gives a fair indication of the seriousness of the Government's intention to achieve parity over the shortest possible time. Viewed in conjunction with the increase in expenditure on non-formal education ($\pm$ R3 000 million in 1980/81 and $\pm$ R8 000 million in 1985/86), the growth of education as a national priority is evident. And these figures do not include the growth in informal education, which is hardly quantifiable

but is a direct result of greater awareness of the critical importance of this mode of education.

The financing of tertiary education is now based on a revised formula for universities and technikons foreshadowed in the White Paper, but has not been fully implemented due to the economic recession.

- The recommended *compulsory nine-year learning period*, of which at least six years must be within the formal system, was accepted with the proviso that this would have to be phased in after consultation with local communities. Subsystems could, by their own choice, extend the nine-year period.
- The *admission of students* to autonomous tertiary institutes such as universities at the discretion of the Councils of such institutes was accepted in principle and over a short period during 1983/84 the Government moved from a quota stance to a position of negotiation at the initiative of the institutions' Councils. All 'White' universities now admit people of colour to a greater or lesser degree. All 'Black' universities admit other population groups to some degree. There are no fully-closed universities left.
- With some reservation, the Government accepted the recommendation that in the formal system a better balance between generally formative preparatory academic and vocational education should replace the present very strong academic bias.
- On the whole, the recommendations regarding the language medium, third language (local) instruction, education for children with special needs, curriculum services, guidance services, educational technology, health services in education, the training of teachers and the provision of physical facilities were accepted.

After the appearance of the White Paper, a report on the role of *computers* in education was presented to the Government. The recommendations regarding computer awareness, computer literacy, computer science, computer-assisted teaching and computer-assisted administration were accepted and a first budgetary provision was recommended to the treasury. As yet the outcome is unknown. A report on the role of *radio and television* in education has, as already indicated, led to acceptance by the SABC of growing involvement in education.

The HSRC report, *Investigation into the Training of Artisans in RSA*, is presently under consideration. The great support this report has from the labour sector is a strong indication that a major restructuring of this important area is in the offing. An essential element of the original view that non-formal and formal education should be more closely aligned can be achieved if the recommendations made in this report are accepted to a sufficient degree.

CONCLUSION

Redesigning the provision of education in a society across the board at all levels and all modes (informal, non-formal and formal) is no mean undertaking, but the groundwork has been done. Some with ultra-conservative political orientations regard the changes and impending changes as catastrophic. Some with extreme leftist views believe that the fact that racially integrated education was not enforced makes all the changes useless. Some having subversive motives use the slowness of physical and manpower changes in education as triggers for discontent leading to unrest, violence and the destruction of the very facilities that are necessary to the development of potential and movement towards parity. The majority sense that constructive reform is under way and that once change is under way, the tempo tends to accelerate. They realise, too, that some of the instruments for supporting responsible change have been created: the single ministry dealing with macro-policy matters which are fundamental to achieving parity; the racially mixed South African Council for Education as a high level advisory body; and many more of the structural changes listed in the previous pages. Of great importance is the fact that men of goodwill, urgency and serious intent are willing to serve education in the public and private sectors.

Education cannot prescribe the course of political development, but it can provide men and women with the necessary skills and value orientation to improve the viability of our society, given the chance.

BIBLIOGRAPHY

HSRC. *The Provision of Education in the RSA*. Pretoria: 1981.
— *White Paper on the Provision of Education in the Republic of South Africa*. Pretoria: Government Printer, 1983.
HSRC. *The use of Radio and Television in Education and Training*. Pretoria: 1984.
HSRC. *The Computer in Education and Training*. Pretoria: 1983.
HSRC. *Investigation into the Training of Artisans in the RSA*. Pretoria: 1984.
National Policy for General Education Affairs Bill, Pretoria: Government Printer, 1984.

9 Freedom of the press in South Africa

YM Burns

THEORETICAL FOUNDATIONS

What does the term 'freedom of the press' entail? Is it merely an expression used by the public to express its views on matters of topical interest, or does it have deeper legal significance?

The man in the street generally sees the 'freedom of the press' as the unrestricted right on the part of the newspaper press to print at will; to report on and discuss all matters of topical interest of a political, cultural, religious, sporting, etc nature. This 'popular' view of press freedom must, however, be distinguished from its legal counterpart. Within the framework of the legal system, 'press freedom' is a composite legal concept. It is not an absolute concept in the sense that it is free from all legal restraint, but is rather a common law freedom which has been recognised by South African courts.[1]

Freedom of the press forms a subsection of freedom of speech, which in turn forms part of freedom of expression. This general freedom of expression may, in a narrow sense, be restricted to verbal and written forms of expression. In the modern world, however, it has been expanded to include, for example, freedom to participate in a protest march, or freedom to demonstrate.

It may be said that freedom of speech (i.e. the verbal and written forms of communication) and freedom of the press are synonymous, for freedom of the press is nothing but a concrete manifestation of freedom of speech. Originally, communication between people was confined to either written or verbal forms, but with the development of the printing press this sphere of communication was extended and the press took over as the largest medium of communication. Thus, the products of the printing press may be seen to be no more than an outward manifestation of speech. As a logical consequence, the protection of freedom of speech was extended to include the protection of the freedom of the press.

Initially, Man lived in a close-knit family community, but in the western world this arrangement changed gradually and the family community expanded into a democratic form of government. This democratic system provides the framework in terms of which the individual can, in theory, satisfy all his individual, spiritual, emotional and psychological needs, as well as his social, economic and political needs. A free press is recognised as playing an essential role in the satisfaction of these needs in western democratic societies.

It may be said that freedom of expression has existed since the existence of Man as a social animal and is not something that has developed from an initially negative position. This approach may be substantiated by reference to the freedom of expression still to be found between clansmen of equal status in primitive tribes (Myburgh in Hammond-Tooke 1971: 289).

In legal nomenclature, freedom of speech and freedom of the press may be categorised as fundamental freedoms or basic human rights. To date the concepts 'freedom', 'liberty' and 'human rights' have no fixed juridical meaning in South Africa, but in the context of the modern world these concepts have become synonymous with the claims of the individual against the state (Van der Vyver 1976: 57). South African jurisprudence does not distinguish clearly between these concepts and in *Simonlanga and Others* v *Masinga and Others*,[2] the court held as follows:

> Now as I understand the law, human rights or fundamental freedoms in our country are principles which are firmly embedded in our common law. In many countries these so-called human rights are contained in bills of rights or declarations of human rights, mostly forming part of the constitutions of those countries. In South Africa, as in England, these freedoms are not listed in the constitution or contained in a piece of legislation by Parliament. These freedoms, and the correlative rights flowing from them, are interwoven into our common law which affords the necessary control and protection to the citizen as a possessor of the rights flowing from these freedoms.

The court, therefore, referred to human rights in the context of a bill or declaration of rights, while it approached freedoms in the context of countries, such as South Africa and the United Kingdom, where no codification of these freedoms exists. Freedom of speech and freedom of the press are recognised as forming part of the democratic rights of the citizens of the Republic of South Africa.[3]

Contrary to the position in the Federal Republic of Germany and the USA, where freedom of the press is constitutionally recognised and protected, no constitutional protection of the rights embodied in this concept exists in South Africa. The protection of fundamental freedoms in South Africa, including the right to freedom of speech and freedom of the press, derives from common law and, more specifically, English common law.

222

Although the so-called 'declaratory acts' of English law (viz the Magna Carta, Petition of Right, Bill of Rights and Act of Settlement) did not contain a schedule of human rights, they did confirm the rights and freedoms of the English people as handed down from one generation to the next. The natural law theory developed by John Locke, which was based on Man's natural, inborn right to his life, liberty and property, provided the theoretical basis for reaction against absolutism in England; it prepared the way for parliamentary democracy and, most important of all, it emphasised the inalienable rights of the individual. Once the king acknowledged a limit to his power and Parliament was accepted as the highest legislative authority, the guarantees contained in the declaratory acts remained as part of English law. Since South African constitutional law is based largely on English law, it may be said that the fundamental freedoms and liberties of South African citizens derive originally from the English 'declaratory acts'.

However, the individual has also acquired certain basic rights or freedoms from Roman-Dutch law. Unfortunately, the basis of these rights is often traced back to the existence of a presumption — the presumption that an individual has a particular right or freedom to the extent that it has not been curtailed by any legal provision.[4]

Freedoms, liberties and human rights are not constitutionally protected in South Africa and such protection as there is takes place via the common law. As a result, these freedoms, liberties and rights may at any time be validly amended by Parliament since, in accordance with the doctrine of the sovereignty of Parliament, it is at liberty to alter or even totally remove individual rights, freedom and liberties.

The question is whether there is any legal restraint whatsoever whereby Parliament may be restrained from infringing upon these rights. In the United Kingdom there is a restraint placed on Parliament via the rule of law (Dicey 1965: 188). The rule of law protects the fundamental freedoms of the individual by acting as a 'political and moral restraint on Parliament' (Dugard 1978: 39). In the South African context reference is very often made to the rule of law, but the effect of this rule as a restraint upon Parliament has not been strikingly significant, as is evidenced by the steady erosion of individual rights by legislative enactments such as the Internal Security Act, 1982 (Act 74 of 1982), the Police Act, 1958 (Act 7 of 1958) and the Publications Act, 1974 (Act 42 of 1974).

The scope and content of freedom of speech in South Africa, although not clearly demarcated, has been referred to as a residual freedom (Mathews 1971: 32). Bearing in mind that the freedom of the press may be seen as an extension of freedom of speech, it may be said that the residual freedom of the freedom of speech includes freedom of the press. It appears that freedom of the press falls into the category of the common law freedoms, powers and privileges of the individual.[5] These rights are protected by public law, must be respected by the State and may be infringed only where statutory authority to that effect exists. It is in this context that the common law rule of minimum infringement by the legislature upon existing rights, freedoms and privileges comes into play (Steyn in Van Tonder et al 1981: 238).

The right to freedom of the press and freedom of speech is not unlimited. Although the right must be respected by the State in the absence of statutory authority to the contrary and although freedom of speech and freedom of the press are recognised as forming part of the democratic rights of the individual, the rights are not absolute in the sense that they are free from legal restraint. The effect hereof is that the press and the individual have the right to free expression, but this right is subject to the rights of others. As we shall see, freedom of the press is subject to a number of legal limitations such as the law of defamation and the law of privacy (by private law), as well as a number of extra-legal controls of an economic, political, social, etc nature.

HISTORICAL BACKGROUND TO PRESS FREEDOM IN SOUTH AFRICA

During the Middle Ages, censorship of the press was imposed by both Church and State to prevent the spread of opposing religious and political viewpoints. This censorship was abolished in England during the 17th century and in America during the 18th century.

In South Africa, freedom of the press became a reality in the Cape Colony during the 19th century and may be ascribed mainly to the efforts of Pringle and Fairbairn. The first publication in the Cape — The Cape Town Gazette — was a Government-sponsored publication and the first independent newspaper to be established was the South African Commercial Advertiser (De Kock 1982: 43). This newspaper became involved in a number of disputes with Lord Charles Somerset, which resulted in its being banned on a number of occasions. A press ordinance (Ordinance 60 of 1829 (Cape)), based on that of English law was eventually promulgated in 1828. The roles played by Pringle and Fairbairn in bringing about a free press cannot be underestimated, as they both opposed Government restriction vehemently.

De Zuid-Afrikaan was established in the Cape Colony in an attempt to resist anglicisation. This newspaper, which eventually amalgamated with Volksvriend in 1870, may be seen as the first official opposition newspaper in South Africa. Die Afrikaanse Patriot, under the influence of two brothers, Stephanus Jacobus du Toit and Daniel Francois du Toit (Oom Lokomotief), played a significant role in the development of Afrikaans (De Kock 1982: 91). Newspapers were also published in Natal during the period

224

1831 to 1854 and in the Transvaal and Orange Free State Republics in 1858 and 1893 respectively.

The first South African printing company, The Argus Printing and Publishing Company, was established in 1886. This venture was followed by the establishment of South African Associated Newspapers (SAAN) in 1905, Nasionale Pers in 1915 and Perskorporasie van Suid-Afrika in 1971.[6]

Right from the outset, English and Afrikaans newspapers had different objectives. The English-language newspapers followed the example set in England; most journalists were of British descent and adopted the Fleet Street approach to journalism and, except for the newspapers published by Pringle and Fairbairn, the campaigners for free speech and a free press in the Cape, English-language newspapers have always been profit-oriented and the direct instruments of financial and commercial power (Williams 1969: 48). On the other hand, the Afrikaans press was not founded as a commercial enterprise, but was aimed at promoting the Afrikaans language and culture. This approach has changed over the years, with the result that the Afrikaans press is now also profit-oriented.[7]

The press industry has always been characterised by fierce commercial competition between the various printing companies. For example, The Sunday Express, owned by the SAAN group, recently suffered a financial set back when The Star, owned by the Argus group, offered reduced advertising rates to estate agents who had formerly placed their advertising with The Sunday Express. The two major Afrikaans printing companies recently became involved in a struggle for commercial supremacy in the Transvaal. When Nasionale Pers withdrew its claim for compensation against Perskor (Perskor had published incorrect circulation figures), a re-shuffle of the Afrikaans newspapers took place. As a result, Beeld (owned by Nasionale Pers) acquired a monopoly of the Johannesburg morning market; the two Pretoria dailies owned by Perskor, viz Hoofstad and Oggendblad, were closed down; and Die Transvaler was moved from Johannesburg to Pretoria to become an afternoon paper.

Attempts at creating a newspaper for Black readers have not been altogether successful. The Township Mail was started by the SAAN group in 1965 and was followed in 1971 by the Extra Mail. Neither of these newspapers proved to be very successful and were followed by The World and The Post. In 1977 The World was banned under the Internal Security Act and when The Post's registration lapsed the Government decided against its re-registration.[8]

THE ROLE OF THE PRESS

Before discussing the role of the press in South Africa, it is interesting to examine the position of the press in other western societies.

225

In the Federal Republic of Germany, press freedom is protected by Article 5 of the Basic Law. The Federal Constitutional Court has emphasised that freedom of expression has both an individual and a social dimension. The individual dimension flows from personal individuality and the social dimension forms the basis of ordered liberty and democracy since it permits public discussion and the exchange of ideas on subjects of general and political importance which are essential to democracy.[9] The press plays a constitutive role in the democratic system by virtue of the fact that it assists in the creation of public opinion and therefore the institutional independence of the press is guaranteed.[10]

The freedom of the press in the USA is protected by the *First Amendment to the Constitution*. It is a fundamental personal right and is part of the natural freedom of persons.[11] Press freedom permits the individual to participate in public life, particularly in the creation of public opinion, for freedom of the press is indispensable to the building of free political opinion in a democratic society[12] and the main function of the press is to control and criticise state action.[13]

In the United Kingdom, freedom of speech, including freedom of the press, is recognised as a residual freedom deriving from common law, that being permitted which is not expressly forbidden. Press freedom is not, therefore, a constitutionally protected right, but is characterised by the limitations placed on it by common and statutory law. The courts have also recognised that freedom of discussion is essential to the perpetuation of a democratic society.[14]

Historically, relations between governments and the press throughout the world have been characterised by tension and conflict. This pattern is reflected in South Africa, as may be seen from the Government bannings and detention orders, etc placed on reporters. On one hand, reporters claim that the Government suppresses information of a political nature, whilst on the other the Government has frequently warned the press to put its house in order and to avoid sensational and distorted reporting. Whilst one must agree with the Government that 'cheque-book' journalism (i.e. paying criminals for their life stories) should not be permitted, investigative journalism should not only be tolerated, but actively encouraged. Investigative reporting plays a very definite 'watch-dog' role in western democratic societies, a role particularly well-suited to the press with its personnel and financial resources.

In South Africa the press not only carries out investigative journalism, but also provides the individual with an information service covering a wide range of topics. Thus, the individual is provided with certain daily needs — information on all topical issues and entertainment. The press has a cultural role — it provides information and comment on matters of cultural importance to the various language and population groups — and articulates public opinion by commenting on and criticising news items. It gives expression to the diverse political views held in the country — ranging from White radicalism to White conservatism and from Black or Coloured radicalism to a more moderate position — and provides surveillance of Government activity, i.e. it carries out the watch-dog function of keeping the public informed of Government malpractice or incompetence.

In South Africa, the legal position relating to freedom of the press is similar to that in the United Kingdom. This means that in theory a South African newspaper or private publisher is free to publish what it chooses, subject to certain legal and extra-legal limitations. The scope and content of the right to freedom of the press has not been clearly demarcated or defined in South African legal theory and in order to determine the scope, content and extent of the freedom, the limitations thereto must be scrutinised. These limitations include legal restrictions such as the protection of the security of the State and control measures such as those exercised by the administrative censorship machinery.

RESTRICTIONS ON PRESS FREEDOM IN THE INTERESTS OF THE STATE

The restrictions on the press in the interests of the State are not confined to 'internal' security legislation, but include 'external' security restrictions such as the Defence Act and the Protection of Information Act. Furthermore, the legal restrictions to be discussed are not only statutory restrictions, but include the common law restriction on the violation of the dignity, repute or authority of judicial bodies or interference with the administration of justice in pending judicial matters.

The Internal Security Act, 1982 (Act 74 of 1982)

This consolidating Act[15] provides for the prohibition of certain publications, the restriction of certain persons under house arrest, preventive detention and the declaration of certain organisations as unlawful.

The provisions of the Act effectively silence any person (and the press) from quoting any person whose name appears on the consolidated list;[16] persons convicted of sedition, treason or sabotage;[17] persons under house arrest;[18] persons whose names appear on a list under the repealed Internal Security Act; persons prohibited from attending gatherings;[19] persons whose speeches have been restricted by the Minister of Law and Order;[20]

227

and persons under preventive detention.[21] Thus, the Act not only prohibits the quoting of persons convicted of treason or sedition, but also the quoting of persons detained at the instance and discretion of the executive and not afforded the opportunity of being heard or brought to trial.[22] Not only the freedom of speech of the individual in question is restricted, but the freedom of the press is also curtailed.

The Minister may restrict the freedom of the press further by prohibiting (or prohibiting for a specified period) the printing, publication or dissemination of a periodical or other publication where he is satisfied that it expresses views or conveys information calculated to endanger the security of the State or the maintenance of law and order, or where it professes by its name or otherwise to be a publication which propagates the principles of or promotes the spread of communism, or expresses the views of an unlawful organisation, or expresses views which are calculated to encourage hostility between different population groups.[23]

The Minister may have the activities, purposes or identity of an organisation investigated where he has reason to suspect that it ought to be declared an unlawful organisation. Where he is of the opinion that the circumstances connected with the printing, publication or dissemination of material warrant prohibition under section 5 of the Act, he may prohibit the printing, publication or dissemination of such material.[24]

The press may also not print, publish, distribute or circulate a notice convening or advertising a gathering, or in any manner making it known, where the gathering has been prohibited under section 46 of the Act.[25] The words 'or in any other manner make(s) it known' have a broad meaning and it appears that any report on such an intended gathering, or the circumstances surrounding the prohibition, or any discussion of the gathering itself, is prohibited.

The Act provides that a consolidated list comprising the names of all those persons and organisations who may not be quoted must be published at regular intervals in the *Gazette* and it is essential therefore that before quoting a 'banned' person or a person suspected of being banned, a journalist consults the consolidated list in order to avoid the danger of prosecution.

The Defence Act, 1957 (Act 44 of 1957)

In terms of this Act, the Minister of Defence has power to restrict or prohibit access to military areas,[26] with the result that the press is unable to comment on military matters without the co-operation of the Defence Force in the form of official statements. In view of the sensitivity of defence and security matters, the Minister of Defence and the Newspaper Press Union have entered into an agreement[27] to ensure regular contact between the Defence Force and the Newspaper Press Union. In terms of this agreement, regular meetings must take place between the two bodies so that issues of policy and principle may be discussed. News liaison takes place via the Media Liaison Section of the Defence Force and certain accredited military correspondents who must be well-equipped and knowledgeable reporters.[28]

The examination of the specific provisions of the Act reveals that it is an offence to publish in any newspaper, magazine, book or pamphlet (or by radio or any other means), any information relating to the composition, movement or disposition of the South African Defence Force, South African or allied ships used for naval or military purposes, or any transport system or air service over which the Defence Force has control.[29] Furthermore, any statement, comment or rumour which is calculated directly or indirectly to convey such information is also forbidden, unless expressly authorised by the Minister of Defence.

Any statement, comment or rumour relating to any member of the South African Defence Force or its activity, or to that of any force of a foreign country, which is calculated[30] to prejudice or embarrass the Government in its foreign relations or to alarm or depress members of the public, except under approval of the Minister, is also punishable.[31] It is apparent that the ambit of this provision is very wide indeed, for a great deal of information relating to State activity may seriously alarm or depress the general public. For example, the mismanagement of funds, such as occurred during the Information scandal, may seriously alarm and depress the public, but it is essential that the public be made aware of such mismanagement.

Any proprietor, printer, publisher or editor of a newspaper, magazine, book or pamphlet in which secret or confidential military information is published, as well as any person responsible for the publication of secret or confidential information relating to the defence of the Republic, is guilty of an offence.[32] No secret or confidential information relating to the defence of the Republic, or information relating to fortifications for the defence of the Republic, may be published.[33]

As was pointed out above, the press is dependent upon the co-operation of the Defence Force with respect to military information. In the event of the Defence Force refusing to divulge information for whatever reason, the press cannot rely on the provisions of the agreement to compel the Defence Force to provide information. This fact, coupled with the fact that the press may not enter a military area or a prohibited place as defined in the Protection of Information Act, means that the freedom of the press to report on military matters is very limited.

The Protection of Information Act, 1982 (Act 84 of 1982)

This Act, which has repealed the Official Secrets Act, deals with espionage, sabotage and the use of official information for the benefit of a foreign power or hostile organisation, or the use of information in a manner which is prejudicial to the safety or interests of the State.

The Act prohibits the approach, inspection, passing over, or being in the neighbourhood of, or entrance into any prohibited place[34] for any purpose prejudicial to the security or interests of the Republic, as well as the obtaining or receiving of any secret or official code, password, documents, model, article or information used, made, or obtained in a prohibited place, for the purpose of disclosure to any foreign state or its agent, or any hostile organisation.[35]

It is also an offence to prepare, compile, make, obtain or receive any document or information relating to prohibited places, armaments, the defence of the Republic, military or security matters, the prevention or combating of terrorism, or any other article which may directly or indirectly be of use to any foreign state or hostile organisation.[36]

Persons in possession or control of official secret codes, passwords, documents or information, which they know or should reasonably know relate to prohibited places, armaments, defence, military or security matters, or the prevention or combating of terrorism, may not disclose, publish, retain or neglect, or fail to take proper care of such information.[37]

It is also an offence for any person to receive secret information knowing, or having reasonable grounds to believe at the time that he receives such information, that its disclosure is contrary to section 4(2) of the Act.

The Police Act, 1958 (Act 7 of 1958)

This Act prohibits *inter alia* the sketching or photographing of persons detained in lawful custody with a view to criminal proceedings, or the sketching or photographing of an escaped fugitive, or the publication of a sketch or photograph of an accused person prior to his trial and, in the case of a witness, a sketch or photograph may be published only at the commencement and not prior to the commencement of the trial.[38]

A provision of the Act which has a direct effect on the freedom of the press is that of section 27B(1). In terms of this section, the publication[39] of any untrue matter in relation to any action by the Force or part thereof, or any member of the Force in relation to the performance of his functions as such a member, without having reasonable grounds for believing the statement to be true, is an offence.[40] The offence is committed by any person who publishes untrue matter regarding any *action* by a member of

230

the Police Force in connection with the performance of his function as a *policeman*. It is submitted that an omission on the part of a policeman will not fall within the definition of the crime.

The effect hereof is that a journalist is forced to verify the truth of any report dealing with police action. Although it is conceded that the publication of untrue statements is undesirable, it is not always possible for the media to confirm the veracity of reports made to it by members of the public, for example.

The Prisons Act, 1959 (Act 8 of 1959)

The court has found that the object behind the prohibition on the sketching or photographing of prisoners is to prevent the humiliation of the prisoner, or his friends and relatives, whilst he is in prison.[41]

The Act prohibits the making of a sketch or taking of a photograph and the publishing or causing to be published of a sketch or photograph of any prison or portion thereof, or of the burial of an executed person.[42] Sketching or taking photographs of a prisoner or group of prisoners is also forbidden, unless it is a sketch or photograph done or taken at any court or adjacent premises in which the prisoner appeared as an accused and was done or taken at the time of the prisoner's appearance. Publishing, or causing a sketch or photograph of any prisoner or group of prisoners to be published, is also forbidden unless it is a sketch or photograph taken at a court or adjacent premises at the time of the prisoner's appearance, or was made or taken before the arrest of the prisoner or group of prisoners and is published within 30 days of the prisoner's conviction or acquittal.[43]

The word 'prison' has a broad meaning in the Act and refers to a place for the reception, detention, confinement, training or treatment of prisoners.[44]

In order to constitute a contravention of the Act, the sketch or photograph must be published while the prisoner is in prison. In S v SAAN, Ludorf J found that a prisoner remains a prisoner whilst in transit from one place to another, or whilst outside a gaol for any lawful police purpose (it makes no difference whether he is in the custody of police or prison officials), but that he ceases to be a prisoner if he escapes.[45]

For the purposes of the Act, a person takes on the quality of a prisoner upon his arrest and retains that status until such time as he is lawfully discharged, granted bail, pardoned, granted parole or escapes.[46]

Section 44 of the Act prohibits the publication of false information concerning the behaviour or prison experiences of any prisoner or ex-prisoner, or relating to the prison administration, when it is known to be false or when reasonable steps to verify the information are not taken. This section has been strictly interpreted by the courts, as is evident in S v

Associated Newspapers Ltd and Others.[47] In this case the editor of the *Rand Daily Mail*, who published a series of articles about prison conditions, required each informant to reduce his statement to writing, to take an oath as to the veracity of the statement and to be subjected to interrogation by an attorney. Despite this procedure, the court found that the accused had failed to prove that he had taken reasonable steps to verify the information of the four informants.[48]

Since journalists fear prosecution for the publication of any information relating to prisoners, the only prison news published is that which emerges during the course of court proceedings or is given official sanction. The onerous requirement that information be verified prevents any adverse information about prison conditions from being published. This stringent statutory provision must be re-examined, particularly in view of the events which occurred at the Barberton Prison during 1983, which resulted in a number of prisoners dying violent deaths and certain warders being convicted of brutality at the Leeuwkop Prison.[49]

Further statutory restrictions on press freedom in the interests of State security

There are a number of statutes which restrict the freedom of the press in the interests of State security. These include the Nuclear Energy Act,[50] the National Key Points Act,[51] the Petroleum Products Act,[52] the Armaments Development and Production Act,[53] the National Supplies Procurement Act,[54] the Intimidation Act,[55] the Advocate-General Act[56] and the Demonstrations in or Near Court Buildings Prohibition Act.[57]

CONTEMPT OF COURT

The common law restriction of contempt of court is directed towards the need to ensure the fair and effective administration of justice. Contempt of court has been defined as the unlawful, intentional violation of the dignity, repute or authority of a judicial body, or interfering in the administration of justice in a matter pending before it.[58]

From this definition it becomes clear that the elements of the offence are unlawfulness, *mens rea*, the existence of a judicial body and *actus reus*, i.e. the violation of or interference with the judicial body.

Privileged statements,[59] for example statements made by parliamentarians acting within the scope of their privilege and statements by judges sitting in appeal or review of proceedings from lower courts, will not constitute unlawfulness.

In a number of early South African decisions, strict liability was applied to the so-called 'newspaper' cases,[60] with the result that intention did not have to be proved and lack of negligence was no defence (Hunt in Milton 1982: 185). This approach was rejected by the courts in *S v Gibson NO & Others*,[61] where it was found that the three essential features of the offence of contempt of court are that it is a crime of intention; it is a crime which relates to the administration of justice and not generally; and is designed to prevent or punish violations of the dignity or authority of the courts and not mere criticism of the administration of justice in the courts.

The violation of the dignity, repute or authority of some organ of the administration of justice other than a judicial body does not constitute contempt of court.[62] The term 'court' includes the Supreme Court, Magistrates' Courts, Commissioners' Courts, etc and it is irrelevant whether the court has criminal or civil jurisdiction.[63]

The question whether contempt of commission will amount to contempt of court has served before the courts on a number of occasions[64] and in *Erasmus & Others NNO v SA Associated Newspapers Ltd*[65] the court found that there is no reason to refer to a commission headed by a judge or magistrate as 'a judicial commission of inquiry'. In *S v Sparks NO & Others*[66] the court came to the following conclusion with regard to contempt of commissions:

- It is not an offence to publish information relating to a matter which falls within the commission's terms of reference.
- An enquiry before a commission does not involve a proceeding between individual parties who are entitled to a hearing and verdict on the evidence led. A commission of enquiry deals with matters of public interest — matters which may already be the subject of public knowledge.
- The *sub iudice* rule does not apply to commissions, since a commission of enquiry cannot be equated with a court of law.
- A court of law is bound by rules of evidence and the pleadings in question, but a commission is not. It may inform itself via facts gleaned from newspaper reports, or via submissions or representations, etc.

As far as *actus reus* (the violation or interference with the judicial body) is concerned, there are three main categories of contempt. These are contempt *in facie curiae*, contempt *ex facie curiae* with reference to pending judicial proceedings and contempt *ex facie curiae* which does not relate to pending proceedings (Hunt in Milton 1982: 198).

Contempts *in facie curiae* must take place in the presence of the court which is sitting and usually take the form of misbehaviour, insults or interruptions.[67]

Contempts *ex facie curiae* with reference to pending proceedings[68] restrict the freedom of the press greatly in that comment is limited and only fair reporting which does not obstruct the administration of justice is permissible. The object behind the creation of this offence is to ensure that an accused is afforded a fair and unprejudiced trial. Examples of potentially prejudicial publications include comments in newspapers or magazines to the effect that a person is guilty of the offence charged,[69] the publication of a photo and any comment during a preparatory examination which prejudges the issue[70] and pleading with the judiciary to disregard evidence given in the course of judicial proceedings.[71]

Criminal proceedings are pending from the moment of their commencement, e.g. arrest, summons, or notice to appear and the matter is *sub iudice* from that time onwards, although the actual trial need not have started (Hunt in Milton 1982: 198). Civil proceedings are pending once they commence, for example by the issue of a summons, although the summons need not have been served (Hunt in Milton 1982: 198). Civil and criminal proceedings terminate when the ultimate court of appeal delivers its judgment, or when the time available for the noting of an appeal has expired, or no appeal has been noted (Stuart 1982: 114, 117). However, the press must be given a fair amount of latitude to report on a judgment, despite the fact that leave has been granted, in order to keep the public informed of the outcome of matters heard in court.

The test for contempt of court (relating to the obstruction of the course of justice) is not whether the words used actually influence the judge, but whether the statement tends to prejudice or interfere with the administration of justice in a pending proceeding.[72] This test may be criticised, since it fails to take judicial training and background into account and the unlikelihood of the judicial mind being influenced by comment on pending proceedings.[73]

When Commodore Gerhardt and his wife were arrested on a charge of espionage, the Government relied on section 118 of the Defence Act to silence the media[74] by the imposition of a type of prior censorship. The correct approach would have been for the Government to invoke contempt of court proceedings, i.e. the obstruction of the fair administration of justice. This would have ensured that the media published fair and accurate reports on trial proceedings and speculative reporting about the Gerhardts' motives, background, etc would have been punishable.

The importance of a fair trial cannot be underrated and the question is whether all matters *sub iudice* should be subjected to a blanket ban on news coverage other than the factual report of court proceedings. The question of public interest must be taken into account and although it may be argued that in these circumstances the public is not being deprived of information, but merely subjected to a postponement thereof, the public interest must be considered.[75]

Contempts *ex facie curiae* which do not refer to pending proceedings relate to the scurrilous abuse of a judge or judgment as a whole, or the imputation of bias, partiality or improper motives to a judge or the courts in their administration of justice.[76]

The law of contempt is not aimed at the protection of the personal dignity or character of a judge or judiciary, but relates to any action which lowers the esteem in which the judicial administration is held in the public gaze.[77]

RESTRICTIONS ON PRESS FREEDOM IN THE INTERESTS OF THE INDIVIDUAL

Although the press is recognised as a corner-stone of democracy and the champion of the individual's rights and liberties, press freedom must be limited in certain instances to protect the individual. The legal system must constantly weigh up and balance conflicting rights, duties and liberties within the democratic system in order to maintain peace, good order and peaceful co-existence within the community. This is done by an independent judiciary.

The State recognises the need to protect personality rights[78] and an infringement of the *dignitas*, *fama* or physical integrity of the individual constitutes a crime. Personality rights are also protected by the law of delict and a person whose rights of personality have been infringed may rely on the *actio iniuriarum* to protect these rights (Joubert 1953: 53).

Although a number of personality rights are protected by the *actio iniuriarum*, this section will be confined to a discussion of defamation and privacy, since these branches of the law are the most relevant to a discussion of the limitation of press freedom in the interests of the individual.

The restrictions imposed under the Copyright Act, being restrictions on the product of the individual's mind, will also be examined in this section.

The delict defamation

The law of defamation is aimed at the protection of the individual's reputation or *fama* as a right of personality.

The unlawfulness of the delict lies in the publication of defamatory matter relating to the good name or reputation of the plaintiff. The court has found that proof of publication of defamatory words gives rise to two presumptions, namely a presumption of unlawfulness and a presumption of *animus iniuriandi*.[79]

Unlawfulness is the objective element of delictual action and proof of circumstances excluding unlawfulness takes place by means of an objective criterion, i.e. the standard of the reasonable man, or a general standard of reasonableness.[80]

Defamation must serve to lower the reputation of the person in the estimation of society generally and not merely a section of society[81] and the lowering of esteem includes imputations against moral character, statements which reflect on office, profession or occupation, statements reflecting on political character and statements involving financial embarrassment such as insolvency.[82] A trading corporation cannot sue for defamation, but may recover damages for patrimonial loss where it has suffered such loss on account of an unlawful attack on its integrity.[83] A voluntary association which is a *universitas* may sue in its own name and may sue for defamation.[84] The State does not have an action for defamation, but an individual minister may have such an action.[85] In *Universiteit van Pretoria v Tommie Meyer Films (Edms) Bpk*,[86] Mostert J found that a *universitas* does not have rights of personality and that the *actio iniuriarum* is not available to a *universitas*. The Appellate Division did not decide on the question whether a university possesses a *dignitas* which can be assailed, or whether a juristic person other than a trading company can be defamed, but upheld the decision by the Transvaal Provincial Division on the facts of the matter.[87]

In the law of defamation, publication means the communication of a defamatory statement to a third person or persons. Publication occurs as soon as the statement has been conveyed to a third person and where the defamatory statement is contained in a book or newspaper of which a number have been sold,[88] a presumption of publication arises.[89]

Every person who contributes to the publication of a defamatory statement is liable, which means that the writer, editor, printer and publisher can all be held liable.[90] The writer of a letter which is published in a newspaper is *prima facie* liable for its publication, but the editor, printer, publisher and proprietor may also be liable.[91]

Although *animus iniuriandi* is generally a requirement for liability based on defamation, the liability of the press has, under the influence of English law, developed along a different path. The courts have found that the editor's ignorance of a defamatory newspaper statement is no defence to a defamatory action.[92]

In *Suid-Afrikaanse Uitsaaikorporasie v O'Malley*,[93] Rumpff CJ stated *obiter* that strict liability should, in his opinion, apply to the owner, printer, publisher and editor of a newspaper. In *Pakendorf en Andere v De Flamingh*,[94] the court found that strict liability should attach to defamatory matter published by the press, i.e. owners, printers, publishers and editors. Chief Justice Rumpff found that the press can always fall back on defences such as truth and public interest, even where strict liability is accepted.[95] The effect of this decision is that the press is held strictly liable for defamatory statements and although the larger newspaper organisations may be in a position to shoulder their losses, the position of the parochial and student newspapers is particularly precarious.[96]

In certain instances, viz proof of privilege, fair comment and truth and public interest, the press will not be liable for statements which are defamatory. These grounds of justification (which remove the element of unlawfulness) merely constitute *prima facie* proof of a ground of justification and where the defendant exceeds the bounds, or has acted with improper motive, the proof may be rebutted.[97] The presumption of unlawfulness may be rebutted by proof of the truth of the words and proof that the publication is in the public interest.[98]

The press may, in certain instances, rely on the defence of privilege to rebut the presumption of unlawfulness. Reports on legal proceedings, parliamentary debates and proceedings[99] are provisionally protected where they are reasonable and accurate, but reports on legal proceedings held *in camera* are not protected.[100] Reports on parliamentary speeches are protected, provided that they are substantially correct.[101] Reports of the proceedings of public bodies which have been instituted by statute and which perform public functions are also privileged.[102]

Fair comment is also a defence to a defamatory action provided that the allegation concerned amounts to comment, the comment is fair and does not exceed reasonable limits, the allegations of fact commented on are true and the comment refers to matters of public interest.[103]

The press may not raise mistake as a defence, since mistake rebuts *animus iniuriandi* and as fault is no longer a requirement for liability of the press, it is pointless to raise this defence.

Liability for defamatory statements is not confined to civil liability, but may also be the subject of criminal liability. The most important distinction between criminal and civil defamation lies in the fault requirement. In an action based on criminal liability, the State must prove *animus iniuriandi* on the part of the press, whereas in civil actions strict liability applies to defamatory statements made by the press.[104]

Privacy

A further right of personality which restricts the freedom of the press is the individual's right to privacy. Although the need for privacy is a phenomenon of modern society, the courts have found that the right to privacy may be included in the concept of *dignitas* and thus find protection via the *actio iniuriarum*.[105] The right to privacy and the right to identity have been identified and recognised as distinct rights of personality in *Universiteit van Pretoria v Tommie Meyer Films (Edms) Bpk*.[106]

Where, for example, a newspaper company published a photograph of the plaintiffs, without their consent, under the title '97 Lonely Nurses Want

Boy Friends', the court found that the publication of the article constituted an insult or *contumelia* to the young married plaintiff.[107] In *Mhlongo* v *Bailey*,[108] the court found that the publication of a photograph of the plaintiff with an article about a singer constituted an invasion of his privacy 'which, because of the article to which the photographs formed a background, constituted an aggression upon his dignitas'.

The wrongfulness of an action infringing privacy is determined in accordance with the *boni mores*,[109] but proof of the existence of a ground of justification, such as a state of emergency, self-defence, consent and the exercise of a statutory right or an official power, removes the unlawfulness of the action (Neethling 1979: 198-212).

Animus iniuriandi is also a requirement to establish liability for invasion of privacy.

The infringement of *dignitas* does not only lead to a civil action, but is also protected by criminal law.[110]

Copyright

It has been pointed out that not only the individual's personality rights are protected against infringement by the press, but the products of the mind, viz Man's intellectual and artistic creations, are also protected.[111]

Copyright consists primarily of a legal relationship between the legal subject (author) and the legal object (his creation) and the content of the right is the author's use and enjoyment of his creative work within the limits of the legal order.

There is no copyright on ideas and in order to qualify for protection under the law an idea must be presented in a physical or material form.[112]

In terms of the Copyright Act, 1978 (Act 98 of 1978), copyright extends to work of an original nature only. This means that literary, musical and artistic works, cinematograph films, sound recordings, broadcasts, programme-carrying signals and published editions must be original in character.[113] Although the Act makes no reference thereto, it is a requirement that the content of the work on which copyright is claimed should not conflict with public morals.[114] The provisions of the Copyright Act which affect the freedom of the press most are those which protect the copyright on literary[115] and artistic works.[116] Infringement of copyright takes place where any person who is not the owner of the copyright carries out, or causes any other person to carry out, any act which the owner must authorise, without the consent of the owner.[117]

The press may rely on certain statutory defences to refute an allegation of infringement of copyright. For example, where the work is used for research purposes, private study, criticism, review, or the reporting of

238

current events in a newspaper, magazine or similar periodical and such use does not involve the making of a copy of the whole or a substantial part of the work, there is no infringement of copyright. Should the work be used for criticism, review or the reporting of current events, the source and the author must be acknowledged.[118]

There is also no infringement of copyright where work is used for the purposes of judicial proceedings or the reporting thereof, or where literary or musical works which are lawfully available to the public are quoted. Quotations from articles in newspapers or periodicals in the form of summaries of such articles do not constitute infringements of copyright provided that such quotations are compatible with fair practice.[119] The press may reproduce a public lecture, address or similar work for the purpose of public information.[120] Any article on current economic, political or religious topics, if first published in a newspaper or periodical or broadcast (and provided the reproduction was not expressly reserved), may be published in the press or broadcast, provided that the source is clearly mentioned.[121]

Copyright does not extend to official texts of a legislative, administrative or legal nature (or official translations thereof), to speeches of a political nature, speeches made during the course of legal proceedings, or in the news of the day which are nothing but items of press information.[122]

Where the employee of the proprietor of a newspaper, magazine or periodical, under contract of service or apprenticeship, produces a literary or artistic work for publication in the newspaper or magazine, the proprietor is the owner of the copyright as far as the publication of the work in any newspaper, magazine or similar periodical is concerned.[123]

The copyright on a letter written to the editor of a newspaper and subsequently published vests in the writer as author, but the writer implicitly authorises the editor to publish the letter as his agent and the editor may alter or shorten the letter, provided that the credit or literary reputation of the writer is not affected.[124]

News contained in a newspaper is protected by copyright provided that the manner of expression is original and the copyright subsists in the news report itself and not in the information contained in the report.[125]

CONTROL OF PRESS FREEDOM IN SOUTH AFRICA

There are a number of legal and extra-legal controls, ranging from judicial, parliamentary and administrative control to financial control and control via labour law, which limit the freedom of the press. These controls will be discussed briefly in this section.

Although the South African judiciary has not played as markedly creative a role in developing freedom of speech and freedom of the press as the judiciary in the Federal Republic of Germany and the United States of America and although Parliament is at liberty to alter or even totally remove freedom of speech, the Supreme Court is regarded as the protector of the rights of the individual. The court's role of protector of individual rights and freedoms means that on one hand it will protect the individual from the unlawful infringement of his rights by the press and, on the other, protect the right of the press to freedom of speech. There are a number of judicial remedies available to the individual or the press where freedom of speech or freedom of the press is infringed, viz an interdict, a summons for recovery of damages and judicial review of administrative action. The purpose of review proceedings is to ensure that administrative action is valid in that all the requirements for the validity of action have been complied with.

The important role played by judicial review of administrative action (in the sphere of press law) may be seen clearly in the case of *Human & Rousseau Uitgewers (Edms) Bpk v Snyman NO*.[126] In this case the Appeal Board had found in its investigation (in terms of the Publications Act, 1974 (Act 42 of 1974)) of what was improper, indecent and offensive to public morals, that the likely reader could not be considered. On review, the Supreme Court found that the Appeal Board had improperly limited its investigation by disregarding the likely reader of the book in question. As a result of this decision, the Appeal Board has since determined that the likely reader must constantly be taken into consideration in investigations relating to public morality.[127]

Court proceedings

The general rule is that the administration of justice is open to the general public, including the press, but in certain circumstances the judicial officer may exclude the public and the press. These circumstances include the protection of the identity of a juvenile offender, the concealment of the identity of a complainant in cases of indecency or extortion and the interests of State security, good order, public morality or the administration of justice.

The press may not publish information which reveals the identity of an accused person or a witness under the age of 18 years in a criminal trial.[128]

Where proceedings in a criminal trial are held behind closed doors, the court must make a further order prohibiting the publication of information relating to the proceedings, but this prohibition will not prevent the press from publishing the name and personal particulars of the accused, the charge against him, the plea, the verdict and the sentence.[129]

The court may order that the proceedings be held behind closed doors where the accused is charged with indecency or extortion.[130]

The Internal Security Act provides that the presiding officer may order that a matter relating to section 54 (terrorism) be heard behind closed doors.[131]

The Divorce Act 70 of 1979, section 12(3) and (3) also curtails the right of newspapers to report on court proceedings. Particulars of the action may not be published, apart from the names of the parties to the action, the fact that a divorce action is pending and the judgment or order of the court.

Administrative control

Registration of newspapers

All newspapers printed and published in South Africa must be registered in terms of the Newspaper and Imprint Registration Act and in order to qualify as a newspaper for the purposes of registration a newspaper must be intended for public sale and dissemination, the greater part of it must consist wholly or for the greater part of political or other news or current topics and it must be published at least once a month.[132]

Registration takes place by application to the Secretary for the Interior in the prescribed form accompanied by the prescribed fee.

In terms of the Internal Security Act, a newspaper shall not be registered under the Newspaper and Imprint Registration Act within a period of 21 days of receipt of the application for registration.[133] Furthermore, the proprietor must deposit an amount to be determined by the Minister of Internal Affairs (not exceeding R40 000) where the Minister is not satisfied that a prohibition in terms of section 5 of the Act will not become necessary.[134] In practice, newspapers which do not have a political content are usually not required to pay a deposit and it is submitted that the criterion on which the Minister bases his decision regarding a deposit is whether the newspaper will constitute a threat to State security.[135]

The registration of a newspaper will lapse under the following circumstances: (a) where printing and publishing is not commenced within one month of registration; (b) where the newspaper is not printed or published during a period exceeding one month; and (c) if the newspaper changes hands.[136]

In terms of the Newspaper Imprint and Registration Act, every copy of a newspaper must bear the full and correct address at which it is published and the full and correct names and addresses of the proprietor, printer and publisher. The editor or acting editor, or the responsible or chief editor of a newspaper must be resident in the Republic. There are, however, no formal statutory requirements relating to the publication of printed matter other than newspapers, save that the full and correct name and address of the printer of any printed matter must appear in legible type in either of the official languages on all such printed matter.[137]

Section 3 of the Registration of Newspapers Amendment Act, 1982 (Act 98 of 1982) (not yet in operation) provides that any newspaper published by a publisher who is not the holder of documentary proof that he subjects himself for disciplinary purposes to an independent and voluntary body recognised by the Minister by notice in the *Government Gazette*, will be included within the definition of 'publication or object' as defined in the Publications Act. The effect of these provisions is that all newspapers will be subject to some form of control, either that provided for in the Publications Act or in the form of a disciplinary body as determined by the Newspaper Registration Act. The Minister may cancel registration of a newspaper where he is satisfied that a newspaper is not subject to discipline as set down in section 3.

Publications Act, 1974 (Act 42 of 1974)

This Act is relevant to the concept of the freedom of the press insofar as the provisions of the Act apply to all newspapers published by a publisher who is not a member of the Newspaper Press Union and to all books, magazines, pamphlets and posters. Although the Publications Act controls undesirable publications or objects, films and public entertainment, this discussion will deal with publications and objects only.

The majority of newspapers are members of the Newspaper Press Union and are thus not subject to control via this Act, but magazines such as *Scope*, which also provides news of a current, political and economic nature, fall within the ambit of the Act.

The Act prohibits the production of any undesirable publication or object and a notice in the *Government Gazette* stating that the publication or object has been found undesirable by a committee is sufficient proof of undesirability.[138]

In S v Moroney,[139] the court found that the decision by a committee merely constituted *prima facie* proof of undesirability. To decide whether the State had proved its case beyond reasonable doubt, the magistrate should have weighed this proof, together with any other proof adduced by the appellant or which emerged from the publications themselves. The omission on the part of the magistrate was a fatal irregularity and the conviction and sentence were set aside.

In S v *Roodt*,[140] the appellant had been convicted of unlawfully producing an undesirable publication. On appeal it was found that in order to secure a conviction, the State had to prove that the accused had produced the publication in question, that the publication had been found undesirable by a publications committee, that notice to this effect had been published in the *Government Gazette* and that the accused had the necessary *mens rea* to commit the offence charged.[141]

The distribution of a publication or object declared undesirable by a committee, notification of which has been published in the *Government Gazette*, is also prohibited.[142]

In terms of section 9(1), a publications committee may declare every edition of a periodical publication or object undesirable if, in its opinion, each subsequent edition is likely to be undesirable. Section 9(2) empowers a committee to prohibit distribution except under authority of a permit of subsequent editions of a publication, where any edition thereof is declared undesirable. This measure amounts to prior censorship in that the approval of the Director must be obtained before publication.

The possession of any publication or object, where such possession has been prohibited under the Act and notice thereof published in the *Government Gazette*, is also prohibited.[143]

The importation of any publication prohibited under the Act after notice to this effect has been published in the *Government Gazette* is prohibited, except when the importation is under permit.[144]

Section 47(2) of the Act defines undesirability as that which

(a) is indecent or obscene or is offensive or harmful to public morals;

(b) is blasphemous or offensive to the religious convictions or feelings of any section of the inhabitants of the Republic;

(c) brings any section of the inhabitants of the Republic into ridicule or contempt;

(d) is harmful to the relations between any sections of the inhabitants of the Republic;

(e) is prejudicial to the safety of the State, the general welfare, or the peace and good order.

The legal objects protected by section 47(2) of the Act relate to the protection of public morality, the religious feelings and convictions of the inhabitants of the Republic, the honour and dignity of the inhabitants, public order and the safety of the State. In view of the disparity between the different legal objects to be protected by the Act, the control of undesirable matter via the Publications Act has not proved altogether successful. The censorship of political matter, for example, has been the subject of a great deal of criticism, since censoring bodies are seen as no more than an extension to and implementation of Government policy.

Although social units such as the family, the school and the church play a role in curbing the production, publication and dissemination of undesirable matter, the only effective way of controlling undesirable matter is via legal measures, i.e. via the State.

Since 1982, the Appeal Board has adopted a more lenient approach towards the banning of undesirable literature in terms of section 47(2)(e) (the safety of the State) and section 47(2)(a) (public morality) are concerned, but it appears that the Directorate of Publications still adheres to its strict approach.[145]

Internal control

Another form of control which limits the freedom of the press is the control exercised by the Media Council. The nature of this control is not administrative, since the legal basis for this type of internal control is contractual agreement and membership is voluntary.

The objects of the Council are set out in article 1 of its constitution and include the upholding and maintenance of the freedom of the media; ensuring that proprietors, editors, journalists, directors, producers and others involved in the media adhere to the highest professional standards; the consideration and adjudication of alleged infringements of the code by members; and considering and enquiring into reports by non-members, etc.

The procedure adopted by the Media Council in the event of an alleged infringement of the code is that of conciliation. A conciliator first attempts to settle the dispute by holding informal discussions with the parties concerned and, if unsuccessful, he refers the matter to the Council. The Chairman of the Council may appoint a committee to investigate any matter of public importance concerning the conduct and repute of the media. On completion of such an investigation the committee must submit a written report to the Council, which then considers and votes thereon. The essence of the Council's proceedings is that complaints are considered and adjudicated upon as soon after publication as possible, they are adjudicated upon in an informal manner and the Council and parties strive to achieve a speedy and amicable settlement.

Members of the Media Council must adhere to the code of conduct as set out in the constitution. In terms of this code the media are obliged to report news truthfully, accurately and objectively, in the correct context and in a balanced manner. The media must distinguish clearly between factual reports and reports based on opinion and, in the event of a published report being incorrect, it must be rectified immediately, without reservation or delay. The media must present reports, photographs or sketches relating to indecent or obscene matters with due regard and sensitivity to the prevailing moral climate. The media shall exercise exceptional care and consideration, bearing in mind the individual's right to privacy, when publishing news or commenting upon the private lives and concerns of individuals. The media must also exercise due regard and care in respect of matters which may cause enmity or give offence in racial, ethnic, religious or cultural matters or incite persons to contravene the law, matters that may affect the peace and good order of the safe defence of the Republic and in the presentation of brutality, violence and atrocities.

The first report by the Media Council concerned a complaint made against the South African Broadcasting Corporation by the Jockey Club. The complaint was about the television programme *Midweek*, broadcast on 1 February 1984.

Although the SABC is not a member of the Media Council, the enquiry was held in terms of section 1(5) of the Council's constitution, whereby the Council undertakes to consider and enquire into reports in the media by non-members of the Newspaper Press Union where matters of importance to the public are concerned. After viewing the programme twice and considering all the evidence, the Council found that the programme had exceeded the bounds of fairness and balance in that the Jockey Club had not been afforded the opportunity of refuting the statements against it. The Council's report was published on 12 April 1984 and an apology to the Jockey Club was broadcast by the SABC on the *Midweek* programme of 18 April 1984. Although the Corporation specifically stated in its apology that the apology was not the result of the findings of the Media Council, it is apparent that the publicity given to the Media Council's report played a part in prompting the Corporation to broadcast an apology.

Economic control

Although the press is recognised as the champion of the rights and freedoms of the individual, the press industry is first and foremost a commercial enterprise which aims at making a financial profit. As a result, the press is subject to the financial and economic restraints of a business striving to make a profit, which in turn has the effect of limiting or restricting the freedom of the press.

Since advertising plays an essential role in maintaining the profitability of a newspaper, it may very often determine the political policy of the newspaper in question, as advertisers consider the editorial policy of the newspaper before placing their advertisements. In order to attract advertisers a newspaper must have a reasonably high circulation. This circulation figure and reasonable advertising rates determine the advertising placed with a particular newspaper. A healthy advertising market is essential to a

245

newspaper's profitability, since advertising is its primary source of revenue.

The accuracy of circulation figures is extremely important to advertisers, because an advertiser obviously wants to promote his product to as large a consumer readership as possible. The importance of this accuracy became apparent in the dispute between Perskor and Nasionale Pers Beperk. Nasionale Pers instituted a R12 million claim against Perskor as compensation for its having fraudulently inflated the circulation figures of *Die Transvaler* and *Die Vaderland* for the period January to June 1980. Nasionale Pers eventually withdrew its claim for compensation in exchange for certain concessions by Perskor, viz the closing down of two Pretoria newspapers owned by Perskor and the transfer of *Die Transvaler*, which was a Johannesburg morning newspaper, to Pretoria, where it was to appear as an afternoon edition. This agreement has secured the monopoly of the Afrikaans morning newspaper market for Nasionale Pers.[146]

The price war between Argus group and SAAN — i.e. between *The Star*, *The Sunday Star* and *The Sunday Express* — illustrates the importance of advertising further. This is also illustrated by Perskor's approach to advertising in the recent election, when it informed its rural newspapers in Pietersburg and Middelburg that they need not support the National Party editorially and that they could accept advertisements from opposition parties. Perskor had previously refused to publish Progressive Federal Party advertisements on the grounds that it would be unethical to publish advertisements conflicting with the newspaper's editorial stance.

Apart from the possibility that freedom of the press may be limited in the pursuit of advertising custom, there are a number of other restrictions which limit the freedom of the press via the 'law' of advertising. There are statutory restrictions such as the Trade Practices Act, 1967 (Act 76 of 1967), common law restrictions known as 'unlawful competition' and restrictions of a voluntary nature, viz the voluntary subjection of the press to the body known as the Advertising Standards Authority of South Africa. This body has laid down a code of advertising practice, its purpose being to ensure that the public and the consumer are protected from dishonest and fraudulent trading practice.

Labour control

The printing industry and newspapers are subject to the provisions of labour law. For example, labour law exerts control over press activity in the sphere of the individual employment relationship between the editor and the publisher through the terms of their contract. The editor is contractually bound to adhere to a certain editorial policy where this has been stipulated in his employment contract. This means that he may not publish

246

any article or editorial which conflicts with this approach and if he does so, he breaches the contract.

Collective labour law, which regulates the relationship and collective bargaining between unions and employers' organisations, may limit the freedom of the press in the sphere of 'closed shop' provisions. The basic terms of a closed shop provision are that an employee is compelled to join a specific union if he wishes to obtain employment with an employer or within an industry and that he must remain a member of the union whilst he is so employed. The specific section of the Labour Relations Amendment Act, 1982 (Act 51 of 1982) is extremely complicated, but is to the effect that certain employers are prohibited from continuing to employ certain employees. There is one registered trade union in the press industry, viz the South African Typographical Union, as well as a number of unregistered trade unions, viz the South African Society of Journalists (SASJ), the Media Workers' Association of South Africa (MWASA), the Magazine Publishers' Association of South Africa and the South African Printing and Allied Industries.

A dispute between an unregistered trade union, SASJ, and the Argus and SAAN groups came before the Industrial Court in February 1983. In this case, *Bleazard & Others v Argus Printing & Publishing Co Ltd & Others*,[147] the Industrial Court decided that in certain circumstances employers may be ordered to bargain in 'good faith' with a union.

Monopolies

The Maintenance and Promotion of Competition Act, 1979 (Act 96 of 1979)[148] regulates *inter alia* the promotion and maintenance of competition in the economy and prevents and controls restrictive practice and the acquisition of controlling interests in business and undertakings. During 1973 the Government thwarted an attempted take-over of a majority shareholding of South African Associated Newspapers (the SAAN group) by the Argus group. The Government was opposed to the take-over because it would create a monopolistic situation and, as a consequence, the Argus group relinquished its board representation on and its rights in SAAN on all matters excepting those relating to finance.

As has already been mentioned, the recent dispute between Nasionale Pers Beperk and Perskor has, in effect, left Nasionale Pers Beperk with the monopoly of the Afrikaans morning newspapers. Jim Bailey's recent sale of a Black newspaper and two Black periodicals has also limited freedom of the press, as these publications are now controlled by a company which supports the Nationalist Party and it can hardly be imagined that strong criticism of Government activity will be the order of the day.

CONCLUSION

The South African Government has repeatedly stated that the press in South Africa is free. Although this statement is essentially true — in the sense that prior censorship of news is not the order of the day — it is also true that South African reporters and editors are obliged to exercise a great deal of self-censorship in order to avoid prosecution under the numerous statutes which impinge upon press freedom. This self-censorship may very often be attributed to wide legislative provisions which do not define prohibited criminal conduct clearly. As a result, the press has adopted a cautious approach to the reporting of matters relating to the security of the State, the defence of the Republic, police and prison matters, etc. This caution has had the effect of depriving the public of a great deal of current news and information of national importance.

As we have seen in the discussion above, some of the most stringent restrictions on the press emanate from legislation and the question is how the conflicting interests of press freedom and other factors such as State security may be reconciled. The ideal situation would be for the press to have unrestricted access to all news and information, but as we have seen this is not always the position.

It is submitted that press freedom could best be reconciled with other conflicting interests by rationalising (and in some instances repealing) a number of statutory provisions. This statement is best illustrated by reference to security legislation.

The best method of reconciling freedom of the press with the conflicting interests of security of the State is to ensure that the legal object protected by the legislative measure, viz the protection of the State from internal and external attack, is the object protected and the only objective pursued. The State has the right to ensure its safety and a duty to protect its subjects from revolution and violence and the provisions of the Internal Security Act, for example, should be directed towards ensuring the security of the State and the maintenance of law and order. The objective should not be the protection of some other object such as the prevention of the publication of information which criticises or embarrasses the Government.

The prosecution of the editor of *The Star* for a contravention of section 56 (1)(p) of the Internal Security Act may serve as an example. This section, which prohibits the quoting of a 'banned' person by any means whatsoever, resulted in the prosecution in question. The prosecution related to the publication of no more than 20 words uttered by a banned person in reply to questions put to him about an interview which the SABC allegedly intended having with him. Since the object behind the prohibition on the quoting of a banned person must surely be to prevent the publication and dissemination of his political views and objectives, prosecution for a statement unrelated to any political event is not acceptable. The total ban on all statements by a banned person is contrary to the legal object behind the statutory measure and the ban should relate to statements of a political nature only.

A further example which may be quoted to illustrate the point that the press is very often silenced on matters of national importance concerns section 4 of the Petroleum Products Act. As has already been shown, the press was not in a position to publish details of the Salem Affair and the resulting fraud when the event occurred, since the Act prohibits the disclosure of information relating to the acquisition or transport of petro-leum products. At the time in question (1983) the Government stated that it was not in the national interest to disclose the information, despite the fact that the fraud had been exposed and was common knowledge in the outside world.

It is suggested that security and other legislation restricting the freedom of the press should be closely scrutinised by the legislature with a view to amendment and abolition where necessary. Easing the restrictions upon press freedom and providing the press with greater access to information would put it in a better position to exercise its function in the democratic process, i.e. the provision of social and individual needs of an educational, informative, cultural, etc nature, the provision of an information service, surveillance over Government activity and assistance in the protection of the rights and freedoms of the individual.

It is conceded that it is not only restrictions in the interests of the State which curtail freedom of the press, since economic restrictions and restrictions in the interests of the individual also limit press freedom. The press is at liberty to publish information regarding individuals and social groups, providing that rights to reputation, honour, dignity and privacy, etc are respected. In the event of a claim for defamation, the press may rely on the defence of truth and public interest, but our courts have adopted the requirements of strict liability in respect of private law defamatory state-ments by the press. No doubt the rationale behind this approach is the protection of the individual, as he is in an inferior position *vis-à-vis* the press and strict liability prevents the press from avoiding liability by raising mistake as a defence.

The present political climate in South Africa and the increasing demands of the unenfranchised are such that an active and ongoing debate on political issues and Government activity is essential. The press is one of the institutions (by virtue of its economic structure and its personnel) best-equipped to provide a forum for this debate. The new constitutional dispensation also highlights the importance of a free press. The Government has stated repeatedly that the 1983 Constitution is based on consensus. This consensus on legislative and other matters will be obtained via negotiations and discussions at committee level. Committee members must be constantly aware of the views of the diverse social and population groups and it is here that the press plays an important role, since it is in a position to canvass and discuss these diverse views and to provide comment and criticism on proposed Government activity. In this way the public is kept informed of proposed legislative and Government activity and Members of Parliament and committee members are kept in touch with prevailing public opinion.

In conclusion it must be pointed out that a more open society in which individual, social and political issues and issues relating to Government activity are canvassed and discussed openly, will strengthen democratic principles such as the support and protection of individual rights, liberties and freedoms. The greater the area of criticism and the freer the exchange of ideas, the more open the society. The more open the society, the stronger the democracy.

NOTES

1 *Simonlanga and Others v Masinga and Others* 1976 2 SA 732 (W).
2 *Supra* at 740.
3 *S v Turrell and Others* 1973 1 SA 248 (C). See too *Publications Control Board v William Heinemann Ltd & Others* 1965 4 SA 137 (A).
4 See J Neethling 'Enkele Gedagtes oor die juridiese aard en inhoud van menseregte en fundamentele vryhede' (1971) 34 *THRHR* 240.
5 Wiechers (1984: 80). See too Van der Vyver, JD. *Die Juridiese Sin van die Leerstuk van Menseregte*. Pretoria: 1973. (Ongepubliseerde tesis.)
6 See Potter (1975: 38 and 66). See too South Africa (Republic). Commision of Inquiry into the Mass Media. (Chairman: MT Steyn.) *Report*. Pretoria: Government Printer, 1981. (RP 89/81). (Steyn Report.)
7 Steyn Report, *op cit* 970.
8 The Argus group eventually withdrew the application for registration of these two newspapers. See *Argus Printing and Publishing Co Ltd v Minister of Internal Affairs* 1981 (2) SA 391 (W).
9 7 *BVerfGE* 198 (1958), 20 *BVerfGE* 162 at 174 (1966).
10 10 *BVerfGE* 118 at 121 (1959).
11 *Schneider v New Jersey* 308 US 147 (1939), *Douglas v City of Jeannette* 130F 2d 652 (1942).
12 *Pennekamp v Florida* 328 US 331 (1945).
13 *New York Times v Sullivan* 376 US 254, 266 (1964).
14 Private ownership is considered essential to avoid political pressure being exerted on a particular newspaper, Hall, S. Newspaper, Parties and Classes in *The British Press: A Manifesto*.
15 The Act consolidates existing security legislation, namely the Internal Security Act, 1950 (Act 44 of 1950), the Criminal Law Amendment Act, 1953 (Act 8 of 1953), the Riotous Assemblies Act, 1956 (Act 17 of 1956), the Unlawful Organisations Act, 1960 (Act 34 of 1960), the General Law Amendment Act, 1962 (Act 76 of 1962) and the Terrorism Act, 1967 (Act 83 of 1967).

16 S 16 requires that a consolidated list be published in the *Government Gazette* at regular intervals in order that a list of office bearers, office members, or supporters of unlawful organisations, persons convicted of sedition or treason, persons restricted to certain places and persons whose names have appeared on a list referred to in s 8 of the Internal Security Act may be compiled and up-dated. The Act prohibits the recording or reproduction (by mechanical or other means) and the printing, publishing or dissemination of any speech, utterance, writing or statement (or extract therefrom) by any person whose name appears on the consolidated list, except for the purposes of court proceedings or where the Minister of Law and Order consents thereto — s 56(1)(*p*).

17 S 54.

18 S 19.

19 S 56 read with s 20 relates to persons who endanger the security of the State, or whose names appear on the consolidated list; or who cause, encourage or foment feelings of hostility between the various population groups.

20 S 23(1). The Minister may prohibit the publication or dissemination of speeches by persons whom he believes endanger the security of the State or the maintenance of law and order, or who are involved in communist activity.

21 S 28.

22 See *S v Ravan Press (Pty) Ltd & Others* 1976 1 SA 929 (T).

23 S 5(1).

24 S 6(1).

25 S 57(1)(*b*).

26 S 89(1). A military area includes a military camp barracks, dockyard, installation or other premises of any land or area of water used for military or defence purposes, or which is under military control.

27 Dated 17 September 1980. Agreements between these bodies have existed since 1967 and their inefficacy is clearly illustrated by referring to the South African invasion of Angola during the 1970s. The Defence Force did not impart this news to the South African media, despite the fact that reports of the attack had been published in overseas newspapers. The Defence Force declined to comment on the matter when approached by the media.

28 Clause 6.2.1.

29 S 118(1)(*a*). In terms of this section, the word 'publish' bears its 'ordinary' meaning, namely 'to make publicly or generally known'. This is made clear by the list of publications referred to and the words 'or any other means must be interpreted' *eiusdem generis. S v du Plessis* 1981 3 SA 382 (A) at 403.

30 The word 'calculated' has been interpreted by the courts as a reasonable probability that the statement, commentary or rumour will alarm the public or cause it to be dejected. See *Minister van Verdediging v John Meinert (Edms) Bpk* 1976 4 SA 113 (SWA).

31 S 118(1)(*b*).

32 S 118(3).

33 S 118(2).

34 Prohibited place does not relate to a military establishment only, but includes factories, dockyards, camps, ships, vessels or aircraft, telegraphy, telephone and radio stations, etc. S 1.

35 Ss 2 and 3(*a*).

36 S 3(*b*). A hostile organisation is one declared so by Parliament or in terms of s 14 of the Act.

37 S 4. Security matter is defined as any matter which is dealt with by the National Intelligence Service or which relates to the functions of that service or to the relationship existing between any person and that Service.

38 S 27A(*a*) and (*b*). See *S v Perskorporasie van Suid-Afrika Beperk* 1979 4 SA 476 (T), which dealt with the publication of a prisoner's photograph prior to the commencement of his trial. The Commissioner of Police may consent to the sketching or photographing of persons referred to in s 27 or the publication of sketches or photographs.

39 It is submitted that the word 'publishes' bears the same connotation as in the law of defamation, viz that communication to one person will not suffice and 'publish' will thus mean communicating with the public generally.

40 No prosecution may be instituted in terms of this section without the written consent of the Attorney-General concerned. S 27B(2).

41 *S v SAAN* 1962 3 SA 396 (T).

42 S 44(1)(e)(i) and (ii).

43 S 44(1)(e)(iii) and (iv).

44 S 1.

45 *Supra* at 398.

46 See *S v SAAN ibid.* The term 'prisoner' includes a person serving a death sentence, or a person declared a President's patient who is being detained in custody within or outside any prison, and the corpse of any such person mentioned — s 1.

47 1970 1 SA 469 (W).

48 The court found *inter alia* that those steps which a reasonable and prudent man in similar circumstances would have taken to ensure the accuracy of the information must be taken; that regard should be had for the character and history of the information and the nature of the information, etc. *Id* at 479-480.

49 Total secrecy relating to prison conditions cannot be justified on the basis of the interest of State security or the defence of strategic positions and the question must be asked whether it is not on the grounds of expediency that prison conditions are clothed in secrecy.

50 92 of 1982. This Act *inter alia* prohibits the disclosure of information relating to reserves of ores and information relating to source materials, etc.

51 102 of 1980. This Act, which was promulgated after the terrorist attacks at Silverton, Sasol, Secunda, Natref and Booysens, provides for the declaring of certain areas as 'national key points' with the object of safeguarding these areas.

52 120 of 1977. The Act provides measures to conserve petroleum products as well as the control of information regarding these products.

53 57 of 1968. The Act prohibits the disclosure of any information relating to the acquisition, supply, marketing, importation, export, development, manufacture, maintenance or repair of, or research in connection with armaments, by, for, or on behalf of the Armaments Corporation (or subsidiary), without written authority by the minister in question.

54 89 of 1970. The principal and amending Acts deal with the stockpiling of strategic commodities and the disclosure of information relating to goods or services.

55 72 of 1982. Any person who compels or induces a particular person to do or refrain from doing any act, or to assume or abandon a particular standpoint, and who assaults or injures or causes damage to such person, or threatens to kill, assault or injure or cause damage to such person, is guilty of an offence under the Act. See *S v Mohapi en Andere* 1984 1 SA 270 (O), in which the court found that, in regard to persons, the word 'particular' points to definite and specific persons and not to a large number of persons. The court found that the Internal Security Act covers intimidation of the general public or of a large group of people.

56 118 of 1979. This Act relates to the investigation by the Advocate-General of the dishonest use or misappropriation of public funds. The Advocate-General may recommend that publication of the content of his report be prohibited where he is of the opinion that its publication is not in the interests of State security. The effect hereof is that his report is laid before the House of Assembly as a confidential paper. Although the purpose behind the Act is to provide for the investigation of the dishonest use of public monies, it is apparent that unless the Advocate-General co-operates with the press in providing information, the press will not be in a position to comment on such matters. Had the Advocate-General Act been in operation at the time of the Information Scandal, for example, the Advocate-General could legally have ensured that the entire affair be kept secret.

57 71 of 1982.

58 See PMA Hunt in *South African Criminal Law and Procedure*, vol. II. See too *S v Gibson NO & Others* 1979 4 SA 115 at 120.

59 S 2 of the Powers and Privileges of Parliament Act, 1963 (Act 91 of 1963) provides that there shall be freedom of speech and debate on proceedings before Parliament and any committee and that such freedom shall not be liable to impeachment or question in any

court or place outside Parliament. See R v Torch Printing and Publishing Co Ltd & Others 1956 1 SA 815 (C) at 821.

60 See In re Blanch & Richardson 1882 1 HCG 83 at 90; Dempster v Robinson 1907 28 NLR 128 at 133; Makiwame v Die Afrikaanse Pers Beperk en 'n Ander 1957 (2) SA 560 (W) at 562.
61 Supra at 121.
62 See R v Robberts 1959 3 SA 706 (SWA); S v Tromp 1966 1 SA 646 (N).
63 Makapan v Khope 1923 AD 551.
64 Erasmus and Others NNO v SA Associated Newspapers Ltd 1979 3 SA 447 (W); Smalberger and Another v Cape Times Ltd and Others 1979 3 SA 457 (C) and S v Sparks NO & Others 1980 3 SA 952 (T).
65 Supra at 456.
66 Supra 959-961.
67 R v Magerman 1960 1 SA 184 (O). Disobedience which occurs in the same building, not far from the court, will not constitute contempt in facie curiae — Louw v Verster NO 1962 PH F101 (O). Section 108 of the Magistrate's Court Act 32 of 1944 lists three species of contempt in facie curiae, viz insults, interruptions and misbehaviour and this list may be extended to the common law in other courts. See Hunt, op cit 197.
68 In Afrikaanse Pers-Publikasies Bpk en 'n Ander v Mbeki 1964 4 SA 618 (A), the court decided that the proceedings are not pending when a person has been taken into custody for interrogation and not as a step in lawfully commenced proceedings which would terminate in an eventual trial.
69 Ibid.
70 Makiwame v Afrikaanse Pers Beperk en 'n Ander supra.
71 S v Van Niekerk 1972 3 SA 711 (A).
72 S v Van Niekerk supra.
73 See J Dugard 'Judges, Academics and Unjust Laws. The Van Niekerk Contempt Case' (1972) 89 SALJ 271.
74 Rand Daily Mail, 7/2/1983.
75 The extensive press coverage given to the assassination of Dr Verwoerd by Demitrio Tsafendas, despite the fact that criminal proceedings would obviously be instituted in the future, may be justified on the ground of public interest. In this instance public interest outweighed the consideration that the proceedings would be prejudiced and would, in effect, amount to contempt of court.
76 Hunt, op cit 202. See too S v Oliver 1964 3 SA 660 (N).
77 In S v Van Niekerk supra, the court found that the true basis of punishment for contempt of court lies in the interest of the public as distinct from the protection of any particular judge or judges.
78 Personality rights are those rights which are closely tied up with the legal subject as a person, e.g. the right to his good name, the right to dignity and honour and the right to privacy.
79 SA Uitsaaikorporasie v O'Malley 1977 3 SA 394 (A) at 402. See too Suttonmere (Pty) Ltd and Another v Hills 1982 2 SA 74 (N).
80 SA Associated Newspapers Ltd v Schoeman 1962 2 SA 613 (A); SA Uitsaaikorporasie v O'Malley supra; Coulson v Rapport Uitgewers (Edms) Bpk 1979 3 SA 286 (A); SA Associated Newspapers Ltd v Samuels 1980 1 SA 24 (A); and Marais v Richard en 'n Ander 1981 1 SA 1157 (A).
81 Prinsloo v SA Associated Newspapers Ltd 1959 2 SA 693 (W) at 659.
82 Schoeman v SA Associated Newspapers 1962 1 PH J714 (T); Gelb v Hawkins 1960 3 SA 687 (A); Channing v SA Financial Gazette 1966 3 SA 470 (W); Kritzinger v Perskorporasie van SA (Edms) Bpk 1981 2 SA 373 (O).
83 Church of Scientology in SA Incorporated Association not for Gain and Another v Reader's Digest Association SA (Pty) Ltd 1980 4 SA 313 (C).
84 Aail (SA) v Muslim Judicial Council 1983 4 SA 855 (C).
85 Die Spoorbond v SAR 1946 AD 999, Pelser v SA Associated Newspapers Ltd and Another 1975 1 SA 34 (N).

86 1977 4 SA 371 (T).

87 1979 1 SA 441 (A).

88 See *Kritzinger v Perskorporasie van Suid-Afrika supra*, in which the court did not place too much reliance on the fact that relatively few copies of the newspaper had been distributed.

89 Strauss, Strydom en Van der Walt (1976: 229). Repetition or re-publication of defamatory statements give rise to further causes of action for defamation. *Mograbi v Miller* 1956 4 SA 239 (T).

90 *Potter v Badenhorst* 1968 4 SA 446 (E).

91 *Ibid.*

92 *Hill v Curlewis* and Brand 1844 Menzies 520.

93 *Supra*

94 1982 3 SA 146 (A).

95 *Id* at 156.

96 See Coenraad Visser 'Valediction of a Chief Justice, Strict Liability of the press for defamation' (1983) *SALJ* 3 at 9.

97 See Visser, *op cit* 105.

98 Strauss, Strydom en Van der Walt (1976: 264). See too *Johnson v Rand Daily Mail* 1928 AD 190 and *Smit v OVS Afrikaanse Pers Bpk* 1956 1 SA (O).

99 Strauss, Strydom en Van der Walt (1976: 271).

100 *Murdock and Another v Ellis and Others* 1955 2 PH J18 D72.

101 *Hearson v Natal Witness Ltd and Another* 1935 NPD 603. See too *Benson v Robinson and Co (Pty) Ltd and Another* 1967 1 SA 420A, which dealt with the question whether a newspaper report regarding the procedure of a foreign parliament was privileged or not.

102 *Smith & Co v SA Newspapers Co* (1906) 23 SC 310.

103 *Marais v Richard & Another supra* at 1167.

104 *S v Gibson NO & Others supra.*

105 Neethling, J. in *Persoonlikheidsreg* relies on *O'Keeffe v Argus Printing & Publishing Co* 1954 3 SA 244 (C) as authority for his view that *dignitas* includes all personality rights worthy of protection, with the exception of *corpus* and *fama*, which have emerged as specifically defined and demarcated rights. See too *S v A* 1971 2 SA 293 (T), in which the court found that *dignitas* is wide enough to include a right to privacy. *Dignitas* may thus be seen as a collective name for a number of personality rights which are as yet undefined, but which include the right to privacy.

106 *Supra.*

107 *Kidson & Others v SA Associated Newspapers Ltd* 1957 3 SA 461 (W).

108 1958 1 SA 370 (W) at 373. See too *Mr & Mrs 'X' v Rhodesia Printing & Publishing Co Ltd* 1974 4 SA 508; *R v A supra* and *Ramsay v Minister van Polisie en Andere* 1981 4 SA 802 (A).

109 *Universiteit van Pretoria v Tommie Meyer Films (Edms) Bpk supra* at 387.

110 See Hunt, *op cit* 536, where he says that although *dignitas* is a somewhat vague and elusive concept, it can broadly be described in terms of a person's right to self-respect, mental tranquility and privacy.

111 The distinction between copyright and rights of personality has tended to blur as a result of the recognition of a copyright holder's rights of personality. See Neethling, 'Outeursreg en Persoonlikheidsregte: 'n Teoretiese Analise met Verwysing na Outeursregbevoegdhede in die Suid-Afrikaanse Reg' (1975) 38 *THRHR* 333 in this regard.

112 See *Natal Picture Framing Co Ltd v Levin* 1920 WLD 35, in which the court found that the idea represented has an important bearing on the question whether one artistic work is a copy or imitation of another.

113 S 2(1). See *Kalamazoo Division (Pty) Ltd v Gay & Others* 1978 2 SA 184 (C). The originality refers to original skill or labour in execution, not to original thought or expression of thought.

114 Copeling (1978: par. 15). See *Goeie Hoop Uitgewers (Edms) Bpk v Central News Agency and Another* 1953 2 SA 843 (W).

115 A literary work, irrespective of literary quality and the mode of expression, includes

novels, stories and poetic works, dramatic works, stage directions, cinematographic film, scenarios and broadcasting works, textbooks, treatises, histories, biographies, essays and articles, encyclopaedias and dictionaries, letters, reports and memoranda, lectures, addresses and sermons and written tables and compilations. S 1(1).

116 Artistic works, irrespective of the artistic quality, include paintings, sculptures, drawings, engravings and photographs, works of architecture and works of artistic craftmanship. S 1(1).
117 S 23. This infringement of copyright may also take the form of importation, selling or distribution of a work without the consent of the owner. See too Copeling op cit par. 23.
118 S 12(1).
119 S 12(2).
120 S 12(6).
121 S 12 (7).
122 S 12(8)(a).
123 S 21(1)(b).
124 See Stuart, op cit 204.
125 Ibid.
126 1978 3 SA 836 (T).
127 See Publications Appeal Board (PAB) 43/82 (Heartland).
128 S 154(3) of the Criminal Procedure Act 51 of 1977. See too S v Citizen Newspapers (Pty) Ltd en 'n Ander. S v Perskorporasie van SA Bpk en 'n Ander 1981 4 SA 18 (A).
129 S 154(1) Act 51 of 1977. See too Stuart, op cit 149.
130 S 153(3).
131 Act 74 of 1982. S 154 of the Criminal Procedure Act also provides for the protection of a person's identity where the presiding officer is of the opinion that the proceedings should be held behind closed doors in the interests of State security, good order, public morals, or the administration of justice.
132 Ss 1 and 2 Act 63 of 1971. See S v Davidson & Bernhardt Promotions (Pty) Ltd & Others 1983 1 SA 676 (T).
133 S 15 of Act 74 of 1982.
134 The object behind these requirements appears to be to enable the authorities to scrutinise the particulars furnished and to ensure that the application is genuinely directed towards the establishment of a newspaper.
135 S 15(4). This is borne out by the fact that the proprietor of the newspaper runs the risk of forfeiting the deposit where the minister finds it necessary to prohibit the newspaper in terms of s 5 of the Internal Security Act.
136 S 15(5). See Argus Printing & Publishing Co Ltd v Minister of Internal Affairs 1981 2 SA 391 (W).
137 Ss 8 and 9.
138 S 8. No prosecution may be instituted unless the publication or object has been declared undesirable by a committee, the period of appeal has expired and the Attorney-General has consented thereto in writing. S 8(4).
139 1978 4 SA 389 (A).
140 1983 3 SA 382 (T).
141 Franklin J assumed, without deciding, that for purposes of the judgment, proof of mens rea in the form of dolus was a requirement.
142 S 8(1)(b). In S v Potgieter 1983 4 SA 270 (N), the court found that mens rea was essential in order to secure a conviction under this section.
143 S 8(1)(d). See S v Cleminshaw 1981 3 SA 685 (C).
144 S 8(1)(e).
145 This approach is substantiated by the large number of appeals initiated by the Directorate against findings of non-desirability by various committees. See for example, PAB 1/83, 2/83 (The Girls of Stag and Stag).
146 Over and above the delictual claim for compensatory damages, a criminal charge was laid against Perskor for fraudulently inflating the circulation figures of the two newspapers. The court imposed a fine of R20 000 against Perskor.

147 Industrial Law Journal including Industrial Law Reports 1983 vol. 4 Part 1, 60.
148 Act 96 of 1979.

BIBLIOGRAPHY

Copeling, AJ. *Copyright and the Act of 1978*. Durban: Butterworths, 1978.

Curran, J (Ed.) *The British Press: A Manifesto*. London: Macmillan, 1978.

De Kock, W. *A Manner of Speaking*. Cape Town: Saayman and Weber, 1982.

Dicey, AV. *Introduction to the Study of the Law of the Constitution*. 10th ed. London: Macmillan & Co Ltd, 1965.

Dugard, J. *Human Rights and the South African Legal Order*. Princeton, New Jersey: Princeton University Press, 1978.

Hammond-Tooke, WD. (Ed.) *The Bantu-speaking Peoples of Southern Africa*. 2nd ed. London: Routlege and Kegan Paul Ltd, 1974

Joubert, WA. *Grondslae van die Persoonlikheidsreg*. Kaapstad: AA Balkema, 1953.

Mathews, AS. *Law, Order and Liberty in South Africa*. Cape Town: Juta, 1971.

Milton, JRL (Ed.) *South African Criminal Law and Procedure*. vol. II, 2nd ed. Cape Town: Juta, 1982.

Neethling, J. *Persoonlikheidsreg*. Durban: Butterworth, 1979.

Potter, E. *The Press as Opposition: The Political role of South African Newspapers*. London: Chatto & Windus, 1975.

Strauss, SA, Strydom, MJ en Van der Walt, JC. *Die Suid-Afrikaanse Persreg*. 3de uitg. Pretoria: Van Schaik Bpk, 1976.

Stuart, KW. *The Newspaperman's Guide to the Law*. 3rd ed. Durban: Butterworth, 1982.

Van der Vyver, JD. *Seven Lectures on Human Rights*. Cape Town: Juta, 1976.

Van Tonder, SIE, Badenhorst, NP, Volschenk, CH en Wepener, JN. *Die Uitleg van Wette*. Kaapstad: Juta, 1981.

Wiechers, M. *Administratiefreg*. 2de uitg. Pretoria: Butterworth, 1984.

Williams, F. *The Right to Know: The Rise of the World Press*. London: Longman's, 1969.

10 Sport and change in South Africa

JL Olivier

INTRODUCTION

The importance of sport in society has increased considerably since the beginning of the century. Various factors, of which the following seem to be the most important, have contributed to this:

- Industrialisation with concomitant urbanisation
- Increased prosperity which results in the individual having more spare time
- The extent of the development of the sports industry
- The extent to which sport has been politicised.

Since 1900, sport has been increasingly politicised and has become an important bargaining instrument in the hands of interested groups. Loy et al (1978: 288) stated the following on the relation between sport and politics: '. . . sport is definitely not apolitical, nor is politics free of sport'. Anderson (1979: 6) is of the opinion that 'the survival of sport is dependent on its acceptance of this politicisation'.

The sporting event that illustrates the politicisation of sport most forcibly is probably the Olympic Games. Today almost no Olympic Games takes place without being marred by political incidents. South African sport became one of the first victims (both internationally and locally) of the politicisation of sport.

South Africa's internal policy, traditionally known as apartheid, was formally established in 1948. This policy had implications for all aspects of society, including the way in which South Africans could practise their sport. The policy of no contact between Whites and other population groups (Blacks, Indians and Coloureds) was strictly applied until the end of the sixties. Since 1967, however, there has been a gradual move away from strict apartheid to a more flexible approach, which has resulted in members of the various population groups making increasing contact with one another both on and off the sports field. However, the first steps in this

257

direction were taken on the sports field. A distinct move away from apartheid sport as it was practised until the end of the sixties, towards non-racial sport, which is generally accepted in South Africa today, took place. However, the implementation of non-racial sport was to have implications reaching much further than the sports field.

The aim of this chapter is to place the development of non-racial sport in historical perspective and to determine what served as the impetus to change. Some remarks about the implications of non-racial sport for South African society in general will also be made.

FROM APARTHEID SPORT TO NON-RACIAL SPORT

The development of South Africa's sports policy may be divided into three distinct phases, namely the periods 1900 to 1956, 1956 to 1967 and 1967 to 1980 (Scholtz 1983: 124-132).

The establishment of an ideology

The period 1900 to 1956 was characterised politically by the rise of Afrikaner nationalism, which led to the development of group cohesion amongst the Afrikaans-speaking Whites who had been dominated by the British at the turn of the century and, ultimately, to the National Party's political victory in 1948 and the formation of the Republic in 1961.

White perceptions of other population groups in South Africa during this period should also be seen in a historical context. Social contact between Whites and Blacks especially, the consequence of Jan van Riebeeck's establishment of a refreshment station at the Cape in 1652, resulted in each race developing distinct perceptions of each other. The Whites' perception was of people who were heathen, uncivilised, inferior labourers, poor and battling to survive. The Blacks saw the Whites as Christian, civilised, superior labourers, rich and successful in their self-preservation. By 1800 these differences had become associated with race and the colour of a person's skin came to be of crucial importance. In the course of time these perceptions developed into traditional stereotypes and today differences in economic and social status, religion, labour competition and literacy are to a large extent linked with the colour of an individual's skin. The White man saw himself as the guardian of the Non-White groups. This implied that Whites should take certain decisions on behalf of Blacks, guarantee them certain freedoms and privileges and handle certain matters for them.

The rise of Afrikaner nationalism, together with a particular perception of Non-Whites, had definite implications for the way in which South Africans would practise their sport. Although sports events in which members of the different race groups participated occurred during this period, such occasions were the exception rather than the rule. Anderson (1979) is of the opinion that by 1920 an unofficial colour bar was already being established. 'Interracial sport was still played, but with the concurrent development of White Afrikaner nationalism interracial contact decreased' (Anderson 1979: 36).

The victory of the National Party in 1948 established the apartheid ideology formally. Up to that time apartheid had been the traditional way in which sport was practised, but it did not have official status. Anderson (1979: 60) described the effect of the National Party's victory on politics and inevitably on sport in South Africa as follows: 'The election to power in 1948 of the Nationalist Party saw racial discrimination given reality. Legislation was enacted to propagate an ideology of segregation of the races. Sport as had been its destiny since earlier times, followed party policy.'

The development of a sports policy

The first of a series of policy statements that was to have an effect on sport was made in 1956 by the then Minister of Internal Affairs, Dr TE Dönges. The practical implication of this policy statement was that the successful sportsman could progress until he became champion of his own population group. Blacks, Indians and Coloureds, however, could not become their country's champions or representatives. That privilege was reserved for Whites only. This policy was confirmed on 4 February 1964 by the new Minister of Internal Affairs, Senator Jan de Klerk, and on 4 September 1965 by the then Prime Minister, Dr HF Verwoerd.

Changes in sports policy

Although the first changes in South African sports policy were introduced in 1967 by the then Prime Minister, Mr BJ Vorster, it was only in the second half of the seventies that noteworthy changes occurred and gained momentum.

Within a period of ten years, South Africa's sports policy changed from a strict apartheid approach to one which recognised the autonomy of sports bodies and allowed them to decide for themselves who they wished to admit to their clubs.

In 1978 Springbok colours were awarded to a Black athlete for the first time. In the same year the Minister of Sport and Recreation, Dr Piet Koornhof, announced that in future there would be no impediment to any sportsman/woman competing at any level or becoming a member of any club.

259

During the first nine months of 1978 there were 2 615 mixed sporting events, of which 2 325 were at club level, 178 at provincial level, 68 at national level and 44 at international level. There are no statistics available since that date, as mixed sport has become an everyday event.

The stimulus to change

From the fifties onwards, international and internal resistance to South Africa's domestic policy began to gather momentum. Sport was the ideal instrument by means of which the international community could express its disapproval of South Africa's domestic policy. This disapproval led to boycotts, demonstrations and also to the suspension of South Africa by international sporting bodies. South Africa has not competed in the Olympic Games since 1964 and by 1978 the country had been suspended from 25 international sporting bodies. Demonstrations became a familiar sight to South Africans competing overseas.

The Gleneagles Agreement of 14 July 1977 committed members of the Commonwealth to '. . . a policy of non-involvement in sport in South Africa' (Anderson 1979: 178). In the late seventies South Africa was also subjected to indirect pressure. Individual sportsmen and women, as well as countries which had sporting links with South Africa, were victimised more and more. Mention can be made of the so-called Black List, which contains the names of those sportsmen who have competed against South Africans.

Until the mid-sixties, internal resistance came predominantly from Black sportsmen who felt that they had the right to be considered for national teams and to participate in the administration and control of sport. Various organisations were established to promote their aims. The most important one was the South African Sports Association (SASA), which was established in 1959. SASA was the forerunner of two other organisations, namely the South African Non-Racial Olympic Committee (SAN-ROC), established in 1961 and the South African Council on Sport (SACOS), established in 1973.

Initially, internal resistance came from so-called radical elements, but in the late sixties moderates also started to call for change. White sportsmen played a major part in this. There can be no doubt that internal and external pressures were important factors contributing to change not only in the field of sport, but also in South African society in general.

This pressure also had an effect on public opinion. Since the beginning of the seventies the public's views on sport have changed dramatically.

Attitudes towards non-racial sport

Various investigations of individuals' views on non-racial sport have been undertaken since the late sixties. These include Market Research in Africa (in Anderson 1979) and those of Lotz (1968), Scholtz (1975), Williams (1976), Pretorius (1978) and Rhoodie and Le Roux (1983).

Although the scope of these investigations was limited (samples included Whites only), it is evident from the findings that views on non-racial sport were becoming increasingly liberal.

The first extensive survey involving all population groups was the HSRC Sports Investigation (Report No. 5, 1982). More than 6 000 respondents (1 500 from each of the four population groups) were involved in a country-wide survey and for the first time it became possible to determine the views of Non-Whites (Blacks, Coloureds and Indians) on mixed sport.

In 1983 a follow-up investigation was undertaken as part of the HSRC's investigation into intergroup relations. This survey was also country-wide (N = 4 000) and members of all population groups were involved.

These two investigations led to important insights. Although the emphasis in this contribution is on the findings of the most recent survey, the most important findings of the HSRC Sports Investigation will be mentioned briefly.

Findings of the HSRC Sports Investigation

Overwhelming support for non-racial sport at all levels was found to exist among all population groups.

Attitudes towards mixed sport at national, provincial and club level and applicable to rugby, cricket, soccer, tennis and swimming were determined. The attitude profile of Coloureds, Indians and Blacks was particularly homogeneous: mixed sport was highly acceptable to all these groups. Of the Indians, 90,8% were in favour of mixed sport at all levels for the five types of sport mentioned. The corresponding preferences were 88,2% for Coloureds; 73,7% for Blacks; and 79,9% for Whites. The weighted mean was 78,9%. From the foregoing it is clear that by 1980/81 mixed sport was highly acceptable to the urban population of South Africa. However, some hesitancy was still perceivable amongst Blacks and Whites.

Great heterogeneity was evident in the attitude profile of Whites. Two factors in particular were responsible for this, namely level of participation and home language of respondent. Whereas mixed sport at national level was acceptable to 89,6% of respondents, this figure declined to 83,4% for mixed sport at provincial level and 66,7% as far as club level was concerned. This is a statistically significant drop which was not apparent in the attitudes of the other three population groups. Scholtz (1983) interpreted this finding according to the theories of social distance and ambivalence.

For Whites the three dominant predictors of attitude preference were sex, age and language. Women and older respondents were generally more conservative, whilst Afrikaans-speaking persons were more conservative than English-speaking persons or members of other population groups. However, the general finding was that non-racial sport is acceptable to most Whites.

As far as the normalisation of sport is concerned, that is, the rate at which discrimination in sport is being abolished, only a small minority (11,8%) indicated that the rate was too fast, 38,2% accepted the rate as 'just right' and 49,8% thought that it was too slow. Differences in emphasis were noted among the different population groups. For most Indians and Coloureds (69%) the rate of normalisation in sport was too slow, for 51,2% of the Blacks the rate could be increased and for 37,1% it was acceptable. Whites' attitudes differed considerably; 47,3% considered the rate to be 'just right', 35,9% thought it too slow and to 16,8% it was unacceptable. These data indicate that 83% of Whites were in favour of the normalisation of sport. This figure reflects a great change from the attitude patterns of the late sixties. Sports autonomy, namely the right of clubs and sports bodies to take decisions on sports matters themselves, was quite acceptable to the public. Eighty-five per cent of all urban South Africans supported this view.

Findings of the 1983 investigation

(a) *Mixed sport at national and club level*

From the figures in table 10.1 it is evident that the percentages of persons preferring multiracial sport were fairly high: 59,9% of Whites; 85,9% of Indians; 83,6% of Coloureds; and 76,6% of Blacks.

Indian, Coloured and Black respondents had strong positive feelings towards non-racial sport, irrespective of the level of participation. Coloureds and Indians were especially homogeneous in their attitudes — to them multiracial sport was almost a matter of course. Black respondents found non-racial soccer, rugby and tennis highly acceptable, but were less certain about non-racial swimming, which accounts for the relatively high proportion whose attitudes were either neutral (12%) or negative (17,5%).

Level of participation and type of sport did not seem to play a highly significant role in determining Black respondents' attitude preferences, but did in the case of Whites. The percentages in table 10.1 indicate that Whites preferred non-racial sport at national rather than club level. Their multiracial sports preferences were determined by the degree of intimacy resulting from participation in a particular sport. Attitude preferences declined once the focus changed from soccer and rugby to swimming and tennis. The findings (table 10.1) indicate that in general

Table 10.1 Percentage of respondents in favour of, indifferent to, or opposed to multiracial sport

Level and type of sport	Population group and attitude preference											
	Blacks (N = 956)			Coloureds (N = 787)			Indians (N = 940)			Whites (N = 690)		
	In favour	Neutral	Opposed	In favour	Neutral	Opposed	In favour	Neutral	Opposed	In favour	Neutral	Opposed
National soccer/rugby teams	79,4	6,4	12,5	84,7	3,6	6,4	87,3	5,4	3,2	74,9	10,6	13,3
Club soccer/rugby teams	82,6	7,3	8,8	85,8	5,0	4,4	87,9	5,4	2,7	61,0	14,1	23,3
National tennis teams	81,6	7,5	9,3	84,3	4,8	5,6	88,3	5,4	2,3	70,1	12,5	15,9
Club tennis teams	84,6	6,4	6,6	84,1	6,1	4,5	88,1	6,3	1,9	54,5	15,8	28,1
National swimming teams (men and women)	65,1	12,9	17,8	81,1	6,2	6,6	82,5	7,5	6,0	56,5	11,5	30,0
Club swimming teams (men and women)	66,0	11,5	17,2	81,8	7,0	5,4	81,2	8,3	6,6	42,6	13,9	40,7
Total	76,6	8,7	12,0	83,6	5,5	5,5	85,9	6,4	3,8	59,9	13,1	25,2

263

White respondents were more conservative in their attitudes to non-racial sport than Indian, Coloured and Black respondents, which is in accordance with the findings in 1980/81. A comparison with the data of 1980/81 shows a slight but general regression in attitude preference which is more noticeable among Whites than the other groups. This may be ascribed partly to the structure of the questions in the investigation of 1983 and partly to a swing to a greater degree of conservatism, or to other reasons.

(b) *Mixed sport at school level*

Respondents were asked how they felt about their school-going children competing against sports teams consisting of members of other population groups. (If respondents had no children at school, they had to reply to the questions as if they had.) These mixed situations included athletes competing against White, Coloured and Black school teams and swimming against White, Indian, Coloured and Black school teams. Attitude preferences were measured in terms of the following: 'strongly in favour of, in favour of, indifferent, against, strongly against and do not know'. The results appear in summary in table 10.2. 'Do not know' responses have been left out, but can be calculated by subtracting the applicable percentages from 100.

Indians, Coloureds and Blacks were generally in favour of non-racial sport at school level. Approximately 85% of respondents preferred this, whilst approximately 6% revealed 'indifferent' and 'uninvolved' attitudes. For the rest it was evident that the particular sports situation (athletics and swimming in this case) and degree of concomitant social intimacy had only a slight effect on the attitudes of Indians and Coloureds towards non-racial school sport.

Blacks showed some hesitancy towards non-racial school sport as far as swimming was concerned, but found non-racial athletics at school level highly acceptable. It was also apparent that the attitude profiles of Blacks, Coloureds and Indians with regard to non-racial school sport was basically similar to their attitude profiles concerning non-racial sport at national and club level.

The attitude of Whites towards non-racial sport in schools was, on the other hand, far more reserved than their attitude towards mixed sport at national and club level: 47,5% supported it, 38,6% were indifferent and 1,3% did not know. The high 'indifferent' response indicates that they found it difficult to make a decision. The data in table 10.2 show that in the case of Whites, the level of intimacy associated with a sport contributed to the different responses. About 54% were prepared to accept non-racial school athletics while only

Table 10.2 Percentage of respondents in favour of, indifferent to, or opposed to multiracial school sport

Sports activity and population group involved	Population group and attitude preference											
	Blacks (N = 958)			Coloureds (N = 787)			Indians (N = 942)			Whites (N = 697)		
	In favour	Neutral	Opposed	In favour	Neutral	Opposed	In favour	Neutral	Opposed	In favour	Neutral	Opposed
Athletics against a White school team	89,9	4,0	5,7	84,2	5,3	7,1	89,4	5,4	2,8	91,6	3,9	3,9
Athletics against a Coloured school team	87,7	4,3	7,7	93,0	2,5	1,3	86,0	6,9	4,5	56,7	12,1	30,3
Athletics against an Indian school team	86,4	5,0	7,7	89,7	4,1	2,8	93,5	3,6	1,0	55,7	13,1	30,2
Athletics against a Black school team	94,1	2,5	2,6	85,3	5,9	5,1	83,5	7,1	6,8	49,3	12,1	37,4
Swimming against a White school team	79,2	8,2	10,5	83,7	5,6	7,5	85,8	7,4	3,8	88,7	4,7	5,9
Swimming against an Indian school team	78,7	8,6	10,9	91,4	3,7	1,9	91,8	4,0	2,1	42,2	13,2	42,8
Swimming against a Coloured school team	79,3	9,2	9,9	89,7	3,3	3,5	83,5	8,2	5,4	43,2	12,5	43,4
Swimming against a Black school team	91,4	4,2	3,3	84,2	6,1	5,8	79,8	8,3	8,9	37,6	12,3	48,2
Total (other and own groups) Total (other groups)	85,8 83,5	5,8 6,6	7,3 8,7	87,7 86,4	4,6 5,9	4,4 5,0	86,7 84,7	6,4 7,2	4,4 5,4	58,1 47,5	10,5 12,6	30,2 38,6

265

41% were prepared to accept mixed swimming at school level, the latter being the most intimate sporting activity. The data indicate that as far as Whites were concerned, non-racial sport should be handled tactfully and would always be a socially sensitive matter.

(c) *Mixed recreation*

Sport and recreation are often considered to be similar activities, sport being a subdivision of recreation.

Recreational activities are less structured and subject to rules than sports activities. Recreation relates more closely to the intimate personal level, to the individual's freedom of choice and the satisfaction resulting from the particular recreational activity. Respondents were asked how they felt about the opening of all public facilities to all races: school and public sports facilities; parks in central urban or municipal areas; theatres (e.g. cinemas) and drive-ins; beaches and holiday resorts; and public libraries, swimming-baths and transport. Respondents' feelings towards the non-racial use of facilities could be expressed in terms of the following: 'strongly in favour of', 'in favour of', 'indifferent', 'against', 'strongly against', or 'do not know'. Naturally this kind of attitude determination includes cognitive and volitional components, all essential for establishing attitudes.

A summary of the findings appears in table 10.3. Trends found to exist in the attitude profiles for non-racial national, club and school sport were also found to exist with regard to mixed recreation. Conspicuously, Whites remained the most conservative group with regard to the non-racial use of facilities.

Only about 30% of the White respondents were in favour of the opening of all public facilities to all races. Of the rest, 13,7% were indifferent and 56% opposed. As far as the other population groups were concerned, 84,8% of the Indian, 91,5% of the Coloured and 84,8% of the Black respondents supported the non-racial use of recreational facilities.

White support for non-racial swimming was 14,2%, whilst 17,7% of respondents supported mixed holiday resorts, 18,6% were in favour of open beaches and 45,8% in favour of non-racial public libraries. Thus, the opening of public swimming-baths, holiday resorts, beaches, public recreational facilities and even parks in central or municipal areas to all races produced strong resistance among Whites, although they showed less opposition to the non-racial use of public libraries and thus to sharing the sources of knowledge. It was these latter facilities that the other population groups were most anxious to share (Indians — 91,8%, Coloureds — 93,8% and Blacks — 92,3%).

Table 10.3 Percentage of respondents in favour of, indifferent to and opposed to the non-racial use of certain recreational facilities

Facilities involved in non-racial use	Blacks (N = 958)			Coloureds (N = 787)			Indians (N = 942)			Whites (N = 697)		
	In favour	Neutral	Opposed	In favour	Neutral	Opposed	In favour	Neutral	Opposed	In favour	Neutral	Opposed
School sports facilities	93,4	2,3	3,7	92,8	2,7	2,3	91,5	3,6	3,1	37,6	12,1	49,5
Public recreational facilities	89,4	4,1	5,3	91,5	3,8	2,4	88,6	4,8	3,6	25,9	14,2	59,2
Public sports facilities	89,6	4,4	4,9	92,3	3,2	2,8	90,3	4,5	3,3	36,6	17,0	46,0
Parks in central urban or municipal areas	86,9	5,6	5,8	90,6	5,2	2,3	85,6	7,1	5,5	27,9	14,2	56,8
Theatres(e.g. cinemas)	82,2	7,4	8,2	88,7	5,7	3,4	77,6	9,5	10,6	29,0	14,7	55,8
Drive-in theatres	78,8	9,4	8,5	92,0	4,5	1,4	79,7	10,1	8,3	42,4	19,4	37,7
Beaches	76,7	9,5	11,1	88,8	5,5	3,5	79,9	6,7	11,4	18,6	9,2	71,6
Holiday resorts	81,8	8,1	6,5	87,7	6,0	4,2	83,9	6,1	7,6	17,7	8,9	72,4
Public libraries	92,3	2,9	2,8	93,8	2,2	2,1	91,8	3,2	3,2	45,8	16,7	36,8
Public swimming-baths	75,8	9,0	12,9	84,0	7,6	6,2	76,1	8,7	12,4	14,2	7,5	77,2
Public transport	86,3	3,2	7,5	93,8	2,5	2,2	87,4	5,3	5,0	30,8	16,2	51,8
Total	84,8	6,0	7,0	91,5	4,5	3,0	84,8	6,3	6,7	29,7	13,7	55,9

Population group and attitude preference

Whites might feel that because they contributed financially and through their own efforts to the establishment of their own recreational facilities, they are entitled to the sole use of these facilities. Other race groups, on the other hand, might feel that because they are doing without these facilities they would prefer to share existing facilities.

Whatever the reasons for the existing attitude preferences, one trend was most prominent: the attitude profile for the Non-White groups differed completely from that for Whites. From this it follows that Non-White groups would be inclined to resist segregated recreation more strongly and might even be unprepared to regard recreation as an 'own affair'. According to their attitude profile, recreation may also be regarded as a group activity. The attitude profile for Whites, on the other hand, suggested that recreation should be regarded as an 'own affair' and that this group was not keen on sharing it with other races. A latent potential for tension and conflict became clear, emphasising the need for comprehensive and adequate provision for recreation.

Discussion of results

It is clear from the foregoing that Whites' attitudes towards social distance are much stronger than those of the other population groups. This is particularly noticeable where non-racial recreation is concerned.

In contrast, the preferences of Indians, Coloureds and Blacks regarding non-racial sport and recreation remained high throughout and it appears that their perception and experience of social distance differs from that of Whites. It is quite possible that social distance is irrelevant in this case and that other motives are involved, for example that non-racialism in sport is regarded as a right which is demanded in a community that is not prepared to grant this to all its members in all fields. The findings do not offer final solutions to these matters. If the findings of the 1983 investigation are compared with those of the HSRC sports investigation, it appears that the attitudes of Blacks, Coloureds and Indians concerning non-racial sport have remained unchanged, whilst those of Whites, especially Afrikaners, have regressed somewhat.

Towards the end of 1983 Whites were more conservative in their attitude to non-racial sport (at national, club and school level) than was the case in 1981. There are two obvious reasons for this.

Firstly, it must be pointed out that this study is the result of an investigation which took place in the spring of 1983, a crucial period in the constitutional history of South Africa. Early in November 1983 a national referendum was held on the desirability of a new political alliance with Coloureds and Indians. This alliance implied power-sharing. The political climate was charged with racial issues; sport at club and school level was bound to be included in the fierce, and at times racial, political campaign. An awakening of greater political activism, the direct opposite of political conservatism, was observed. That national issues would have an effect on attitudes to non-racial sport was to be expected. The regression or decline that occurred, however, may be regarded as moderate and it may be expected that Whites' attitudes to non-racial sport will return to what they were in 1981.

A second possible explanation for the regression in Whites' attitudes at the end of 1983 lies in the historical context of sport-political events. During the past ten years Whites' attitudes towards non-racial sport have become increasingly positive and non-racial sport has occurred more frequently. It was hoped that an increase in non-racial sport would lead to local and international breakthroughs against isolation, but this did not prove to be the case. Expectations were frustrated by increasing international pressure, exclusion and boycotts. The motivation to further adjustments by Whites began to decline, as did the motivation to change. Consequently, a return to more conservatism, that is to say more sport apartheid, is not inexplicable.

NON-RACIAL SPORT AND SOUTH AFRICAN SOCIETY

Sport cannot be isolated from the society in which it is practised. What takes place in the field of sport has implications for the rest of society, whilst what happens in the other institutions of society can, in turn, have implications for sport.

In the beginning of the seventies socio-political changes were instituted and are continuing today. The question arises whether sport contributed to these in any way. Scientists agree that sport conveys values and that it has an important socialising function in society. Seen in this way, sport can 'also be an agent to change within society' (Snyder and Spreitzer 1978: 27). Apart from its supportive function, sport may also play an activating function in society.

It has already been stated that international and internal pressure were important reasons for the move away from apartheid sport to non-racial sport. In South Africa values have changed to such an extent that not only mixed sport, but also other forms of mixed contact, have become acceptable. The abolition of job reservation and other labour reforms, as well as the new constitutional dispensation according to which Whites share political power with Indians and Coloureds for the first time are examples that can be mentioned. In turn, the new constitutional dispensation has implications for society. Examples are the efforts to repeal the Group Areas

Act, section 16 of the Immorality Act and the Prohibition of Mixed Marriages Act.

Without stating categorically that sport played the most important role in achieving change, it is doubtful whether South Africa would have entered a new era if the implementation of non-racial sport had failed. The first steps taken in the field of sport led to the gradual breakdown of resistance and other forms of contact across the colour bar became acceptable.

CONCLUSION

The following conclusions may be drawn:

- Distinct changes in South Africa's sports policy occurred. There was a move away from the rigid apartheid approach to one which allowed autonomous sports bodies to take their own decisions. The past 15 years are noted for the privatisation of South African sport.
- This changed policy was particularly noticeable in the increasing extent to which non-racial sport occurred. Non-racial sport, except in schools, is an everyday occurrence in South Africa today.
- White South Africans' perceptions of non-racial sport have changed dramatically over the past 15 years. Thus, non-racial sport has had a considerable impact on society. The greatest resistance to non-racialism is to be found in recreational activities.
- South African sport has made an important contribution to other changes in South African society.

BIBLIOGRAPHY

Anderson, PG. *An investigation into the effect of race and politics on the development of South African sport.* Stellenbosch: University of Stellenbosch, 1979. (Unpublished D.Phil. thesis.)

Lapchik, RE. *The politics of race and international sport: the case of South Africa.* London: Greenwood Press, 1975.

Loy, JW, McPherson, BD and Kenyon, G. *Sport and social systems.* London: Addison-Wesley Publishing Co, 1978.

Olivier, JL. *'n Sosiologiese studie van die verband tussen sport en sosiale verandering in Suid-Afrika.* Pretoria: University of South Africa, 1984. (Ongepubliseerde M.A.-verhandeling.)

Pretorius, KJ. *Die invloed van een seisoen van sportkontak op die rassevooroordeel van Blanke sportlui.* Stellenbosch: University of Stellenbosch, 1978. (Ongepubliseerde M.A.-verhandeling.)

HSRC Sports Investigation. *Sport in the RSA* (No.1). Pretoria: Human Sciences Research Council, 1982.

HSRC Sports Investigation. *Sportbetrokkenheid en houdings* (No.5). Pretoria: Human Sciences Research Council, 1982.

Rhoodie, NJ and Le Roux, WL du P. *A sample survey of the attitudes of White residents in Randburg towards the opening of public/municipal amenities to all races.* Pretoria: Human Sciences Research Council, 1983.

Scholtz, GJL. *Perspektiewe oor sport, politiek en menseverhoudinge.* Potchefstroom: Institute for the advancement of Calvinism, University of Potchefstroom, 1975.

— *Voorkeurpatrone vir sport en rekreasie in die RSA.* Pretoria: SAASPER publikasies, nr. 4/83, 1983.

Scholtz, GJL and Olivier, JL. Attitude of urban South Africans towards non-racial sport and their expectations of future race relations — a comparative study. *International Review for Sociology of Sport,* vol. 19, no. 2, 1984.

Snyder, EE and Spreitzer, E. *Social aspects of sport.* New Jersey: Prentice-Hall Inc, 1978.

Williams, JG. *'n Sosiologiese ondersoek na bepaalde aspekte van die maatskaplike milieu en leefwyse van 'n groep provinsiale rugbyspelers.* Pretoria: Universiteit van Pretoria, 1976. (Ongepubliseerde M.A.-verhandeling.)

11 Church, theology and change in South Africa

JA Loader

INTRODUCTION

Has there been any change recently in the theological scene in South Africa? If so, was it in any way penetrating? What was affected by it? Has it been significant in the broader context of recent developments in South Africa? In order to answer these questions — or as I intend to do in this chapter, to help the reader to answer these questions for himself — we will have to bear several points in mind.

First, the different meanings of the terms 'theology' and 'theological' must be clarified. They are often used in a restricted sense, but also in a wider, more popular sense. On one hand, 'theology' can mean reflection on what Religious Man believes about God. In a Christian context this would be *reflection on what the Church believes* about God and the relationship between Him and Man. On the other hand, people often use the term to refer to *anything that relates to the Bible and the Church*. We will pay attention to developments that could be called 'theological' in both the restricted and the wider senses. Because of the topicality and importance of the Church's involvement in public life, including social and political matters, we will concentrate on the debate concerning these fields as it has been developing in the churches of South Africa — even though much of this would not be 'theological' in the technical sense (neither would the participants necessarily be 'theologians' in the scholarly sense). Nevertheless, this is not the only field in which change may have taken place and in which important shifts of emphasis may have occurred in recent years. So we will also pay some attention to the question of change in the broader context of church life.

STATISTICS

The most recent census data about church membership in South Africa are to be found in the 1980 census figures (church membership was not

272

incorporated in the 1985 census). One has to bear in mind that census figures cannot truly reflect church affiliation because of ignorance, non-chalance and nominal membership. Many people are not sure what the church to which they regard themselves as belonging is called (cf. the different names by which the Anglican churches are known). Others are careless about what they claim regarding their church membership (which is reflected in the fact that official denominational figures do not tally with census figures). One of the greatest problems, from a statistical as well as an ecclesiastical perspective, is nominal membership. Many people regard themselves as members of a church and indeed have some remote relation with a denomination, such as having been baptized in a Christian church or having been entered on the list of congregants, but do not participate in the activities of that church.

Another fact which should be borne in mind in the interpretation of religious and theological change in South Africa against the backdrop of numbers is that resolutions adopted by synods and stances taken by denominational leadership do not necessarily reflect the views of the membership at grassroots level. In fact, there are indications of actual discrepancies on this count. One example may illustrate this. During the lead-up to the 1983 referendum on constitutional change in South Africa, leaders and prominent clergy of most 'English-speaking churches', the Hervormde Church and the Roman Catholic Church were either officially opposed to the implementation of the Government's proposals or conspi-cuously vocal in criticising them. Had the members of these churches who could vote followed the official line of their churches or the sentiments popularised by clergy, they would have needed no or almost no support from other groups to bring about a victory for the 'no' lobby. Or, to put it another way, had the total 'no' vote come from these churches, a mass of almost 400 000 would still have ignored the call or advice of their spiritual leaders. Whichever way one looks at it, the massive victory for the 'yes' lobby is clear evidence of a discrepancy between the thinking of the clergy and that of general membership. Therefore, it would be unwise to project official church policies or the views of prominent clergy and theologians on to the rank and file members of the churches.

Nevertheless, statistical figures give a general idea of the relative strength of the various churches in South Africa.

Without regarding these denominations as monolithic entities, some interesting perspectives can be gleaned from the figures. Of the total population, 76,7% are prepared to call themselves Christians and among the remaining 23,3% there may be more. Some 92% of the Whites, 87% of the Coloureds and 74% of the Blacks regard themselves as Christians (the last figure is mistakenly given as 76% by Meiring in Van Vuuren 1983: 292).

Table 11.1 Church membership of the South African population according to the 1980 census (in thousands).

Denomination Group name	White Adherents	%	Coloured Adherents	%	Asian Adherents	%	Black Adherents	%	Total Adherents	%
NG Church	1 694	37,4	678	26,0	2	0,3	1 104	6,5	3 478	14,0
Gereformeerde Church	128	2,8	8	0,3	1	0,4	65	0,4	202	0,8
NH Church	246	5,4	3	0,1	1	0,1	26	0,2	276	1,1
Church of the Province	94	2,1	149	5,7	3	0,4	162	1,0	409	1,6
Church of England in SA	31	0,7	13	0,5	1	0,1	51	0,3	96	0,4
Church of England	111	2,5	19	0,7	0	0	132	0,8	263	1,1
Anglican Church	219	4,8	170	6,5	5	0,6	452	2,7	845	3,4
Methodist Church of SA	414	9,1	140	5,4	4	0,5	1 554	9,2	2 113	8,5
Presbyterian Church of SA	129	2,8	8	0,2	2	0,2	361	2,1	499	2,0
United Congr. Church of SA	24	0,5	170	6,5	5	0,6	208	1,2	407	1,6
Lutheran churches	40	0,9	96	3,7	1	0,1	698	4,1	835	3,4
Roman Catholic Church	394	8,7	265	10,1	21	2,6	1 677	9,9	2 356	9,5
Apostolic Faith Mission	126	2,8	49	1,9	3	0,3	126	0,7	303	1,2
Other Apostolic churches	145	3,2	199	7,6	3	0,3	281	1,7	627	2,5
Baptist churches	75	1,7	16	0,6	3	0,4	161	1,0	255	1,0
Christian Science, etc	38	0,8	21	0,8	0	0	14	0,1	77	0,3
Faith healers	1	0	1	0			7	0	8	0
Full Gospel, etc	63	1,4	22	0,8	23	2,8	62	0,4	169	0,7
Orthodox churches	28	0,6	0	0	0	0	2	0	31	0,1
Mormons	6	0,1	1	0	0	0	4	0	11	0
Pentecostals	11	0,2	14	0,6	3	0,4	25	0,1	53	0,2
Salvation Army	5	0,1	2	0,1	2	0,2	44	0,3	51	0,2
Seventh Day Adventists	16	0,4	13	0,5	3	0,3	50	0,3	81	0,3
SA Gen. Mission, etc	0	0	0	0	0	0	8	0	8	0
Swiss Mission	0	0	0	0	0	0	83	0,5	83	0,3
Assemblies of God	19	0,4	11	0,4	2	0,3	100	0,6	133	0,5
Zion Christian Church	0	0	4	0,2	0	0	764	4,5	769	3,1
Independent Black Churches	0	0	114	4,4	0	0	4 190	24,8	4 304	17,3
Other Christian churches	95	2,1	86	3,3	12	1,5	139	0,8	333	1,3
Jewish faith	119	2,6	0	0	1	0,1	5	0	125	0,5
Buddhists	1	0	0	0		0,1	9	0,1	11	0
Confucians	0	0	0	0	1	0,1	15	0,1	16	0,1
Hindus	1	0	2	0,1	512	62,4	3	0	519	2,1
Islam	2	0	164	6,3	154	18,8	8	0	328	1,3
Other faiths	22	0,5	27	1,0	11	1,3	61	0,4	121	0,5
Objectors	34	0,7	11	0,4	4	0,5	592	3,5	641	2,6
No church/faith	44	1,0	14	0,5	3	0,3	532	3,1	592	2,4
Unknown	150	3,3	120	4,6	33	4,0	3 153	18,6	3 456	13,9
Total	4 528 18,2%	100,0	2 613 10,5%	100,0	821 3,3%	100,0	16 924 68,0%	100,0	24 886 100,0%	100,0

274

It is difficult to determine the 'biggest' churches in South Africa. One can claim that the Nederduitse Gereformeerde Church (the NGK) is the biggest church in South Africa, but that would be misleading in view of the polarisation of tension between the white NG Church on one hand and the Black NG Churches on the other. These are four autonomous churches and for years the White church has been resisting moves towards structural unity between the churches of the so-called NG family. So the separate NG churches cannot be regarded as one for demographic, organisational and even theological reasons — a fact that is obscured by the columns in the census table.

On the other hand, it is difficult not to regard the Black independent churches as a unit, in spite of the many groups among them. Denominations in the usual sense of the word are not found among these people and they form a homogeneous group in that they strive to indigenise Christianity in Africa. There seems to be no clear-cut criterion according to which the different denominations may be demarcated and counted. Much depends on the way in which church membership is or is not affected by race. If we take this into account (as the segregationist churches would insist we should) and if we regard the independent Black churches as a unity, the following list of the 15 most popular churches in South Africa can be drawn up:

1 The Black independent churches (5,07 million)
2 Roman Catholic Church (2,35 million)
3 Methodist Church (2,11 million)
4 Nederduitse Gereformeerde Church (for Whites) (1,69 million)
5. Anglican Churches (1,61 million)
6. NG Church in Africa (for Blacks) (1,11 million)
7. Lutheran Churches (0,83 million)
8. NG Mission Church (for Coloureds) (0,67 million)
9. Apostolic churches (excluding the Apostolic Faith Mission) (0,62 million)
10. Presbyterian Church (0,49 million)
11. Congregational Church (0,40 million)
12.   Apostolic Faith Mission (0,30 million)
13. Baptist churches (0,25 million)
14. Nederduitsch Hervormde Church (for Whites) (0,24 million)
15. Gereformeerde churches (for Whites) (0,20 million).

If the two largest non-Christian groups were slotted into their appropriate positions on the list, the Hindu group (0,51 million) would occupy tenth position and the Muslim group (0,32 million) would come 13th. It is a rather sobering thought that the Hervormde and Gereformeerde Churches, for all their prominence in the media and the minds of Afrikaners, would not even make the 'top 15'.

When one looks at membership figures as they appear in a racial breakdown, it becomes obvious that there is no predominant Christian denomination in any group. In fact, the Hindus constitute the only religious majority in one racial category, making up 62,4% of the Asians in South Africa (which equals only 2% of the total population).

The three largest denominations among *Whites* remain minorities within the White group: NGK (37,4%); Anglican (10,1%); and Methodist (9,1%). Among *Coloureds* much the same situation prevails: NG Mission Church (26%); Anglican (13,4%); and Roman Catholic (10,1%). Of all the *Asians* in South Africa, only 12,8% belong to a Christian church, whilst 62,4% are Hindus and 18,8% Muslims. In the *Black community*, the three largest groups are: Independent churches (29% — not of Black *Christians* as Meiring claims in Van Vuuren 1983: 294, but of *all* Blacks in South Africa); Roman Catholic (9,9%); and Methodist (9,2%).

This picture reveals that as far as denominational affiliation is concerned, South Africans are totally divided. The only group whose percentage runs into double figures on a national scale, the Black independent churches (with 20,4% of the population), is itself divided into some 4 000 groups. The second and third largest denominations on our list make up only 9,5% and 8,5% of the population respectively, whereas the NGK, which is reputed to be the most influential church in South Africa (cf. Meiring in Van Vuuren 1983: 303), can lay claim to a meagre 6,8% of South Africans in its fold. Although we will come to the question of ecclesiastical power and influence later, this denominational jigsaw with its multitude of minute pieces must be kept in mind when one judges the influence and representativeness of opinions voiced by synods and spokesmen for churches. If, for instance, the three Afrikaans 'sister churches' had unanimously come out in favour of the retention of the Act on the Prohibition of Mixed Marriages and related acts, they would have been speaking for a mere 8,3% of the population. In additon (as we have seen), there is no reason to imagine that official top-level views are shared at the grassroots level. It should be obvious that the churches, if they are to speak with anything approaching a unified voice, will have to find each other in ecumenical consultation.

HISTORICAL NOTES ON THE MAJOR CURRENTS

The first Whites in South Africa were *Roman Catholics*. In 1501 Joao da Nova, a Portuguese, erected the first church building at Angra de Sao Bras, later Mossel Bay. However, this was intended only as a stopover for travellers between Europe and East India and thus did not represent a permanent church settlement. During 1635 a second Portuguese chapel was built near the Umzimkulu River on the Natal coast. After the arrival of the Dutch at the Cape there were always Catholics among the Reformed majority. They were given equal rights only in 1804 and the first active Apostolic vicar, Bishop Raymond Griffith, started work among his flock of 700 in April 1838. The Church grew steadily in the Cape Colony, Natal, the Orange Free State and the Transvaal. In spite of initial opposition there were about 25 000 Catholics in South Africa during the early nineties. It took the Roman Catholic Church less than another century to become the largest church in the country, next to the independent Black group (cf. Brown 1960).

The *Protestant tradition*, although not the first to arrive in South Africa, was the first to strike root here. When the first permanent settlement of Dutch Christians was established at the Cape of Good Hope in 1652 there were Lutherans, Mennonites and Roman Catholics among them, but the main brand of Protestantism was the Reformed faith. This was a form of Calvinism characterised by the rigid and dogmatic orthodoxy then prevailing in the Netherlands. However, a pietistic reaction to this kind of rationalistic faith also had influence among the settlers.

There was a *Lutheran* minority among the Dutch at the Cape, but the Reformed numbers were augmented by the arrival of the French Huguenots in 1688. The Lutherans were tolerated, but there were some disagreements with the Calvinist authorities because of discrimination against them. Their organisation improved after 1780 and their numbers were boosted in the next century by new arrivals from Lutheran countries.

The Reformed church obtained the service of *Scottish Calvinists* in several Cape congregations, which should be regarded as part of the British role in South African church history. After the Great Trek of 1836, when farmers who were dissatisfied with British rule left the eastern districts to make a new life for themselves, three different Calvinist churches grew out of the original one. These were the Nederduitse Gereformeerde, the Nederduitsch Hervormde and the Gereformeerde Churches.

The English-speaking denominations arrived at the Cape during the 19th century. The *Anglican tradition* came with the British occupation in 1806, but the first bishop was appointed only in 1847. Its history during the latter half of the century was restless, if not turbulent, with quarrels centring around Bishop JW Colenso of Natal and discord in the diocese of Grahamstown, not to mention the upheavals as a result of the Anglo-Boer War (1899-1902).

The *Methodists*, too, came with the occupying forces. At first they were openly discriminated against, but they persevered in ministering to

277

soldiers and slaves while paying much attention to missionary activity in the interior.

There were *Presbyterians* among the British soldiers as well. Initially they held church services with Congregationals, but after 1829 they had their own church. The Scottish contingent among the 1820 Settlers from Britain included a large Presbyterian community. This Church spread northwards when diamonds and gold were discovered and also established itself in the mission field.

Also amongst the British settlers were *Baptists*. In spite of disunity because of strife between ultra-Calvinist elements and others in the Baptist Church, it spread all over South Africa. Baptist numbers were strengthened by missionary work and even by German immigrants, who were predominantly, but not exclusively, Lutheran.

The *Pentecostal tradition* made its appearance in South Africa within Congregational circles during the 1870s. Later, Pentecostals from America came to South Africa and in 1910 they founded the Apostolic Faith Mission with the support of former NG missionaries. During the same year another group, which came to be called the Full Gospel Church in 1920, was constituted. These and other Pentecostal churches steadily increased their membership, both White and Black.

The *Black independent churches* are a unique phenomenon in Africa. There are three basic varieties of these churches, namely Ethiopian, Zionist and Messianic. The Ethiopian variety dates from 1872 and is more orthodox than the others; the Zionist group is charismatic and dates from the turn of the century; and the Messianic group reveres a new, Black Messiah sent by God. These churches are Black Christians' response to White Christianity in the light of the economic implications of the social set-up in South Africa (cf. Sundkler 1961: 32-33). Their expansion has been phenomenal, as can be seen from the fact that their numbers have swollen from a mere 25 000 in 1904 to more than 5 million in 1980.

THE CHURCHES' PARTICIPATION IN A CHANGING SOUTH AFRICA

The question whether the churches *should* play a role in the field of socio-politics may be a theologically valid one, but it is really irrelevant from the perspective of a *description* of the church's involvement in this field. In actual fact the churches *do* participate actively in a variety of ways. Even those churches or theological currents which advocate a withdrawal of the church from the realm of 'the world' participate in that they decide not to criticise the *status quo*. Others make open pronouncements about public matters in their very condemnation of 'activism' by churches. Thus, they attack participation in debates by denying their opponents the right to do so at all, but in this way actually participate in the controversies themselves. Still others are deeply committed to working for change in the socio-political field and are very active in trying to do something about it. Whether any of this is very influential or effective is not clear, but the fact is that churches across the spectrum are involved in a changing process and enjoy a high profile as far as this is concerned, which calls for a description. We will go about the task by discussing the active or passive participation of the churches in terms of several categories, namely those churches who participate *passively*, those who are predominantly *critical* of government policies (the anti-apartheid churches) and those who have traditionally been *supporters* of these policies.

The 'passive' participants

At least four branches within the ecclesiastical community in South Africa may be said to be 'passively' taking part in the churches' involvement in a changing situation. This means that they concentrate on 'spiritual' matters and avoid participating in the 'political' debate taking place in theological and church circles. However abstinent they endeavour to be, by their very reluctance to address the controversial issues they do, in fact, play a part and sometimes are even forced to make at least a statement about relevant topics.

The first branch of the so-called 'passive' churches consists of the *Pentecostal group*, in which the Apostolic Faith Mission and the Full Gospel Church are the most prominent. In this tradition all the emphasis is on the experience of the Holy Spirit, becoming a re-born Christian and personal salvation. Therefore in religious life attention is focused on issues like conversion, being born again, baptism and so on. This reflects the influence of the anabaptist tradition of the 16th century, viz that the world stands irreconcilably counterpoised to the church and that Christians should forsake the sinful world (including its socio-political and cultural dimensions) and live 'spiritual' lives. In the long run this separatist stance can be maintained only by radical withdrawal from cultural life altogether, which these churches do not propagate (actually there has been criticism from within some of these churches that they have become too institutionalised and for conforming to establishment standards). Therefore their implicit support for the *status quo*, although it cannot be called active, occasionally turns out to be endorsement of a political position. For instance, the Apostolic Faith Mission has found itself forced to account for 'the race policies of this country'. Its official view is that people of all races are to be kept within the framework of one church, but that the different 'race groups' should have separate congregations and ministers (Apostolic

279

Faith Mission Yearbook 1964). This comes very close to the view held by the three Afrikaans 'sister churches', but it must be added that joint worship and membership are possible. This kind of ambivalence is illustrated further by the controversy that surrounded Pastor GR Wessels, a pastor of the Apostolic Faith Mission who went into politics and became a senator of the governing National Party. One group in the Church felt that it was a good thing and that the influence of the Church would be enhanced by such a step, while another was opposed to this kind of compromisation of the traditional anabaptist principle. The Full Gospel Church provides another example. Although it has always maintained its character as a single church, there have always been different sections for the four main racial groups in South Africa. However, at its 1985 synod, the Church decided to establish an overarching body that is capable of taking binding decisions for all the groups.

The second branch of the 'a-political' group is made up of the so-called *conservative evangelical churches*. These are mainly small English-speaking churches, which are generally fundamentalist in their religious outlook. They include the Church of the Nazarene, the Baptists, Free Methodists, Free Lutherans and the evangelical wing of Anglicanism in South Africa (the Church of England in South Africa). A strong trend of personal pietism and conservatism in matters such as inspiration, inerrancy and the authority of the Bible fulfils essentially the same function here as the typical Pentecostal spiritual experience in the previous group — interest is focused on religious fundamentals. However, here, too, a tacit and sometimes even explicit tendency to support the powers that be is found. These churches are not members of the South African Council of Churches (SACC), which is outspoken in its opposition of Government policy. Often the conservative evangelicals are as outspoken in their criticism of the SACC as the Council is of the Government and often they are given a high profile in the media for this. So, once again we have to conclude that even focusing heavily on traditional religious issues (the so-called 'vertical' dimension, i.e. between God and Man) in itself constitutes a clear position on 'worldly' matters (the so-called 'horizontal' dimension, i.e. between human beings and their fellow human beings). On the other hand, it must be pointed out that internationally the evangelical movement has become more aware of socio-political issues in recent years. As far as South Africa is concerned this resulted in conservative evangelical representatives taking part in the South African Christian Leadership Assembly (SACLA) held in Pretoria in 1979. However, this has not proved to be a trend-setting development in evangelical ranks and, apart from a statement by the Baptist Union calling for adequate political representation of all races (Meiring *et al* in Van der Horst 1981: 200), there has been no major change in the predominance of the 'vertical' interests of these churches.

Thirdly, we should take note of the *charismatic movement* in South Africa. This is not so much a group of churches as a trend within several churches (cf Lee 1983: 98). The charismatic phenomenon is characterised by emotional response to the feeling of being grasped by God. At the centre of interest are the doctrine of baptism in the Holy Spirit, the conviction of regeneration (being born again) and phenomena like glossolalia (speaking unintelligible words), healing, fellowship and growth in discipleship. There are various charismatic currents in South Africa (cf Lederle 1982: 36-38). It stands to reason that their interests will centre on the 'charismatic experience' rather than on involvement in socio-political affairs. However, many charismatics belong to denominations which are involved in such issues and have influenced their churches without opposing the social awareness of these churches. Others are developing into denominations or functioning as independent groups.

The last branch of politically 'passive' churches is by far the largest of all religious groups in South Africa; it comprises the *Black independent churches*. Paradoxically, these churches came into existence because of the political and concomitant social and economic developments which changed the face of Africa when the colonial powers stepped in. They exist because of changes that occurred in the past, but have little practical influence on the changes taking place now or being called for. An example of how far removed from the political activism of many other ecclesiastical organisations these churches are, is the fact that President PW Botha was enthusiastically received at the Easter gathering of more than 2 million* Black members of the Zion Christian Church at Pietersburg in 1985 only a few days after the demand made in Cape Town by Dr Allan Boesak, Assessor of the NG Mission Church, that the State President 'remove himself' from office. These churches have become a refuge for thousands of Blacks who have been uprooted by urbanisation and its social, economic and cultural effects. Therefore, the independent churches started functioning as agents of acquiescence rather than of change. They have assumed the role of helping their adherents to cope with the *status quo*, not of changing it. Karl Marx would have considered these churches a text-book example of his idea of religion as the 'opiate of the people'. Much attention is paid to ceremonies, rites, the healing powers of leaders and respect for authority (for which latter reason some employers prefer the services of these Christians). Although the leaders of the independent churches are not

---

*The large number of members present shows that the 1980 census figures should be amended considerably.

involved in the socio-political debate in South Africa, there has been the odd exception and they do care for the economic welfare of their members. To regard the independent churches as standing outside the mainstream of church activities in South Africa is possible only on the basis of a particular (Western) definition of 'church activities' and if the sheer number of their adherents is ignored.

The 'critical' churches

The churches belonging to the SACC are the Methodist Church, the Anglican Church, the Presbyterian Church, the Congregational Church (commonly called the 'English-speaking churches', but this is not accurate in view of the many Blacks in these denominations), the NG Church in Africa, the NG Mission Church and the Reformed Church in Africa. Together they have a membership exceeding 7 million people. These churches have been severely critical of the *status quo* in South Africa and have been supported in this by the Roman Catholic Church, with its membership of over 2 million. This makes the 'critical' churches the strongest lobby (in terms of members) on the South African scene, despite the huge number of adherents of the Black independent churches. Whether White membership identifies with the church leaders or not, this makes the critical voice in South African church circles a force to be reckoned with.

The SACC and its forerunner, the Christian Council of South Africa, have always been at odds with the governing National Party. They have always claimed to be opposed to the policy of apartheid on biblical grounds (just as the Afrikaans churches have claimed biblical support for the defence of apartheid). As a result the 'English-speaking churches' have often clashed with the National Party leaders, who consistently regarded the protests of Council leaders as political activism 'under the cloak of religion'. In the early days of National Party government, Dr DF Malan refused to receive a delegation from the Christian Council on such grounds, as did Dr HF Verwoerd when the SACC requested an interview with him in 1964. In 1968 Mr BJ Vorster rejected the SACC's 'Message to the people of South Africa' as an attack 'under the cloak of religion' (Thomas 1982: 53) and President PW Botha used the same phrase in March 1985 in a dramatic address to the joint session of the three chambers of Parliament which was taken to refer *inter alia* to the General Secretary of the SACC, Dr CF Beyers Naudé and the President of the World Alliance of Reformed Churches, Dr Allan Boesak, who had just led an illegal protest march to Parliament. Nevertheless it was Mr Botha who, in 1980 as Prime Minister, took the surprising step of inviting the SACC to talks and in 1982 invited all churches, including the SACC members, to advise him on the possible repeal of the highly controversial Mixed Marriages Act and Article 16 of the Immorality Act. This showed a more flexible attitude than that of his predecessors and gave the SACC an opportunity denied it by previous government leaders.

Since their confrontation with Dr Malan in the late forties, the SACC churches have followed a course of continual opposition to the Government's apartheid policies. When Dr Verwoerd, as Minister of Native Affairs, tried to prohibit 'Non-Whites' from attending church services in a predominantly White area (the so-called 'church clause' in the Black Laws Amendment Act of 1957), there was a storm of protest. Spokesmen for these churches even resolved to revert to civil disobedience if the law was passed. The success of the protest was probably ensured by the fact that this was one of the very few cases in which the NG Church also opposed a Government measure (Hansard 1957: 4 519).

The anti-apartheid stance of the critical churches surfaced prominently at several occasions after this. At a leaders' conference in Bloemfontein in 1965 a call was made for united action by all churches in South Africa in protest against the growing number of race barriers separating people in the country and in 1968 a commission was appointed to investigate the racial issues in church and country. This emanated in the SACC document entitled 'Message to the people of South Africa', in which the whole constellation of apartheid philosophy and measures was strongly rejected. Next, the SACC embarked on its Study Project on Christianity in Apartheid Society (Spro-cas). All aspects of life in South African society were investigated and it was found, interestingly, that the blame could not be laid entirely on others, because discrepancies in their own ranks were not totally lacking.

In fact, the context within which this history of protest against apartheid has taken place has changed to such an extent that today much of the early opposition is regarded as unacceptable because of its paternalistic flavour. In 1946, for instance, the Christian Council testified to the Fagan Commission on Native laws (appointed by the governing United Party) in favour of gradual 'education' of the 'uncivilised' for a common citizenship and the 'advance' of individuals of different races (Thomas 1982: 55). While the General Secretary of the Christian Council went so far as to call for a trade boycott of South African exports in the fifties, the former President of the SACC, Rev. Peter Storey, came out against disinvestment in South Africa as a means of forcing change (at a seminar of the University of South Africa, March 1985). It is noteworthy that these opinions differ despite the fact that the confrontation between the critical churches and the Government has intensified rather than abated. However, it should be added that other leaders in the critical camp would probably differ on this score and that the issue is determined by the consideration of the viability or otherwise of disinvestment.

The confrontation between the critical churches and the National Party Government escalated in the early sixties, which were traumatic years for South African political and ecclesiastical life. Like the unrest in Black townships during 1976 and 1985, that of 1960 came in the wake of an economic recession. On 21 March 1960 the police shot dead 69 Blacks and wounded many more at the Sharpeville township. This created an uproar in South Africa and internationally. A state of emergency was declared and the atmosphere in the whole country was tense. In December of the same year the World Council of Churches (WCC) organised a conference of its member-churches in South Africa. Most of the delegates were from the English-speaking churches, but a number from the NG Church of the Cape and the Transvaal and from the Hervormde Church, were present. This conference, subsequently called the Cottesloe Conference, dealt with many controversial topics such as mixed marriages and land tenure. The conference was highly critical of some cornerstones of Government policy and the name 'Cottesloe' became a symbol of church opposition to apartheid. The English-speaking churches were not alone in their criticism, but they were prominent participants.

The criticism of Government policies by clergymen took yet another form when the Christian Institute for South Africa was established in 1961. Although this was not a representative body like the Christian Council or the SACC, it became prominent because of its criticism of the South African *status quo*. It was taken so seriously that the NG and Hervormde Churches officially rejected the Institute and even saw fit to forbid their members to join it. In 1977 it was declared an affected organisation by the Government, while the director, Dr Beyers Naudé, was banned until 1984. The Christian Institute and Dr Naudé became international symbols of church rejection of apartheid, particularly in the Netherlands. After his unbanning Dr Naudé became General Secretary of the SACC, succeeding Bishop Desmond Tutu, who had become the Anglican Bishop of Johannesburg.

The international reputation of the SACC has been greatly enhanced by the fortunes of two of its prominent leaders. In 1982, in the wake of severe criticism of apartheid and those churches who supported it, Dr Allan Boesak was elected President of the World Alliance of Reformed Churches. In 1984 Bishop Tutu was awarded the Nobel Peace Prize for his endeavours to rid South Africa of apartheid without recourse to violence. Both events met with sharp reaction in South Africa, but certainly promoted the interests of the SACC and its member churches. On the other hand, the SACC's image has been damaged greatly by internal problems, particularly with regard to financial administration and there have been criminal charges against Mr John Rees, a former Secretary-General, as well as a judicial inquiry into its financial affairs (the so-called Eloff Commission). A scandal concerning Dr Boesak's private life and involving a Council official rocked the SACC in 1985. On account of this Dr Boesak was temporarily suspended by his church.

These two Black church leaders illustrate the movement away from White domination and paternalism in the SACC and its member churches. This goes hand in hand with the emergence of the so-called Black Consciousness Movement and Black Theology during the sixties (Meiring 1983: 322). As the influence of these movements and their exponents (like Steve Biko, Manas Buthelezi and Elliot Mgojo) and that of related organisations (e.g. the South African Students' Organisation) increased, the influence of Black moderates waned. Co-operation with the Government is scorned and every vestige of paternalism both in the political field and in the churches is resented. Blacks have assumed leading positions in the executives of not only the SACC, but also of its member churches (e.g. the Methodist and Anglican Churches). However, there has been resistance in some of these churches to the leadership of certain SACC officials. This became apparent in the NG Mission Church, where Dr Boesak lost the run for the moderatorship to a moderate in spite of having just been elected to the presidency of the World Alliance of Reformed Churches, and in the Anglican Church, where there was much opposition to the election of Bishop Tutu as Bishop of Johannesburg, notwithstanding his having just received the Nobel Peace Prize. In the English churches especially an ever-widening cleft between the clergy and White membership seems to be developing. This could be seen clearly in the referendum of 1983, when English-speaking Whites obviously discarded the counsel of their spiritual leaders, but it also appears in letters to the press and in the public criticism of church leadership by associations within churches (e.g. in the Roman Catholic Church during 1983). If anything, this state of affairs exemplifies the hardening of attitudes and growing polarisation in South Africa.

The three 'Black Reformed churches' which emanated from the mission work of the NG Church, viz the NG Church in Africa, the NG Mission Church and the Reformed Church in Africa, are not only members of the SACC, but also very vocal and active in their rejection of both apartheid and ecclesiastical support of the ideology. The White NG Church officially opted for independent church structures for the different race groups which form part of the so-called 'NG family', but the 'younger churches' judged differently. In 1978 they asked for an overarching synod as the first step on the road to unity. Later in the same year the synod of the NG Church rejected the idea out of hand and polarisation began in earnest. Predictably, the often faltering criticism of apartheid from within the ranks of these churches became more articulate and continued in a growing crescendo which was to reach a climax in 1982.

In 1978 the NG Mission Church officially declared apartheid or, as it is also called, separate development, to be 'contrary to the gospel' (NG Mission Church 1978: 399, 559). Four years later this unequivocal statement was underlined in no uncertain terms. The three 'Black Reformed churches' participated actively in the condemnation of apartheid at the meeting of the World Alliance of Reformed Churches in Ottawa. Delegates from these churches were instrumental in bringing about the suspension of the Hervormde Church and their own spiritual mother, the NG Church, for supporting apartheid. Some of these delegates also refused to take part in a communion service with delegates from the 'apartheid churches', thereby demonstrating most dramatically their abhorrence and utter condemnation of the system supported by the Afrikaans churches. Next, one of the most outspoken of these delegates, Dr Allan Boesak, was elected president of the world body — an occurrence that obviously stunned the White churches in question. As if this was not clear enough a message to the White churches, the NG Mission Church declared at its synod later in 1982:

> Because the secular gospel of Apartheid is a serious threat to the testimony of reconciliation in Jesus Christ and the church of Jesus Christ, the NG Mission Church in South Africa declares that it presents the church of Jesus Christ with a status confessionis (that is a matter on which it is impossible for believers to differ without coming into conflict with the testimony of the church). We declare apartheid or separate development to be a sin, that moral and theological validation thereof makes a mockery of the gospel and that its sustained disobedience to the Word of God is a theological heresy (NG Mission Church 1982: 3).

In effect, this meant that the Mission Church was accusing the Afrikaans 'sister churches' of having left the fold of the true faith. The implication is that these churches now become objects of mission work instead of subjects. There are also other implications, inter alia that apartheid becomes a matter of doctrine and that it is singled out as a watershed affecting brotherhood in Christ, whereas other doctrinal differences with non-apartheid churches like the Lutheran and Roman Catholic churches are not regarded as seriously. This should probably be explained in the light of the existential involvement of the Mission Church in an unbearable situation which renders theological discrepancies and implications relatively unimportant.

The largest single denomination in South Africa, the Roman Catholic Church, became articulate in its criticism of the Government, apartheid and the status quo only after the Second Vatican Council of the early sixties. At this council, usually referred to as Vaticanum II, powerful pronouncements on human rights and the evils of discrimination were made. Step by step the hierarchy in South Africa joined the chorus of international Christian condemnation of apartheid: in 1972 they issued a 'Call to Conscience'; in 1977 they rejected the socio-political system in South Africa as 'oppression'; and in 1983 the Conference of Bishops rejected the Government's plans for constitutional reform as inadequate (although this was not left unopposed by Roman Catholic laymen). Senior Catholic spokesmen, including the Archbishop of Durban, Denis Hurley, and Owen Cardinal McCann, Archbishop of Cape Town, have been noted for their critical stance and have thrown their church's weight in behind the SACC in these matters, but have remained outside the Council for theological reasons (cf Meiring in Van Vuuren 1983: 323-324).

The churches supporting apartheid

In effect, the three Afrikaans 'sister churches' have supported racial segregation for many years. Sometimes spokesmen for the NG and Hervormde Churches are even heard boasting that their churches had already developed the policy when the National Party came into existence. There have been differences between the three churches on this issue, but these have been mainly in style, theological substantiation and points of detail. It cannot be denied that the three Afrikaans churches have provided the Government with religious legitimation for its racial policies, particularly since 1948, when the National Party won the elections on an apartheid ticket.

Because of its size the NG Church has been the most prominent of the three 'sisters' as far as the debate about the relations between the Church and the National Party is concerned. It is often said that there could be no change in South Africa without the co-operation of the NG Church (cf Meiring in Van Vuuren 1983: 303, O'Brien Geldenhuys 1982: 38). This claim is certainly exaggerated; history has shown that revolutionary change, once it gains momentum, sweeps away all powerful church structures associated with the old order. If such forces were unleashed in South Africa, the change would come not only in spite of the NG Church, but also at its cost. What is true, however, is the fact that the NG Church is a power base of the National Party government. This government will not be removed at the polls or be able to change the face of South Africa if the majority of NG members decide otherwise. Therefore, the NG Church is a force of major importance due to its close association with the National Party over the years and because of its links with present power structures.

Many parliamentarians, cabinet ministers and even one prime minister started their careers as ministers of the NG Church and South Africa has never had a prime minister who was not a practising member of this church. There have also been important members of the Hervormde and Gereformeerde Churches in the government benches and in the Cabinet. Until 1982 it could be said:

> The D(utch) R(eformed) Church is much more than a denomination in the ordinary sense of the word. It functions as the key institution in sustaining and developing the Afrikaans language and culture. This had led to a closeness of relationships between church, language, culture, and people that would be difficult to equal anywhere else. To be a true Afrikaner means to speak Afrikaans, to belong to one of the Dutch Reformed churches, and to support the National Party. When one of these three elements is missing in any specific individual, he or she can hardly claim to be a *true* Afrikaner (Bosch 1979: 13).

This has been the generally accepted establishment view, but it has always been denied by those Afrikaans speakers who belong to other churches and/or oppose the National Party. However, in 1982 a major split in the National Party (much more serious than the splintering-off of the HNP in 1969) took place and as a result, the Conservative Party was established. This has made it possible for Afrikaans speakers not only to belong to different churches, but *also* to oppose the National Party. As a consequence, the solid monolith of language, church and party in Afrikanerdom has been broken. There has been speculation in the media that this situation might develop into a realignment of membership in the three 'sister churches' along the lines of political sympathies, e.g. that the Hervormde Church might become the 'church of the right' by providing a refuge for disgruntled members of the other churches. Although this speculation is not without basis in fact, a grandscale landslide is only a remote possibility because of the very conservatism of Afrikaners when their church is concerned. Above all, there is still a major conservative component in the other two churches around which sympathisers can rally. Although the close ties between church and party have been severed in recent years, the factors involved have not combined — nor are they likely to combine — in such a way that the huge political resources of the NG Church could be consolidated on the side of the lobby for change vis-à-vis the forces resisting it. It is this which makes the debate on change in South Africa within the NG and the other two churches so interesting and, one may add, so crucial.

As a result of the expansion of the Dutch Reformed Church in the Cape Colony during the 18th and 19th centuries, many members of the Church were not White. Blacks and Coloureds simply attended the same services as Whites. However, some Whites started objecting to these people sharing the table of Holy Communion with them. In 1857 the synod of the 'Cape Church' (as it is popularly called) decided to concede to the wishes of those who 'as a result of weakness' could not bear the presence of people other than Whites at their Communion table. It is important to note that this was a *concession* and not the formulation of a principle. On the contrary, the resolution expressly stipulates the 'scripturally correct' procedure: the incorporation of converted 'heathens' into existing (White) congregations. Only where the 'weakness of some members' caused embarrassment were these converts to have services in separate buildings (NG Church 1857: 171). In due course this concession 'strengthened' the 'weakness' of Whites in the sense that it became accepted policy not only to hold separate services, but for all mission work and all the churches established to be completely separate. Ironically, therefore, the 16 churches founded in Southern Africa as a result of this policy, including the NG Church in Africa for Blacks and the NG Mission Church for Coloureds, exist due to the 'weakness' of some Whites. In fairness it should be added that the missionary zeal of the NG Church, especially during the following century, sprang from a sincere concern for the spiritual needs of people who were not White. Nevertheless, racial segregation was part and parcel of the policy whereby these spiritual ends were to be achieved. What is more, it became part and parcel of the political philosophy which was to be applied in the interests of the socio- economic survival of the Afrikaner after his crushing defeat by British imperialism at the beginning of the 20th century.

The first half of this century was characterised by many synods and congresses at which the Afrikaans churches played a prominent role and where the principles of 'classic apartheid' were hammered out. Biological integration was anathematised, separate churches and schools were fervently championed and it was seen as a viable goal to involve Blacks in separate development within the context of their ethnic origins. Long before the Act on the Prohibition of Mixed Marriages found its way into the statute books, the NG Church actually requested that the Government prohibit marriages not between the different race groups, but only between Whites and people who were not White. This was done by the Federal Council of the NG Church in 1937. It had its way after several congresses concerning the interests of Afrikaner nationalism and the vicissitudes of the urban Afrikaner. In 1948 the National Party narrowly won the general election by capitalising on the rampant apartheid issue and immediately started translating promises into acts. Mixed marriages between Whites and other race groups were prohibited in 1949 and existing Acts of Parliament were extended and altered in order to fit the apartheid ideology. The group areas (where different races may live), labour relations (including the reservation of some jobs for Whites), separate Black education, separate amenities for different races (meaning the White race as opposed to all others), scores of laws regulating the movement of Blacks and the prohibition of sexual intercourse between Whites and people of other races, were introduced.

The Afrikaans churches consistently and adamantly supported these measures by providing the politicians with religious legitimation. Time and again the apartheid laws were defended in terms of a basic underlying principle, viz that diversity was God's will. Texts like Genesis 11: 1-9 (the tower of Babel and the dispersion of people into groups which spoke different languages), Deuteronomy 32: 8 (about God having determined the boundaries between peoples), Acts 17: 26 (about God having made all races from one blood [sic!] and having fixed territories for them), the 'apartheid measures' found in the Books of Ezra and Nehemiah and similar passages were constantly invoked in the attempt to justify apartheid biblically. An ever-present theme was the identification of the Afrikaner people with ancient Israel (just as the theme is now being exploited by liberation theologies). Tours de force and inconsistencies in interpretation have been the order of the day ever since, because the 'prophetic' character of the Old Testament had to be preserved in the service of traditional protestant theology, and the disasters that befell the Israelites had to be ignored whilst their being a 'separated' people had to be exploited. Many examples of this kind of argument have been given by critics of the proponents of an 'apartheid theology'.

The NG Church accepted the principle of 'separate development' as its official policy at the general synod of 1974 (NG Church 1973). The Hervormde Church has never needed such an official formulation of its policy in racial affairs, since it is the only church in the world to be White by definition. Its Church Order specifically states that only Whites may become members of the Church. The stipulation is formulated as follows in Article III:

> The Church, conscious of the dangers of the admixture of White and non-White for both groups, allows no admixture in its midst but envisages the formation of national churches (volkskerke) in each of the various national communities in the conviction that in this way the command of our Lord — 'Make disciples of all nations', Mt. 28: 19 — will be best executed and that the unity in Christ will not be harmed by such a working arrangement.

This view was strongly criticised by a small minority of theologians and ministers during the sixties. Some of the critics participated in the activities of the Christian Institute and either contributed to or supported the booklet *Delayed action* (1961/2). This caused a storm in all three 'sister churches', because the very foundation of apartheid theology was questioned by theologians from all three denominations. Public frenzy was vented in the press and critics like Professors BJ Marais and BB Keet (from the NG Church) and AS Geyser and A van Selms (from the Hervormde Church) were ostracised by their communities. The Hervormde Church went further and forbade its members to enrol with the Christian Institute, as a result of which several ministers left the Church (to join the Presbyterian Church). Moreover, this Church also deemed it necessary to forbid its members to criticise 'the Church's policy in these matters' anywhere except at some official bodies within the Church (Resolution 61 of the 1961 General Assembly). The 'apartheid article' was again seriously criticised by the memoranda of a minority serving on a commission appointed in 1978 to study the Church's policy, but the critical voices in the ensuing debate could be counted on one hand.

In the NG Church, critical opinion has always been more strongly represented. 'There is strength in numbers' is an adage that applies to the Afrikaans churches, because group dynamics work effectively in relatively small communities. Because of the size of the NG Church, there has always been more than a handful of dissenters and therefore the need for change has always been pointed out with greater effect by NG theologians. From the late forties onwards, the professors mentioned above and others in the NG Church questioned the validity of the Church's sanctioning of segregation, but never achieved any success apart from keeping the debate going — which in itself is noteworthy in the light of the great controversy that has taken hold of ecclesiastical South Africa today. The fifties were not conspicuous for any progress or change in these matters, notwithstanding the fact that the NG Church of the Transvaal and the Cape and the Hervormde Church were still members of the World Council of Churches and took part in various ecumenical conferences.

It was against the background of these circumstances that the Sharpeville tragedy and the Cottesloe Conference took place. The riots in the Black townships, the killings and the resultant state of emergency declared by the Government created an extremely tense situation which was aggravated by the universal condemnation of international church bodies, theologians and politicians. It was predictable that any conference under the auspices of the World Council of Churches would be regarded with more than superficial animosity in South Africa. At the Cottesloe Conference vital aspects of apartheid policy were criticised on theological grounds. NG participants were associated with the critical tone of the Cottesloe resolutions, but the Hervormde delegates took a strong stand in defence of apartheid. This resulted in the Hervormde Church not only leaving the conference, but withdrawing from the World Council. The two participating NG synods condemned the resolutions in which their own delegates had played a role and in 1961 followed the Hervormde Church in withdrawing from the WCC. Much of this was effected by the furore created by the interference of politicians, particularly the then Prime Minister, Dr HF Verwoerd, who (probably correctly) realised the dangers of the theological opposition to apartheid, especially if this could be associated with the NG Church (cf Serfontein 1982: 62, Lückhoff 1978).

During the turbulent sixties the Christian Institute, founded in 1961, continued to question the *status quo* in its mouthpiece *Pro Veritate*. In this it was supported by Afrikaner theologians, particularly from the NG and Hervormde Churches, including those who had left these churches either because of pressure from within or because of active disciplinary action taken against them by their churches. The Institute gradually became more radical in its pronouncements and the Government clamp-down on the organisation and its director was widely expected when it took place in 1977. PGJ Meiring's assessment of the era inaugurated by the events of 1960 is largely accurate:

> For nearly 20 years the ghost of Cottesloe haunted the Church and the storm of 1961 exercised a paralysing effect on its actions. The initiatives of the fifties, with the subsequent ecumenical congresses and lively debates, were as good as done for (Meiring in Van Vuuren 1983:309).

In general this would be true of the Hervormde, as well as the NG Church.

The debate on the Church's role in society, with its particular bias towards race relations so typical of the South African scene, gained momentum at the end of the seventies and the beginning of the eighties. An important characteristic of the debate is that much of it took place on the theological level (as opposed to the ecclesiastical level) in that the views of individual theologians and groups were weighed against each other in public declarations, press debates and conferences rather than in the form of official synod resolutions (although the latter were, of course, not lacking).

Much of the debate was sparked by the NG Church's acceptance, in 1974, of a report, *Human relations in the light of Scriptures*, which made apartheid official NG policy. This report came in for a lot of criticism for using the Bible to support a political ideology and for the questionable use of biblical texts. This criticism came largely from within the NG Church, but it is interesting to note that several Hervormde ministers derided the document for not being staunch enough in its defence of apartheid.

Following the debate on Article III in Hervormde circles, which was given much publicity by both the Afrikaans and English press and even by the SABC during 1979, the so-called Reformation Day Testimony of 31 October 1980 took centre stage. In this document, eight important NG theologians voiced their dissatisfaction about racism and the 'apparent powerlessness of the institutionalised church in South Africa' and spoke out against polarisation between population groups and the lack of visible church unity in South Africa. Although the Testimony did not go far enough according to some observers (e.g. Serfontein 1982: 156-157), it caused such an uproar that after four months the moderatures of several regional synods called a joint meeting of ministers in order to calm the opposing factions.

This was quickly followed in 1981 by a book, *Storm-kompas* (Smith *et al* 1981), the title of which is readily understandable even to those who do not know Afrikaans. Again there was a storm in the media. This time there was no question of ambiguous statements and criticism not going far enough. The book, although it contained contributions by some conservatives, clearly voiced criticism of what was amiss in South African society and of the NG Church's support of the *status quo*. It had become clear that the advocates of change in church and society were not going to be intimidated by the fear of rejection any longer. The contributors to *Storm-kompas* were all sincere NG churchmen and several took pains to stress their loyalty to the Church. This was a note that had already been struck in the earlier Hervormde debate, but which had not been appreciated or widely noticed. 'Criticism in solidarity' now became a more frequently heard dictum.

While the *Storm-kompas* storm was still raging, an interdenominational committee from various theological societies was arranging a conference called 'Church in the Eighties', which was held in Pretoria early in 1982. This was an interdenominational conference which addressed the same basic issues on church and society and the need for change in South Africa. The chief ecumenical executive of the NG Church took part (and caused a stir among Black, NG and English participants alike with his obviously pro-apartheid paper), but there was harsh rejection of the conference by several church leaders even before it started. Again a war of words in the press ensued, particularly in the Afrikaans daily, *Beeld*, which regularly shows intense interest in church affairs.

All of this was tame in comparison with the 'Open Letter' signed by 123 NG ministers, which followed in 1982. In this document specific apartheid laws and measures were named and rejected. One of the signatories, PGJ Meiring, writes the following about the document:

This (i.e. the Pretoria conference, 1982) was followed by what is probably one of the most dramatic events in the history of the NG Kerk of the past few decades, namely the publication of the so-called 'Open

Letter' (1982), in which 123 ministers of the NG Kerk (this number later grew to 148) clearly and concisely expressed their convictions: 'We, ordained ministers of the NG Kerk, express it as our conviction that true reconciliation in Christ between individuals and groups is the greatest single need in the church and therefore also in our country and our society. We believe that the church of Christ in South Africa has a particular contribution to make in this regard . . .'. It then frankly states that 'a social order which elevates irreconcilability to a principle of societal living and which alienates the different sections of the South African population from one another, is unacceptable'. It was no longer possible to remain silent about the discriminatory laws, symbols of such a system (Meiring in Van Vuuren 1983: 310).

This letter caused one of the lengthiest and most heated debates within church circles ever witnessed in Afrikanerdom. Church officials, laymen, members of other churches, people of other races and newspaper editors all took part. With a few exceptions, even Afrikaans newspapers which supported the National Party commented favourably on this outright rejection of what had for decades been looked upon as inspired doctrine. This time no measure comparable to Dr Verwoerd's energetic opposition to the Cottesloe Conference was forthcoming from the Government. If one places the Open Letter next to comparable statements of a decade earlier, the difference is striking. For instance, the 1973 synod of the Hervormde Church issued an official 'Pastoral Letter' in which it was blandly stated that apartheid was 'a permanent, unchanging ruling which is scripturally founded' [sic] and the NG synod declared officially in 1974 that 'a political system built on autogenous development in different population groups can, in the light of the Bible, be justified in principle'. Of course these are official documents and the Open Letter was not, but the difference in contents highlights what it had become possible to say openly and with considerable support in Afrikaans church circles. Officials of the NG Church tried to suppress the Open Letter when they were approached by the leading authors. The signatories wanted the letter to be discussed at the 1982 synod, but the church leadership prevented this. The letter was handicapped by stumbling blocks put in its way on procedural grounds and after publication the signatories were accused of not following the 'correct channels' and the loyalty of the 123 was questioned. This official reaction is typical of Afrikaans church leadership, which often reacts unfavourably and ad hominem when criticism arises from within.

The Open Letter was noticed overseas and regarded as a sign that there is hope for change in South Africa if such manifestly critical things can be said freely in the church (cf Coetzee 1983: 33). In spite of the positive reaction generated overseas by the Open Letter, the two Afrikaans members of the World Alliance of Reformed Churches experienced no patience at the assembly of the world body in 1982 (cf Coetzee 1983: 38-49). Both were conditionally suspended and required to discontinue their support for apartheid and help those who suffer as a result of the system.

The General Executive tendered the Hervormde Church's resignation from the Alliance forthwith, refusing to bow to what it regarded as a humiliating threat. The NG executive (Moderature) took no similar step, but the General Synod of October 1982 reacted to this issue as it did to many other controversial matters — a decision was postponed for four years and a 'wait-and-see' attitude was adopted. The same happened about the debates on mixed marriages and Article 16 of the Immorality Act and the serious tension caused by the declarations of the NG Mission Church referred to above. The synod seemed to be paralysed by the emotions that had been reverberating throughout Afrikaner church life for some two years. The uneasy balance of the 'conservatives' and the 'enlightened' group meant, in effect, that no step was taken on the road to change, which meant that the supporters of the *status quo* could regard the synod as a victory for themselves. Many representatives of the other wing regarded the synod as proof of the inability of the NG Church to contribute to meaningful change in South Africa and of the alarming petrification of group prejudices and irreconcilability in the country (cf Coetzee 1983: 65-73).

During 1983 the synod of the Hervormde Church (called its General Assembly) and the Western Cape regional synod of the NG Church took place. The former summarily endorsed the Executive's withdrawal from the World Alliance and reiterated the Church's allegiance to its traditional stand on the ever-troublesome issues of mixed marriages, 'mixed immorality' and related matters. A feature of this synod, as opposed to that of the NG Church, was the small number who differed from the majority sentiment and the irritation shown at their dissent, from both the floor and the chair. It was obvious that speculation about a spiritual home for the 'really conservative' in the Hervormde Church, though exaggerated, had its origins in this kind of climate. The Cape synod of the NG Church, which took place later in the year, had a completely different attitude to current social issues. In fact, it unambiguously declared the Mixed Marriages Act and 'its appendix in Article 16 of the Immorality Act' to be directly 'in conflict with the biblical and Christian-ethical principles on marriage'. Although it was not prepared to state categorically that 'separate development' should be condemned (because the Church, in its view, should refrain from justifying *any* political blueprint on biblical grounds), it clearly condemned racial discrimination (Resolution 328) and was much more sensitive to the seriousness of Mission Church criticism than the

General Synod (Resolution 338), which was even criticised directly by the Cape synod (Resolution 336.4.2).

As yet, little attention has been paid to the third Afrikaans 'sister', the Gereformeerde Church. This is not only because of its small numbers (just more than half the size of the Hervormde Church, as far as Whites are concerned), but mainly because of its independent style. The Gereformeerde Church is a strictly Calvinistic and theologically extremely conservative religious community. Though this can lead to intransigence in doctrinal matters, it can just as easily lead to a sincere willingness to change a stand once the conviction that 'scriptural grounds' make it necessary is reached. This is what happended at the January 1985 synod at Potchefstroom.

The Gereformeerde Church has always identified with the Afrikaner people and certainly does not take a back seat to either the NG or the Hervormde Churches in this. Like its bigger 'sisters', the Church has also backed apartheid. A number of important political figures have come from Gereformeerde ranks, e.g. Minister Jan de Klerk, a former cabinet minister closely related in politics to Dr Verwoerd; his son, Minister FW de Klerk, leader of the Transvaal National Party; and Dr CP Mulder, former minister and now senior member of the Conservative Party. However, a number of significant contributions to the debate on change in South Africa have been forthcoming from Gereformeerde circles.

First, a number of Gereformeerde academics, associated mainly with the Potchefstroom University for Christian Higher Education, have, over the years, been subjecting the socio-political situation in South Africa to incisive investigations. In the process they have come up with most disquieting criticism and frank questioning of the *status quo*, mostly published in the Potchefstroom journal *Woord en Daad*. Next, in 1977, a number of Gereformeerde members issued a declaration which criticised major aspects of Government policy. The principle of multiracial co-operation was accepted in the declaration and the repeal of a number of controversial acts was called for (e.g. immorality laws and, significantly, much security legislation). Though Gereformeerde church leadership was not officially involved in these developments, the Church obviously found no fault with their taking place.

The Gereformeerde synod of 1970 openly took an apartheid stance by accepting a resolution that 'also the church will promote the policy of geographical separation' (i.e. of the races). However, the synod of 1985 repealed the resolution in a show of readiness to practise self-criticism extremely rare in Afrikaans church circles. It was resolved *inter alia* that the Bible did not warrant a resolution like the one taken in 1970 and that the latter was actually out of step with earlier Gereformeerde convictions (cf

Gereformeerde Church 1985: 6-7). Overseas theologians representing other reformed churches welcomed the repeal of the 1970 resolution when they addressed the synod. It must be conceded that this kind of impression has not been made on overseas observers by either of the other Afrikaans 'sister churches'. In spite of the 1983 synod of the Cape NG Church (which is only a regional synod), the NG and Hervormde Churches have never conceded that their support of apartheid may have been wrong. The Gereformeerde Church has not said that apartheid (i.e. the total dispensation involving the socio-political situation of the races in South Africa) is *wrong*, but it has sounded a critical note which shows that the traditional massive support of the *status quo* in the Afrikaans churches is being eroded.

Later in 1984 the most recent row in the NG Church was caused when the moderature decided to suspend the Church's membership of the Reformed Ecumenical Synod (RES), an ecumenical body of much smaller proportions than the World Alliance of Reformed Churches and more parochial in character. This dismayed many NG theologians, because the last remaining link with an ecumenical body had been severed by the NG Church of its own accord. Whereas the Gereformeerde Church decided to remain a member of the RES, the NG Church, like the Hervormde Church, now stands completely isolated within world Christianity. In both the latter churches, the situation is often rationalised by the claim that ecumenicity (an important concept to the church) is still possible without membership of an ecumenical body. The fact that theologians all over the world continually point out the underlying grounds for the isolation very rarely seems to prompt Afrikaans theologians to consider the possibility that Christianity at large may be right and we wrong.

When we review the above sketch, it seems reasonable to state that there *has* been change in South Africa in recent years. On one hand, criticism from World Christianity and from critical churches within South Africa, especially the 'daughter churches' of the NG Church, has created an unbearable situation. In earlier years it was possible for the Afrikaans churches to live with criticism without paying too much attention to it. It is clear that this situation has changed and that sooner or later the granite must crack. This impression is enhanced by the fact that the critical voice within Afrikaans churches has become much more articulate and fearless, which is a significant change compared to the isolation of critics in the early years. It is now possible to criticise official church policies on socio-political matters without being subjected to the severe censures that were standard practice in the sixties, although such criticism is still not welcomed. This is also a change. *But in 1985 the major and basic controversial issues concerning official church policy of interest to us have not changed.* It is possible to put a positive complexion on the situation by saying that there are *many more people than previously in the Afrikaans churches who work for change within these churches while opting for solidarity with their spiritual mother.* This became visible in January 1985, when an organisation called 'Reforum' was established by hundreds of clergymen and ordinary members in Pretoria. Reforum, its name a pun on 'reform' and 'forum', is a non-racial organisation committed to constructive dialogue in search of reconciliation, justice and peace in South Africa. Whether it will be successful remains to be seen; its birth is a sign of modest change — modest, but not to be scorned for that reason.

SOME THEOLOGICAL TRENDS

It would be impossible to treat the vast subject of theological change in the more technical sense of the word within the scope of this chapter. Nevertheless, there are some significant trends that relate to the main interest of our survey to a greater or lesser extent.

The most remarkable of these is probably the almost perfect *criss-cross pattern of conservatism and progressive thinking in the Hervormde and Gereformeerde traditions.* For more than a century the Hervormde Church has been described as 'theologically liberal' by other reformed groups in South Africa. Though Hervormers have always denied this (mainly due to the emotional quality of the term 'liberal'), there has been reason for the label. The Hervormde Church has never forsaken its Dutch tradition where there has been room for the less rigidly orthodox and more modern currents of protestantism. The so-called 'modernism', i.e. the left wing of 19th century Dutch theology, could not work its way into the South African Hervormde Church, but the moderately critical school, the so-called Dutch ethicals, exercised a profound influence on local Hervormde theology. As a result, biblical criticism and its implications are freely practised and applied to theology in general and to preaching. Therefore, Hervormde theology is traditionally much more open to other theological influences, predominantly from Germany but also from the Anglo-Saxon world, than the gereformeerde (note: not written with a capital G) currents. Hervormde theology is by very nature and tradition not congenial to fundamentalism. On the other hand, the Gereformeerde Church, both here and in the Netherlands, came into existence because of unease with Hervormde 'liberalism'. In fact, the break-away took place in terms of the Calvinistic conviction that true Christians should separate themselves from the 'false church'. On this standpoint the Hervormde Church in the Netherlands and in South Africa is technically a false, i.e. a non-Christian, church. Therefore it is not surprising to find ultra-conservatism rampant in the Gereformeerde Church. The same synod that took such bold steps concerning racial segregation in 1985 took extremely conservative views on biblical criticism and voiced uneasiness about 'liberal' theological tendencies in the new Afrikaans translation of the Bible. So we end up with a cross-pattern: the church which is by far the most conservative of the three concerning socio-political matters (the Hervormde Church) is also the church with the most liberal theological tradition and therefore the church with the most potential for development in this direction; on the other hand, the church which harbours some of the most progressive or 'liberal' political forces on the Afrikaans ecclesiastical scene (the Gereformeerde Church) is also the church with the most conservative theological orientation.

A tendency that can be related to this kind of paradox is to be seen in both NG and English-speaking theological circles. On one hand *many of the influential and even internationally recognised advocates of change in South Africa are theologically conservative*, although not necessarily fundamentalist. An elegant example of this brand of theologian is David J Bosch, Dean of the theological faculty at the University of South Africa, who is a world-famous missiologist. His theology is of the conservative reformed type and even contains a measure of pietism, but at the same time he is internationally regarded as one of the most important progressive theological forces in the country. In principle, the same could be said of Beyers Naudé, although he is more of a church leader than a professional theologian. On the other hand, *there is basically no difference in the techniques of biblical interpretation and concept of scriptural authority found among theologians advocating both the right and the left of the political spectrum.* Figures like Dr Dirk Fourie and the late Dr Koot Vorster (both happen to be NG men) are not essentially different from figures like Dr Allan Boesak and Bishop Desmond Tutu when the theological issues are examined. They all use the same appeal to Scripture, the same type of hermeneutics, the same kind of exegesis and sometimes even the same texts, in the defence of their socio-political views. Only their politics seem to differ. This phenomenon, which is by no means confined to the few examples just mentioned, has been epitomised by the dictum that 'Black and White theology are blood brothers'.

South Africa has not been conspicuous for its *contribution to theology on an international level.* However, a handful of Europeans who emigrated to South Africa have developed into important scholarly theologians (as opposed to church leaders who are often called 'theologians' too). The most important of these was Bishop John William Colenso (1814-1883), who worked as an Anglican missionary in Natal during the second half of the 19th century. He published in the fields of mathematics, classics, New Testament and others, but became world-famous for his work on Old Testament studies — particularly on the Pentateuch. About half a century later the Dutchmen Berend Gemser and Adrianus van Selms arrived to embark on their careers of Old Testament and Semitic learning. Van Selms's scope of interest was just as wide as Colenso's and, like Gemser, he became an internationally recognised expert whose writings are still read in many countries. Today there are some ten or twelve South African theologians who publish internationally and whose works are noted and reviewed in internationally important scholarly journals. Obvious features in this regard are the preponderance of biblical specialists among these scholars and the small number of English-speakers and Blacks in their midst (two or three at most).

In Gereformeerde and NG circles there is often *uneasiness about critical scholarship, especially in the biblical disciplines.* This was again apparent at the 1985 synod of the Gereformeerde Church, which followed a long and heated debate in the 'Kerkbode' (official mouthpiece of the NG Church) about the 'dangers' of scholarly exegesis. A large meeting of NG ministers was held in April 1985 in order to restore calm. In these debates especially, though not exclusively, scholars from the non-denominational theological faculty of the University of South Africa were attacked for their 'liberal' views. It should be added that Hervormde members usually do not take part in this kind of thing, although they do sometimes voice their opposition to other Unisa theologians for *political* 'liberalism'.

This is not to say that little of importance is being done in the field of South African scholarly theology. There are signs that many of *the younger generation of theologians* are developing into established scholars in their own right. On the other hand, it is a remarkable though explicable fact that individuals involved in the upper echelons of church leadership and ecclesiastical decision-making are, with perhaps one or two exceptions, making no serious contribution to learned theology. This can be attributed to an old tradition of patriarchal society, viz that leadership is based on social seniority and standing and that criticism by inferiors is presumptuous. Nevertheless, this is changing slowly and younger theologians are no longer silent for fear of being labelled 'arrogant'. In this way they are asserting what could be called 'ecclesiastical freedom of speech' (for want of a better expression), which should be regarded as a healthy development.

The *contribution to theology by the pentecostal movement* has been minimal. The lack of serious theological reflection is understandable in the light of the character of the movement and its early history, but in recent years a change in these quarters has become apparent. There has been an obvious desire among pastors of churches like the Apostolic Faith Mission and even the Full Gospel Church to study theology at university level and this has led to an appreciable number of them working on programmes for

300

master's and doctoral degrees, while a few have already graduated as doctors of theology. There is now also some tension within the movement between the 'original' pentecostal ideal and the 'new' drive for scholarly respectability.

CONCLUSION

South Africa is a land of bewildering diversity, complexity and polarisation, not least in the field of church, religion and theology. Diversity can be very enriching and positive, but the condition is that it should not converge with polarisation. The pity of religious diversity and theological debate in South Africa is not only that it has converged with polarisation, but that the divisions have widened almost beyond repair. Churches, groups, councils and creeds have become symbols of political forces and are now assuming the stance of irreconcilable phalanxes. If this continues, theology and religion will be completely annexed by other forces, losing their independence, relevance and vitality. Some people are of the opinion that this point has already been reached. There are those who are bellowing at the fires and those who are sealing the cauldron's lid. There are still others who cannot give up hope that the inevitable and fundamental change approaching South African society will come about neither in spite of the churches nor as victory for some of the churches, but as a result of the churches proving how reconciliation can mould a society.

BIBLIOGRAPHY

Bosch, DJ. Racism and revolution: responses of the churches in South Africa. *Occasional Bulletin of Missionary Research*, vol. 3, no. 1, 1979.
Brown, WE. *The Catholic Church in South Africa*. London: Burns & Oats, 1960.
Coetzee, JK. *Die kerk as begeleier van sosiale verandering — 'n studie van twee groepe*. Bloemfontein: Universiteit van die Oranje-Vrystaat, 1983.
Geldenhuys, FE O'B. A house divided. *Leadership South Africa*, vol. 1, no. 2, 1982.
Gereformeerde Church. *Die Kerkblad* (official mouthpiece of the church), vol. 87, no. 2 710, 1985.
Geyser, AS et al. *Delayed action*. Pretoria: NGK, 1961.
Lederle, HI. Be filled with the Spirit of love: An update on the state of the charismatic renewal and some reflections on its central experiential teaching. *Theologia Evangelica*, vol. 15, no. 3, 1982.
Lee, P. The new christianity. *Leadership South Africa*, vol. 2, no. 3, 1983.
Lückhoff, A. *Cottesloe*. Cape Town: Tafelberg, 1978.
NG Church. *Acta Synodi*. Cape Town: 1857. *Human relations in the light of Scriptures*. Cape Town: NGK, 1973.
— *Minutes of the Western Cape Synod*. Cape Town: 1983.
NG Mission Church. *Handleiding van die Sinode*. Kaapstad: 1978. *Die NG Sendingkerk en apartheid* (Report to synod), 1982.

Serfontein, JHP. *Apartheid, change and the NG Kerk.* Johannesburg: Taurus, 1982.

Smith, NJ et al. *Storm-kompas. Opstelle op soek na 'n suiwer koers in die Suid-Afrikaanse konteks van die jare tagtig.* Kaapstad: Tafelberg, 1981.

Sundkler, BGM. *Bantu prophets in South Africa.* London: Butterworths, 1961.

Thomas, D. Church-state relationships in South Africa: uncomfortable bedfellows. *South Africa International,* vol. 13, no. 1, 1982.

Van der Horst, ST (Ed). *Race discrimination in South Africa.* Cape Town: David Philip, 1981.

Van Vuuren, DJ et al (Eds). *Change in South Africa.* Durban: Butterworths, 1983.

12 White perceptions of socio-political change in South Africa

Nic J Rhoodie, CP de Kock and MP Couper

INTRODUCTION

It is generally acknowledged at virtually all levels of South African society that the socio-political changes in South Africa over the last three years have been historically more significant than any that have occurred during the almost four decades of National Party (NP) rule. The majority of these changes are linked to the NP Government's redefinition of the so-called race problem and re-evaluation of a race policy that could manifestly no longer withstand the pressures of contemporary realities. The NP Government's current stance on political and constitutional reform is a direct function of this process, the constitution of 1983 being the most obvious and concrete manifestation of socio-political renewal. To a large extent, socio-political change in South Africa mùst be seen against the background of the new constitutional dispensation — not merely as a change of laws, but as a wide spectrum of potential change stemming from the spirit, as well as the substance, of the new constitutional system.

Included in the new constitutional dispensation are various concrete, or at least implicit, directional adjustments and shifts in emphasis in both formal government policy and the NP's socio-political philosophy, which underline the historical importance of current socio-political change in South Africa. To name but a few, there are the repeal of the Mixed Marriages Act and the race clause in the Immorality Act; the abolition of statutory job reservation in practically all occupational sectors; tangible attempts to ease the most demeaning and humiliating aspects of influx control; greater willingness to repeal all racially discriminatory statutory legislation, or to amend these laws in such a way that the discriminatory aspects of such laws or measures are eliminated (for example the Reservation of Separate Amenities Act, the Group Areas Act and even the Political Interference Act); the Government's viewpoint that Blacks who do not have permanent homes in a national Black State can be recognised as permanent residents of South Africa, as illustrated by the granting of permanent residence status

303

to the Black squatters of the Western Cape; the Government's undertaking that Black aspirations for South African citizenship will have to be accommodated democratically — a matter closely linked to a further undertaking that will make provision for Blacks domiciled in South Africa to participate in the central decision-making institutions of the State where their interests are affected; the undertaking that the principle and practice of joint decision-making which cuts through racial and colour barriers will also be extended to general affairs at second and third tier levels of government; a formal undertaking not to resettle any Black community against its collective will; State President PW Botha's announcement that he wants to enter into dialogue with Blacks with a view to a preliminary unstructured exchange of opinion on ways in which the latter's rightful political aspirations may be satisfied, as well as his invitation to all White opposition parties to co-operate with the cabinet committee specially appointed to give attention to the political and constitutional accommodation of Blacks; and finally, the extension of the principle of joint decision-making and mutual responsibility to a new set of second tier government bodies which will replace the Provincial Councils, thereby establishing the practice of 'colour blind' joint government in respect of 'general affairs', an area of decision-making traditionally the exclusive prerogative of Whites.

The abovementioned reformist initiatives, which can be regarded as the NP Government's collective response to contemporary historical realities in South Africa, are not, however, the central focus of this chapter. What will be discussed is, more specifically, White perceptions (particularly those of White Afrikaans-speakers) of socio-political change and the future implications of these changes in terms of critical White interests. It is self-evident that the changes are directly linked to the NP's reformist initiatives and thus to a large extent they can be regarded as concrete manifestations of this reform process.[1]

Furthermore, the aim is not to analyse the specific reformist initiatives in terms of the latest theories and models designed to explain social phenomena such as change, conflict, order and stability. What is offered here are the findings of an empirically based analysis of urban Whites' perceptions of certain comtemporary socio-political changes in South Africa, which was undertaken with the aid of a national probability sample survey.

The rest of the chapter may be summarised as follows: After a brief exposition of the survey design and the most important social and demographic characteristics of the sample, the main findings of the investigation, based on a broad overview of the respondents' perceptions of the general state of affairs in South Africa, will be given. Then the respondents' perceptions of more specific issues and problem areas will be examined. These include the Government's reformist actions, the new constitutional

304

dispensation, racially discriminatory laws, leadership and party preferences and White (particularly Afrikaner) responses to socio-political
change (including Afrikaner conservatism regarding conventional apartheid institutions). Special attention is given to the respondents' perceptions of the Mixed Marriages Act and the race clause in the Immorality Act.
Finally, there is a short discussion of the role of the Afrikaans-English
language differential as the predictor variable explaining most of the
variation in the sample's responses.

THE SAMPLE DESIGN AND CHIEF CHARACTERISTICS OF THE SAMPLE

The survey was undertaken nationally in February/March 1984 among a
probability sample of adult (18 years and older) urban Whites. Interviews
were conducted with 1 024 respondents out of a target sample of 1 500. The
response rate was 68,3%, which can be regarded as quite favourable for a

Table 12.1 Primary socio-demographic characteristics of the sample

Characteristics	% *
SEX	
Male	42,3
Female	57,6
AGE	
18-34	35,5
35-49	28,6
50-64	24,0
65+	11,8
EDUCATIONAL LEVEL	
Std 7 or lower, or equivalent	14,8
Std 8 or 9, or equivalent	27,1
Std 10 or equivalent	28,2
Std 10 with up to 2 years further training	8,4
Std 10 with 3 or more years further training	21,6
MARITAL STATUS	
Married	71,0
Never married	13,6
Divorced/estranged/widow/widower	15,3
LANGUAGE	
Afrikaans	51,8
English	39,7
Other	8,6
ANNUAL INCOME	
R0–R7 000	18,5
R7 001–R15 000	31,9
R15 001–R25 000	26,2
R25 001 and more	23,4

*Because of rounding, the totals will not always add up to 100. The same applies to the other tables
in this chapter.

survey of this type. The fieldwork was done by trained and professionally supervised co-workers of the HSRC's Opinion Survey Centre.

The primary socio-demographic characteristics of the sample are presented in table 12.1. The basic biographical attributes (sex, age, marital status, language and educational level) correspond, broadly speaking, with those of the White urban population of South Africa. The sample was constituted according to recognised statistical procedures in order that it would be broadly representative of the target population (adult urban Whites). The responses were satisfactory and the non-responses did not vary significantly in terms of the geographical distribution of the sample. Thus there are grounds for assuming that the collective opinions of the adult urban White population on specific socio-political changes are, generally speaking, reflected in the sample.

PERCEPTIONS OF SPECIFIC NATIONAL PROBLEM AREAS

Slightly more than half (50,7%) of the sample (54,3% of the Afrikaans speakers and 44,5% of the English speakers) were 'very satisfied' or at least 'satisfied' with the current state of affairs in South Africa in general, in contrast to 21,7% who were 'dissatisfied' or 'very dissatisfied'. The rest (27,6%) were either neutral (and categorised as 'neither satisfied nor dissatisfied'), or 'did not know'.

While 52,5% of the respondents (48,8% of the Afrikaans speakers and 54,6% of the English speakers) believed that the general political situation had improved over the past few years, 20,0% were of the opinion that it had deteriorated, 18,2% thought that it had remained unchanged and 9,3% did not know. As far as the current political situation was concerned, 47,0% were 'satisfied' or 'very satisfied' as opposed to 21,2% who were 'dissatisfied' or 'very dissatisfied'. The rest (31,8%) were either neutral, or did not know. Just over half of the respondents (51,9%) were of the opinion that the general political situation would improve over the next few years. Of the rest, 15,6% expected a deterioration in the situation, 13,6% foresaw no change and 19,0% did not know.

Proportionally fewer respondents were satisfied with the current economic situation. Less than one third (31,8%) were satisfied with the country's economic position, while 40,5% expresssed dissatisfaction. The remainder (27,7%) were either neutral or ignorant. The economic situation was regarded by most respondents as the country's 'number one problem'. Practically the same proportion of Afrikaans (25,2%) and English speakers (28,0%) expressed this opinion.

The fact that only 13,5% felt that the South African Government was spending too much on defence (as opposed to 21,3% who thought that too little was spent) can be taken as an indication that the legitimacy and credibility of the SA Defence Force was accepted by the great majority of respondents. Almost 80% felt that there was either too little or just enough being spent on defence. Almost three times as many English speakers (19,4%) as Afrikaans speakers (7,8%) felt that the Government was spending too much on defence, although practically the same proportions of each language group (58,9% and 58,4% respectively) felt that the right amount was being allocated. As far as the Black homelands were concerned, 44% of the sample (58,8% of the Afrikaans speakers and 33,7% of the English speakers) felt that too much money was being spent. Only 9,9% felt that too little was spent on them, while 35,0% believed the amount to be right and 11,1% did not know.

More than half (52,6%) of the respondents (58,3% of the Afrikaans speakers and 44,8% of the English speakers) regarded communism as the greatest threat to peace and prosperity in SA. Black nationalism of the Black Power type was seen as the greatest threat by the second largest number of respondents (24,3%). In the latter case, slightly more English speakers (26,1%) than Afrikaans speakers (23,5%) were of the opinion that Black nationalism posed the greatest threat. The Government's 'race policy' was considered to be the greatest threat by 7,3% of the sample. Communism was seen as South Africa's biggest problem by only 3,6% of the respondents, the indication being that communism is still regarded primarily as a potential and external threat and not so much as a real internal problem for South Africa.

The respondents' opinions on ten important problem areas are collated in table 12.2. The most negative evaluations were in respect of inflation and the influx of Blacks into the cities. The Government was considered to have fared 'poorly' or 'very poorly' in each of these two matters by 34,2% and 30,6% of the sample respectively. The most positive evaluations concerned the protection of South Africa's borders and the combating of terrorism. In both cases more than 90% of the respondents expressed the opinion that the Government had fared 'extremely well' or 'well'. This finding can be interpreted as proof that the legitimacy of the Government's handling of the security question — as far as external attacks on the political and constitutional integrity of SA is concerned — is supported by the large majority of Whites. (The deduction is supported by the finding that about 80% of the respondents felt that the Government was either spending too little or just enough on defence.)

The obvious difference between the two main language groups on the issues of the national economy and the curbing of inflation is particularly striking, English speakers being clearly more sensitive to economic issues.

Table 12.2 Respondents' opinions on the Government's handling of specific national affairs

	Response categories											
	Very good or good			Neutral			Very poor or poor			Uncertain/Don't know			Total (all respondents)
National affair	Afr speakers	Eng speakers	All respondents	Afr speakers	Eng speakers	All respondents	Afr speakers	Eng speakers	All respondents	Afr speakers	Eng speakers	All respondents	
						Percentage							
National economy	63,4	41,4	53,6	22,7	35,2	28,5	8,9	16,7	12,3	4,9	6,9	5,7	100,1
Protection of national borders	94,1	92,9	93,7	2,8	4,2	3,2	2,3	0,3	1,5	0,8	2,7	1,6	100,0
Combating terrorism	92,2	87,7	90,6	3,8	5,9	4,6	2,9	3,0	2,8	1,1	3,5	2,1	100,1
Influx of Blacks into cities	31,8	25,4	29,3	30,7	31,0	30,6	28,8	32,5	30,6	8,7	11,1	9,6	100,1
Constitutional reform	57,6	45,8	52,2	20,5	30,3	24,9	10,2	10,6	10,5	11,7	13,3	12,4	100,0
White education	80,3	71,4	76,4	11,0	18,5	14,0	7,6	6,4	7,4	1,1	3,7	2,3	100,1
Curbing inflation	38,8	21,9	31,2	26,7	33,0	29,3	29,2	39,2	34,2	5,3	5,9	5,3	100,0
Promotion of South Africa's image overseas	54,5	31,3	43,3	24,8	30,5	27,5	13,4	26,1	19,5	7,2	12,1	9,7	100,0
International sporting ties	57,6	44,8	51,9	21,4	25,4	22,8	15,2	24,4	19,5	5,9	5,4	5,8	100,0
White self-determination	62,9	50,7	58,5	20,5	29,1	23,7	9,1	8,4	8,8	7,6	11,8	9,1	100,1

Somewhat unexpected is the comparatively small gap between the two language groups in their views on constitutional reform, as well as the fact that relatively more English speakers than Afrikaans speakers felt that the Government was faring well in combating terrorism.

More than a third (34,2%) of the respondents (38,5% of the Afrikaans speakers and 29,3% of the English speakers) indicated that they accepted the new Constitution *completely*, 42,3% accepted only *certain sections* of the Constitution, 9,4% (10,6% of the Afrikaans speakers and 9,1% of the English speakers) rejected it *completely* and 14,1% were uncertain or did not know. It would appear that almost the same proportion of Afrikaans speakers as English speakers (76,5% and 76,9% respectively) accept the new Constitution in part at least.

Sixty per cent of the respondents (55,3% of the Afrikaans speakers and 65,4% of the English speakers) were of the opinion that relations between Whites, Coloureds and Indians would improve under the new Constitution, 10,8% (14,6% of the Afrikaans speakers and 6,6% of the English speakers) believed that relations would worsen, 16,4% felt that relations would neither improve nor worsen and 12,8% were uncertain or did not know. The fact that proportionally more English speakers than Afrikaans speakers felt that relations between these three groups would improve can possibly be ascribed to relatively more English speakers being traditionally opposed to apartheid and therefore supportive of any measures that might at least soften the classic apartheid system.

LEADERSHIP AND PARTY PREFERENCE

Asked whom they would choose to lead South Africa politically at the present time, 38,0% of the sample nominated the current State President, Mr PW Botha, 30,1% nominated Mr Pik Botha, 4,4% chose Dr Van Zyl Slabbert, 2,5% Dr AP Treurnicht and 9,5% diverse leaders who each received less than 1% support, while 15,4% were uncertain or did not know. Of the respondents who did mention a candidate by name, about 45% chose Mr PW Botha.

If we look at the two main language groups, we find that 39,5% of the Afrikaans speakers and 36,2% of the English speakers chose the current State President. The corresponding proportions in the case of Mr Pik Botha were 33,8% and 24,9% respectively. (It is noteworthy that the abovementioned 36,2% approximates the 40,8% of English speakers who indicated that they supported the NP.) In view of the traditionally sharp political division which has prevailed between the two language groups regarding leadership preference until fairly recently, it is remarkable that about equal proportions of English and Afrikaans speakers chose Mr PW Botha.

Further, it appears that the trend towards parity between the two language groups in their choice of a national (not necessarily NP) leader, is manifestly not repeated in their attitudes towards basic apartheid institutions (see table 12.4).

The party-political preferences of the respondents are set out in table 12.3. If we look at the response patterns in this table, it is notable that the proportional support for the New Republic Party (NRP), Conservative Party (CP) and Progressive Federal Party (PFP) was, at the time of the survey, lower than that calculated by political analysts and organisers for these parties at about the same time. It is justifiable to ask whether or not the explanation for this discrepancy lies in the particularly large proportion of respondents (27,2%) who did not indicate a choice at the time of the survey. Judged superficially, it would appear that a sizeable proportion of this 27,2% were respondents who at the time of the survey were inclined to support the PFP, CP or NRP, but for one or other reason did not indicate a preference for a particular party.

Table 12.3 Whites' party-political preferences (by language)

Language	NP %	PFP %	CP %	HNP %	NRP %	No response %	Total %
				Political party			
Afrikaans	69,3	1,5	8,2	4,2	0,6	16,2	100,0
English	40,8	13,9	1,7	0,3	4,2	39,1	100,0
Total sample	56,4	7,0	5,1	2,4	2,0	27,1	100,1

As far as the PFP is concerned, the relatively large proportion of English-speaking respondents who did not indicate a party preference (or did not want to) can be regarded as significant. At the time of the survey, about 40% of the English-speaking respondents did not indicate a party preference. The chances are strong, therefore, that a large proportion of these respondents supported the PFP, but for some reason did not mention (or want to mention) such support. The fact remains that the 7,0% support of the PFP is decidedly lower than the figure accepted at that time by most politicians.

SUPPORT FOR OR REJECTION OF SPECIFIC APARTHEID MEASURES

Tables 12.4-12.6 represent an exposition of the respondents' relative support for (or rejection of) 21 apartheid institutions. The seven policy areas cited in table 12.5 represent seven fundamental (macro) apartheid structures which, with the exception of *separate public amenities*, have traditionally been regarded as 'grand' apartheid. The 14 measures that appear in table 12.6 represent specific micro-apartheid structures. They are largely an itemisation of the aforementioned separate public amenities or services normally entrusted to or administered by a local authority and commonly referred to as 'petty' apartheid. In the case of the seven macro-apartheid structures, the respondents were asked to indicate whether they supported or opposed the structures and in the case of the 14 micro-apartheid structures, the respondents were asked to what degree they were in favour of the desegregation of such structures. For both the seven macro- and 14 micro-apartheid measures, the three Non-White population groups were regarded as a single entity.

Even a superficial glance at tables 12.4 and 12.5 will reveal a strong conservative trend in the responses. It is being assumed that a respondent's

Table 12.4 Respondents displaying polar conservatism — by language, sex, age, educational level, income and party preference

Variables	Respondents who indicated their support for:			
	All 21 apartheid practices*	All 14 micro-apartheid measures**	All seven macro-apartheid structures***	All five sensitive micro-apartheid measures†
	%	%	%	%
All respondents	19,4	29,2	39,4	52,7
LANGUAGE				
Afrikaans	30,2	42,2	57,9	71,3
English	6,9	13,8	20,1	31,4
SEX				
Male	17,7	24,9	36,2	47,2
Female	20,5	32,0	41,9	56,2
AGE				
18-34	18,5	24,8	41,3	47,4
35-49	18,4	27,6	37,2	54,3
50-64	19,9	29,3	40,2	53,7
65+	22,3	43,8	37,2	61,2
EDUCATIONAL LEVEL				
Nil to Std 9	28,3	44,4	46,0	66,8
Std 10 and more	12,8	17,8	34,6	42,2
POLITICAL PARTY				
NP	20,6	30,4	43,5	57,0
CP	34,6	55,8	59,6	86,5
PFP	4,2	7,0	11,3	14,1
HNP	58,3	75,0	66,7	91,7
NRP	5,0	20,0	25,0	45,0
None and uncertain	15,6	23,9	33,0	44,6

*Seven macro-measures and 14 micro-measures. See tables 12.5 and 12.6.
**See table 12.6. Only 'never' responses.
***See table 12.5.
†Creches and nursery schools, hospital wards, public toilets, swimming-baths and beaches. Only 'never' responses.

311

degree of socio-political conservatism will be in direct relation to the extent to which he or she supports the 21 apartheid institutions in question or, to put it the other way round, the respondent's degree of support for reform will correlate with the degree to which he or she opposes these apartheid structures. In other words, for analytical purposes the supposition is made that opposition to or support for the aforementioned apartheid practices is an indicator or index of socio-political conservatism as opposed to a socio-political desire for reform. A response which indicates support for a specific macro-apartheid measure is regarded as a conservative response. Similarly, a response indicating that the respondent feels that a particular micro-apartheid practice should *never* be desegregated is regarded as a conservative response.

Support for all, or at least the large majority of the 21 apartheid measures is indicative of a fundamental conservative disposition (*polar conservatism*). However, for the purposes of statistical analysis it has been decided that those respondents who adopted a conservative stance towards *all 21* apartheid measures should be categorised collectively as polar conservatives. A strong case could, however, be made for a conservative response to all seven macro- or all 14 micro-apartheid structures also being regarded as a measure of polar conservatism. Indeed, an equally strong argument could be that as such the criteria are still too narrow and that those who supported at least three-quarters of the seven macro-apartheid or 14 micro-apartheid measures could also be regarded as socio-politically conservative. Accordingly, it must be borne in mind that for the purpose of this analysis only polar (extreme) conservatism is being taken into account. In all likelihood, a considerable proportion of the sample will qualify as simply less extreme or less rigidly conservative. Thus, as far as the apartheid institutions in question are concerned, the focus is on polar conservatism and not on conservatism as a continuum ranging from less or more extreme positions across the attitudinal spectrum.

Furthermore, if the abovementioned approach is inverted, it can be argued that the measure of support accorded to the apartheid measures by the respondents could be taken as a general index of reformist ideology, *increasing* reformism being associated with *decreasing* support for apartheid. In other words, a *decreasing* frequency of support for the particular apartheid measures may be regarded as a rough indicator of a corresponding increase in support for reformist change.

If we take the seven macro- and 14 micro-apartheid measures together (see table 12.4), it appears that 19,4% of the respondents (30,2% of the Afrikaans speakers and 6,9% of the English speakers) held a conservative viewpoint on *all 21* measures — a tendency which confirms the strong historical correlation between the Afrikaans language variable and socio-political conservatism. Table 12.4 also indicates the tendency for the younger, more educated and higher-income respondents to adopt a less conservative outlook than the older, less educated and lower-income respondents. Women are clearly more inclined towards polar conservatism than men. These broad tendencies associated with language, sex, income, age and educational level come to the fore whichever of the three groupings of apartheid measures (seven, 14 or 21) is used as the point of departure.

The relationship between socio-political conservatism and party-political support is analysed in the section entitled 'The connection between socio-political conservatism and (political) party preference'. The question which of the aforementioned variables (socio-demographic characteristics) explains the greatest measure of variation in the sample's responses, is examined in more detail under the heading 'Variables that determine the greatest measure of variation in the sample's perceptions of socio-political change'.

From table 12.5 it appears that the proportion of the total sample that rejected the seven macro-apartheid structures never exceeded 28% in the case of any one of these structures. In all seven cases more than 60% of the respondents were in favour of the particular measure, the greatest support being for separate voters' rolls (78,6%) and Black homelands (75,7%). The strongest measure of rejection was directed at the Mixed Marriages Act (27,7%) and the Group Areas Act (26,5%). The proportion of Afrikaans speakers who supported the seven macro-structures was not *lower* than 76% in any one case, whilst the English language group indicated less than 65% support throughout. Among Afrikaans speakers, support for the seven measures ranged between 76,8% (Group Areas Act) to 92,1% (separate voters' rolls). The comparable proportions for English speakers were 37,8% (the Immorality Act) and 64,3% (separate voters' rolls). For both language groups, the *least opposition to* and the *most support for* an apartheid measure was recorded for separate voters' rolls — a response pattern which has significant implications for political reform in South Africa.

Table 12.6 shows that as far as the desegregation of public facilities is concerned, in the case of 11 of these 14 amenities/services more than half of the respondents felt that such facilities should 'never' be opened to all races. The three exceptions were public transport, hotels and libraries, where 47,8%, 48,8% and 42,3% of respondents respectively felt that the services concerned should 'never' be desegregated. The strongest opposition to desegregation was directed at public swimming-baths (71,3% 'never' response), public toilets (68,1% 'never' response), hospital wards (66,7% 'never' response), nursery schools and crèches (66,4% 'never' response) and beaches (65,6% 'never' response).

A comparison of the responses given by members of the two language

Table 12.5 Afrikaans-speaking and English-speaking Whites' attitudes towards seven fundamental apartheid structures

Apartheid structure	White language group	Respondents' attitudes (%)				Total
		In favour	Neutral*	Opposed	Uncertain or do not know	
Mixed Marriages Act	Afrikaans speakers	78,9	3,8	16,6	0,8	100,1
	English speakers	41,3	15,2	41,3	2,2	100,0
	Total sample	61,3	9,4	27,7	1,6	100,0
Immorality Act (prohibition of sexual relations between Whites and Non-Whites)	Afrikaans speakers	81,3	4,9	13,4	0,4	100,0
	English speakers	37,8	16,5	41,0	4,7	100,0
	Total sample	61,1	10,4	25,9	2,5	99,9
Group Areas Act (prohibition of multiracial residential areas)	Afrikaans speakers	76,8	6,1	16,1	1,1	100,1
	English speakers	42,4	15,5	38,4	3,7	100,0
	Total sample	60,2	10,9	26,5	2,4	100,0
Separate schools for Whites	Afrikaans speakers	90,2	4,2	5,1	0,6	100,1
	English speakers	55,4	13,1	28,3	3,2	100,0
	Total sample	73,4	8,6	15,7	2,2	99,9
Separate public amenities/services	Afrikaans speakers	84,9	5,3	8,1	1,7	100,0
	English speakers	50,5	16,8	30,1	2,7	100,1
	Total sample	68,1	11,3	18,1	2,5	100,0
Black homelands	Afrikaans speakers	89,6	2,6	4,2	3,6	100,0
	English speakers	60,3	10,8	19,7	9,1	99,9
	Total sample	75,7	7,1	11,0	6,2	100,0
Separate voters' rolls	Afrikaans speakers	92,1	2,6	2,5	2,8	100,0
	English speakers	64,3	11,1	17,7	6,9	100,0
	Total sample	78,6	6,6	9,8	5,0	100,0

* Not in favour of or against.

Table 12.6 Respondents' viewpoints with regard to the desegregation of 14 public amenities/services

Public amenities/ services	When should an amenity/service be opened to all races?															Total (all respondents)
	Now			In the near future			In the distant future			Never*			Uncertain			
	Afr-speakers	Eng-speakers	All respondents	Afr-speakers	Eng-speakers	All respondents	Afr-speakers	Eng-speakers	All respondents	Afr-speakers	Eng-speakers	All respondents	Afr-speakers	Eng-speakers	All respondents	
	Percentage															
Crèches and nursery schools	1,0	13,5	7,1	3,2	18,2	10,0	5,9	15,7	10,5	86,6	44,5	66,4	3,4	8,1	6,0	100,0
Hospital wards	1,9	14,5	7,6	3,2	14,3	8,9	5,7	16,5	10,3	85,3	45,5	66,7	4,0	9,3	6,5	100,0
Public swimming-baths	1,5	17,0	8,2	1,3	11,3	6,5	5,9	12,5	8,8	88,3	51,4	71,3	3,0	7,9	5,2	100,0
Bars	4,9	15,5	9,8	2,1	13,0	7,3	7,8	15,2	11,3	78,3	45,2	62,6	7,0	11,1	9,0	100,0
Public beaches	2,1	19,4	10,0	2,3	14,5	8,2	7,9	12,0	10,1	84,5	44,7	65,6	3,2	9,3	6,2	100,1
Health clinics	4,4	18,9	10,9	5,5	17,4	11,7	9,1	18,2	12,7	74,9	38,1	57,5	6,2	7,4	7,1	99,9
Public toilets	4,7	17,7	10,9	3,0	13,0	7,7	7,6	10,6	9,0	82,2	52,3	68,1	2,5	6,4	4,3	100,0
Cinemas	5,7	23,6	14,2	3,8	15,5	9,6	12,1	16,0	13,2	73,4	37,6	56,8	5,1	7,4	6,3	100,1
Hotels	6,1	26,5	15,8	8,3	18,4	12,9	11,2	16,0	13,1	65,0	30,5	48,8	9,5	8,6	9,4	100,0
Restaurants	6,4	25,8	15,8	5,3	17,2	10,9	10,4	15,0	12,3	73,0	33,2	54,2	4,9	8,9	6,7	99,9
Parks	9,5	31,2	19,7	6,8	15,5	11,1	9,1	13,3	11,1	68,3	34,6	52,3	6,3	5,4	5,9	100,1
Cemeteries	10,4	30,7	20,1	4,0	13,0	8,4	10,0	13,0	10,9	69,4	31,2	51,4	6,2	12,0	9,2	100,0
Public transport	10,0	33,9	20,7	8,5	15,0	11,6	10,8	14,0	12,3	63,5	30,2	47,8	7,2	6,9	7,5	99,9
Public libraries	12,3	34,6	22,9	11,2	19,9	15,2	11,9	14,7	13,1	58,6	24,3	42,3	6,1	6,4	6,5	100,0

* Described in this section as an indication of polar conservatism.

groups reveals that Afrikaans speakers have a more conservative response pattern than their English-speaking compatriots. For example, the proportion of Afrikaans speakers who felt that particular facilities should 'never' be opened ranged from 58,6% (public libraries) to 83,3% (public swimming-baths). The comparable figures for English speakers ranged from 24,3% (public libraries) to 52,3% (public toilets). In contrast, more than half of the English speakers felt that only *two* amenities, namely public swimming-baths (51,4%) and public toilets (52,3%) should 'never' be opened. (The importance of the language differential is considered again in the section entitled 'Variables that determine the greatest measure of variation in the sample's perceptions of socio-political change'.)

From table 12.6 it would be justifiable to ask whether a 'never' response should be used as the only measure of conservatism. Many experts would argue that the option *'in the distant future'* could just as well be taken as a measure of conservatism. If so, the sum of the 'never' and 'in the distant future' responses would raise the conservative response rate by between 8,8% (public swimming-baths) and 13,2% (cinemas) for the 14 apartheid measures specified. If this method of calculation were used, the Afrikaans-speaking respondents would, in each case, return a conservative response rate of more than 70%. In the case of the five most sensitive contact situations (crèches and nursery schools, hospital wards, public swimming-baths, public toilets and public beaches), the English-speakers' conservative response would exceed 50% throughout.

The interpretation of the response patterns in tables 12.4 to 12.6 must take another factor into account, namely that no differentiation between the three Non-White race groups was made. If, however, one were to pose this series of questions with respect to Coloureds and Indians on one hand and Non-Whites (including Blacks) on the other, it could be safely accepted that there would be a consistent variation in the conservative response rates, the greatest measure of White resistance being directed at the opening of facilities to Blacks.

The tendency to differentiate between Coloureds and Indians on one hand and Blacks on the other is a general one among Whites. Many White respondents argued that the politically dominant White group's policy of excluding Blacks from the central power institutions of the State, as witnessed in the new constitutional dispensation, was strongly supported by White public opinion that critical White interests necessitated the differential treatment of Black interests. In the present survey almost two thirds of the respondents (77,7% of Afrikaans speakers and 47,0% of English speakers) agreed with the argument that Blacks should not serve in the same government with Whites, Coloureds and Indians, while 29,6% rejected this argument and 6,3% were uncertain or did not know. This

Table 12.7 White perceptions of a future under a White government, a mixed government including Coloureds and Indians and a Black government*

Positive Characteristics	White perceptions expressed as positive, middle** and negative responses in respect of:												Negative characteristics
	White government				Mixed White, Coloured and Indian government				Black government				
	Positive response	Middle response	Negative response	Total	Positive response	Middle response	Negative response	Total	Positive response	Middle response	Negative response	Total	
	Percentage												
Good	81,9	7,5	10,6	100,0	56,3	16,1	27,5	99,9	3,0	3,3	93,6	99,9	Bad
Relaxed	56,5	8,6	35,0	100,1	37,0	14,9	48,1	100,0	1,9	2,0	96,1	100,0	Tense
Easy	55,9	12,3	31,8	100,0	29,6	19,7	50,6	99,9	1,0	2,5	96,6	100,1	Difficult
Orderly	80,2	7,3	12,4	99,9	50,3	17,9	31,8	100,0	4,0	3,4	92,6	100,0	Chaotic
Prosperity	80,7	9,0	10,4	100,1	53,3	19,5	27,3	100,1	4,2	4,1	91,7	100,0	Decline
Safe future	71,3	11,2	17,6	100,1	46,8	19,0	34,3	100,1	3,7	3,6	92,8	100,1	Unsafe future
Peace	60,5	16,3	23,2	100,0	48,6	22,8	28,5	99,9	5,6	10,9	83,4	99,9	War

* HSRC Institute for Historical Research, 1982.

** Responses regarded as neither positive, nor negative.

317

tendency among Whites to differentiate between Blacks on one hand and Coloureds and Indians on the other was further reflected in the finding that Whites were appreciably less optimistic that relationships with Blacks would improve.

The available empirical evidence indicates that the White (and especially the Afrikaner) tolerance threshold for reformist initiatives in intergroup relations is considerably higher with regard to Coloureds and Indians than it is with regard to Blacks. A nation-wide HSRC survey in July 1982 aimed at an analysis of urban Whites' perceptions of a future under a 'mixed' government highlighted this differentiated approach. The relevant findings are set out in table 12.7. One fundamental deduction that can be made from the table focuses on the pertinent manner in which Whites indicated that they had little enthusiasm for Black partnership in a mixed government. The rate at which the positive responses decline and the negative responses increase as soon as the Blacks are taken into account is so drastic that there is little room for doubt regarding the Whites' relatively low tolerance threshold for power-sharing with Blacks in an integrated political system.

The abovementioned tendency was confirmed in April 1984 during a survey conducted by the HSRC in three strongly conservative Afrikaner-dominant communities, namely Pietersburg, Delmas and Barberton (see Rhoodie and Couper 1984). In Pietersburg and Barberton an average of 34% of the respondents who supported the new constitutional dispensation maintained that they would withdraw their support should Coloureds and Indians receive representation in White local government. Almost two thirds (65%) said they would react in this way if *Blacks* were drawn into local government bodies. It was calculated that 35% of the respondents who were against *Black* representation in local bodies were not opposed to Coloured and Indian representation in these bodies. This empirical evidence is collectively significant for the Government's present initiatives on constitutional reform in general, as well as for the debate in both specialist and lay circles on the future accommodation of Black political aspirations.

THE CONNECTION BETWEEN SOCIO-POLITICAL CONSERVATISM AND (POLITICAL) PARTY PREFERENCE

One would expect that a markedly conservative response to the 21 apartheid institutions set out in tables 12.4-12.6 could be regarded as a clear indicator or predictor of (political) party preference and, conversely, that party preference could be used as an indicator of conservatism. If the justifiable assumption is made that support for *all 21* apartheid institutions, or *all seven* macro-apartheid structures, or *all 14* micro-apartheid

318

measures, can be regarded as a broad measure of polar conservatism, one could expect that a relatively small proportion of PFP supporters and a relatively large proportion of HNP supporters would be found in the ranks of such polar conservatives. Furthermore, most analysts would certainly concede that today White voters associate the NP with an ultra-conservative image as little as they associate the CP with a moderate or 'enlightened' image. This argument incorporates a further implicit assumption: Afrikaans speakers in particular who qualify as polar conservatives should identify with strongly right-wing parties, the converse being equally true of the relation between opposition to apartheid on one hand and support for more reformist-inclined parties on the other. Thus, the degree of symmetry between ideology and party will be determined largely by the degree to which the Whites' formal party support is consistently in agreement with their position on the reformism-conservatism spectrum. The question is whether formal party support can be regarded as a predictor of the particular party's position on the ideological spectrum and vice versa.

In the sample a symmetrical relationship between party preference and ideological position definitely exists with regard to the PFP and HNP. As can be gathered from table 12.4, there is an obvious symmetry between polar reformism/conservatism and party support. Only 4,2% of PFP supporters (compared with 58,3% of HNP supporters) were in favour of *all 21* apartheid institutions, while 7% and 75% respectively of these two parties' supporters supported *all 14* micro-apartheid measures and 11,3% and 66,7% supported *all seven* macro-apartheid institutions. In other words, the average PFP supporter is ideologically 'liberal' and formally supports a party with an obviously reformist credo, while the average HNP follower is polar conservative and formally supports a party with a decidedly ultra-conservative policy. In contrast, as table 12.4 underlines, the same symmetry (between party preference and reformism/conservatism) does not exist in the case of NP, CP, or NRP supporters. We see, for example, that 20,6% of the NP supporters and 34,6% of the CP supporters qualify as polar conservatives in respect of *all 21* apartheid institutions, while 43,5% (NP) and 59,6% (CP) supported *all seven* macro-apartheid institutions. Respectively, 30,4% and 55,8% of the NP and CP supporters expressed opposition to the desegregation of all 14 local amenities/services.

Measured by the criteria for socio-political conservatism set out above, the relative distance between the NP and CP respondent categories is, generally speaking, smaller than that between the NP and PFP. Judged by the respondents' party preference on the whole, the relative gap between the NP and the CP is not much greater than that between the CP and the HNP. (See table 12.4.) What should not be lost sight of, however, is that these deductions are not based on an analysis of formal party policy, but on the opinions of respondents who supported all 21, or all 14, or all seven apartheid institutions and who, on the grounds of their preference for the NP, PFP, CP, NRP or HNP, were categorised as sub-samples for the purposes of analysis.

For the purposes of comparison, the relative gap between the five categories of party supporters can be arranged on a scale between 0 and 100. The zero value means that no supporters of a particular party supported all 21, or all 14, or all seven apartheid institutions. Generally speaking, the scale represents an ascending order of conservatism from 0, the minimum degree of conservatism, to 100, the maximum degree. Conversely, the polar values (0 and 100) can be regarded as a rough index of the respondents' support or rejection of socio-political reform, with the 0 and 100 values indicating maximum and minimum support for reform respectively.

Measured by the percentage of respondents who supported all 21, all 14, or all seven apartheid institutions, the relative gap between the respondents according to party preference is shown in figure 12.1.

For PFP and HNP supporters, the trend towards a more symmetrical relationship between party preference and socio-political ideology is clearly underlined by the three scales. In contrast, a greater measure of ambivalence is revealed by those respondents indicating a preference for the NP or the CP. There is a greater proportion of polar conservatives among NP supporters than might be expected when the increasingly 'verligte' (literally: enlightened) image of the party is taken into account. Among the CP supporters, on the other hand, there are fewer polar conservatives than might be expected if that party's political credo is taken into consideration. On all three scales the NP supporters take the middle position, the suggestion being that, broadly speaking, the NP party is considered to be the 'middle of the road' party by Whites. In terms of party co-operation, coalition government and policy options, in the South African power constellation a 'middle of the road' party can enjoy certain strategic and competitive advantages beyond the reach of ideologically more extreme parties.

The asymmetrical relationship between ideological orientation and formal party preference in the case of NP and CP supporters repeats itself when this relationship is analysed for *Afrikaans-speaking* NP supporters in particular. From the survey data it would appear that 27,3% of this category supported *all 21* apartheid institutions, 38,0% *all 14* micro-apartheid measures and 55,9% *all seven* macro-apartheid structures, compared with 32,6%, 55,8% and 60,5% respectively for CP supporters. Thus a White Afrikaans speaker's formal party preference cannot simply be taken as a reliable measure of his or her degree of socio-political conservatism. The converse is probably equally true.

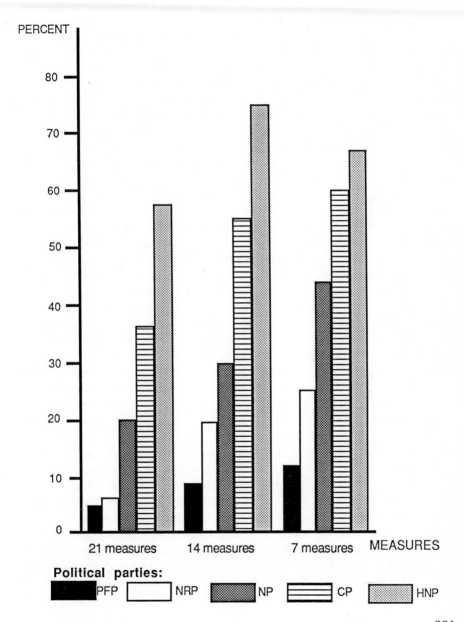

Fig 12.1 Level of conservatism of supporters of specific political parties in terms of support for various apartheid measures

What ought to be clear at this stage is that the preceding analysis has bearing on the question whether degree of socio-political conservatism can be regarded as a reasonably accurate predictor of formal *party preference* and *not* on the question whether socio-political conservatism is an accurate predictor of the White respondent's support for or rejection of the new *constitutional dispensation* as such. Although support for the 21 apartheid institutions can be taken as a measure of polar conservatism, they cannot be used as a predictor of support for or rejection of the new constitutional dispensation, because they include various institutions or structures not directly or immediately affected by the new dispensation.

In other words, even a polar conservative can support the new constitutional system without implying that by doing so he is in favour of the abolition of all 21 apartheid measures. Thus, polar conservatism and acceptance of the new constitutional system do not necessarily contradict each other. Table 12.8, which refers to the proportions of the respondents who accept or reject the new constitutional plan, shows that support for the particular apartheid measures is only to a slight degree an indicator of support for or rejection of the new dispensation. For example, the new Constitution was accepted *in its entirety* by 28,3% of the respondents who supported *all 21* apartheid institutions, by 28,6% of those who supported *all 14* micro-apartheid measures and by 33,0% of those who supported *all seven* macro-apartheid institutions.

Because the new Constitution is associated to a greater or lesser degree with socio-political reform, one would expect it to be rejected by a greater proportion of polar conservatives than was the case with the sample as a whole. According to table 12.8, no such tendency is revealed by the survey data. In fact, the proportion of polar conservatives who support or reject the Constitution does not differ significantly from that of the sample as a whole.

ATTITUDES TOWARDS MARRIAGE AND SEXUAL RELATIONS ACROSS THE COLOUR BAR AS MEASURES OF REFORMISM/CONSERVATISM

Many experts on intergroup relationships in South Africa subscribe to the hypothesis that for many years Whites' opinions on marriage and sexual relations across the colour bar have served as a reasonably reliable indicator of their positions on the reformism/conservatism spectrum. Support for the two statutory measures which prohibited marriage and sexual contact between White and Non-White (the Mixed Marriages Act and section 16 of the Immorality Act) has traditionally been interpreted as a relatively reliable index of socio-political conservatism and, conversely, rejection of these two laws has traditionally been interpreted as a relatively reliable index of socio-political reformism. In spite of the repeal of these

322

Table 12.8 The proportion of polar conservative respondents who support or reject the new Constitution

Response	Respondents who support all 21 apartheid measures*	Respondents who support 14 micro-apartheid measures**	Respondents who support seven macro-apartheid measures***	Total sample
		Percentage		
Accept the Constitution in its entirety	28,3	28,6	33,0	34,2
Accept some parts of the Constitution	39,9	36,7	42,4	42,3
Reject the Constitution in its entirety	16,7	17,5	11,9	9,4
Uncertain or don't know	15,2	17,2	12,7	14,1
Total	100,1	100,0	100,0	100,0

* See table 12.4.

** See table 12.6.

*** See table 12.5.

323

laws, the original rationale behind them is rooted in an ideology still widely regarded as one of the corner-stones of White (and especially Afrikaner) conservatism.

As far as the results of the present study are concerned, it appears from table 12.5 that a clear majority of Whites support the retention of both the Mixed Marriages Act and section 16 of the Immorality Act (61,3% and 61,1% repectively). The response patterns of the sample underline a tendency already apparent in a number of surveys on socio-political change in South Africa, namely that Whites do not think or act as a homogeneous group where opinions or attitudes on the socio-political accommodation of Non-Whites are concerned. This trend is clearly reflected in table 12.5. The level of support for or opposition to these two apartheid laws among Afrikaans speakers was roughly equal. The same tendency was found among English speakers. The big difference emerges when the degree of support or opposition found among the two language groups is compared. What is especially noticeable is that Afrikaans-speaking respondents are, comparatively speaking, more in favour of the two laws than English-speaking respondents and in the former group far fewer respondents were neutral ('neither for nor against'), 'uncertain', or in the 'did not know' category. Proportionally, almost twice as many Afrikaans speakers as English speakers were in favour of the two laws. In contrast, compared with Afrikaans speakers, almost two-and-a-half times as many English speakers opposed the Mixed Marriages Act and about three times as many rejected the Immorality Act.

More specifically, as far as the Mixed Marriages Act and Immorality Act are concerned, it can be deduced from table 12.5 that the Afrikaans-speaking respondents' support for these two laws was approximately on the same high level as their support for the other five apartheid structures. In the case of English-speaking respondents, we find that the support they lent to the aforementioned laws was less than their support for the other five apartheid structures.

VARIABLES THAT DETERMINE THE GREATEST MEASURE OF VARIATION IN THE SAMPLE'S PERCEPTIONS OF SOCIO-POLITICAL CHANGE

As a further step in the analysis of the relevant data, an attempt was made to determine which socio-demographic variables explained most of the variation in the respondents' perceptions of socio-political change. To this effect, the variation in the sample's responses on two key questions, namely support for or rejection of, firstly, the race clause in the Immorality Act and, secondly, the new constitutional dispensation, was subjected to a Multiple Classification Analysis (MCA).[2] Six primary socio-demographic variables were selected for this purpose, namely sex, age, educational level, marital status, income and home language.[3] Application of the MCA technique produced basically the same results for the Immorality Act and the new constitutional dispensation. However, due to shortage of space it was decided to focus on the Immorality Act.

With regard to the sample as a whole, the relationship between five of the six socio-demographic characteristics and respondents' attitudes towards the Immorality Act proved to be statistically significant. These five variables were sex, educational qualification, marital status, income and home language. Taken together,[4] these five characteristics explain a total of 19,2% of the variation in a particular attitude. That is to say, the other approximately 80% of variation in an attitude is attributable to either uncontrolled or unknown characteristics of the respondents and their social milieu. It can also be stated that the five controllable socio-demographic characteristics reflect about 20% of the relevant social reality. At first glance it might appear that nothing much has been achieved by this analysis, but this 20% is relatively high for the sciences/disciplines that address very complex social realities. Given the five socio-demographic characteristics, a social scientist should be correct in 20 out of 100 predictions pertaining to attitude towards the Immorality Act.

The percentage variation in the attitude concerned explained by *each* of the five characteristics *in isolation*[5] is as follows:

Home language	16,3%
Education level	3,0%
Marital status	2,3%
Income	1,6%
Sex	1,1%

From the evidence it is clear that home language accounts for most of the variation. (See also tables 12.4-12.6.) Indeed, the major disparity between the two main White language groups' perceptions of socio-political change is a central theme in the survey. It can be argued that this gap indicates the existence of two different social collectivities, each socialised in a characteristic normative direction. In the final instance it is not a question of language as a sensory communication medium, but of language as both a function and a determinant of a particular lifestyle, normative orientation and culture base and of fundamental socialising processes in the parental home, in broader family relationships and in the school, the church, and the friendship group. Broadly stated, Afrikaans speakers respond differently from English speakers — not so much because they speak Afrikaans, but because their social personalities are different and because they have been socialised to respond differently to the adaptive demands of their social milieu.

Table 12.9 Attitudes towards the Immorality Act (section 16) analysed according to home language, marital status, income, educational qualifications and sex

Socio-demographic characteristics (in order of importance according to MCA)	Attitude towards the Immorality Act					
	Support the Act	Reject the Act	Neutral	Uncertain	Total	N**
	%	%	%	%	%	
HOME LANGUAGE*						
Afrikaans	78,9	16,6	3,8	0,8	100,1	530
English	41,3	41,3	15,2	2,2	100,0	407
EDUCATIONAL QUALIFICATIONS						
Low educational quali- fications (no schooling to Std 9)	67,8	21,0	7,9	3,3	100,0	429
High educational quali- fications (matric and further qualifications after matric)	56,3	29,4	12,3	2,0	100,0	595
MARITAL STATUS						
Married	62,1	23,9	11,4	2,6	100,0	728
Never married	48,2	41,0	7,9	2,9	100,0	139
Was married and now divorced or widow/ widower	68,1	21,7	8,3	1,9	100,0	157
INCOME						
R0 to R15 000 per annum	66,6	21,3	9,1	3,0	100,0	503
R15 001 and more per annum	56,0	30,2	12,2	1,6	100,0	493
SEX						
Male	56,2	30,4	11,8	1,6	100,0	434
Female	64,8	22,5	9,5	3,2	100,0	590

*The 'other' and 'both' categories were not included in the analysis.
**The N will not always total 1 024, because not all the respondents answered all the questions.

In table 12.9 the relationships between the various socio-demographic characteristics and attitudes towards the relevant Act have been tabulated. The ideal would be to identify the relationship between all the socio-demographic characteristics — in interaction — and attitude towards the Act. Unfortunately, the latter is impossible when a single multi-directional table is used, because the cell values will become too small and lead to invalid conclusions. Therefore, four multi-directional tables have been drawn up (see tables 12.10 to 12.13). *Home language* (which in isolation explains 16,3% of the variation) has been used as divider in each case.

Table 12.10 Afrikaans-speaking and English-speaking Whites' attitudes towards the Immorality Act (section 16) analysed according to educational qualifications

Attitude towards the Immorality Act	Afrikaans speakers		English speakers	
	Low educational qualifications (none to Std 9)	High educational qualifications (matric and post-matric qual.)	Low educational qualifications (none to Std 9)	High educational qualifications (matric and post-matric qual.)
	Percentage			
Support the Act	84,0	79,2	46,8	32,2
Reject the Act	13,1	13,7	32,1	46,6
Neutral	2,1	7,2	14,7	17,5
Uncertain	0,8	0,0	6,4	3,6
Total	100,0	100,1	100,0	100,0

From tables 12.9 to 12.13 it can be ascertained that Afrikaans-speaking married women having low educational qualifications and low incomes are more inclined to support the Immorality Act. In contrast, unmarried English-speaking men who earn high incomes and have high educational qualifications are more inclined to reject the Act. It seems, therefore, that over and above home language (as an indicator of ethnic and thus cultural differences), socio-economic class (as deduced from educational qualifications and income), marital status and sex affected attitudes towards the Immorality Act. (Note: The term class is not used in its Marxist sense, but merely as an abbreviation for the concept of socio-economic category.) Various factors and combinations of factors can contribute to these response patterns and one must be careful not to attempt an explanation of such factors in terms of a simple non-causal process. It can be argued that certain social categories are more exposed to the detrimental consequences of immorality or marriage across the colour bar than others and that lower-class married White women's relatively stronger support of the laws in question can be explained in this context.

It is universally evident that lower-class people are more conservatively oriented towards changes in conventional behavioural patterns than people in the higher professional, income and educational strata are. Ignorance and faulty insights into the ways in which society functions and changes, coupled with a tendency to cling to any custom or system that protects survival-related interests, influence lower-class people to oppose radical social change to a greater degree than higher class persons.

Table 12.11 Afrikaans-speaking and English-speaking Whites' attitudes towards the Immorality Act(section 16) analysed according to marital status

Attitude towards the Immorality Act	Afrikaans speakers			English speakers		
	Married	Never married	Once married	Married	Never married	Once married
	Percentage					
Support the Act	80,4	80,0	87,0	36.7	28,8	50,7
Reject the Act	13,2	20,0	10,4	39,8	54,8	32,0
Neutral	6,0	0,0	2,6	18,2	12,3	14,7
Uncertain	0,5	0,0	0,0	5,4	4,1	2,7
Total	100,1	100,0	100,0	100,1	100,0	100,1

Table 12.12 Afrikaans-speaking and English-speaking Whites' attitudes towards the Immorality Act(section 16) analysed according to income

Attitude towards the Immorality Act	Afrikaans speakers		English speakers	
	Low income (R0 to R15 000 per per annum)	High income (R15 001 and more per annum)	Low income (R0 to R15 000 per annum)	High income (R15 001 and more per annum)
	Percentage			
Support the Act	85,5	77,7	44,4	30,5
Reject the Act	10,8	15,1	32,3	50,3
Neutral	3,0	7,2	17,2	16,8
Uncertain	0,8	0,0	6,1	2,5
Total	100,1	100,0	100,0	100,1

In conclusion, it must be emphasised that as far as differences in attitude towards the Immorality Act in terms of education, marital status, income and sex are concerned, the survey clearly reveals that smaller differences exist within the Afrikaans-speaking community than within the English-speaking community. Afrikaans speakers probably comprise a more homogeneous group and are bound by stronger communal values. For this reason, subcultural, class and sex differences within the Afrikaner community do not lead to large differences in attitudes towards fundamental social values such as those relating to immorality or marriage across the colour bar.

Analysis of the sample's attitudes towards the new constitutional dispensation by means of the MCA technique produced results confirming the above tendency. There is also sufficient empirical evidence to support the deduction that, for almost all the questions concerning socio-political change, the relative importance of the five socio-demographic variables (as predictors of variation in the sample's responses) will broadly follow the same pattern identified above for the Immorality Act.

CONCLUSION

The relatively high incidence of socio-political conservatism among White Afrikaans-speaking respondents (and, by extrapolation, among White Afrikaans speakers in general), holds important implications for the future distribution of political power in general and White political power in particular. The tolerance threshold of many NP-inclined Afrikaners with regard to socio-political change is coming increasingly under pressure, especially as the Government's reformist initiatives are extended to Blacks.

Indeed, it is clear that an Afrikaner's formal party preference can no longer be taken as a reliable predictor of his or her position on the reformism/conservatism spectrum. On the other hand, the possibility exists that the tolerance threshold of many conservative NP-inclined Afrikaners can be raised by the pursuasive power of realpolitik to such an extent that they may accommodate new socio-political change without switching party preference.

As for the present survey, it is difficult to explain why so many Afrikaners who can be identified as polar-conservatives still support the NP. Political behaviour is never easy to comprehend and because it frequently contains strong emotional, even irrational components, it cannot be analysed exactly. Political behaviour (for example voting for a party) is commonly determined by a complex combination of social and psychological variables and therefore it is difficult to isolate any one fundamental variable responsible for most of the variation in a particular political behaviour pattern.

There must be many reasons why so many conservative Afrikaners support the NP at a stage when the party is associated with socio-political reform and policy initiatives which cannot reasonably be reconciled with polar conservatism. One of these reasons, which is at least partially verifiable empirically, is the significant support given to State President PW Botha as head of government and the large measure of legitimacy his leadership enjoys in White, Indian and Coloured circles — a legitimacy largely built into the South African political fabric as a result of 37 years of NP hegemony. Many polar conservatives who have confidence in the State President will therefore continue to give the NP formal support in spite of 'liberal' adjustments to party policy, provided that these amendments do not test the tolerance ceiling of polar conservative NP-supporters too often. Obviously, polar conservative Afrikaners will differ in their individual tolerance ceilings and some will possess a greater absorption capacity than others, provided of course that socio-political change does not lead to a drastic frontal attack on the group's fundamental interests.

Support for and loyalty to a party that has been in power for almost four decades may also have a strong sentimental basis, hence the term 'bloed-natte' ('die-hard' NP supporters) in popular parlance. Many Afrikaners are historically conditioned to regard the NP as the 'natural' party political home of Afrikanerdom, hence their considerable tolerance for reformist policy adjustments within the party. Furthermore, there may be a large number of Afrikaners who really believe that the NP is still fundamentally a conservative party and support it as such. Then there will be Afrikaners who are essentially polar conservative and believe either that the direction the NP is currently taking is historically unavoidable, or that the more extreme conservative parties such as the CP and HNP would fare no better, for instance because their leaders are perceived as less competent or less charismatic than those of the NP.

In the cultural, ethnic and racially segmented South African society (with its distinctive group-stratified distribution of power), the institutional structures of social inequality and political domination are rooted in complex historical processes. This has a psycho-sociological equivalent in the form of the perceptions and attitudes the dominant White segment maintains with regard to the socio-political distance between itself and the outgroup(s). Empirical research shows, however, that it is risky to regard the dominant group's perceptions of socio-political distance as a reliable indicator of how individual group members would actually react should circumstances decree that members of the out-group(s) be accommodated in the dominant group. Because the individual finds it more difficult to change the realities of the social, economic and political order than to modify his or her own attitudes and perceptions, these attitudes are often overestimated as a predictor of actual social behaviour.

For example, in the specific context of changing race relations in South Africa there are many Whites who talk in a particular direction to indicate their resistance to certain changes. Under pressure of social, economic and political realities, however, they rarely resort to protest or resistance action. A good example of this is White reaction to the repeal of the Mixed Marriages Act. The present survey showed that, measured in terms of attitudes and perceptions, 61% of the White respondents were in favour of the retention of this apartheid law. Based on empirical evidence regarding the relationship between attitude and behaviour, there is no reason to accept that the repeal of this law will lead to actual protest action (for example, change of party preference) on the part of most Whites. During a follow-up survey in February 1985, the present authors found, for example, that only 21% of the White respondents who at that stage supported the new constitutional dispensation said that they would withdraw their support if the Mixed Marriages Act was repealed. A survey (Rhoodie and Couper 1984) conducted by the HSRC in the three Transvaal towns of Pietersburg, Barberton and Delmas in March/April 1984 showed that even in an overwhelmingly conservative Afrikaner community like that of Pietersburg, about half of the Afrikaans-speaking respondents who supported the new dispensation in broad outline would continue to do so even if the Mixed Marriages Act was scrapped.

The individual's tolerance threshold for accommodating even comparatively weighty socio-political changes is a complex psycho-social phenomenon. In the context of White South Africans' perceptions of change, it will not easily occur that a single social, economic or political event will place this tolerance threshold under such pressure that the Whites in question will react with a strong behavioural response (such as changing party preference). This does not mean that they would welcome or embrace such socio-political changes. Rather, as far as the Afrikaner is concerned, it would be more a case of the majority acquiescing in a process seen as historically unavoidable — a realisation that the winds of change did not conveniently blow themselves out on the banks of the Limpopo. Basically, here one is dealing with a pragmatic response to the adaptive demands of historical realities that can no longer be accommodated in a traditional apartheid society.

Table 12.13 Afrikaans-speaking and English-speaking Whites' attitudes towards the Immorality Act (section 16) analysed according to sex

Attitude towards the Immorality Act	Afrikaans speakers		English speakers	
	Male	Female	Male	Female
	Percentage			
Support the Act	77,5	84,1	33,5	41,1
Reject the Act	15,3	12,0	47,7	35,9
Neutral	6,8	3,6	15,9	16,9
Uncertain	0,5	0,3	2,8	6,1
Total	100,1	100,0	99,9	100,0

Today most Whites realise that there is a price they will have to pay for a White/Black accommodation which will enable them to retain control over at least their own vital interests. Support for or acquiescence to socio-political reform is thus born from the need for an investment in survival rather than from some or other moral compulsion to compensate the Non-White community for the hardship it experiences under an apartheid regime. For most Afrikaners it is an accepted fact that classic apartheid is not the best investment in survival, hence the obvious swing to a compromise policy which, many people hope, will guarantee that communal decision making by all the main population groups about general affairs on one hand and White sovereignty over own affairs on the other, can be reconciled in a joint state system.

The current reform process is altering the old order fairly radically in the sense that most Whites are coming to feel that the ideal of a White/Black power distribution based on separate sovereignties, with each sovereignty politically and spacially established in a discrete State territorium, is no longer tenable. Instead, the politically relevant power groups will have to accommodate each other in a common State entity. Consequently, the Whites — the Afrikaner-dominant NP Government in particular — are increasingly prepared to extend the basis of democratic power-sharing to Black power groups which realise that they will fare better in terms of cost-effectiveness if they seek an accommodation with Whites through consensual and co-operative relationships instead of by means of a zero-sum revolutionary confrontation aimed at attaining total Black hegemony.

Considering the political arithmetic of Black demographic domination, in the foreseeable future socio-political reform in South Africa will focus increasingly on the accommodation of Blacks in the traditionally White-dominated social and political order. As for power-sharing, it is inevitable that Blacks will not easily swallow a constitutional dispensation that does not reflect the demographic reality of Black numerical preponderance. Ultimately, with the accommodation of Coloureds and Indians in the current dispensation, demographic ratios (roughly 4:2:1 for Whites, Coloureds and Indians respectively) were accepted as the basis for 'power-sharing' in the allocation of parliamentary seats and the composition of both the President's Council and the Parliamentary Electoral College that elects the State President. Thus, a precedent has already been created and therefore it is highly unlikely that Blacks will accept a political formula which means that they voluntarily become party to their own devaluation in the political market. Should the existing demographic ratio of Blacks be accepted as the basis for power-sharing, the question arises whether the compromise model will, in the long term, render results any different from the extreme revolutionary Black majority model.

A more immediate question, however, is whether the present reform process will keep pace with rapidly accelerating Black aspirations. What will the White response be if Black and White perceptions of 'reasonable' aspirations differ radically? Speculatively or hypothetically, various future scenarios can be considered in this context. The answer to this question is locked in a history still to be written.

NOTES

1 For more details on these reformist initiatives, see *inter alia* Breytenbach 1984; Rautenbach 1984; Welsh 1983 and 1984; De Villiers 1983; Stultz 1983; Boulle 1984; Wiechers 1984; Schlemmer 1984; and Van Vuuren *et al*, 1983. See also other chapters referring to constitutional change.
2 For a full technical description of this technique, see Andrews *et al*, 1973.
3 It must be continually borne in mind that there can be x number of variables in a real-life social situation which determine variations in attitudes towards this law. It is, however, impossible to control all of these variables and therefore the social reality has to be reduced to these socio-demographic characteristics and certain concomitant social structures for the purpose of this analysis. For example, income and educational levels (which indicate class strata) and age (which can determine generational differences in respect of values, norms and socialisation).
4 To be more precise, when the interaction between these five characteristics and attitudes towards the relevant Act are taken into account. Naturally, the interaction between these six factors and all the other unknown or uncontrolled variables (the number of variables mentioned in the previous footnote) is unknown.
5 That is to say, the unique contributions of each of the five biographical characteristics to the explanation of variation in attitude towards the Act, without controlling for the effect of the other four characteristics in the model.

BIBLIOGRAPHY

Andrews, FM and Messenger, RC. *Multivariate nominal scale analysis*. Ann Arbor: Institute for Social Research, University of Michigan, 1973.
Boulle, LJ. *South Africa and the consociational option: A constitutional analysis*. Johannesburg: Juta & Co Ltd, 1984.
Breytenbach, WJ. The new South African Constitution and its implications for development. *Development Southern Africa*, vol. 1, no. 1, May 1984.
De Villiers, Fleur (Ed.) *Bridge or barricade. The constitution: A first appraisal*. Johannesburg: Jonathan Ball Paperbacks, 1983.
Rautenbach, IM. *Die politieke ontwikkeling van en deelname deur die Swartes buite die nasionale state en die TBVC-state*. Paper read during symposium of the Institute for Political and African Studies, Potchefstroom: PU vir CHO, 24 August 1984.
Rhoodie, Nic J en Couper, MP. *'n Vergelykende ontleding van drie Afrikaner-dominante gemeenskappe se persepsies van Wit-Swart-verhoudinge in Suid-Afrika*. Memorandum prepared for HSRC Investigation into Intergroup Relations, Pretoria: HSRC, 1984.
Schlemmer, Lawrence. *The carrot or stick: Reflections on the reform process*. Johannesburg: South African Institute of Race Relations, 1984.
Stultz, Newell M. Consociational engineering in South Africa. *Journal of Contemporary African Studies*, vol. 2, no. 2, 1983.
Van Vuuren, DJ *et al*. (Eds.) *Change in South Africa*. Durban: Butterworths, 1983.

Welsh, David. South Africa: Power, process and prospect. *Journal of Contemporary African Studies*, vol. 2, no. 2, 1983.

— The 1983 constitutional referendum and the future of South Africa after the vote. *South Africa International*, vol. 14, no. 3, January 1984.

Wiechers, Marinus. The 1983 constitutional referendum and the future of South Africa: View Two — Motor for change or retardant? *South Africa International*, vol. 14, no. 3, January 1984.

13 Black views on socio-political change in South Africa

CP de Kock, Nic J Rhoodie and MP Couper

INTRODUCTION

On 3 September 1984, serious and widespread rioting erupted in Black residential areas in the Vaal Triangle and subsequently spread to other parts of South Africa. Now, many months later, daily reports of unrest in various parts of the country are still being received and the extent and intensity of the unrest show no signs of diminishing.

The question asked on previous occasions of large-scale and prolonged manifestations of conflict in violence (such as Sharpeville 1960 and Soweto 1976) is being asked once more: 'South Africa — revolution or reform?' (For earlier arguments on this issue see Callinicos and Rogers 1978; Herbstein 1978; Hitchcock 1977; Johnson 1977; and Kane-Berman 1978.) It should be rephrased thus: Will the Blacks ultimately effect a violent overthrow of the White power structure, take over the government and establish a new social order, or is there going to be a gradual movement — through more or less organised protest action (both violent and non-violent) on the part of Blacks, negotiation between White and Black and reform of the social structure — towards assuring and maintaining an optimal balance between freedom and order (see Dahrendorf 1979 and De Kock 1984) for all interest groups in South Africa?

In either event (revolution or reform), the possibility of violence is by no means excluded. Rather, the difference between the two alternatives lies in the end result — the post-revolution or post-reform society. A post-revolution society created by a group (whether a specific ethnic or racial group, a class, an elite, or a dictatorship and its henchmen) which seized political and military power through violence is potentially less able to guarantee freedom and order for all interest groups. Consequently, it would start off with a situation of latent conflict which could later manifest itself in violence. It is logical that such a social structure would have been created not through consensus, but by coercion. Even if the Blacks in South Africa managed to stage a successful revolution, there is no guarantee that the Whites in the country would not launch a counter-revolution. Moreover, this argument presupposes that Blacks have identical interests and the same social structure as their ideal and that Coloureds and Indians will remain neutral, passive onlookers.

A post-reform social structure would be the product of negotiation between all interest groups, which would ensure that all parties would abide by the outcome. In such a social structure, the use of force would be limited and legitimate and the potential for non-violent and violent conflict would be largely lacking. Order would be maintained by mutually persuasive communication and consensus, rather than by brute force leading to a lack of freedom. (For a more detailed exposition of this argument, see De Kock 1984.)

Whatever theoretical model or framework one uses to interpret current events in South Africa, the conclusion that conflict is manifest and erupts sporadically into violence and that the chances of a revolution are considerable, is inescapable. One could analyse the South African situation in terms of various macro-level, meso-level and micro-level theories derived from diverse sociological and socio-psychological traditions.[1] Whichever theory one opts for, the conclusion remains the same, namely that all the conditions for manifest conflict — particularly in its violent forms — are present and continue to develop and expand. The exact form in which violence is manifested (terrorism, civil war, revolution, revolutionary war, riots, rebellion, etc — often a mixture of all of these) is determined by a host of factors such as the oppressed masses' access to arms, the strength of the security system, the extent of popular political awareness and the involvement of third parties. To the social scientist, however, this is of less concern than the conditions under which violence (in whatever form) is manifested. Violence is extremely dysfunctional[2] for conflict regulation and hence for reform, since it may trigger a cycle of revenge and counter-revenge, result in more negative stereotypes on both sides, escalate the use of force by the dominant group, diminish the value of peaceful mutually persuasive communication and stimulate the escalation (both in scope and number) of demands and minimum terms for agreement (people who have shed blood for a cause will want enough in return to make the sacrifice worthwhile). Hence, the more conflict is manifest in violence, the harder it will be to get the conflicting parties to meet around a conference table.

In the light of the above, it should be evident that realistic negotiation politics has become an urgent necessity in South Africa — a country which over the past three decades has witnessed several manifestations of political violence (such as rioting and sabotage in the early sixties; Soweto

336

1976; the present wave of unrest; and the wave of terrorism which began with the Silverton hostage drama in 1980). The critical questions facing social scientists in South Africa today are no longer whether there is macro-societal conflict in the country, what its sources are and what conditions favour it, but rather how conflict can be regulated in such a way that reform can take place with a minimum of violence and achieve optimal results (results that will satisfy the maximum number of interest groups).

Many factors can hinder or facilitate the regulation (or accommodation) of conflict.[3]

Dahrendorf (1959: 225-227) and Deutsch (1973: 377-378) outline the principal factors in the facilitation of conflict regulation. (These factors are, in fact, so important, they should be seen as pre-conditions for conflict regulation):

(a) Both conflicting parties must appreciate the reality of the conflict situation and, in this sense, the fundamental justice of the opposition's cause. In this context, acknowledgement or insight implies that both parties recognise the true nature of the conflict, namely that it is a product of the power structure of the particular association. Conflict cannot be regulated effectively if the opponent's case is denigrated as unrealistic or never given a fair hearing. On the other hand, effective conflict regulation is impossible if the conflict is not acknowledged as such and common interests are overemphasised. On this latter point, Dahrendorf (1959: 225-226) writes as follows:

> Without doubt, there are 'common interests' in any conflict situation; without community, no conflict, and vice versa. However, the crucial factor for effectively regulating conflict is recognition, and even emphasis, of systematic divergence and opposition. The attempt to obliterate lines of conflict by ready ideologies of harmony and unity in effect serves to increase rather than decrease the violence of conflict manifestations.

(b) The interest groups must be organised. While the conflicting forces remain diffuse it is virtually impossible to regulate the conflict. Deutsch (1973: 377) puts it thus:

> Unless each party is sufficiently internally coherent and stable to act as an organized unit so that the actions of its components are controlled and unified in relation to the conflict, it is evident that regulation cannot be effectively developed and maintained.

(c) Each party must be prepared to accept the outcome of the negotiations (conflict regulation) even if the terms are not fully compatible with his interests (see Deutsch 1973: 378).

(d) For effective conflict regulation, the opposing parties must agree on certain formal rules of the game. Deutsch (1973: 379) writes:

> A duel of honour presupposes that the duelists have a common code of honour, a code to which all members of a given community will adhere if they want to be esteemed within that community. It also presupposes a set of social roles and procedures that have been carefully articulated within the community and that help to limit and specify the actions that may be taken by the adversaries.

One could pose the question: to what extent do these pre-conditions for conflict regulation exist in South Africa? The answer can only be ascertained through empirical research among all interest groups in the country. At this critical hour, when South Africa is faced with the alternatives of revolution or relatively peaceful reform, it is essential that the popular opinion of the various interest groups[4] should be constantly monitored and publicised. After all, the future of the country will be determined not by a handful of leaders sitting around a conference table as delegates of the various groups, but by the popular opinion of their followers. Whatever plans or negotiations are thrashed out around the conference table, they must continually be tested against popular opinion lest the negotiators find, when it comes to implementation, that the outcome lacks legitimacy.

This is the background against which the Division for Group Interaction of the Institute for Sociological and Demographic Research of the Human Sciences Research Council (HSRC) has been conducting annual[5] national monitor surveys among the four main population groups in the country since 1982.

The initial research projects (1982 and 1983) were confined to Whites, Coloureds and Indians. The reasons for the exclusion of Blacks were organisational (for instance the lack of manpower and funds); the rapid developments attending the new constitutional dispensation for these three groups, which demanded considerable attention at that time; and the hesitancy among Blacks to take part in empirical research of a political nature (which resulted in certain methodological problems).

In July 1984 the first (experimental) socio-political monitor survey among Blacks was launched in the Pretoria-Witwatersrand-Vaal Triangle (PWV) area. A second survey has just been completed and the data collected are at present being processed. The first survey was not focused specifically on the pre-conditions for conflict regulation outlined above, although certain guidelines for conflict regulation can be inferred from the data. The second survey among Blacks, and the one shortly to be conducted among Blacks and other population groups, are aimed more specifically

338

at negotiation politics and seek to probe popular opinion on political questions such as the following:

- Should there be negotiation? (Or is violence the preferred option?)
- With whom should there be negotiations? (That is, the identification of all possible interest groups.)
- What should the nature of the negotiations be? (e.g. how binding should the outcome be?)
- What issues should be negotiated?
- What should be the minimum conditions for negotiations to take place?
- What are the minimum demands of the various interest groups (the so-called 'bottom-line')?

No doubt the findings of such research will be helpful to the leaders of interest groups but should also stimulate public dialogue between these groups, thus creating the pre-conditions for effective conflict regulation — or at least the first two discussed above.

OBJECTIVE

The aim of this study is to infer some general guidelines for negotiation politics from the data gathered in the first monitor survey among Blacks in the PWV area. It should be borne in mind that the data were collected in the PWV area only, the data were collected before the present wave of unrest and this was the first (experimental) survey on socio-political matters in the monitor series. The general guidelines inferred from the data are presented in the section entitled 'Guidelines for negotiation politics in South Africa'.

RESEARCH DESIGN

The survey in which these data were collected was conducted among an effective sample of 1 478 Blacks aged 18 and over in the PWV complex in the course of June and July 1984 — that is, just before the September 1984 riots. Initially, a sample of 1 500 residential addresses was drawn. These addresses were visited with the object of conducting 1 500 interviews (i.e. one at each address). Of the 1 500 questionnaires completed, 1 478 could be processed — the other 22 (1,5% of the proposed sample) were incorrectly completed.

Target population

The target population was Blacks aged 18 and over residing in the PWV metropolitan complex. The PWV was selected as the target area for the following reasons:

- It accommodates the largest and densest concentration of Blacks in the RSA — 2 705 819 Blacks live in the area (Van der Merwe and Steenekamp 1982: 30). Expressed as a percentage of all Blacks living in White urban areas, this number represents 50,8% of such Blacks and 26,7% of all Blacks in 'White' South Africa. (See South Africa 1980a: 1.)
- The Black population of the area is ethnically heterogeneous (see table 13.1), making it particularly suitable for research in which ethnicity could be a significant independent variable. If, say, the Port Elizabeth-Uitenhage or Durban-Pinetown metropolitan complexes were to have been selected as target areas, the populations studied would have been almost exclusively Xhosa or Zulu.
- Blacks in the PWV area have proved historically that they wield an important influence in political events. The events in Sharpeville (1960) and Soweto (1976) have already been recorded in history books and have since played a decisive role in the development of Black/White relations. Shortly after this survey was conducted, conflict in the area manifested in violence once more.
- Logistically, it was easier and cheaper to concentrate on this area because of its proximity to HSRC headquarters. *Inter alia* it assured better control over the fieldwork.

Sample

Sampling technique

The target sample of 1 500 addresses was drawn according to the guidelines for drawing a Black sample in the PWV area laid down by Van der Merwe and Steenekamp (1982: 27-29). Briefly, it meant that districts in the target area, the enumerator subdistricts (ESDs) for census surveys by the Central Statistical Services within these districts, addresses within the ESDs and respondents at the relevant addresses were all drawn on a random basis.

A number of additional addresses (over and above the original 1 500) were drawn randomly and some of these were visited in instances where the original addresses proved unsuitable (for instance where there were refusals or nobody qualifying as a respondent).

How representative was the sample?

A comparison between certain biographical characteristics of the sample and the 1980 census data (5% sample) for both the PWV urban area and the RSA urban areas is provided in table 13.1. Males, people with low educational qualifications and people with no church affiliation are

340

underrepresented in the sample, while females, people with high educational qualifications and Zulus are overrepresented. Minor discrepancies between the sample and the census data may also be detected in respect of Xhosas, Swazis and members of the Roman Catholic Church. These discrepancies are probably attributable to a combination of the following factors:

- The sample does not include Black labourers residing in compounds belonging to their employers. These compounds are certainly occupied mainly by males who have low educational qualifications. Since compound residents tend to be predominantly migrant labourers and some employers tend to recruit workers from specific ethnic areas (homelands), the exclusion of the compounds could cause an ethnic imbalance in the sample. It should be borne in mind that there are 110 compounds in the 26 districts of the PWV area and 42 in the districts specifically included in the sample. Residential figures of several thousand per compound are not unusual.
- Blacks living 'illegally' in White areas often include large numbers of women who have followed their husbands. Such women would be more wary of revealing their presence in an official census than in the case of a survey not associated with influx control. This may cause the sex distribution in the sample to differ from that in the census statistics.
- Respondents may tend to present their biographical particulars in a more favourable light. Thus they could indicate a church affiliation and high educational level rather than admit to the fieldworker that they do not belong to a church or have poor educational qualifications. In a census, on the other hand, people may be more accurate because they know that the survey is official and fear the consequences of supplying false information.
- Some categories of people are more inclined to refuse an interview than others. Experience has shown that men returning home weary from work (particularly Black men who, due to great distances and poor transport, arrive home very late) and people who, being poorly educated, are ill-informed about and indifferent to current events, are more likely to refuse an interview. Such refusals can cause distortions in a sample. Although the refusal rate for this survey was below 10%, it should be pointed out that every fieldworker received a few additional addresses and may have visited some of these in cases where their visit to the original address was unsuccessful.

Despite the discrepancies between the characteristics reflected in the sample and those in the census data, it would seem, nevertheless, that the

341

sample provides a fair reflection of the principal biographical and socio-demographic attributes of the Black population in the PWV area, especially if the foregoing explanations are taken into account. In some respects the sample may even afford a fairly accurate reflection of the entire urban Black population of the RSA. (See the third column in table 13.1.) It should be noted, however, that it would be invalid to make an unqualified generalisation from the data of this study to the whole of the RSA. It is primarily a *sample* of Blacks in the PWV area and in generalising inferences from the sample to the whole of the RSA, one must exercise extreme caution.

Table 13.1 Comparison between features of the HSRC sample and 1980 Census data (5% sample) PWV urban and RSA urban*

Characteristic	HSRC sample	Census (PWV urban)	Census (RSA urban)
	%	%	%
SEX			
Male	38,5	54,4	56,8
Female	61,5	45,6	43,2
AGE**			
20-24 years	23,6	21,1	21,2
25-34 years	29,9	33,7	32,5
35-44 years	19,0	21,1	21,2
45-54 years	12,6	13,7	13,7
55-64 years	9,2	7,1	7,3
65-74 years	4,8	2,4	2,8
75 years +	0,9	1,0	1,2
EDUCATION**			
None	8,7	–	23,0
Gr.I/Sub A to Std 3	10,7	–	20,5
Std 4 to Std 6	37,1	–	36,3
Std 7 to Std 9	31,5	–	15,3
Matric	8,5	–	2,4
Post-matric	3,6	–	1,3
Unspecified	–	–	1,2
ETHNIC GROUP#			
Xhosa	7,3	12,8	25,2
Zulu	32,7	20,6	27,0
Swazi	1,9	6,8	5,5
Ndebele	2,3	5,8	3,6
Sotho	31,5	28,3	21,1
Tswana	15,7	14,8	11,3
Shangana/Tsonga	6,5	6,7	4,0
Venda	2,2	2,9	1,5
Other	0,0	1,2	0,8

CHURCH AND/OR FAITH			
Dutch Reformed Church	6,1	5,1	5,8
Anglican	8,3	7,0	7,0
Methodist	10,8	9,6	13,0
Presbyterian	1,9	1,9	2,8
Congregational	0,3	0,6	1,4
Lutheran	7,2	5,8	4,6
Roman Catholic	15,0	10,1	11,0
Other Christian churches	44,6	40,1	38,1
Non-Christian churches	0,0	0,5	0,5
No church	5,7	19,2	15,7

* Compiled from South Africa (1980b).

** The sample includes respondents of 18 and 19 as well, but since the census age category is 15 to 19, only respondents aged 20 or over could be included in the comparison and the age distribution had to be recomputed. However, the findings discussed in this study are based on the full sample.

*** Age-specific educational distribution (i.e. distribution for persons aged 18 and over) for the PWV area could not be computed. Hence, age-specific distribution of education is given for
. RSA urban areas only.

In the case of the sample, home language = ethnic group.

Survey procedure

Black fieldworkers from the HSRC's section for Indigenous Languages visited the previously selected addresses (see the paragraph entitled Sampling technique), where they used a random sampling grid to determine which person to interview and then conducted the interview according to a structured schedule. During the course of the survey, a sample of the addresses where interviews were conducted was visited by Black HSRC officials to check whether interviewing and sample regulations had been properly observed. The fact that the Black fieldworkers concerned were highly experienced definitely contributed to the smooth progress of the operation.

Questionnaire

The questionnaire was specifically compiled to allow for the fact that in 1980 some 80% of urban Blacks in the RSA had educational qualifications of standard 6 or lower (the percentage of urban Whites who had this qualification was about 38%).

Thus every effort was made to avoid complicated questions or terms and to include 'not certain' and/or 'don't know' response options throughout the questionnaire. After the questionnaire had been compiled and finalised by the researchers, it was submitted to an anthropologist and certain Black

343

HSRC officials for comment and 'translation' into simpler idiom. The compilers also tried to keep the questionnaire brief, since 'respondent resistance' is common among people who have low educational qualifications.

FINDINGS

Black perceptions of the new constitutional dispensation for Whites, Coloureds and Indians

Almost half (48,8%) of the respondents admitted to having heard about the 'new parliament' for Whites, Coloureds and Indians. Of those who knew about it, 23,8% (11,6% of the total sample) felt that it was a 'good thing', while 60,5% (29,5% of the total sample) believed it to be a 'bad thing' and 15,7% were uncertain or did not know.

Asked about their main reason for regarding the 'new parliament' as either a 'good thing' or a 'bad thing', respondents who knew something about the new constitutional dispensation answered as follows:

Why the new parliament is a 'good thing'	%
Because Blacks will eventually be admitted to the new parliament	30,2
Because Indians and Coloureds in the new parliament can act in the interests of Blacks	34,0
Because it will improve the lot of Blacks	15,4
Because it gives Coloureds and Indians a say in government	9,3
Other reasons	11,2
Total	100,1*

* Because percentages were rounded to the nearest decimal, the subtotals do not always add up to 100.

Why the new parliament is a 'bad thing'	%
Because Blacks are excluded and discriminated against	87,6
Because it promotes apartheid	5,3
Because Indians and Coloureds should not be in the new parliament	3,7
Because it means more power for the Whites	1,2
Other reasons	2,3
Total	100,1

In answer to another question, more than one third (35,1%) of the respondents who knew something about the new dispensation felt that Indian and Coloured participation in the new dispensation would eventually lead to

344

Black representation in the new parliament, slightly over half (51,3%) did not subscribe to this view and 13,6% was unsure or did not know. In addition, 45,2% (21,8% of the total group) believed that Coloureds and Indians should refuse to be involved in the new dispensation because Blacks are excluded, roughly the same proportion (43,2% or 20,9% of the group as a whole) did not feel that Coloureds and Indians should withdraw and 11,6% was uncertain or did not know.

Although in July 1984 the majority of Blacks in the PWV area were unaware of the new constitutional dispensation for Whites, Coloureds and Indians, the majority of those who knew about it were opposed to it. (They believed that it was a 'bad thing', that it would not lead to Black representation in the new parliament and that Coloureds and Indians should boycott it.) Of course it was to be expected that political reform which did not represent a very definite move away from group differentiation (apartheid and separate development) and which did not offer Blacks very real political rights would not be acceptable to the majority of Blacks. One must even consider whether the new dispensation did not in fact contribute towards the present unrest.

Perceptions of the nature of greatest problems facing Blacks

In answer to an (open) question as to what was the greatest problem experienced by Blacks in South Africa today, the total sample mentioned the following difficulties:

Problem	%
Economic pressure (including too little money, housing problems, inflation, the drought and unemployment)	64,0
Diverse apartheid measures such as influx control, job reservation, resettlement and lack of political rights	21,3
Educational problems, including school boycotts	5,7
Lack of freedom	2,2
Lack of Black unity	0,7
Crime	0,5
Other problems, or none specified	2,1
Don't know	3,4
Total	99,9

A striking feature is the great importance attached to economic problems and the lack of emphasis on educational questions. Crime and the lack of freedom and political rights also received remarkably little emphasis. If one were to regard lack of freedom as an aspect of 'apartheid', then less than a quarter (23,5%) of all respondents identified apartheid as their greatest problem. Of course, this figure should be treated with great circumspection, since many analysts will quite rightly point out that many of the problems which Blacks perceive as *economic* in nature are in fact caused by apartheid measures. From the data available, however, it is not possible to infer to what extent a particular economic problem is in fact a direct function of 'apartheid'. Moreover, it is doubtful whether such a causal relationship will ever be measurable, if one takes into account the question of what *apartheid* in fact entails and how it contributes to a particular economic problem — in other words, which apartheid measures are manifested in a specific economic problem.

Innumerable indepth interviews and group discussions conducted by various researchers of the HSRC Division for Group Interaction over the past two months (March/April 1985) with Blacks from all socio-economic strata have shown quite clearly that although poverty and concomitant socio-economic problems are the principal difficulties of everyday life, Blacks ascribe these problems to the political structure. (Hence they see their poverty as structural rather than personally fortuitous.) Accordingly, the solutions to the problems are also considered to be political. The Blacks' ideal is freedom and equality, something that can be achieved only through equal political power. The redistribution of wealth alone will afford temporary economic equality, but will not assure freedom or equal opportunities, since the latter entail far more than just material possessions (for instance education).

In the context of the recent unrest in Black residential areas, it is also remarkable that high rent was cited as the greatest problem by a mere 3,3% of the 1 478 respondents. Although rent is mentioned as a direct cause of the unrest, the percentage of Blacks who mentioned it as their greatest problem is negligible. This would indicate that rent, a problem affecting everyone and universally understood, was used as an instrument for mobilisation in the unrest.

Choice of leadership

In answer to the unstructured (open) question, 'If you could choose one person from *any* population group to lead South Africa in these times, whom would you choose?', respondents answered as follows:

	%		%
Mr Nelson Mandela	9,7	People who insisted on a Black	
Mr PW Botha	7,5	leader but did not specify whom	19,7
Bishop Desmond Tutu	3,2	People who insisted on a White	
Chief Minister Gatsha Buthelezi	2,4	leader, including others	
Mr Ephraim Tshabalala	1,8	mentioned by name	15,7

Pres Lucas Mangope	1,2
Dr Nthato Motlana	1,0
Dr Cedric Phatudi	0,9
Mr Oliver Tambo	0,5
Mr Tsietsi Mashinini	0,4
Dr Robert Mugabe	0,3
Mr Pik Botha	0,3
Mr MC Botha	0,3
Mr Walter Sisulu	0,3
Pres Kaiser Matanzima	0,2
Prof Hudson Ntsanwisi	0,2
Other Blacks mentioned by name	0,7

An Indian person	0,3
A Coloured person	0,1
Uncertain/don't know	23,2
There is no such person	8,2
Other	1,6
No answer	0,2

Total	99,9

To another open question — 'If you had to choose one *Black person* to lead South Africa in these times, whom would you choose?' — respondents answered as follows:

	%		%
Mr Nelson Mandela	17,2	Mr Walter Sisulu	0,3
Chief Minister Gatsha Buthelezi	5,7	Pres Lennox Sebe	0,3
Bishop Desmond Tutu	5,1	Mr ZZ Mashao	0,3
Mr Ephraim Tshabalala	3,1	Chief Leabua Jonathan	0,2
Pres Lucas Mangope	2,5	Pres Samora Machel	0,2
Dr Cedric Phatudi	2,4	Other Blacks mentioned by name	5,5
Dr Nthato Motlana	2,0	Insist on Mr PW Botha	2,1
Mr Oliver Tambo	0,9	Insist on a White	2,1
Mr Tsietsi Mashinini	0,8	Uncertain or don't know	27,8
Mr Robert Mugabe	0,7	There is no such person	16,9
Pres Kaiser Matanzima	0,6	Other	1,6
Prof Hudson Ntsanwisi	0,4	No answer	0,5
Mr Robert Sobukwe	0,4		
Pres Patrick Mphephu	0,3		

Total	99,9

The responses to these two questions permit the following conclusions:

- There are signs of a leadership problem among Blacks in the PWV area. Given a choice out of all population groups, the percentage for 'uncertain/don't know' is 23,2 and that for 'there is no such person' 8,2 (that is, 31,4% altogether). When the choice is limited to a Black person, the 'uncertain/don't know' category comprises 27,8% of the sample and the 'there is no such person' category 16,9% (44,7% altogether). Thus, almost one third of the respondents could identify no leader, even when given an unrestricted choice.
- The degree of consensus about a specific leader is not particularly high

for either question. The 30,2% who indicated specific leaders (these include leaders who received 0,2% or more support only) in response to the first question identified 16 leaders altogether, whilst the 45,5% who indicated specific leaders (once again only those who received 0,2% or more support) in response to the second question identified 20 leaders altogether.

- The four Black leaders who emerge as the strongest leaders in both cases are Mr Nelson Mandela, Bishop Desmond Tutu, Chief Minister Gatsha Buthelezi and Mr Ephraim Tshabalala. The combined support enjoyed by these four leaders is 17,1 and 31,1% for the first and second questions respectively. It could be that these four leaders — the head of a national 'liberation organisation' (Mandela), a well-known spiritual leader (Tutu), a well-known ethnic leader (Buthelezi) and a prominent local community leader (Tshabalala) — are very familiar to people in the PWV area and therefore enjoy greater support than other Black leaders.

- Mandela definitely enjoys greater support than any other Black leader. For every one person supporting Chief Minister Buthelezi, there are three Mandela supporters and this despite the fact that Mandela is a member of a prohibited organisation and that to support him openly is in fact an indictable offence (hence the percentage response in favour of Mandela must be regarded as 'conservative').

- When the respondents' choice of a leader is confined to Blacks it would seem that the support for various broad political groupings or ideologies is as follows:

Various broad political groupings or schools of thought	%
ANC (Mandela, Tambo, Mashinini, Sisulu, Winnie Mandela)	19,3
PAC (Sobukwe)	0,4
Leaders of neighbouring states (Sobhuza, Mugabe, Samora Machel, Leabua Jonathan)	1,3
Leaders of independent national states and homelands within South Africa's historical international boundaries (Mangope, Phatudi, Mphephu, Ntsanwisi, Sebe, Matanzima)	6,5
Internal leaders operating outside the system (Motlana, Tutu, Nkondo, Mkatshwa)	7,3
Internal leaders operating inside the system (Tshabalala, Mashao)	3,4
Inkatha/Buthelezi	5,7
Insist on PW Botha	2,1
Insist on a White	2,1
Other Black names with very little support	5,0
No person, no choice	16,9
Uncertain or don't know	27,8
No answer	0,5
Other	1,6
Total	99,9

Once again the 'uncertain' and 'no choice' responses (jointly 44,7%) are in the majority, followed by responses in favour of the ANC (19,3%) and internal leaders who are strongly opposed to the White Government and who operate outside the system (7,3%). Of the respondents who registered a choice, the ANC managed to secure the support of 35,4%, whereas homeland and national state leaders received a mere 11,7% support from the same group. Hence, for every supporter of a homeland leader, the ANC has three supporters — and, as mentioned earlier, this latter percentage must be seen as an absolute minimum. The 44,7% who were either unable to choose or uncertain about their choice should be regarded as a reservoir of potential support for other groups. How this support is to be divided will depend on various factors such as the rate, depth and direction of political change in South Africa, which group features most prominently in such change (the 'strong man' image) and the nature of the relations between White and Black. At the moment many factors favour the ANC. For instance, in this survey 50,4% of Blacks believed that relations between Black and White were either deteriorating or unchanged, while 43,2% believed that they were improving. Furthermore, because of the support the ANC enjoys (the roughly 20,0% mentioned above, to be regarded as a minimum, plus a possible additional 30,0% of sympathisers — see the section entitled 'The ANC') and its continued activities in spite of the Nkomati Accord between South Africa and Mozambique, it already has a 'strong man' image. In addition, social change in recent years has brought little significant change to the Black man's position in the South African power structure.

• Finally, mention should be made of the nearly one quarter (23,8%) of respondents who, in answer to the first question, preferred a White leader. What makes this percentage even more noteworthy is the fact that less than half (42,5%) of the respondents preferred Black leaders (22,8% identified more than 13 different Black leaders, whilst a further 19,7% insisted on Black leaders without mentioning names). According to the responses, Mr PW Botha was the single individual who received the second-greatest amount of support (7,5%). In fact, this 7,5% brings him very close to Mr Mandela (who received 9,7% support), while the third strongest leader (Bishop Desmond Tutu) received 3,2% support. However, Mr Botha did not receive nearly as much support from Blacks as studies over the past two years show him to be enjoying among Coloureds and Indians. Among these two groups his average support was about 40% — more than the combined support given to all other leaders (from any population group).

One would expect those respondents who prefer White leaders to be the less radical Blacks (those with low educational qualifications and elderly people) and members of ethnic minorities. Such people might feel that

White leadership affords them security. Many Blacks have also been socialised to take the legitimacy of White political dominance more or less for granted. However, statistical analysis provides no significant corroboration for such conjectures about the nature of Black support for White leadership.

Knowledge of and support for various social movements

The survey determined the respondent's knowledge of and support for various Black or multi-ethnic social movements. The organisations were the African National Congress (ANC), the Azanian People's Organisation (AZAPO), the United Democratic Front (UDF) and Inkatha.[6]

The ANC

Respondents were asked three questions concerning the ANC. The three questions with the response options and percentage responses were as follows:

'Do you think most of the leaders of the African National Congress (ANC) are Black or White?'

Not applicable — does not know about ANC	19,5%
Black	47,5%
White	13,8%
Black and White	6,1%
Uncertain or don't know	13,0%
Total	99,9%

'The ANC claims that it is fighting not only for certain groups in South Africa, but for all the peoples of South Africa. Do you agree or disagree with this claim?'

Not applicable — does not know about ANC	19,5%
Agree	51,8%
Disagree	12,7%
Uncertain or don't know	16,1%
Total	100,1%

'Some people claim that the Russians make most of the important decisions for the ANC. Do you agree or disagree?'

Not applicable — does not know about ANC	19,5%
Agree	26,4%
Disagree	23,3%
Uncertain or don't know	30,8%
Total	100,0%

Respondents were not asked whether they supported or were members of the ANC, since it is a prohibited organisation and no valid answers could have been expected to such questions.

From the three questions reproduced above, the following indirect conclusions may be drawn:

- About two out of every ten respondents either are or claim to be totally ignorant about the ANC. (The category 'don't know about ANC' comprises 19,5% of the respondents.) The UDF, AZAPO and Inkatha are unknown to 51,2, 36,7 and 19,0% of the respondents respectively.
- A further one to three out of every ten respondents did not know enough about the ANC to answer the questions put to them. (The 'uncertain or don't know' category ranges from 13,0% to 30,8% of the respondents.) It is interesting that the 'uncertain/don't know' categories are much the same for the first two questions — 13,0 and 16,1% — but that it soars to 30,8% for the third question. Of course it must be remembered that the leaders of the ANC and its declared multiracial policy are fairly widely known, whereas the possible covert role of the Russians and, more specifically, the influence of the Communist Party is at this stage still largely conjectural and is strongly associated with the anti-Communist propaganda of Western interest groups. These factors could cause a greater or lesser degree of uncertainty among Blacks.
- The rest of the respondents — about six out of every ten (the group varies from 49,7% to 67,4%) — expressed their views on the ANC. It appeared that 53,6% of the *total* group of respondents were of the opinion that the ANC's leadership was predominantly Black or a multi-ethnic balance, while 51,8% believed that the ANC was fighting for all people in South Africa and 23,3% believed that the ANC was not a pawn manipulated by Russia. These percentages represent 79,5, 80,3 and 46,9% respectively of the respondents *who actually expressed a viewpoint.* In contrast, 13,8% of all respondents believed that the ANC's leadership was predominantly White, 12,7% that the ANC was fighting for certain people in South Africa only and 26,4% that it is a Russian pawn. These figures represent 20,5, 19,7 and 53,1% respectively of the respondents who expressed a viewpoint at all. The responses to the first two questions in particular seem to indicate that the vast majority of Blacks who know about the ANC have no doubts about its credibility. Of course this does not mean that some 50% of the respondents (53,6% for the first question and 51,8% for the second) in fact support the ANC, but it does bear out the conclusion that the ANC can count on at least 50% potential support.
- There is a striking similarity between the foregoing 50% and the 48,8% who maintain that it is *wrong* for Swaziland and Mozambique to expel the ANC from their countries in keeping with the peace treaties between these countries and South Africa. Of the respondents, 26,6% felt these countries were *right* to expel the ANC from their territory, while the

351

remainder (24,6%) was uncertain. Cross-tabulation of this question about ANC residence in neighbouring states and the question concerning the ANC's struggle for all people in South Africa shows that 41,3% of the respondents believed that the two neighbouring states in question were wrong to expel the ANC and that the ANC was fighting for everyone. Only 7,3% of the respondents believed that these countries were right to expel the ANC and that the ANC was fighting for certain groups only. A further 13,7% of the respondents' reaction to at least one of the two questions was 'positive' towards the ANC, whilst they were uncertain about the other question. In other words, 55% of the respondents held generally positive perceptions of the ANC in response to these questions, once again confirming the roughly 50% of the sample which was sympathetic towards this organisation.

Finally, it should be noted that the ANC managed to attract almost 20% of the leadership support (see the section entitled 'Choice of leadership'). This is the largest single block of support for leaders subscribing to roughly the same political ideology. This figure is extremely high if one bears in mind that Blacks would not easily mention an ANC leader as a possible leader for South Africa for fear of prosecution. Hence, the 20% cited here is a conservative estimate.

From these data the conclusion may be drawn that there is a strong possibility that at least 20% of the Blacks in the PWV area support the ANC, whilst at least another 30% have ANC sympathies. In a recent survey among Black workers, Professor L Schlemmer, head of the Centre for Applied Social Sciences at the University of Natal (see *Sunday Times* 23/9/1984), identified ANC support as being 27% in the PWV and PE metropolitan areas. At the end of this section there will be a brief comparison between Schlemmer's data and those of the HSRC.

AZAPO

Almost two thirds of the research group was aware of the existence of AZAPO. Hence this organisation was better known to Blacks in the PWV area than the UDF (63,3% as opposed to 48,8%). Of the respondents who knew of its existence, 31% (19,6% of the total sample) supported it, 60,1% (38% of the total sample) did not support it and the rest (8,9%) were uncertain. To the question, 'Do you think that AZAPO will have a *good* or a *bad* effect on relations between Blacks and Whites?', respondents answered as follows:

Good influence	44,7%
Bad influence	19,3%
Uncertain or don't know	36,0%

Hence, for every one respondent who believed that AZAPO would have a detrimental effect on intergroup relations, there were more than two who believed the opposite. On the whole, however, it would seem that at this stage Blacks in the PWV area are still largely ignorant about AZAPO. Only 40,5% of the total sample were able to express a definite view in response to the above question, the remainder (59,5%) either did not know of AZAPO's existence, or knew too little about it to express a view on its influence on intergroup relations.

The UDF

Nearly half of the research group (48,8%) knew of the existence of the UDF. Of these, 40,6% supported it, 48,7% did not and the rest (10,7%) were uncertain. Of the research group as a whole, 19,8% supported the UDF and 23,7% did not. More than half of the respondents (56,5%) either did not know about the organisation, or were uncertain about supporting it. Asked why they were UDF supporters, the 19,8% gave their principal reasons as follows:

Reasons for supporting the UDF	%
Fights for democracy	35,6
Solves our problems	17,1
Represents all groups	12,7
Makes people aware of their rights	8,6
Helps people fight for their rights	5,8
Will help Blacks	5,8
Does nothing wrong	2,4
Will bring peace to South Africa	2,4
Unites Blacks	1,4
Represents students	0,7
Other reasons	6,2
No reason	1,4
Total	100,1

UDF supporters phrased their reasons for backing the organisation very simplistically and it would seem that often they were simply expressing the same idea in different words, namely that the UDF might one day obtain rights for Blacks. Interestingly, 12,7% of the supporters specified that they supported this organisation because it is not ethnically or racially based, but represents all groups. The 23,7% who indicated that they did not support the UDF gave the following reasons:

353

Reasons for not supporting the UDF	%
Don't know what it stands for	37,1
Don't agree with its aims	6,3
Too exclusive/elitist	5,1
All talk and no action	4,0
Scared of being arrested	3,7
Because Whites are involved	2,0
They do not help the people	2,0
They are responsible for boycotts	1,1
Other reasons	9,4
No reason	29,2
Total	99,9

Almost two thirds (66,3%) of respondents who claimed to know about the UDF but did not support it could either give no reason for their non-support, or maintained that they did not know what the organisation stood for and therefore would not support it. Slightly more than one fifth (20,5%) advanced specific objections to the UDF as their reasons for non-support. Of these, the three most important objections were disagreement with UDF objectives, its exclusiveness and its lack of action.

Clearly the UDF, like AZAPO, was not well-known among Blacks in the PWV area at the time of the survey.

Inkatha

More than half (58%) of the respondents said that they did not support the Inkatha movement, whilst 18,9% indicated support for it. Nineteen per cent of the sample said that they had never heard of Inkatha and 4,1% were uncertain about supporting it. Of the respondents who did know about Inkatha, 71,7% did not support the organisation, 23,3% supported it and the rest (5%) were uncertain. When one compares the support for Inkatha with support for the ANC, the UDF and AZAPO (see table 13.2), it appears that Inkatha has much the same degree of support in the PWV area as the UDF and AZAPO, but considerably less than the ANC. This finding is corroborated by the data on leadership choices (see the section entitled 'Choice of leadership'). Only 5,7% of respondents chose Chief Minister Buthelezi as the *Black* leader of South Africa, whereas 17,2% opted for Mandela — this despite the fact that the ANC is a banned organisation and supporting it is, in fact, illegal.

Table 13.2 Support for the ANC, the UDF, AZAPO and Inkatha expressed as percentages of the research group as a whole and as percentages of respondents who knew about the *relevant organisation*

Organisation	Support as % of total research group	Support as % of respondents who knew about the organisation
ANC*	Between 20,0% and 50,0%**	Between 36,0% and 65,0%**
UDF	19,8	40,6
AZAPO	19,6	31,0
Inkatha	18,9	23,3

* Nobody was directly questioned about supporting the ANC, hence the percentages were inferred indirectly. (See the section entitled 'The ANC'.)
** Response rates for different questions.

The explanation for Inkatha's poor support in the PWV metropolitan area could lie in its reputation as an exclusively Zulu cultural organisation and hence may be associated with the ethnic structure of the Black population of the PWV area. One could justifiably assume that the movement enjoys far greater support among the Zulu communities in Natal, especially in rural areas and among the more traditionally-minded Zulu. In a recent survey, Professor L Schlemmer of the University of Natal found that Inkatha/Buthelezi enjoyed 54% support in Durban as opposed to 14% in the PWV/PE areas, while analyses of the HSRC data on support for Inkatha indicated that 30,4% of Zulu speakers in the PWV area supported the movement as opposed to 16,8% of Xhosa speakers and 10,4% of Tswana speakers. In the PWV region (a multi-ethnic area) and the PE region (a predominantly Xhosa area), Inkatha will inevitably have fewer supporters than in the predominantly Zulu Durban area. Inkatha has never managed to rid itself of its image as a Zulu cultural-cum-political movement with strong nationalist aspirations. Any South African Black political movement or party with a strong ethnic basis will have problems in gaining acceptance outside its own ethnic borders because of the country's history of ethnic conflict and because the White Government's policy of separate development has made any ethnically based policy or system unpopular among Blacks.

In response to the question 'Do you believe that Inkatha is being used by the Zulus to increase their own power', respondents answered as follows:

Yes	39,0%
No	20,1%
Uncertain/don't know	21,0%
Never heard of Inkatha	19,8%
Total	99,9%

Less than half (48,2%) of the respondents *who knew about Inkatha's existence* believed that the Zulus were using it to strengthen their own political power base, 24,9% did not believe this and the rest (26,9%) were uncertain. A fairly large percentage of respondents therefore regarded Inkatha as a Zulu nationalist movement. Further analysis of all responses to this question indicated that it was predominantly Zulu speakers who believed that the Zulus were using Inkatha to extend their power (46,3% Zulu as opposed to 37,1% Sotho and Tswana). It should be pointed out, however, that non-Zulus obviously know less about Inkatha than the Zulus themselves. For instance, 51,1% of the Tswana and 44% of the Sotho had either never heard of Inkatha or knew too little about it to answer this question. In contrast, only 28,3% of the Zulus were either totally ignorant of Inkatha or not knowledgeable enough to answer the question.

Support for various political movements: HSRC findings contrasted with those of the Schlemmer study

Table 13.3 gives a comparison of the foregoing data on the support enjoyed by various organisations with the findings of Schlemmer (1984).

Table 13.3 Support among urban Blacks for various political groups: A comparison between the HSRC survey and the Schlemmer study

Political group	HSRC survey*	Schlemmer survey (only Tvl/PE data)
ANC/Mandela	20,0% +**	27,0%
UDF	19,8%	11,0%
AZAPO	19,6%	5,0%
Inkatha/Buthelezi	18,9%	14,0%
Other/None	55,0%	43,0%

* Because respondents indicated their support for each organisation in turn, these percentages do not add up to 100.
** The 20,0% + was inferred indirectly from questions on leadership, support and sympathy with the ANC.

The table shows that

- the relative support for the ANC, the UDF and Inkatha is broadly the same. The 'other' and 'none' category in the HSRC survey (55% of the sample) is also much the same as the corresponding category in the Schlemmer survey (43% of his sample); and
- in both studies the ANC emerges as the strongest group — the two surveys affirm each other's findings in this respect.

356

Note, however, that the above data are not always strictly comparable for the following reasons:

- The samples differ considerably. The HSRC survey made use of a sample of 1 478 Blacks aged 18 or over in Black residential areas in the PWV (compounds excluded). Schlemmer's sample consisted of 551 Black workers from eight different areas (Johannesburg, Pretoria, East Rand, West Rand, the Vaal Triangle, Port Elizabeth, Durban and Pinetown). Although Schlemmer's data (quoted in table 13.3) are only from the Transvaal and Port Elizabeth, it should be borne in mind that the ethnic composition of the populations of these two target areas differs greatly. Thus 98,1% of the Black population of Port Elizabeth are Xhosa, whereas only 12,8% of the Blacks in the PWV area are Xhosa (South Africa 1980a: 143). Quite apart from this ethnic difference, it stands to reason that there must be sex, age, income, educational and occupational (e.g. economically active as opposed to economically inactive) differences between a sample drawn from the entire adult population and one drawn only from workers.
- The two surveys also used different methods to determine support for the various political groups. Schlemmer's survey made use of a single question, in answer to which respondents had to make their political choice. (Hence they could indicate only one political group.) The HSRC survey used several questions to determine whether or not respondents supported each *individual* political group (permitting them to indicate support for *more than one* group). Thus they were asked each time (with reference to the UDF, AZAPO and Inkatha): 'Do you support . . .?' Support for the ANC was inferred from a variety of other questions (including the respondent's choice of a leader).

In view of these differences, the extent of mutual corroboration in the two sets of research findings is all the more remarkable.

Multiparty support

Finally, we should briefly note the respondents' support for more than one political group. Table 13.4 indicates how many respondents support more than one political group.

Table 13.4 Multiparty political support

Number of groups supported by respondents	%	Number
Respondents supporting neither the ANC, UDF, AZAPO, nor Inkatha	55,0	813
Respondents supporting only 1 of the 4 groups	22,5	333
Respondents supporting 2 of the 4 groups	13,5	200
Respondents supporting 3 of the 4 groups	7,6	112
Respondents supporting all 4 groups	1,4	20
Total	100,0	1 478

Thus 22,5% of all respondents support more than one group — in fact, the same percentage as that for respondents supporting only one group. This trend may be attributed to the basically powerless situation of Blacks within the South African political structure. People in this position will resort to every means outside the formal decision-making bodies of the RSA in order to secure power, particularly since the essential aim and aspirations of all the groups are the same. The trend will be manifested particularly if the groups in question do not differ appreciably as far as their secondary aims and aspirations are concerned. Thus one may accept that the ANC and Inkatha are both striving for effective political power in South Africa, but that the differences between them are more significant (e.g. in their views of ethnicity and the method of effecting socio-political change) than those between the ANC, AZAPO and the UDF. In terms of this argument, Blacks who support more than one party would be more inclined to give their allegiance to combinations of organisations which do not include both the ANC and Inkatha. Of the 332 respondents who supported more than one party, 33,7% supported the ANC but not Inkatha, 32,8% supported Inkatha but not the ANC, 18,7% supported both the ANC and Inkatha and 14,8% supported other combinations excluding both Inkatha and the ANC. These data confirm the argument that the ANC and Inkatha are less frequently combined than other groups and hence enjoy a lesser degree of multiple support. It would also seem that the ANC enjoys a significant degree of acceptance from supporters of South Africa's internal political organisations.

Probability of support for various organisations

With a view to a more searching analysis of differential support for the various interest groups in terms of certain background variables, the Multivariate Nominal Scale Analysis (MNA) technique was employed.[7] Since a number of analyses were undertaken and different combinations of predictor (independent) and response (dependent) variables were used, it is not possible to tabulate the results of the analyses here. For this reason, only a few of the observations will be discussed.

With regard to prediction of support for the UDF, it was found that a combination of the ten background variables used in the survey, plus leadership choice as an 11th variable, accounted for 21,4% of the variation in the response variable. In the case of the 'support the UDF' category, the best predictors (with Beta-square values[8]) were the following:

Choice of a national leader	5,7%
Educational level	2,4%
Residential area	1,3%

None of the other predictor variables had a Beta-square value above 1%.

With the aid of the MNA technique one can predict the *probable* attributes of a UDF supporter. Thus, the probability that a male in the 18 to 24 age group living in Mamelodi and having an educational level of Std 10 will support the UDF is 0,40. This means that four in every ten predictions that such a person will support the UDF will be correct, or that 40% of all persons possessing these characteristics will be UDF supporters, as opposed to only 20% of the sample as a whole. If, in addition to the aforementioned background variables, one were to include the fact that the person selected an ANC member as the leader of South Africa, then the probability that he will support the UDF increases to 0,55.

Analysis of ANC support reveals a similar pattern with regard to the identification of the most likely ANC supporters. The same ten background variables, plus an eleventh (leadership choice) were used in the model. This combination accounts for 17,9% of the variation in the dependent (response) variable. The best predictors of ANC support were the following:

Educational level	2,9%
Preferred newspaper	2,1%
Sex	1,3%
Income	1,1%

The other variables all had Beta-square values of below 1%. There is a 0,69% probability of correctly predicting that a male in the 18 to 24 age group who has an educational level of Std 10 or higher earns R300 or more per month and prefers to read White-controlled newspapers will support the ANC. In other words, seven out of every ten Blacks in the sample possessing this combination of attributes were ANC supporters. (Without prior knowledge of the respondent's party or group preference, the probability of correctly predicting ANC support is 0,28.)

In the case of AZAPO, it is again young, educated males who are most likely to support the organisation.

To sum up the results of the aforementioned analyses, one may infer that the three organisations concerned draw most of their support from the ranks of young Black males who have comparatively high educational qualifications. These findings, together with Schlemmer's conclusion (1984) that younger and better-educated persons tend to be more militant, support the conclusion that the generation gap may possibly play a significant role among the Black population.

If one considers that 61,3% of Blacks were born after Sharpeville (1960), there should be no doubt about the revolutionary potential of Black youth. They grew up in an era marked by better educational opportunities, political struggles and aspirations (particularly in view of the fact that most African states became independent under indigenous Black governments during the late fifties and early sixties and liberation movements in Southern Africa gained momentum), greater physical and psychological estrangement between Black and White as a result of apartheid, etc. Hence, in addition to the natural desire of youth to change the status quo to their own taste, there are a number of political factors peculiar to the period during which South Africa's Black youths grew up, all of which motivate them to alter the status quo. Moreover, the age distribution of Blacks has certain economic and demographic implications which will gravely affect the future of Black youths both now and in the future (for instance, rising unemployment if it proves impossible to create sufficient job opportunities for such a flood of work seekers).

Viewed collectively, these factors make Black youth a revolutionary force to be reckoned with. On the other hand, the power to which Black youth aspires is in the hands of an elderly White power elite. These are the people who created the present order and they will not readily change it, since nobody likes to change something that he has created and older people, in terms of the assumption made in this argument, will be even less inclined to do so. Thus, the phenomenon of a generation gap can potentially intensify intergroup conflict (for instance between Black and White).

GUIDELINES FOR NEGOTIATION POLITICS IN SOUTH AFRICA

On the basis of the preceding discussion of data collected among Black adults in the PWV area in July 1984 (i.e. before the most recent spate of unrest), the following general guidelines for negotiation politics in South Africa may be laid down:

- Blacks will not accept any constitutional reform which does not grant them an effective say in government. In fact, any dispensation (no matter how good it is) implemented without their co-determination is doomed.
- Because of South Africa's history of apartheid, Blacks will not accept any constitutional reform which has too strong a group basis.
- Economic reform (e.g. a socialist economic system which purports to provide an equal distribution of wealth) without political reform will not succeed. The notion that a Black middle class could prevent revolution is fallacious, since economic equality does not necessarily ensure freedom in the broad sense. That same Black middle class will insist on equal political rights as well. Economic reform will have to be effected in conjunction with political reform.
- Blacks have a clear leadership problem which could be extremely

dysfunctional for conflict regulation. Few leaders emerge with strong popular support. In fact, the only leader who significantly outranks the large number of persons cited as potential leaders is Nelson Mandela. The Government will also have to start negotiating with leaders who they consider to be non-legitimate or less legitimate. These leaders may eventually, by virtue of their very non-legitimacy vis-à-vis the 'apartheid regime', enjoy such popular support that they may be unwilling to confer with the Government.

- There is still an appreciable percentage of Blacks who prefer White leadership. These people's confidence should not be disappointed by unwise official action.
- The various Black interest groups (e.g. political parties and pressure groups such as the UDF and AZAPO) were, at the time of the survey, less widely known among the Black public than is necessary for effective negotiation politics. Moreover, there is a considerable number of Blacks who support two or more parties simultaneously. This indicates great diffuseness in Black viewpoints and approaches concerning the political future of the country. As mentioned in the introduction, such a state of affairs is not functional for negotiation politics.
- The younger generation of Blacks (25 years or younger — a category which includes 61,3% of all Blacks) is politically the most radical. This should definitely be taken into consideration in future negotiations. If the younger generation were to be excluded from such negotiations, the chances of success would be slender indeed.

NOTES

1 See for instance Rhoodie (1983), Schlemmer (in Van Vuuren *et al* 1983) and Bekker (1974) for the conditions of conflict in deeply segmented societies; Davies (1962 and in Graham and Gurr 1969) for his J-curve of rising expectations and declining satisfaction; the frustration-aggression theory postulated by Dollard *et al* (1969); the social change/systematic frustration theory of Feierabend, Feierabend and Nesvold (in Graham and Gurr 1969); Gurr's (1971) theory of relative deprivation; Galtung's (1974, 1978) structural theory of revolutions; Smelser's (1970) theory of collective behaviour; the conflict theories of Karl Marx (1951a, 1951b, 1952) and Dahrendorf (1958, 1959); Duke's (1976) theory of the legitimacy of power; and De Kock's (1984) power conflict model.
2 Violence can also be functional. Thus it could be seen as symptomatic of grave structurally generated conflict within an organisation or society and as such may expedite change (reform). On the whole, however, violence is more dysfunctional than functional.
3 For brief, systematic expositions of some of these factors, see De Kock (1984: 310-314); Rhoodie (1983: 146-163); Deutsch (1973: 351-400); Himes (1980: 167-276); Kriesberg (1973: 204-246); and Oberschall (1973: 242-277).
4 The various groups themselves and their popular support cannot be established without such research.
5 The eventual aim is to conduct more frequent surveys.

6 For further information regarding the origin and development of the ANC, UDF, AZAPO and Inkatha, the following sources can be consulted: Carter (1980: chapter 4), Laurence (in Hellman et al 1979), South African Institute of Race Relations' surveys of race relations in South Africa from 1977 to 1983 (SAIRR (1978: 31-39), SAIRR (1979: 27-38), SAIRR (1980: 40-57), SAIRR (1981: 48-65), SAIRR (1982: 24-31), SAIRR (1983: 32-42), SAIRR (1984: 43-63)) and the South African Reviews (volumes I and II) published by the South African Research Service (SARS (1983: 6-30), SARS (1984: 6-25)).

7 For a detailed exposition of the MNA technique, see Andrews, FM and Messenger, RC. *Multivariate Nominal Scale Analysis.* Ann Arbor: Institute for Social Research, University of Michigan, 1973. This is a useful technique for analysing the relation between a set of categorical predictors and a single categorical (nominal) dependent (response) variable.

8 Beta-square values are criteria of the significance of the relevant independent variable as a predictor of the dependent variable category concerned when all other independent variables in the model are kept constant.

BIBLIOGRAPHY

Andrews, FM and Messenger,RC. *Multivariate nominal scale analysis.* Ann Arbor: Institute for Social Research, University of Michigan, 1973.

Bekker, S. *The plural society and the problem of order.* Cape Town: University of Cape Town, 1974 (unpublished Ph.D. dissertation).

Callinicos, A and Rogers, J. *Southern Africa after Soweto.* London: Pluto Press, 1978.

Carter, GM. *Which way is South Africa going?* Bloomington: Indiana University Press, 1980.

Dahrendorf, R. Toward a theory of social conflict. *Journal of Conflict Resolution,* vol. 2, no. 2, June 1958.

Dahrendorf, R. *Class and class conflict in industrial society.* London: Routledge & Kegan Paul, 1959.

Dahrendorf, R. *Life changes: Approaches to social and political theory.* Chicago: University of Chicago Press, 1979.

Davies, JC. Toward a theory of revolution. *American Sociological Review,* vol. 27, no. 1, February 1962.

De Kock, CP. *Die sosiologiese begrip konflik: 'n Kritiese evaluering van enkele bydraes.* Pretoria: Universiteit van Suid-Afrika, 1984 (ongepubliseerde D.Litt. et Phil.-proefskrif).

Deutsch, M. *The resolution of conflict: Constructive and destructive processes.* New Haven: Yale University Press, 1973.

Dollard, J et al. *Frustration and aggression.* New Haven: Yale University Press, 1969.

Duke, JT. *Conflict and power in social life.* Provo: Brigham Young University Press, 1976.

Galtung, J. *A structural theory of revolutions.* Rotterdam: Rotterdam University Press, 1974.

— *Peace and social structure.* Copenhagen: Christian Ejlers, 1978.

Graham, HD and Gurr, TR (Eds.) *The history of violence in America.* New York: Bantam,1969.

Gurr, TR. *Why men rebel.* Princeton: Princeton University Press, 1971.

Hellman, E and Lever, H (Eds.). *Conflict and progress: fifty years of race relations in South Africa.* Johannesburg: Macmillan South Africa, 1979.

Herbstein, D. *White man, we want to talk to you.* Harmondsworth, Middlesex: Penguin, 1978.

Himes, JS. *Conflict and conflict management.* Athens: The University of Georgia Press, 1980.

Hitchcock, B. *Flashpoint South Africa.* Cape Town: Don Nelson, 1977.

Johnson, RW. *How long will South Africa survive?* Johannesburg: Macmillan South Africa, 1977.

Kane-Berman, J. *Soweto: Black revolt, White reaction.* Johannesburg: Ravan Press, 1978.

Kriesberg, L. *The sociology of social conflicts.* Englewood Cliffs, New Jersey: Prentice-Hall, 1973.

Marx, Karl. *Karl Marx and Fredrick Engels: Selected works in two volumes,* Volume 1. Moscow: Foreign Languages Publishing House, 1951a.

— *Karl Marx and Fredrick Engels: Selected works in two volumes*, Volume 2. Moscow: Foreign Languages Publishing House, 1951b.

— *Revolution and counter-revolution or Germany in 1948*. London: George Allen and Unwin Ltd, 1952.

Oberschall, A. *Social conflict and social movements*. Englewood Cliffs, New Jersey: Prentice-Hall, 1973.

Rhoodie, Nic J. *Intergroup conflict in deeply segmented societies: An introductory conceptual framework*. Pretoria: Human Sciences Research Council. (Report GR-W-1), 1983.

SAIRR. *Survey of race relations in South Africa: 1977*. vol. 31. Johannesburg: South African Institute of Race Relations, 1978.

SAIRR. *Survey of race relations in South Africa: 1978*. vol. 32. Johannesburg: South African Institute of Race Relations, 1979.

SAIRR. *Survey of race relations in South Africa: 1979*. vol. 33. Johannesburg: South African Institute of Race Relations, 1980.

SAIRR. *Survey of race relations in South Africa: 1980*. vol. 34. Johannesburg: South African Institute of Race Relations, 1981.

SAIRR. *Survey of race relations in South Africa: 1981*. vol. 35. Johannesburg: South African Institute of Race Relations, 1982.

SAIRR. *Survey of race relations in South Africa: 1982*. vol. 36. Johannesburg: South African Institute of Race Relations, 1983.

SAIRR. *Survey of race relations in South Africa: 1983*. vol. 37. Johannesburg: South African Institute of Race Relations, 1984.

SARS. (South African Research Service). *South African Review I*. Johannesburg: Ravan Press, 1983.

SARS (South African Research Service). *South African Review II*. Johannesburg: Ravan Press, 1984.

Smelser, NJ. *Theory of collective behavior*. London: Routledge & Kegan Paul, 1970.

South Africa (Republic). 1980a. Central Statistical Services. *Population census 80: Sample tabulation, geographical distribution of the population*. Pretoria: Government Printer. (RP 02-80-01).

South Africa (Republic). 1980b. Central Statistical Services. *Population census 80: Sample tabulation, social characteristics*. Pretoria: Government Printer. (RP 02-80-02).

Van der Merwe, CF en Steenekamp, CS. *Riglyne vir die gebruik van die panele van die RGN-Meningspeilingsentrum*. Pretoria: Raad vir Geesteswetenskaplike Navorsing. (Verslag 1982-09).

Van Vuuren, DJ, Wiehahn, NE, Lombard, JA and Rhoodie, Nic J.*Change in South Africa*. Durban: Butterworths, 1983.

14 Socio-political perspectives on change in the Coloured sector of the South African population

De Wet Schutte

INTRODUCTION

Any study of change presupposes the existence of some trend or other in a context of time. Because of the topicality of the subject of this article, anyone writing about it now runs the risk of lapsing into anachronistic rhetoric. On the other hand, he may concentrate so much on contemporary events that he ventures into speculations about the future — which as a rule merely make interesting (sometimes amusing) reading, depending on how close to the mark the author manages to get (Keppel-Jones 1949). This article proposes to examine the latest events associated with the implementation of the so-called 'new dispensation', yet to avoid both excessive anachronism and speculation about the future. The two epochs relevant to the discussion are those prior and subsequent to the implementation of the new dispensation.

My frame of reference may be described as general, sometimes even amorphous. The views expressed were confirmed empathically and by numerous conversations with members of the Coloured sector of South African society. The reader will notice that there is little reliance on empirical data and this is largely for two reasons. Firstly, in this field few data are available in processed form because of the recency of the new dispensation and secondly, there is considerable confusion among the different population groups as to the implications the Constitution of September 1984 has for them. Both prior to and since the implementation of the new Constitution there have been so many 'influential voices' for and against it, and the content of this rhetoric has been so divergent, that the opinion of the average Coloured voter — who, mainly for historical reasons, takes comparatively little interest in current political affairs — may be described as fluid and hence not readily fathomable by empirical means. The large percentages of 'uncertain' and 'don't know' responses recorded in HSRC surveys confirm this fluidity of opinion (Rhoodie 1983; Roothman and Schutte 1982).

To complicate the matter even further, experience has shown that as a whole the Coloured public is highly suspicious of surveys and in empirical studies the researcher cannot always distinguish between *evasive responses* and *ignorance* or *lack of interest*.

For all these reasons my approach will be largely descriptive and not every phenomenon will be substantiated by statistically verified explanation. The methodological basis for Coetzee's paper to a South African Sociological Association (SASA) congress is applicable to this article as well. He said:

> Hence what I am presenting is intended simply as tentative statements based on observations — partly questions, partly postulates, but always with the aim of serving as a starting point for closer enquiry, testing and correction. I regard what I am presenting in acquitting myself of my commission not as answers to questions, but as tentative questions awaiting answers from scientific research (Coetzee 1982:4 (translation)).

At the outset I should mention that I am fully aware of the controversy (mainly in the Afrikaans language) about labelling people 'brown' or 'Coloured'. I have settled for the term 'Coloured', because in my experience this term (in English) evokes less resentment among the majority of people, although neither designation is universally acceptable. It would seem that in Afrikaans the term 'Bruin' (Brown translated) evokes least resentment. My use of the term does not stem from a conviction that the Coloured sector of the South African population should be designated as a separate, identifiable 'nation', nor from a desire to conform to any official classification, but is simply a convenient way of observing the logical demarcation implied in the topic under discussion.

Note also that the term 'new dispensation' consistently refers to the RSA constitution of 1984, which came into effect on 3 September 1984. No attempt will be made to provide a detailed chronological survey of what the Coloured population regards as 'positive change' — rather this article is intended to discuss the whole polemical issue, according due regard to the political and socio-economic *Umwelt* of the Coloured sector of the South African population today. The premise of the discussion is that of Moore and many other social scientists, namely that nothing in the social sciences may be regarded as static (Moore 1967; Jessop 1972; Parsons in Etzioni and Etzioni 1964; and Eisenstadt 1966).

It is difficult for any person to make value-judgments about how another population or ethnic group views matters and in South Africa this difficulty is exacerbated by the fact that for several years statutory measures have governed and controlled association between certain population groups. Today, a White speaking on behalf of the Coloureds about socio-political change could easily be accused of paternalism or totally false perceptions, an accusation which would have been unfounded a few decades ago. From an Afrikaner's point of view, the principal single reason for this situation is that the Coloured population has come of age and should be permitted to speak for itself. Of course this view is based on the assumption that the Coloured population of former times was immature, a notion which is anything but the truth.

The facts show that the criticism of the socio-political order voiced by Coloured politicians, academics and members of the public today is substantially the same as that expressed by Coloured people during the fifties. In essence, the criticisms levelled against the political system in the RSA up to 2 September 1984 (the pre-new dispensation era) have not changed at all and some of the criticisms against the 'former dispensation' are still being applied to the new by some leaders (this will be discussed more fully later). Hence, it would seem that the 'immaturity' was not so much on the part of the 'orators' as on the part of the 'audience' — those for whom the message was intended.

Today there is such a large body of published data on the Coloured population that people have become more outspoken about its situation. Moreover, association between Whites and Coloureds is much freer than it used to be, so that it is possible for people having the capacity for emphatic observation and open minds to contribute meaningfully to the debate on the Coloured population's perceptions of socio-political change in the RSA.

It should be remembered that only those facets of change affecting the Coloured sector of South African society will be dealt with here. Because of the interdependence of the ethnic/racial groups in South Africa there will be frequent references to the White sector, but only where it has bearing on the subject under discussion. The article could be criticised for this because, as acknowledged earlier, in some respects the Coloured sector is closely interwoven or even totally integrated with the other Non-White population groups. In fact, in some instances the statutory measures embodied in laws and regulations are applicable to all Non-Whites in South Africa, whereas others (e.g. the Group Areas Act) differentiate between Whites and certain Non-White groups. Hence, all along there was the temptation to incorporate the Indian or Black population groups. However, in order to confine the discussion to the prescribed topic and for the sake of logical order, it was necessary to observe a drastic discipline.

The Coloured sector is amongst South Africa's most researched population groups (as the many official and unofficial reports and publications to be found in libraries testify) and there are any number of in-depth studies of the history and origins of the Coloured people, probably the most authoritative being those by Marais (1939) and Cilliers (1963). Therefore, this article will not deal with the Coloured people's origins.

Several official commissions have reported to the government of the day on matters affecting the Coloured population, but a study of the various reports reveals that very few 'new' findings or perspectives have emerged from the successive enquiries.[1] Apart from a difference in slant, the principal contributions to the comprehensive Theron Report may be seen as 'official' confirmation of the conclusions of innumerable formal and informal studies on these and allied matters by social scientists, expressed by word of mouth or published in theses, dissertations, reports and articles. This 'official' confirmation is manifestly a tribute to the scientific integrity of the many researchers and academics who fearlessly submitted their objective findings to commissions of which they were sometimes members. The facts remain the same, but it would seem that the attitude that some Whites and certain politicians had towards Coloureds has changed, possibly for the very reason that they were constantly being confronted with the same facts about the Coloured population.[2] Minister Hendrickse put it thus:

> I am happy to observe a dramatic change in Afrikaner thinking, views and attitudes. I experience this not only as a member of the Cabinet, but I discern an overall change in their thinking (*Die Burger* 4/1/1985 (translation)).

In a sense the subject of this discussion is ever so simple, yet at the same time it is vastly complicated (Leistner 1980). To condense the Coloured population's perception of positive change into a single credo would be to say quite simply that all forms of statutory discrimination based on colour should be abolished. One of the most important (and perhaps most essential) steps towards achieving this would be the abolition of a measure such as the Group Areas Act. This Act has been and always will be the *locus focus* of the socio-political aspirations of the majority of Coloured people. Rhoodie's press statement about South Africa's most pressing problem confirms this. Of a Coloured sample population asked to name South Africa's most serious problem, 30% cited apartheid practices, 26% the economic situation and 14% housing matters (Rhoodie 1984). However, it must be acknowledged that in the eyes of the average Coloured respondent, economic and housing matters are largely influenced by apartheid practices.

The complexity of the problem is evident from the fact that since their arrival at the Cape in 1652, Whites have wielded political sovereignty (the final say) over all the other peoples in South Africa. Thus they have the most to lose should the franchise be extended to all inhabitants in a unitary South African state, whilst the other population or ethnic groups (in the present instance the Coloured population) can only gain by such a move.[3] This 'gain-loss' syndrome has become institutionalised in South African society, which is why the problem may be regarded as so simple, yet so complicated and why conflict regulation has become such a complex matter. Rhoodie and De Kock maintain that 'in societies deeply segmented in terms of cleavages that are relatively enduring and survival related, people aggregate around these cleavages with the result that competition for the *society's* scarce resources manifests itself structurally and organisationally as conflict between the interest groups' (Rhoodie and De Kock 1983:345; also see Bekker 1974). The present ruling party in the House of Representatives appears to be stressing the complicated side of the situation, for example, at a meeting in Danielskuil, Minister Hendrickse rejected the idea of one man one vote in a unitary state, yet adhered to the ultimate aim of the abolition of all discriminatory statutory measures (*Die Burger* 21/5/1985).

MAJOR THEMES IN THE DEBATE ON CHANGE

At present, the debate on change in South Africa is conducted chiefly in the socio-political sphere and hinges on the nature of the change initiatives accepted by the Government and the rate at which it launches them. Obviously there is a logical connection between the rate and reality of change and any distinction between the two concepts must be theoretical. Occasionally in this article, when specific change initiatives are examined more closely, some hint of such a distinction will be discernible.

Grievances and discrimination

When one talks to Coloureds about grievances and discrimination, it appears that what they interpret and experience as discriminatory was not changed in any way by the measures implemented by the ruling National party in its search for a solution up until the late seventies. The apartheid-conditioned White response to the Coloured population's outspoken experience of discrimination — namely the creation of more separate amenities and the mere upgrading of existing separate amenities — did not reach the root of the problem (see the Theron Report (RP 38/1976); see also Theron and Du Toit 1977). Pleas for the abolition of discrimination and the creation of equal opportunities in society almost invariably met with such measures as the upgrading of the existing separate facilities and/or infrastructure in residential areas. For example, in some instances institutions such as the University of the Western Cape and, at a non-government level, the NG Sendingkerk were granted autonomy (Schwartz, in Rhoodie 1973). However, with very few exceptions these measures failed to change the negative experience of 'being Coloured', since they did not come to grips with the most essential and basic element of this experience, namely the misprision of the Coloureds' basic freedoms, rights and privileges as native citizens of the country. This point is made very clearly in Curry's article in *South African Dialogue* (in Rhoodie 1973).[4]

Numerical proportion

The question of population numbers appears to be focal to White (and particularly Afrikaner) attitudes towards socio-political matters. When this deep-seated White attitude is probed more deeply, one finds that in almost all instances the criterion for opening up or upgrading certain amenities for all races is demand in terms of *numbers*. By this is meant the number of people appealing for the use of certain facilities hitherto reserved for Whites. An argument commonly heard in White circles is that they (the Whites) cannot understand why there is so much fuss about, say, 'open' cricket, since only one Coloured cricketer has ever managed to earn provincial colours.[5] Thus, the small number of people on behalf of whom the appeals are made is taken as the justification for this attitude and used by some Whites to substantiate the argument in favour of separate amenities for Coloureds.

Ironically, this same 'frequency argument' is used to justify the opening of certain Whites-only facilities or institutions. In such a case it is argued that because there are not enough Coloureds appealing for a separate amenity or institution, the existing White one should be opened up to them.

In both of the above arguments one observes an underlying *numerical* reasoning.

In my conversations with Coloured people it emerged that the mere upgrading of existing facilities or the creation of separate, equivalent facilities (so-called parallel development) does *not* alleviate the negative sense of discrimination experienced by the Coloured population. Essentially, the Coloured sector has never seen it solely as a matter of having inferior amenities upgraded (although that was part of it), but primarily as the *violation of the Coloured population's human dignity*, even when only one individual (or no one at all) was affected (Theron and Du Toit 1977; Cilliers 1963). Hence this may be seen as the Coloured population's chief criterion for the evaluation of the reality of socio-political change in South Africa. It also explains the continued dissatisfaction of some Coloured sportsmen, even though they may have equal sporting facilities and/or at this stage may not even have the calibre of sportsmen who can compete with Whites on an equal footing. As long as Coloured sportsmen have a chance of competing for a place in, say, a Springbok rugby team, an all-White team will not be interpreted as discriminatory and will therefore enjoy the support of the entire body of rugby fans, irrespective of race or colour. This has been proved in practice in such sports as rugby, soccer, boxing, athletics and tennis.

From the foregoing it is obvious that Coloured people will not feel any less aggrieved if a Whites-only facility is opened up to all races only on certain occasions on the grounds that the demand (numbers) does not justify opening it up to everyone permanently. The fact is that even if not one Coloured person was ever to stay overnight in a White hotel in the RSA, the mere idea that Coloured people are statutorily prohibited from doing so is experienced as discriminatory (see the Theron Report (RP 38/1976), chapter 22.15).

THE NEW DISPENSATION

Indisputably the greatest single development in the sphere of socio-political change in the 1980s was the implementation of the so-called new dispensation. This measure was directly responsible for involving the Coloured population in central political decision-making once more. The new dispensation has been operative for only a few months and any observer who ventures at this stage to predict its implications for the Coloured population in microcosm, or for the RSA as a whole, will soon find himself in deep water — as was the case with the many political commentators, politicians and theorists who tried to predict developments when the National Party came to power in 1948.

A crisis of legitimacy

Ever since the commencement of the sessions of the Houses of Representatives, Delegates and Commons in January 1985, decisions having direct implications for the direction and rate of change have been made almost daily. Certain observers in particular describe the present (introductory) phase 'tense' — an evaluation that could perhaps be ascribed to the fact that these individuals made explicit comments for or against the draft constitution or certain of its elements prior to its implementation and are watching the situation like hawks so as to prove their own comments right or to disprove those of other observers.

As has been said, developments in the constitutional sphere are proceeding literally day by day and as yet the 'basic' plans (premises) for reform have not all been tabled. Thus there is currently enquiry into a formula for the granting of political participation in central decision-making to the so-called urban Black population and the reorganisation of third-tier government is also under discussion. Hence any comment on or prediction about the implications of specific measures for the public is a risky exercise at present, since new norms and values are emerging as the result of, for instance, ever-changing political aspirations and it should be borne in mind that politics is a power game not always characterised by rationality. There is no doubt, however, that the RSA has embarked on a new dispensation and one which, despite all criticism of detail, is a reality. Ever since 3 September 1984, Whites simply no longer have sovereign trustee- ship over the Coloured and Indian population groups, nor, in a sense, over Blacks either.

I shall not dwell on the Constitution of the new dispensation, but would rather shift the emphasis to the 'crisis of legitimacy' into which the new dispensation itself and some members of the House of Representatives are apparently plunged. It must be accepted that in the eyes of the people, legitimacy of a government is essential to their submission to the powers vested in the elected members in terms of the Constitution. Judge VG Hiemstra said in this regard:

> Before one considers the possibility of a manifesto of human rights, or, to use the Continental term, a *declaration of human rights*, one must realise that a constitution has to undergo a process of acceptance by the population. Only thus will the necessary respect, loyalty and trust be engendered (*Beeld* 24/8/1984 (translation)).

If one considers the recent election among the Coloured population, the question of its legitimacy arises at once. The basic problem is whether a 30% vote may be interpreted as a mandate for a number of Coloured politicians to lead the entire Coloured population alongside Whites and Indians (*Beeld* 24/8/1984). If one were to argue that this percentage vote does *not* afford legitimacy, the logical question would be what percentage does constitute legitimacy. An examination of the percentage votes obtain- ed in elections in highly developed countries such as the USA (and even in certain past elections in South Africa) reveals that a 30% vote, although relatively low, is by no means exceptionally so. In fact, when one looks at elections for members of town and city councils, 30% seems comparatively high!

Support for the New Dispensation

Some observers maintain that the comparatively low percentage poll implies that the majority of the Coloured population reject the new dispensation (*Rand Daily Mail* 24/8/1984). Observers have advanced various explanations for the low percentage vote, the most important being the poor infrastructure of the competing parties, the intimidation of prospective participants and a deliberate abstention vote.[7] It must be remembered that the competing parties had comparatively little time to get their electoral machinery going and that they did not have recent address lists of supporters for canvassing purposes. In fact, it was a 'first' election, since the Coloured Representative Council (CRC) had operated in a totally different situation. Hence it came as no surprise that the party with the best residual infrastructure (the Labour Party) and the best-known candidates (dating from the days of the Coloured Representative Council) won the election (Theron and Du Toit 1977:93). Another reason why this should be regarded as a 'first' election is that the candidates for whom people were asked to vote did not have relevant 'track records' to assist voters in the exercise of their choice.

When one examines the various political parties, policy statements, one finds that the differences between them would not have been at all clear to the average voter. Thus all four party leaders

- spoke out against apartheid;
- saw the new dispensation purely as a beginning;
- rejected the United Democratic Front's extra-parliamentary methods;
- pleaded for the relief of the housing shortage; and
- regarded the elimination of the Coloured population's socio-economic backwardness (with the accent on equal education) as the top priority (*Rapport* 20/2/1984; *Beeld* 21/2/1984; *Beeld* 22/8/1984; *Beeld* 23/8/1984; *Rapport* 26/8/1984).

If, in addition to the aforementioned factors, one allows for a strong intimidation factor, then one obviously has the general climate for a low percentage vote. A further contributory factor was that the Coloured population had no tradition of voting, largely because Coloured voters have been deprived of effective participation in the democratic political system since 1956.

Registration versus voting percentage as barometer

In view of the fact that apart from the election itself, no referendum was held among the Coloured population to gauge the legitimacy of the politicians' participation in the new dispensation, the general registration of voters could perhaps serve as a barometer to measure Coloured support for such participation. Note that here we are not concerned with the legitimacy of the elected persons.

The rationale for considering the percentage of registered voters as a measure of support is the argument that this should be considered a 'first election'. It was essential that voters registered in order that they might vote in the general election. This registration process took place in a particular historical situation in which, unlike in White elections, there were two camps. On one side were the officially participating political parties who appealed to voters to register so that they might take part in the new dispensation and on the other the so-called UDF group, which actively sought to dissuade voters from registering so that by desistence (and consequent non-participation in the election) they could demonstrate their rejection of the so-called new dispensation. What it amounted to was, in fact, a referendum, with participation and non-participation in the new dispensation as the options. The registration process took place over a certain period and not at specific public polling venues, with the result that intimidation played a less forceful role during this phase of the proposed election than on the actual election day, 22 August 1984 although the preparatory phase was highly politicised and rumours of intimidation to prevent registration were circulating even then.

If one accepts the validity of registration as a barometer, then one must accept that some 65% of Coloured voters expressed, to a greater or lesser extent, their willingness to participate in the new dispensation. At the same time, one must allow for the fact that voters were legally obliged to register (*Rand Daily Mail*, 9/8/1984). It is difficult to assess what percentage of voters registered solely for this reason — just as it is difficult to gauge what percentage of voters abstained from voting because of intimidation on 22 August 1984.

A more reliable indicator of Coloured support for the new dispensation than the percentage vote seems to be a combination of the percentage vote and the percentage of registered voters. Thus it follows that conclusions such as Dr Boesak's, namely that '82% of so-called 'coloureds' wanted nothing to do with the Constitution or apartheid' (*Rand Daily Mail* 24/8/1984:1), appear to be unfounded. A more accurate figure would be in the region of 48%.[8]

Legitimacy of elected members

It would seem, however, that there is an even greater crisis of legitimacy among the Coloured people than the one we have just discussed, namely that of the elected members in the light of the number of votes they polled. Although there is an obvious connection between the causes of the two 'crises', it seems that in the case of some elected members the legitimacy crisis involves their persons rather than the overall cause of participation in the new dispensation. In any event, the fact is that the elected members represent the various constituencies in Parliament, will pass or reject legislation and will take decisions on what is known as 'own affairs'.[9]

It is evident that the solution to the legitimacy crisis presently confronting some members of the House of Representatives lies, to a great extent, in the hands of White politicians and, by implication, White voters (*Die Burger* 22/4/1980 and 4/1/1985). There are so many alarming parallels between the criticism of the abortive CRC and that of the current new dispensation that only actual, palpable and relevant reforms could possibly 'buy time' to permit the evolutionary achievement of the eventual goal of justice, equality and brotherhood among all the population groups in the country.

The main reason why the solution lies with the Whites is that in the historical course of the institutional political system (particularly since 1948) Whites have arrogated the task of sovereign trusteeship over the Coloured population. Unlike the Whites, the Coloureds have no direct executive powers and therefore have everything to gain. The whole problem of relations with the Coloured population (if a second impasse after the abortive CRC is to be avoided) hinges on the *rate* and *reality* of reform measures. One may expect the new dispensation to place all the population groups in South Africa into a new frame of reference from which new horizons will be observed and studied. This in itself is a necessary step for positive evolutionary socio-political reform initiatives in the South African context. Because this represents virgin territory, any future projections (as was pointed out earlier) are a risky enterprise.

There are indications that the legitimacy crisis is already being relieved. Section 16 of the Immorality Act, the Political Interference Act and other rankling Acts are being scrapped from the statutes and Coloured MPs are able to claim credit for their share in the abolition, irrespective of whether some of these laws had a direct influence on the daily lives of Coloureds. Often symbolic significance is what really matters. But the crisis will only be resolved in subsequent elections, when the present candidates may be expected to account to their constituents for what they have managed to achieve during their term in office.

To the Coloured and White politicians remains the challenge of interpreting the abolition of certain Acts in a manner acceptable to their respective electorates, for what is acceptable to the majority of the Coloured electorate is not necessarily acceptable to the majority of the White electorate. As a result, on occasion Coloured and White politicians will be compelled to adopt different viewpoints to substantiate a particular move in order to ensure their legitimacy among their respective electorates. Thus, when section 16 of the Immorality Act was scrapped, White voters were assured that it would have few, if any, implications for Whites, whilst Coloured politicians told their constituents that it was a 'great stride'.

The new dispensation has irreversibly become part of South African constitutional politics and in future, as now, voters will be able to effect change in the country via the ballot box only. The alternative is extra-parliamentary action — something which has traditionally been rejected by the majority of Whites as well as by all the participating Coloured political parties in the first general election. An interesting consequence of this situation is that an extra-parliamentary pressure group such as the UDF now has constitutional channels at its disposal for expressing its condemnation of the new dispensation. All that is required is that it participates in future elections. The only question is whether leaders who lay claim to legitimacy in their community will be prepared to demonstrate this at a ballot box. If they are not, the UDF and similar organisations run the risk of continuing to be branded extra-parliamentary pressure groups.

LEADERS AMONG THE COLOURED POPULATION

The Coloured population has not found a symbolic leader such as the Indians appear to find in Mahatma Gandhi and there has been enquiry into the reasons for this. HSRC surveys including questions about leadership show consistently that when respondents are asked to select someone from any population group to lead the country, White politicians receive overwhelming support (Rhoodie 1984). This implies that currently Coloured politicians and other charismatic leaders do not enjoy as much support among their 'own people' as White politicians. One could discern in this an element of 'self-hate' (Rajab and Chohan 1980), but the phenomenon should be viewed in a historical context. In any event, it seems that at this stage the Coloured people in general is 'colour blind' when it comes to choosing a political leader. In the aforementioned HSRC surveys, 48% of the respondents chose White leaders and a total of 17% settled for Coloured, Indian or Black leaders for the country.

As mentioned, the principal reason for this phenomenon must be sought in historical determinants, including the removal of Coloureds from the voters' roll in 1956. This meant that Coloured people identified with White politics and their fate was intimately linked with the decisions taken by White politicians. One result could have been that Coloured political leadership and its participation in the politics of the day dwindled systematically because of the futility of participating by constitutional means. At the same time, the media reported mainly 'White' politics (because it was topical news), which meant that this became the political *Umwelt* of the politically-minded Coloured citizen.

Therefore, one may infer that the era from 1956 up to the early eighties, during which the Coloureds wandered in a political wilderness, effectively caused them to become politically colour blind — the exact opposite, in fact, of what the philosophy of apartheid had envisaged, namely that each group would choose leaders from its own ranks.

It also had the opposite effect of what British rule over the Afrikaners achieved. When making such a comparison, one must bear in mind that the Coloured population, unlike the Afrikaners, did not have the motivation of a common culture, religion, language or a country which they had 'civilised'. The Coloured people have never seen themselves as possessing a distinctive cultural identity, with the result that isolation or oppression has not affected them in the same way as, for instance, the Afrikaners or the Zulu.

Thus, the extent to which the new dispensation manages to maintain its present character will depend on whether the elected members of the House of Representatives manage to convince their electorate that their handling of 'own affairs' can at least secure them a better deal in terms of the abolition of discriminatory legislation. Ironically, this conviction requires the reversal of the process which occurred when the Coloured people were removed from 'White politics'.

Among the various parties in the House of Representatives at present, there was initially unanimity on the principle that the new dispensation was no more than a starting point on the road to a unicameral parliamentary system. Whether the new dispensation in its *present* form will satisfy the expectations of the majority of Coloured South Africans as far as timely and actual change are concerned will depend partly on the extent to which it manages to disentangle the Coloured people's political aspirations (at least as far as their own affairs are concerned) from those of Whites, as well as on the extent to which and the rate at which Whites will be prepared to relinquish their sovereignty of decision-making for Coloured (and other) population groups.

Because of the phenomenon of 'colour blindness', however, it seems unlikely that a White State President will have any problems (at least in the short and medium term) with legitimacy among the majority of Coloured voters — something which redounds to the credit of the Coloured public at large.

NOTES

1 In this connection see also Cruse 1947; Van der Ross 1984; Van den Horst (ed.) 1976; Heese 1984; Du Toit 1964; Theron and Du Toit 1977; Cilliers 1964; and Terblanche 1977.

2 See Leistner (1980), who gives a detailed exposition of change and stagnation in the ranks of the ruling Afrikaner government. HJ Kotze (1982) also contributed an article to *Humanitas*, in which he reveals patterns of leadership norms that by and large govern policy-making and the spectrum of inter- and intraparty relations.

3 The same undertone may be observed in Venter (1984), in his cryptic article entitled 'Die einde van die eerste — en die begin van die tweede Republiek van Suid-Afrika'.

4 See also *Coloured Viewpoint*, compiled by Hatting and Bredenkamp, in which Van der Ross' articles in the *Cape Times* during the period 1958-1965 appear.

5 This does not imply that there is currently any discrimination on racial or national grounds in cricket — in fact, the reverse is the case.
6 Stern (1985) cites the same parallel between the theoretical criticism of the German Constitution prior to its implementation and the present situation in South Africa. See also his warning in this regard in his paper, 'The South African constitution — an external appraisal'.
7 See Venter (1984) and Coetzee (1984) and *Rapport* (26/8/84) for detailed analyses of the election.
8 Two HSRC surveys on this issue by Rhoodie showed that 40% and 46% of respondents supported the new dispensation. See the HSRC press releases of 13 March 1983 and 1 September 1985. The 48% was obtained by halving the sum of the percentage vote and the registered voters.
9 For an exposition of identified own affairs, see the Constitution of the Republic of South Africa, Act 110 of 1983, p. 62-66.

BIBLIOGRAPHY

Bekker, SB. *The Plural Society and the Problem of Order.* Cape Town: University of Cape Town, 1974 (unpublished D.Phil. thesis).
Coetzee, HJ. Veranderende Menseverhoudinge in Suide-Afrika. *Die Suide-Afrikaanse Tydskrif vir Sosiologie,* vol. 13, nr. 1, 1982.
Coetzee, JH. Die Kleurling- en Indiërverkiesings. *Oënskou,* jg. 2, nr. 8, 1984.
Cilliers, SP. *The Coloureds of South Africa.* Cape Town: Bannier Publishers (Pty) Ltd, 1963.
Cilliers, SP. *Wes-Kaapland. 'n Sosio-ekonomiese Studie.* Stellenbosch: Kosmo Uitgewery (Edms) Bpk, 1964.
Cruse, HP. *Die Opheffing van die Kleurlingbevolking.* Stellenbosch: CSV-Boekhandel, 1947.
De Kiewiet, CW. *The Anatomy of South Africa Misery.* London: Oxford University Press, 1956.
Du Toit, AS. *Kontak en Assosiasie van Kleurlinge met Bantoe in die Kaapse Skiereiland.* Stellenbosch: Universiteit van Stellenbosch (ongepubliseerde D.Phil.-tesis).
Eisenstadt, SN. *Modernization: Protest and Change.* Englewood Cliffs, New Jersey: Prentice-Hall, 1966.
Etzioni, A and Etzioni, E(eds). *Social Change.* New York: Basic Books, 1974.
Heese, HF. *Groep Sonder Grense.* Bellville: Wes-Kaaplandse Instituut vir Historiese Navorsing, Universiteit van Wes-Kaapland, 1984.
Jessop, RD. *Social Order, Reform and Revolution.* London: The Macmillan Press Ltd, 1972.
Keppel-Jones, A. *When Smuts Goes: History of South Africa from 1952 to 2010.* Pietermaritzburg: Shuter and Shooter, 1949.
Kotze, HJ. Die Politieke Oortuigings van Suid-Afrikaanse Volksraadslede. *Humanitas,* vol. 9, nr. 4, 1982.
Leistner, GMF. Change in Afrikaner National Life. *Africa Insight,* vol. 10, no. 2, 1980.
Marais, JS. *The Cape Coloured People 1652-1937.* London: Longmans, Green and Co Ltd, 1939.
Moore, WE. *Social Change.* Englewood Cliffs, New Jersey: Prentice-Hall, 1967.
Rajab and Chohan. Extrapunitive, Intrapunitive and Impunitive Response of Indian Students to Different Racial Groups in South Africa. *South African Journal of Psychology,* vol. 10, no. 315, 1980.
Roothman, S en Schutte, De W Ondersoek na die aanvaarbaarheid van die Presidentsraad onder 'n groep Kleurlinge in die RSA. Pretoria: RGN. *Verslag,* 1982 (K-16).
Rhoodie, NJ (Ed.) *South African Dialogue.* Johannesburg: McGraw-Hill Book Company, 1973.
Rhoodie, NJ. Voorlopige verslag van 'n opname van Kleurling- en Indiervolwassenes se persepsies van sosiaal-politieke verandering na aanleiding van die Regering se riglyne vir grondwetlike hervorming. Pretoria: RGN. *Persverklaring* 13/3/1983.

377

Rhoodie, NJ. Coloureds and Indians — Perceptions of specific socio-political issues. Pretoria: HSRC. *Press release.* 1/9/1984.

Small, A. *Die Eerste Steen*, Kaapstad: HAUM, 1961.

Editorial. South Africa: Towards a Junta? *Africa Confidential*, vol. 25, no. 20, 1984.

Suid-Afrika (Unie). Kommissie van Ondersoek na die Kaapse Kleurling Bevolking van die Unie. *Verslag.* Pretoria: Staatsdrukker, 1937. (Nr. 39/394 UG Nr. 54).

Suid-Afrika (Republiek). Kommissie van Ondersoek na aangeleenthede rakende die Kleurlingebevolkingsgroep. (Theron Report.) *Verslag.* Pretoria: Staatsdrukker, 1976. (RP 38/1976).

Suid-Afrika (Republiek). *Grondwet van die Republiek van Suid-Afrika, 1983* (Wet 110 van 1983).

Stern, K. *The South African Constitution — An External Appraisal.* Pretoria: Referaat gelewer voor RGN-simposium oor die Grondwet, 1985.

Terblanche, SJ. *Gemeenskapsarmoede, Perspektief op kroniese armoede in die Kleurlinggemeenskap na aanleiding van die Erica Theron-Verslag.* Kaapstad: Tafelberg, 1977.

Theron, E en Swart, MJ (Eds). *Die Kleurling van Suid-Afrika.* Stellenbosch: SABRA Universiteitsuitgewers en -boekhandel, 1964.

Theron, E en Du Toit, JB. *Kortbegrip van die Theron-Verslag.* Kaapstad: Tafelberg,1977.

Van der Horst, ST (Ed.) *The Theron Commission Report: A summary of the findings and recommendations of the Commission of Inquiry into matters relating to the Coloured population group.* Johannesburg: SAIRR, 1976.

Van der Ross, RE. *Myths and Attitudes.* Cape Town: Tafelberg, 1984.

Van Vuuren, DJ, Wiehahn, NE, Lombard, JA and Rhoodie, NJ (Eds). *Change in South Africa.* Pretoria: Butterworths, 1983.

Venter, F. Die einde van die Eerste en die begin van die Tweede Republiek van Suid-Afrika. *Oënskou*, jg. 2 nr. 8, 1984.

15 Indian attitudes towards the new constitutional dispensation and related issues

MP Couper, NJ Rhoodie and CP de Kock

INTRODUCTION

When the new Constitution of South Africa came into effect on 3 September 1984, a new chapter in the history of the country's Indian community began. Whether the new dispensation will bring real benefits to the Indian community in terms of political power, or whether it will remain apartheid under a different guise, is yet to be seen. Indian responses to the new Constitution have ranged from enthusiastic support, through cautious optimism and cynical distrust, to outright rejection.

In the light of the chequered political history of the Indians in South Africa, such a range of reactions is understandable. Indians first came to South Africa in the 1860s to work as indentured labourers on the sugar and cotton plantations in Natal. After working for three years, such labourers were given the option of repatriation or becoming free men with full citizenship rights. The majority opted for the latter. Increased Indian immigration and negative White reactions to the Indian presence in the Transvaal and Natal eventually resulted in the disenfranchisement of Indians in Natal in 1896.

Following this, concerted efforts were made to repatriate large numbers of Indians. This period was also marked by an increase in discriminatory legislation which culminated in the statutory adoption of apartheid as a national policy in 1948 when the National Party came into power. In 1961 the Government finally recognised the failure of the repatriation policies and agreed to accept Indians as a permanent part of the population. The period after 1961 was characterised by various attempts to solve the question of Indian representation, such as the creation of the purely advisory National Indian Council (later replaced by the South African Indian Council (SAIC)) in 1964, as well as increasing opposition to the Government's apartheid policies. Indians have a history of protest against National Party Government policy, beginning with non-violent protest in

379

the Ghandian tradition, but later becoming increasingly militant in their opposition to the Government.

Eventually, in 1983 the new Constitution came into effect and South African Indians were offered the opportunity not only of obtaining the right of self-determination within the boundaries of their own community, but also of making decisions together with Whites and Coloureds in a single parliament (albeit with separate chambers) on matters of national importance. Being an extremely vulnerable minority group (Indians formed only 3,3% of the total population of South Africa in 1982), in view of their doubly inferior position of power (relative to both White national hegemony and Zulu regional pre-eminence in Natal, where more than 90% of South Africa's Indians are concentrated), the Indian community is faced with the choice of entering into a political coalition with Whites and Coloureds, or refusing to participate in any system which excludes Blacks from central government.

For all practical purposes the Indians have, for almost the full period of their residence in South Africa, been exposed to the same basic segregation practices as the Coloureds and the Blacks. With the advent of statutory apartheid in 1948 no special dispensation was made to the Indians in this regard: statutory measures such as the Population Registration Act, the Mixed Marriages Act, the Reservation of Separate Amenities Act and the Group Areas Act were aimed at Non-Whites, whether they were Indian, Coloured or Black. Only with regard to the so-called pass laws, which affect Blacks only, was any real distinction made between the three Non-White groups. The inclusion of Indians and Coloureds in the new dispensation could possibly alter this traditional distinction between White and Non-White (and maybe even result in a distinction between Black and Non-Black). Whatever the effect of the new dispensation, it will certainly result in changes to the traditional alignments among the four race groups in South Africa.

In view of the fact that socio-political change in South Africa over the past five years has, in historical terms, been more far-reaching than that over the previous 70 years, it is self-evident that this change is likely to stimulate a rapidly rising spiral of expectations within the politically disadvantaged Non-White communities, especially with regard to socio-political reform. Equally unavoidable is the fact that the rising tide of expectations will make the members of these communities more aware of their role and place in the socio-political framework of this country. The average Indian is certainly no exception to this phenomenon of rising expectations and socio-political sensitisation. Indians' perceptions of socio-political change are thus also in the process of becoming more sharply focused, more clearly delineated and cognitively more specific.

380

Since July 1982 the Division for Group Interaction of the HSRC's Institute for Sociological and Demographic Research has undertaken a series of nation-wide sample surveys among urban Indians aimed at ascertaining trends in Indian attitudes towards socio-political change. The following analysis is based mainly on the most recent of these surveys, namely a national survey among urban Indians undertaken in March 1984 under the direction of the authors. This analysis focuses on certain important contemporary problems which are closely linked to current socio-political changes in general and the Government's constitutional reforms in particular. This survey formed part of the Division for Group Interaction's annual monitor surveys on various aspects of intergroup relations among all population groups in South Africa.

RESEARCH DESIGN

Sample

A national sample of 1 500 adult (18 years and older) urban Indians was selected. A probability sampling technique was applied. The various census enumeration districts, addresses within each district and the respondents at these addresses were randomly selected.

Survey procedure

Indian fieldworkers of the HSRC's Opinion Survey Centre visited the sampled addresses and interviewed the respondent selected at each address according to a structured interview schedule (questionnaire). During the survey the addresses visited by fieldworkers were again visited by supervisors to check whether the questionnaires had been completed according to instructions and whether all the relevant requirements of a sample survey had been met. Of the 1 500 respondents visited, 1 406 completed the questionnaire. This represents a response rate of 93,7%, which for this type of survey can be regarded as particularly favourable.

Representativeness of the sample

Some of the main socio-demographic characteristics of the sample are given in table 15.1. The survey was constituted according to recognised statistical procedures in order to be broadly representative of the target population (adult urban Indians). The responses were generally satisfactory and did not vary significantly in terms of the geographical distribution of the sample. It can thus be assumed that the sample reflects the collective

381

opinion of the adult urban Indian population of South Africa on various socio-political issues. Furthermore, in view of the fact that urban Indians represent 90% of the South African Indian population, these findings can also, with caution be generalised to the entire adult Indian population of this country.

Table 15.1 Socio-demographic characteristics of the sample

Characteristic	%
Sex	
Male	47,0
Female	53,0
Age	
18-24	20,4
25-34	31,3
35-49	34,5
50-64	12,8
65+	1,0
Education	
Std 3 or less	10,1
Std 4 or 5	13,4
Std 6 or 7	26,7
Std 8 or 9	24,9
Matric	15,9
Matric plus further education	9,1
Marital status	
Married	74,8
Unmarried	18,1
Divorced/separated	2,1
Widow/widower	5,0

The questionnaire

The questionnaire was fully structured. It was discussed with Indian personnel of the HSRC's regional office in Durban during training sessions and the wording of certain questions was altered where necessary. At no stage of the fieldwork did the questionnaire present any problems.

DISCUSSION OF THE FINDINGS

General satisfaction and future expectations

In response to a general question on the way things are going in South Africa today, 48,3% of the respondents indicated that they were either satisfied or very satisfied, 24,9% of the respondents were dissatisfied or very dissatisfied and the remaining 26,8% were either neutral (neither satisfied nor dissatisfied) or uncertain. When asked about the present economic situation, 39,9% expressed satisfaction, 34,6% were dissatisfied and the remaining 25,5% were either neutral or uncertain. With regard to the present *political* situation, the corresponding percentages were 35,8% satisfied, 27,5% dissatisfied, and 36,7% neutral or uncertain.

It can thus be seen that although the number of satisfied respondents is roughly the same with regard to the economic and political situations, there are more Indians dissatisfied with the current economic situation than with the political situation. It must be remembered that although South Africa is currently experiencing an economic recession, there is a climate of political expectation regarding the new Constitution. The large number of respondents (more than a third of the sample) who were uncertain or neutral concerning the political situation is also significant.

A similar tendency is observed when the responses regarding the future are compared. Forty-two per cent of the respondents felt that the *economic* situation will improve over the next few years, whereas 22,3% felt that it would deteriorate. With regard to *political* change over the next few years, 47% felt that the situation in South Africa would improve, whilst 10,9% felt that it would worsen.

To summarise, there appears to be less pessimism among Indians regarding the political future than the economic future of South Africa. However, Indians are also more uncertain about the political future than the economic future of the country. It must be remembered that the survey was conducted roughly midway between the White referendum on the new Constitution in November 1983 and the election of Indian representatives to the new tricameral parliament in August 1984. This period was characterised by much political manoeuvring in preparation for the elections by both those intending to participate and those opposed to such elections. In addition, the implications and possible workings of the new Constitution were still unclear to many South Africans of all groups. In such an atmosphere it could be expected that many respondents would react cautiously with regard to questions about the political future of this country.

However, when one compares these results with those from similar questions in a survey conducted in 1981 by Dostal, Vergrani and Gagiano (n.d.: 59-61), one finds that Indians were generally more satisfied with both the economic and political situation in 1984 than in 1981. Of the respondents in the 1981 survey, 26,1% claimed to be satisfied or highly satisfied with the current *economic* situation, compared to 39,9% of the respondents to the 1984 survey. No less than 58,7% were dissatisfied or highly dissatisfied with the economic situation in 1981 (34,6% in 1984), whilst 15,2% did not know (25,5% in 1984). Those satisfied with the *political* situation in this country constituted 13,5% of the sample in 1981 (35,8% in 1984), whilst 69% expressed dissatisfaction (27,5% in 1984) and 17,5% did not know (36,7% in 1984). In a similar vein, in 1984 almost 20% more people felt that the political situation would improve over the next few years. Thus, although in 1984 there was much more uncertainty among Indians with regard to their political situation because of the major political changes taking place, there was also significantly more optimism with regard to the political future of this country.

Major problems facing South Africa

By means of a series of open questions, respondents were asked to name the three most important problems facing South Africa today in order of importance. The largest group of respondents (30,3%) named various apartheid practices as the most pressing problem facing this country. General economic problems were named by 26,5% of the sample, housing was mentioned by 11,6%, unemployment by 10,6%, crime by 2,7% and educational problems by 2,5%. The remaining 15,9% either named various other problems or could not respond to the question. When the three most important problems are combined, 50,6% of the sample mentioned apartheid at least once and 48,4% general economic problems. More than a third of the sample (37,6%) mentioned housing as one of the three most important problems.

Later in the questionnaire, respondents were asked to select from a list the one thing they regarded as the greatest threat to peace and prosperity in South Africa. The responses to this question are given in table 15.2.

Table 15.2 Greatest threat to peace and prosperity in South Africa

Poverty and unemployment	31,7%
The Government's race policies	19,6%
Black nationalism	18,0%
Communism	17,8%
Conservative Whites who refuse power-sharing	7,0%
Crime	6,0%
Total	100,1%

Although South Africa is experiencing an economic recession of major proportions at present, it is the distribution of wealth among various groups rather than the scarcity of resources in general that seems to be of primary concern. In response to a series of questions on Government expenditure, the majority of Indians felt that too little was spent on housing (79,9%), pensions (79,8%), education (66,7%) and health services (59%) for their own group. Less than 4% said that the Government spends too much on any of these services. The remaining respondents either felt that the right

384

amount was spent in each case, or did not know. In contrast to this, only 15,5% felt that too little was spent on defence (59,4% felt that too much was spent) and 19% felt that too little was spent on the promotion of South Africa's image abroad (30,8% felt that too much was spent).

Political leadership

With regard to the question of political leadership in South Africa, a remarkable pattern of responses emerges. When asked (by means of an open question) to choose one person from any population group to lead South Africa politically in these times, the respondents answered as follows:

Table 15.3 Choice of political leader for South Africa

Mr PW Botha	41,5%
Dr F Van Zyl Slabbert	5,7%
Mr RF (Pik) Botha	5,0%
Dr JN Reddy	0,8%
Mr A Rajbansi	0,4%
Whites	7,0%
Other	5,7%
Do not know/none	33,9%
Total	100,0%

It is interesting to note that in a survey conducted among Indians in November 1982 (Rhoodie, De Kock), Mr PW Botha received almost the same amount of support (40%) as in March 1984. In the November 1982 survey a further 3% named White Government leaders, 11% named other White leaders and 10% named Indian leaders. The remaining 36% either named various other persons, or were undecided.

Further evidence of support for Mr PW Botha can be seen in the responses to a question in which the respondents were asked to rate the performance of the Prime Minister over the past year. The results were as follows: 15,4% responded that he had fared extremely well, 34,5% that he had fared well and 32,6% that he had fared averagely. Only 3,6% felt that he had fared poorly and 3,3% that he had fared very poorly. The remaining 10,8% of the sample were uncertain about the matter. Thus just less than half of the sample responded favourably with regard to PW Botha's performance as Prime Minister whilst only 6,9% responded unfavourably.

A combination of the responses to these two questions (choice of leader and rating of the Prime Minister's performance) shows that 65,6% of those who named PW Botha as their choice of leader for South Africa felt that he had fared either well or extremely well in response to the latter question. A further 27,6% of this group said he had fared averagely. This supports the notion expressed below that PW Botha's support among Indians is directly linked to his performance as head of government. A further analysis of leadership choice by means of a Multiple Classification Analysis (for a full description of this technique see Andrews et al, 1973) reveals that support for PW Botha is significantly associated with general satisfaction, trust in the Government and support for the new Constitution.

There are a number of possible explanations for the high degree of support the then Prime Minister enjoyed at the time of the survey. Firstly, Mr Botha is the de facto leader of the RSA and as incumbent of such a position holds a number of advantages over other possible candidates for such a leadership position. One of these is the amount of media exposure he enjoys as head of government. This is confirmed when one looks at the support enjoyed by other White leaders such as Mr Pik Botha and Dr F Van Zyl Slabbert. In addition, as Prime Minister and now President, Mr Botha is seen making decisions which affect the lives of all South Africans. In other words, he has far more opportunity to demonstrate his leadership abilities. Another reason for Mr Botha's popularity is the fact that in the minds of many people he is associated with the current reform initiatives. Although such initiatives do not have the unqualified support of the Indian community, he is at least being given due credit for the steps he has taken thus far.

Many of the above reasons may also account for the lack of support shown for leaders from within the Indian community. Even when the respondents were asked to restrict their choice of leader to Indians only, the two most popular persons, Mr A Rajbansi and Dr JN Reddy, received only 14,4% and 11,3% of the support respectively and 63,1% of the respondents still could or would not name their choice of leader. The remaining responses (11,2%) were distributed among a number of other leaders. Thus it is evident that at the time of the survey no clear political leader had emerged from the ranks of the Indian community.

Those Indian leaders named have either never held political office, or have held office in a body with little real power (such as the SAIC). Not only has this severely restricted media coverage of such personalities; it has also given them no real opportunity to demonstrate their leadership abilities. It is felt that as the Indian leaders become more active in central government, whether in the House of Delegates or in the Cabinet itself, and as they begin to achieve tangible gains for their communities, the amount of support for these leaders will increase considerably, thus effectively reducing the support currently enjoyed by various White politicians. Of course, the opposite is also true. If the new tricameral parliament does not result in any significant power gains for Indians, the task of those opposing the Government's current reforms will be made that much easier.

Attitudes towards the new Constitution

In response to a question on the extent to which the new Constitution was accepted or rejected, the following responses were elicited: 16,7% accepted the new Constitution completely, 40,4% accepted only certain parts of it, 14,8% rejected it completely and 28,1% were uncertain, or did not know. When one excludes the large number of respondents who were either uncertain or had mixed feelings about the new Constitution, approximately the same proportion of respondents supported the new Constitution as rejected it.

In response to similar questions in three previous surveys on the constitutional proposals by the HSRC in November 1979 (Lötter and Schutte, 1980), November 1982 (Rhoodie and De Kock, 1982) and March 1983 (Rhoodie, 1983), the following patterns of support emerged:

Table 15.4 Support for constitutional proposals: Previous surveys

	November 1979 (N = 998)	November 1982 (N = 1 247)	March 1983 (N = 1 420)
Support	26,7%	43,8%	43,5%
Reject	38,8%	14,4%	23,8%
Uncertain	34,6%	41,8%	32,7%
Total	100,1%	100,0%	100,0%

Unfortunately, exact comparison is not possible as the wording of the question in the present survey differs from that in the previous three surveys. The respondents who accept only certain parts of the new Constitution (40%) cannot be regarded as completely supportive of the Constitution, neither can they be regarded as opposed to the new system of government. What is possible is that the large number of supporters in the November 1982 and March 1983 surveys in particular may include a number of people who are not entirely convinced of the merit of the new system, but are at least prepared to give it a chance.

Another indicator of tacit support can be seen in the responses to a question on whether relations between Whites, Coloureds and Indians would improve as a result of the new Constitution: 45,3% of the respondents felt that relations would improve, 12,1% felt that they would deteriorate and the remaining respondents either felt that such relations would remain unchanged (18,2%) or were uncertain about the matter (24,4%).

During the elections for the House of Delegates on 28 August 1984, 20,3% of the registered voters and an estimated 15,5% of eligible voters (Magyar and Ranchod 1985:32) in the Indian community voted. Numerous explanations, ranging from massive intimidation to outright rejection of the new system, have been given for the low poll. Based on the above results and on an analysis of the Coloured elections for the House of Representatives (in which there was a percentage poll of 30,9%) by the authors (Rhoodie, De Kock and Couper, 1985), it appears that about half of the Indian community in South Africa was apathetic or neutral towards the new Constitution at the time of the survey, with the remainder being almost equally split between those who support the new system and those who reject it.

According to Magyar and Ranchod (1985:32), the anti-constitutionalists may be grouped into three categories:

1. The Natal Indian Congress (NIC) and the Transvaal Indian Congress (TIC) offered the most visible organised opposition to the tricameral parliamentary election. Their efforts at persuading the Indian community to boycott the election matched in intensity the efforts of any party vying for parliamentary seats.
2. An undetermined portion of the 80 per cent of non-voters demonstrated the usual democratic characteristic of voter apathy. The lack of participatory history, uncertainty, social pressure, confusion, etc may have been contributing causes.
3. The moderate anti-constitutionalists likewise comprised an undetermined block. Members of this group followed closely the unfolding pro- and anti-constitution debate, but rejected the opportunity to vote. Their reasons were not shaped by the campaign of the NIC or the TIC, nor were there many concerted organisational efforts by the moderates to persuade people to boycott the election. For the most part, members of this group made individual assessments and opted for the decision to abstain from voting.

It must also be noted that support for or opposition to the new Constitution is not necessarily a good predictor of participation in the elections. For instance, those opposed to the new Constitution were faced with two choices: to advocate a total boycott of the system or to participate in the new parliament with a view to bringing about change from within.

Not only was the percentage poll for the Indians much lower than expected by proponents of the new system, it was also significantly lower than that for the Coloured elections (20,3% as opposed to 30,9%). There are a number of possible reasons for this, three of these being: Firstly, the Coloured elections preceded the Indian elections by six days. The poor turnout for the former might have caused a number of Indians to think twice about participation. A second factor could have been the dominant presence of Zulus in Natal. Indians and Zulus have a history of uneasy co-existence in the province and Zulu threats against Indian participation (mainly from Inkatha) may have had a profound effect on electoral participation. In response to a question posed in the November 1982 survey, 59,7% of the Indian respondents felt that the Zulus would one day take revenge on the Indian community if they were to agree to the Government's constitutional proposals, while 11,3% of the sample disagreed with this view and 29% were uncertain. The third possible factor affecting the percentage poll in the Indian elections was the arrest of 18 prominent members (including a number of Indians) of organisations opposed to the new system of government (see also Lemon 1984:100-101). These factors should be assessed against the background of two trends summarised by Magyar and Ranchod (1985) as follows:

1. The political parties failed to align along perceptible ideological lines.
2. The effort of the Congresses (Natal Indian Congress and Transvaal Indian Congress) soon made the contest one between those who accepted and those who rejected the Constitution.

However, despite the lower percentage poll for Indians, it cannot be said that support for the new Constitution in the Indian community is substantially lower than in the Coloured community.

The success or failure of the new system will, in large measure, depend on the extent to which the interest and support of those indifferent or undecided members of the Indian community can be mobilised. In the same way that support for Indian leaders can be expected to increase with real gains achieved through participation in the new parliament, so too should support for the new system increase. The opposite is also true. For many Indians the choice may be one between possible present socio-economic advantages resulting from participation in central government and possible future political disadvantages resulting from their alienating themselves from the struggle for Black freedom. Gann and Duignan (1981:37) feel that the former course of action will be chosen:

> ... given the numerical weakness of the Indian community, existing tensions between Indians and Zulu, and the Indians' fear of losing their stake in the event of an African take-over, the Indians are most likely, in the long run, to side with the Whites.

However, one cannot ignore the vital historical role Indians have played in Non-White liberation movements and their continued alignment with Black organisations in opposition to the Government.

CONSTITUTIONAL REFORM AND INDIAN-BLACK RELATIONS

Contrary to the belief that granting political rights to Coloureds and Indians would buy some time for the Government with regard to the political future of Blacks, the new Constitution has had the effect of accelerating Black demands for political rights at the highest level. The floodtide of rising Black expectations and demands for inclusion in decision-making processes at all levels means that the Indians may again become a marginal group in terms of power politics in South Africa. Blacks must, of necessity, command the Government's full attention at this stage, but the process of winning over the support of the Indians cannot be ignored. Although there is a reservoir of potential supporters of the new system, these people could just as easily be regarded as potential opposition. The process of co-optation of the Indian community is thus far from over.

Lemon (1984:105) notes that

> . . . the Government's credibility at home and abroad would be critically damaged by the withdrawal of Coloureds and Indians from parliament. They must therefore be given at least enough evidence of achievement to present to their constituents in justification of their continued participation. For the Government this will not be easy.

Lemon goes on to point out that the Government has two basic strategic options available for winning over Indian and Coloured support for the new Constitution: legislative reforms and economic advancements. Given the present economic conditions in South Africa and the focus of attention on the socio-economic demands of Blacks, the possibilities within the latter option are extremely limited and could possibly be carried out only at the expense of Whites. It appears that the Government has opted for the former strategy for the present. The last few months have seen announcements regarding the repeal of the Mixed Marriages Act and Section 16 (the race clause) of the Immorality Act, the relaxation of certain influx control regulations, the repeal of the Political Interference Act and the relaxation of the Group Areas Act to allow Non-White businesses to be re-established in the central business districts of certain metropolitan areas.

The question of the exclusion of Blacks from the new parliament has been a major point of contention during the months leading up to the first elections for the House of Delegates. With regard to the inclusion of Blacks in central government, 30,1% of the respondents felt that Blacks should not participate in the same government as the Whites, Coloureds and Indians, 56,5% disagreed with this statement and 13,5% were uncertain. Virtually the same percentage (30%) said that they were in favour of the homelands policy for Blacks. Only 33,8% claimed to oppose the homelands policy, while the remaining 36,2% were either neutral or uncertain about the issue. In the November 1982 survey, 63,6% of the sample disagreed with the following statement: 'A Black majority government in South Africa will be more advantageous to me than the current White government.' Only 21,2% of the respondents agreed with this statement.

Indians are all too aware that they will remain a captive minority regardless of whether South Africa is ruled by Whites or Blacks. Especially in Natal, where the Indians are subject to a double minority status *vis-à-vis* the Whites and the Zulus, they will always have to consider their political options with great circumspection. Especially now that the Political Interference Act has been repealed, Indians will be faced with a difficult choice: whether to align themselves politically with the White Progressive Federal Party; to throw their weight in with the Blacks; or, as a separate minority, to keep their options open with a view to possible strategic alliances with either the Whites or the Blacks, or even concurrently with both. In this way the Indians can play an important catalytic function in South African politics and by means of strategic alignments can play a significant role in decision making at all levels of government. In the meantime, a significant proportion of the Indian power elite will be prepared to operate within the current constitutional dispensation in a pragmatic manner — as long as it offers them certain competitive advantages in the opportunity system.

The fact that Indians regard the threat of Black domination in a serious light is evidenced in the findings of the survey in November 1982, which revealed that they were less willing than Coloureds to grant residence rights to Blacks in their residential areas. Respondents were asked whether they agreed or disagreed with the following statement: 'Blacks should be able to live in our residential areas.' The responses were as follows:

Response	Indians	Coloureds
Agree	28,9%	35,5%
Disagree	57,9%	46,9%
Uncertain	13,2%	17,6%
Total	100,0%	100,0%

A clear majority of both the Coloured and Indian samples were opposed to Blacks being allowed to live in their residential areas, with the Indian sample clearly less prepared to grant such rights to Blacks in Indian residential areas. Fear of Black domination thus appears to be more widespread and more substantial in the Indian community than in the Coloured community. A comparable tolerance differential occurs with

391

respect to the desegregation of public facilities and amenities. The November 1982 survey nevertheless showed that the majority of Indian and Coloured respondents felt that Black influx control should be more strictly applied. Almost half of the Indian (47%) and Coloured (49,5%) samples supported this view, whilst 30,8% and 31,7% respectively were not in favour of stricter control.

The above-mentioned findings confirm the dilemma facing the Indian community with regard to the dismantling of apartheid measures. It cannot be denied that apartheid measures such as the Group Areas Act and the Reservation of Separate Amenities Act are stumbling-blocks for the vast majority of Indians and that they have been fighting for the repeal of these Acts for a long time. There is little doubt among Indians that the repeal of statutory apartheid measures will lead to great improvements in their living circumstances. On the other hand, they realise that the dismantling of apartheid will also raise the socio-economic and spatial mobility of Blacks. The threat which an increased Black mobility could pose to their critical survival interests must be self-evident to many Indians. Some will even argue that Blacks will be the most advantaged by the general elimination of apartheid, possibly at the cost not only of White interests, but also of Indian interests. The dilemma facing Indians as seen in the findings of the November 1982 survey discussed earlier must thus also be interpreted in the context of the Indian community's ambivalence concerning certain statutory apartheid measures. Further evidence of this is the not insubstantial number of Indians who expressed support for various apartheid measures in the March 1984 survey: 26,9% for the Mixed Marriages Act, 27,8% for separate education and 30% for the homelands policy.

However, the Group Areas Act and separate amenities are seen by Indians as integral components of the apartheid system as a whole. In spite of the price which will have to be paid in terms of a possible drastic increase in Black competition for scarce resources, it is virtually a foregone conclusion that the vast majority of Indians will not allow their opposition to these two apartheid structures to be bought off merely because the increasing socio-economic mobility (and thus competitive power) of Blacks (which would be a function of the elimination of these two apartheid structures) would probably generate, to a greater or lesser degree, social conflict between Blacks, Coloureds and Indians.

CONCLUDING REMARKS

The accommodation of Indians and Coloureds in the new constitutional dispensation is, without doubt, seriously eroding the traditional role of race and colour as the final criterion for the granting of political rights. Van der Merwe (*The Star*, 16 February 1985) writes in this regard:

> The incorporation of Coloured people and Indians into the central Parliament and the prospects of some kind of accommodation of Africans in the Government are evidence that race ceases to be the major criterion for discrimination and division in our society. New alliances across racial lines and new divisions within racial groups suggest that there are other issues than race that constitute sources of division among some and grounds for common cause among others.

The next few years will probably be characterised by a degree of political manoeuvering and the formation and re-formation of alliances based on interest group divisions rather than on purely racial differentials.

Although opposition to the new parliament is not as widespread among Indians as opponents of the new system would have one believe, it would be naïve to expect a flood of enthusiastic support for the current constitutional reforms. In the past Indians have experienced too much alienation and rejection regarding the question of political representation and power-sharing to greet the new dispensation with anything but a noncommittal and cautious attitude. Magyar and Ranchod (1985:34) conclude:

> Eyes will also be focused on the long-range future. While the present dispensation was the unilateral offer by an increasingly embattled power-wielding minority, the Indians and Coloureds in the present parliament may be able to engineer their own prominence as initiators for the next constitutional system.

It is thus impossible at this stage to attempt an accurate prediction of future Indian attitudes towards the new system of government and participation in future elections. There are just too many factors (such as the Indian MP's performance in the new parliament, Black demands for political rights, further major socio-political reform and the possibility of a conservative White backlash) that could alter the whole picture in the space of a few months. The success or failure of the new parliamentary system still hangs in the balance and only time will tell which way the pendulum will swing with regard to Indian involvement in the new constitutional dispensation.

BIBLIOGRAPHY

Andrews, FM et al. *Multiple classification analysis*. 2nd ed. Ann Arbor: Institute for Social Research, University of Michigan, 1973.
Bhana, Surenda and Pachai, Brigdal (eds). *A documentary history of Indian South Africans*. Cape Town: David Philip, 1984.

Dostal, E, Vergnani, T and Gagiano, JIK. *A survey of socio-political attitudes among White, Coloured and Asian South Africans.* Stellenbosch: Institute for Futures Research, University of Stellenbosch, n.d.

Gann, LH and Duignan, Peter. *Why South Africa will survive.* Cape Town: Tafelberg, 1981.

Lemon, Anthony. The Indian and Coloured elections: Co-optation rejected? *South African International,* vol. 15, no. 2, October 1984, pp. 84-107.

Lötter, JM and Schutte, CD. *Enkele politieke orientasies van Indiër-Suid- Afrikaners.* Pretoria: Raad vir Geesteswetenskaplike Navorsing, 1980 (navorsingbevinding S-N-191).

Magyar, KP and Ranchod, B. South Africa's new constitution: The Indian perspective. *Africa Insight,* vol. 15, no. 1, 1985, pp. 31-34.

Pachai, Brigdal. *The international aspects of the South African Indian question 1860-1971.* Cape Town: Struik, 1971.

Pachai, Brigdal (Ed.). *South Africa's Indians: The evolution of a minority.* Washington: University Press of America, 1979.

Rhoodie, NJ. *Provisional report on a survey of the perceptions of adult Coloureds and Indians of sociopolitical change on the basis of the Government's proposals for constitutional reform.* Pretoria: Human Sciences Research Council, 1983 (unpublished research finding).

Rhoodie, NJ and De Kock, CP. *Provisional report on a survey of the perceptions of adult Coloureds and Indians of socio-political change on the basis of the Government's proposals for constitutions reform.* Pretoria: Human Sciences Research Council, 1982 (unpublished research finding).

Rhoodie, NJ, De Kock, CP and Couper, MP. *Findings of sample surveys among Coloureds and Indians.* Pretoria: Human Sciences Research Council, 1984 (unpublished research finding).

Rhoodie, NJ, De Kock, CP and Couper, MP. *Kleurlinge se persepsies van die eerste verkiesing van die Huis van Verteenwoordigers: Verslag van 'n steekproefopname onder stedelike Kleurlinge woonagtig in die Kaapprovinsie.* Pretoria: Raad vir Geesteswetenskaplike Navorsing, 1985 (ongepubliseerde navorsingsbevinding).

South Africa (Republic). Central Statistical Services. *Population census 1980: Sample tabulation — geographical distribution of the population.* Pretoria: Government Printer, 1982 (report no. 02-80-01).

16 The role of Blacks in politics and change in South Africa

L Schlemmer

INTRODUCTION

The most obvious feature of South African society at present is the absence of opportunities for Black people to participate formally in the central decision making processes of society. Indeed, this issue lies at the heart of the international controversy surrounding South Africa. It is also the issue which dominates the internal political debate in South Africa. For example, the clearest differentiation between the policies of the various parties in Parliament concerns the nature of future franchise rights for Black people.

Political participation is not merely a matter of formal franchise rights, however, and a range of informal pressures and forms of political action must also be taken into account in addressing the topic of this chapter. In fact, in some ways the informal responses of Blacks in the South African political system are the most significant dimension of social action in South Africa at present.

Blacks have a franchise at the third tier of government in local communities and in the national states or 'homelands', which are either formally independent of South Africa (the so-called TBVC states) or not independent, but almost fully autonomous political regions situated outside the core areas of industrial, commercial and agricultural activity.

Because interaction between Black local authorities, 'homelands' and the central government takes place on terms which are defined by the relevant cabinet ministers and senior bureaucrats in the central government, it cannot be said that the political participation of Blacks in these institutions constitutes an exercise of effective power in the South African Government as such. This political participation, in a formal sense, is highly marginal to the affairs of state.

At present the major influences of Blacks on the South African polity have to be exercised through extra-parliamentary organisations, trade unions, popular demonstrations, public dissidence, insurgency and appeals to the international community. The informal role of 'homeland'-based political movements is also of some significance. Of all the types of activity of an informal kind, the most dramatic has been the public dissidence and demonstrations which have occurred from time to time. It is necessary, therefore, to commence this analysis with a brief historical overview of open protest among Blacks in South Africa.

CYCLES OF ACTIVE POLITICAL PROTEST

At the time of writing South Africa is experiencing what is perhaps the most serious and sustained internal dissent and political unrest in its entire history. Since September 1984 violent clashes between Black protesters, police and rival groups in the townships have left more than 700 people dead.

Most observers in South Africa and abroad have broad notions that inequality between Black and White and poor conditions in Black communities make our society vulnerable to instability. In addition, there have always been predictions of revolution or crippling instability by a variety of political observers. These loose predictions have reached a crescendo in the past few months.

Yet, assessed by world standards over time, South Africa has not been a particularly unstable country. Most of the assessments of business risk made by international organisations have placed South Africa among the 20 or so most risk-free countries in the world. Obviously this is not the case at the moment, but it has been the general trend in the modern history of the country.

The past few decades have been characterised by the following broad patterns (see Walshe 1971 and Gerhardt 1978): After the Second World War up until the early fifties South Africa was a very well-controlled system, the Blacks being very quiescent although in a far worse material position relative to Whites than they are today. In the late forties, however, radical pressures had emerged in the then legal ANC. Black leadership up until then had adopted a basically moderate, Christian stance of moral protest. Boycott resolutions by the youth wing of the ANC led to the adoption of a 'programme of action' in 1949, followed in 1951/52 by the well-known 'defiance campaign' of the fifties committed to the mobilisation of Blacks through mass action in the form of boycotts, demonstrations and general non-collaboration. An alliance between the ANC, the South African Indian Congress, the South African Coloured People's Organisation and the very small White SA Congress of Democrats, many of whose members were former members of the Communist Party, resulted in the political thinking of Black leaders acquiring a much more radical ideological flavour. Generally, however, no large-scale open conflict occurred.

A dramatic turn of events occurred in 1958 when the more youthful Africanists in the ANC broke away to form the Pan African Congress (PAC), producing a very militant and confrontationist leadership among Blacks for the first time. These developments culminated in what was South Africa's first taste of overt and violent political action from Blacks. In the late fifities there were stonings of buses and beerhalls and limited marches or demonstrations in the major cities, but the calls for stay-at-home strikes were generally only partly successful, except in one or two townships. Where developments appeared dangerous, the authorites quelled the action with determined counteraction and arrests. Still the resistance mounted and finally reached a peak in March and April 1960, the time of the Sharpeville killings.

The PAC had prepared for massive nation-wide action, but officially strictly along the lines of passive resistance. It even informed the police of its plans in some cases. However, the participation of less organised youthful elements made the situation unpredictable. While most of the Witwatersrand was quiet, there were massive encounters with the police in Cape Town, the Southern Witwatersrand (where the Sharpeville incident occurred) and in Durban. Elsewhere thousands burned their passes, even in Bloemfontein. A march of 15 000 people to the centre of Cape Town, where political stay-away strikes were also well supported, was perhaps most threatening to Whites.

After a short period of uncertainty the authorities reacted decisively. An emergency was declared and somewhere between 11 000 and 18 000 people were arrested in the period which followed — a figure amounting to over 25% of the 70 000 formal membership of the PAC and ANC combined, although by no means all of the arrests were on political grounds.

New legislation was passed to control dissidence and the ANC and the PAC were banned. Subsequent calls by the underground ANC for stay-at-home strikes were largely ignored and Blacks started queuing to replace their burned passes. As Gail Gerhardt observed, 'The myth that the African masses were a volcano on the verge of an explosion had itself been exploded' (1978: 251). Two major lessons were learned: Firstly, the majority of Black people were not prepared to risk their security and meagre privileges in any sustained active political engagement with the authorities and secondly, the South African State was easily able to control and repress the most determined public dissidence from the radical wings of Black society. Following the emergency of 1961 there were some 200 incidents of underground action and insurgency up to the end of 1964, but the police steadily tracked down and destroyed the underground formations responsible (Horrell 1971).

A period of quiet followed during the rest of the sixties and early seventies. From 1968 onwards, however, a new political consciousness had begun to take form — Black consciousness. Originating in the United States (although with Africanist roots), the movement first gained momentum among Black theology students and a Black student group which broke away from the predominantly White student organisation, NUSAS. A movement dedicated to all Black (i.e. none-White) solidarity, by the mid-seventies it had produced a fair number of strongly ideological organisations, including the South African Students Organisation (SASO) and the Black Peoples Convention (BPC). The political culture of Black solidarity and the spirit of independence from and, in part, hostility towards Whites held sway over Black students and high school leadership groups. From 1972 onwards there were numerous demonstrations and boycotts on Black campuses throughout the country.

In 1976 Black and Coloured educational facilities were becoming increasingly over-stressed as a result of the rapid increase in pupil numbers. The independence of Transkei created insecurity with regard to citizenship status among the predominantly Xhosa-speaking youth leadership on the Witwatersrand. Real growth rates in the economy of 2,6% in 1975 (compared with 8,2% in 1974) produced a spurt in Black youth unemployment. The authorities' insistence on the use of Afrikaans as a medium of instruction in Black schools was perceived by pupils as a political imposition and made them fear even greater difficulties in passing examinations than they already had. Against the background of the youth political solidarity produced by the Black consciousness movement, this final frustration resulted in the June 1976 youth uprisings on the Witwatersrand, which spread to over 160 communities in other parts of the Transvaal, to Coloured and Indian pupils, to university students and even to the Inkatha-dominated Natal township of KwaMashu, although the scope was very limited there. (See Cillie Commission 1980 and Kane-Berman 1978.)

On occasion these youth uprisings led to marches by tens of thousands on Johannesburg and into the centre of Cape Town, where large-scale confrontations with the police occurred. Several calls for sympathy stay-away strikes by adult workers were made. The first was partly successful because of picketing by the demonstrators, the second and particularly the third gained the co-operation of adult workers in Johannesburg and were 50 to 70% successful, but later calls for strikes were unsuccessful because of a tougher attitude to absenteeism among employers. The disturbances claimed the lives of 575 people (137 in Cape Town, the rest mainly on the

Witwatersrand), with an additional 3 900 people injured. The police made nearly 6 000 arrests over the period. Many hundreds, if not thousands, of young people fled the country. In June 1978 the Chief of the Security Police estimated that some 4 000 Black South Africans were undergoing insurgency training abroad and said that he expected the number to increase as a result of the 'Soweto' uprisings.

The disturbances may not have started as a fundamentally political event, but after the first clashes with the police soon took on a markedly rhetorical political flavour. There was clearly organised leadership by students' councils and for a while their leadership was readily replaced after arrests. The focus of violence was generally State property and liquor outlets which the students claimed weakened the political will of the victims of apartheid.

These disturbances continued, with outbreaks in 1979, particularly in the Cape. In 1980 there were once again boycotts and demonstrations among the school-going youth, with hundreds of arrests and some violent confrontations with police. The school boycotts in 1980 in Natal brought the youthful demonstrators into conflict with Inkatha, the mass Black organisation that will be discussed presently. The restlessness among Black youth subsided during 1981, with the exception of ongoing tension on Black university campuses.

Despite the widespread scope of these events, it was clear that yet again the Black political protest from 1976 onwards was no match for the controlling power of the State. Indeed, the police were able to cope relatively easily and it was not necessary for the army to become involved in any significant way. Some support from workers was forthcoming, but was never likely to be sustained. In Soweto in 1976 the young peoples' demonstration against rent increases won them considerable sympathy, but the majority of Black adults remained judiciously uninvolved. In late 1976 two Government cabinet ministers were able to claim that only 20% or less of Soweto had in any way shown themselves to be supporters of the disturbances (Kane-Berman 1978: 6). Of course, this did not take account of hidden sympathies. The German investigating team from the Arnold Bergstraesser Institute found in sample surveys that some 57% of urban Blacks declared themsleves to be in sympathy with the Soweto disturbances. While less well-educated workers outside Soweto generally condemned the disturbances (less than 30% were in favour), in Soweto itself, even among the lower working class, 62% sympathised with the radical youth (Hanf et al 1978: 335-6). It is also worth noting that not all the participants in the Soweto disturbances were youths. The SA Institute of Race Relations estimated that roughly one-third of casualties were over 26 years of age. (See also Kane-Berman 1978: Ch 1.)

Nevertheless, the much feared escalation of mass Black political action did not occur; White lives and property were never in danger and the loss of life, although substantial and tragic, never looked like becoming a bloodbath. Furthermore, serious divisions in Black political responses were revealed once again; in Soweto, Cape Town and Durban there were instances of migrant blue-collar worker action against the more radical youth.

In February 1984 school boycott activity among Black pupils intensified once again and has continued, with fluctuations in activity, until the present. In August 1984 vehement protests occurred, mainly among Coloured and Indian supporters of extra-parliamentary opposition movements, as a consequence of the elections for the Coloured and Indian houses in the new tricameral parliament. For some months open protests by Blacks had been taking place in specific areas like Lamontville and Sobantu in Natal. In September 1984, however, open dissidence in townships began to occur in the Transvaal, starting in the Vaal Triangle area (Sharpeville and Sebokeng) and spreading to the Witwatersrand, the Northern Free State, the Eastern Cape and, most recently, the Western Cape and KwaZulu.

The current unrest is more serious than previous cycles (for descriptions and analyses see *Indicator SA*, 1985). In the 15-month period covering the unrest (up until the end of September), 722 people have died. This figure exceeds the total for both the 1976-77 disturbances and the 1960 events. According to the Minister of Law and Order, Mr Le Grange, the same period has seen over 10 000 arrests for political offences, here again exceeding the number of political arrests in 1976-77 and roughly equalling the political arrests in the post-Sharpeville period in the sixties. While the unrest of 1976-77 acquired a political character in the course of its development, a political dimension has been clearly evident from the start of the current unrest. Although more mundane forms of discontent have certainly constituted triggers and flashpoints (e.g. rent increases in the Vaal Triangle and Natal townships, bus fare boycotts in these areas and the Eastern Cape, etc) the most noteworthy characteristic of the present unrest is the fact that it had its origins in the protest organisations formed at the time of the introduction of parliamentary reform for Coloureds and Indians (but not Blacks) and, earlier still, in the resistance to the Government's proposals to modify and streamline the system of influx control.

Another contrast between previous cycles of unrest and the current phenomena is the depth of intra-Black conflict which has been brought into the open by the unrest. In the late fifties and sixties there was a sharp division of opinion between ANC-oriented action and PAC-organised strategy, but neither directed their strategies against each other to any significant degree. In 1976-77 the ideological basis of the protests was not sufficiently crystallised to allow for ideological camps to emerge; it was conducted under the very broad inspiration and stimulus of the 'Black consciousness' movement (see Gerhardt 1978).

The current protests have taken place in the context of two clearly distinctive liberation ideologies. The major one is that broadly propounded by the United Democratic Front (UDF) and owes its basic conceptualisation to the Kliptown Freedom Charter of the ANC. Perhaps the major activist grouping in the current unrest, COSAS, is an affiliate of the UDF. The other ideology has been broadly conceptualised within the National Forum Movement and is a development of the older Black consciousness movement. The current unrest for a while subsumed under the major conflict with the authorities a minor conflict between UDF and Black consciousness groupings, with suspected killings on either side, particularly in the Eastern Cape.

The most open and serious Black on Black conflict, however, has been systematic violence directed against Blacks perceived to be agents or hirelings of 'the system': Black town councillors; unsympathetic shopkeepers; Black policemen; and, in Natal, persons or properties connected with Inkatha, the KwaZulu-centred Black political-cultural movement which controls the KwaZulu legislature and hence is branded as being an extension of the government system. Some three days after the current unrest commenced in the KwaZulu-Natal townships, the conflict between protesters and the State had become secondary to a confrontation between the dissident factions and Inkatha.

The current unrest, more than previous cycles, has had a major impact on the economy. It has provided immensely valuable propaganda for the pro-sanctions and disinvestment campaign abroad and has also led to a sharp fall in overseas risk-assessments of the South African economy and hence to a sudden demand for foreign-exchange credit repayments and a consequent fall in the value of the rand on international money markets. These factors have also sharply intensified a related economic problem which has been developing for some time, i.e. a difficulty in attracting foreign capital at favourable rates.

As before, however, the current unrest has not constituted a direct threat to the ability of the State to govern in a general sense. The death toll, although tragically high, could have been of infinitely greater magnitude had the authorities been sufficiently threatened to use sharp ammunition and automatic weapons instead of tearsmoke, plastic bullets and buckshot (see also Du Toit 1985). Only in a few, isolated incidents in which Black protesters have been active in White areas or along major thoroughfares, and in one successful but brief general strike on the Witwatersrand has it had a significant *direct* impact on Whites or the orderly pattern of life in the

401

core centres of industry and administration. Unrest, as a form of political participation calculated to achieve change in South Africa, is very largely an indirect weapon, exercising an effect through the economy, through raising the costs of social control and through the demonstration effect it has on White political sentiments and morale.

This assertion, however, relates to unrest which has clearly been more limited in scope than it could be if a militant solidarity were to develop among a *majority* of Blacks. There can be no doubt that South Africa's police force of under 50 000 and its army of 85 000 would be overwhelmed if Blacks were to mobilise by the millions. Here one is thinking in terms of wholesale revolution, not unrest. The analysis in the next section will consider the prospects of Black action on a massively larger scale.

THE PROSPECTS OF LARGE-SCALE REVOLUTIONARY VIOLENCE

Needless to say, there is a common perception both abroad and in South Africa that a revolution, sooner or later, is not only highly possible, but perhaps inevitable. The stark separation of the races in residential and educational spheres, the White domination of political decision making and the refusal of the White Government to concede political rights at parliamentary level to Blacks, the per capita income gap of roughly 9 : 1 between Whites and Blacks (Loubser 1985) and the fact that roughly three out of ten Black families in urban areas and six to seven out of ten in rural areas live below subsistence level (McGrath and Jenkins 1985) are all blatantly obvious factors which would justify expectations of revolutionary upheaval. Predictions of impending revolution in South Africa have been fairly commonplace both within the country and abroad. Over past decades the relative circumstances of Blacks have tended to improve in aggregate terms. The frequent predictions of revolution are made largely on the basis of a moral assessment of the South African situation and, no matter how justified such an assessment may be, the perceptions of the situation which the predictions reflect are inevitably facile and superficial.

At present, however, predictions of revolutionary violence are more compelling. Firstly, the current unrest and the fact that on 21 July of this year the Government had to declare an official state of emergency covering 36 magisterial districts in the most highly-populated, industrial regions are pointers to the possibility of revolution. Furthermore, the fatality rate has risen from a daily average of 1,65 in the two months preceding the declaration of the emergency to 3,8 in the two months following the declaration (*Sunday Times* Editorial Comment, 29 September 1985), indicating that the unrest is persisting in the face of massive attempts to damp it down (the unrest tends to escalate in areas other than those subject to a state of emergency).

Secondly, it can be assumed that Black expectations have been stimulated by the introduction of a parliamentary franchise last year for Coloureds and Indians and by repeated Government promises of negotiated reform. Such negotiations have not appeared to commence and do not even seem to be possible, given the refusal of most Black spokesmen of repute to enter into negotiations. The imprisoned ANC leader, Nelson Mandela, has recently signified his unwillingness to negotiate with the present government; an event which was widely reported to South Africa at large.

Thirdly, the material conditions experienced by Blacks have probably also had the effect of raising expectations of increased material welfare which have been sharply frustrated by the current downturn in the economy. Average real wages for Blacks grew at a rate of 2,5% per annum between 1971 and 1981 and between June 1980 to June 1982 at a rate of 6,6% per annum, both rates being significantly higher than White wage increases. Since the onset of the recession last year, however, in real terms Black wage increases have declined sharply. In the period of favourable economic growth from 1980 to 1982 employment grew at only 1,5% per annum, well below the growth of demand, and over the past two years the average growth in employment has been negative, thus sharply stimulating unemployment, particularly among the younger Black school-leavers. (Statistics obtained from *Indicator SA*, all issues from 1983 to the present.) Hence, a period of rising prosperity for those Blacks in employment has been followed by a sharp deterioration in circumstances, thus producing the classic conditions for a rise in feelings of relative deprivation.

Finally, since the South African Government signed the Nkomati peace pact with Mozambique, thereby making it impossible for the external wing of the ANC to maintain bases for guerilla insurgency, that organisation has been forced to adopt a strategy of encouraging internal dissent with a view to creating a situation of ungovernability and internal revolution. This view is widely propagated by word of mouth as a consequence of frequent broadcasts to South Africa which can be heard in any Black home with a short-wave radio. The very significant focused political content in the present unrest referred to in the preceding section is of relevance in this regard as well.

One must accept, therefore, that the prospects of a spread of revolutionary unrest are very much higher at present than they have been for some time. Ignoring for a moment the possibility of reform altering the basic constellation of factors, the issue of the possibility of revolutionary violence must be carefully considered.

There is a remarkable broad congruence between the various theories of revolution or rebellion which have appeared in the literature (for example Davies 1962 and 1979; Galtung 1974; Gurr 1970; Gurr and Duvall 1973; and

Muller 1979). Muller's (1979) propositions provide a useful scheme in terms of which to assess the various indications of revolutionary violence which can be adduced in South Africa.

Stated very simply and briefly, Muller's major proposition, which he termed the 'Expectancy-Value-Norms Theory', suggests that predisposition towards political aggression is the outcome of interaction between

(a) the extent of people's alienation from the political system and the degree of their radical commitment (Normative Justification for Aggression), amounting to the extent that people regard political aggression as justifiable;

(b) the degree of people's exposure to social norms favourable to aggression (Facilitative Social Norms), as for example when a person exists in a left-leaning radical university community;

(c) the extent to which a large number of people are available for political behaviour in terms of age, their lack of dependants, their being unemployed, etc; and

(d) the extent of people's beliefs that political aggression have produced benefits and that they have the capacity to act influentially in political confrontation (Muller terms this Utilitarian Justification for Aggression).

Muller also presents a series of secondary propositions which relate to factors which operate to increase the strength of (a) above, 'Normative Justification for Violence'. They include political dissatisfaction, relative deprivation and disequilibrium in rank, i.e. when people are accorded a lower status than their objective achievements would indicate. One may assume that all these factors are present among a majority of Blacks in South Africa. He also presents several more factors which bear upon the likelihood of violence actually occurring if the major factors listed above are sufficiently strongly present. These additional factors will be discussed presently.

Turning to the four major factors which Muller argues to be the key variables determining attitudinal willingness to participate in revolutionary violence, the following can be said to be the case among Blacks in South Africa at the present time.

Normative justification for violence

It is frequently assumed that Blacks are convinced of the justifications for violence in the present order. Yet Government spokesmen equally frequently state the view that the majority of Blacks reject violence as a solution in South Africa and are peace-loving, law-abiding, respectable people.

404

Some survey evidence is available to elucidate this issue. For example, this author conducted a survey among Black male industrial workers in the Witwatersrand, Eastern Cape and Durban-Pinetown areas in early to mid-1984, in which spontaneous answers were obtained on what respondents felt Blacks in Namibia should do in that situation of White political domination (Schlemmer 1984).

Roughly 55% of respondents freely mentioned armed confrontation or violence as a solution to the Namibian problem. In 1981 this author included a very similar question in survey research for the Buthelezi Commission (1982) which referred not only to Namibia, but to Israel and the former Rhodesia as well. Among Black male respondents on the Witwatersrand and in KwaZulu-Natal, an average of some 29% considered violence and armed confrontation to be desirable. It would seem that an increase in the perception of moral justification for violence has taken place.

A major political survey undertaken by the Human Sciences Research Council for the Investigation into Intergroup Relations in early 1984 produced results similar to my most recent findings. Some 50% of the sample of 961 Blacks in major centres agreed or strongly agreed with the statement 'Religious movements can condone violence when people's rights and dignity are restricted'.

A snap survey undertaken among 300 Blacks on the Witwatersrand and Durban by the firm Markinor in August 1985 for the London *Sunday Times*, reported here in the *Sunday Tribune*, 25 August 1985, established that 43% held the view that 'violence is justified in order to end Apartheid'. The fact that the item was very directly phrased may have resulted in a degree of caution in answering, and hence the 43% may be taken as a minimum indication of a moral justification for violence. Even more recently, in September 1985, Mark Orkin (1985) undertook a survey in conjunction with Research Surveys (Pty) Ltd among 800 Blacks in major centres. A question concerning strategies considered to be appropriate if the Government 'refused to end apartheid' was posed. Some 66% of the respondents endorsed 'direct action by Blacks . . . such as strikes, boycotts of White businesses, and protests', 36% supported an 'armed struggle against the government's security forces' and 28% 'attacks on Blacks who work for the system . . .' The 66% above does not necessarily refer to violence, but the presence of that alternative with its strategy of boycott and strike may have drawn support away from the item on 'armed' confrontation.

In reviewing these diverse results obtained by researchers and authors who are often vehemently opposed to one another in the political debate on South Africa, a remarkably consistent pattern emerges in terms of which it would be fair to say that roughly between four and five out of ten Blacks in urban industrial areas feel that violence is justified in opposing the system. This may not constitute a clear majority, but it is a very large minority amounting to between two and three million people. One must conclude that there is ample support for violence in the system.

Exposure to norms justifying violence

The evidence on this precondition for conflict is not conclusive. On one hand some 70% of Black homes in metropolitan areas own TV sets and are therefore massively exposed to the SABC counter-revolutionary propaganda (study by Research Surveys (Pty) Ltd, reported in *Saturday Night Star*, 20 April 1985). On the other hand, however, all the surveys referred to under the previous heading revealed that the ANC is currently the political grouping with the greatest popular support. Since the strategy of the ANC is one of armed struggle at present, there is powerful normative reinforcement for political violence simply in the political identification pattern of most urban Blacks. Furthermore, it has become commonplace for prominent Black spokespeople like Bishop Desmond Tutu to warn of the inevitability of violence and revolution should 'apartheid' not be dismantled soon. Generally, one must assume that normative support for violence in the political environment of Blacks effectively countervails the normative opposition to violence emanating from establishment South Africa media.

Availability for violence

There is little doubt that a relatively high 'availability' for violent confrontation exists in South Africa at present, mainly due to high unemployment among Blacks. In the past unemployment and under-employment among Blacks has been estimated at roughly 20% of the adult labour force. With the current recession it has undoubtedly risen substantially (McGrath and Jenkins 1985). No recent systematic estimates of unemployment exist, but, based on the assumption of an absence of formal or full-time employment among those who seek such employment, a figure of 25% would not be surprising at present. Among younger adults and school-leavers the figure could be much higher, exceeding 30%. Given this fact and the fact that young people have fewer family responsibilities, it is obvious that South Africa has a relatively high availability of able-bodied, alienated young adults who have nothing to lose.

Utilitarian justification for violence and revolution

Muller's fourth proposition is that would-be revolutionaries need to have formed a reasonably convinced perception that violence will succeed in achieving the goals they set for it. This is the essential element in all motivational chains, a positive expectation of the outcome of action.

In the past this expectation has probably been the one major factor constraining the Black population from wholesale participation in pre-revolutionary turmoil. The established order in South Africa has been rock-like in its image of determination, strength and immalleability (Schlemmer 1976).

It is not surprising that a small but representative survey conducted by the present author in 1979 (sample 150 personal interviews with Black adults, Durban Metropolitan area, stratified random selection of clusters, quota-controlled final selection) yielded the following results:

Percentage endorsement of alternative-choice statements relating to Black political strategy (Zulu-speaking men, n 150)

(Statements are paraphrased, uncertain responses omitted)

	%
A leader must act strongly to win support	22
He should wait in order to form a strong organisation	76
A Black leader should never co-operate with the government	11
He should criticise, but co-operate where beneficial	85
Being patient does not help, a leader must make strong demands now	30
He must be patient and work with the tools he has	61
There is no longer anything to be gained by being patient	19
It pays to be patient and plan carefully	81

The manifest caution displayed by this sample of men, who were otherwise deeply discontented and rejecting of the system in South Africa, can only be explained with reference to a low expectation of a positive outcome for violence and insurrection.

However, the survey above was conducted in 1979, since which time a great deal has changed. The Government has introduced certain reforms, most notably the legislation recognising Black trade unions, the abolition of the prohibition of mixed marriages, the recognition of urban Africans in the common area of the country as a permanent part of the population and a municipal franchise, thereby modifying its previously granite-like image and raising expectations of further reform. There has also been a period of some three years during which activists, extra-parliamentary organisations like the UDF, the Congress of South African Students and others operated without being cowed or silenced by security action, that is until very recently.

Hence, one might expect that the consciousness of rank and file Blacks regarding the likely outcome of militant action has altered. Evidence bearing upon this question is available from a very recent (September) survey (referred to earlier) conducted by Orkin (1985) among a sample of 800 Blacks in metropolitan areas (undertaken with the assistance of Research Surveys (Pty) Ltd).

In the earlier reference to this survey it was mentioned that 66% of the respondents felt that militant action such as strikes and boycotts was justifiable and 36% considered the 'armed struggle' to be justifiable. A follow-up question was 'which one strategy do you think will work best in pressurising the government?' Some 50% of the respondents chose 'public demands for negotiation . . .', 19% 'Foreign or overseas pressure...', the same proportion (19%) 'Direct action by Blacks such as strikes, boycotts of shops...' and only 11% endorsed 'Armed struggle against the government's security forces'.

Hence, from this one piece of survey evidence it would appear that public violence is not assessed at all positively as a lever against the Government. However, if one were to include strikes and boycotts, as well as 'attacks on Blacks who work for the system', under the general heading 'revolutionary' activity, then some one-third of urban Blacks would be positively motivated to engage in militant or fairly militant confrontation of the system.

Comparing this broad estimate of one-third oriented to and believing in militant action with earlier research other than that already mentioned above (see Schlemmer 1983), then it would seem that the proportion of Blacks having militant sentiments and beliefs has not altered much during the current unrest.

Obviously there are parts of the country where this general comment would not hold, for example the Eastern Cape, an area in which violent activity has been particularly prominent and enduring in all three major phases of violence; 1958-61, 1976-77 and 1985 onwards. A real life assessment of the validity of the more general pattern, however, is to be found in the outcome of attempts to mount a general 'political' consumer boycott of White shops in various parts of the country. While the consumer boycott in the Eastern Cape gathered momentum soon after it was launched in mid-July and has been sustained and substantially effective up until the present, leading to negotiations between the representatives of commerce and the UDF in some areas, the boycott strategy in the Transvaal and Natal has been markedly less successful. The boycott in Natal was called off, without ever really having succeeded, on 4 October (*Daily News*, 3 October 1985) after encountering resistance from the Black traders organised under the Inyanda Chamber of Commerce. In the Transvaal attempts to mount the boycott have, after an initial spurt of success in some areas, apparently been undermined by security action including the closing of some Black shops, the detention of certain shopkeepers and interference with the supply of goods to township commerce. A detailed report in the *Weekly Mail* (20-26 September 1985) concluded that '. . . it will take a long time and a great deal of hard work. The boycott may or may not be an eventual success'. The Natal and Transvaal reactions to the consumer boycott do not suggest a highly motivated Black mass public willing to make sacrifices in the expectation of change, and boycotts are a far cry from violent rebellion.

OTHER STRUCTURAL FACTORS

The issue of negative expectations of revolutionary violence exists at the level of mass psychology. Even more powerful constraints on or encourage- ment of overt violence exist in the structures of control and mobilisation. Muller (1979) mentions, *inter alia*, the following factors which contain overt political violence: The strength, consistency and scope of sanctions or repression (violence may be exacerbated in the short-term by strong counter-reaction, but is usually suppressed by such sanctions in the long run, according to Muller); the flexibility and adaptability of Government reactions to violence; the strength of dissident organisation; and the proportion of people in the categories from which dissidence emanates.

In South Africa the highly solidary army and police force can be counted on to impose sanctions of great consistency and strength if necessary, but the odds in terms of ratios of system to antisystem-oriented people are enormous. The flexibility of the Government in responding to violence is also vitiated by foreign pressures and ideological constraints within its own ranks. Strategies of co-optation and incorporation of Black leadership able to countervail dissident leadership have tended to be subject to tortuous constitutional planning and elaborate safeguards for White con- trol because of the highly structured perception of the racial order within the governing National Party.

The cohesiveness and effectiveness of Black political organisation in the face of security sanctions is a vital issue affecting the outcome of conflict in South Africa. It is, after all, only organisation which can transform the cycles of riots and turmoil into effective leverage and capacity for tough but peaceful negotiation. To quote Martin Luther King, 'The limitations of riots, moral questions aside, is that they cannot win and their participants know it. Hence, rioting is not revolutionary, but reactionary because it inspires defeat. It involves an emotional catharsis, but it must be followed by a sense of futility.' This is precisely what appears to have happened after each previous cycle of turmoil.

The Black political organisations involved in the current conflicts reveal dramatic differences in the coherence of their organisation. The most prominent, the UDF, is in fact a loose network of 600 affiliated organisations united by common sentiment rather than a binding structure and discipline. Among its ranks COSAS, the pupil-based organisation, has proved to be most effective in mounting collective action, perhaps because the organisation of schools gives it a natural branch structure (or cell structure), with regular meetings and face-to-face interaction controlled by an age-based hierarchy. Its great weakness is that it could not function effectively without usurping the very routine in which it was rooted, school attendance. For that reason an uneasy flirtation with school premises continued, even during boycotts in many cases. Ultimately it is vulnerable to sanctions because its points of organisation can be monitored and controlled, albeit with difficulty.

Black trade unions, some of which have become involved in the consumer boycott of White shops and in the successful but short stay-away strike of November 1984, have exactly the same difficulty in achieving high-key political involvement. Their greatest organisational strength lies in factory-based organisation, but any move towards active militancy involves putting the factory-base and the reason for the continuity of the organisation — workplace negotiation — at risk. For this reason the more successful industrial unions have tended to avoid too much overt political involvement.

Inkatha, the political-cultural movement under Chief Buthelezi, has been most successful in maintaining an organisation of huge size (over one million members at present). Like any organisation it cannot exist only on the basis of voluntarism and idealism, and hence it has chosen to institutionalise itself in the KwaZulu Government, but could move into local community politics outside of KwaZulu. It has the advantage of being able to practise politics without usurping some other more formal role. Its participation in a homeland government has also given it invaluable experience in administration and exposure to the challenges of development. Its weakness lies in its vulnerability to accusations of lending credibility to apartheid structures and the fact that its official status causes it to become the target of dissidence along with the South African Government. The challenge for Inkatha is how to move beyond the institutions of homeland government. If this can be achieved, the cohesiveness of its internal structure could make it a very major factor in the balance of forces in the country. For this reason its participation (with the Progressive Federal Party) in the recently-established convention alliance should be watched with great interest.

CONCLUDING COMMENT

In the recent round of National Party congresses held during August and September, the governing National Party, under pressure from Western governments and the disinvestment campaign, has moved to a bolder position on reform than it has ever held previously. The State President has committed himself to power-sharing on matters of common concern between the races, to a common citizenship for all Blacks, to inclusive negotiations with all peacefully-oriented Black leadership and to the inclusion of Blacks on the President's Council. Yet so far his signals of reform have met with rejection from all Black spokesmen and leaders, Chief Buthelezi included. The major reason for this is that the various Black political leader-figures are in intense competition with one another, some in rather premature anticipation of assuming control of government. In this competition political credibility can be lost by participating too closely in Government reform programmes and in negotiations in which the agenda is so structured as to make racial categories the basic political units. Race classification is anathema, not only because it has meant structured inequality in the past, but because, by implication, it is a value judgement about identity and hence a badge of honour or dishonour.

The Government, on the other hand, like all political formations, will continue to be concerned primarily with protecting its power-base, which is a complex interaction of race and ethnicity (Schlemmer and Committee, forthcoming). There is not likely to be a move away from race as an ordering principle and group autonomy as a principle in government policy in the near future. The State President's recent categorical commitments to separate Group Areas at the Party congresses confirms this.

Black political participation and organisation, therefore, will have to survive and endure a good few years of protest and opposition politics if it chooses not to compromise on race classification and the principle of group autonomy. The analysis presented in this chapter suggests that in this period dissidence and turmoil could be serious because of fairly substantial moral endorsement of revolutionary violence, a ready army of alienated, unemployed people and a constant ideological stimulation to active dissent from highly-respected externally-based political 'champions'.

Nevertheless, there are also clearly-defined factors which, on present evidence, would appear to make an escalation of revolutionary activity to

411

a point at which the system would collapse highly unlikely. These include a low popular expectation of success, weaknesses in the structure of dissident organisation and powerful security forces, the full capacity of which to impose crippling coercive sanctions has not yet been tested.

In what can be predicted to be a protracted period of low-level instability manifested in cycles of unrest, South Africa will pay the price in economic growth for the imperfections in both its White and Black politics.

BIBLIOGRAPHY

Buthelezi Commission. *The Requirements of Stability and Development in KwaZulu and Natal.* Durban: H & H Publications, 1982.

Cillié Commission. *Report of the Commission of Enquiry into the Riots in Soweto and Elsewhere from June 16, 1976 to February 28, 1977.* Pretoria: Government Printer, 1980.

Davies, JC. Towards a Theory of Revolution. *American Sociological Review,* vol. 27, no. 1, February 1962.

Galtung, J. *A Structural Theory of Revolutions.* Rotterdam: Rotterdam University Press, 1974.

Gerhardt, Gail. *Black Power in South Africa.* Berkeley: University of California Press, 1978.

Graham, HD and Gurr, TD (Eds). *Violence in America.* London: Sage Publications, 1979.

Gurr, TD. *Why Men Rebel.* Princeton: Princeton University Press, 1970.

Gurr, TD and Duvall, R. Civil Conflict in the Sixties. *Comparative Political Studies,* vol. 6, July 1973.

Hanf, Theodor *et al. Südafrika: Friedlicher Wandel?* Munchen/Mainz: Kaiser-Grünewald, 1978.

Horrell, Muriel. *Action, Reaction and Counter-Reaction.* Johannesburg: SA Institute of Race Relations, 1971.

Howe, G, Schlemmer, L *et al* (Eds). *Indicator SA.* Durban: Centre for Applied Social Sciences, University of Natal, 1983 — 1985.

Kane-Berman, John. *Soweto: Black Revolt, White Reaction.* Johannesburg: Ravan Press, 1978.

Loubser, M. *Address to the Black Market Convention.* Johannesburg: SA Advertising Research Foundation, 1985.

McGrath, MD and Jenkins, C. *The Economic Implications of Disinvestment for the South African Economy.* Durban: Paper presented to the Economic Society of South Africa, 19 September 1985.

Muller, EM. *Aggressive Political Participation.* Princeton NJ: Princeton University Press, 1979.

Orkin, Mark. *Black Attitudes to Disinvestment: The Real Story* (News release). Johannesburg: Community Agency for Social Enquiry/Institute for Black Research, 1985.

Schlemmer, L. Black Attitudes: Adaptation and Reaction. *Social Dynamics,* vol. 2, no. 1, 1976.

Schlemmer, L. *Conflict in South Africa: Build-up to Revolution or Impasse?* (Indicator SA Issue Focus Series.) Durban: Centre for Applied Social Sciences, 1983.

Schlemmer, L. *Black Attitudes, Capitalism and Disinvestment.* (Indicator SA Issue Focus Series.) Durban: Centre for Applied Social Sciences, University of Natal, 1984.

Schlemmer, L and Committee. *Report of the Working Group on Race, Ethnicity and Culture.* Investigation into Inter-Group Relations, Pretoria: Human Sciences Research Council (forthcoming).

Walshe, Peter. *The Rise of African Nationalism in South Africa.* Berkeley: University of California Press, 1971.

NEWSPAPER ARTICLES

Daily News. Report on Natal Consumer Boycott. Durban: Argus Co, 3 October 1985.

Natal Mercury. André du Toit, 17 September 1985.

Sunday Times. Editorial Comment. Johannesburg: SA Associated Newspapers, 29 September 1985.

Sunday Tribune. Report on London Sunday Times Poll. Durban: Argus Co, 25 August 1985.

Saturday Night Star. News report on Survey of TV Ownership. Johannesburg: Argus Co, 20 April 1985.

Weekly Mail. Report on consumer Boycott in Transvaal. Johannesburg: WM Publications, 20-26 September 1985.

17 Foreign policy 1983-85: The regional context

J Barratt

INTRODUCTORY SUMMARY

In both regional and wider international relations, South Africa's fortunes have fluctuated wildly during the period mid-1983 to mid-1985. In the former year it seemed that conflict in Southern Africa was escalating steadily and internationally the South African Government was increasingly accused of pursuing a policy of destabilising its neighbours. Then in early 1984 the Lusaka Agreement and the Nkomati Accord aroused new hopes of détente, while Prime Minister PW Botha's visit to Europe in June of the same year appeared to mark a breakthrough in South Africa's relations with the West. It was hoped that this was the beginning of the end of South Africa's political isolation. These new hopes were furthered by the fact that the world was taking notice of the Government's reform initiatives within South Africa and encouraging Mr PW Botha to continue along the path of reform.

In the second half of 1984, however, this promising scenario began to unravel. The agreements with Angola and Mozambique were not producing the expected positive results and within South Africa serious unrest erupted during the election campaigns for the two new Houses of Parliament created for the Coloured and Indian communities by South Africa's reformed Constitution. These disturbances, the resultant low percentage polls in the elections and the rise of the United Democratic Front (UDF), which articulated militant Black opposition to the new Constitution, raised doubts internationally about the viability of the Government's plans for constitutional reform. This negative reaction was aggravated by various other events during the second half of the year, including the detention of UDF and Black trade union leaders under security legislation, the British Consulate affair (in which six UDF leaders sought asylum in the Consulate in Durban), the South African retaliatory decision not to allow four South Africans to return to Britain for trial on charges relating to attempts to break the British trade embargo, a two-day 'stay away' by Black workers in the

414

Witwatersrand area in early November and the award of the Nobel Peace Prize to Bishop Desmond Tutu in November.

November marked the beginning of an intense anti-apartheid campaign in the United States. This has continued and grown in 1985 and has included proposals for sanctions legislation in the US Congress, wider support for disinvestment by American companies in South Africa, continuous protest demonstrations and a high level of media attention to South African affairs. The intensity and widespread nature of this campaign are unprecedented in the history of relations between the United States and South Africa and it has put severe pressure on the Reagan Administration's policy of constructive engagement.

The American campaign and the wider international criticism of the South African Government, for instance in Western Europe and the United Nations, intensified during the first half of 1985 as a result of several other events in Southern Africa and within South Africa. In particular, there were the tragic incident in a Black township near Uitenhage in March, the continuing unrest in Black townships throughout South Africa, the incident involving a South African military unit in Cabinda (Angola) in late May and the military raid on ANC targets in Gaborone (Botswana) in June.

By mid-1985, therefore, South Africa's regional and wider external relations appeared to have deteriorated considerably, in spite of the important advances made during the earlier part of the period under review. The Nkomati Accord and the Prime Minister's European visit were the highwater marks of these advances regionally and internationally and, in spite of the subsequent decline in South Africa's international fortunes, their significance for the future has not been obliterated.

It is intended in this chapter to review the developments over the past two years, focusing on the main issues which have dominated South African foreign policy-making during this period and which have substantially affected and will continue to affect South Africa's external relations generally. The issues relate primarily to regional relations within Southern Africa and the Government's attempts to develop and apply an integrated regional policy, the outlines of which have become clearer over the past two years. The Nkomati Accord is the core of this policy and therefore special attention will be paid to the implications of Nkomati as the Government's main achievement in its regional policy to date. As relations with the United States became a matter of special concern in the first half of 1985, brief attention must also be given to the reasons for the critical state of these relations.

Although it is not the purpose of this chapter to discuss domestic developments, mention of them cannot be avoided because they are (and will continue to be) the main issue in South Africa's international relations.

415

Similarly, although the focus is on political and security factors, it is important to recognise that economic considerations cannot be neatly divorced from politics. Thus, South Africa's current domestic political problems have been compounded by deteriorating economic conditions and the American anti-apartheid campaign, although politically motivated, is attempting to use economic weapons. Within Southern Africa economic factors are of fundamental importance to the relationships between South Africa and its neighbours and in a sense constitute a potentially stabilising counter-force to the destabilising effect of political and security problems.

REGIONAL RELATIONS

1983 — Spreading conflict

On 23 May 1983 a South African air strike was carried out on targets in the outskirts of Maputo, the capital of Mozambique. It was aimed at buildings occupied by the African National Congress (ANC) and the South African Defence Force claimed that 41 members of the ANC were killed in the raid, together with 17 Frelimo soldiers. This occurred immediately after 17 people were killed in a car-bomb blast in the centre of Pretoria, for which the ANC claimed responsibility, and was widely interpreted as retaliation for the blast. In January 1981 South African troops had attacked ANC houses in the Matola suburb of Maputo and in September 1982 South African forces attacked ANC houses in Maseru, the capital of Lesotho, an attack in which 42 people died. There was also a smaller commando raid on an ANC house in the centre of Maputo in October 1983. These strikes into neighbouring territories drew considerable criticism from within the region and internationally. All had been aimed specifically at the ANC and, according to the South African Government, were justified in the interests of the security of the people of South Africa and because the ANC was being allowed to use the territory of neighbouring countries as bases for the launching of sabotage and terrorist incursions into South Africa.

In 1983 South Africa was also criticised for other types of intervention in neighbouring countries. These criticisms related inter alia to material and training support provided to the resistance movement Renamo (also referred to as the MNR (Mozambique National Resistance) opposed to the Frelimo Government of Mozambique, similar support for Unita in Angola and dissidents in Matebeleland in Zimbabwe and to various economic pressures on these countries and Lesotho. All of these actions were perceived as part of an aggressive South African policy aimed at the destabilisation of her neighbours in order to create a weak bank of states around the country and/or force them to comply with her demands.

416

Conflict was also prevalent within several other countries in the region. Mozambique and Angola in particular were affected by spreading anti-government guerrilla movements and in Zimbabwe the Government was attempting to repress violent dissidents among the Matabele who were supporting the opposition movement, ZAPU. In addition, the Namibian dispute was unresolved and conflict between the South African Defence Force and SWAPO across the border from northern Namibia into southern Angola continued.

The American policy of constructive engagement initiated by the Reagan Administration in 1981 was aimed at reducing conflict and promoting stability in the region, but by 1983 had achieved little in the way of demonstrable results. Only on the Namibian issue were negotiations known to be continuing, but even there no breakthrough was in sight. However, in spite of the evidence of widening conflict, talks were proceeding in an attempt to defuse the conflict and introduce greater stability to regional relationships.

The first change in the picture of escalating regional conflict came on 16 February 1984, when the South African and Angolan Governments reached an agreement in Lusaka which provided for co-operation between them to reduce the level of conflict in the south of Angola. The Lusaka Agreement was promoted by the United States with the assistance of President Kaunda of Zambia and was the fruit of a long process of negotiation over Namibia's future. It was not intended as an end in itself, but rather as a confidence-building measure and a step towards the resolution of other problems standing in the way of agreement on Namibian independence. (The Lusaka Agreement and subsequent developments with regard to Angola and Namibia will be examined further below.)

The Nkomati Accord and its aftermath

However, it was the Nkomati Accord between South Africa and Mozambique which marked a dramatic change in the Southern African scene and created a new and hopeful mood of détente. In the Accord, which was signed on 16 March 1984 at a highly publicised ceremony on the border between the two countries, the two Governments undertook 'to respect each other's sovereignty and independence, and in fulfilment of this fundamental obligation, to refrain from interfering in the internal affairs of the other' (Article One). More specifically, they agreed not to allow their respective territories to be used in any way by organisations or individuals planning 'to commit acts of violence, terrorism or aggression' against the other party. The Accord went on to specify in detail the various types of acts which the two parties undertook to prevent or eliminate.[1]

417

The signing of the Nkomati Accord drew world attention to what was a very significant change in the regional configuration. As indicated above, in 1983 the South African Government's regional policy was widely perceived simply as one of destabilising its neighbours and international criticism of the Government mounted, not only in Africa and the United Nations, but also in Western capitals. Against this background, the Lusaka Agreement and the Nkomati Accord in particular appeared to indicate that the South African Government had changed its policy, or had at least added the element of negotiation to the military and economic pressure it had been using. This latter interpretation was referred to by the *Economist* as the 'thump and talk' approach.[2] From another viewpoint it could be said, in the case of Mozambique at least, that the South African Government was now trying to wean Mozambique away from the Soviet camp instead of to subvert or even overthrow the Marxist government of that country. This interpretation placed South Africa in line with American policy regarding the region, which was designed to increase Western economic and political influence in Southern Africa at the expense of Soviet influence. There is no doubt that American negotiators strongly encouraged the process which led to the Nkomati Accord, since for some time they had been working to improve the United States' own relations with Mozambique.

The South African attitude towards Marxist governments, particularly those having clear links with the Soviet Union, was well known. Over the years public statements by political and military leaders referred frequently to the concept of a 'total onslaught' on South Africa promoted by Moscow with the assistance *inter alia* of neighbouring 'Marxist' states. In Mozambique's case, the Frelimo Government proclaimed itself Marxist and had a Treaty of Friendship and Co-operation with the Soviet Union. Its main supplier of weapons was the Soviet Union, whilst other Eastern bloc states assisted it in the security and economic fields. However, by 1983 it was clear that Mozambique's alignment with the Soviet Union was weakening, particularly because of Soviet ineffectiveness in helping the Frelimo Government to deal with its country's increasingly severe economic problems. As the Soviet influence declined, American relations with Mozambique gradually improved. Full diplomatic relations were established and ambassadors were exchanged between Washington and Maputo. In addition to its willingness to provide economic aid, Washington encouraged the American private sector to take a greater interest in Mozambique. In mid-1983 President Samora Machel visited countries in Western Europe and gave clear signals that Mozambique was open to Western assistance. Notably, relations with Portugal, the former colonial power, were significantly improved.

In all of these moves President Machel demonstrated the pragmatism for which he has become well known and did not allow ideological considerations to prevent him from facing up to the desperate economic situation of his country, which was being compounded by the rapidly deteriorating security situation. Without reducing the spreading security threat from Renamo, he could not hope for any meaningful economic reconstruction and development and to this end a deal with South Africa, Renamo's main supporter, was required.

Although the Nkomati Accord made no specific reference to either the ANC or Renamo and no explicit admission that Mozambique had been supporting one and South Africa the other, it was clearly intended to end the support which the two parties had been giving to these movements. Therefore, if the terms of the Accord were fully implemented, the South African Government would achieve its aim of closing the Mozambique corridor to the ANC and President Machel's Government would succeed in greatly reducing Renamo's ability to continue its subversive and disruptive campaign. It was hoped that greater stability would lead to economic improvement in Mozambique. Although the Nkomati Accord was purely a security agreement, no reference being made to economic co-operation, the hopes and expectations aroused on Mozambique's part were clearly related to its potential economic benefits, including benefits to be gained from closer links with South Africa.

In these circumstances it may seem that the Mozambique Government had little choice, but was driven into this agreement by its desperate economic and security situation coupled with increasing pressure from South Africa. Given Mozambique's weakness, which in a real sense South Africa exploited in order to achieve its primary aim of stopping ANC operations, there is considerable truth in this assessment. However, South Africa also had other needs which Mozambique could help to meet through the Accord.

Although South African willingness to sign a security agreement with a self-confessed Marxist government caused considerable surprise within South Africa and abroad, the Government has adopted a fairly pragmatic approach towards links with Mozambique ever since Frelimo took power from the Portuguese in 1975. At that time Prime Minister John Vorster spoke of a policy of co-existence in spite of political and ideological differences.[3] The main elements of the economic link between the two countries, established when the Portuguese were in control, continued (although at a somewhat reduced level) without either side officially trying to end them. These links were the provision of labour for South African mines and other industries, South African use of the port of Maputo and the railway link to that port, the purchase of power from Cahora Bassa and the supply of electricity to Maputo from the South African grid and some trade

419

and investment. It is one of the paradoxes of the Southern African scene that these links were maintained in spite of the fact that the ANC was using Mozambique territory to infiltrate into South Africa and in spite of the South African military strikes into Mozambique. In the case of the Cahora Bassa power line, there was the added irony that this line was constantly sabotaged by the South African-supported Renamo, so that for long periods South Africa was denied the extra power it needed from that source.

The Nkomati Accord was seen as the basis upon which these links could be strengthened and new forms of co-operation developed. One immediate step was the re-negotiation of the Cahora Bassa Agreement between South Africa, Portugal and Mozambique. This agreement holds out the promise that South Africa will receive a regular supply of power from that source and the Mozambique Government will derive income from the supply, provided that it flows regularly. However, this promise has not yet been fulfilled, because Renamo has continued to interrupt the supply and the Mozambique Government has not been capable of protecting the power line effectively. The two Governments established a joint committee to work on other aspects of economic co-operation and the South African private sector has been encouraged to take more interest in trade, tourism and other links with Mozambique.

Unfortunately, as with the Cahora Bassa power supply, little meaningful development has resulted from all these efforts because, in spite of Nkomati, the security situation has continued to deteriorate. In fact, during the second half of 1984 and in early 1985, Renamo sabotage and terrorist activities increased greatly around Maputo in the southern part of Mozambique. The rail link with South Africa has been cut several times and travel by road is unsafe, thus making the route to Maputo unreliable for South African exports and imports.

Another major advantage which South Africa stood to gain from the Nkomati Accord was less quantifiable than potential economic benefits. This related to the question of the international credibility to be derived from an agreement with a formerly hostile neighbour state and to the precedent it might set for similar agreements with other states in the region. In fact, once the Nkomati Accord was signed the Government of Swaziland felt free to announce that it had signed a security agreement with South Africa two years previously. The way seemed open for similar arrangements, either formal or informal, with Lesotho and Botswana, while a more relaxed relationship with Zimbabwe was even becoming apparent. The trend, therefore, was towards greater stability in Southern Africa and away from the pattern of conflicting relationships and the perception of South Africa as an aggressive power in the region. This changed perception of South Africa's role in Southern Africa was one of the main factors which made the Prime Minister's visit to several important European countries in June 1984 possible.

However, as the year passed the South African Government's credit was dissipated to some extent when it became clear that the anticipated positive effects of Nkomati were not being realised within Mozambique. The South African Government made a major effort to bring about a reconciliation between Renamo and the Frelimo Government through negotiation and an agreement in principle to end the violent conflict was reached in Pretoria on 3 October. However, further negotiations towards the implementation of this declaration of intent were broken off by Renamo and the conflict has worsened.

The Mozambique Government, it is generally agreed, fulfilled its side of the bargain in curbing ANC operations. But it is widely believed that although the South African Government took a policy decision to give effect to its undertakings in the Nkomati Accord, this decision was not immediately implemented at all levels. As a result, support from within South Africa was not entirely cut off, even if such support — from private sources and perhaps even lower level official and military sources — was not condoned by the Government. Early in 1985 this situation was seen to be threatening to bring an end to the agreement between the two Governments. At a reception for the diplomatic corps in Maputo at the beginning of January, President Samora Machel stated: 'There are facts which indicate the existence of violations of the Nkomati Accord from South African territory and from other countries which are Mozambique's neighbours.' He did not accuse the South African Government of being directly responsible.[4] A few days later President Machel met in Maputo with the representatives of the five permanent members of the UN Security Council (China, France, the United Kingdom, the United States and the Soviet Union) and after the meeting he was reported to have said: 'Everyone agreed the Nkomati Accord was not being fully implemented in letter or in spirit. However, we also agreed that Mozambique had carried the Accord out fully.'[5] South African spokesmen denied that the Government was in any way involved in contraventions of the Accord and the Joint Security Commission, which had been created in terms of the Accord, was asked to investigate the allegations.

The spreading concern about the future of the Nkomati Accord led to a strong statement by President PW Botha that the Government would not tolerate violent action against Mozambique from South African territory. He said that the Government would not hesitate to act 'efficiently' against persons who planned or perpetrated violence from South African territory or who fled to South Africa after they had carried out violent activities in Mozambique.[6]

421

Meanwhile, the South African Government was continuing its efforts to bring an end to the civil war in Mozambique through agreement between Renamo and President Machel's Government. However, by the end of January 1985 very little hope that these efforts would bear fruit remained. At a press conference on 31 January, Foreign Minister RF Botha said that peace had been frustrated by 'unreasonable' demands from the rebel movement. 'The last demands of the MNR I have not even passed on to President Machel, because they are so unreasonable that he would think that something was wrong with me if I transmitted them', he said. 'The MNR believes it is on the point of winning, but I told them they could stay like that for ten years, while destroying the country in the process.'[7]

On the same occasion Foreign Minister Botha repeated the South African Government's categorical denial that it was still giving clandestine support to the MNR. But he added: 'I do not deny that there might be elements within South Africa and further afield from where individuals do take or plan actions in support of the MNR.' He added that South African security forces and the police were under strict instructions to act against suspected individuals. Without naming specific countries, he said: 'I believe assistance is being rendered to the MNR from countries in Europe and the Middle East and who knows from elsewhere.'[8] Reports at the time indicated that Portuguese sources, including politicians and businessmen who formerly had interests in Mozambique, were among those responsible for continued aid to Renamo.

On 15 March, the eve of the first anniversary of the signing of the Nkomati Accord, a high-level ministerial delegation visited Maputo for discussions with the Mozambique Government in what was seen as a final effort to save the Accord from collapse. In a communiqué issued at the end of the discussions, which took place in the context of a meeting of the Joint Security Commission, the two parties 'reiterated their governments' continued commitment to, and full support for, the Accord'. Further, the communiqué said that 'both delegations agreed it was essential for the development of the whole Southern African region that the Nkomati Accord should be fully implemented'. Significantly, the communiqué also said that the two Governments were 'concerned at the increase in violence in Mozambique, and proposals were discussed as to ways and means of bringing an end to it'.[9]

On the following day, at a widely publicised press conference, Foreign Minister RF Botha announced that the police had uncovered a 'Renamo-connected criminal gang' based in Johannesburg and that several people had been arrested and would soon appear in court. Quantities of counterfeit money and propaganda material had been seized. Mr Botha also referred to an 'international web of bankers, financiers and businessmen with Renamo connections intent on turning Mozambique into their own private economic preserve'.[10]

By this demonstration of firm action within South Africa, the collapse of the Nkomati Accord was avoided. As one commentator concluded: 'It seems to have taken a near-ultimatum from Mozambique's Samora Machel — coupled with a strong condemnation from the Presidents of frontline states — to galvanise South Africa into action over the failing Nkomati Accord. However it seems the Accord has been salvaged.'[11] At the same time, there was no doubt that the threat from Renamo was still very real and the activities of this movement indicated that in fact it was stronger than it had been a year previously. Therefore, more had to be done in order to reduce this threat and there was speculation that South Africa might even send troops into Mozambique to assist Frelimo. When this suggestion was put to President PW Botha in an interview, he said that South Africa would be prepared to consider military intervention in Mozambique 'on merit' and if asked to do so publicly by the West and President Machel's Government.[12] In the circumstances this was not, and still is not, a serious option for the South African Government for various reasons, including domestic political reaction in South Africa and the unlikelihood that President Machel could afford the domestic and international political risk of asking for overt South African military assistance. The reason for President Botha's inclusion of the proviso that the West should ask publicly for South African military intervention was, of course, the South African experience in Angola in 1975, when the Government regarded itself as having been 'let down' after a private request from the West (for 'West' read 'United States') to intervene. Nevertheless, when South Africa made its re-commitment to the Nkomati Accord, it was clearly recognised that something more effective had to be done to deal with the security situation in Mozambique. This was the main subject of discussion at the meeting in Maputo on 15 March and since then various actions which indicate that South Africa agreed to take certain meaningful steps to give effect to its commitment have been taken.

One course of action has aimed at cutting off the sources of support for Renamo and at persuading other governments — in Europe and elsewhere — to assist to this end. For instance, according to reports, in December 1984, while on an unpublicised trip to East Africa, Foreign Minister Botha asked at least two heads of state for assurances that they were not allowing their countries to be used as supply bases for the rebels in Mozambique. The states were not named, but one was reported to be the Comores. In an interview published in London in late March, individual Portuguese businessmen living in Portugal and Brazil were specifically named by Deputy Foreign Minister Louis Nel as being amongst the 'most important' financial backers of Renamo.[13]

Another course of action has aimed at stopping any South African sources of support. Thus, for instance, the border area between South Africa and Mozambique in the Eastern Transvaal has been declared 'a special restricted airspace' with the aim, according to the Minister of Defence, of preventing private interests from giving logistical support to any rebel movement in Mozambique and of curtailing smuggling. This means that pilots need official permission to fly in the designated zone, which is monitored by the South African Air Force using 'all possible technological aids'.[14] It is also noteworthy that the services of five members of the South African Defence Force have been terminated following an investigation to determine whether they were Renamo sympathisers. On 14 May 1985, the Defence Minister, General Magnus Malan, informed Parliament that the investigation had been carried out after an undertaking given to the Mozambique Government during the meeting on 15 March and he added that the investigation was still continuing. General Malan also said that certain units had been reorganised to allow for the transfer of a number of Portuguese-speaking members to another station to prevent any suspicion of contact with Mozambique and conceded that it was possible that individual members or employees of the Defence Force could be Renamo sympathisers. However, he said that since the signing of the Nkomati Accord, the Government's standpoint that no support of any nature might be given to Renamo had repeatedly been brought to the attention of Defence Force staff.[15]

As far as security assistance for Mozambique within that country is concerned, there have been discussions with the Mozambique authorities about the establishment of units of private security guards which would be used primarily to protect the rail and road link between South Africa and Maputo and the power line between Cahora Bassa and South Africa. As yet, there has been no formal announcement in this regard, but it seems that the South African Electricity Supply Commission (ESCOM) is giving particular attention to means of repairing and protecting the 900 km of power line within Mozambique. No significant supplies of electricity have been received from Cahora Bassa for nearly two years, mainly because of Renamo sabotage.

Whatever may be said about South Africa's failure to take firm practical action during the first year of the Nkomati Accord while attempts were being made to effect a reconciliation between Renamo and Frelimo, these more recent actions demonstrate the Government's renewed determination that the Accord should be maintained. The Accord is seen not only as the basis for the development of co-operative relations with Mozambique for security and economic reasons, but also as the basis for the further development of regional policy in Southern Africa generally. In addition, the collapse of the Accord would have an extremely negative effect on South Africa's wider international relations: the return to a confrontational position vis-à-vis Mozambique would put more pressure on the American policy of constructive engagement; it would create the risk of Mozambique turning back to the Soviet Union for assistance and away from the West; and it would destroy the South African argument that understanding, co-existence and even co-operation can be achieved with neighbouring states. The maintenance of the Nkomati Accord becomes even more important when the deadlock over Namibian independence, the deterioration in relations with Angola and the new conflict with Botswana are taken into account.

The Lusaka Agreement and relations with Angola

The Lusaka Agreement of 16 February 1984 was reached through the mediation of the United States. As indicated above, it was not an end in itself; the United States Government saw it as part of a process, as one step along the path towards the eventual goals of Cuban withdrawal from Angola and an independent Namibia. The Agreement was intended to end the conflict in southern Angola involving South Africa, SWAPO and Angolan forces and to create a climate of trust between the South African and Angolan Governments. Hopefully, this improved climate would allow for further constructive steps to be taken in the ongoing process of negotiation.

The Lusaka Agreement provided for the creation of a joint South African/Angolan Commission to monitor the disengagement process in southern Angola, including the withdrawal of South African forces from and the cessation of hostilities in the area. It was envisaged that the Angolan armed forces would take the responsibility for ensuring that this area of southern Angola was not used by SWAPO for launching incursions into Namibia — the reason for the South African military presence in Angolan territory. The Agreement was seen, in the words of an official statement issued in Lusaka by the representatives of Angola, South Africa and the United States, as 'an important and constructive step towards the peaceful resolution of the problems of the region, including the question of the implementation of UN Security Council Resolution 435 (on Namibian independence)'.[16]

The Joint Monitoring Commission (JMC) was composed of South African and Angolan military officers and after its first meeting in Lusaka on 16 February, it was established within Angola. The Agreement provided that 'a small number of American representatives could participate in the activities of the Joint Commission at the request of the parties' and in order to facilitate this participation an American mission was established in Windhoek. The continued involvement of the United States was thus assured. (The Windhoek mission was closed in February 1985, when it appeared that the work of the JMC was nearing completion.)

At the time it was hoped that the various stages of the South African military withdrawal from the south of Angola and the establishment of Angolan Government control over the area would be completed within a few months. The Agreement provided that the JMC would not only monitor this 'disengagement process', but 'detect, investigate and report any alleged violations of the commitment of the parties'. Although SWAPO did not participate in the Lusaka meeting and was not referred to in the Agreement, it became clear from comments by the parties involved that one of Angola's commitments was to take responsibility for keeping SWAPO forces out of the area evacuated by the South Africans. For instance, the day after the Agreement the South African Administrator-General of South West Africa/Namibia, Dr Willie van Niekerk, said: 'The Angolans have undertaken to keep SWAPO out of southern Angola, and that is a fact.'[17] While SWAPO did not publicly endorse the Agreement, a spokesman claimed that they had 'no more interest in preventing the South African troops from withdrawing from Angola than we have in prolonging the armed struggle in Namibia itself' and reiterated SWAPO's willingness to sign its own cease-fire agreement with Pretoria as a first step towards implementing the UN independence plan.[18] Moreover, the SWAPO leader, Mr Sam Nujoma, claimed that 'SWAPO never fights inside Angola, it fights within Namibia'. At the same time he pledged to continue the war, regardless of the disengagement or cease-fire agreement between South Africa and Angola.[19] In any case, whatever SWAPO's public position, it was assumed that the frontline states, particularly Angola and Zambia, would put pressure on SWAPO to prevent it from wrecking the Agreement.

However, within less than two weeks of the signing of the Agreement a problem arose between the South African and Angolan Governments over the South African claims that SWAPO had begun an infiltration of 800 men into northern Namibia. The South African Government claimed that these SWAPO activities were contrary to the Lusaka Agreement and at an urgent meeting of the JMC the Angolan delegation was reported to have undertaken to consider concrete ways of carrying out the principles of the Agreement.[20] President Kenneth Kaunda of Zambia called for patience from South Africa and asked the South African authorities to give the Angolans all the information about the movement of SWAPO guerrillas. He said: 'All of us working together can, through persuasion and other measures that are non-confrontational, bring this under control. We must not resort to attack and counter-attack.'[21]

This incident, which did not lead to the breakdown of the Agreement as some expected it would do, served to illustrate both the problem of SWAPO's position (as a non-signatory of the Agreement) and the strong desire of the Governments directly concerned (Angolan, South African, Zambian and American) that the Agreement should work. While the question of SWAPO's presence in the area during the withdrawal of the South African forces to the south continued to pose a problem, the Agreement did not collapse and the difficulties associated with its implementation were dealt with realistically. In fact, it is surprising that it was ever expected that the Angolans, or even the Angolans and the South Africans together, would be able to keep SWAPO forces out of the area entirely. As a South African official source is reported to have said: 'You mustn't forget we are not operating in a block of streets. It is a vast area and to find the SWAPO troops is like searching for a needle in a haystack.'[22]

The result was that it took over 14 months for the JMC to complete its work. It was not until 17 April 1985 that the last contingents of South African troops were finally withdrawn across the border into Namibia, in accordance with the Lusaka Agreement. The JMC was dissolved a month later, having completed its work, although it was agreed that contact between South African and Angolan officers on either side of the border should be maintained.

The delay in the implementation of the Lusaka Agreement was unfortunate, particularly because the momentum behind improving the relations between South Africa and Angola was lost. Therefore, the Agreement did not adequately serve the purpose intended by the Americans at least, namely that a basis of trust which would advance the negotiation process towards the withdrawal of Cuban troops from Angola and the independence of Namibia should be laid. During 1984 and early 1985, proposals and counter-proposals on the Cuban issue were made by Angola and South Africa, with American mediation. However, so far the positions of the two parties appear to have remained far apart. Moreover, the related question of Unita's role remains in the background as a vital factor yet to be dealt with.

The incident in the northern Angolan enclave of Cabinda on 22 May 1985, in which two South African military personnel were killed and one captured by Angolan forces, complicated the negotiations still further. It resulted in a considerable setback in relations between South Africa and Angola and in a flood of international criticism of the South African Government. Among the strong critics was the United States Government and the incident marked the beginning of a deterioration in relations between the Reagan Administration and the South African Government which was aggravated by domestic pressures on the former and by subsequent developments in Southern Africa relating to Namibia and Botswana, which will be dealt with further below.

The official Angolan version of this incident is that the South Africans' mission was to sabotage the oil refinery run by the American company, Gulf Oil, whose operations in Angola provide a major portion of the Angolan Government's revenue. This version was corroborated by the statement of the captured South African at a press conference in Luanda. The South African explanation, on the other hand, is that the South African group was there on an intelligence-gathering mission in connection with the existence of ANC training bases and official spokesmen for South Africa have admitted and defended, on the grounds of security, the presence of other South African units in Angola for the same purpose. It has been specifically denied that there was any intention of sabotaging the Gulf Oil refinery or any other installation. The right to operate in Angola for intelligence purposes has been defended on the grounds that South African and Namibian security is involved and the Government maintained that the Angolan Government has been warned many times not to allow the establishment of ANC bases on its territory.

Given the nature of these covert activities and the lack of adequate reliable information, it is difficult to come to an objective conclusion regarding this incident. But, whatever the truth, there is no doubt that internationally the Angolan version has been widely accepted and that South African credibility has been negatively affected. The result is that, for the time being at least, South African/Angolan relations have again taken a turn for the worse, in spite of the hopeful expectations aroused by the Lusaka Agreement. This deterioration was reflected in the Security Council debates on the Namibian issue and the Cabinda incident in June. Judging by the rhetoric from both sides in these debates, the relationship has again become confrontational, which further reduces the chances of any early agreement on the withdrawal of Cuban forces and independence for Namibia.

South West Africa/Namibia

In the meantime, Namibia has moved no nearer to internationally acceptable independence than it was two years ago. However, this two-year period has culminated in a significiant change in the internal administration of the territory. Over the past ten years the South African Government has promoted several attempts to put together an internal political force, comprising parties and ethnic group representatives, as a counter to SWAPO. This began with the Turnhalle Conference in 1975 and the internal elections in December 1978. The last attempt ended with the dissolution of the National Assembly in January 1983. A State Council with appointed members was envisaged, but never met because of lack of agreement among those who were to be invited to sit on the Council. Instead, a Multi-Party Conference (MPC) was formed in November 1983 on the initiative of several movements and parties in the territory, including the Democratic Turnhalle Alliance (DTA) and the National Party of South West Africa, as well as parties not previously involved such as SWANU and the SWAPO Democrats. SWAPO was invited to join, but refused. In January 1984 the MPC issued a statement of intent committing the parties involved to work out a political and constitutional system acceptable to the people as a whole, which would fit into the framework set out by South Africa and the Western Contact Group. Then, in February 1984, the MPC issued a declaration of basic principles and in April came to agreement on a Charter of Fundamental Rights and Objectives. But it was not until March 1985 that it was eventually agreed to ask the South African Government to transfer powers to a transitional government to be formed by the members of the MPC.

This Transitional Government was formed on 17 June and legislative and executive powers were transferred to it by proclamation of the South African Government, whilst external defence and foreign affairs were reserved to South Africa. In addition to its responsibility for governing South West Africa/Nambia, over the next two years the Transitional Government will undertake the drafting of a Constitution for an independent Namibia.

The South African Government has stated categorically that the creation of the Transitional Government does not mean that it has given up its commitment to seek an international agreement for independence. But there have been strong hints that if at the end of these two years the Cubans have not left Angola and the necessary conditions for the implementation of Security Council Resolution 435 have not been met, another solution will have to be found. In a speech on the occasion of the inauguration of the new legislative and executive authorities for SWA/Namibia on 17 June, the State President, Mr PW Botha, said: 'The fact that South West Africa has not yet acceded to independence may be ascribed to the deviations by the United Nations and SWAPO from the original Contact Group proposal, to the United Nations' continuing bias in favour of SWAPO and to the continuing threat posed by the presence of more than 30 000 Cuban troops in Angola.' After explaining that the establishment of this new government was 'simply a stage on the road of South West Africa's constitutional development and not its culmination' and that it should be seen as 'an interim mechanism for the internal administration of the territory pending agreement on an internationally acceptable independence', Mr Botha continued:

For as long as there is a possibility that the present international negotiations hold any realistic prospect of bringing about the genuine withdrawal of Cuban forces from Angola, the South African Government will not act in a manner irreconcilable with the international settlement plan. However, the people of South West Africa, including SWAPO, cannot wait indefinitely for a breakthrough on the withdrawal of the Cubans from Angola. Should it eventually become evident, after all avenues have been thoroughly explored, that there is no realistic prospect of attaining this goal, all the parties most intimately affected by the present negotiations will obviously have to reconsider how internationally acceptable independence may best be attained in the light of prevailing circumstances.[23]

Not surprisingly, the establishment of the Transitional Government has been condemned by the United Nations Security Council and the United States and other members of the Western Contact Group have also strongly criticised the move as being, at best, 'unhelpful'. They see this as a unilateral move by South Africa which will complicate international negotiations and put Namibia on a different road to independence, without participation by SWAPO and without international acceptance.

It is clear that although the South African Government has been committed in principle to Security Council Resolution 435 since 1978, it is not enthusiastic about this plan for independence, which includes the withdrawal of South African forces and an election for a constituent assembly, monitored by a United Nations group. Moreover, most parties in the Multi-Party Conference (and now in the Transitional Government) are not in favour of the UN plan and would strongly prefer that a constitution was drafted and accepted before any election and independence. Such a process is unacceptable to SWAPO, which maintains that there must be no deviation in this regard from the 435 plan, which provides for the drafting of the Constitution after the UN-monitored election. Thus, SWAPO would hope to gain a majority in the constituent assembly and have a decisive say in drafting the independence Constitution. It is interesting to note that in the case of Zimbabwe, the independence Constitution was drawn up and accepted at Lancaster House before the elections in April 1980, which were won by Mr Robert Mugabe's party. MPC leaders have used this example to reinforce their own arguments.

While the South African Government no doubt sympathises with the views of the MPC, it is well aware that any move which constitutes a unilateral declaration of independence will simply mean a continuation and even intensification of the international dispute over Namibia and that there will be strong opposition from the Western powers too. Therefore, the

Transitional Government will be encouraged to seek internal and external support for its view, including support in Africa in particular, in the hope that its success will demonstrate that there is a viable alternative to the plan laid down under Resolution 435.

The Government has already made attempts to explore the possibilities of a settlement which would be supported within Southern Africa and which would, in effect, bypass Resolution 435. After the release on 1 March 1984 of Mr Herman Toivo ja Toivo, a founder of SWAPO who had been in prison for 16 years, Foreign Minister Botha proposed a regional peace conference to be attended by governments and parties directly concerned in Southern Africa, including SWAPO, the internal Namibian parties and Unita. This proposal was not acceptable to Angola or SWAPO; apart from any other reason, the inclusion of Unita would legitimise its position in Angola and acknowledge the link between the Angolan and Namibian issues. The United States Administration was also opposed to the proposal, which it perceived as an obstacle to its own step-by-step negotiations. Instead, later in March, a conference between SWAPO and the MPC, which was jointly chaired by the Administrator-General of SWA/Namibia and President Kenneth Kaunda, was held in Lusaka, Zambia. The SWAPO delegation was joined by the representatives of several internal political parties which had not joined the MPC. However, no agreement was reached, not even on a final communiqué.

In July 1984 a meeting between the Administrator-General and SWAPO President Sam Nujoma was held on the Cape Verde Islands. These were the first direct talks between SWAPO and the South African Government, but again no compromise agreement was possible. SWAPO insisted that it would only agree to stop its 'armed struggle' if South Africa agreed to the immediate implementation of the UN settlement plan. Although these initiatives aimed at effecting some form of reconciliation between SWAPO and the internal groups involved in the MPC have failed, the door has been left open for SWAPO participation. However, it is highly unlikely that this will occur, as it would mean that SWAPO would have to play a relatively minor role as only one of many parties and it regards itself as 'the authentic representative' of the people (and has been so designated by the UN General Assembly). In any case, no doubt the South African Government hopes that if the new Transitional Government in Namibia is successful, there will be a reduction in popular support for SWAPO, which has already had its military activities severely curtailed. As a result, it is hoped, a weakened SWAPO — or at least some of its leaders — will see the necessity of taking part in the political developments within Namibia.

By opening up this alternative option, in effect the South African Government is pursuing what has often been termed its 'two-track' policy in Namibia, i.e. an internal and an external course simultaneously. So far it has managed to maintain the external track of international and regional negotiations, at the same time experimenting with forms of internal government which could be relied on should a dead-end be reached in international negotiations.

It is also important to recognise that Namibia is not dealt with as an issue on its own; the South African Government has increasingly come to view it in a regional context. The indications are that the South African Government wishes to see this issue settled as part of a regional settlement involving Angola and Botswana, which assures stability in the region and takes into account not only the security needs of Namibia, but in particular the security and political interests of South Africa itself.

RELATIONS WITH THE UNITED STATES

The above discussion of certain key developments in the relations between South Africa and its neighbours has already indicated the central role which the United States has come to play in Southern Africa. This role has been increasing since 1976, when Dr Henry Kissinger, then Secretary of State in the Administration of President Ford, made an intensive diplomatic effort to resolve the Rhodesian conflict. His initiatives followed the Angolan war, the outcome of which, in his view, had been detrimental to the interests of the United States and favourable to the Soviet Union's ambitions. In the global context, he saw Southern Africa as an important region in which growing Soviet influence was challenging the interests of the United States and, in addition to Rhodesia, he began to pay closer attention to the unresolved Namibian dispute. But Dr Kissinger had limited time, for he went out of office after the defeat of President Ford by Mr Jimmy Carter at the end of 1976.

The Carter Administration continued to pay attention to Southern African issues. Although there was a shift in the American approach, with more account being taken of regional factors peculiar to Southern Africa and of South Africa's own domestic racial situation (following the severe unrest of 1976/77), the aim of countering Soviet influence was still an important element motivating the Carter Administration. During this period, the Americans co-ordinated their activities closely with those of their Western allies. Thus, on the Rhodesian issue they were supportive of the British in the negotiations which led to Lancaster House and Zimbabwe's independence in early 1980. A new initiative regarding Namibia began in 1977, with the United States and four other Western states (who were then members of the UN Security Council) forming the so-called Contact Group to negotiate with South Africa, SWAPO and the African frontline states. After the parties concerned had accepted the Contact Group's proposals for a Namibian independence settlement and the UN Security Council had endorsed the plan in Resolution 435 (September 1978), the Group continued what became the much more difficult task of obtaining agreement on the implementation of Resolution 435. By the end of the Carter Administration's four-year term of office, it was clear that a deadlock had been reached on the Namibian issue.

When the Reagan Administration came into office at the beginning of 1981, an even closer involvement in Southern African affairs developed with the appointment of Dr Chester Crocker as Assistant Secretary of State for Africa and the adoption of the policy of 'constructive engagement'. Since then, the United States has been acting independently to a greater extent in taking initiatives to achieve the aims of the policy, which are to reduce conflict generally and to bring greater stability and development to the Southern African region.

It is important to note that the constructive engagement policy was designed as a policy for the region as a whole and mention has already been made above of America's initiatives with regard to the Namibian and Angolan issues and of its active support of the Nkomati Accord between South Africa and Mozambique. But constructive engagement has also included support and encouragement (with some quiet pressure) for the process of substantive reform in South Africa and clear opposition to the use of violence to bring about change.

During President Reagan's first term of office, criticism of the policy of constructive engagement increased gradually within the United States and among Black groups within South Africa on the grounds that it was too supportive of the South African Government and was not achieving demonstrable progress in resolving the Namibian issue. On the latter issue, opposition groups in the United States were particularly critical of the link created between the Cuban military presence in Angola and the Namibian independence negotiations. Besides this criticism of constructive engage-ment, there was a growing anti-apartheid campaign in the United States which advocated the disinvestment of American companies in South Africa. This campaign was focused on state legislatures, city governments and universities, its aim being to obtain the disinvestment of the funds of these bodies from American companies doing business in South Africa as a means of pressure on them to withdraw from the Republic. At the Federal level there were also attempts, largely unsuccessful, to have legislation of a punitive nature adopted in the United States Congress.

However, since the re-election of President Reagan to a second term in November 1984, the attacks on his Administration's policy have taken on a new and greater intensity and the South African issue has moved much higher on the agenda of American concerns than ever before. Sustained attention to South Africa in the American media has also been much greater than during any previous period.

In attempting to answer the question why this intense concern with South Africa should have developed at this particular time, one obviously has to see it, to a considerable extent, as a response to disturbing events within South Africa since the middle of 1984 in particular, including Black opposition to the new Constitution, urban Black unrest, the tragic shootings at Uitenhage, etc. But the same intensity of concern and high level of activity regarding the South African question has not occurred in other Western countries (although there is a growing level of negative criticism in Europe, too) and therefore it is necessary to identify certain factors peculiar to the United States' approach to South Africa and the Southern African region generally. These factors can be seen both in terms of US domestic politics and in the context of American foreign policy.

Domestic political considerations account to a great degree for the active role being played by leaders of the Democratic Party with regard to legislation on South Africa in the Congress. Following their overwhelming defeat by Mr Reagan in the Presidential elections of November 1984 and given the resulting tensions within the Democratic Party, the South African issue has proved a useful one on which to present a largely united front against the President. Moreover, it is an issue which can be presented in simple moral terms in order to gain public support. In a similar way, Black leaders and groups have added their criticism of the Administration's policy towards South Africa to their attacks on President Reagan's domestic, social and economic policies, which they regard as insensitive to the needs of Black Americans.

Underlying the American attention to South Africa is the fact that any question of racial discrimination and conflict touches a sensitive nerve in American society. Their own experience of severe racial problems is a matter of recent memory and in some areas racial tensions are still fairly close to the surface. It is inevitable, therefore, that the racial issue singles out South Africa for special attention, even though infringements of human rights and political disorder may be much greater and more serious in many other countries in Africa and elsewhere.

Looked at from the point of view of American foreign policy, there are several other factors which serve to explain the current special interest in Southern Africa and South Africa in particular. Firstly, there is the fact that the United States is a global power with interests in many regions of the world. Southern Africa is regarded as a region of importance to the United States for economic and strategic reasons. Therefore, the United States sees any extension of the influence and power of its global adversary, the Soviet

Union, in the region as contrary to American interests and will seek to protect and advance its perceived interest in the region, as it does elsewhere, with or without the co-operation of the South African Government.

Secondly, it must be recognised that the question of human rights, or simply the moral position, has been a strong element in American foreign policy ever since the Revolution. The moral element is strongly mixed with pragmatic self-interest and it is sometimes stronger and closer to the surface, as during the Carter years, than at other times. Almost unavoidably, the South African issue lends itself to fairly simple definition in moral terms.

Thirdly, the Reagan Administration set itself rather ambitious goals — some would say that they were unrealistic and even unattainable — in its policy of constructive engagement, which sought to achieve the resolution of long-standing and deep-seated disputes and conflicts and the promotion of stability, co-operation and economic development in Southern Africa. Because the achievements have fallen so far short of these high aims, the policy has become an easy target for critics inside and outside the United States. Even though official spokesmen have acknowledged the limited leverage available to the United States to give effect to its policies in Southern Africa, the stated objectives of the policy (and, for that matter, the statements of the previous Administration) were bound to raise expectations which could not be fulfilled.

A fourth factor which has contributed to the intensification of the controversy over the South African issue has been the assertiveness of the US Congress in the field of foreign policy. Since Vietnam and Watergate, Congress has been taking stronger initiatives on foreign policy issues, thus limiting the freedom of action of the President and his Administration in the formulation and implementation of foreign policy (which traditionally, in terms of the American Constitution, has been primarily the responsibility of the Executive Branch of government). In recent times President Reagan has come up against Congress because of this policy towards Central America as well, but there can be few, if any, cases in American history where so many proposals for legislation have been made in Congress on a strictly foreign policy issue, as is now the case for South Africa. This onslaught on the Administration's policy of constructive engagement has come mainly from the Democratic Party, but many members of the President's own Republican Party have also been involved. Because of the fact that this foreign policy issue strikes a chord in American domestic politics, there is a stronger motivation than with many other foreign policy issues for politicians to take a position on it in Congress and thus gain political credit in their constituencies. It must be added that there is no credit to be gained by taking a contrary position on South African legislation; instead there is the great risk of being labelled 'pro-apartheid'.

At the time of writing some of the proposed legislation has passed through its initial stages in the House of Representatives and the Senate and it is probable that legislation with mild sanctions against South Africa will be passed by the Congress in 1985. The question is whether the President will agree to sign it, or decide to veto it in the belief that it will undercut his policy. To date, all statements by the Administration indicate that the policy of constructive engagement will be retained in its essentials, but clearly adaptations are being made to take into account the domestic pressures and events in Southern Africa. A more critical attitude has already been adopted in public towards the South African Government and the recall of the American Ambassador to South Africa for consultations after the military raid on ANC targets in Gaborone, Botswana on June 14 is a clear sign that the US Government sees the need to demonstrate its displeasure, at least, with certain South African actions.

The South African Government's response to the growing pressures from the United States and to the recent deterioration in relations with the Reagan Administration has been mixed. There does not seem to be a clear co-ordinated response, but rather a tendency to react to developments in different ways. On one hand, there have been clear signs of concern over the implications of disinvestment and sanctions for South Africa should they succeed and recognition of the importance of continued economic and political links with the United States. Every effort has been made to present the Government's reform initiatives and the legislative reforms adopted in the first session of the new Parliament to the American public, Congress and Administration as arguments against sanctions and disinvestment. In this sense, the American pressures and the desire to help the American Administration to maintain its policy of constructive engagement have probably served to advance the reform process. In other words, the threat of drastic action, such as sanctions, has had some positive effect. On the other hand, there are now indications of a reaction and of resistance building up in Government circles and the White electorate in general to what is seen as excessive American interference in South Africa's domestic affairs. This reaction, should it develop further, may well have a negative and counter-productive effect on the reform process and greatly reduce the influence built up by the Reagan Administration through its policy of constructive engagement.

The South African Government's reluctance to bow to overt American pressures has been clearly demonstrated recently in its regional policy.

While the Government has co-operated with the United States in several initiatives to bring greater stability to Southern Africa, the Lusaka Agreement and the Nkomati Accord of 1984 being notable examples, it is clear that when the Government considers that its own interests demand a different approach, it goes ahead with little regard for contrary American views. The Cabinda incident in Angola, the Botswana raid and the inauguration of the Transitional Government in SWA/Namibia are illustrations of this tough and independent external policy in the Southern African region.

The indications in mid-1985 are that a critical stage is being reached in relations between the United States and South Africa and that attitudes are hardening on both sides. However, given the importance for the Republic of its links with the United States and the recognition of the dangers of international isolation from the West, as well as the American desire to protect and promote its interests in Southern Africa, it is unlikely that either side will allow a serious and lasting disruption of the relationship to occur.

CONCLUSION: THE DEVELOPMENT OF SOUTH AFRICAN REGIONAL POLICY

It is not possible to discuss here in any detail the background to South Africa's current regional policy, but one may recall that there have been various stages in the development of this policy in response to the changes in Southern Africa over the past two decades. From the mid-1960s, as the immediate neighbour states of Botswana, Lesotho and Swaziland, all closely tied to South Africa, moved to independence, Dr Verwoerd's Government made clear its willingness to accept their independence and to co-exist with them as sovereign states. This realistic acceptance of the first products of the rapidly spreading movement of African nationalism and independence constituted a change from the Government's former policy, which had been to seek the incorporation of these three territories into South Africa and which was generally opposed to what was regarded as the over-hasty capitulation of the colonial powers in Africa. This willingness to co-exist and even co-operate with Black-ruled states, in spite of strong political differences, has been maintained as a basic element of regional policy ever since, but with the important proviso that there should be no interference in South Africa's domestic affairs.

However, as the region continued to change there was growing concern, firstly regarding the potential political threat posed to South Africa's internal apartheid system by these manifestations of nationalism and independence. This perception of political threat was aggravated by the spread of a Marxist-inclined ideology and the growing links between countries in the region and the Soviet Union. Secondly, there emerged growing concern about a potential security threat and after the independence of Mozambique and Angola in 1975 these security concerns came to dominate South African official thinking on regional issues. The perception of threat was reinforced in 1980 by Zimbabwe's independence, which was seen as completing the band of hostile states around South Africa.

In the mid-1970s, the Government of Prime Minister John Vorster attempted to promote a policy of détente and negotiation, primarily with regard to the escalating Rhodesian conflict which was threatening to involve South Africa more directly. But from the Government's point of view this policy did not succeed, in halting the growth of the threat to South Africa's political and security interests. A different approach was adopted in the case of Angola, where South Africa undertook direct military intervention to try to prevent the MPLA, supported by Russia and Cuba, from taking absolute power instead of sharing it with the two other liberation movements, the FNLA and Unita. That policy did not succeed either and South Africa was forced to withdraw from Angola for international political reasons.

However, the Angolan war proved to be the precursor of what was to become a major element of regional policy after Mr PW Botha became Prime Minister in 1978, namely the use of military force, when this was considered necessary, as a means of protecting and asserting South African regional interests, particularly security interests. By 1983, various illustrations of this element of South African regional policy, referred to earlier in the chapter, had demonstrated that international reaction would not deter the South African Government from using its military strength in the region, particularly to counter threats from the ANC, which was becoming more active with sabotage attacks within South Africa and from SWAPO, which was operating in South West Africa/Namibia from Angola.

As an extension of this military element in regional policy, the South African Government became involved in providing various forms of support to insurgent movements within neighbouring countries as a means of further pressure on the relevant governments. The two main instances, which were dealt with earlier in this chapter, were Renamo in Mozambique (more or less from the time of Zimbabwe's independence in 1980) and Unita in Angola (probably from the time of the 1975 war). In addition, there have been allegations of South African support for dissident movements in Zimbabwe and Lesotho. Forms of economic pressure were added to this policy, notably in Zimbabwe and Lesotho and as a result accusations that the South African Government was engaged in a policy of destabilising the region were being voiced strongly from many quarters by 1983.

This widely held impression of an aggressive, hardline posture completely overshadowed South African statements about the Government's willingness to co-exist peacefully and to co-operate economically with its neighbours in the region. Little notice was taken of any diplomatic efforts and negotiations, for instance with Angola and Mozambique. Then, at the beginning of 1984, the conclusion of the Lusaka Agreement and the Nkomati Accord caused considerable surprise and they were interpreted as demonstrating the reversal of South African regional policy, a move away from the use of force towards negotiation and co-operation. While commentators recognised that, to a large extent, the Nkomati Accord was the product of South African military pressures and relative economic strength coupled with Mozambique's desperate economic state and security situation, there was a tendency for them to assume that, having achieved its objective, the South African Government would sheath its sword and pursue the more internationally acceptable path of negotiation and compromise. It was also assumed that, although military influence had previously been dominant in Government decisions, the diplomatic approach, as represented by the Foreign Minister and his Department, had now asserted itself in regional policy.

This perception of a significant change in policy may have been strengthened by the impression given that the South African agreements with Angola and Mozambique were largely the result of the American policy of constructive engagement. As discussed above, this policy has been directed at ending confrontation and conflict and at promoting negotiated settlements and regional stability. It has been consistently opposed to any South African military action against its neighbours. There is no doubt that American influence played an important role in persuading South Africa to pursue the negotiations which led to the two agreements of early 1984, but this does not mean that the South African Government gave up the military option because of American disapproval. It never changed its position on the overriding importance of security considerations, nor its belief that the use or threat of military action was a decisive factor in Mozambique and Angola's willingness to conclude the agreements. In fact, it was even claimed that the agreements proved the success of South Africa's regional policy, with its elements of both force and negotiation, rather than simply the success of American diplomacy.

The perception that policy had changed to exclude the use of force underestimated the continued significance of the security factor in South African thinking. In fact, it has been strengthened even more by the growing Black unrest since mid-1984. As a result, the Botswana raid caused considerable surprise and consternation in many quarters, particularly in the West. The extent to which the Reagan Administration believed that

South African regional policy had changed since the Nkomati Accord was reflected in the American reaction to the Botswana raid, including the comment by Dr Chester Crocker that there is now 'a new pattern of negative decisions incompatible with American goals'.[24]

With regard to Dr Crocker's comment, it is worth recalling the statement made by Mr PW Botha on 31 August 1984 on the eve of his becoming State President under the new Constitution, when he addressed himself to the role of the Super Powers in Southern Africa. He acknowledged that they had 'justifiable interests' in the region as global powers and said that South Africa would not exert itself against such interests, provided that 'they in turn would not endanger South Africa's essential regional interests'. He continued:

> However, should the super power involvement be conducted in a manner which the RSA perceives as threatening these essential regional interests . . . then the RSA will continue to safeguard and advance its essential and legitimate interests by all means at its disposal.[25]

South African regional policy was clarified further in various official statements made in June 1985 following events (the Cabinda incident, the Botswana raid and the establishment of the Transitional Government in Namibia) which caused strongly critical international reaction. In particular, State President PW Botha annunciated five ground rules which the Government believes all countries in the region must accept if relations are to be normalised. In a statement to Parliament on 19 June, the State President summarised these ground rules. First he defended the right of the Government to take action against ANC 'terrorists' in Botswana and concluded: 'It is and remains the responsibility of each government to ensure the security of its peoples. My Government will not abdicate this responsibility.' He continued:

> On behalf of the South African Government I once again offer to all our neighbours a hand of friendship and a readiness to come to an understanding on the basis of certain ground rules which in my opinion ought to form the guidelines for regulating and normalising our relations. These ground rules include an unqualified prohibition on support for cross-border violence or the planning of such violence; the removal of foreign forces from the region; the peaceful resolution of disputes; regional co-operation in meeting common challenges; and toleration of the different socio-economic and political systems within our region.[26]

From this and many other Government statements it can be concluded that the goal of South African policy is the achievement of a co-operative regional arrangement which allows for the co-existence of differing independent political systems, extensive economic interchange between them, but no interference by any state in the domestic affairs of another. However, if there is to be stability this co-operative dispensation must be based, in the Government's view, on a recognition of South Africa's dominant role as the major regional power and on respect for South Africa's interests. As Foreign Minister Botha said in August 1984 in a typical statement on this theme: 'The fact of the matter is that we are a regional power in Southern Africa . . . Any country wishing to deal with us will have to take this reality, as well as our reasonable concerns, into account.'[27] Earlier, in February 1984, Prime Minister PW Botha, arguing in Parliament in favour of co-operative relations in the region, said: 'South Africa is a major force in the region and has no intention of apologising for its economic, industrial and military strength.'[28]

In the concluding section of this chapter an attempt has been made to clarify the nature of South African regional policy, particularly as it has emerged over the past two years. This has not been intended as a comprehensive analysis of the making and implementation of policy and few critical viewpoints have been included. However, one must add, finally, that several objective questions could be raised about this policy and its implications. These include questions about the long-term effects on attitudes to South Africa and thus on regional relationships, about the use of force in neighbouring countries and about the effects on the attitudes of South Africa's own Black population. Further, there is the question whether calculations are made of other potential costs such as damage to wider international and political relations and whether these are balanced against the advantages gained in terms of internal security.

There is also the matter, which is now being raised, of the credibility of South African negotiators. In other words, have other parties in negotiations, including the Americans, been misled at all about South African intentions and has the Government, in effect, been saying one thing and doing another in some cases? The impression that this may have happened may simply be the result of wishful thinking by other parties at the time, particularly the Americans (who seem to be so surprised by recent events). But it is a legitimate question to ask about the practice of all parties in negotiations on bilateral relations or on the Namibian issue, because misunderstanding of the intentions of others can lead to serious miscalculations in policy making. Moreover, if there is to be any hope of negotiations leading to fruitful results, the creation of a basis of trust between the parties involved is of fundamental importance. In South Africa's case this applies as much to relations with its neighbours as it does to relations within the country, where attempts are being made to settle deep-seated differences and conflict through a process of negotiation.

NOTES

1 For full text of Nkomati Accord, see *Southern Africa Record* (SAIIA), no. 35, April 1984, pp. 6-10.
2 *The Economist* (London), 24 March 1984, p. 13.
3 *Southern Africa Record* (SAIIA), no. 1, March 1975, p. 5.
4 *Sunday Express*, 6 January 1985.
5 *The Star*, 8 January 1985.
6 *Beeld*, 18 January 1985.
7 *Financial Times* (London), 1 February 1985.
8 *Financial Times* (London), 1 February 1985.
9 From text of communiqué as supplied by Department of Foreign Affairs, Pretoria.
10 *Sunday Express*, 17 March 1985.
11 *Financial Mail*, 22 March 1985.
12 *Rand Daily Mail*, 16 March 1985.
13 *The Citizen*, 30 March 1985.
14 *The Citizen*, 21 March 1985.
15 *The Citizen*, 15 May 1985.
16 *Southern Africa Record*. (SAIIA), no. 36, August 1984, pp. 35 and 36.
17 *Pretoria News*, 18 February 1984.
18 *The Star*, 25 February 1984.
19 *Pretoria News*, 18 February 1984.
20 *Beeld*, 27 February 1984.
21 *The Star*, 25 February 1984.
22 *Sunday Tribune*, 26 February 1984.
23 From text of Windhoek speech on 17 June 1985, made available by State President's Office.
24 *Business Day*, 27 June 1985.
25 Address by the Hon. PW Botha, Johannesburg: SAIIA (Occasional Paper), September 1984, p. 4.
26 A long extract from the State President's speech to Parliament, including these quotations, was reproduced in a letter from the South African Foreign Minister, the Hon. RF Botha, to the Minister of External Affairs of Botswana, the Hon. GKT Chiepe, on 20 June 1985. Text made available by Department of Foreign Affairs.
27 *Rand Daily Mail*, 14 August 1984.
28 South Africa (Republic). Parliament, House of Assembly Debates, no. 1, 1984, col no. 124.

18 The federal option

JA du Pisanie and L Kritzinger

The State President of the Republic of South Africa made some very important statements on the future direction of change in South Africa (including Transkei, Bophuthatswana, Venda and Ciskei) on 30 September 1985. He told the National Party Congress at Port Elizabeth that all groups and communities in the RSA should receive representation at the highest level, without domination of one another (Botha 1985: 46) and that the National Party rejects discrimination on the basis of race, ethnic connection and origin (ibid: 7, 33 and 54). The self-governing national states form part of the RSA, while the Government of the RSA accepts that co-operation with Transkei, Bophuthatswana, Venda and Ciskei can take place within a common framework (ibid: 44).

Given the rejection of discrimination on the basis of race, ethnic connection and origin, it follows logically that the groups and communities to which the State President referred will no longer be defined by ascription in statutes, but will be formed by voluntary association.

Because of the above, it is assumed in this chapter that statutory discrimination by race has to be replaced by free association among individuals and that all citizens will be represented at all levels of government in the Republic of South Africa. It is accepted throughout that Transkei, Bophuthatswana, Venda and/or Ciskei could once again become part of a single system of government in the original areas of the RSA. Given these assumptions, the chapter addresses the question of how different minority groups — to be formed by free association — can be protected against domination by other groups. It is contended that a government structure built on federal principles can best achieve this goal.

THE NATURE OF FEDERALISM[1]

Political systems can be classified into two families based on two different underlying philosophies. The philosophy underlying unitary systems of government presumes that there must be some single, ultimate centre of

443

authority in any society — the central government. Such a government typically holds the final legislative and executive power. While the judicial power may be effectively separated from these, no legislation by the central government — not even legislation altering the national constitution — is subject to revision by a court of law. In such a system there can be no competing sovereign body. In fact, the central government has unrestricted monopoly of power. The two essential qualities of a unitary state may be said to be the supremacy of the central parliament and the absence of subsidiary sovereign bodies. The practical implication of this is that any group which has legitimately captured the central and single source of authority can legitimately dominate the whole society by exercising ultimate control over each and every subnational unit of government in the whole country.

The alternative philosophy accepts that the government sector may be *polycentric* in structure, with several concurrent and competing sources of power, each limited to particular fields of competence by a constitution or social contract which is enforceable by the courts of law. The relevant fields of competence may be defined in terms of functions, geographical areas and/or groups of persons, while legislative, executive and judicial powers would ideally be separated at all levels of government. The two essential qualities of a federal state may be said to be the absence of a single supreme body and divided sovereignty. The practical implication of this is that no single group would be able to dominate the whole society unless it captured each and every unit of government in the whole country. This is the *federal alternative*.

The federal alternative finds its intellectual origins in the teachings of Judaeo-Christian theology, Greek philosophy and Roman law (Ostrom 1983: 128). Perhaps the most basic principles upon which federalism is built is that the individual is 'the best and sole judge of his own private interest, and that society has no right to control a man's actions unless they are prejudicial to the common weal or unless the common weal demands his help' (De Tocqueville 1945: 67, originally published in 1835). This maxim follows from the belief that the individual 'is free, and responsible to God alone, for all that concerns himself' (loc cit).

The principle of *individual freedom* of decision making already implies that all forms of co-operation among individuals will necessarily flow from agreements, contracts or covenants among individuals. In fact, the term 'federal' is derived from the Latin term 'foedus', meaning to covenant (Ostrom 1983: 129; Kriek 1978: 189). De Tocqueville (loc cit) eloquently explained the relationship between the individual and government 150 years ago: 'In the nations by which the sovereignty of the people is recognised, every individual has an equal share of power and participates equally in the government of the state. Why then, does he obey society, and what are the natural limits of this obedience? Every individual is always supposed to be as well informed, as virtuous, and as strong as any of his fellow citizens. He obeys society, not because he is inferior to those who conduct it or because he is less capable than any other of governing himself, but because he acknowledges the utility of an association with his fellow men and he knows that no such association can exist without a regulating force.'

Communities established by means of *covenants or social contracts* among individuals can themselves enter into contracts with one another to form a community of communities. In the same sense that the freedom and different personalities of individual persons can be preserved within a community, the autonomy and diversity of individual communities can be preserved within a community of communities.

Ostrom (1983: 127) points out a further principle underlying the covenantal concept of community: 'Fashioning a community of communities which allows for autonomy and diversity depends, in some fundamental sense, upon a *shared conception of right*. Human societies that aspire to be self-governing can only be constituted in relation to moral principles of self respect and mutual respect for one another . . . People must share some fundamental understanding about principles for the right ordering of human relationships; and, as Alexis de Tocqueville has put it, some basic ideal of right. There can be no shared communities of interest unless those diverse interests comprising such a community possess a shared idea of right as it is relevant to political experience' (our emphasis).

Needless to say, definitions of federalism abound in political science literature. One of the weakest definitions is that of Riker (1964: 11), which has only three elements, namely that a federal state is one in which (1) at least two levels of government exist; (2) each government level has at least one area of functional jurisdiction in which it is autonomous; and (3) a guarantee exists that each government can act autonomously in its own sphere of jurisdiction (Kriek 1978: 190).

Federalism is a logical alternative when different communities have common interests as well as interests which they regard as their own. Kriek (1978: 192) points out two basic preconditions for the existence of a federal state: Firstly, the communities involved must have a strong need to manage their common affairs collectively. Secondly, an equally strong need must exist to manage the own affairs of the communities separately. If the first need, resulting from centripetal forces, does not exist, no association will be established (or an existing association might crumble and eventually disappear). If the second need, flowing from centrifugal forces, does not exist, a centralised union rather than a federation will be established.

445

In order to accommodate both needs in a federation, those affairs which are common to all the federating units may be entrusted to the national government, while matters required for the maintenance of an own identity will be left to the individual units. This means that *the very sovereignty of the state will be divided*. The national government will be sovereign in respect of the matters entrusted to it and the federating units will be sovereign in their areas of jurisdiction (*ibid*: 191).

These fields of sovereignty are agreed to in *a written constitution or social contract* between the federating units. In the same way that a buyer and seller may be irrevocably bound to a contract between them, so the different units of government are irrevocably bound to the constitution and just as private persons entering into a contract have to recognise the arbitration of the courts when disputes arise, so the different units of government must subject themselves to an objective arbiter, usually the Supreme Court. The arbiter has the *jurisdiction to test the decisions and legislation of the federal government as well as the federating units against the constitution* and to declare them null and void should they be in conflict with the constitution. In unitary systems such as the Republic of South Africa, the courts may declare legislation null and void only if the government officials failed to follow the *procedure* laid down in the constitution. They have no jurisdiction to rule on the *contents* of the legislation, except when the constitution explicitly provides for such control by the Supreme Court, as in the case of the entrenchment of the two official languages in the Constitution of the Republic of South Africa.

It follows from the above that another principle of federalism is that *the federating units have the right of concurrence in the process of amending the national constitution*. The procedure for such amendment is one of the most important elements of the contract between the federating units. Changes in the constitution need not necessarily require the consent of each and every federating unit. Amendments may, for instance, require the consent of the national government plus the consent of the governments of a stated number or a certain proportion of the federating units. A constitution is established through processes of constitutional decision making which are exercised by the people and are *unalterable* by a government acting upon its own prerogative. The basic foundation of republican or democratic self-government therefore depends upon citizens reserving unto themselves the ultimate authority of constitutional decision making. As long as a people can reserve prerogatives of constitutional decision making to themselves and can enforce the terms of constitutional law, they retain ultimate authority to modify and alter the terms and conditions of government.

The federating units can have *a territorial or a corporate base* (or a

446

combination of both). Their jurisdiction may be defined in terms of geographical areas so that they will have authority over all persons within the geographical area. A corporate base means that the jurisdiction of the federating units is defined in terms of a particular group of persons, irrespective of where they may happen to be in geographic space.

Corporate federations are often referred to as consociations. According to Lijphart (in Rhoodie 1980: 29-41), this is not necessarily the case. Consociations occur in plural societies and rest on four principles, all of which deviate from the Westminster model of majority rule. The two most important, complementary principles are *grand coalition* and *segmental autonomy*. Grand coalition means that the political leaders of all the segments of a plural society govern the country jointly and may also be called the principle of power sharing. The principle of segmental autonomy means that decision making authority is delegated to the separate segments to the maximum possible extent. The idea is that each segment rules itself in all matters that are not of common interest and therefore they are not decided upon jointly by the segments' leaders. The third consociational principle is the mutual or minority veto, which may be either a formal of an informal rule. The purpose of this is to provide a guarantee that no segment can be outvoted on the central political level when its vital interests are at stake. The fourth principle is proportionality of political representation, civil service appointments and the allocation of public funds. When the segments are very unequal in size, small minorities may be afforded special protection by means of overrepresentation or parity of representation (*ibid*: 29-30).

From the above it is clear that a consociation need not necessarily conform to the covenantal concept of community and the underlying principles of individualism and a shared conception of right which form the basis of federalism, nor to the resulting principle of the ultimate authority of the constitution as interpreted by the courts. Likewise, corporate federations need not conform to the consociational principles of mutual or minority veto, proportionality in respect of civil service appointments and the allocation of public funds.

To people who have been brought up in a country with a unitary system of government, federations often seem disorderly. Federal systems necessarily consist of multiplicities of government units that have overlapping jurisdictions and that have to resort to contracting and other market-like means of co-ordination amongst themselves. This contrasts sharply with the seemingly neat, triangular structure of command in a unitary system (Ostrom 1983: 146).

In the case of federal systems, order, like beauty, is in the eye of the beholder. A market system seems utterly disorderly. In fact, it took a philosopher of the stature of Adam Smith to discern order in the market place. Similarly, a federal system possesses an order which may not be conspicuous, but which cannot be denied.

Economists have devised concepts and methods to discern and analyse market structure, conduct and performance in the private sector. Similar concepts and methods are being devised to discern and analyse the structure, conduct and performance of public-sector industries such as the police industry, the water industry, the education industry, the welfare industry and the health industry (Ostrom 1983: 146-7).

A point related to the problem of order is the idea that subnational authorities necessarily have to be controlled from above. Many South Africans simply accept that local authorities have to be controlled by the provincial councils or the central government and the provincial councils by the central government. This idea is foreign to federations. Each authority in a federal system is sovereign in respect of its functions and is not controlled from above, but from below. It is *controlled by its own citizens* through their contact with representatives, through the ballot box and through court action.

This book focuses on change in South Africa. In this context it is important to point out that federalism should not be seen only as a static pattern of design characterised by a particular and precisely fixed division of powers between governmental levels. Federalism is also and perhaps primarily the process of federalising a political community, that is to say the process by which a number of separate political communities enter into arrangements for working out solutions, adopting joint policies and making joint decisions on joint problems and, conversely, also the process by which a unitary political community becomes differentiated into a federally organised whole. By their very nature, federal relations are fluctuating relations. Any federally organised community must therefore provide itself with instrumentalities for the recurrent revision of its pattern of design. For only thus can the shifting balance of common and disparate values, interests and beliefs be reflected effectively in more differentiated or more integrated relations. In short, we have federalism only if a set of political communities co-exist and interact as autonomous entities, united in a common order with an autonomy of its own (Friedrich 1968: 7-8).

Federalism refers to an evolutionary process, to the structures and patterns which the process creates and to the ideas and ideologies which it presupposes and generates. The flexibility of a federal structure can accommodate life as a process of reform and change referred to by the State President (Botha 1985: 29).

In conclusion, it should be pointed out that all the principles set out in the above are applicable to federations as well as to confederations. The most important difference between the two is that confederating units retain the right to withdraw from the confederation unilaterally, while federating units do not.

The question how these abstract principles may be applied to the reality of the South African situation is addressed in the rest of this chapter.

THE FEASIBILITY OF A FEDERAL OPTION IN SOUTH AFRICA

The degree to which South African society meets some of the preconditions for the success of federalism, as well as certain arguments against the federal option, are discussed briefly in this section.

Simultaneous need for self-determination and for joint decision making

The federal option will be taken only if two needs exist simultaneously in a society: the need for autonomous decision making in some spheres of life must exist among some or all segments of the population and the need for joint decision making in other spheres of life must exist among all the segments of the population (compare p. 4).

Probably the most important characteristic of the population of South Africa (i.e. the Republics of South Africa, Transkei, Bophuthatswana, Venda and Ciskei) is its *cultural plurality*. The large number of groups shown in table 18.1 testify to this. While the Black population is shown by major language groups (nine languages are distinguished), the Whites, Coloureds and Indians are shown as such. They, too, can be further disaggregated by major language groups. Whites and Coloureds mainly use Afrikaans and English, while about one third of the Indians use English as their home language and the rest use several Indian languages.

The cultural plurality of South African society indicates the existence of a need for autonomous decision making or self-determination in respect of culturally sensitive affairs on the part of most of the groups. In fact, White politics is dominated by arguments about ways of protecting their self-determination.

Each of the Black nations originally settled in a more or less geographically definable area; the Xhosa in the Eastern Cape, the Zulu in Natal, the South-Sotho in and around the highlands of the Malutis, the North-Sotho north of the Magalies mountains in the Transvaal and the Tswana in the Northern Cape and Western Transvaal. The territorial bases of the Sotho, Swazi and Tswana peoples were in fact politically split up by the decision of the British colonial office in the late 19th century to grant crown colony status to the chiefdoms of these nations in territories that did not fully embrace the whole area of settlement of all the tribes belonging to these nations.

The remarkable fact is that this geographic distribution of the Black population is still more or less intact (see table 18.1). Since the foundation of the Union of South Africa three quarters of a century ago, considerable migration of people from these 'homelands' has taken place, particularly to farms and towns in their vicinity, but also on a very large scale to the so-called PWV (Pretoria-Witwatersrand-Vereeniging) industrial metropole on the Transvaal Highveld and on a much smaller scale to the industrial metropole of the Cape Peninsula. The migration of Zulus to the Durban metropolitan area was equally heavy, if not more so than in the other cases, but like the migration of Xhosas to Port Elizabeth, this movement may be regarded as having taken place within the subregional base of the particular nation.

The Coloured and Indian populations of South Africa also have relatively clear geographic bases. The Coloureds are confined largely to the Cape Province and the PWV region and the Indians to Natal and the PWV region.

While the Whites have spread into all parts of the RSA, they have respected the national states as the exclusive domain of the Black nations. They tend to concentrate in the PWV region to a greater extent than any other group, but because of their minority status in the total population, they still form a minority in this region. In fact, the Whites do not form a majority in any sub-region of South Africa, save in White municipal areas. The same goes for the Indians.

It is clear that while the various ethnic groups in South Africa each have a relatively clear geographical base, some degree of overlap of the geographical areas where different groups are most frequently found, occur. This overlap is the result of economic interdependence among the various population groups. Different occupations are pursued by members of different groups in the same places of employment.

The concentration of culturally divergent people in the same geographical areas commenced at the time of the discovery of diamonds and gold and gained momentum during the Great Depression of the early thirties and especially in the process of industrialisation since the Second World War. The process of urbanisation took place mainly outside the national states.

About 27,8% of the urban Blacks outside national states were under the age of 15 in 1980. The comparable figure for their non-urban counterparts were 41,1% (RSA 1982b). These figures imply that many Blacks are living outside the national states on a permanent basis and that many Black children are born and brought up outside the statutory homelands.

Both the economic interdependence and the resulting overlap of areas of

Table 18.1 The geographic distribution of South Africa*, 1980

Population group	Transvaal		Cape		Natal		OFS		Kwazulu		Transkei		Lebowa		Bophuthat.		Ciskei		Gazankulu		Venda		Kangwane		Qwaqwa		Kwandebele		Total	
	'000	%	'000	%	'000	%	'000	%	'000	%	'000	%	'000	%	'000	%	'000	%	'000	%	'000	%	'000	%	'000	%	'000	%	'000	%
White	2 362	52,1	1 264	27,9	562	12,4	326	7,2	4	0,1	6	0,1	5	0,1	2	–	2	–	2	–	1	–	–	–	1	–	–	–	4 537	100,0
Coloured	228	8,7	2 226	85,0	91	3,5	56	2,1	3	0,1	7	0,3	2	0,1	–	–	6	0,2	1	–	–	–	–	–	–	–	–	–	2 620	100,0
Indian	116	14,1	32	3,9	665	80,7	–	–	7	0,8	2	0,2	1	0,1	–	–	1	0,1	–	–	–	–	–	–	–	–	–	–	824	100,0
Zulu	924	16,1	12	0,2	1 189	20,7	181	3,2	3 316	57,8	5	0,1	14	0,2	52	0,9	–	–	5	0,1	–	–	10	0,2	23	0,4	8	0,1	5 739	100,0
Xhosa	603	10,8	1 279	23,0	118	2,1	270	4,9	44	0,8	2 500	45,0	3	0,1	70	1,3	664	11,9	–	–	–	–	1	–	3	0,1	2	–	5 558	100,0
North-Sotho	847	34,6	7	0,3	3	0,1	13	0,5	2	0,1	1	–	1 406	57,4	99	4,0	–	–	46	1,9	4	0,2	2	0,1	1	–	19	0,8	2 449	100,0
Tswana	962	40,8	213	9,0	3	0,1	155	6,6	8	0,3	–	–	11	0,5	998	42,4	–	–	2	0,1	–	–	1	–	1	–	3	0,1	2 355	100,0
South-Sotho	632	33,2	40	2,1	27	1,4	874	45,0	21	1,1	101	5,3	11	0,6	61	3,2	4	0,2	2	0,1	–	–	1	–	125	6,6	5	0,3	1 904	100,0
Shangaan/Tsonga	390	35,2	1	0,1	5	0,4	10	0,9	3	0,3	–	–	121	10,9	103	9,3	–	–	440	39,7	10	0,9	21	1,9	1	0,1	5	0,4	1 109	100,0
Swazi	649	74,0	1	0,1	7	0,8	11	1,3	10	1,1	–	–	29	3,3	24	2,7	–	–	11	1,3	–	–	124	14,1	–	–	10	1,1	877	100,0
Venda	174	32,8	1	0,2	1	0,2	2	0,4	–	–	–	–	6	1,1	12	2,3	–	–	5	0,9	328	61,9	–	–	–	–	1	0,2	530	100,0
South-Ndebele	247	57,7	–	–	1	0,2	23	5,4	1	0,2	–	–	29	6,8	36	8,4	–	–	–	–	–	–	1	0,2	2	0,5	88	20,6	428	100,0
North-Ndebele	141	46,2	1	0,3	–	–	4	1,3	1	0,3	–	–	104	34,1	39	12,8	–	–	–	–	–	–	–	–	–	–	15	4,9	305	100,0
Other	75	58,6	14	10,9	5	3,9	6	4,7	1	0,8	2	1,6	6	4,7	15	11,7	–	–	1	0,8	2	1,6	1	0,8	–	–	–	–	128	100,0
Total	8 351	28,4	5 091	17,3	2 676	9,1	1 932	6,6	3 433	11,7	2 623	8,9	1 747	6,0	1 511	5,1	678	2,3	514	1,8	345	1,2	161	0,6	158	0,5	156	0,5	29 365	100,0

Header: Province (White areas only) or national state

* Republics of South Africa, Transkei, Bophuthatswana, Ciskei and Venda.
– less than 500, or less than 0,05%.
Totals sometimes do not tally, due to rounding.

Sources:
RSA. 1982. Central Statistical Service. *Population Census 80. Sample Tabulation. Geographic distribution of the population.* Report no. 02-80-01. Pretoria: Government Printer.
Republic of Transkei. Department of Trade, Industries and Tourism, Unpublished statistics.
Republic of Bophuthatswana. Department of Economic Affairs. Unpublished statistics.
Republic of Venda. Department of the President. Unpublished statistics.

residence of different cultural groups indicate the existence of common interests and the need for joint decision making on related public matters.

Costs associated with federalism

It is often claimed that federal systems of government are more expensive than unitary systems. This statement can have at least three different meanings. Firstly, it may be taken to mean that direct government expenditure is higher in federal than in unitary systems; secondly, that federal systems make greater total demands on the resources of the relevant society; and thirdly, that some average level of need satisfaction is lower in a federal than in a unitary system of government. Answering the first allegation is a purely empirical question which can be resolved fairly easily by a study of the government accounts of various countries. The second allegation, however, cannot be satisfactorily addressed by such a study and the third to an even lesser extent.

Political processes are supposed to articulate the demands of the relevant community for government services in the most efficient way. At least two categories of cost are associated with the process of political interaction which such articulation requires, viz political decision making costs and political external costs (Buchanan & Tullock 1962).

Political decision making costs consist of the opportunity costs of the resources that citizens invest in organisational activities by moving or not moving to more congenial jurisidictions, or signalling their contentment or discontentment in order to improve their welfare (by achieving a better trade-off between the public goods they receive and the taxes they pay for them). Included in the activities in which citizens engage when they participate in the political process are mobility — the act of moving from one jurisdiction to another — and signalling. Signalling is *inter alia* '(1) participating in efforts to influence the actions of lobbies and large pressure groups; (2) engaging in actions to influence politicians directly; (3) joining social movements; (4) regulating one's own private economic behaviour; (5) organising the private provision of public and non-private goods and (6) voting or the act of giving one's support to or withholding it from a candidate of a political party or, in very special cases, a policy' (Breton and Scott 1978: 32).

It is clear that few of these costs will be included in accounts of government expenditure. Furthermore, the costs are extremely difficult to quantify, because citizens do not always incur them by spending money. More often than not they take the form of lost production or consumption. Given the built-in protection of minority groups in federal systems and given a particular rule to reach a decision (e.g. simple majority), it is

452

probably reasonable to expect that decision-making costs are typically higher in federal than in unitary systems. However, these constitute only part of the costs of political interaction.

Investment in political participation by a citizen is not only a function of his own contentment with public policies and the benefits he derives from them, but also of expected contentment. The latter is the result of the effect of the migration of other citizens and of their signalling. Put differently, a citizen bears political external costs whenever these processes result in decisions that differ from his own preferences. These costs are probably even more difficult to measure than the costs of political decision making. It seems reasonable to expect, however, that they will increase with increasing cultural heterogeneity of the society and with a decreasing proportion of votes required to carry a motion. A unitary system based on the principles of one man one vote and of simple majority decisions would clearly bring about very high levels of political external costs for members of minority groups (at least in respect of decisions on culturally sensitive matters, on redistribution of income and wealth and on nationalisation of private property). In South African society these costs could exceed the increased decision making costs of a federal system by far. The adamant rejection of one man one vote in a unitary system by all the White political parties is a strong indication that most Whites in fact hold the view that this is the case.

The African experience

Sceptics argue that 'federations do not work in Africa' and to support their view they can refer to a number of failures in Central, East and North Africa. But when the reasons for these failures are studied, it transpires that the particular federal structures imposed failed precisely because they were imposed from above upon an unwilling populace in terms of the last wills and testaments of colonial powers, and not negotiated *inter vivos* by the domestic vested interests. There was no 'state-idea' — perhaps the single most crucial prerequisite for successful federation — on the part of the majority of the inhabitants.

At the same time, federal principles of government stood in the way of the totalitarian ambitions of the newly emergent domestic leaders. These post colonial leaders could justify their totalitarian ambitions in terms of ideals such as 'building one nation' or 'building a socialist order' — aims which appear to require a concentration of power at the centre. Whether these motives were genuine or not is not important. What is important is that these power-seeking leaders commanded enough support for their aims among the people to secure possession of the instruments of government.

453

In other words, the real alternative to federalism in Africa was not the Westminster system of parliamentary democracy. Nor was it a South African-style separation of political power in independent states within an economic union. The real alternative to federalism was totalitarian dictatorship. Insofar as people in Africa naturally applied and voiced federal ideas in the organisation of their social life at grass roots level, these tendencies were adamantly suppressed from above.

Are these experiences good reason to believe that federal structures will also fail in South Africa? On the contrary, precisely because there are such powerful political forces in South Africa which refuse to submit to totalitarian government, whether in the form of a majoritarian government in a unitary system or a dictatorship in a non-system, the federal alternative to them as the basic principle of government is far stronger in South Africa than anywhere else on this continent.

Federal principles have always applied to a host of the most important institutions in the social system of South Africa. In the field of labour relations, the system of industrial conciliation was quoted earlier as being typically federal. In sport, most governing bodies, including the South African Rugby Union, are federally constituted. So is the governing body of the Dutch Reformed Church. At least among Whites, the system of primary and secondary education has a strongly federal governing principle. Even the National Party is governed on federal principles.

Conclusion

The brief discussion of some of the preconditions for and arguments against federalism leads to the conclusion that a federal option is indeed feasible in South Africa. The present system of government in South Africa is, however, typically non-federal, save for the series of multilateral agreements that have come into being since the independence of Transkei in 1976. It is therefore legitimate to ask at this point 'How will South Africa get from here to there?' This question is addressed in the next section.

POSSIBLE IMPLEMENTATION OF FEDERALISM IN SOUTH AFRICA

In view of the above, expansion of democracy to include Blacks in such a way that the self-determination of all minority groups is guaranteed, requires prior or simultaneous implementation of a federal system in South Africa. If one agrees with the State President that new structures of government should be implemented through negotiation with the leaders of all the communities (Botha 1985: 48-9), one cannot be prescriptive as to the process of implementation or the exact structures that are to evolve from the processes of negotiation. In order to provide further proof of the feasibility of federalism in South Africa, one may suggest, however, that such a system might be implemented by a series of four steps, namely

(1) entrenchment of individual rights
(2) devolution of power to local authorities
(3) establishment of regional governments and cultural authorities
(4) establishment of structures for general affairs of national interest.

These steps are outlined in the following subsections.

Entrenchment of the common law foundations of the South African private enterprise economy

The first step in the implementation of a new, non-racial political dispensation in the Republic of South Africa should be the recognition and entrenchment of the basic norms of the common law of South Africa. They are the foundation of the rights and responsibilities of individuals in the private enterprise economy of the Republic. This step will accomplish, firstly, immediate and unfettered participation by all South Africans in market processes and, secondly, an atmosphere of goodwill in which negotiations about their full participation in political processes at all levels can take place.

'Common law' is understood to mean non-statutory law, the legal norms developed by society and the case law developed by the court in response to particular conflicts and other problems requiring a ruling. Rulings which turn out to be of general practicability become law. Thus the common law of a community grows 'organically' as the characteristics of social life develop, relationships among individual members of society become increasingly complicated and new experiences and new institutions arise.

The core of the common law of South Africa is the so-called Roman-Dutch Law. Since the middle of the 19th century these Roman-Dutch norms have been extensively amplified by English jurisprudence, particularly in regard to the concept of joint stock companies as legal entities, instruments of financing commerce, and industrial labour relations.

Over the past two centuries or more the Black communities of South Africa also developed common laws, whose concepts differed in many respects from the norms of Roman-Dutch and English jurisprudence. In the case of the Zulu, for instance, these principles have been codified and given legal force in terms of the so-called Natal Code. Seeing that large numbers of Blacks are migrating from social systems governed by such codes to the cosmopolitan areas of economic activity governed by Roman-Dutch and English concepts, a conflict of law may exist, if not in the formal sense of recognition in the courts, then in the minds of the newly urbanised

455

migrants who have to adjust to the rules of the new society (Lombard *et al* 1980: 17).

The question arises on what level of detail such a formal recognition and entrenchment should take place. Detailed recognition raises the suggestion of codification of the South African common law. However, it seems that most jurists, including most academics, believe that codification would seriously undermine the remarkable ability of the South African civil law to move soundly with changing circumstances in the capable hands of the judges of the South African Supreme Court. Be that as it may, the level of recognition of the common law need not be nearly as detailed as would be required by codification, while it should be much more articulate than a simple reference to 'the common law of the country'. The instrument of recognition must therefore make its impact on the general level of politics, or public law, rather than on the level of the interpretation of the details of civil law by the courts.

For the Blacks, the reaffirmation of the basic norms of individual freedom underlying and permeating the jurisprudence of the common law holds the very great advantage that the Government publicly subjects itself to objective criteria by which discriminatory laws and regulations in civil affairs can be identified. Such a document might provide the Magna Carta in civilian affairs for the removal of such laws and regulations. For the Whites, the document could become the basic protection of their legitimate interests as individuals or groups in civil affairs when, some time in the future, their political power becomes much less absolute than it has been hitherto.

'Private enterprise economy' as a description of the way economic behaviour in our society is conducted serves to juxtapose the *basically* free, private and competitive economic system of the Republic of South Africa with centrally planned socialist systems — to which there is widespread opposition among the present citizens of the Republic. *Why is it so fundamentally important that the character of this economic system does not change radically towards a centrally planned socialist democracy? And in what way is the basic character of our present system being preserved by the fundamental norms of our common law?*

While most White citizens of the Republic oppose socialism, it is seen by many prospective Black citizens of the Republic as the true harbinger of economic security, freedom and prosperity. Their support for socialism stems from the kind of rules of economic behaviour they currently have to face in South Africa. It is obvious that what Blacks in the South African economy experience as 'the rules of the game' — the almost innumerable restrictions on their economic freedom — is the *antithesis* of a free, private enterprise economy! It is not sufficiently recognised that these restrictions

456

do not arise from the principles of the market economy, but from the completely different ideology of 'statutorily enforced separate development', derogatorily referred to as 'Apartheid'.

The explicit identification of the true and pure principles of the market orientated, competitive economy will enable Blacks to base their case for the removal of statutory discrimination on these principles rather than on those of socialism. It seems to be vitally important to clarify the political climate on this level, i.e. to remove the grave misunderstanding among most Blacks about what the two opposing ideologies of the market economy versus socialism stand for and to make it clear that neither in any way supports the ideologies of statutorily enforced separate development. Only then will it be at all possible to properly address the real issue, namely the preferability of the decentralised market economy over centrally planned socialism as a system of regulaton of people's economic behaviour.

Why is it so fundamentally important that the character of this private enterprise market economy of South Africa, having rid itself of discrimination against Blacks, does not change radically towards a centrally planned socialist democracy?

The short answer to this question is that central economic planning in the heterogeneous community of all South Africans will not work at all. Serious attempts at central planning of the production and distribution of income in South Africa would produce disastrous results, as it has patently done in so many other African communities.

However, there is little in the basic macro-economic laws of productivity, stability, growth and distribution that necessarily favours the market system over the centrally planned system. The laws of 'optimum allocation of productive resources' and specialisation according to least comparative costs, the laws of rapid growth on the basis of savings and capital accumulation and the minimising of the costs of ignorance, uncertainty and risk all apply in both systems with equal force. *The superiority of the market economy over the centrally planned economy does not lie in these laws, but in the philosophical outlook and jurisprudential approach which prevail in the community and which give rise to the former rather than the latter economic system.* It is, accordingly, fundamentally important to us that the market economy system be preserved in the Republic of South Africa. The market economy is the product of human nature and the politico-economic system patronising the market economy is based on a more realistic and consequently superior understanding of human nature. The superiority of the market system in the production of income stems from this basic realism about human nature; the competitive processes of the market are better able than the bureaucratic processes of central planning to minimise the cost of human failings while maximising the value of their excellence.

The perception of human nature implied in market orientated political constitutions is that of individuals who tend to pursue their own objectives in the light of their own knowledge and to the best of their own abilities. Market-orientated constitutions leave people basically free to do so, subject only to the maxim that the limits to one man's freedom is the recognition of that of another. Freedom is therefore a market-related concept. Freedom exists whenever individuals may, unhindered by the state, exploit whatever market opportunities lie open to them. The style of government policy inspired by this view is, accordingly, also that of limited intervention with the operation of the spontaneous market processes.

That the market economy copes with social pluralism in a way centrally planned systems cannot possibly emulate is obviously doubly important in the Republic of South Africa, where the heterogeneity and consequent divergence of preferences of the various population groups is the outstanding socio-political characteristic of the country.

These philosophical foundations of our economic system find practical expression in the system of civil law. The exceptional power of the law to restrain and guide the behaviour of people in society derives from the fact that the law is a set of behavioural rules acknowledged by the sovereign and enforced by it.

Individual choice in markets is based mainly on the common law principles of

- equality before the law
- private property and the right of contract
- legal culpability of the individual.

These are discussed briefly in the following subsections.

The status of the individual: equality before the law

The essential character of the common law of the Republic is its emphasis on the legal status of the individual as a person, as an owner of both material and immaterial property and as a party to binding contracts and other voluntary agreements giving rise to rights and obligations. These common law norms constitute the 'Bill of Rights' of *personal freedom* in South Africa.

The common law in South Africa protects the fundamental right of the individual to exist (the 'right to life') and to acquire other rights. It determines his competence to enter into obligations and to defend his rights in a court of law. The citizenship issue begins at this point. The basic principle is that such competences rest on *the degree of responsibility that can be expected of individuals.*

458

According to Friedrich von Hayek, a famous philosopher of the idea of liberty as developed in European cultural history, '*liberty and responsibility are inseparable*' (Hayek 1972: 71) and the greater part of the moral philosophy, as well as the jurisprudence in this field of rights, is concerned with the nature of individual responsibility rather than with freedom as such. In this connection, the importance of a proper general education for every person, before he seeks industrial or professional training in a specific occupation, is stressed. This primary emphasis on the individual does not, however, exclude the legal recognition of collective entities such as the family, joint stock companies in trade and industry and municipalities.

Private property and the right of contract: freedom of opportunity

In principle, the owner of a thing, whether immovable (such as land), movable (such as sheep), or immaterial (such as a man's reputation), may treat such a thing as he likes — provided his actions do not unduly constrain or interfere with other rights in that thing or in other related things possessed by other people. While ownership is the most important recognised right in things, there are also other rights, such as the right of succession, the right of servitude and the right of pledge or mortgage.

Next to these rights in things, the common law of South Africa recognises so-called personal rights, from which personal liabilities or obligations also necessarily arise. The more general and economically most important personal rights and obligations are those arising from transactions which are given the force of law in the form of contracts. All such contracts derive their validity from the mutual and free consent of the contracting parties, and contracts may be declared invalid if certain requirements pertaining to such free consent have not been met. Personal obligations are clearly distinguished from punishments resulting from the rules of the criminal law as such.

The recognition of personal property rights is also regarded by philosophers of civilisation as an essential element of personal freedom in general. The famous anthropologist, Malinowski, maintained that '*the roots of property as a legal principle which determines the physical relationships between man and his environmental setting, natural and artificial, are the very prerequisites of any ordered action in the cultural sense*' (Malinowski 1944: 132-3 as quoted by Hayek 1972: 140).

The important idea in this connection is not that every single, competent member of society must own property to support the principle of freedom. Political freedoms in modern democracies are distributed on strictly egalitarian presumptions. In contrast, the pattern of resource ownership is unequal. Consequently, although each individual possesses the same market freedoms, the incidence of material return from them is unequal. Hayek shows that what is important is that everyone has a right to own property and that the ownership of property is sufficiently dispersed to ensure that 'the individual is not dependent upon particular persons to trade or to seek employment. Freedom requires a competitive situation. In turn, the system of competitive trade (including the selling of skills or labour), requires the legal framework of the law of contracts. The whole network of rights created by contracts is as important a part of our protected sphere . . . as any property of our own' (Hayek 1972: 141).

The fact is that in the course of this century the legislature of the RSA has interfered considerably with the freedom of persons to enter into contracts. This interference has been politically justified on various grounds such as the protection of the interests of sections of the community who are particularly vulnerable to exploitation. Whatever the merits or demerits of these inroads into the freedom of contract may be, Blacks will be able to challenge the validity of regulations preventing the operation of the informal business sector and even the practice of influx control through the invalidation of employment contracts involving persons from non-scheduled areas.

Legal culpability of the individual

The idea of individual responsibility and of rights and obligations arising from it extends to obligations arising from wrongful acts by persons which harm the interests of other members of the community. Various remedies involving appropriate compensation to the persons who sustained the losses are provided in the law of delicts, which extends beyond civil law to include damages from violations of criminal law as well.

Recognition of collective bodies as legal persons

The common law of South Africa, having been recognised by the sovereign, also constrains the sovereign from interfering with the rights of the individual. That South African parliaments have in the past often broken the Rule of Law is true, but that is one of the main reasons why this question of the formal entrenchment of true rules should be addressed. In general, however, it is still the case in South Africa that the government does not have the right to interfere arbitrarily with the individual in the management of his own affairs. With regard to his 'internal' affairs, e.g. his own property (and in a family context with regard to his wards) he is an autonomous, quasi-sovereign entity. With regard to his external relations, he is protected as well as constrained by the legal system.

460

This protection by the Rule of Law also extends to *groups of individuals* who constitute themselves into bodies recognised as legal persons in terms of the provisions of the legal system. Perhaps the most commonly known example is the joint stock company with limited liability. The Companies Act, 1973 (Act 61 of 1973) is an enabling charter for the creation of companies as legal persons. Another major example of a subsystem of collective bodies *with internal autonomy and external status in law* whose right to exist and to function has had to be recognised by the sovereign are the trade unions and the industrial conciliation councils, on which trade unions are represented. In terms of the Labour Relations Act, 1956 (Act 28 of 1956), an industrial council is an autonomous body with legal status externally, i.e. towards the rest of society, and with autonomous powers internally, i.e. over those matters about which agreements were reached between its members, the representatives of the workers and the employers in the industrial sector or the occupation concerned. It is a notable feature of this system that the Government has no right to interfere with the process of collective bargaining conducted under the auspices of an industrial council. This system of industrial councils, which has worked so well in the maintenance of industrial peace in South Africa, is a good example of the political philosophy of 'grass roots autonomy'. The contention of the section entitled 'Devolution of power to local authorities in a uniform system' is indeed that this philosophy can be further extended into the public sector, particularly at the level of the formation and functioning of local authorities.

Procedures for entrenchment

The fundamental common law norms should be so entrenched in the constitutional charter of the Republic that they cannot be rejected or eroded by future governments without substantial consensus of the population groups who originally reached consensus on their recognition. The danger of a total or categorical rejection of these fundamentals of the South African economic system by temporary, simple majorities in any future Parliament of the Republic is obviously not very real under the present constitution of the Republic. The extent of the danger may, however, have to be reconsidered once the terms of Black participation in politics are clear. This is so simply because it will take some time before the majority of Blacks come to a firm acceptance of the private and competitive enterprise economy as the natural expression of their ideas of human dignity and rights. In the meantime, should the forces of national and international politics bring about the kind of constitutional changes that allow unlimited, simple majoritarian government of South Africa, these foundations of the private enterprise economy will obviously be exposed to rejection. Under such circumstances, it would be highly desirable for those inhabitants of the Republic who continue to value these foundations to be able to fall back on the protection of a specific clause or clauses in the constitution that explicitly prevent the Government from acting in ways which deny the validity of these foundations.

Should the present references in the preamble to the Constitution Act, 1983 (Act 110 of 1983) of the RSA be expanded to include specific references to these fundamental norms of the common law, it would have a certain political value but no decisive legal significance, since it plays no role in the interpretation and application of the Constitution. To acquire direct constitutional meaning these principles would have to be taken up as specific articles of the Constitution itself. Such articles could be seen as a 'Bill of Rights' and could be entrenched, e.g. by the two-thirds majority procedure presently applicable to the official languages of the Republic (sections 89 and 99(2)).

Another possibility is to entrench these principles in important economic and social legislation. In this connection a precedent exists in the Act on a National Policy for General Educational Matters, 1984 (Act 76 of 1984). Section 2(1)(d) of this Act lays down 11 policy principles that have to be followed by the Minister in the administering of the rest of the Act. Such a framework of policy principles is of great significance in terms of administrative law and will greatly support the legitimacy of the future administration of education in the Republic. This procedure can be expanded to introduce the common law principles into the most important pieces of legislation dealing with economic and social affairs.

The entrenchment of common law principles in particular pieces of legislation may be accompanied by the expansion of *judicial control*. Such control might extend not only to the revision of administrative actions in terms of the Acts concerned, but also to the validity of subsequent amendments should such amendments impinge upon or negate the common law principles. South African constitutional law already recognises the principle of judicial control of legislation in the case of the entrenched language rights.

Whether such a procedure provides any real protection in practice is a moot point, with most competent commentators on the side of scepticism. Under circumstances in which a hostile parliamentary majority moves towards total conflict with the entrenched values protecting the politically powerless minority, these values have little chance of being upheld. The most the deprived minority could make of the situation is to have it declared a 'revolution against the state', but since the revolution would be perpetrated by the majority, backed by the military and administrative

462

powers of their government, the 'revolution' would most probably simply be condoned by international opinion.

The chances of the values of individual freedom, property and contractual rights being upheld by the citizens of the future Republic of South Africa would be considerably enhanced *if this Republic could rest on federal constitutional foundations.*

Devolution of power to local authorities in a uniform system[4]

Analysis of the geographical distribution of the various population groups in South Africa indicates that if regional authorities on the basis of one man one vote should be established in any set of regions bigger than individual municipal areas, a single group would dominate political processes in most of them. It follows that the political problems associated with the pluralism of South African society as a whole would also occur in each of the regions. *Local authorities, with extensive powers covering as many culturally sensitive government functions as possible, will be most important in safeguarding the autonomy and self-determination of the various population groups.*

The norms of private property ownership and freedom of individual decision making on the allocation of production factors, embodied in South African common law, are the corner-stones of the free market economy. A free market can provide packageable goods and services efficiently. Some goods and services, however, cannot be packaged and sold to particular individuals to the exclusion of others. Such goods are commonly referred to as public or collective goods.[5] The fact that public goods are not packageable *necessitates their provision by some kind of authority with coercive powers.* Such coercive powers are needed to force people who receive benefits from public goods to help pay for the provision of these goods.

While many public goods cannot be packaged and sold to individual persons, households or firms, *the benefits from their provision are limited to a group of persons consisting of a much smaller number than all the people in the country.* The benefits might accrue mainly to the residents of a town or city. A local authority with coercive powers limited to the boundaries of the town or city would be quite competent to provide the public goods concerned.

Once established, local authorities take part in market transactions just like households and firms. A system of local authorities can be viewed as an extension of the market system principles into the public sector. A local authority has coercive power over its constituents, but so does the head of a household and the management of a firm. The coercive powers of household heads and firm managements have their origin in voluntary contracts which are enforced by the law. People can therefore leave households and firms should they become dissatisfied with the way the household head or firm management treats them. The same principle applies to local authorities. By taking up residence or buying property in the area of jurisdiction of a local authority, a person subjects him- or herself to the coercive power of the local authority, just as a person taking a job with a firm subjects him- or herself to the coercive power of the management. Both actions are the result of voluntary decisions on the part of the person joining the group. In both cases, the coercive power of the managing body is limited by law, the managing body becomes obliged by law to treat the person joining the group in certain ways, and the latter person can leave the group. *Local authorities can thus be regarded as firms in a municipal services industry.*

An enabling act for the establishment of local authorities

Given the above, *local authorities could function in terms of the principles of South African common law* as set out in the previous section. They could be established by groups of interested persons in much the same way as companies or industrial councils are established.

The Companies Act, 1973 (Act 61 of 1973) and the Labour Relations Act, 1956 (Act 28 of 1956) state which persons are allowed to create companies or industrial councils, under what circumstances they may do so and what procedure should be followed in order to obtain juristic standing for the entity being established. The Companies Act also states for what purposes companies can be formed, to what formal requirements the name and statutes must conform and what kinds of companies may be formed, and contains various other requirements to prevent damage to un- or misinformed shareholders or other parties dealing with the company. In other words, a company or industrial council can be formed by any group of persons conforming to a set of objective requirements that may be tested in a court of law. *No discretion to allow or not to allow the establishment of a company or industrial council conforming to the objective requirements is afforded a minister or other government official.* Furthermore, the group of persons forming a company decide for themselves who the directors will be, what line of business they will undertake, what internal rules they will follow and what transactions they will enter into with other parties, limited only by general rules of the law and the powers afforded the company in terms of the relevant Act and its own statute.

As in the case of companies and industrial councils, *there is no need to have different systems of local authorities for different race groups.*

Uniform rights to establish local governments can be extended to all persons, irrespective of race. This can be done by promulgating an enabling Act comparable to the Companies Act. This Act should lay down uniform and objective rules or criteria for the establishment and operation of a local authority by any group of persons (i.e Whites, Coloureds, Indians and/or Blacks). It should contain a list of possible forms and a list of obligatory and optional functions from which a statute or constitution for a particular local authority (including composite local authorities such as regional services councils) may be compiled by the persons establishing the local authority, not by some higher authority.[6] The procedure to be followed and the minimum requirements to which the statute must conform will naturally have to be set out in the enabling Act. Such an Act will also have to provide for a register of local authorities serving as proof of the existence and legal status of the local authority, as in the case of companies, co-operatives, financial institutions and other legal persons.

The operation of a local authority does differ, however, from the operation of a business in one important respect. All people in the geographical area of jurisdiction of the local authority will receive benefits from the authority's actions. If their contributions to the cost of these actions are completely voluntary in the same sense that no individual can be compelled by a company to become a shareholder or a client of that company, many people will elect to be 'free-riders'. Obviously, ways and means of compelling all residents or property owners in the area of jurisdiction of a local authority to contribute to the costs of its actions are needed, as is the case in the existing system.

These procedural ideas are not new or foreign to democratic societies. In the USA the procedure for establishing a local authority follows these lines almost exactly. The existing procedures for establishing local authorities in South Africa are often very similar, the major difference being that in South Africa the provincial administrator or a minister has discretion as to whether a local authority should be established in response to an application and, if established, whether the area of jurisdiction, form and powers of the authority will be as set out in the application. The authority is not automatically established, provided only that stated, objective criteria are conformed to.

In principle, co-ordination among local authorities can be effected by means of either central control or voluntary contracts between two or more local authorities. The creation of regional bodies consisting of representatives of local authorities in the region can also be classified under either of the former headings, depending on whether the regional bodies are established through directives from above or through the automatic market-orientated discipline of voluntary contracts among participating local authorities. In the latter case, local authorities need to be empowered to enter into such contracts. Such empowerment in a central government Act does not necessarily imply central control. The relevant Act might simply be an enabling measure, such as an Act enabling private persons to form companies for business purposes.

The distinction between the provision and the physical production of goods and services is important in this regard. Local councils clearly have two quite distinct functions, namely on one hand to articulate the demand of the community they represent for various municipal services and on the other hand to provide services to meet the demand. Once the local council has decided which municipal services are to be provided, several possibilities are open to it. These options provide ample opportunities for co-ordination among local authorities without any interference by higher authorities. This usually occurs in large urban or metropolitan areas, in which several local authorities operate in close proximity to one another.

The process of true devolution of power

Given the present, unitary system of government in the Republic of South Africa, the Government can delegate freedom to take decisions on particular functions without changing the Constitution, but it retains ultimate responsibility for the performance of the functions as well as the right to revoke the freedom of decision unilaterally. A person or group who is dissatisfied with the way in which the delegated functions are handled at the subnational level will certainly put pressure on the national Government to intervene or even to revoke the function — and this may happen even before the dissatisfied party has exhausted its influence in local politics.

Moreover, a change in the South African Constitution in order to assign one or more government functions to a subnational level will not necessarily amount to devolution in the true sense of the word. One reason is that the national Government can change the Constitution on its own, without having to solicit the agreement of any subnational unit of government. Secondly, no legislation by the South African Government is subject to revision by a court of law. Consequently, in the final analysis no subnational government has any constitutional right to prevent the national Government from revoking a delegated function, even if such delegation took place by means of a change in the national Constitution. The national Government can simply change the Constitution again.

True devolution of some (as opposed to all) government functions requires a change in the very nature of the Constitution. It requires that the Constitution be changed in such a way that future changes to it will be subject to agreement by the subnational government institutions to which political power is devolved and it requires that in future the latter must have recourse to a court of law should the national Government unilaterally change the Constitution in order to revoke the devolved functions. In fact, it means that the very sovereignty of the national Government will be divided. It will have sovereign power over the functions it retains in terms of the Constitution, but the subnational governments will have sovereign power over the functions which will have been devolved to them. In other words, South Africa will no longer have a unitary system of government, but a federal or confederal one.

Regional and cultural authorities[7]

Some government services, such as education and hospital services, are rendered to particular individuals. Even if people live in the same area they can be provided with these services by different institutions. However, many government services, including the making and enforcement of regulations, are rendered in particular areas. Everyone in such an area receives the benefits and carries the indirect costs associated with such a service. Should such services be rendered in the same area by more than one cultural authority, each of these authorities could state that its constituents do not want tarred roads, streetlights, kerbstones or whatever service might be under discussion, knowing that if the service is rendered by another authority its own constituents would receive the benefits without paying for the service. The result might be that the service is not rendered at all. The other possibility is that more than one authority might provide the same service, for instance a siren to warn people of oncoming natural disasters, military attacks, etc, and each siren would be heard by all the people in the area. Thus, there would be unnecessary duplication of services.

The devolution of the power to perform government functions that are area-bound rather than person-bound to authorities for members of cultural groups who live in the same geographical areas is therefore impractical or economically non-justifiable. Area-bound functions — general affairs in the jargon of the present Constitution of the RSA — have to be entrusted to regional authorities with jurisdiction over particular areas, irrespective of who lives in those areas. Some area-bound functions might be of national interest in the sense that their direct benefits extend to all persons in the country. However, the benefits of many government services do not extend that far, while many make themselves felt in areas larger than the areas of local authorities with culturally homogeneous populations.

It is clear that regional authorities for general affairs of regional interest will be needed. The question is how to protect minority groups in such regions from domination by other groups. One possibility is to organise the regional governments on a basis similar to the present central government. In other words, a regional government consisting of chambers for the cultural groups present in appreciable numbers may be formed to manage their own affairs separately and general affairs jointly. Cultural groups need not be defined in terms of race, but could be defined by means of other criteria, e.g. home language and religion.

Where applicable, the present national state governments and provincial councils could become chambers within states in a federation or confederation. The national state governments already have jurisdiction over particular geographical areas and some jurisdiction over their citizens living outside these geographical areas. Thus, extra-territorial or ethnic-based jurisdiction is not a new principle in their case. Where necessary, the boundaries and number of the provinces and national states might have to be adjusted. Persons residing in a particular state and who are not members of a group for which a chamber exists in the state government could be allowed to apply for membership of one of the groups which does have such a chamber. Should the group applied to reject the application, the applicant could apply for membership of another group. Again, this principle is not new. At present, members of one Black national unit living in the national state of another national unit may apply for citizenship of the national state in which they reside.

The areas of jurisdiction of possible state governments will have to be decided upon at the negotiating table. Whether negotiators will seek to combine or to divide existing regions such as provinces and national states will obviously depend upon the structures negotiated for the states in the federation or confederation. Should they consist of chambers for different cultural groups, rather large states might be acceptable, even to negotiators stressing self-determination of groups. If not, such negotiators will obviously opt for smaller states with more homogeneous populations.

Whatever regions are to become states in a federation or confederation, it is clear that members of a single cultural group will probably be spread over a number of the states. They might feel that they need an interregional, cultural authority to handle their common, culture-related interests. In order to provide Zulu primary schools to a large percentage of the Zulu population of South Africa, the majority of Zulus might be convinced that they need a Zulu primary school board operating in several states. Alternatively, the majority of Zulus might be satisfied with a separate Zulu primary school board in each of the states that might be formed. A third possibility is that each of the relevant states might have a single department of education providing primary schools with similar curricula, but differ-

468

ent languages of instruction for all population groups of significant size within its area of jurisdiction. Yet another possibility would be for special local authorities or school boards to provide education in areas of jurisdiction that may be much smaller than the areas of jurisdiction of the states and which may have populations that are practically homogeneous in respect of culture.

It is quite possible that the legal competence of state governments consisting of chambers for the most important cultural groups in the geographical area of each could be limited to decisions on general affairs taken on the basis of consensus among the chambers. All own affairs could then be taken care of by complementary, interregional, cultural authorities, each representing all members of the cultural group concerned. The members of the cultural authorities could be chosen independently of the members of the chambers in the territorially-based government units. The seat of each cultural authority would probably be in the state where most members of the group concerned are concentrated. They would, however, be allowed to operate in other states as well, but obviously only within the limits of the functions allotted to them by the constitution.

Possibilities for structuring the national government in a federation or confederation

From the discussion in the previous sections, it follows that in South Africa it might be possible to create a federation or confederation consisting of territorially-defined states as federating or confederating units, which in turn consist of corporately-defined federating entities or chambers. Decisions on general affairs could be taken on the basis of consensus among the corporate units, while decisions on own affairs could be taken independently by the corporate units.

Alternatively, territorial state governments or regional authorities responsible for general affairs and corporate units or cultural authorities for own affairs could be elected independently.

Whatever the case, these government units' responsibilities and powers should be strictly limited to non-local affairs. Local affairs should be the entrenched functions of local authorities which are established independently and elected in terms of an enabling act, as set out in the section entitled 'Devolution of power to local authorities in a uniform system'.

The legislative, executive and judicial powers of the national government of such a federation or confederation should be strictly separated in terms of the principles put forward in the section entitled 'The nature of federalism'.

The legislature could consist of two chambers, one representing the territorial states and the other the cultural authorities, which could either be chambers in the regional governments or cultural authorities handling their groups' own affairs in more than one region.

The executive could be chosen by popular election or by an electoral college consisting of representatives of the chambers of the national legislature or of the territorial states and cultural authorities.

For the sake of completeness, it should be mentioned that a number of federations could be formed in South Africa and that all or some of them could form a confederation (which could include other countries as well). It is possible, for instance, that Venda, Lebowa, Gazankulu and a state consisting of areas surrounding them could form a federation and that such a federation of Northern Transvaal could become a member of a confederation of Southern Africa.

It is obvious that each level of government should have its own sources of revenue and should not be dependent on transfers from other authorities, because then it could lose its *de jure* independence by having to conform to conditions set by the authorities transferring the funds. Division of tax sources among the different levels of government will consequently be an immensely important aspect of negotiations on the constitutional future of South Africa. This issue is discussed in the next section.

FEDERAL FINANCE

A specific principle of development aid

A regional basis for federalism in the Republic of South Africa seems practical, particularly if coupled with cultural authorities, but may require a specific principle of development aid to compensate for fiscal imbalances.

Residents of large regions and members of large groups at the lower end of the income scale might oppose a federal system for a future South Africa, because a unitary system might afford them a better opportunity to redistribute income and wealth in their own favour. Consequently, a precondition for their acceptance of a federal model will probably be agreement on a specific principle of development aid. The national Government will certainly be required to give aid to the poorer regions and people if it is to fulfil its mandate of promoting well-balanced development.

As long as the basic gaps in social and economic conditions between people exist, the stability of the order in the country will be in question. Assistance by leading individuals and groups to their lagging associates in society is as much a matter of enlightened self-interest as it may be the

470

manifestation of altruistic motives. When, however, the initiative in closing the gap is taken by the poor by means of political power used intra- or extra-constitutionally to coerce a redistribution of produced income, the outcome will be a serious deterioration of the productivity and the stability of the entire economy.

A strategy of full participation of all South Africans in the opportunities of the economic system of the country should, accordingly, be regarded as much more than a matter of occasional charity. It should be a fundamental element of the character of relationships at all levels of public (and indeed even private) affairs.

Allocation of income sources and income transfers

The problem of the optimum allocation of tax rights between national and regional governments is common to federations at all stages of development. Securing sufficient tax rights for the national government to look after national policy may imply allocating to the regions (or at least some of them) less than they need to carry out their powers and duties effectively.

The negotiations on income transfers may be simplified greatly by the allocation of substantial sources of income to each level of government in a federal South Africa, which could be embodied in the constitution. A possible allocation of major sources of income (1981/82 figures are shown to indicate relative importance) is:

- National government
  customs and exise duties   R2 200 million
  company taxes   R5 400 million

- Regional governments
  personal income tax   R3 200 million
  general sales tax   R2 100 million

- Local governments
  user charges   R3 200 million
  property taxes   R 700 million

There is no once-and-for-all solution to the problem of revenue allocation, because of changing conditions. The constitutions of the new federations contain mainly provisions which recognise the need for financial adjustment. Such clauses could also be built into the future South African constitution. It is particularly important that these possible built-in provisions should work, because the rapid rate of economic development that is hoped for may (if it is achieved) make some of the financial clauses obsolete in the future. It would be unfortunate if such clauses were built into a system in ways which created vested interests in their continuance and so made them an irremovable part of a constitution which might be difficult to amend.

National grants can play a very important part in accelerating development in general and in seeing that it is distributed over the whole country in such a way that the initial differences between the regions tend to diminish rather than to widen and that these aims can be secured without imperilling the political integrity of the regions or their essential budgetary freedom. The necessary conditions for success along these lines are that national-regional financial relations should be flexible and that the transfer structure should be subject to periodic review, with adjustment where necessary.

After the desirability of transfers has been established, the question arises how it should be calculated and on what conditions it should be paid. The most appropriate institution for national-regional financial co-operation problems would be an impartial, independent and non-political body with a firm statistical foundation for its work, for example the Commonwealth Grants Commission of Australia. The latter body handles this matter impartially and objectively by changing laid-down formulas from time to time. The problems with which such a body might deal could be listed under six general headings, namely tax distribution, transfers distribution, loan co-ordination, social services, economic development and intergovernmental disputes not appropriate for court jurisdiction.

The institutions required for this strategy of development co-operation must emerge from a proper definition of the form of assistance and the functions to be performed.

The principles that should guide the system of development co-operation should harmonise with those discussed above. In other words, the aim of development co-operation should be (a) to promote among people as widespread a distribution of private economic power as possible, a sense of personal responsiblity among as many South Africans as possible and an ability and a propensity to economise among as many economically active people as possible, and (b) to promote among regions or smaller areas a balance of economic activity in keeping with the relative social and political significance of the region or area, but with due regard for the limits to effective intervention in the market processes of industrial location.

Participation by the people concerned in the policies of the development agencies is a matter of fundamental importance. Where the agencies are ordinary private persons or corporations, the participation by recipients of assistance should ideally be couched as a private contractual relationship. Private charity blatantly administered does not improve the self-respect of the recipient. Where the relationship cannot, by its very nature, be contractual in the commercial sense, but must be handled as a 'collective good', for example basic health and education or improvement of the physical infrastructure, the institutions responsible should be the creation of all of the parties concerned. As soon as development assistance is presented as one-way charity (which it is not) rather than as two-way co-operation, it loses the greatest part of its potential strength.

Redistribution of income

Economic arguments suggest that control of most sources of revenue should be given to the national government (for purposes of economic development and economic stability), but the political argument (wherever possible the responsibilities for raising and spending money should rest with the same authority) suggests that it should be given to the regions. If some regions are poorer than others, so that the standards of their local services (e.g. health and education) are substantially below the national average, or if the tax system is designed so that one level receives less than it needs, the real complications of federal finance emerge. The fiscal capacity of a region is not only a function of the tax system, but also of the incomes of the members of the relevant community. These problems might be solved by the redistribution of income through the subsidisation of objects, persons and authorities, the re-allocation of functions among authorities with larger and smaller areas of jurisdiction and the assumption that the principle of 'fiscal equivalence' might apply in the government system envisaged here.

Distribution and redistribution of revenue: Subsidisation of objects, persons and authorities

The demarcation of local authority areas on the basis of ethnicity results in different local authorities possessing vastly different fiscal resources. Even if they all had access to the same forms or sources of income, it is clear that the ultimate source of income would be the relevant community. Therefore, a standardised enabling act for local authorities would not diminish the need for income redistribution from high-income communities to low-income communities.

It is important, however, to pay close attention to the differential effects of various methods of income redistribution. Grants to local authorities, for instance, have effects which are vastly different to those of grants to deprived individuals.

Every community, no matter how low its average level of income and wealth, will include high-income persons and families. This is clearly applicable to Black local authorities in South Africa as well. To the extent that wealthy Blacks within Black local authorities possess property, they (and not the poor for whom the relief is intended) might be the people capturing the benefits of intergovernmental grants. The argument is that the grants will enable the local authority to provide better services while keeping taxes and user fees to its citizens constant, or even reducing them. This will cause property prices to rise, so that those who already own property will receive a one-time benefit to the detriment of those who still have to purchase property (see Bish 1983: 122-5 for a more extensive treatment).

Similar effects occur when objects rather than persons are subsidised. Many wealthy people in South Africa receive subsidies on bread daily — while the subsidy is clearly intended to assist the needy. The same applies to housing subsidies or subsidised house rents, transport rates and medical fees, which are common in Black townships.

The conclusion is that it would be much better to subsidise the expenditure on certain goods by persons in low-income groups by means of tax allowances, vouchers, or direct cash grants. Such vouchers or cash grants received from regional authorities or the national Government could be used to pay for local authority services, thereby supplementing their fiscal resources without unintended effects on income distribution within the local communities.

Redistribution of income through allocation of functions among authorities with larger and smaller areas of jurisdiction

Appreciable redistribution of income is not feasible in local authority areas, because those being taxed may leave. The local authority may consequently be left with an even less adequate fiscal base than before. At the same time, people eligible for receipt of redistributed funds or benefits will tend to move into local authority areas where substantial redistribution of income takes place. This will obviously aggravate the situation. In fact, a situation of 'unstable equilibrium' will result. The local authority's financial position will go from bad to worse, as has happened in the case of the City of New York.

Should the redistribution of income be regarded as desirable, it must of necessity take place in relatively large regions, or preferably nationally, so that the cost of leaving becomes at least as high as the tax burden. (Note that the possibility of out-migration places an effective limit on the extent of taxation, provided that freedom of movement exists.)

The redistribution of income could be effected by regional or metropolitan authorities responsible for the provision of region-wide infrastructure

474

and with the power to impose region-wide taxes. Such authorities will obviously receive most of their tax income from the more affluent communities, but will be able to spend it to the benefit of less affluent communities as well. Redistribution does not necessarily imply direct cash grants to persons or local authorities in the area of the regional or metropolitan authority.

The principle of fiscal equivalence

One of the most desirable features of the market system is its self-correcting behaviour. When shortages or surpluses occur, prices rise or fall, thereby indicating quickly and efficiently how buyers and producers should respond.

If the government system is to be self-correcting, the principle of 'fiscal equivalence' (Olson 1969, as quoted by Bish 1983: 116) must apply. This principle requires that those who decide, benefit and pay should be the same group of people. The citizens who make decisions on programmes (or directly influence representatives who act on their behalf) will be those who benefit from the programme and those who pay the cost of the programme (Bish 1983: 116).

Fiscal equivalence is usually self-correcting because the decision makers consciously compare benefits with costs, both of which accrue directly to them, when making decisions. At the same time, fiscal equivalence may be considered equitable because beneficiaries pay the costs of obtaining their benefits rather than shifting the costs to third parties (ibid: 117).

When the activities of government involve providing products or services such as water supply or public transport to identifiable individuals, the fiscally equivalent way to finance such activities is through user charges (ibid: 117).

Temporal fiscal equivalence requires that capital expenditures, which give rise to a benefit stream in the future, should be financed from borrowed funds, with beneficiaries repaying the debt over the life of the project. Operating expenditures, in contrast, should be financed from an annually balanced budget (ibid: 118).

Spatial fiscal equivalence means that people in the geographic area in which the benefits of a public project are concentrated, should pay for the project. Given that the benefits of different projects extend over different geographical areas, spatial fiscal equivalence can be attained by the simultaneous use of local, regional and national authorities. Some of these may best be functionally specialised. Large, consolidated local authorities can hardly meet the requirements of spatial fiscal equivalence unless rates may be differentiated by neighbourhoods within their area.

475

POWER VERSUS PRINCIPLES: THE POLITICAL BOTTOM LINE[8]

The approach to political reform proposed in this chapter stresses the reliance on people's automatic respect for basic principles. That is why it was considered so important to rediscover those basic norms which have guided the social order in South Africa and most other states in Western civilisation for the past three centuries.

However, it cannot be denied that a widespread scepticism about the validity of such an approach to political stability in a democracy exists, particularly with reference to Black African democracies. How reliable is the respect for the Rule of Law among the people of South Africa? The sceptics suggest that, on the contrary, *people basically respect power —* economic power and political power. Under these circumstances, political stability in South Africa will ultimately require a dictatorship of some kind or another, but it is obvious that such an outcome will be preceded by tremendous disruption, including a great deal of bloodshed.

Unfortunately, we know of no authoritative examination of the extent to which respect for the Rule of Law as an important precondition for a stable democracy is already present among the masses of South Africa. Even under a federal constitution, given the economic, social and political realities of South Africa as they probably will remain over the next decade or two, entrenchment of the common law foundations of the economy might not suffice. To protect these foundations reliably against categorical rejection by hostile political majorities, even in the context of federal political and administrative structures, a much more sophisticated pro- gramme, not only of legal reform, but also of *educational enlightenment and economic assistance,* will be required.

In the meantime, it would obviously be unwise to dismantle the existing political power structure in one fell swoop without any idea of the nature of the power structure to take its place or the way in which the battle for power should be waged. Evolutionary change from the existing political dispensation to a fully legitimate new dispensation therefore requires that the existing power structure should be dismantled gradually, since power can devolve fairly safely upon new structures supported by the people involved. It is emphasised throughout this chapter that the political bottom line of the stability of the order is a balance of powers in the system, so that those groups of people who insist upon government according to the common law norms of this country remain in a sufficiently strong position to keep the enemies of the system from destroying it.

To conclude, the maintenance of federalism in the social order of society depends upon a number of conditions, the most important of which are (a) the people's respect for the Rule of Law, (b) the competence of the Supreme

Court to review Acts of Parliament in the light of the constitution, (c) the vertical decentralisation of power to authorities of subnational communities, (d) the horizontal separation of political power between the executive and Parliament and (e) the maintenance of a balance of physical (military) and economic power among the different political groups who agreed to enter into the federal political contract.

The fifth condition may be regarded as a last-ditch condition for the protection of the federal character of the state. It might be said that if matters have degenerated to the point where this condition has, in fact, to be relied upon, the survival of the federation has become questionable. On the other hand, the mere fact that power can, if necessary, be exercised legitimately by a constituent of the federation against the central government to protect the constitution, may go a long way to prevent matters from degenerating that far.

NOTES

1 This section consists mainly of slightly revised excerpts from Lombard *et al* (1985: 74-75 and 83-89).
2 This section consists mainly of excerpts from Lombard *et al* (1985: 88-89).
3 This section consists mainly of excerpts from Lombard *et al* (1985: 12-26).
4 This section consists mainly of excerpts from Lombard *et al* (1985: 33-61).
5 Other classes of goods (externalities and common pool resources) have similar characteristics and create similar problems. See for instance Bish (1983: 22-27 and 32-33).
6 Of course, this does not exclude the possibility that a higher authority might publish a standard statute to serve as a guide-line for people establishing a local authority.
7 The latter part of this section consists of excerpts from Lombard *et al* (1985: 91-93).
8 This section consists of excerpts from Lombard *et al* (1985: 26 and 93-94).

BIBLIOGRAPHY

Bish, RL. *Basic principles of political decentralisation to local authorities.* Pretoria: Bureau for Economic Policy and Analysis, University of Pretoria, 1983.
Botha, PW. *Speech by State President PW Botha DMS on occasion of opening of the National Party Congress.* Port Elizabeth, 30 September 1985. Pretoria: Office of the State President, 1985.
Boulle, LJ. *South Africa and the consociational option. A constitutional analysis.* Cape Town: Juta, 1984.
Breton, A and Scott, A. *The economic constitution of federal states.* Toronto: University of Toronto Press, 1978.
Buchanan, JM and Tullock, G. *The calculus of consent. Logical foundations of constitutional democracy.* Ann Arbor: Ann Arbor Paperbacks, 1965.
De Tocqueville, A. *Democracy in America.* Vol. 1, New York: Vintage Books, 1945.
Du Pisanie, JA. *Streeksekonomiese beleid in die RSA: 'n Beskrywing en ontleding.* Pretoria: Buro vir Ekonomiese Politiek en Analise, Universiteit van Pretoria, 1981.
Friedrich, CJ. *Trends of federalism in theory and practice.* New York: Praeger, 1968.

Hayek, R. The constitution of liberty. Indiana: Gateway, 1972.

Hobbes, T. Leviathan: Or the matter, forme and power of a commonwealth ecclesiastical and civil. New York: Collier Books, 1962.

Juta, H. (Translator.). Van der Linden's Manual, commonly known as the institutes. Cape Town: Juta, 1920.

Kriek, DJ. Enkele gedagtes oor die teorie en praktyk van federalisme. Politikon, jg. 5, no. 2, 1978.

Lombard, JA and Du Pisanie, JA. Removal of discrimination against Blacks in the political economy of the Republic of South Africa. A memorandum for ASSOCOM. Johannesburg: ASSOCOM, 1985.

Lombard, JA, Du Pisanie JA, Olivier, GC and Vosloo, WB. Alternatives for the consolidation of KwaZulu. Special Pretoria: Bureau for Economic Policy and Analysis, University of Pretoria, 1980.

Malinowski, B. Freedom and civilisation. London: 1944.

Olson, M. The principle of fiscal equivalence: The division of responsibility among different levels of government. American Economic Review, May 1969.

Ostrom, V. Reflections on public administration in Europe. The development of research and training in European policy-making. Maastricht: European Institute of Public Administration, 1983.

Ostrom V. Empirical theory and methodology: The comparative study of public institutions. Indiana: Indiana University, 1984. (Unpublished class notes for course Y773.)

Parsons, RWK. The relationship between the Reserve Bank and the Central Government. A memorandum to the Commission of Inquiry into the Monetary System and Monetary Policy.

South Africa (Republic). 1982a. Central Statistical service. Population census 80.Sample tabulation. Economic characteristics. Pretoria: Government Printer, 1982. (Report No. 02-80-02).

South Africa (Republic). 1982b. Central Statistical Service. Population Census 80. Sample tabulation. Social Characteristics. Pretoria: Government Printer, 1982. (Report No. 02-80-02).

Tullock, G. Tiebout squared. Virginia: Center for Study of Public Choice, George Mason University, 1984. (Unpublished paper.)

Wiechers, M. Private communication. 1985.

Short profile on contributors

Adlem, WLJ

WLJ Adlem read for the degrees B Admin (1967), B Admin (Hons) (1968) and M Admin (1975) at the University of Pretoria. He obtained the D Admin in Public Administration from the University of South Africa in 1979.

He has been connected with the Department of Political Science and Public Administration at the University of South Africa since 1973 and in 1980 was appointed Joint Professor in Municipal Government and Administration.

Professor Adlem is a committee member of the Northern Transvaal regional branch of the South African Institute of Public Administration and serves on the editorial committee of the Institute of Public Administration. Various articles by him on municipal government and administration have appeared in technical magazines.

Backer, W

W Backer holds a D Phil degree from Potchefstroom University for CHE and a D Litt and D Phil on the subject of job motivation from the University of South Africa. He has also worked with Professor Fred Herzberg in Salt Lake City.

Professor Backer has worked in the textile industry as a personnel manager and for seven years was Managing Director of one of the industry's training organisations, the Timber Industry Manpower Services.

Formerly a lecturer at Potchefstroom University, the University of Fort Hare and Rhodes, he is now Professor of Manpower Strategies and Labour Relations at the Rand Afrikaans University.

Professor Backer is a registered industrial psychologist, acts as labour relations consultant for various organisations and serves on a number of boards. He is the author of three books and a considerable number of articles on job motivation and training.

Barratt, J

J Barratt was born in Transkei and educated at St Andrews College, Grahamstown, the University of the Witwatersrand and Oxford University.

He was a member of the South African Foreign Service for 13 years, seven of which were spent serving with the South African Mission to the United Nations in New York.

Since 1967 he has been Director, and since 1980 Director General, of the South African Institute of International Affairs at Jan Smuts House in Johannesburg.

In 1981 he was awarded an honorary professorship in International Relations by the University of the Witwatersrand. He is the author of articles and chapters in books on South Africa's foreign relations and Southern African developments and has co-edited several books on these subjects.

Boulle, LJ

LJ Boulle holds the degrees LLB (Stellenbosch, 1972), LLM (London, 1975) and Ph D (Natal, 1982).

From 1973 to 1976 he served as a State Advocate. In 1976 he was appointed Senior Lecturer at the University of Natal and in 1983 became Associate Professor. He was a visiting Research Scholar at the University of Michigan Law School, Ann Arbor, USA, during 1983/1984.

Professor Boulle's main fields of interest are constitutional and administrative law, statute law, the criminal process and comparative law. Besides having written a few chapters in books, various articles and case notes, he is co-editor of *Natal and KwaZulu: Constitutional and Political Options* (Juta 1981) and author of *South Africa and the Consociational Option: A Constitutional Analysis* (Juta 1984) and *Constitutional Reform and the Apartheid State: Legitimacy and Control in South Africa* (St Martins Press 1984).

He has also acted as constitutional consultant on various occasions.

Burns, YM

Yvonne M Burns holds the degrees LLB (1975), LLM (1978) and LLD (1984). During 1981 she spent a year at the Max Planck Institute in Heidelberg, Germany, researching press freedom in that country. This comparative research formed part of her doctoral thesis, which was entitled *Freedom of the Press: A comparative legal survey.*

She has been in the employ of the University of South Africa for the past 11 years and was appointed Senior Lecturer in 1977 and Associate Professor in 1984.

Coetzee, SF

SF Coetzee is Head of Regional and Urban Development, Department of Policy Research, in the Development Bank of Southern Africa.

He is a graduate of the University of Stellenbosch (MA) and the University of the Orange Free State (D Phil).

From 1974 to 1981 he was a lecturer/researcher and then Senior Lecturer/ Researcher in Economics at the Institute of Economic and Social Research at the University of the Orange Free State and from 1982 to 1983 he was Associate Professor in Economics at the University of South Africa.

Dr Coetzee joined the Development Bank of Southern Africa in 1984. He is currently Chairman of the Development Society of Southern Africa, a member of the Head Committee for Economic Sciences of the Human Sciences Research Council and assistant editor of *Development Southern Africa*, a quarterly journal of the Development Bank. During 1980/1981 he paid a research visit to the University of Manchester in England on a British Council Bursary.

Dr Coetzee has written numerous articles and research reports on development themes and is co-author of three chapters in a forthcoming book — *Development is for people* (edited by JK Coetzee). His main interests are regional and urban development, with special reference to South Africa.

Corder, HM

HM Corder obtained the B Comm and LLB degrees from the University of Cape Town. He subsequently obtained an LLB from Trinity Hall, Cambridge (1979) and a D Phil from Keble College, Oxford (1982).

He has taught at the University of Cape Town and has been Senior Lecturer in Public Law at Stellenbosch since 1983.

Dr Corder is the local chairman of Lawyers for Human Rights and a member of the editorial board of *The SA Journal on Human Rights* and of the Regional Committee of the SA Institute of Race Relations. He is the author of *Judges at Work* (1984) and several articles.

Couper, MP

MP Couper obtained a M Soc Sc from the University of Cape Town. He is a Ph D candidate at Rhodes University, his topic of study being immigrant adaptation in South Africa.

Mr Couper is a Senior Researcher in the Division for Group Interaction of the Human Sciences Research Council in Pretoria. His main interests are research methodology and social conflict.

De Kock, CP

CP de Kock is a graduate of Stellenbosch University (BA Hons) and the University of South Africa (MA and Ph D). He is Senior Chief Researcher in the Division for Group Interaction of the Human Sciences Research Council.

Dr De Kock's main interest is intergroup conflict in plural societies and the violent manifestations of conflict and his publications deal with problems in this field.

De Lange, JP

JP de Lange was educated at the Universities of Stellenbosch and Pretoria, the University of South Africa and the Rand Afrikaans University. He is now Principal and Vice-Chancellor of the latter, serves *inter alia* on the Councils of Goudstad College of Education and the Rand Afrikaans University and is Chairman of the Council of the Vista University.

Professor De Lange is also a member of the Joint Matriculation Board and the Scientific Advisory Council to the Prime Minister and is Chairman of the National Education Council. He was Director of the HSRC Investigation into Education in South Africa and was appointed Chairman of the Education Working Committee. He is presently Chairman of the HSRC Main Committee on Research into Education and Chairman of the interim South African Council for Education.

Du Pisanie, JA

Johann du Pisanie obtained the degrees B Com, M Com (Economics), D Com (Economics) and M BA at the University of Pretoria. He lectured in economics at the same University from 1969 to 1970, moved to the Board of Trade and Industries in 1971 and returned to the University of Pretoria in 1973 as Senior Lecturer in Economics. He was promoted to Professor in Economics in 1980.

His current interests are micro-economics, urban and regional economics, development economics and public economics and public economics. He has published in all of these fields. The best known of the publications to which he has contributed are *Alternatives to the consolidation of Kwazulu* (the so-called Lombard report which was completed in 1980) and a recent memorandum for Assocom, *Removal of discrimination against Blacks in the political economy of South Africa.*

482

Kok, PC

PC Kok holds the degrees BA (1970) and Master in Town and Regional Planning (1973) and the Diploma in Datametrics (with distinction) (1981).

He has worked as a town planner for the Provincial Administration of the Cape of Good Hope and at the Borough of Newcastle.

In 1980 he was employed as Chief Researcher, responsible for immigration research, by the HSRC's Institute for Sociological and Demographic Research.

Since 1973 he has produced various published and unpublished reports (amongst which were contributions to the Science and Constitutional Committees of the President's Council and to the HSRC's national investigations into education and sport), as well as a number of articles and papers.

Kritzinger, L

Lolette Kritzinger obtained the B Com (Economics) and the B Com Hons (Economics) degrees from the University of Pretoria in 1979 and 1980 respectively. At present she is completing her M Com dissertation in Political Economy.

She joined the Bureau for Economic Policy and Analysis at the University of Pretoria in 1981 as research assistant and was promoted to research officer in 1983. Her interests in Economics include political economy, economic development and public finance. She is co-author of several research reports and articles. Recent publications include *The tax burden* and *The logic of the federal option*, published by Mercabank in its *Focus on Key Economic Issues* series.

Ligthelm, AA

AA Ligthelm is a graduate of the University of Pretoria (B Comm (Hons)) and Potchefstroom University for CHE (D Comm).

He was a Senior Economist at the Bureau for Economic Research: Co-operation and Development, but is presently Manager: Policy Research at the Development Bank of Southern Africa. His research contributions concern the economic development of the less developed areas of Southern Africa and particularly the design of appropriate development strategies for these areas.

He has written numerous magazine articles and research reports and is co-author of three chapters in a forthcoming book — *Development is for people* (edited by JK Coetzee).

Loader, JA

JA Loader studied at the University of Pretoria (D Litt), the University of Groningen, Netherlands (Th D), and the University of South Africa (D Th). He did research work at Cambridge University and several Dutch institutes and took part in various congresses of the International Organisation for the Study of the Old Testament, the British Society for Old Testament Study and of South African Societies for Old Testament Studies, Judaic Studies and Church History.

He is the author of approximately 200 articles and three books, co-author of four books, editor of the quarterly, *Theologia Evangelica* and a regular columnist and commentator on ecclesiastical and religious affairs.

He is ordained a minister of the Nederduitsch Hervormde Kerk.

Lombard, JA

JA Lombard obtained a BA degree in Economics and Law from the University of Pretoria (1947) and an MA in Economics (1950). In 1954 he obtained a Ph D in Economics (Finance and Banking) from the University of London.

He was an economist in the public service until 1959, Deputy Economic Adviser to the Prime Minister in 1960 and Professor in Economics at the University of Pretoria from January 1961. He also served on various committees concerned with fiscal, monetary and development policy.

Mostert, WP

WP Mostert worked as a teacher before he joined the Bureau for Social and Educational Research during 1965. He obtained a D Phil degree in Sociology in 1968 and was sent to Paris, France by the Human Sciences Research Council during 1971-1972 to study demographic research methodology at l'Institut National d'Etude Demographie and l'Université de Paris (Sorbonne).

In 1974 he joined the Department of Health and Welfare and was responsible for the development of the motivational programme of the National Family Planning Programme. He returned to the Human Sciences Research Council during 1981.

He is author and co-author of approximately 60 reports and articles and assisted the Science Committee in the writing of the *Report on Demographic Trends in South Africa* (1983).

Olivier, JL

JL Olivier is a Senior Researcher at the Human Sciences Research Council and was research co-ordinator of the HSRC Investigations into Sport (1980-1982) and Intergroup Relations (1982-1985).

He holds a BA (Hons) degree in Sociology from the University of Pretoria and an MA degree from the University of South Africa. At present he is studying at Cornell University in the USA.

Rhoodie, NJ

Nic Rhoodie is a Senior Research Specialist in the Institute for Sociological and Demographic Research at the Human Sciences Research Council. The current President of the South African Sociological Association, he is a graduate of the University of Pretoria (MA and Ph D), where he was Professor in Sociology before joining the HSRC in 1981.

Specialising in group conflict in plural societies, Dr Rhoodie has written extensively on various aspects of intergroup relations, particularly in the context of South Africa's race problems. In 1967 and 1969 he visited the UK and the USA as a guest of the Government.

Schlemmer, L

Lawrence Schlemmer studied at the University of Pretoria and the University of South Africa. At present he is reading for a doctorate at the University of Natal. He lectured in Sociology at the University of the Witwatersrand and was a Senior Researcher at the Institute of Social Research at the University of Natal. Since 1973 he has been Professor and Director of the Centre for Applied Social Studies at the University of Natal.

He has about 85 publications to his credit, *inter alia* articles in scientific reference works and chapters in books, such as part 4 of Theodor Hanf *et al*, *Südafrika, friedlicher Wandel?* (1978) and *Change, reform and economic growth in South Africa* (1977). He is a council member of the Human Sciences Research Council and of the KwaZulu Development Corporation, and serves on the Planning and Co-ordinating Council of the KwaZulu government. He is a part-time director of the Inkatha Institute and Vice-President of the South African Institute of Race Relations, as well as being a member of the Natal executive of the Urban Foundation. He has read papers at 12 overseas conferences.

Schutte, De W

De Wet Schutte is a Research Officer at the Human Sciences Research Council and was attached to the former Division of Conflict Studies of the Council before being appointed Head of Research at the Cape Town branch of the HSRC. He holds a Master's degree in Sociology from the University of Stellenbosch and a diploma in labour relations (DPLR) from the Institute of Labour Relations of the University of South Africa. He is the author and co-author of several publications. His main interest is socio-political change in South Africa.

Van Vuuren, DJ

DJ van Vuuren was awarded the MA and D Phil degrees by the University of the Orange Free State and has won various bursaries. He studied at the University of Leyden on a national scholarship and thereafter became Senior Lecturer in Political Science at the University of Port Elizabeth. At present he is Head of the Division for Political Science Research of the Human Sciences Research Council.

He is the author and co-author of several publications and co-editor of *Politieke Alternatiewe vir Suider Afrika — Grondslae en Perspektiewe* (MacMillan 1982) and the English edition, *Political Alternatives for Southern Africa — Principles and Perspectives* (Butterworths 1983), *Change in South Africa* (Butterworths 1983) and *Constitutions of Transkei, Bophuthatswana, Venda and Ciskei* (Butterworths 1985). In 1983 he visited the United States of America on a grant from the Human Sciences Research Council.

Wiehahn, NE

NE Wiehahn holds the degrees BA, LLB (University of the Orange Free State) and LLD (University of South Africa). He did research work at universities overseas and was professor in Labour and Industrial Law at various universities. He has held various posts in the civil service, *inter alia* full-time Labour Adviser to the Minister of Manpower Utilisation (1977-1979). At present he is Professor and holder of the Siemens Chair of Industrial Relations in the School of Business Leadership at the University of South Africa. Professor Wiehahn was or still is a member of various committees, commissions and councils such as the Cabinet Committee on Legislation concerning Black Community Development (Grosskopff Committee, 1981/1982), the Tomlinson Commission on the constitutional development of the Ingwavuma area (1982-), the Rumpff Commission of

Inquiry into the problem of the Ingwavuma and Kangwane areas with Swaziland (1982-), the Prime Minister's Economic Advisory Council (1977-) and the council of the University of the Orange Free State. He is also Chairman of the council of the University of Zululand. He is probably most well known as Chairman of the Commission of Inquiry into Labour Legislation (Wiehahn Commission, 1977-1980).

He has received the following awards and bursaries: the Golden Award as Man of the Year (1979) from the Institute of Personnel Management (Southern Africa), an award from the United Nations International Business Council for contribution to sound relations between peoples and countries, an award as one of the Top Five Business Men of 1981 and the Claude Harris Leon Foundation Award for 1982 for contributing to the design and structure of a new labour system for South Africa.

Professor Wiehahn is director of the School of Business Leadership at the University of South Africa.

INDEX

general affairs 8, 62
own affairs 8, 62, 63
own departments 62
regional offices 64, 66, 67-68
Depoliticisation 1
Destabilisation 34, 414, 416, 418, 438
Detente 438
Detention 22, 42, 226
preventive 227, 228
Developed countries 182
Developing states 33
Development —
appropriate strategy 187-195
communities 190
development decades 185-186
endogenous 188-189
from within 188-189
gap rich and poor 185-186
grass roots 190-192
interdependent 192
interplay of forces 187-188
leaders 190
local physical and human resources 189
multidimensional nature 188, 195
new approach 187-195
people for people by people 189-190
political aspirations 188
public/private sector 192
redistribution with growth 190, 192
self-generated efforts 190
self-reliant 188-189
self-sufficiency 195
servitude and dependence 190
socio-cultural setting 188
TBVC countries 196
traditional society 194-195
Development agencies 472
Development and Services Board 66
Development aid 55, 177, 470-471
Development Bank of Southern Africa 20
Development Board 19, 21
Development Co-operation 472
Development corporations 203
Development councils 53
Development economics 186-187
Development experience 173, 174-181
Africa 174-175
national states 175-181
Development projects 173
Development regions 203, 204
Development strategy 173-209
appropriate strategy 173, 193-205
capital 198
collective political will 197
comprehensive approach 196
conventional approach 173
development from below 197
economic and non-economic factors 206
economic growth 198, 200
economic structural change 198, 200
education 198
employment 198, 200, 201
endogenous 197
funds 197
health 198
income 197, 198, 200, 201
infrastructure 198
interdependent development in Southern Africa 196
integrated rural development 197
interrelationships 199
investment 197
labour 199, 201
unutilised 197
less developed countries 173
local resources 197
unutilised 197
national states 196
people by people for people 197
production factors 198
production structure 199, 200
productivity 197, 201-202
programme 200
public services 205, 206
public works programmes 198, 201
raw materials 199
redistribution of income 206
self-reliance 200
small business/sector 198
smaller undertakings 199
social structures 200
TBVC countries 196
technology 198, 199, 201, 206
trade 198
Development theories —
agriculture 183
capital accumulation 182-184
conventional approach 181-185
disenchantment 185-187
exogenous 184
rural sector 183
Devolution of power see Power
Dictatorship 30, 454, 476

individual rights and freedom 249
internal control 244-245
Internal Security Act, 1982 227-228
judicial control 240
labour control 246-247
legal and extra-legal control 239
legal limitation 224
legal theory 227
legislative measures 248
minimum infringement 224
Police Act, 1958 230-231
political issues 249
Prisons Act, 1959 231-232
privacy: individual right 245
Protection of Information Act, 1982
    230
public law protection 224
reports based on opinion 244
residual freedom 223
restrictions in interests of individuals
    235-239
    copyright 238-239
    defamation 235-237
    privacy 237-238
restrictions in interests of state
    227-232
self-censorship 248
state security 248
United Kingdom 226
United States of America 226
Pressure groups 34, 375, 452
Pretoria car-bomb blast 416
Printing 225
Prisoners: information 231, 232
Prisons —
    conditions 232
    information 231
    population 89, 90
Privacy 237-238, 245, 249
Private enterprise economy 455-458
Private law 224
Privatisation 1
Privileged statements 232
Production 187, 205
Productivity 55, 120, 188, 197, 198, 200,
    201-202, 471
Progressive Federal Party 310, 319-320,
    391, 411
Prohibited place 230
Property 456, 458, 459-460, 463, 474
Prosperity 44, 53
    redistribution 38
Protestant tradition 277

Provincial Councils 21, 25, 64-66, 304,
    468
    abolished 65
    Administrators 47, 65, 66
    autonomy 65
    centralisation/decentralisation 47
    constitutional control 74
    control 448
    decision-making processes 47
    executive committees 47, 65, 66
    functions 64
    general affairs 47, 65, 66, 74
    own affairs 47, 65, 66, 74
    legislative functions 65
    provincial departments 65
    revenue 65
    vacancy 65
    Whites only 65
Public amenities 311, 313, 316, 391 see
    also separate amenities
Public opinion 226, 227, 250
Public service 121, 126, 136, 447
    general affairs 47
    integration 8
    own affairs 47
Public services 205, 206
Public toilets 313, 316
Public transport 313, 475
Publications —
    prohibition 227, 228
    undesirable 242-244
    Appeal Board 244
    distribution 243
    possession 243
PWV area 116, 450

Q

Quail Commission 20
Qwaqwa see National States

R

Race 17, 35, 411, 443
Race policy 303, 307
Racial discrimination 51, 93, 367, 368,
    369, 379, 434, 443 see also Apartheid
    labour relations 121
    laws 81, 303, 305, 456
Racial segregation 287
    Nederduitse Gereformeerde Kerk 289
    mixed marriages 289
Rajbansi, A 385, 386
Rand 44

Rand monetary union payments 178
Reagan administration *see* United States
Rebellion 336
Recognition agreements 151
Recreation —
  mixed 266-268, 270
  own affair 268
  social distance 268
Reddy, JN 385, 386
Referendum, 1983 41, 60, 268, 273, 285
Reform 335, 337, 338
Reform initiatives 304, 329, 414, 436
Reform measures 374
Reform option 2, 17
Reform/control paradox 25
Reformed Church 277, 287-298
Reformed Church in Africa 275, 282, 285, 286
Reformed Ecumenical Synod 297
Reformism 312, 318-324
Reforum 298
Refuse dumps 73, 77
Regional authorities/government 21, 46, 63-64, 455, 465, 466, 474
  general affairs 467, 468, 469
Regional co-operation 48
Regional Courts 87, 88
Regional Courts Advisory Board 86
Regional development policy 177
Regional development strategy 52, 192, 203-204
  capital-intensive 204, 205
  economic aspects 203
  employment creation 205
  harmonising of programmes and instruments 204-205
  labour-intensive 204
  raw materials 205
  technology 204
Regional government 21
Regional policy *see* Foreign relations
Regional power 441
Regional Services Boards 71
Regional Services Councils 21, 25, 47, 52, 64, 68, 74, 76
  boundaries 76
  composition 77
  decision-making 47
  finance 76
  functions 68
  group domination 77
  provincial control 47

services 76-77
Renamo 416, 419, 420, 421, 422, 423, 424, 438
Repression 409
Republics 34
Research 184
Residential areas 53, 54, 291, 402
  segregation 54
Resources 28, 184
Revenue 473-475
Revolution 43, 248, 335, 336, 338, 360, 402, 462, 463
  justification 407
Revolutionary violence 402-409
  see also Political violence; Violence
  moral endorsement 411
Riekert Commission 38
Right to life 458
Right to work 52
Right(s) and liberties 30, 34, 44, 240, 249, 445, 447, 455, 458, 459
Riots 335, 336, 339, 409-410
Roads 64, 66, 73, 76
Roman Catholic Church 273, 275, 276, 277, 282, 285, 286-287
Roman-Dutch law 455
RSA constitution *see* Constitution
Rule of law 51, 223, 460, 461, 476
Rural co-operation 67
Rural development 185, 192-194, 201
  goals 193
  interplay of forces 193
  organisational structure 193
  people 193
  political sphere 193
  territorial plan 193
Rural economy 184
Russia *see* Soviet Union

S
SA Christian Leadership Assembly 280
SA Council for Education 215, 217, 220
SA Council for Teachers 215
SA Council of Churches 41, 42, 43, 280, 282-287
  finances 285
  Message to the People of South Africa 282
SA Council on Sport 260
SA Federation of Labour 127, 129-130
SA Indian Council 379
SA Non-Racial Olympic Committee 260
SA Sports Association 260